Project Management and Appraisal

SITANGSHU KHATUA

Associate Professor
Management Education Centre
Heritage Institute of Technology, Kolkata

OXFORD
UNIVERSITY PRESS

OXFORD
UNIVERSITY PRESS

Oxford University Press is a department of the University of Oxford.
It furthers the University's objective of excellence in research, scholarship,
and education by publishing worldwide. Oxford is a registered trademark of
Oxford University Press in the UK and in certain other countries

Published in India by
Oxford University Press
22 Workspace, 2nd Floor, 1/22 Asaf Ali Road, New Delhi 110 002

ISBN-13: 978-0-19-806690-3
ISBN-10: 0-19-806690-2

Typeset in Baskerville
by Recto Graphics, Delhi 110 096
M P Printer (a unit of D B Corp. Ltd.), Noida 201 305

For product information and current price, please visit www.india.oup.com

To Ma and Baba
And to Suparna, my wife

PREFACE

The world today is constantly witnessing completion of ambitious projects—be it the construction of Burj Dubai or the world-class Terminal 3 at IGI Airport New Delhi, the ultra-modern Delhi Metro, or the launch of the Large Hadron Collider beneath Franco-Swiss border near Geneva. All such projects have been possible due to tremendous human efforts coupled with appropriate technological and financial investments. The operations and logistics aspects involved in all such projects are perhaps more overwhelming (and less talked about) than the visualization of the projects themselves. Resource utilization, working under numerous constraints, deadlines, deliverables, outputs, risk, man management, etc. are the aspects that actually form the crux of all the work that happens (or is planned for) during any project.

Management of all available resources and bringing them together within a time frame for a desired result is called project management. It is a coordinated and planned effort that deals with the four stages of a project, beginning with defining the specifications and technical inputs, to planning the project, followed by executing the project, and finally delivering the output to the customers.

Since the 1950s, when quality of a product was the only objective of organizations, project management has come a long way. Its significance has become vital in today's global business environment. Organizations now have to deal with fierce competition, not only at the domestic but also at the international level. To capture the maximum market share and sustain growth and profit, they have to create new and complex products, services, and processes. This in turn means that project managers have to minutely work out the cost and time overrun of projects. Thus, project management has evolved as a separate discipline in management education to tackle the long-felt need for developing technical and human skills in project managers.

Multiple risks are involved in implementing a project, and project management is a powerful tool that is used by firms to monitor a project, overcome risks, and accomplish the objectives. Accurate financial decisions and selection of the right tools and techniques is central to project success. Proper execution of the plan is also essential.

This textbook will be useful to all aspiring managers, who would, at one point or the other, undertake projects in various organizations. It also highlights the integrated aspects of operations and financial issues suitably, making it valuable to practising professionals.

About the Book

Project Management and Appraisal has been specially designed to fulfil the needs of MBA students studying project appraisal and specializing in finance or operations. The basic aim behind developing this book has been to help readers understand and appreciate the integrated aspects of the subject and have a better understanding of project management processes. Efforts have also been made to address the need for a book that is comprehensive, relevant, and current.

The book is divided into four parts and provides an overview of project management theories, various appraisal techniques, and guidelines for evaluating a project. The principles and concepts, though universally applicable, have been illustrated keeping the Indian context in mind. Current emerging concepts of real option, international project appraisal, detailed project reports, e-projects, and the future of project management have also been dealt with lucidity.

Pedagogical Features

This book attempts to strike a balance between the two dimensions—the operational and the financial—of project management. The key features of the book are as follows:

- It explains comprehensively the concept of financial appraisal in project scanning and selection, including the fundamentals of capital budgeting decisions
- The future of project management and e-projects has been discussed in detail to help train future professionals
- The concepts have been aptly illustrated with Indian examples, such as the Tata Nano and Delhi Metro projects, which will help readers to relate to the concepts better
- Critical thinking exercises and project work have been provided to enhance the managerial skills of students
- Numerous solved and unsolved numerical questions included throughout the book for readers to test their understanding

Coverage and Structure

This book is laid out in four parts. Part I, Introduction to Project Management, consists of Chapters 1 and 2; Part II, Project Appraisal, consists of Chapters 3 to 12; Part III, Project Planning, Execution, and Control, of Chapters 13 to 15; and Part IV, Project Management—The Future, of Chapters 16 and 17.

Chapter 1 discusses the attributes of a project and project life cycle. It also describes the role of a project manager in different functional areas and gives a holistic perspective of project management.

Chapter 2 describes the phases of project management and project scheduling techniques with constrained resources. Crashing of a project network and graphical evaluation and review techniques (GERT) also find a mention in this chapter. It also gives an introduction to Microsoft Project 2010.

Chapter 3 focuses on the generation of project ideas and opportunities as well as how to allocate resources at corporate and business unit levels. It also explains various models, such as PEST, Porter's five forces, value chain analysis, BCG matrix, etc., that aid managers in making sound strategic decisions.

Chapter 4 deals with different appraisal methods—market, technical, and environmental. It also includes various social appraisal approaches like UNID and LM and explains linkages between corporate social responsibility and project management.

Chapter 5 elaborates on the basic concepts of time value of money, cost of capital, and the fundamentals of capital budgeting decisions. It also provides various DCF and non-DCF methods of financial appraisal techniques of a project, with the pros and cons of each.

Chapter 6 explains the selection of the exact discount factor for any project and various other concepts related to IRR, APV, WACC, interest, and depreciation.

Chapter 7 focuses on the risk analysis models of capital budgeting, such as probability, sensitivity, scenario, break even, Hiller model, simulation, etc., and analyzes decision tree, capital rationing, the portfolio theory, and the capital asset pricing models.

Chapter 8 discusses financial forecasting techniques and explains ways to estimate the future sales revenue.

Chapter 9 includes discussions on financing strategies of projects and the components of a project capital mix.

Chapter 10 illustrates the importance of real options in project evaluation and discusses various models and formulae of real options. It also describes the evolution of real options, the link between financial options and real options, and the exact reality of real options in the real world.

Chapter 11 deals with the constraints of carrying out multiple projects at a particular time, ranking conflict of projects and solutions, and various other programming approaches like linear programming, integer programming, and goal programming.

Chapter 12 focuses on appraisal of international projects and the various approaches and formulae involved.

Chapter 13 explains the need for, the inputs, and the process of project planning. It also discusses the reasons for cost and time overrun in a project. It also looks at the key factors for a project's success or failure.

Chapter 14 discusses the steps in project execution: organization, staffing, budgeting, and scheduling.

Chapter 15 focuses on the process of controlling and monitoring of projects, along with an insight into project audit.

Chapter 16 explains the planning, resourcing, and financing involved in e-project management.

Chapter 17 looks at the future of project management. It talks about the career opportunities in project management and the contemporary issues that impact project success.

The book also contains three appendices on the regulatory framework in project appraisal, tables of several discounted and compounded factor values for different rates and time periods, and the format of a DPR (detail project report).

ACKNOWLEDGEMENTS

First, I would like to gratefully acknowledge the contribution of all my teachers and professors at XLRI Jamshedpur for their inputs at various levels of my learning. I would like to particularly mention and thank Prof. S. Sengupta, Prof. H.K. Pradhan, Prof. P. Mohanty, and Prof. U. Damodaran for their invaluable contribution. My inspiration to write this book came from attending Prof. Sengupta's CAPEX course at XLRI during my fellowship.

I am also thankful to my colleagues at NIT Durgapur, IBS Kolkata, and JSB Kolkata for being a steady source of support in completing this endeavour. I humbly acknowledge the learning and inputs received from my students as well.

My sincere thanks to the editorial team of Oxford University Press, New Delhi, for their constructive criticism and continuous follow-ups during the course of writing this book. I also wish to thank my research assistant Mr Joydeep Sengupta for his assistance.

I must acknowledge the relentless support and co-operation of my wife, Suparna, who helped me with her valuable inputs and suggestions, without which this book would never have seen the light of the day. I would also like to thank my children—Noton and Buntun—for their support.

I wish to thank all my readers—teachers and students. I shall look forward to your valuable comments and suggestions at sitangshu_k@yahoo.com.

Sitangshu Khatua

BRIEF CONTENTS

DETAILED CONTENTS

....

PART II   Project Appraisal

3. Generation of Project Ideas

4. Various Appraisal Methods in Project Scanning and Selection

PART I
INTRODUCTION TO PROJECT MANAGEMENT

1. Project Management—Functions, Attributes, and Processes
2. Project Management—An Overview

PROJECT MANAGEMENT— FUNCTIONS, ATTRIBUTES, AND PROCESSES

A project is a combination of human and non-human resources pulled together in a temporary organization to achieve a specific purpose.

— CLELAND AND KERZNER

LEARNING OBJECTIVES

After studying this chapter, you will be able to

- Define project and project management
- Understand the various attributes of a project
- Explain the different phases in the life of a project
- Understand the role of project managers
- Formulate an overall view of modern project management

Hard Work vs Smart Work

Rakesh and Sameer are from the same engineering college. They are not exactly friends, but know each other quite well. So, when they joined SRM Construction in 2003, they were happy to share a room in their executive hostel. However, after initial training, they were put in different projects.

Now, after putting in 6–7 years of service, Rakesh and Sameer are part of the same assignment: a mega project for setting up an IT hub on the top floor of City Heights Tower. Rakesh is in charge of construction and Sameer is heading the electrical group.

At 6 p.m. on a Saturday, Rakesh goes to Sameer's office, hoping to discuss certain issues over coffee. He is surprised to find Sameer at the table, surrounded by files, circuit diagrams, sketches, etc.

RAKESH: Hi! What's up? Haven't finished yet?

SAMEER: Oh, it's you! No, it's only 6 p.m. How do you expect the head of the Electrical Department to pack up so early? You see, I have to finalize this part of the circuit layout before leaving for the weekend. I don't think I can afford to chat with you now.

RAKESH (taken aback): Well, all right then, I will leave. But tell me one thing Sameer. When you are finalizing the circuit, don't you need to discuss the exact requirement with the functional manager? I find it easier to do it this way.

SAMEER: My God! What does any functional manager know about electrical circuits? It is my subject.

RAKESH: Yes, I agree. But he is an important part of the project as well. We have to design the project in such a way that it meets requirements, and inputs by the functional manager can be of great help in this regard. I have taken all the concerned people into confidence at every step of the construction project, and, I believe, the result will speak for itself. The construction part is so designed that it is tailor-made for the IT hub, and the people working there will find all their needs met. Moreover, I can also be tension-free and finish the job within schedule.

SAMEER: I don't like leisuring around like you. I shall overstay and come on Sundays, if required, and finish my job as I feel is right. You please leave me alone.

RAKESH: Ha Ha! You workaholic! You dump yourself in this office for as long as you want. If you finish, come over to the club. I'll be on my way.

1.1 PROJECT AND PROJECT MANAGEMENT

In layman's terms, a project is a specific task that has a beginning and an end.

According to ISO 8402, a project is defined as a unique process, consisting of a set of coordinated and controlled activities with start and finish dates, undertaken to achieve an objective conforming to specific requirements including constraints of time, cost, and resources. Therefore, it can be seen as a complex, non-routine, one-time effort to complete a particular task.

The term 'project management' is used for defining the process of executing a project in a systematic and scientific manner.

The Manhattan Project, which created the first atom bomb, is considered to have put to use, for the first time, the modern methods of project management. The Taj Mahal, the Great Wall of China, the Parthenon (Greece), and the Pyramids are some of the ancient examples and results of project management.

1.2 PROJECT ATTRIBUTES

Most of the modern successful projects, such as the Tata Nano project, have all been made possible by the careful implementation of project management techniques. Let us try to understand the various attributes of a project on the lines of the famous Tata Nano car project.

Target   A project works towards a specific goal or target. Cost considerations and time management are some of the important issues associated with setting up of a project and achievement of targets. For example, in the case of the Singur Nano car project, the objective was to establish an automobile plant to produce a small and inexpensive car, targeting potential consumers both in domestic and foreign markets.

Unique   Every project has certain unique characteristics that set it apart from similar initiatives. This unique nature, most of the times, is the driving force behind the conception and completion of a project. For example, the Singur Nano car project was unique because at the highly affordable price of Rs 1 lakh, it was the first automobile unit in India that aimed at catering to the middle-income group in India (and abroad), a hitherto unexploited section in the four-wheelers market.

A start and an end   Since a project means accomplishing of a certain task, it has to have a beginning and an end. Meeting the beginning and end deadlines adds to the reputation of the final output, and restricts, in most cases, exceeding of assigned budget. In the case of Nano, impressive preparations and publicity were carried out even before its manufacturing had begun. So, by the time the cars were ready for delivery, considerable public interest about it had been generated. Tata's promise to deliver within deadlines, despite the relocation of the manufacturing plant to Sanand in Gujarat, added to its high reputation and ensured a good market.

Complicated   A project involves coordination, integration, and management of several complex processes. These processes may have various technical, environmental, socio-economic, and political implications. For example, the Singur Nano project had to be called off as a result of serious political protests due to certain land acquisition issues. Eventually, the project had to be shifted to Gujarat. Such events, often unforeseen, add to the complexity of a project.

Time, cost, and resource requirements   The three core factors that define a project include time, budget, and resources. Proper utilization of these three interdependent components determines the value of the final product, i.e., the success of the project (Figure 1.1).

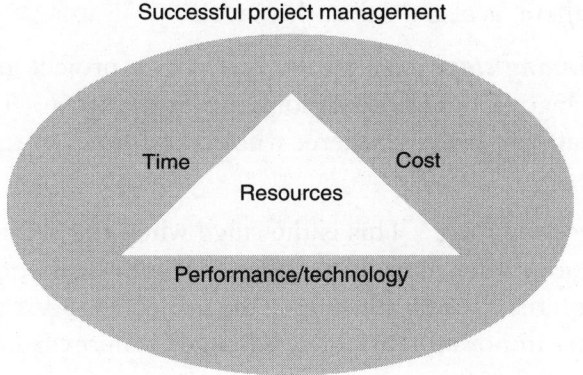

FIGURE 1.1   Time, cost, and resources chart

In case of the Nano project, Tata Motors announced in March 2006 that it would roll out the car by 2008 and it would be priced at $2,000 (approx. Rs 1,00,000). They also specified that the Singur plant would have a capacity of 2.5 lakh vehicles per annum, with flexibility to raise it to 3.5 lakh per annum from the second year.

Uncertainty and risks   In the planning stage of a project, the time schedule for completion, cost, and resource requirements are planned based on prediction, anticipation, and earlier experience. However, actual conditions are likely to be different. Hence, uncertainty or risk is an integral part of project management. In case of the Nano project, there was significant skepticism among some sections of the media and the public regarding safety features of the car. It was assumed that a small, low-cost car would compromise on safety and quality. It posed a significant risk to the value of the project. However, inclusion of impressive safety features by the company helped minimizing the uncertainty, and thus ensured better receptivity of the car.

1.3 PROJECT LIFE CYCLE

Spatial and temporal limitations are characteristic of every project and define its life cycle. The nature and magnitude of the constituent tasks tend to vary at different points in the life cycle of a project. For instance, task A may have a smaller budget than task B. However, the former may require more time for completion as compared to the latter. Although, every project is unique in its own way, the following stages (of project life cycle) are common to most of them.

The defining stage   A project commences at this stage. Different project-related requirements, such as commercial specifications, technical inputs, etc., are determined. Formation of different teams, and the division of tasks and responsibilities among them, is also done at this level.

The planning stage   All plans related to a project are conceived and developed at this stage. Critical discussions are organised to find answers to the 5Ws and 1H (what, why, when, where, whom, and how) of the project ands its associated activities.

The executing stage   This is the stage when the actual job is executed, within the framework of the plan. It includes both physical and conceptual initiatives. This level requires close monitoring of the project vis-à-vis the budget, the time schedule, and other important variables. Changes, wherever necessary, are introduced and incorporated at this stage.

The delivering stage   This is the final stage of the project when the ready output is delivered to the customers. Also, the workforce and other resources, which were previously involved with the completed project, are assigned new tasks or programmes.

Thus, a project life cycle represents a temporal and spatial framework of the entire project, along with the constituent tasks that it involves. Success at any stage, to a large extent, is determined by well-executed actions in the previous stage. A typical life cycle for a project is shown in Figure 1.2.

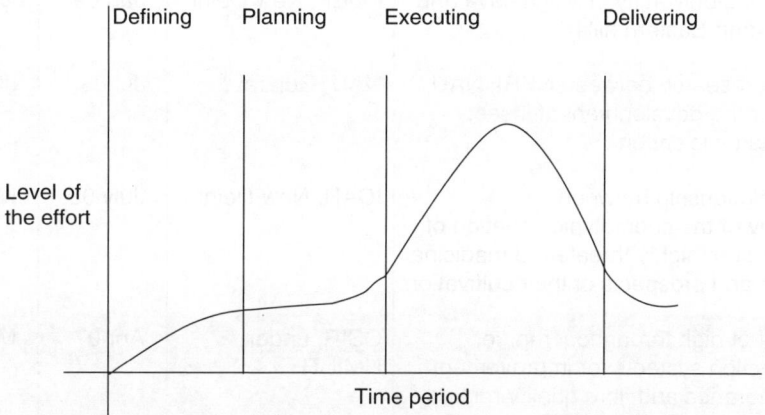

Source: Gray and Larson 2005.

FIGURE 1.2   Project life cycle

Some important completed and on-going projects in India are listed in Exhibit 1.1 and Table 1.1, respectively.

EXHIBIT 1.1   Few recently completed projects in India

1. Indian Patenting Activity in International and Domestic Patent System: Contemporary Scenario
2. Project on preparation of a Road Map for Oil Spill Management for India
3. Project on Information Security
4. Project on the development of GaAs: Epitaxial Multijunction Quantum Well Infrared Photodetectors (QWIPS): Phase-I
5. Project on Modelling of Fluidized Bed Coal Gasifiers
6. Measures of Progress of Science in India: an analysis of the publication output in Science and Technology
7. National Energy Map for India: Technology Vision 2030
8. Project on the Development of a Bulk Encryption Unit and an Algorithm
9. Project on the Development of a Readout Integrated Circuit (ROIC) for an 8×8 QWIP array
10. Measures of Impact of Science and Technology in India: Agriculture and Rural Development
11. Project on the Development of Explosive Detector based on Ion Mobility Spectrometry Technology
12. Production and demonstration of high-quality planting material of Jatropha Curcas
13. Bt-gene stacking and gene targeting in brinjal for resistance to shoot and fruit borer
14. Genomics and biotechnology of fruit quality
15. Identification and role of ethylene response factors in ethylene signalling in tomato
16. Molecular systematics of the genus sapindus L. (Sapindaceae) in India using PCR-based techniques

Source: http://psa.gov.in/uniquepage.asp?ID_PK=6, accessed 6 March 2010.

TABLE 1.1   Few ongoing projects in India (2009–10)

Project title	Funding agency	Month and year of starting	Month and year of completion	Cost of project (Rs in lakhs)
Biodiversity assessment, prospection and conservation of plant of India	CSIR	April 07	March 12	1729.00
Assessment of biodiversity in Meghalaya and Manipur (in North Eastern hills)	MoEF, New Delhi	Jan 09	Dec 11	25.826
Collaborative research between NBRI, NAU, and GSSC for the development of insect resistant transgenic cotton	NAU, Gujarat	Jul 05	June 10	50.00
Studies on relationship between ecogeography of the chemotypic variation of nine important but highly threatened medicinal plant species and prospects of their cultivation	ICAR, New Delhi	July 08	Mar 12	203.1138
Development of high throughout marker assisted selection systems for improvement of drought tolerance and fibre quality related traits in cotton	CSIR, under NMILTI	Apr 07	Mar 12	496.50
Functional analysis of novel petal abscission and senescence related genes from rose and gladioli	DBT, New Delhi	Oct 07	Sept 10	33.28
Regulation of gene expression in plants (JC Bose fellowship)	DST, New Delhi	Jul 07	Jun 12	40.00
Studies on diversity and distribution of pteridophytic flora of Pachmarhi Biosphere Reserve	MoEF	Apr 08	Mar 11	13.338
Advancement in metrology	CSIR	Apr 08	Mar 12	15.00
Screening of herbal drugs used in treatment of hepato cellular carcinoma	DST, New Delhi	Jan 08	Dec 10	22.88
Transgenic crop plant and genes for resistance to insect pests	CSIR	Apr 07	Mar 12	775.00
Rural development programmes: (i) Sustainable development and utilization of sodic wastelands, adopting green technologies, using schools as knowledge dissemination centres, (ii) Dissemination of dry flower/cut flower technologies, and (iii) Remediation of contaminated ground resources	CSIR	Apr 07	Mar 12	350.00

Contd

Table 1.1 *Contd*

Project title	Funding agency	Month and year of starting	Month and year of completion	Cost of project (Rs in lakhs)
Pathway engineering and system biology approach towards homologous and heterologous expression of high-value phytoceuticals (artemisinin, picrosides, morphine, withanolides podophyllotoxin)	CSIR	Apr 07	Mar 12	271.00
Enhancing water utilization efficiency in crop plants: Prospecting plant diversity for genes and systems biology for drought tolerance	CSIR	Apr 07	Mar 12	1000.00
Environmental contaminants: New screening technologies and effect on human health	CSIR	Apr 07	Mar 12	227.00
Remediation, eco-restoration, and clean-up of contaminated ground and water resources	CSIR	Apr 07	Mar 12	345.00
Exploratory studies on climate change and adaptation of species complexes	CSIR	Apr 07	Mar 12	610.00
Genetic improvement of canna by induced mutation and development of core collections	DAE, BRNS, Mumbai	Dec 07	Nov 10	9.11675
Generation of a seed specific EST library in Jatropha and identification of genes for oil biosynthesis pathway	DBT, New Delhi	Oct 07	Sept 10	22.15
Study of herbal acaricides as means to overcome the development of resistance in ticks to conventional acaricides	ICAR, New Delhi	Jul 08	Mar 12	86.32

Source: http://www.nbri-lko.org/List_of_On.pdf, accessed 6 March 2010.

1.4 THE ROLE OF A PROJECT MANAGER

Project managers occupy a challenging office. They coordinate among various functional areas and integrate the diverse processes associated with them. Excellent communication and interpersonal skills, familiarity with the tasks, teams, and technologies associated with the project are some of the prerequisites of the project manager's position. On the downside, project managers' authority is very limited as compared to the range of responsibilities that they undertake. Therefore, they must use negotiation skills to synchronise operations involving the higher management and the functional managers, ensuring optimal utilization of the company's resources. Figure 1.3 illustrates J. Robert Fluor's (1977) description of the responsibilities of project managers at Fluor Corporation.

	Strategic planning	Finanacial management	Resource allocation scheduling and integration • People • Material • Equipment • Money	Management functions • Planning • Staffing • Coordinating • Controlling • Directing	Providing programme and technical direction
Top-level management	↑↓	↑↓	↑↓		
Regions for negotiation	Programme management/project engineering				
Functional management		↑↓	↑↓	↑↓	↑↓

Source: Fluor 1977.

FIGURE 1.3   J. Robert Fluor's description

1.4.1 Responsibilities of a Project Manager

Some of the important responsibilities of a project manager (Wilemon and Cicero 1970) are listed below:

- Project managers are responsible for completion of a specified project within allocated time, budget, and resources.
- They direct, integrate, and co-ordinate the project team. They are responsible for the management and performance of the team members.
- They must involve the most suitable candidates for a given task to ensure the best possible output.
- While operating within the guidelines of the project, they must foster cordial relationship with the customers and ensure their satisfaction.
- A project manager is the common link between various organizations working on a project. Although project management has its own set of specialized tasks, it cannot remain isolated from the processes and structures of the different organizations that it intends to manage. Therefore, a project manager must see his/her role as that of a coordinator and integrator of different forces that contribute to the project at various levels and degrees.

Following are some examples explaining the concept of interface management:

- Managing human interrelationship in the project organization
- Maintaining the balance between technical and managerial project functions
- Coping with the risk associated with project management
- Surviving organizational restraints

1.4.2 Project Manager vs Line Manager

A comparison between a project manager and a line manager will help us better understand the role the project manager. In any organization, where a separate project management department is set up, there is always a constant tussle between the general line managers and project managers. This tussle arises as both compete with each other to share the organization's money, human resource, equipment, facilities, materials, and information technologies. The conflict of interest is further compounded by the fact that some of the important resources, such as human resource, are controlled by line managers.

Project managers inform line managers of their requirements for staff and accordingly appropriate allocation is made by the latter. This also applies to resources that are controlled by specific departments. Project managers are generally not allowed to choose the resources that they want. They have to work with whatever is given to them and can complain only if they come across substandard services or material.

The employees provided to a project manager continue to report to their line managers. Their appraisals are also done by the line managers. Therefore, it is only natural that they give preference to the commands of the line manager over the project manager. In such a situation, the success of a project depends on

(i) Presence of a good working relationship between project manager and line manager and

(ii) Effective handling of cross-reporting by the functional employees (employees sent to work on the project).

1.5 PROJECT MANAGEMENT—AN OVERALL PERSPECTIVE

The pressure for completion of an often almost impossible task is focused on how effectively the project manager carries out his or her job (Stuckenbruck 1978). Today project management is the key to the success of projects that include diverse, multi-disciplinary processes. The greatest strength and weakness of a project manager lies in the single-point authority and responsibility of his or her role.

On the one hand, a single project manager enjoys the right to coordinate and integrate the functions of different teams working on the project. This helps to avoid a lot of confusion and conflict of interests. On the other hand, the project manager must also bear the greater responsibility of project failure, if that occurs. The progress report of a project is made by evaluating the effectiveness and performance of the project manager associated with it.

It is a management axiom that the overall job of every manager is to create satisfaction within the organization and environment, which would facilitate the accomplishment of its objectives (Koontz and O'Donnell 1972). Project management can of course be perceived as just another job requiring an experienced and conscientious manager. But is 'just any experienced manager' prepared for the job of project management?

As shown in Figure 1.4, managers must try to strike a balance between differentiation and integration to achieve high performance and secure a position in high management. They should not only strive to achieve the goals of the organization, but also adopt a unique approach to work in order to stand out in a group.

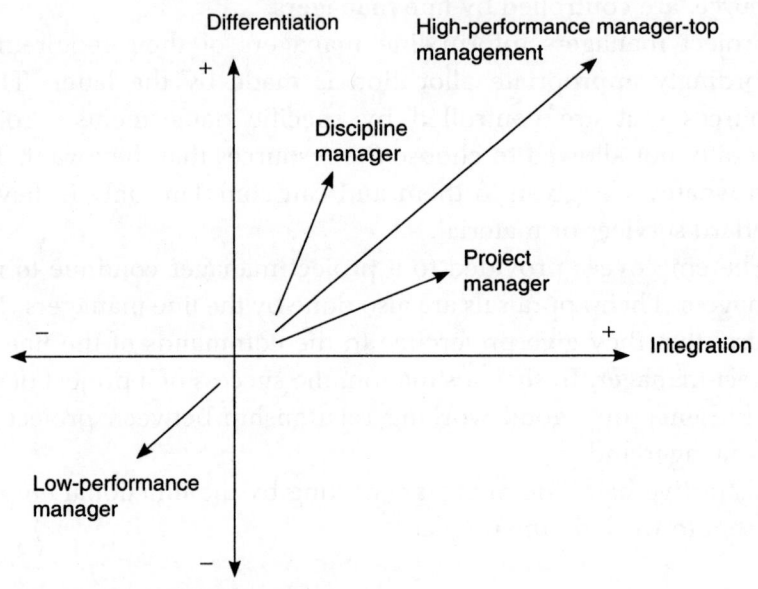

Source: Cleland and King 1975.

FIGURE 1.4   Measuring managerial performance

1.5.1 Project Integration

Project integration occurs when all the constituent units (such as different groups, individuals, supporting organizations, etc.) unite and work as one system to achieve the final output. Several interrelated and interdependent units together form a project. Proper integration of these constituent units is a common feature of all projects, whether simple or complex. The integration of units to form a harmonious and productive system is the main responsibility of the project manager. Of course, all efforts would go in vain if the project manager does not enjoy the confidence of the different team members. This incorporation is not a one-time effort; rather, it is a continuous process and requires constant monitoring as differences among various groups or individuals can occur at any time and at any stage of the project. This makes the task of project management more challenging and rigorous.

A project manager must be sensitive to the diversity of a project system. Every constituent element of a project must be given appropriate time and attention. The loyalty of the project manager must lie with the project as a whole, instead of with any particular team, department, or individual associated with it.

Different units of a project vary in importance. Some are critical to the project, whereas others may be playing an external supporting role. A project manager must exercise discretion while dealing with such units of varied importance. Figure 1.5 shows the diversity of a project system.

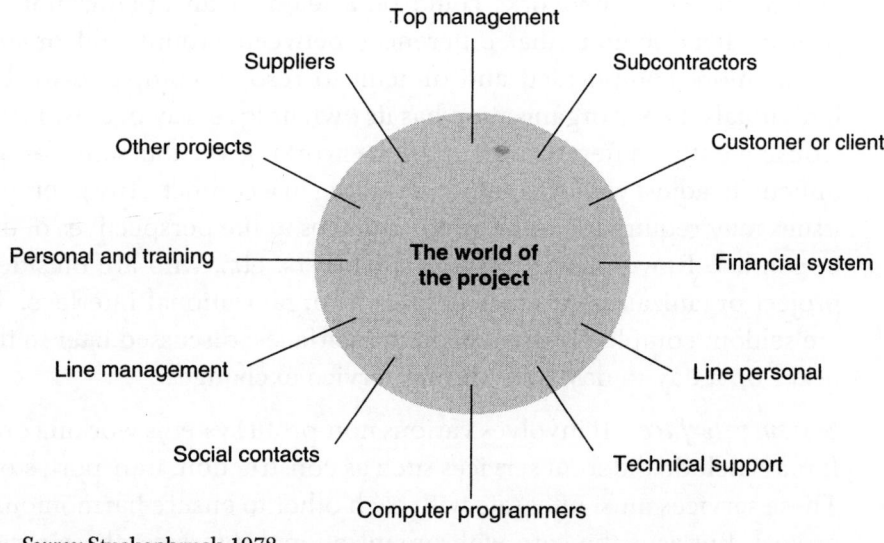

Source: Stuckenbruck 1978.

FIGURE 1.5   Total project system

1.5.2 Project Interfaces

Project interface refers to the links or relationships among the various organizations, units, groups, and individuals associated with a project. Various kinds of project interfaces can be divided, according to Archibald (1977), into product and project types. They have further sub-divisions, of which, management interface is an important one.

Project interface can be understood in terms of three important types of interfaces—personal, organizational, and system interfaces.

Personal interface   It refers to the interactions and relationship among members of a project. Differences in opinion and conflicts are common occurrences when a set of people work together on a project. The differences could range from being trivial to serious in nature. It is the responsibility of a project manager to seek out conflicts in the interest of the project. His or her role becomes all the more important when individuals in conflict belong to two or more different functional lines. However, his or her influence may be restricted if the differences arise in the same functional lines, because the respective line manager would have a greater say in the matter. Also, differences among functional managers may be difficult to resolve, as the office of a project manager does not carry much authority to govern its subordinates.

Organizational interface If personal interface is about individuals, organizational interface refers to the interaction between a network of individuals, both large and small. These networks could be a team or an organization working on the project. It is obvious that differences between groups and organizations would be far more complicated and difficult to resolve compared to those concerning individuals. Every organization has its own unique way of existing and functioning. Consequently, different organizations working on the same project may find it difficult to adjust with each other, resulting in a conflict. Any attempt to resolve such issues may require major or minor changes in the perspectives of the organizations in conflict. Raw material suppliers, bankers, etc., who are outside the immediate project organization, also participate in organizational interface. These interfaces are seldom completely management interfaces (discussed later in the chapter), and occur on a day-to-day basis during service exchanges.

System interface It involves various non-profit systems working on/for the project. It may include different services such as construction, transport, storage, and so on. These services must integrate with each other to ensure harmonious progress of the project. But as is the case with organizational interface, these services are unique in nature and functioning and they are also controlled by different individuals and organizations. Hence, differences may arise in priority, work protocol, etc. when these services are expected to coordinate with each other.

1.5.3 Management Interfaces

Problems may arise in any or all the different interfaces (personal, organizational, and system) mentioned before. In such an event, the project as a whole suffers. Management interface constitutes the features of both personal and organizational interfaces. When different individuals working on the same project interact, they also represent the concerns of their respective teams or organizations. Therefore, a conflict between different workers or managers also shows the larger disconnect among the organizations that they represent.

A conventional organization chart, whether hierarchical or matrix, shows a hypothetical structure of operations. It is, however, not an exact representation of actual processes associated with real organizations.

Several important management interfaces, such as management-leader and management-subordinate relationship, are depicted well in a conventional organization chart.

However, these charts only suggest some of the other really important interfaces. These important interfaces, as shown by the double-end arrows in Figure 1.6, consist of project-functional manager interfaces, project manager-top management interfaces, functional manager-functional manager interfaces, and sometime even project manager-project manager interfaces.

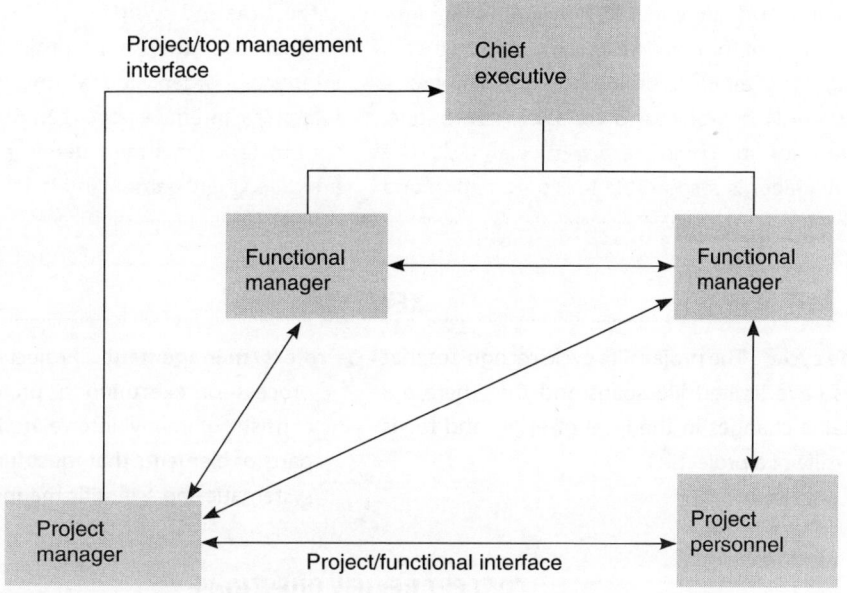

Source: Stuckenbruck 1978.

FIGURE 1.6   The multiple management interface in matrix

Interactions between various project managers and functional managers, particularly those who are operating on the same reporting level, are critical interfaces in a project. Such interfaces are most prone to conflicts as they involve a constant tussle for power and authority between the project managers and the functional managers.

A poor communication network among functional managers is often a source of problems as they are in charge of their respective functional lines. Sometimes, project managers may not be adequately informed about the problems faced by their functional counterparts, and hence are not able to play proper mediators.

Finally, an open and direct interaction between project managers and top management is crucial to the success of a project, as the former is accountable for the project and the latter is the source of all authority and resources. The top management must be accessible to a project manager as and when required to facilitate proper development of the project. Also, clear support from top management empowers project managers to discharge their duties efficiently.

SUMMARY

Project management is a unique process, consisting of a set of coordinated and controlled activities with a beginning and an end, undertaken to achieve an objective conforming to specific requirements including constraints of time, cost, and resources. In other words, a project is a complex, nonroutine, one-time effort to complete a particular task. The project manager is responsible for coordinating and integrating activities across multiple functional lines. In short, a project is a unique task to be completed within time and budget.

There are three types of project interfaces: personal interfaces, organizational interfaces, and system interfaces. Interfaces between project managers and various functional managers supporting the project are called management interfaces.

KEY TERMS

Project life cycle The project life cycle recognizes that projects have limited life spans and that there are predictable changes in the level of effort and focus over the life of a project.

Project management Project management is the process of executing a project, a system which consists of many interrelated and interconnected parts or elements that must function as a whole, in a systematic and scientific manner.

CONCEPT REVIEW QUESTIONS

1. Define the term 'project'. Enumerate the key attributes of a project with suitable examples.
2. Describe different phases of a project life cycle with a suitable example.
3. Enumerate different roles of a project manager in a specific project.

CRITICAL THINKING QUESTIONS

1. Gather information about the Delhi Metro project, one of the recent well-known projects in India. Analyse the type of problems it faced while opening the service to the public.
2. Review the ISO definition of a project. Use the basic features of a project to differentiate a project from a non-project. Try to search for project examples that do not satisfy all project features.
3. Select a project in your neighbourhood and discuss its objectives, scope, and strategy.
4. Gather information about the project of Tollygunge-New Garia Kolkata Metro Rail Extension and try to find out the problems that resulted in its delay?

5. Explain how the following statement can have a bearing upon who is ultimately selected as part of the project team: 'There comes a time in the life cycle of all projects when one must shoot the design engineer and begin production.'

6. How would you defend the statement that project managers must help themselves?

7. Can project life cycles have different shapes? Provide hypothetical examples of projects for which the life cycles follow different paths and discuss their characteristics.

8. Is project management designed to transfer power from line managers to project managers?

9. In a project organization, do you think there might be a conflict in opinions over whether project managers or functional managers contribute to profits?

10. In a project scenario, the cause and effect relationship is always obvious. Some causes and effects are enlisted below. For each one of the effects, select the possible cause or causes:

Effects

(a) Cost overruns

(b) Time overruns

(c) Late start of activities

(d) Substandard performance

(e) High attrition rate of project staff

(f) High turnover in functional staff

Causes

(a) Schedule commitments not matching reality

(b) Too many projects going on simultaneously

(c) Top management not prioritising an activity as a project

(d) Poorly organized project office

(e) No integrated planning and control

(f) No project cost accounting ability

(g) Conflicting project priorities

(h) Wrong person assigned as project manager

(i) No functional input in the planning phase

ASSIGNMENT

Your organization has just assigned you to a newly formed task team which is to take over a secret project presently being handled by R&D. The first task before your team is to design a plan to manage the project.

A list of 20 management activities (A through T) is arranged in random order. Your task is to rank the order of these activities according to the sequence you would follow in managing the project.

Step 1: Without discussing with anyone, go over the risks and rank the order of these activities A through T according to the sequence you think should be followed in managing the project. Assign number 1 for the first activity and 20 for the last.

Step 2: Now, as a team, agree to the sequence of activities shown in the table below.

Labels	Management activities	Step 1: Individual rankings	Step 2: Team ranking	Step 3: Planning expert ranking	Step 4: Absolute difference between steps 1 and 3	Step 5: Absolute difference between steps 2 and 3
A	Find qualified people to fill position					
B	Measure progress and/or deviation from the project goal					
C	Identify and analyse the various jobs tasks necessary to implement the project					
D	Develop strategies (priorities, sequences, and timings)					
E	Develop alternative course of action					

Contd

Table   *Contd*

Labels	Management activities	Step 1: Individual rankings	Step 2: Team ranking	Step 3: Planning expert ranking	Step 4: Absolute difference between steps 1 and 3	Step 5: Absolute difference between steps 2 and 3
F	Arrange appropriate consequences for individual performances					
G	Assign responsibility/authority					
H	Set project objectives (desired results)					
I	Train and develop personnel for new jobs					
J	Gather and analyse facts of current project situation					
K	Establish qualification for new positions					
L	Take corrective actions on project (recycle plans)					
M	Coordinate ongoing activities					
N	Determine allocation of resources (budget, manpower, etc.)					
O	Measure individual performance against performance standards					
P	Identify negative consequences of each course of action					
Q	Develop individual performance standards mutually agreeable to individual and the manager					
R	Define scope of relationship, authorities of new position					
S	Decide on basic course of action					
T	Determine measurable checkpoints for the project and variations expected					
	Total					

SELECT REFERENCES

Archibald, and Russell, D., *Managing High-Technology Programs and Projects,* Wiley, New York, 1977, pp. 66.

Cleland, David, I., and King, W.R., *System Analysis and Project Management,* 2nd edn., McGraw-Hill, New York, 1975.

Fluor, J.R., 'Development of Project Managers', *Ninth International Seminar Symposium,* PMI, Chicago, October 1977.

Gray, C. and Larson, E., *Project Management,* TMH, New Delhi, 2005.

Koontz, H. and O'Donnell, C., *Principles of Management: An Analysis of Managerial Functions,* McGraw-Hill, New York, 1972, p. 46.

Stuckenbruck, L.C., 'Project Manager-The System's Integrator', *Project Management Quarterly,* September 1978, pp. 31–38.

Wilemon, D.L. and Cicero, J.P., "The Project Manager-Anomalies and Ambiguities", *Academy of Management Journal,* September 1970.

Other resources

http://www.nbri-lko.org/List_of_On.pdf; accessed 6 March 2010.

http://psa.gov.in/uniquepage.asp?ID_PK=6; accessed 6 March 2010.

CASE STUDY
The Case of ARTF Corporation

The employees of ARTF Corporation are in a confused state of mind. They know that they ought to be happy and proud as their organization is in the process of implementing a new online SAP system. ARTF will be the first organization in the rubber manufacturing business to have this honour to their credit.

But how will things work from now on? Most of them have practically no exposure to the computerized system, and suddenly everything, every activity has to be done through the new system. The traditional system of working, record keeping, purchasing, financial activity, etc., will stop on 31 December, and on the 1 January, they will have to wake up to a new working style. Across the organization, people are tense and unsure about the whole thing.

The management has appointed M/s KK Systems International, a project consultancy firm, to work out the system for ARTF Corporation. A core group has been constituted with consultants from KK Systems and ARTF departmental officials to study and understand the existing system and map it into the SAP system. This core group is headed by Mr Prakash Jain, Chief of Automation, who directly reports to Mr K. Subramanian, the finance director of ARTF Corporation.

The automation department is also responsible for cross-functional system integration across departments. Many people consider this as a baby project management structure within the parent organization.

The core group is working on the system, and constantly interacting with senior officials of ARTF Corporation at each stage of development to address the issues and bottlenecks faced.

Some of the officials of ARTF feel that it is a waste of their valuable time and energy to explain their working to some third agency who will design a new system for them. They also feel that the third agency will not be in a position to prioritize their work based on importance and urgency. However, the top management team seemed quite satisfied and confident with Mr Prakash Jain monitoring the activities, and giving feedback to Mr Subramanian every fortnight on the progress. The new system was flagged off as per schedule after scrapping off the existing systems.

All users at various ends of the organization are desperately trying to get into the system and start working, but the members are still not sure about how to use it. All employees are suddenly trying to contact the core group members to find out what to do and some of them rush to the automation centre to catch hold of a suitable person who can help them deal with the problem.

Mr Prakash seeks an urgent appointment with Mr Subramanian.

PRAKASH: Sir, I'm afraid things have not worked out as we had expected. People are complaining that all the activities have come to a halt, and that the system is not working.

SUBRAMANIAN: This was bound to happen. When your boys asked for suggestions and solutions, people did not have the time. Now they say that their issues are not taken care of. Now nothing can be done. Everybody has to work on this system.

PRAKASH: These people from functional areas do not have the slightest idea about how long it takes to write, modify, and debug programs to run such sophisticated systems. They can only shout and raise problems.

SUBRAMANIAN: All right, I understand. But do not develop a closed shop in your department. Your team members hardly interact with other groups and members of the organization. You must advise your boys to socialise across the organization. It will help solve problems better.

PRAKASH: Sir, with due respect I have a submission. If my people are not considered as equals vis-à-vis employees of this organization, I am afraid we may lose some of our good people. More so now, with the mass of employees being against us, they think that

we are useless and have created an incompetent system.

SUBRAMANIAN: So, what's your suggestion?

Discussion questions

1. What went wrong? Can you outline the basic reasons for the occurrence of the above mentioned problem?
2. According to you, what will be the arrangement that Prakash may develop?
3. Identify various aspects of project management in the above case and explain the role of project managers in successful completion of a project.

PROJECT MANAGEMENT—
AN OVERVIEW

Project management is like juggling three balls—time, cost, and quality.

— G. REISS

Project Overrun

The Sunshine Project of Axis Corporation was completed three months behind schedule at a cost overrun of approximately 50 per cent. After the completion of the project, Mr M.K. Mehra, the GM (Projects) of Axis Corporation, called Raj Sinha, the project manager, and B. Rajan, the operations manager, for a meeting.

MEHRA: Gentlemen! This meeting is not to blame anybody. We shall discuss what went wrong and try to formulate a policy to ensure that this does not recur in our future ventures.

SINHA: When we accepted the contract, we did not have a fixed delivery schedule as we did not know when the plant would be ready. But midway we were asked to accelerate the production activities. So we put our people on overtime to adhere to their schedule. This was a mistake, as we accepted a fixed delivery date and budget without clearly understanding the details.

RAJAN: Sir, our problem was that the client did not provide us with a fixed set of the specifications at the beginning. Our people were asked to commit to particular man hours, before specifications could be reviewed. It was 6 months after the project go-ahead that the final specifications were issued. We had to re-engineer about 1,00,000 units to match the final specs.

SINHA: The contract provided by the company was for the payment against re-engineered units. Unfortunately, our contract people did not inform me that we were still liable to pay penalty for time overrun.

MEHRA: Don't you feel that proper interpretation of the terms and conditions is your responsibility?

- Describe how to analyse project scheduling with constrained resources
- Understand the concept of critical chain and buffer management approach
- Understand the graphical evaluation and review technique (GERT)
- Understand project management software such as Microsoft Project 2010

SINHA: I accept the responsibility, sir, and am ready to take the blame.

RAJAN: We need clear documentation on what to do in case of specification change. User approval of specifications can come anytime during a project. We must have a system in place for implementing change.

MEHRA: I heard that the operations personnel in the plant are grumbling about the Sunshine Project. What is the issue?

RAJAN: We were directed to cut out all overtime in all projects. But to complete the Sunshine Project, overtime was the only way out. So, for one and a half years, people on the Sunshine Project got as much overtime as they could manage. This made people on other projects very unhappy. Now the people who worked in the Sunshine Project have become used to the fat pay-packet and suddenly, with no overtime, they are unhappy too. They demand that they should be given overtime again. So, everybody is unhappy and they hate us.

MEHRA: Well, now we understand the problem. Let us start working out prevention strategies.

2.1 PHASES OF PROJECT MANAGEMENT

As mentioned in the previous chapter, every project has a life cycle. Each phase of this cycle requires proper management. The project management process constitutes the following phases.

Concept phase   The point at which the customer, i.e., the individual or the organization is willing to provide funds, identifies a need that is to be met. It may be a new product or service, a move from one location to another, a new information system, an advertising campaign, and so on.

Definition phase   Before starting the complex task of planning and executing a project, it is necessary to be clear about what is to be done to fulfil the need, i.e., what exactly is required to be done. Basically, three different elements are needed to define a project: objective, scope, and strategy.

Planning phase   After the project is properly defined, the planning phase starts. The planning process involves these crucial steps—identification of project activities, estimation of time and resources, identification of relationships and dependencies, and identification of constraints.

Scheduling phase   Project scheduling involves preparation of a project-based plan. The plan must specify the sequence of activities, feasible start and completion dates, amount of various resource types required during each time period, and budget for every activity.

Control phase Once a baseline plan is established, it is required to be implemented. As the project starts, the progress must be monitored. This involves measuring actual progress and comparing it with planned progress.

Termination phase This is the last stage of the project and it is as important as the initial phase. The ultimate aim of project management and project scheduling in particular is to have a satisfied customer.

Let's take the example of Kolkata Metro Rail (the first metro rail project of India) to understand all these stages better. Initially, the need for another traffic path was identified for a densely populated and busy city like Kolkata. Existing roads were already overburdened and there was no further space to build new roads within the city. Hence, the idea of a tube rail was conceptualized. Then in the definition phase, three things were to be defined—goal, scope, and strategy.

Next, in the planning phase, a feasibility study for preparation of the entire road map and estimation of time and resources for the metro rail project was completed. The scheduling phase started with the sequencing of various activities for the completion of the metro rail. It also provided feasible start and completion dates and allocated time and budget for each activity. However, the project exceeded the allotted budget due to various reasons. These reasons could be monitored in the control phase of the project management. Finally, the people of Kolkata could avail the benefits of the metro rail. This was the termination phase.

2.2 PROJECT SCHEDULING PROCESS

In this section, we will discuss the basic concept of project (activity) network, the development of work breakdown and organizational breakdown structures, the network representation of activities and events, and the Gantt chart.

2.2.1 Activity Networks

Various interrelated activities together comprise a project. Every activity or task, with exception of dummies, is performed within a limited period of time and resources. Resources may consist of various elements such as capital, human resource, power, machinery, raw material, etc. at any point in time. A completion of a certain activity is called an event.

The various interrelated activities of a project may happen simultaneously or following one another. The latter comes under the category of precedence relationships. A zero time lag between the end of an activity and the starting of another is considered the best precedence relationship. Gantt chart (Clark 1954), line of balance (Lumsden 1968), and track planning (Herroelen et al. 1998) are the other methods of representing a project network, apart from precedence relationship. Graph representation is another way of showing various activities, events, and their respective precedence relationship.

The different activities and events of a project form its project network, represented as a graph that involves a set of nodes (N) and arcs of arrows (A). Thus, a project network can be represented by

1. *The activity-on-arc or activity-on-arrow (AOA)*—In this mode, activities are represented by a set of arcs or arrows marked A, and events by a set of nodes marked N.

2. *The activity-on-node (AON)*—In this mode, activities are represented by a set of nodes marked N, and the precedence relations by a set of arc or arrows marked A.

AOA networks

The drawing of the network, which is termed as network design, comprises of diagrammatic expressions of the sequential relationship between various activities. This is also known as activity-on-arrow (AOA) diagram. An activity is represented as shown in Figure 2.1. It is usually denoted by arrows and circles and is called the events or nodes of the beginning and the end of an activity.

There are some network diagrams where the activity is represented through a node and an arrow only shows the sequential relationship between the two activities. These are called activity-on-node (AON) diagrams. We will first discuss AOA network.

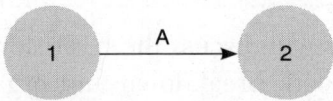

FIGURE 2.1   AOA network

The following example will clarify the difference between an event and an activity.

Activity

Machine installation (activity A)

Event

Start machine installation (event 1)

Completion of machine installation (event 2)

If two activities A and B are carried out in succession (B is started only after A is completed), it is known as a series relationship (Figure 2.2). Here A is the immediate predecessor of B. If A and B can be done simultaneously, it is known as a parallel relationship (shown in Figure 2.3). In both cases, 1, 2, and 3 are the nodes or events.

FIGURE 2.2　Series relationship

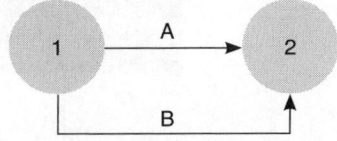

FIGURE 2.3　Parallel relationship

These series and parallel networks are the only two basic relationships used in the generally practised networks. However, if relationships which are not simply series or parallel (as shown below) are to be expressed, they cannot be expressed as in Figure 2.4 because P is not dependent on the completion of M. In such a case, the help of a fictitious or dummy activity is taken. A dummy consumes no time or resources. This relationship is shown in Figure 2.5.

Activity	Immediate predecessor
M	–
N	–
O	M, N
P	N

FIGURE 2.4　AOA network without a dummy activity

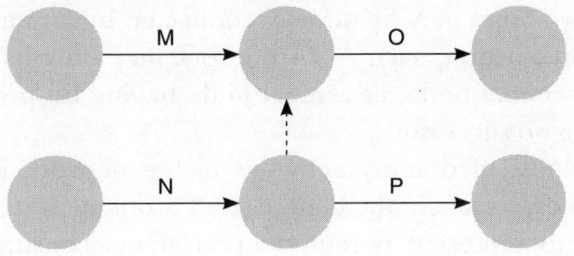

FIGURE 2.5　Use of a dummy activity (broken arrow)

The length of the arrow does not signify the duration of the activity. The importance of an arrow, instead of just a line, can be explained very well by using dummies. For instance, if the direction of the dummy in Figure 2.5 is reversed, we get a diagram, shown in Figure 2.6, which has an entirely different predecessor relationship.

Activity	Immediate predecessor
M	–
N	–
O	M
P	M, N

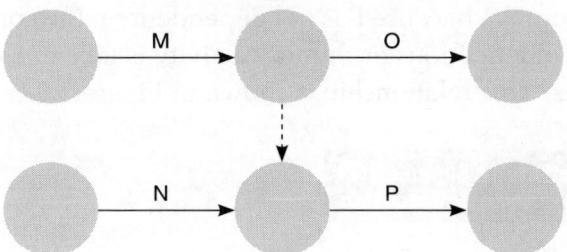

FIGURE 2.6   Change predecessor relationship

Moder et al, in 1983, outlined the key features of an AOA network as
1. An activity can only start if all its predecessor activities are completed.
2. An arrow implies only logical precedence. Neither its length nor its compass direction on the drawings has any significance.
3. Nodes are usually numbered in such a way that no event is duplicated.
4. For computer computation, an activity is defined by its start and end note. But any two notes may be directly connected by no more than one activity.
5. By construction, each AOA network may only have one initial node and only one terminal node, i.e., initial node having no predecessor and terminal node having no successor.
6. Usefulness of dummy activities in the network is to preserve uniqueness of activities, to satisfy the condition of a unique initial and terminal event and to correctly represent all required precedence constraints.
7. Minimizing number of dummy activities. Several algorithms have been developed for constructing AOA network with a minimum number of dummy activities (Corneil 1973).

Example 2.1   Some activities with their immediate predecessors are given in Table E2.1. Draw the corresponding AOA network diagram.

Table E2.1

Activity	Immediate predecessor
P	–
Q	–
R	P
S	P
T	P
U	Q, R
V	R, S, T
W	U
X	V

Solution

If activities R, S, and T are all immediate predecessors of P, then the above relationship can be depicted as in Figure E2.1.

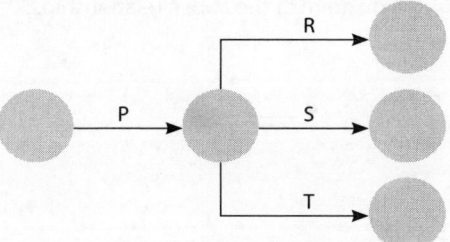

Figure E2.1

Activities U and V have the common activity R. Therefore, the common activity R would be followed by two dummy activities approaching in opposite direction. The exact relationship is shown in Figure E2.2.

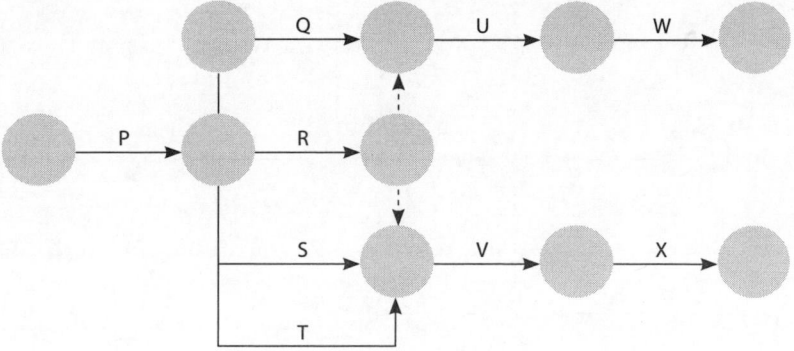

Figure E2.2

Example 2.2   Given the relationship between the listed activities in Table E2.2, draw the corresponding network diagram.

Table E2.2

Activity	Immediate predecessor
P	–
Q	–
R	P, Q
S	–
T	P, S
U	T
V	–
W	V, S
X	–
Y	S, X
Z	Y

Solution

Figure E2.3 depicts the network diagram of the above relationship.

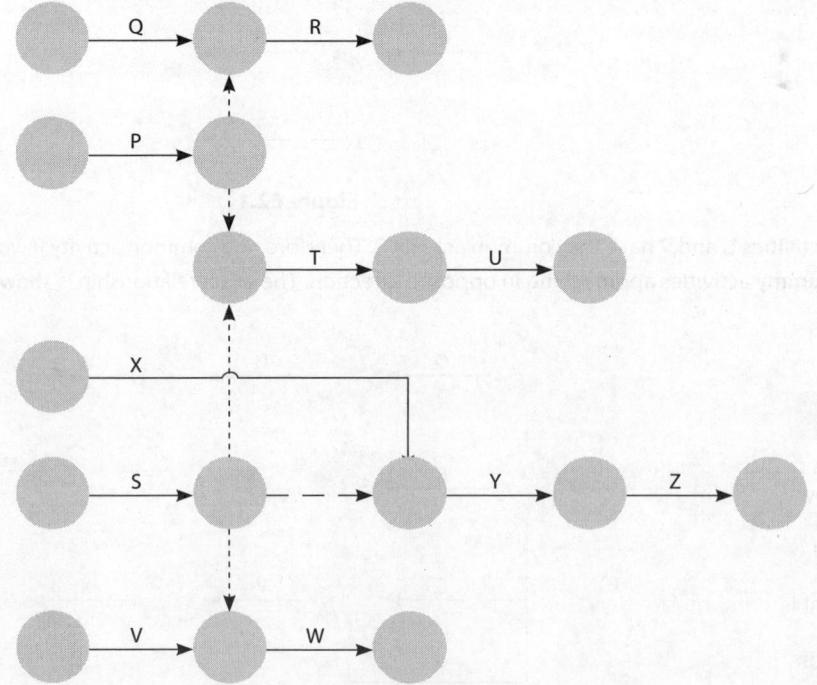

Figure E2.3

Activity-on-node representation

In the activity-on-node (AON) representation, each activity is represented by a node and each event by an arrow. It is a symbolic representation of precedence requirement between two activities. Thus, the AOA diagram (Figure 2.7) would be represented in AON format as shown in Figure 2.8.

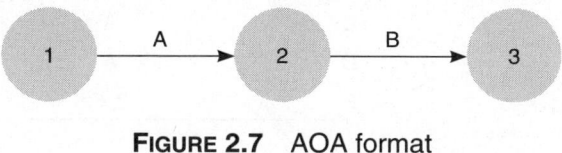

FIGURE 2.7   AOA format

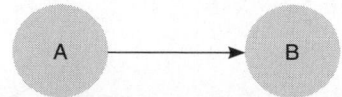

FIGURE 2.8   AON format

In an AON diagram, there is no need for representing events by numbers as in the AOA format. This may be an advantage. The proponents of AON feel that it is a better visual aid because of its closer resemblance to the bar chart. But, in India, AOA is more popular than AON due to its simplicity.

Key features of AON network are

1. In an AON network diagram, each activity is represented by a node.
2. Each event is denoted by a directional arrow which is a symbolic representation of the precedence requirement between two activities.
3. Arrows imply only logical precedence. Neither length nor compass direction on the drawings have any significance.
4. There is no need for representing events by numbers as in the AOA format.
   Table 2.1 Outlines main differences between AOA and AON representations.

TABLE 2.1   The difference between AOA and AON networks

AOA network	AON network
In an AOA network diagram the activity is denoted by an arrow	In an AON network diagram each activity is represented by a node
Nodes are denoted by circles.	Nodes are denoted by arrows.
Each event is numbered	There is no need to number the events.
AOA is more popular and widely used.	It has a better visual aid because of its closer resemblance to the bar chart.

Example 2.3   Draw AOA and AON diagrams for the relationship shown in Table E2.3.

Table E2.3

Activity	Immediate predecessor
A	–
B	–
C	A
D	A
E	B, C

Solution

Figures E2.4 and E2.5 represent AOA and AON networks, respectively.

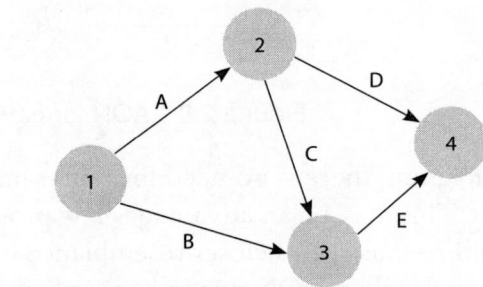

Figure E2.4

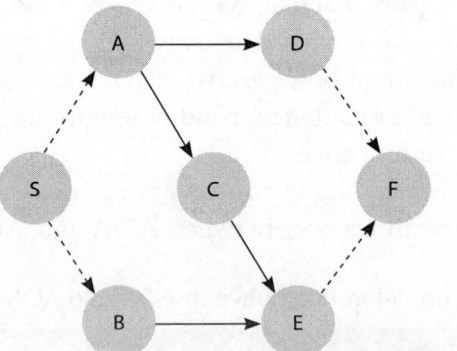

(s–start, f–finish)

Figure E2.5

2.2.2 Work Breakdown Structure

It is important to clearly understand the aim, scope, and strategy of a project before initiating its actual planning and execution processes. For this, a work breakdown structure (WBS) is created. It displays the further sub-divisions of a given project.

The WBS defines the various project sub-activities in relation to the project result. The WBS creates a framework for project control and provides the basis for insight in the time and cost status of a project through various management tools.

Consider the case of the WBS for an institute construction project shown in Figure 2.9. There are five levels in the WBS, and each level is coded. For example, Institute Project is at WBS level zero with code 0. Next, we have three parts at WBS level one—Administrative Block (code A), Academic Block (code B), and Learning Resource Centre Block (Code C). In level two of WBS, there are activities

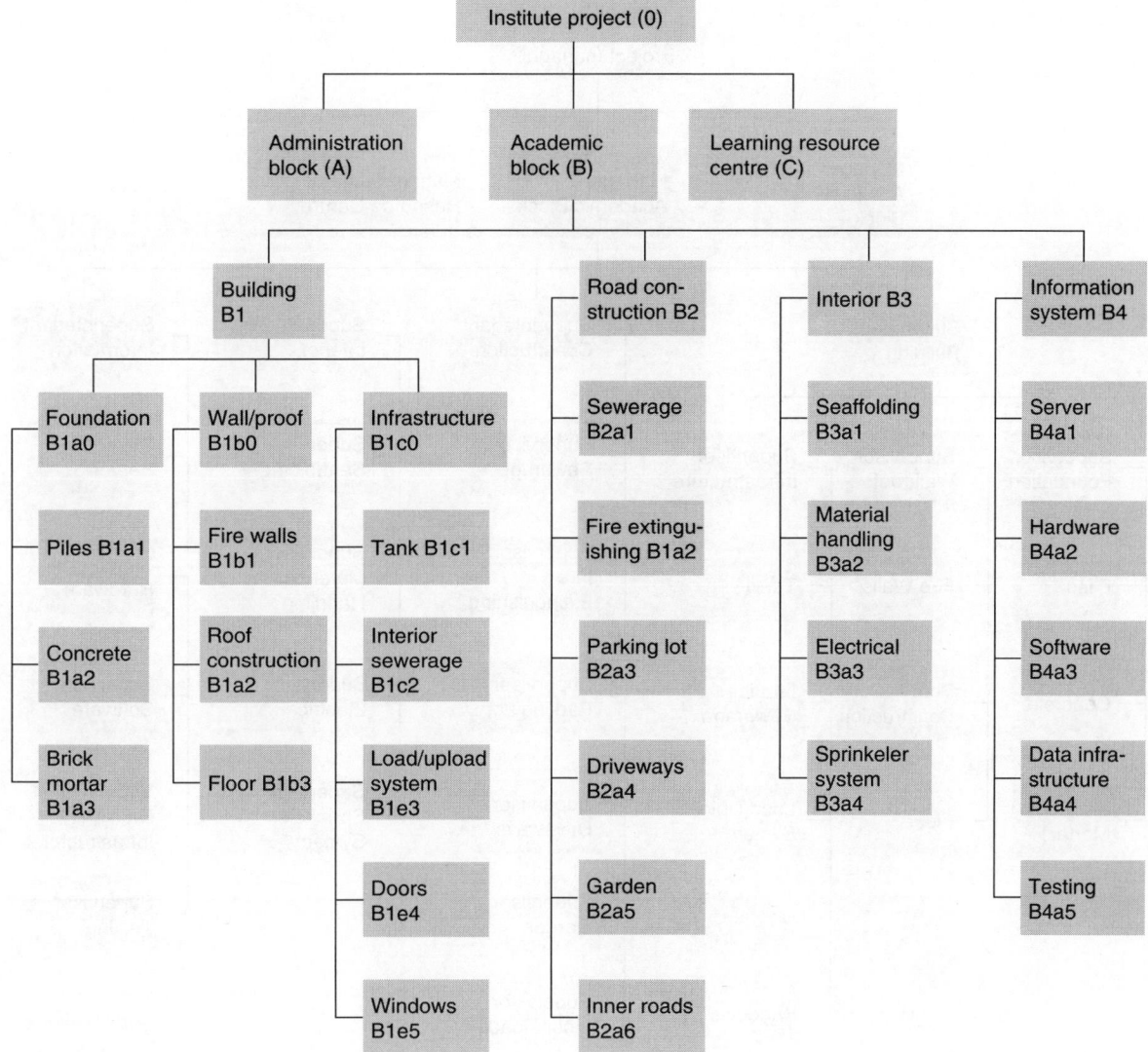

Source: Adapted from Demeulemeester and Herroelen 2002.

FIGURE 2.9   WBS for an institute construction project

with codes B1, B2, B3, and B4. Similarly, at level three, there are elements B1a0, B1b0, etc., and level four has B1a1, B1b1, and so on.

2.2.3 Organization Breakdown Structure

The organization breakdown structure (OBS) is an organizational chart that represents the various constituent units that will work on a given project. The structure links the responsibilities of constituent units to their respective WBS levels. Every unit in WBS finds a unique organizational unit in the OBS with a specific role. Figure 2.10 shows an OBS structure for a construction project.

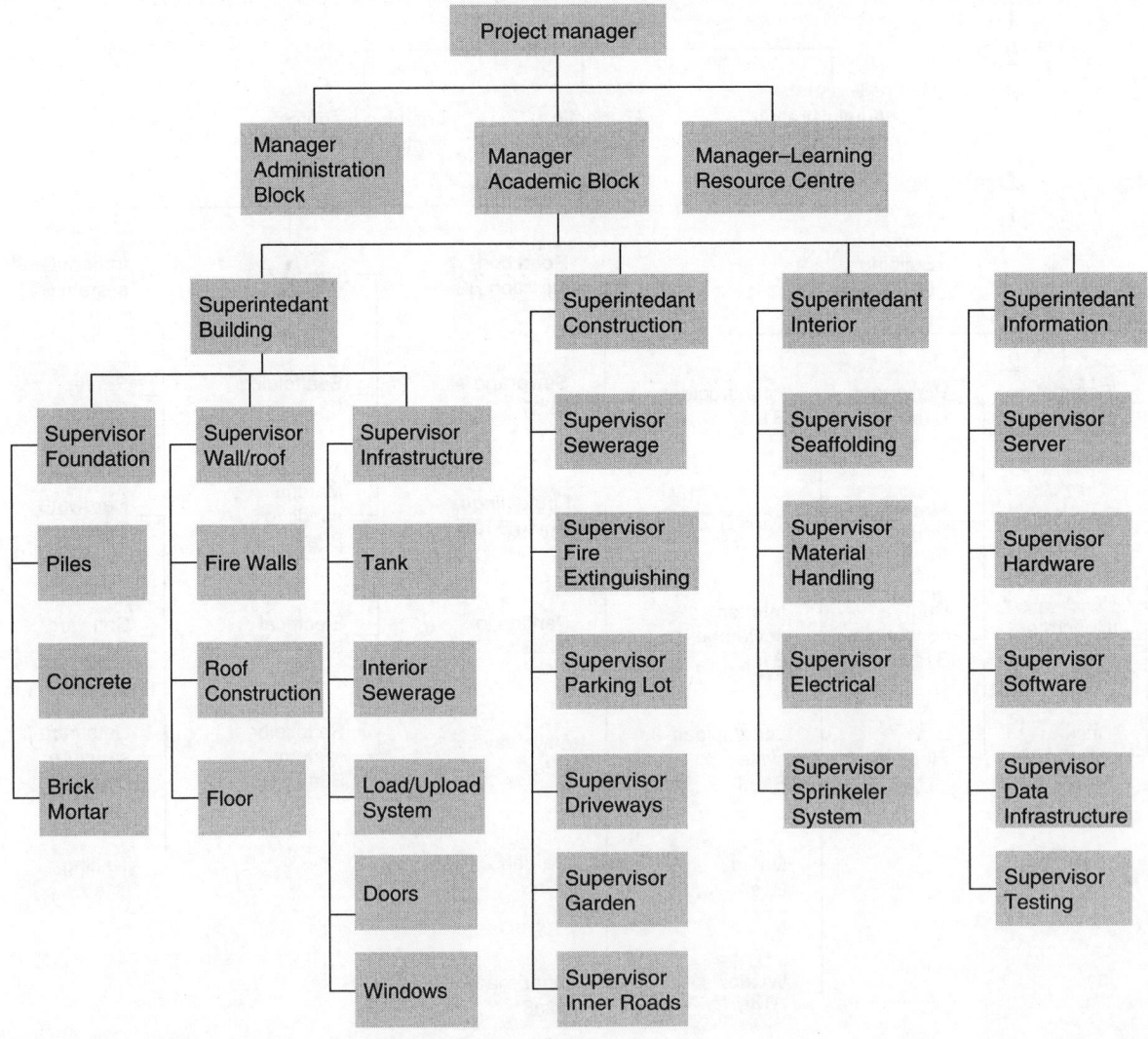

Source: Adapted from Demeulemeester and Herroelen 2002.

FIGURE 2.10 OBS for an institute construction project

2.3 GANTT CHART

The most common type of display is the bar or Gantt chart. It is named after Henry Gantt, who first utilized this procedure in the early 1920s. It is a means of displaying simple activities or events plotted against time. These are commonly used to exhibit programme progress or define specific work required to accomplish an objective. It includes list of activities, activity durations, schedule dates, and progress-to-date. Figure 2.11 shows nine activities required to start up a production line for a new product.

Advantages

1. It is simple to understand and easy to change.
2. It is the simplest and least complex means of portraying progress.
3. It can easily be expanded to identify specific elements that may be either behind or ahead of schedule.

Disadvantages

1. It does not show the interdependencies of the activities, and therefore does not represent a network of activities. For example, it does not explain if the procurement activity (V), in Figure 2.11, requires that the agreement be signed (III) before procurement can begin.
2. It cannot show the result of an early or a late start in activities. How will a slippage of the operation scheduling activity (VIII), in Figure 2.11, affect the completion date of the programme?

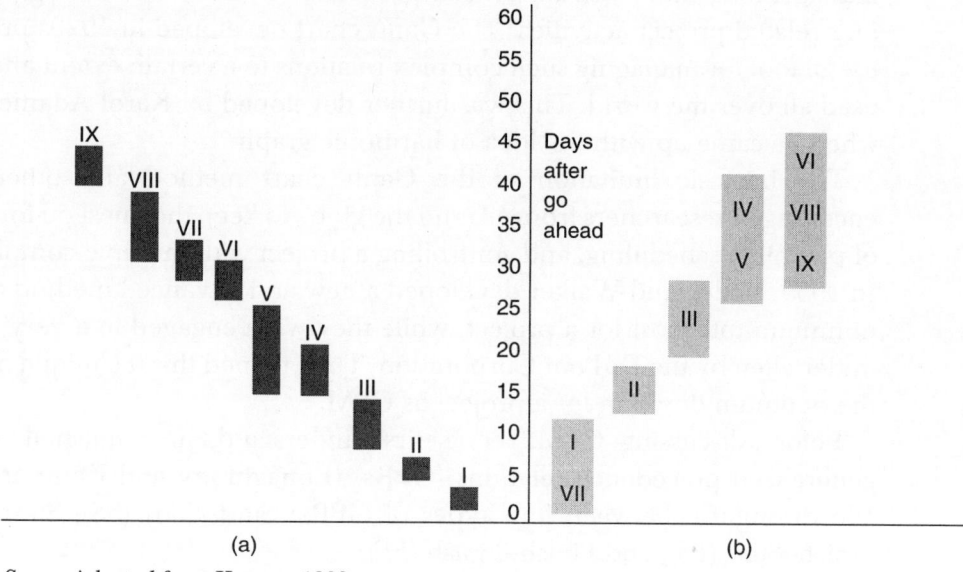

(a)   (b)

Source: Adapted from Kerzner 1992.

FIGURE 2.11   Bar chart activities (a) single (b) combined

3. It does not show the uncertainty involved in performing the activity and, therefore, does not readily admit itself to sensitive analysis. For instance, it can not show the longest time, shortest time, or the average time that an activity might take.

Some of the limitations of the bar chart can be overcome by combining activities as shown in Figure 2.11. For example, activity I and VII, or activity IV and V, or activity VI, VIII, and IX have been combined together.

The activities as illustrated in Figure 2.11(a) and (b) correspond to the list shown in Table 2.2.

TABLE 2.2 List of activities

Activity no.	Activity name	Activity no.	Activity name
I	Tender notification	VI	Receiving of materials
II	Vender selection	VII	Material specifications
III	Agreement signed	VIII	Operation scheduling
IV	Inspection at sight	IX	Start production
V	Procurement		

2.4 CRITICAL PATH METHOD

Till the critical path method (CPM) came into being in the world of project management, there was no official procedure to state and manage the complex interrelated project activities. The Gantt chart developed in 1920s proved to be a useful tool for managing such complex relations to a certain extent and was widely used all over the world. This was further developed by Karol Adameicki in 1931, when he came up with the idea of harmonic graph.

The intrinsic limitation of the Gantt chart method and other techniques encouraged researchers from around the globe to keep the quest on for a better way of planning, scheduling, and controlling a project with multiple complex activities. In 1959, Kelley and Walker developed a new and advanced method of getting the minimum total cost for a project, while they were engaged in a very large project undertaken by the DuPont Corporation. They named this technique of developing the optimum duration for a project as CPM.

Before discussing CPM, let us first understand, in a nutshell, the different generalized precedence relations (GPRs) (Elmaghraby and Kamburowski 1992). We distinguish between four types of GPRs: Start–Start (SS), Start–Finish (SF), Finish–Start (FS), and Finish–Finish (FF).

GPRs represent a minimal or maximal time lag between a pair of activities. A minimal time lag ($SS^{xy}_{min}(a)$, $SF^{xy}_{min}(a)$, $FS^{xy}_{min}(a)$, $FF^{xy}_{min}(a)$) specifies that activity

y can only start (finish) when its predecessor x has already started (finished) for a certain time period, say a time units (Figure 2.12) (Moder et al. 1983). A maximal time lag ($SS^{xy}_{max}(a)$, $SF^{xy}_{max}(a)$, $FS^{xy}_{max}(x)$, $FF^{xy}_{max}(a)$) specifies that activity y should be started (or finished) at the latest possible time period after the start (or finish) of activity x.

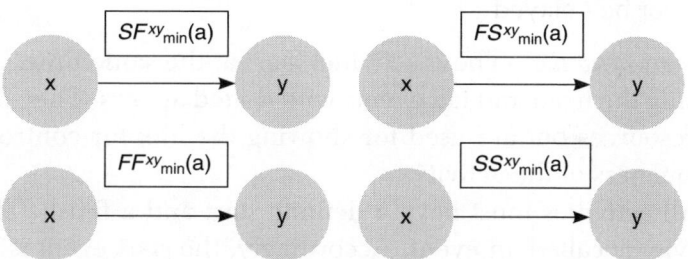

FIGURE 2.12 GPRs with a minimal time lag

GPRs that specify a maximal time lag can be represented by a minimal time lag in the opposite direction. The equivalence between maximal and minimal time lags is shown in Table 2.3.

TABLE 2.3 Equivalence between maximal and minimal time lags

GPRs with maximal time lag	GPRs with minimal time lag
$SS^{xy}_{max}(a)$	$SS^{xy}_{max}(-a)$
$SF^{xy}_{max}(a)$	$SF^{xy}_{max}(-a)$
$FS^{xy}_{max}(a)$	$FS^{xy}_{max}(-a)$
$FF^{xy}_{max}(a)$	$FF^{xy}_{max}(-a)$

CPM is the scheduled technique used to plan, schedule, and control a project consisting of a number of interrelated activities. These techniques provide a frame that defines the job that is to be done, integrates them into a logical sequence, and provides a system of control over the progress of the plan. The CPM procedure, developed by Kelley and Walker, aids in handling a particular problem—the problem that arises when we need the project schedule with minimized total project costs. This is equivalent to the project activity schedule that balances the marginal value of time saved against the marginal cost of saving that time.

2.4.1 Key Aspects of CPM or Other Network Analysis Project

The project to be planned by network technique should consist of clearly specific jobs called activities. Activities are classified as follows.

Critical activities   These activities have the potential to delay the project if they are not completed within their stipulated duration. Therefore, these activities require more attention. These are denoted by thick arrows or double lines.

Non-critical activities   These activities have a provision for float or slack so that even if they consume a specific time over and above the estimated time, the project will not be delayed.

Dummy activities   These activities start at the same time. They are represented by joining the head and tail events with dotted arrows. They do not consume any time or resources but are used for showing the link for controlling or maintaining the uniqueness of the activity.

All activities must have a definite start and a finish. The start and finish of an activity is called an event. Accordingly, the start event is known as tail event and the finish event as head event (Figure 2.13). An event must occur in a definite pattern and must be performed in a technological sequence. Network diagram is a pictorial representation of a project plan showing the interrelationship and interdependencies among the various activities in a sequence in which they are to be performed to complete the project.

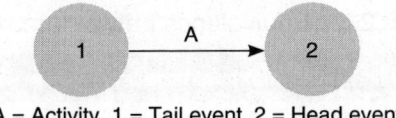

A = Activity, 1 = Tail event, 2 = Head event

FIGURE 2.13   Network diagram

In a sequential project work, operations can be (a) pre-operations, which precede the operation under consideration, (b) post-operations, which succeed the operation under consideration, and (c) concurrent operations, which can be started simultaneously (Table 2.4).
Various times used in CPM are

Earliest start time (EST)   It is the earliest possible time at which an activity can start, and is calculated by moving from first to last event in the network diagram.

Earliest finish time (EFT)   It is the earliest possible time at which an activity can be finished.

EFT = EST + duration of activity

Latest start time (LST)   It is the latest possible time by which an activity can start without delaying the date of completion of project.

LST = LFT – Duration of the activity

Latest finish time (LFT)   It is the latest time by which a project must be completed so that the scheduled date for the completion of the project may not be delayed. It is calculated by moving backward, i.e., from last event to first event of the network diagram.

Float or slack means a margin of extra time over and above its duration which a non-critical activity can consume without delaying the date of the completion of the project.

Float or slack = Time available for completion of the activity – Time necessary
to complete the same

Slack is used with PERT and float with CPM, but in general practice they can
be used interchangeably.

Critical path is formed by a chain of activities that do not have any float, i.e., their earliest and latest finish time is the same. The net project duration, or the maximum project duration, is estimated using the sequence of events represented by the critical path. This path demands close monitoring, as to reduce the net duration of a project, the duration of its various constituent activities (denoted by the critical path) have to be reduced (refer to Table 2.4 and the network diagram in Figure 2.14).

TABLE 2.4   Activity details

Activity	Duration (days)	Pre-operation	Post-operation	Concurrent operation
A	5	None	C	A and B
B	3	None	D	
C	4	A	E	C and D
D	2	B	E	
E	5	C, D	None	None

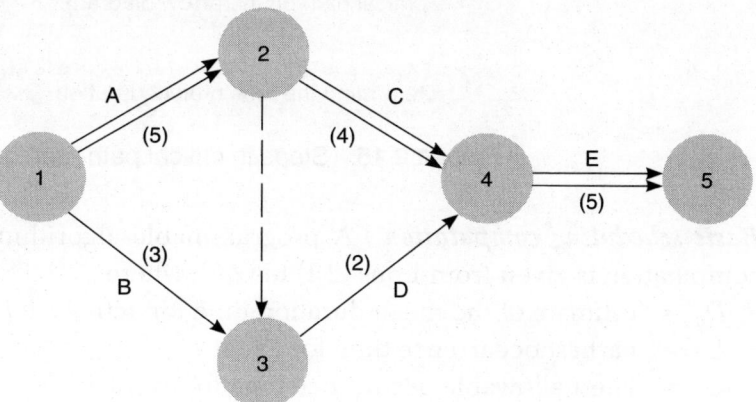

FIGURE 2.14   Critical path (A, C, E)

In Figure 2.14, the longest path is A–C–E, which consumes the maximum time, i.e., 14 days. Other paths, like B–D–E, consume 10 days, whereas, A–D–E consumes 12 days. Hence, the total project duration will be 14 days. Activities A, C, and E are critical activities and have zero float. Activities B and D are non-critical activities, and activity 2–3 is a dummy activity (dotted arrow). Steps of critical path method are given in Figure 2.15.

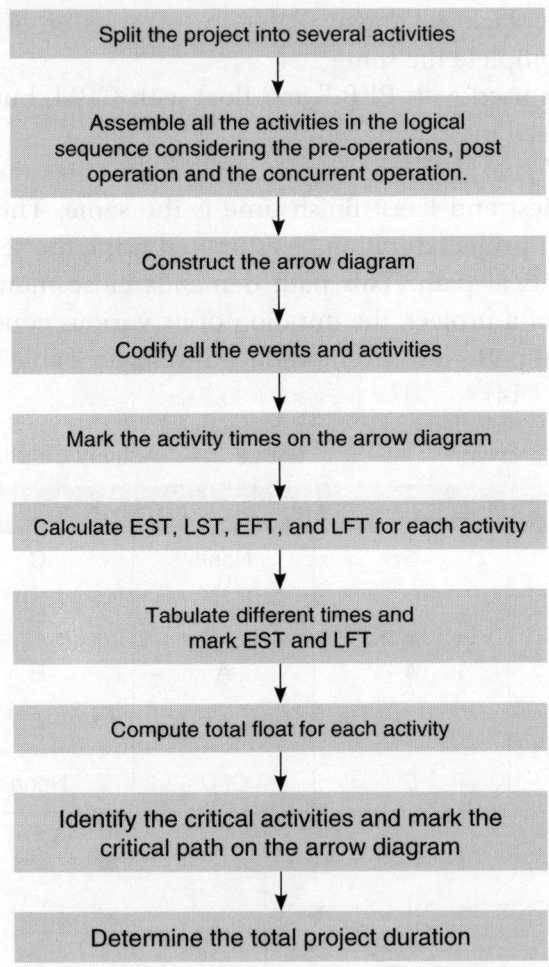

Split the project into several activities

Assemble all the activities in the logical sequence considering the pre-operations, post operation and the concurrent operation.

Construct the arrow diagram

Codify all the events and activities

Mark the activity times on the arrow diagram

Calculate EST, LST, EFT, and LFT for each activity

Tabulate different times and mark EST and LFT

Compute total float for each activity

Identify the critical activities and mark the critical path on the arrow diagram

Determine the total project duration

FIGURE 2.15 Steps in critical path method

Basic scheduling computation A programmable algorithm for basic scheduling computation is given from Eqns (2.1) to (2.7), where

D_{ij} = estimate of the mean duration time for activity i–j

E_i = earliest occurrence time for event i

L_i = latest allowable occurrence time for event i

ES_{ij} = earliest start time for activity $i–j$
EF_{ij} = earliest finish time for activity $i–j$
LS_{ij} = latest allowable start time for activity $i–j$
LF_{ij} = latest allowable finish time for activity $i–j$
S_{ij} = total slack (or float time) for activity $i–j$
FS_{ij} = free slack (or float time) for activity $i–j$
T_s = scheduled time for the completion of project or the occurrence of certain key events in the project

Earliest and latest event times Assume that the events are numbered (or renumbered by a simple algorithm) so that the initial event is 1, the terminal event is t, and all other events $(i – j)$ are numbered so that $i < j$. Now, let $E_1 = 0$ by assumption, then

$$E_j = \max_i (E_i + D_{ij}) \; 2 \le j \le t \tag{2.1}$$

E_t = (expected) project duration, and

$L_i = E_t$ or T_s, the scheduled project completion time.

Then, $L_i = \min_j (L_i – D_{ij}) \; 1 \le i \le t – 1$ $\tag{2.2}$

Earliest and latest activity start and finish times and slack

$$ES_{ij} = E_i \tag{2.3}$$

$$EF_{ij} = E_i + D_{ij} \tag{2.4}$$

$$LF_{ij} = L_j \tag{2.5}$$

$$LS_{ij} = L_j – D_{ij} \tag{2.6}$$

$$S_{ij} = L_j – EF_{ij} \tag{2.7}$$

The above equations embody two basic sets of calculations which are discussed in the next point.

Forward pass and backward pass The forward pass calculations are carried out to determine the earliest occurrence time for each event j (E_j), and the earliest start and finish times for each activity $i–j$ $(ES_{ij}$ and $EF_{ij})$. These calculations are based on the assumption that the activities are conducted as early as possible, that is, they are started as soon as their predecessor events occur. Since these calculations are initiated by equating the initial project events to time zero $(E_1 = 0)$, the earliest time computed for the project terminal (E_t) gives the expected project duration.

The latest (allowable) occurrence time for each event i (L_i), and the latest (allowable) start and finish times for each activity j $(LS_{ij}$ and $LF_{ij})$ are estimated through this set of calculations. Starting at the project end, the backward pass calculation equates the latest (allowable) occurrence time to scheduled project duration. $L = T_s$, if any duration is mentioned, otherwise $(L_t – E_t)$.

This is referred to as a 'zero slack' convention. This calculation then is processed by working backwards through the network, always assuming that each activity is conducted as late as possible.

To facilitate these hand calculations, 'all times will be assumed as the end of times'. Thus, the initial activities, that is, those without predecessors, will have an early start time of zero. This represents the scheduled calendar date for the project start. A start time of zero means end of the day zero, which is the same as the start of day one.

2.4.2 Some Important Definitions

Some other definitions/concepts related to CPM are as follows.

Date convention Activity start time denotes the beginning of the day (or other time period) corresponding to the finish date of the activity.

Again, to simplify calculation, all times will be assumed to be end times. Hence, for an activity, start time of t means the end of working day t or the beginning of the working day $t+1$. For example, an activity start time on Friday means 5 p.m. of Friday or 10 a.m. of the following Monday (assuming 5 working days per week).

Activity float The float values of various network activities, such as total float, safety float, etc., can be calculated by forward and backward computation.

Total float The total float (total slack) of activity j, TS_j, is defined as:

$$TS_j = LST_j - EST_j = LFT_j - EFT_j \tag{2.8}$$

If the earliest possible and the latest allowable start times of a single-end node of the network are equal, the total float indicates the time and activity that can be delayed without delaying the project.

Free float The free float (safety slack) of activity FSj, can be computed as:

$$FS_j = \min\{EST_j\} - EFT_j \tag{2.9}$$

The free float defines the allowable delay in the activity finish time without affecting the possible start time of its immediate successors.

Safety float The safety float (safety slack) of activity j, SSj, is computed as:

$$SS_j = LST_j - \max\{LFT_j\} \tag{2.10}$$

The safety float of activity j represents the number of periods by which the given activity may be prolonged when all its predecessors would start.

Example 2.4 A project schedule has the following characteristics. Refer to Table E2.4.

Table E2.4

Activity	Description	Duration in days
A (1–2)	Start earth work	3
B (1–4)	Vendor selection	2
C (1–7)	Start handling	1
D (2–3)	Continue earth work	3
E (3–6)	Finish earth work	2
F (4–5)	Ordering raw material	4
G (4–8)	Excavation for drains	6
H (5–6)	Receiving raw material	5
I (6–9)	Base concreting	4
J (7–8)	Continue handling	4
K (8–9)	Laying drains	5

Draw the network diagram and trace the critical path of the network. What are the various time estimates and the total duration of the above project?

Solution

EST (earliest start time) is calculated by preceding in the forward pass from the first event to the last event. It is calculated by starting from activity A, i.e., from event 1 where time given is zero.

Now, $EST_A = 0$, $EST_B = 0$, $EST_C = 0$,

$EST_D = EST_A + \text{Duration}_A = 0 + 3 = 3$

$EST_E = EST_D + \text{Duration}_D = 3 + 3 = 6$

Similarly, ESTs of other activities can be calculated.

$EST_F = 2$, $EST_G = 2$, $EST_H = 6$, $EST_I = 11$, $EST_J = 1$, $EST_K = 8$

Paths that can be possible—either A–D–E–I (12 days), B–F–H–I (15 days), B–F–G–K (13 days), or C–J–K (10 days). Out of these, B–F–H–I will be of the longest duration and hence it will be the critical path. Therefore, total project duration will be 15 days.

LFT is calculated in a manner similar to EST but in the backward pass, i.e., by proceeding backward from the last event to the first event. Therefore, $LFT_I = $ total project duration $- \text{Duration}_I = 15 - 4 = 11$.

$LFT_J = \text{Duration of the project} - \text{Duration}_K = 15 - 5 = 10$

$LFT_C = LFT_J - \text{Duration}_J = 10 - 4 = 6$

LST is calculated by the relation $LST = LFT - \text{Duration of that activity}$.
For example, $LST_C = LFT_C - \text{Duration}_C = 6 - 1 = 5$

EFT is calculated by the relation $EFT = EST +$ Duration of that activity.
For example, $EFT_D = EST_D + \text{Duration}_D = 3 + 3 = 6$

Similarly, other LFTs, LSTs, and EFTs will be calculated accordingly.

Total float $= LST – EST$ or $LFT – EFT$
For example, Float$_B = 0 – 0$ or $2 – 2 = 0$ (critical activity) and Float$_D = 6 – 3$ or $9 – 6 = 3$ (non-critical activity).

Table E2.5 shows the different estimated time and Figure E2.5 shows the required network diagram for Example 2.4.

Table E2.5

Activity	Duration	EST	LST	EFT	LFT	Total float	Remarks
A (1–2)	3	0	3	3	6	3	–
B (1–4)	2	0	0	2	2	0	Critical
C (1–7)	1	0	5	1	6	5	–
D (2–3)	3	3	6	6	9	3	–
E (3–6)	2	6	9	8	11	3	–
F (4–5)	4	2	2	6	6	0	Critical
G (4–8)	6	2	4	8	10	2	–
H (5–6)	5	6	6	11	11	0	Critical
I (6–9)	4	11	11	15	15	0	Critical
J (7–8)	4	1	6	5	10	5	–
K (8–9)	5	8	8	13	15	2	–

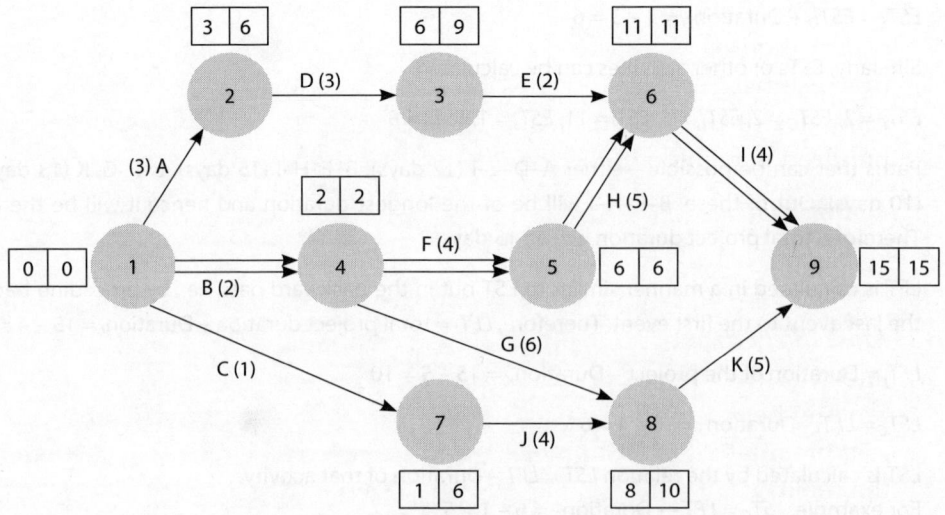

Figure E2.5

2.5 PROGRAMME EVALUATION AND REVIEW TECHNIQUE

Programme evaluation and review technique (PERT) is actually an R&D planning tool and it is used where activity timings cannot be estimated with enough certainty. It can be implemented at those places where a project cannot be easily defined in terms of time and resources required.

One of the major concerns in the development of PERT was to keep the key milestones event on schedule. Because of this event orientation, the activity levels were placed inside the event symbols. These conventions do not have any major difference from the networking procedures described above. The difference arises due to the uncertainty of estimated timings that may or may not be the same as the original plan of timing.

PERT can be applied in the following cases:

- Long-range planning
- Marketing promotional programme
- R&D projects
- Defence projects
- Installation of machinery
- Construction programmes
- Instituting inventory control
- Designing manufacturing prototype products

2.5.1 Three Time Estimates of PERT

In the PERT approach, the actual activity performance time t is assumed to have a hypothetical probability distribution with mean t_e, and variance σ_t^2. It is referred to as deterministic or probabilistic because it is estimated, based on some actual observations, i.e., through sampling of prior work experience. There are three time estimates in PERT called optimistic (a), most likely (m), and pessimistic (b) estimates of time. Statistically, these are the zero percentile, the mode, and the hundred percentile of the hypothetical probability distribution.

Optimistic time   It is the shortest possible time in which an activity can be completed considering that everything goes exceptionally well. It has low probability of occurrence.

Most likely time   It is the most likely time required to complete the activity taking into consideration all favourable and unfavourable conditions. These estimates of time lie between optimistic a time and pessimistic b time. Hence, it is considered as a pragmatic sense of time estimation, which would be to some extent similar to the reality.

Pessimistic time   It is the time which an activity will take to complete if everything turns out against expectation, i.e., in adverse conditions. It is the longest possible time to complete the project. Similar to optimistic, it too has also low probability of occurrence.

A rule of thumb in statistics is that standard deviation can be estimated roughly as one-sixth of the range of the distribution. This follows from the fact that 89 per cent of the distribution lies within three standard deviations from the mean, and for the normal distribution the percentage is more than 99.7. Thus, the estimate of the variance is given by (as shown in Eqn (2.11)).

$$\text{Variance of } t = \sigma_t^2 = [(b - a) / 6]^2 \tag{2.11}$$

The more the uncertainty in estimated time, the more will be the difference in optimistic and pessimistic time. The high value of σ_t represents the high degree of uncertainty regarding the activity times.

To derive an estimate of mean, an assumption of the shape of the probability distribution of t in the development of PERT is required. It is assumed that a plausible (and mathematically convenient) distribution for t is the beta distribution whose standard deviation is one-sixth of its range. For this distribution, Eqn (2.12) gives a linear approximation of the true (cubic) relationship between the mean t_e and the mode m (refer to Figure 2.16):

$$\text{Expected time} = t = t_e = (a + 4m + b) / 6 \tag{2.12}$$

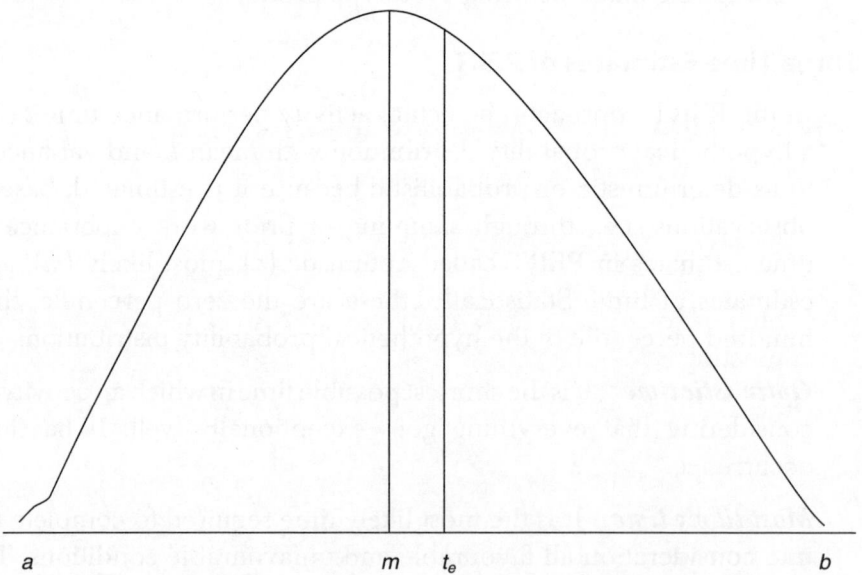

FIGURE 2.16   PERT estimated time distribution

2.5.2 PERT Probability Calculation

At this point, scheduling computation can be carried out using the mean values calculated from Eqn (2.14) for each activity. There is a strong simplified assumption in PERT procedures. It considers activities only on the critical paths through the networks and ignores all others. If there are several critical paths through the network, then the one with the largest variance is chosen to represent the network. Assuming the actual activity performance times for these activities to be independent random variables with mean t_{ei} and σ_{ti}^2, the statistical probability for the project duration directly follow the central limit theorem.

Assuming the critical path consisting of n activities and denoting the sum of their actual durations by T, this can be written as:

$$T = \sum_{i=1}^{n} t_1 \qquad (2.13)$$

$$\text{Mean of } t = T_e = \sum_{i=1}^{n} t_{ei} \qquad (2.14)$$

$$\text{Variance of } T = \sigma_t^2 = \sum_{i=1}^{n} \sigma_{ti}^2 \qquad (2.15)$$

Shape of distribution of T = normal probability of meeting schedule T_s

$$= P\{T \le T_s\} = P\left\{Z \le \frac{T_s - T_e}{\sigma_T}\right\} \qquad (2.16)$$

where Z has normal distribution with zero mean and unit variance, so that the last probability is read from the standard table of the cumulative normal distribution. Steps of PERT are provided in Figure 2.17.

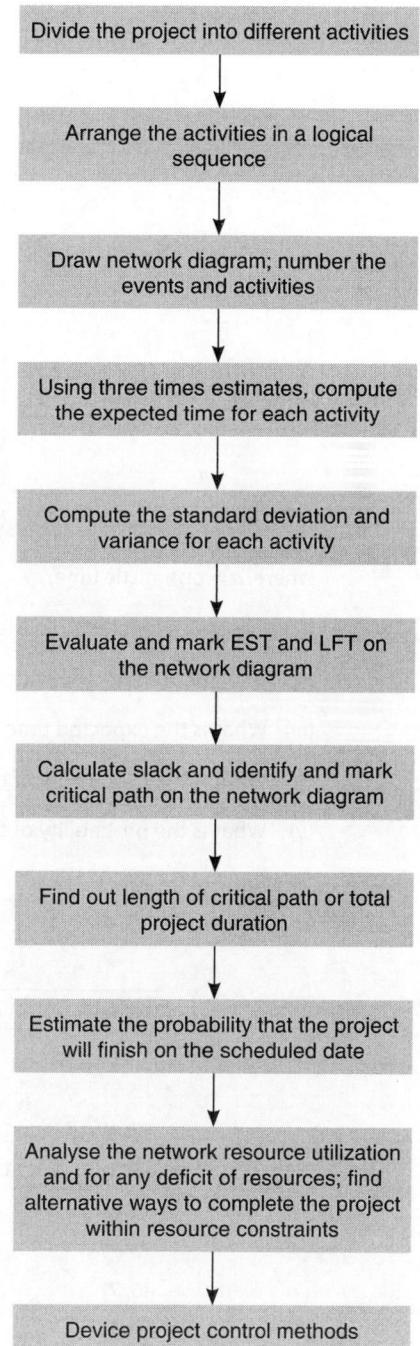

Divide the project into different activities

Arrange the activities in a logical sequence

Draw network diagram; number the events and activities

Using three times estimates, compute the expected time for each activity

Compute the standard deviation and variance for each activity

Evaluate and mark EST and LFT on the network diagram

Calculate slack and identify and mark critical path on the network diagram

Find out length of critical path or total project duration

Estimate the probability that the project will finish on the scheduled date

Analyse the network resource utilization and for any deficit of resources; find alternative ways to complete the project within resource constraints

Device project control methods

FIGURE 2.17   Steps in PERT

Example 2.5   In an assembly line production, time estimate for the activities are as shown in Table E2.6 (per time estimates are given in weeks)

Table E2.6

Activity	a	m	b
(1, 2)	7	11	13
(2, 3)	1	4	7
(2, 4)	10	15	48
(3, 5)	12	20	26
(3, 6)	4	7	16
(3, 7)	4	7	16
(6, 7)	5	8	11
(4, 7)	2	8	14
(7, 8)	9	12	15
(8, 9)	1	4	7

where, a = optimistic time, m = most likely time, b = pessimistic time

(i)   Find the expected time, standard deviation, and variance for each activity.

(ii)   Find the standard deviation and expected time for each event.

(iii) What is the expected time of completion of the project?

(iv)   What is the probability of completing the project in 34 weeks?

(v)   What is the probability of the event 7 being completed in the twentieth week?

Solution

(i)

Table E2.7

Activity	a	m	b	te	SD	Variance
(1, 2)	7	11	13	10.66667	1	1
(2, 3)	1	4	7	4	1	1
(2, 4)	10	15	48	19.66667	6.333333	40.11111
(3, 5)	12	20	26	19.66667	2.333333	5.444444
(3, 6)	4	7	16	8	2	4
(3, 7)	4	7	16	8	2	4
(6, 7)	5	8	11	8	1	1
(4, 7)	2	8	14	8	2	4
(7, 8)	9	12	15	12	1	1
(8, 9)	1	4	7	4	1	1

t_e = expected or mean time = $(a + 4m + b) / 6$, SD = $(b - a) / 6$, Variance = SD^2

(ii)

Table E2.8

Event	Longest path to the event	Expected time	Variance	SD (weeks)
1				
2	1–2	10.66667	1	1
3	1–2–3	14.6667	2	1.414
4	1–2–4	30.33334	41.1111	6.4111
5	1–2–3–5	34.33334	7.44	2.72
6	1–2–3–6	22.66667	6	2.4494
7	1–2–3–7	22.66667	6	2.4494
8	1–2–3–7–8	34.66667	7	2.6457
9	1–2–3–7–8–9	38.66667	8	2.8284

(iii) The expected time of completion of project is Σt_e in the longest path (1–2–3–7–8–9) is 38.66667 = 39 weeks (approx.).

(iv) The probability of the project being completed in 56 weeks for the longest path (1–2–3–7–8–9) is given by

$$Z = \frac{x - \mu}{\sigma}$$

where, x is the given no. of weeks = 34, μ is the mean time = 39 and σ is the standard deviation of the longest path = 2.8284 = 3 (approx.)

$$Z = \frac{34 - 39}{3} = -1.66667$$

Therefore, from standard normal distribution tables,

Probability = 0.5 – 0.4525 = 0.0475 i.e. 4.75 %

(v) The probability of event 7 to be completed in the twentieth week:

Mean time (1–2–3–7) = 22.67 weeks, i.e., 23 weeks, SD (1–2–3–7) = 2.4494 weeks

Therefore, $Z = \frac{x - \mu}{\sigma} = (20 - 23) / 2.4494 = -1.223$

Therefore, probability = 0.5 – 0.3907 = 0.1093, i.e., 10.93 %

Example 2.6   Table E2.9 gives the activities in a construction project and other related information (per time estimates are given in days).

Table E2.9

Activity	a	m	b
(1, 2)	19	29	45
(1, 3)	8	11	20
(2, 3)	2	4	6
(2, 4)	1	2	3
(3, 4)	1	1	2
(4, 5)	11	17	23

where, a = optimistic time, b = most likely time, c = pessimistic time.

(i)   Draw a PERT diagram

(ii)   Calculate total project duration

(iii) Mark critical path

(iv)   Find the probability that the project will be completed in 50 days

Solution

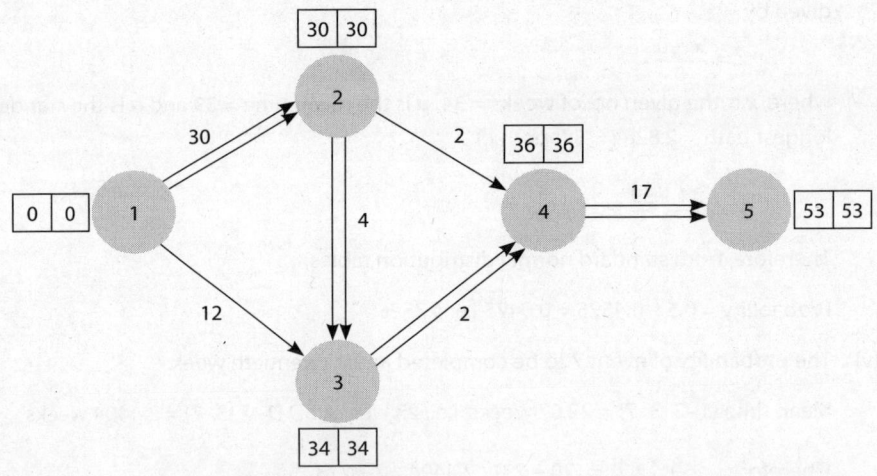

Figure E2.6

Table E2.10

Activity	a	m	b	t_e	Variance
(1,2)	19	29	45	30	18.77778
(1,3)	8	11	20	12	4
(2,3)	2	4	6	4	0.444444
(2,4)	1	2	3	2	0.111111
(3,4)	1	1	2	1.166667	0.027778
(4,5)	11	17	23	17	4

t_e = expected or mean time = $(a + 4m + b) / 6$, SD = $(b - a) / 6$, Variance = SD^2

(i) The total project duration = $\Sigma\, t_e$ in the longest path or the critical path = $30 + 4 + 2 + 17 = 53$ days.

(ii) Critical path will be 1–2–3–4–5 (shown in double arrow in Figure E2.6).

(iii) Expected or mean time = 53 days.

Standard deviation = square root of $(18.77778 + 0.444444 + 0.027778 + 4) = 4.82$ days

The probability that the project will be completed in 50 days

$$Z = \frac{x - \mu}{\sigma} = (50 - 53) / 4.82 = -0.622$$

Therefore, probability = $0.5 - 0.221 = 0.2790$, i.e., 27.9 %

In project scheduling, critical path method is a very well known and widely used technique. But this scheduling has been done on the basis of future estimated time. Since it is based on expected time, there is no certainty that actual time will be as anticipated. In PERT, uncertainty can be incorporated. That is why it gives more accurate results. Table 2.5 discusses the difference between PERT and CPM.

TABLE 2.5   The difference between PERT and CPM

PERT	CPM
It is used when the emphasis is on reducing project execution time without bothering for cost implication.	It is used when the emphasis is on optimizing resource allocation and minimizing overall cost for a given project execution time.
A probabilistic model with uncertainty.	A deterministic model with well-known activity time based on past experience.
Three time estimates (optimistic time, most likely time, and pessimistic time) are used to make allowances for uncertainties.	A single time estimate is used.
An event-oriented technique.	An activity-oriented technique.
The use of dummy activity is required for depicting the proper sequence.	The use of dummy activity is not necessary, making the diagram becomes slightly simpler.
It is suitable in defence projects and R&D, where the activity time cannot be readily predicted.	It is suitable for problems in industrial plant maintenance, civil construction projects, etc.

2.6 CRASHING OF PROJECT NETWORK

Crashing is defined as the shortening of a specific activity. The shortest possible time in which an activity can be realistically completed is called its crash time.

The direct cost to complete an activity in its crash time is called a crash cost. The main concern of a project manager is to choose the activity that is to be shortened and how much it should be shortened. Shortening of a critical activity is highly dependent on the cost factor, i.e., it should be with the smallest possible increase in the cost per unit time.

2.6.1 Guidelines for Network Crashing

The *total project cost* is the sum total of the direct and indirect costs that are related to the project. The direct costs are directly related to the concerned project, such as direct material cost, direct labour cost, etc. The indirect costs are those which are not related directly to the project but without which the project cannot be completed. Examples of indirect cost can be overheads, manager's salary, rent of project office, etc. Thus, with elongation of the project completion time, the total cost of the project increases, mainly due to the increase in the indirect costs rather than the direct costs. Figure 2.18 shows the indirect, direct, and the corresponding total cost curve.

In the total cost curve in Figure 2.18, the optimum time is the point of minimum total cost. The project cost increases with the increase in the project duration beyond optimum time due to the increase in indirect cost. The project cost would increase even if project duration is reduced by using more resources due to increase in direct cost.

The graph depicts the relationship between project cost and its duration. The duration of a project can be shortened by systematic analysis of the critical path activities, crashing cost, and its effect on direct and indirect costs. The time–cost relationship (Figure 2.19) needs to be critically examined to determine the optimum cost (time).

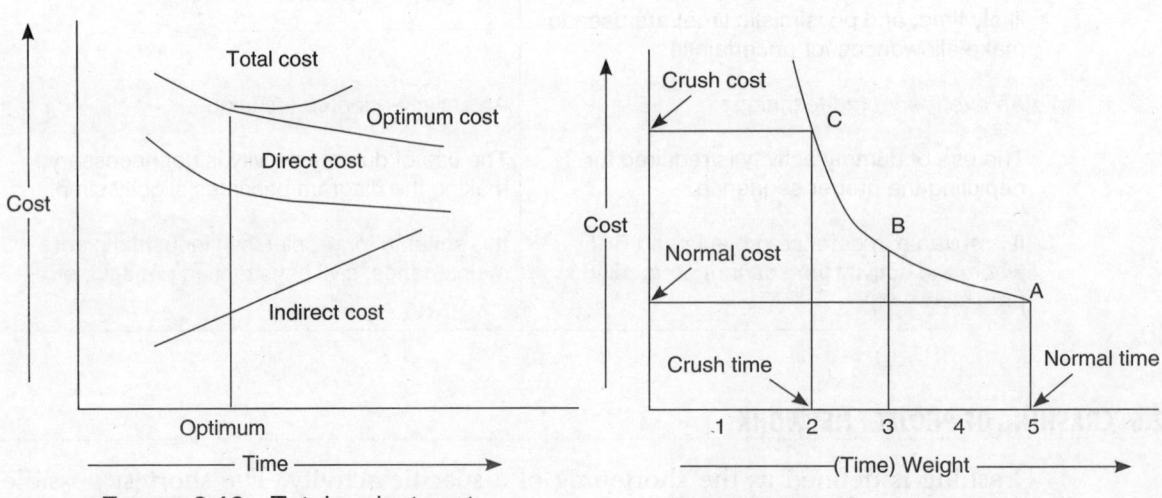

FIGURE 2.18 Total project cost   **FIGURE 2.19** Cost–time trade-off

2.6.2 Crashing of Project Network with Costs Trade-off

The project has the highest correspondence to the cost duration and the nominal cost corresponds to the normal duration. Thus, we have two types of costs and time.

Normal time (N_T)   Normal time is the regular time, related with normal resources of the organization to perform an activity.

Crash time (C_T)   Crash time is the minimum feasible time in which an activity can be completed by employing extra resources. Crash time is that time beyond which the activity cannot be shrunken even if resources are increased.

Normal cost (N_C)   The expenditure incurred on normal resources for completing any activity in normal time is called normal cost.

Crash cost (C_C)   The total expenditure incurred on normal and additional resources for completing any activity in crash time is known as crash cost.

The time–cost relationship is not linear, but the relationship can be approximated by a straight line called the 'cost slope'.

The cost slope formula can be represented as

Cost slope =

$$\frac{\text{Crash cost} - \text{Normal cost}}{\text{Normal time} - \text{Crash time}} = \frac{C_C - N_C}{N_T - C_T} \quad (2.17)$$

Cost slope refers to the additional cost required for decreasing the time limit of an activity by one unit of time. To reduce the duration of an activity, the management may take a decision to incur extra expenditure, but for optimization of the cost, effort is to be made to keep the cost slope at the minimum. Steps of time–cost optimization technique are given in Figure 2.20.

Establish direct cost–time relationships for a variety of activities of the project by analysing past cost records

↓

Determine cost slopes of various activities and arrange them in rising order of cost slope

↓

Compute direct cost for the network and normal duration activities

↓

Crash the activities in the critical path as per ranking, i.e., opening with the critical activity having the lowest slope

↓

Continue crashing the critical activities in the ascending order of slope

↓

Crash parallel non-critical activities that have become critical by the reduction of critical path duration due to crashing in steps 4 and 5

↓

Continue crashing process through steps 4 to 6, till a stage is reached beyond which no further crashing is possible

↓

Find the total cost of project at every step by adding indirect costs to the direct costs determined above

↓

Plot total cost duration curve

↓

Pick up the optimum duration corresponding to which least total project cost is obtained

FIGURE 2.20   Steps in time–cost optimization

Example 2.7   For a network shown in Figure E2.7, normal time, crash time, normal cost, and cash cost are given in Table E2.11. Contract the network by crashing it to its optimum value and calculate the optimum project cost. Indirect cost is given as Rs 100 per day.

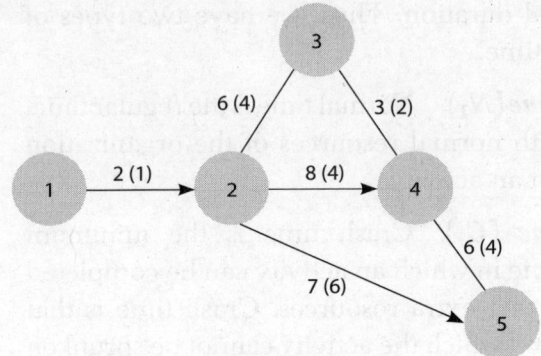

Figure E2.7

Table E2.11

Activity	Normal		Crash	
	Time (days)	Cost (Rs)	Time (days)	Cost (Rs)
(1–2)	2	380	1	400
(2–3)	6	500	4	520
(2–4)	8	2000	4	2500
(2–5)	7	350	6	600
(3–4)	3	350	2	360
(4–5)	6	510	4	520

Solution

From the network diagram (Figure E2.7) the critical path is (1–2–3–4–5) and the project duration is 17 days. To contract the network, in the first stage we must identify those activities on critical path which have cost slopes less than the indirect cost. The slopes are calculated and shown in Table E2.12.

Table E2.12

Activity	Normal		Crash		Crash cost–	Normal time–	Cost
	Time (days)	Cost (Rs)	Time (days)	Cost (Rs)	normal cost	crash time	slope
(1–2)	2	380	1	400	20	1	20
(2–3)	6	500	4	520	20	2	10
(2–4)	8	2000	4	2500	500	4	125
(2–5)	7	350	6	600	250	1	250
(3–4)	3	350	2	360	10	1	10
(4–5)	6	510	4	520	10	2	5

Now for crashing we consider all possible paths in the network and corresponding durations in the tabular form as in Table E2.13.

Table E2.13

Path	Sequence	Target time	Time crashed at various stages		
			(4–5)	(3–4)	(2–3)
p1	(1–2–3–4–5)	17	15	14	12
p2	(1–2–4–5)	16	14	14	14
p3	(1–2–5)	9	9	9	9

Critical path activity (4–5) has least the cost slope. Therefore, crashing the activities (4-5) by two days, project duration will be 17 – 2 = 15 days.

Therefore, Cost of project = Normal cost + Extra crashing cost + Indirect cost

$$= (380 + 500 + 2000 + 350 + 350 + 510) + (2 \times 5) + (15 \times 100) = Rs\ 5600$$

Now in the second stage, crashing the least cost slope activities (2–3) and (3–4) on critical path by two days and one day, respectively, project duration = 15 – 3 = 12 days.

Therefore, Cost of project = Normal cost + Extra crashing cost + Indirect cost

$$= 4090 + (2 \times 10 + 1 \times 10) + 12 \times 100 = Rs\ 5320$$

The total project cost with normal activities (without crashing)

$$= normal\ cost + indirect\ cost\ for\ 17\ days = 4090 + 17 \times 100 = Rs\ 5790.$$

Therefore, the optimum cost of the project is Rs 5320.

2.6.3 Network Cost Control

Network cost control refers to expenditure control as the project progresses in time and execution.

The activity costs and duration are positively associated in an 'enumerative cost model' under network cost control. When different activities receive their share of the project budget, then their respective earliest and latest allowable activity times can be used to plot the cumulative cost versus time curve. The two curves represent the scheduled time for each activity.

The latter one is considered on the target against which progress is measured. This curve is depicted in Figure 2.21 as 'budgeted cost of work scheduled'. Two variances like cost and scheduled variance are defined in Eqns (2.18) and (2.19).

t_0 = Time of update or time now

t_c = Scheduled project completion time

t_f = Forecasted project completion time

$$\text{ACWP} = \text{Actual cost of work in place at } t_0$$

$$\text{BCWS} = \text{Budgeted cost of work scheduled for completion at } t_0$$

$$\text{BCWP} = \text{Budgeted cost of work in place at } t_0$$

Cost variance at $t_0 = (\text{BCWP} - \text{ACWP} / \text{BCWP}) \, 100\%$ (2.18)

Schedule variance at $t_0 = (\text{BCWP} - \text{BCWS}) / \text{BCWP}) \, 100\%$ (2.19)

The net percentage of project cost overrun, up to time t_0, is given by the cost variance. It helps in forecasting the cost of the total project.

The schedule variance helps in differentiating between the calculated and the actual budget cost for the calculation of time position. For instance, if resources are not invested in a given project at the estimated rate, then the project cost exceeds the budget. It is indicated by a negative schedule variance and a positive cost variance.

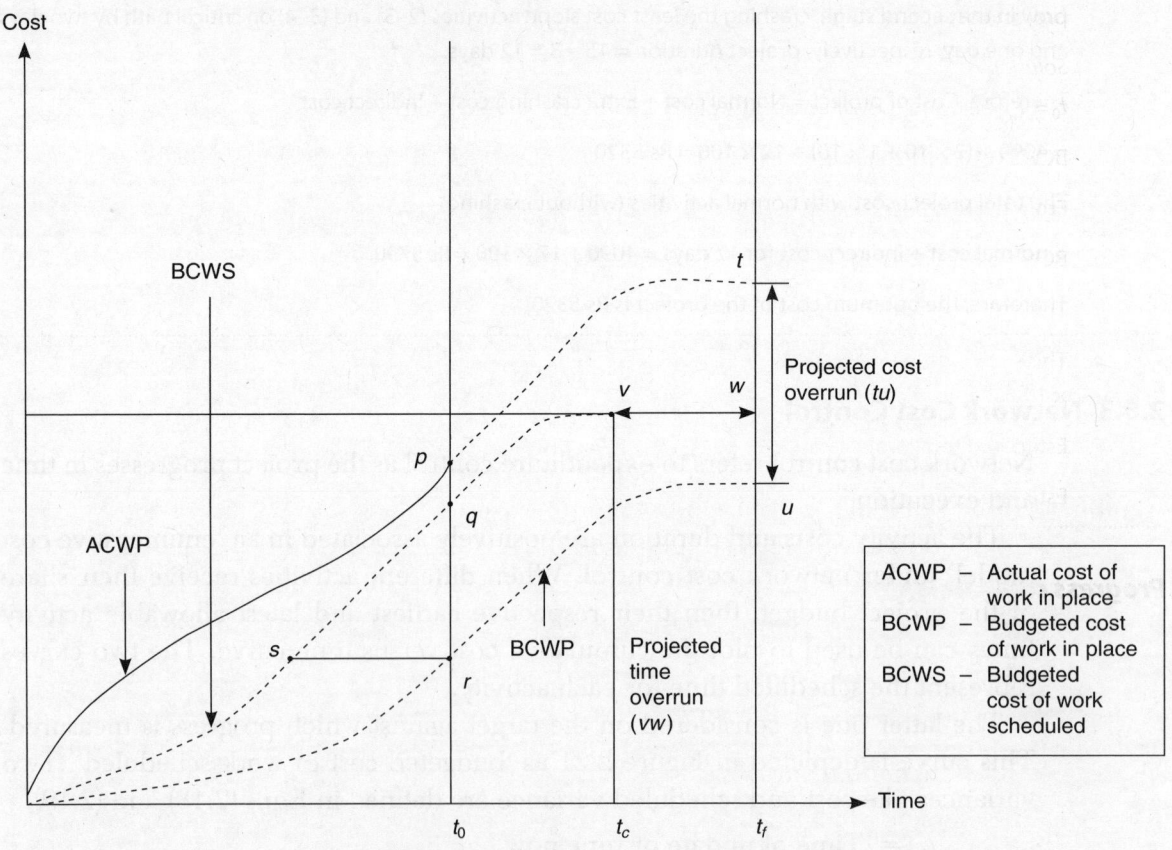

FIGURE 2.21 Project cost versus time curve

This questions the viability of the project in the future. The project is considered desirable if it is under budget and ahead of schedule (i.e., Eqns (2.18) and (2.19) are positive). It is undesirable if it is over budget and behind schedule (i.e., Eqns (2.18) and (2.19) are negative).

Example 2.8 The following example consists of oversimplified settings that involve only one activity rather than the entire network.

Project plan: Construct foundations for 40 identical cube homes in one continuous period.

Schedule plan: Construct 10 foundations per week.

Cost plan: Cost (budget) per each home is Rs 2,000, for a total project cost of Rs 80,000.

Progress report: At the end of one week, 8 foundations have been completed at a total cost of Rs 18,000.

Does this project stand in respect to cost and budget? If the current trend continues, what will be the total project cost and duration?

Solution

$t_0 = 1$ week, and the schedule cost plans, BCWS is computed to be Rs 20,000

BCWS = 10 × Rs 2000 per foundation = Rs 20,000

From the progress report, we determine that ACWP = Rs 18,000 and BCWP = Rs 16,000

BCWP = 8 foundations in places × Rs 2000 per foundation = Rs 16,000

Thus, the cost and schedule variances at $t_0 = 1$ week:

This means, the project is 12.5 % i.e. [(18000 − 16000) / 16000 × 100], over budget and 25 %, i.e. [(10 − 8) / 8 × 100], behind schedule. If this trend continues throughout the project, the following will result:

Estimated total project cost = Rs 80,000 × 1.125 = Rs 90,000

Estimated project duration = 4 weeks × 1.25 = 5 weeks

Progress control signals

Another approach of cost control would be by using value variances. Cost variance and scheduled variance in terms of money are given in Eqns (2.20) and (2.21).

$$\text{Cost variance} = \text{BCWP} - \text{ACWP} \qquad (2.20)$$

$$\text{Schedule variance} = \text{BCWP} - \text{BCWS} \qquad (2.21)$$

Referring to Figure 2.21, the cost variance is the distance between point p and r, which in this case indicates a large negative difference or cost overrun. Similarly, the schedule variance is the distance between point r and q, which is also a large negative difference denoting the time overrun. The time behind can be evaluated approximately by the time difference representing as rs in Figure 2.21.

If the two variances given in Eqns (2.20) and (2.21) are positive, they seem to be good (under budget and ahead of schedule) and if they are negative, they are undesirable (over budget and behind schedule). A powerful set of control signals, suggested by Brown (1985), can be developed by combining this information with the project float on the critical path. The latter can be positive (ahead of schedule) or negative (behind schedule). It can also be denoted as a percentage by dividing the float by the anticipated completion time of the project.

Consider the following definitions for these signals:

C+ Positive cost variance (under budget)
C− Negative cost variance (over budget)
S+ Positive schedule variance (ahead of schedule)
S− Negative schedule variance (behind schedule)
F+ Positive float on the critical path (ahead of schedule)
F− Negative float on the critical path (behind schedule)

The cost variance and schedule variance, expressed in percentages (Eqns (2.18) and (2.19)) or value variances (Eqns (2.20) and (2.21)) are issued at each project updates. They can be used very efficiently and effectively to know the status of the project. C± deals with cost management, F± deals with schedule management of the critical path, and S± deals with schedule management of the entire project and not only for the critical path activities.

For example, (C+, F+, S+) would indicate that project performance is good from all angles, whereas the opposite signal, (C−, S−, F−), might be explained by possible labour problems, budgets and schedules too tight, or just poor overall management. A mixed signal like (C+, S+, F−) might indicate a well-managed project (C+, S+) that needs a recovery plan for the critical path (F−). Similarly, (C+, S−, F+) might indicate a well-managed (C+ and F+) but understaffed project (S−).

There can be another possibility like (C−, F+, S+), which means that the project is an overbudgeted one with running ahead of schedule not only in the critical path but also in the overall project activities. Other possibilities might be (C−, F−, S+), (C+, F−, S−), and (C−, F+, S−). Their meanings are self-explanatory.

2.7 PROJECT SCHEDULING WITH CONSTRAINT RESOURCES

Duration of a project network cannot be scheduled till the required resources have been assigned. A project must face challenging questions, such as are the planned benchmarks feasible? How should the resources be prioritised? Is the supplied manpower enough to handle the task? What can be the critical path? Whether some other ongoing project would have any delaying effect on this one?

Project scheduling system should be well equipped in finding subtle and effective answers to these questions. In reality a project manager could encounter with more grave problems than shortage of resources. It can considerably affect the technical constraints. Resource conflict generally occurs among the activities that are happening parallel to each other. Because of resource constraints it gradually happens that activities that were initially considered as independent are found to be dependent on others as the project progresses.

2.7.1 How to Overcome Resource Constraints

There are many resource constraints. The most important are people, materials, equipment, and working capital.

Resource levelling   There are many activities in a project that require varying levels of resources. In the resource-levelling process, the activities are rescheduled so that the maximum and peak resources requirement does not exceed the limit of available resources. The available resources should not, however, be less than the maximum amount of resources required for any activity of the project. In rescheduling, the available floors are first used. If in doing so, it is seen that the resource demand exceeds the available resources in some activity, the duration of these activities are increased to offset the increase in demand. Thus, by resource levelling, the project duration initially planned might increase.

Resources smoothing   Time allotted and required resource for any activities along with corresponding float, if any, is used for resource smoothing. The periods of maximum demand for resources are allocated and the activities according to their float values are shifted to balance the resource needs and availability. Thus, intelligent utilization of floats smoothen the demand of resources to a great extent. Smoothing techniques delay non-critical activities by using slack, by which they reduce peak demand. Smoothing uses slack to fill in the valleys for increased utilization of resources or reduction of peak demand. Smoothing becomes even more important in a multi-project environment in which a portfolio in a project and resources are classified into skill pools.

Resource allocation   A project is the sum total of a number of interrelated activities. Resources are required to perform each activity. At some point of time, activities may have to be performed simultaneously, requiring common resources, and it may so happen that total requirement of resources exceeds the total available resources. Also, there may be times when the resources are not required to be utilized to the maximum. This being the most important aspect, we will now discuss this in detail.

2.7.2 How to Allocate Resources

Resource allocation is a challenge for project leaders to optimally allocate the available resources to obtain maximum utilization for performing various activities.

PERT and CPM techniques provide valuable guidelines for resource allocation. Slack and float are used to divert resources from non-critical activities to the more critical ones. Resource smoothing and resource levelling techniques are also used. The following are the four major resource allocation scenarios that capture most of the conditions facing project managers. They are also illustrated in Figure 2.22.

1. *Time limited*—These projects have an imposed duration that is considered a must. A time-to-market project is a classic example of time limited (constrained) project. It is assumed that resources will be made available to ensure that the project is completed by deadline. Although time is a critical factor, resource usage should be no more than is necessary and sufficient.

2. *Time is not limited*—In this condition, the project plan duration will be accepted and resources will be made available as and when needed.

3. *Resource limited, but adequate resources*—Resource availability level is limited (fixed). But the resource loading run shows that no resources are over allocated. (Resource loading is the sequence or order in which number of jobs or operations can be assigned to a finite numbers of service facility and accordingly resources are allocated to the assigned job.)

4. *Resource limited and over allocated*—Resource loading run shows that resources are over allocated. Given the limited resources available, the resource conflicts make it impossible to complete the project within the planned time duration.

Steps in resource allocation are depicted in Figure 2.23.

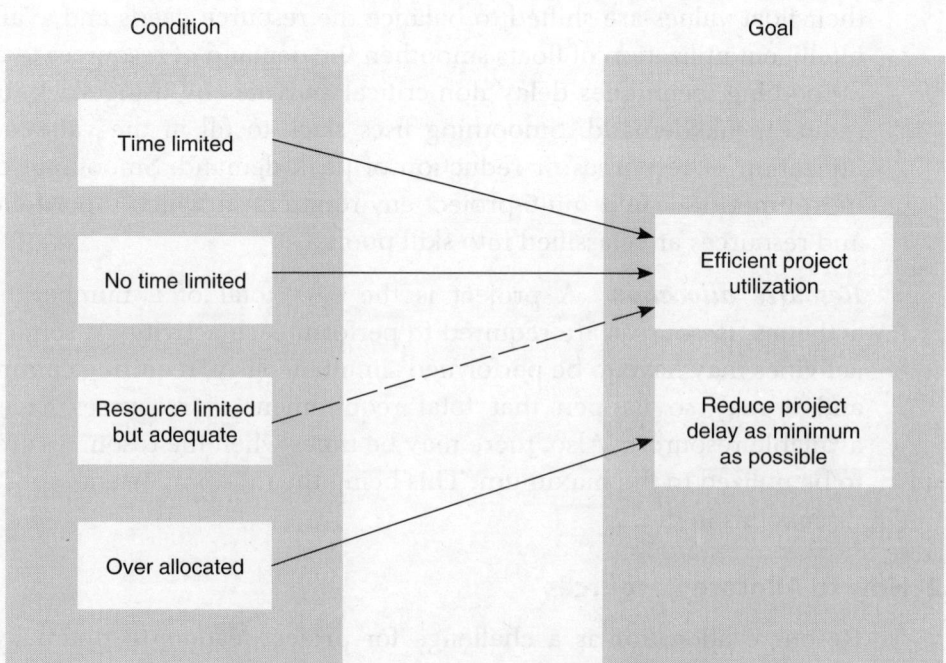

FIGURE 2.22   Resource scheduling conditions and goals

Resource requisite for each activity are enlisted for each item of resource, i.e., men, machine, and material

↓

The type-wise availability of various resources with respect to quantity and time is also enlisted

↓

The distribution of resources to activities lying on the critical path are given the most priorities but for non-critical activities some negotiation can be made. Jobs with least slacks will be preferred more than others in case same resources are required for them

FIGURE 2.23   Steps in resource allocation

2.7.3 Critical Chain and the Buffer Management Approach

Goldratt's Theory of Constraints (TOC) (1997) and its direct application to project management, known as the critical chain scheduling and buffer management, has found its way to project management practice. The fundamentals of critical chain and buffer management are summarized in Table 2.6 (Herroelen et al. 2001).

TABLE 2.6   Critical chain and buffer management fundamentals

Determine a precedence and resource feasible baseline schedule.
Identify the critical activity and the critical chain.
Sum up uncertainty allowances into buffers.
Keep the baseline schedule and the critical chain fixed during project execution.
No multi tasking, activity due dates and milestones exist.
Determine an early start based on buffered projected schedule.
Use the buffers as a proactive warning measure.

Some of the common challenges faced during project execution are
(a)   budget overrun
(b)   time overrun
(c)   compromise of requirement

It is more important to complete projects within their time schedule, as budget overruns do not cause as much damage as time overruns.

Critical chain and buffer management observes and analyse these commonly encountered problems. According to it, uncertainty is the root of all problems faced during project management. In fact, project management acquires meaning due to the presence of uncertainty. Different project management techniques seek to introduce certainty and control over the project. The primary agenda of critical chain and buffer management is to complete a project on time, while dealing with the uncertainty (Murphy's Law) involved in it. It also deals with other factors of project delays as enumerated by Parkinson's law (work expands to fill the time allowed) (Parkinson 1957; Schonberger 1981; Gutierrez and Kouvelis 1991).

Critical chain and buffer management finds out the interdependencies of activity durations, precedence relations, resource constraint, and availability of resources as the factors for project duration. The span of project is fixed by sequences of resource dependent activities. In 1977, Glodratt defined this sequence as a critical chain. Critical chain is defined as a set of activities that fixes up the total project duration considering the precedence and resource dependencies of the activities. To minimize the work in progress (WIP), a precedence feasible schedule is built, wherein activities are scheduled by their latest start time based on their critical path.

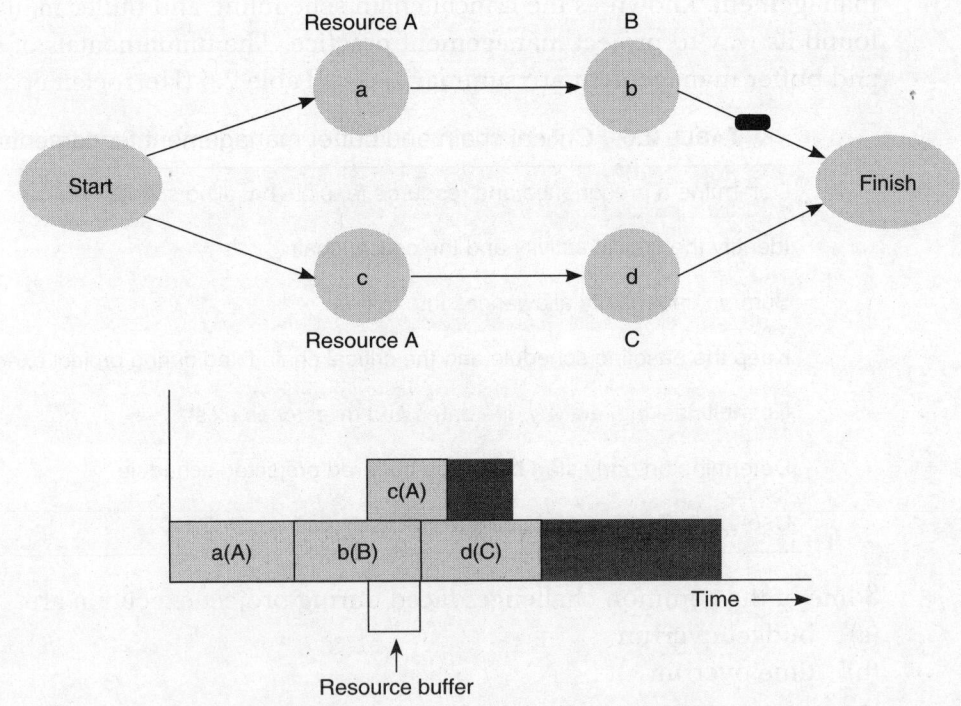

FIGURE 2.24 A critical chain schedule

As there lies a finish–start precedence relationship between activities *a* and *b* and activities *c* and *d*, shown in Figure 2.24, they must be performed in a series. The single renewable resource A must be utilized to perform activities *a* and *c*. The conflict of resource allotment is sorted out by executing the given activities in series. The path Start–*a*–*c*–*d*–Finish represents the critical chain. Thereby, the single renewable source C is allocated to *a*, *c*, and *d*.

Critical chain and buffer management attaches safety associated with critical chain activities to the end of the critical chain. This is known as *project buffer*. A similar practice in the building industry is to add 'weather delay' to the baseline schedule, which is also known as weather contingency (Clough and Sears 1991). *Feeding buffers* are placed whenever the non-critical-chain activity joins the critical chain. It may be noted that a feeding buffer protects the longest non-critical sequence of tasks. Contrary to the critical chain, this longest non-critical sequence is not created from the influence of other sequences of the same length.

The safety associated with the critical chain tasks is shifted to the end of the critical chain in the form of a project buffer (Figure 2.24), the aim of which is to protect the due date promised to the client from variations in the critical chain tasks. Because the targeted durations of activities are 50 per cent of confidence interval, it might be expected that half the time they are finished early while half the time they finish late. The early tasks are expected to offset some of the late ones. Consequently, a project buffer of half the project duration is expected to provide sufficient protection.

Feeding buffers are usually half the duration of the non-critical chain activity. These buffers are placed wherever a non-critical chain activity joins the critical chain. Feeding buffers protect the critical chain from disruptions in the activities feeding it and allow early start of the critical chain activities if the progress is satisfactory.

Informal buffers may be created in the critical chain, in the form of graphs, when there is lack of space to push the chain feeding the buffer to the past. Eventually, the present buffer size must be decreased accordingly to balance the informal buffers or gaps.

Resource buffers (Figure 2.25), usually in the form of an advance warning, are placed whenever a resource has jobs on a critical chain and the previous critical chain activity is done by a different resource.

Thus, the critical chain schedule should aim to avoid expansion of work as per Parkinson's Law, by eliminating activity due dates and milestones, and allowing advantage of early completion of activities. The schedule should be protected by early warnings from preceding activities. The promised project due date should be protected from variation by project buffer, and the critical chain should be protected from variation in the non-critical activities by feeding buffers. If there is more than one critical chain in the schedule, one must be chosen and the others should be buffered.

Execution of projects are not managed by using activity due dates only, but through buffer management. As activities get completed, the manager should keep track of buffers that have been consumed. As long as buffers are not fully exhausted, it is understood that the progress is fine and the buffer consumption is in the green zone. If activity variation consumes a buffer in excess (the yellow or 'watch and plan' zone), a warning is raised to determine what should be done if the situation deteriorates further. If it deteriorates beyond a critical point (the red 'act' zone), action is required to execute the plan.

The execution of the project activities should be done with an athlete's mentality. The basic point is not to create work when there is none and not to question availability of resources. The key in reducing system-wise WIP is to control the flow of work into the system. This means that the activities without non-dummy predecessors (the gating tasks) should not start before the scheduled start time, while non-gating tasks, especially those on the critical chain, be started as soon as they can, when work becomes available.

Multi-projects resource constraints

In multi-project circumstances, critical chain and buffer management depend upon common types of principal constraints. Every individual project is equipped with a critical chain schedule having the project, the feeding, and the resource buffers. The most critical strategic resource is defined as the drum resource.

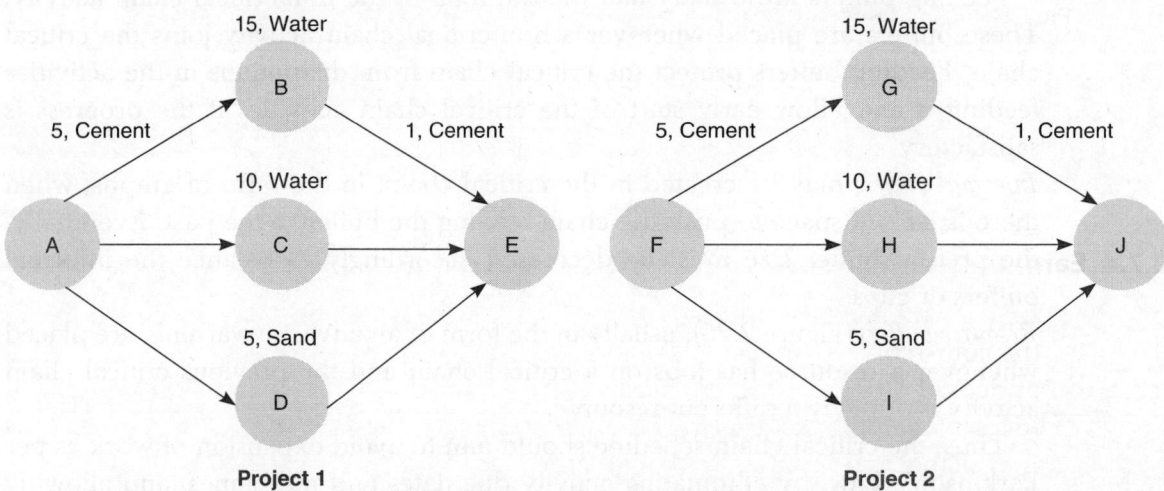

FIGURE 2.25 Two project networks

Out of the two projects, as shown in Figure 2.25, the green resource is considered to be the strategic resource. Therefore, to get the maximum utilization of strategic resource, it must be kept busy.

A strategic resource schedule (the drum plan) is constructed as shown in Figure 2.26, where the drum plan is shown by the bold line. It is important to have a start and finish time in this schedule due to the activities in the strategic resource. The individual projects are subjected to the critical chain calculations as explained above and decoupled by placing a capacity buffer before a strategic resource task. The buffer in front of activity G is a capacity buffer. It can be taken as a protective capacity. The availability of resources for the critical chain (in the strategic resource schedule) is ensured by the creation of idle time or space on the strategic resource. A drum buffer protects the strategic resource from non-strategic resources and other disruptions. The example of drum buffer includes the buffer activity F and the space in front of activity G (as shown in Figure 2.26).

The drum buffer is similar to a feeding buffer that protects the critical chain in the individual projects. However, this buffer ensures availability of work for the strategic resource.

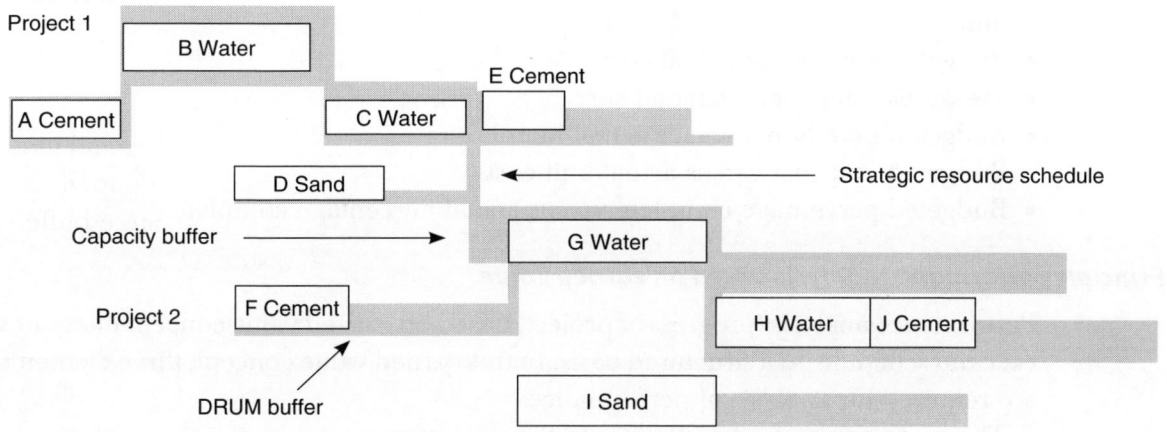

FIGURE 2.26   Multi-project schedule

2.7.4 Earned Value Management

Perhaps the most common questions that a project manager has to answer during the course of any project is along the lines of 'How are we doing? Are we still set to deliver on time? Will we finish within the budget?' Answers to these questions involve analysis, especially for a big project. If a proper critical path network data is available and progress is regularly monitored against it, it would be fairly simple to speculate the completion time. If any critical activity is running behind schedule, it can be said that project completion will be delayed to that extent. But what about the cost? Even if actual expenditure to date or at least up to the end of previous accounting period is known, how can the cost incurred be related to the progress achieved?

The answer to this question is usually more difficult to answer and is complicated for any project of significant size with a huge amount of WIP.

Variance analysis

Variance analysis is the most common method of control analysis. This method evaluates the difference (variance) between the planned result and the actual outcome. The planned (budgeted) and the actual progress (actual costs) can be differentiated using variance analysis. This variance from the actual plan is called 'exception'. It is done by focusing attention on things that actually need attention. The following are certain comparisons where variances (or exceptions) usually occur:

- Scheduled start versus actual start
- Scheduled finish versus actual finish
- Scheduled time for an activity versus actual time
- Scheduled achievement time for any milestone event versus actual achievement time
- Budgeted cost versus actual cost
- Measured value versus actual cost
- Budgeted man-hours versus actual man-hours
- Budgeted unit cost versus actual unit cost
- Budgeted percentage complete versus actual percentage complete

Principle performance analysis based on earned value

Performance analysis (progress of project) based on earned value concept integrates cost and schedule on a structured basis. In this earned value concept, three elements are required for analysis of performance:

1. The budgeted cost scheduled up to the time of measurement
2. The actual cost at the time of measurement
3. The corresponding earned value

The earned value is simply the budgeted value (cost or man hours) of the work actually completed. For example, if a job was budgeted to cost Rs 5,00,000 even if the actual cost of completing the job happened to be Rs 4,00,000 or Rs 9,00,000. Subjectivity problem is minimized in the structured earned value approach, where the work is broken down into WBS elements, cost accounts, and work packages. The total earned value of the work completed at the time of measurement is then based on the budgeted value of all these completed segment of work, plus an estimate to allow for active WIP.

Work package is the performance analysis of a project using the earned value concept on cost centre. It offers effective management of project information. An appropriate work package size can be chosen, one that complements the size of the project and quality of the information system. The scheduled and cost performance indices, together with scheduled and cost variances, provide dependable information on the progress made against the budgeted schedule and cost. The system automatically produces forecasts of the final cost for parts of the project or for the project as a whole. Also, the performance of contributing organization is automatically monitored and gives effective feedback to those responsible.

However, these modes of estimation and analysis require considerable effort. To avoid the complicated terminology, the alternatives given in Tables 2.7 and 2.8 can be used here.

From Table 2.7, the following can be concluded:

1. Remaining estimated cost to completion (ETC) = (BAC – BCWP) / CPI (where BAC is the budget at completion)
2. Forecast final cost or estimate at completion (EAC) = ACWP + ETC

Figure 2.27 is a graphical, S-curve illustration of these quantities for a typical project.

TABLE 2.7 Terminology used in EVM

Item	Equivalence	Meaning
BCWS = Budgeted cost and work scheduled	PV = Planned value	Sum of authorized budget, from start to status date
BCWP = Budgeted cost and work performed	EV = Earned value	Sum of authorized budget for work actually performed
ACWP = Actual cost of work performed	AC = Actual cost	Actual cost incurred, up to status date
BAC = Budget at completion	BAC = Budget at completion	The sum of all authorized budget for the project
CV = Cost variance	CV = Cost variance	CV = BCWP – ACWP (EV – AC)
SV = Scheduled variance	SV = Scheduled variance	SV = BCWP – BCWS (EV – PV)
CPI = Cost performance index	CPI = Cost performance index	CPI = BCWP/ACWP
SPI = Scheduled performance index	SPI = Scheduled performance index	SPI = BCWP/BCWS
CR = Critical ratio	CR = Critical ratio	CR = CPI × SPI

TABLE 2.8 Projected completion time and cost at the end of the project

	Cost at completion		
	Optimistic	Likely	Pessimistic
Formula	Actual cost + (BAC – BCWP)	Actual cost + (BAC – BCWP)/CPI	Actual cost + (BAC – BCWP)/(CPI × SPI)
	ACWP + (BAC – BCWP)	(BAC/CPI)	ACWP + (BAC-BCWP)/(CPI × SPI)
Logic	No further slippage will occur	Balance cost will be incurred at current efficiency	There is a time/cost relation

Contd

Table 2.8   *Contd*

	Time at completion		
	Optimistic	**Likely**	**Pessimistic**
Formula	Scheduled work that should have been completed in elapsed time + time remaining as per schedule	Actual time spent + time remaining as per schedule decided by SPI	Actual time spent + time remaining as per schedule decided by product of SPI + CPI
	Elapsed time/SPI + time remaining as per schedule	Total scheduled time/SPI	Actual time spent + time remaining as per schedule/CR
Logic	Only current delay will spill over, rest will be as per schedule	Further delays will be continued at current efficiencies	Cost efficiency may slow down work

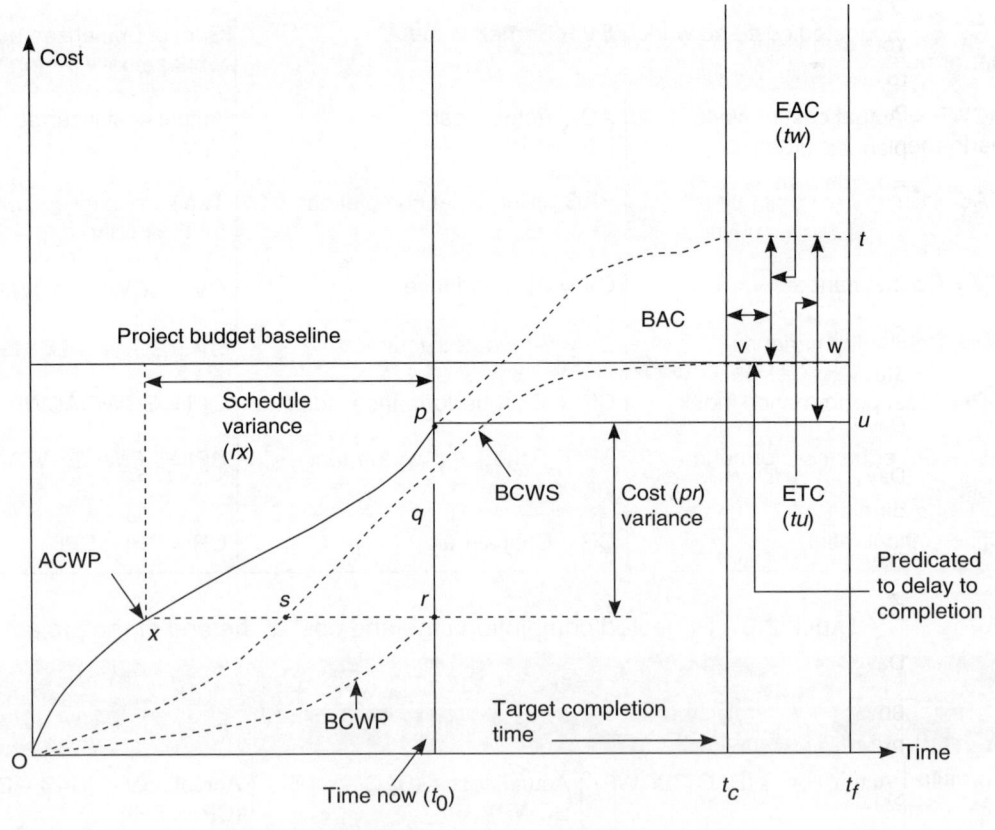

FIGURE 2.27   A project S-curve

Example 2.9   Your task is to get your flat painted. You are required to track the progress and cost for day 1. The total job is estimated to take 5 days (total 50 hours), and requires 10 litres of paint. The requirement of each unit of the flat is shown in Table E2.14. The work schedule is such that each room must be finished before the other can start. The sequence is bedroom, toilet, drawing cum dinning room, kitchen, and study.

Table E2.14

Unit of flat	No. of hours	No. of litres
Bedroom	10	1.8
Toilet	5	1.2
Drawing cum Dinning room	15	3.6
Kitchen	10	1.6
Study	10	1.8

ACWP of day 1 = 2 l (given), the progress of day 1 will be as follows:

Your neighbour's dog overturned the paint while you were preparing your materials. Luckily, you were able to upright the tin before too much paint was spilt. However, you spent half an hour cleaning up the mess. Painting the ceiling proved more difficult than anticipated, and you had to use more paint than you had planned. BCWS (Day 1) = 1.8 l ACWP (dog victims) = 2 l, ACWP (ceiling difficulties) = 2.2 l, project progress = 15 per cent.

1. Determine the BCWS and BCWP and also calculate SPI and CPI.

2. Determine expected cost at completion and expected time at completion for day 1.

Solution

Step 1: Determine BCWP for all 5 days

Day 1 = 1.8 l (Day 1, 10 hours work for bedroom)

Day 2 = 1.8 l (Day1 BCWP) + 1.2 l (Day 2, 5 hours work for toilet) + 1.2 l (Day 2, 5 hours work for drawing cum dinning = 4.2 l

Day 3 = 4.2 l (Day 2 BCWP) + 2.4 l (Day 3, 10 hours work for drawing cum dinning = 6.6 l

Day 4 = 6.6 l (Day 3 BCWP) + 1.6 l (Day 4, 10 hours work of kitchen) = 8.2 l

Day 5 = 8.2 l (Day 4 BCWP) + 1.8 l (Day 5, 10 hours work for study) = 10 l

BCWP = PV – Project progress of ACWP = 1.8 l – 15 % of 2 l = 1.5 l, where ACWP = AC = 2 l (given), BCWS = PV =1.8 l (determined)

SPI = BCWP / BCWS = 1.5 / 1.8 = 0.833

CPI = BCWP / ACWP = 1.5 / 2 = 0.75

CR = CPI × SPI = 0.833 × 0.75 = 0. 624

BAC (time) = 50 hours (given) and BAC (cost) = 10 litres (given)

Cost Projection

Optimistic = AC + (BAC − EV) = 2 + (10 − 1.5) = 10.5 l

Likely = AC + (BAC − EV) / CPI = 2 + (10 − 1.5) / 0.75 = 13.33 l

Pessimistic = AC + (BAC − EV) / CR = 2 + (10 − 1.5) / 0.624 = 15.622 l

Time Projection

Optimistic = Scheduled work that should have been completed in elapsed time + Time remaining as per schedule = Actual time / SPI + Remaining time = 10 / (1.5 / 1.8) + 40 = 52 hours

Likely = Estimated time / SPI = 50 / (1.5 / 1.8) = 60 hours

Pessimistic = Actual time + Remaining time / CR = 10 + 40 / 0.624 = 74.1 hours

2.8 GRAPHICAL EVALUATION AND REVIEW TECHNIQUE

The activity network is of the probabilistic type where the evolution of the corresponding project is not uniquely determined in advance but is stochastic in nature (Neumann 1998). This category encompasses generalized activity network (Elmaghraby 1977) such as GERT (Neumann and Steinhardt 1979). Compared to PERT and CPM networks, GERT network uses the activity-on-arc (A-O-A) network representation. It possesses more general arc weights and cycles to represent feedback. GERT network allows six different node types. A node has three possible entrance sides and 2 possible exit sides.

There is another special entrance called AND-entrance. In a situation, where the node is activated when the incoming activity has been cancelled for the first time, the AND-entrance could be an inclusive (IOR) entrance. However, the AND-entrance is an exclusive (or EOR) entrance when the mode is activated at every cancellation of incoming activities. The exit is deterministic in a situation where every outgoing activity is performed when a node is activated. In case the node is activated during only one outgoing activity, the exit is called stochastic. Table 2.9 briefs about some of the available project management techniques.

2.9 PROJECT MANAGEMENT SOFTWARE

A good plan does not always translate into good project management, unless all the inputs and information are carefully accessed and critically analysed within the constraints of time and resources. There is no dearth of software that can aid in the efficient management of projects. However, according to Kerzner and Thamhain (1986), even the most sophisticated software package is not a substitute

TABLE 2.9 Evaluation of major network-based project management techniques

Criterion	PERT/CPM	PERT/Cost	LOB	GERT	VERT
Project phase acceptability	Prime application to one time projects, largely design and development phase	Same as basic PERT/CPM	Production only	Most value in concept phase; usable in all phases to some degree	Most value in concept phase; usable in all phases to some degree
Parametric focus	Time oriented; treats performance and costs as objectives, constraints or by products	Add cost planning and control feature to basic PERT/CPM	Time-oriented schedule and quantity	Time-oriented add on cost feature, analyses time and cost	Fully treats time costs and various performance measures; analyzes risk in all three.
Preparation requirements	Network and time estimating is significant, but planning should be done anyway	Cost estimating work packages and activity is significant addition to PERT preparation, but should be done anyway	Main requirement is production flow chart and cycle time	Networking requires special familiarity; multitude of features create complexity	Same as for GERT; use of optional features increases requirements
Database	By-product of preparation as is quality of data	Cost accumulation and control requires extensive data input	Requires only time and quantity at selected control points	Direct function of the number of features selected; large if technique fully utilized	Direct function of the number of features selected; large if fully utilized
System operating cost	Programmes easy to use, main cost is effort of preparation and updating	Canned programmes expand basic PERT; largest cost by far is preparation	Practically non-existent, especially if part of MRP or other system	Function of database simulation requires multiple runs; input preparation appreciable	Same as for GERT; to use additional features increases cost
Compre-hensiveness	Limited to time parameter and non-repetitive activities	Limited to time and cost parameter and non-repetitive activities	Limited to repetitive situations only	Accommodates most types of activity	Accommodates most types of activity plus numerous inputs

Contd

Table 2.9   *Contd*

Criterion	PERT/CPM	PERT/Cost	LOB	GERT	VERT
Flexibility	Handles deterministic situations only, no ability to accommodate decision	Deterministic only, same as PERT	Deterministic situations only; fixed production cycle required; learning curve presents problem	Accommodates stochastic and deterministic activities	Significantly more optional input and output features than budgeting capability
Ease of update	Relatively simple, requires discipline to ensure that future activities are re-evaluated; actual times present little problem	Theoretically simple but major efforts in practice; 'estimating actual' cost data and constant changes are problems	Requires only a physical count of cumulative production	Appreciable, but value of technique of planning, rather than control	Appreciable, but value of technique of planning, rather than control
Focus reporting	Highlighting of critical activities and problem areas are strong point; forecasts status at completion	Adds to PERT the ability to trade cost problems to the source	Highlights potential delivery schedule problem areas	Risk analysis focuses attention on hat is likely to occur and its probability	Analyzes and highlights outcomes in time, costs, and performance; can be used in a non-project strategic planning

PERT: Program evaluation and review techniques; CPM: Critical path method; LOB: Line of balance; VERT: Venture evaluation and review techniques; GERT: Graphical evaluation and review techniques

Source: Meredith and Mantel 1999.

for competent project leaders, and cannot, by itself, identify or correct any task-related problems. It can only be an aid to the project manager in tracking the many interrelated variables and tasks that come into play with a modern project.

Some of the relevant project management software are Microsoft Project for Windows application, Project Scheduler 4, Timeline, InstaPlan 5000, Micro-Planner, and PRIMA VERA (refer *Software Digest*, volume 7, November 1990 by National Software Testing Laboratories (NSTL), Pennsylvania). We will discuss Microsoft Project in brief.

Microsoft Project helps project managers in developing project plans, allocating available resources, monitoring progress of projects, and keeping a check on the budget. It supports the managers in creating critical path schedules and defining resources in terms of people, equipment, and materials. Microsoft Project also helps in sharing these among multiple projects using a shared resource pool. It schedules tasks based on resource availability as defined in the resource calendar. Budgets can also be calculated based on assignment works and resource rates. Microsoft Project has been extended with MS Office Project Server and Microsoft Project Web Access. Project Server stores data in a central database, which can be displayed and updated over the Internet through Project Web Access.

The latest version of Microsoft Project Server 2010 unifies project and portfolio management to assist organizations in managing resources and investing with priorities, and helps in visualizing performance through dashboards. The inclusion of a demand management module that captures all the work—from simple tasks to complex projects and programmes—is a new feature. The software also helps organizations in the selection of projects that are aligned to their business goals. It assists in decisions through inbuilt capabilities of prioritizing competition requests, running optimization scenarios under budgetary constraints, and optimizing utilization of resources.

Microsoft Project 2010 ensures a fluent user interface across Project Standard 2010, Project Professional 2010, and Project Server 2010. The additional experience comes through Microsoft's Business Intelligence platform that includes Excel Services, PerformancePoint Services, Visio Services, PowerPivot for Excel 2010, and SQL Reporting Services. The integration of Microsoft Project 2010 with related technologies of Microsoft, such as, Microsoft Exchange Server, Microsoft Visual Studio Team Foundation Server, and SharePoint Server Sync provides a familiar and connected work management platform.

SUMMARY

Project management process constitutes the following phases: concept phase, definition phase, planning phase, scheduling phase, control phase, and termination phase. A project consists of a number of events (milestones), activities, or tasks that have to be performed in accordance with a set of precedent constraints. Each activity has an assigned duration and resources (except dummies). The techniques of WBS and OBS, Gantt chart, bar chart, and line of balance (LOB) help in understanding ways of achieving better results. Some of the other methods used by managers for project scheduling and networking are the critical path method (CPM) and programme evaluation and review technique (PERT).

Crashing of a project network as well as its guidelines explains ways in which project managers would be able to achieve goals as quickly as possible. The sections on project scheduling with techniques about resource levelling, resource smoothing, and resource allocation discuss ways of overcoming the constraints. Microsoft Project 2010 is explained as a project management software.

KEY TERMS

Activity float The result of the forward and backward pass computation allow for the calculation of various float values for the network activities like total float, free float, and safety float.

Activity-on-arrow or activity-on-arc (AOA) The mode of representation that uses a set of arcs or arrows to represent the activities and a set of nodes to represent events.

Activity-on-node (AON) The mode of representation that uses a set of nodes to denote the activities or events and the set of set arc or arrows A to represent the precedence relations.

Backward pass This calculation then processed by working backwards through the network, always assuming that each activity is conducted as late as possible.

Cost slope It represents the extra cost for shortening the duration of the activity by one time unit.

Crash cost (C_C) The total expenditure incurred on normal and additional resources for completing any activity in normal time is known as normal cost.

Crash time (C_T) Crash time is the minimum possible time in which an activity can be completed by employing extra resources. Crash time is that time beyond which the activity cannot be shortened by any amount of increase in resources.

Crashing of project network This is the process by which time for an activity is reduced as much as possible. The shortest possible time in which an activity can be realistically completed is called its crash time. The direct cost for completing an activity in its crash time is called crash cost.

Critical activities In a network diagram, critical activities are those that consume more than their estimated time, thus delaying the project. More attention should be given to the critical activity. It is marked either by a thick arrow or a double line.

Critical chain (CC) It is the set of tasks that determine the overall duration of the project, taking into account both precedence and resource dependencies. In order to minimize work-in-progress, a precedence feasible schedule is constructed in which the activities are scheduled at their latest start times based on traditional critical path calculations.

Critical path A path along which the earliest finish time and latest finish time is equal is known as critical path. It is that sequence of activities which decides the total project duration. It is the longest path and consumes the maximum time.

Critical path method (CPM) A scheduled technique which is used to plan, schedule, and control a project consisting of a number of inter-related activities. These techniques provide a frame which defines the job that is to be performed, integrates them in a logical sequence, and provides a system of control over the progress of the plan.

Dummy activities When two activities start at the same instant of time, the head events are joined by dotted arrows and this is known as a dummy activity. These activities do not consume any time or resources but are used as a link to control or maintain uniqueness of activity.

Earliest finish time (EFT) It is the earliest possible time at which an activity can be finished. EFT is the sum of EST and the duration of the activity.

Earliest start time (EST) It is the earliest possible time at which an activity can start and is calculated by moving from first to last event in the network diagram.

Feeding buffer Feeding buffers are placed whenever the non-critical chain activity joins the critical chain.

Float or slack Float or slack means a margin of extra time over and above its duration which a non-critical activity can consume without delaying the date of the completion of the project. Float or slack is the time available for completion of the activity mine the time necessary to complete the same.

Forward pass The forward pass calculations are carried out to determine the earliest occurrence time for each event j (E_j), and the earliest start and finish times for each activity i–j (ES_{ij} and EF_{ij}), these calculations are based on the assumption that activity is conducted as early as possible.

Free float It defines the allowable delay in the activity finish time without affecting the possible start time of its immediate successors.

Gantt chart/bar chart It is a means of displaying simple activities or events plotted against time. These are most commonly used for exhibiting programme progress or defining specific work requirements to accomplish an objective.

Graphical evaluation review technique (GERT) GERT networks use the activity-on-arc network representation but possess more general arc weights (including the execution probabilities of activities) and cycles to represent feedback.

Latest finish time (LFT) It is the latest time by which a project must be completed so that the scheduled date for the completion of the project may not be delayed. It is calculated by moving backward, i.e., from last event to first event of the networked diagram.

Latest start time (LST) It is the latest possible time by which an activity can start without delaying the date of completion of project. LST is LFT minus duration of the activity.

Most likely time Most likely time m is the time required to complete the activity taking into consideration all favourable and unfavourable conditions. These estimates of time lie between optimistic time a and pessimistic time b.

Non-critical activities These activities have a provision of float or slack so that, even if they consume a specific time over and above the estimated time, the project will not be delayed.

Normal cost (N_C) The expenditure incurred on normal resources for completing any activity in normal time is called normal cost.

Normal time (N_T) Normal time is the standard time associated with normal resources of the organization to perform an activity.

Optimistic time Optimistic time a is the shortest time in which an activity can be completed assuming that everything would go exceptionally well. It has a low probability of occurrence.

Organization breakdown structure (OBS) The decisions about the disintegration or the integration process of a project are intimately tuned with the decision concerning the organization of the project as shown in the organization chart, also called the organizational breakdown structure.

PERT It is a probabilistic event oriented project scheduling technique. It is suitable in defence project, R&D project, where the activity time cannot be readily predicted.

Pessimistic time Pessimistic time b is the time that an activity will take to complete if everything turns out against expectations, i.e., an adverse condition. Similar to optimistic time, it has also low probability of occurrence.

Project buffers The safety associated with critical chain activities to the end of the critical chain is to be provided in the form of project buffer.

Resource allocation Every management wants to allocate the limited resource equipments to various activities in such a manner that there is best possible use of resources at disposal.

Resource levelling In the resource-levelling process the activities are so scheduled that the maximum and peak resource requirement does not exceeds the limit of available resources.

Resources smoothing The time-scaled version of various activities and their resource requirements along with corresponding floats if any, is used for resource smoothing. The periods of maximum demand for resources are allocated and the activities according to their float values are shifted for balancing the resource needs and availability.

Safety float The safety float of the activity j represents the number of period by which the given activity may be prolonged when all its predecessors start as late as possible completion time.

Total float It denotes the time and activity that can be delayed without causing a delay in the project.

Work breakdown structure (WBS) These are the project activities in relation to the project result that creates a framework for project control and which provide the basis for obtaining a relevant insight in the time and cost status of a project through the various management areas.

CONCEPT REVIEW QUESTIONS

1. Differentiate between PERT and CPM.
2. Differentiate between
   (a) AOA and AON network
   (b) EST and LST
   (c) EFT and LFT
   (d) Critical activity and dummy activity
   (e) An event and an activity
   (f) Free float and total float
3. Describe the different types of precedence relations.
4. Consider the following set of activities with their immediate predecessors. Refer to the table below. The precedence relations are of the finish-start type with zero time-lag.

Activity	Immediate predecessors
a	–
b	–
c	–
d	a, b
e	a, c
f	a, b, c

Draw the corresponding AOA network. Reduce the number of dummy activities to the minimum possible. Draw the corresponding AOA network.

5. Draw the Gantt chart for a simple project, say, installing a railway station involving activities as shown in the table below. What is the total project duration?

Activity	Duration (days)	Preceding activities
A	5	–
B	10	A
C	15	–
D	5	B, C
E	10	–
F	5	E

6. What is cost slope? Explain the method time-cost trade-off of a project network.
7. With the help of an illustrative example, explain the resource allocation method.
8. Make a comparative report describing the merits and demerits of different project scheduling methods like PERT, CPM, LOB, GERT, and VERT.
9. Enumerate the features of MS Project 2010 Software.

NUMERICAL PROBLEMS

1. Consider the project activities with corresponding data in the adjacent table. All precedence relations are of the finish-start type with zero time-lag. Draw the network in AOA format. Perform the forward and backward critical path calculations. Derive for each activity the total free and safety float values.

2. Consider the AON and AOA networks shown in the following figure. All precedence relations are of the finish-start type with zero time-lag. Perform the forward and backward critical path calculations in both the format. Derive for each activity the total free and safety float values in both the cases. What are your conclusions?

Activity	Duration (days)	Immediate successors
A	0	B, C, D
B	2	F, E
C	1	I
D	8	J
E	4	G, K
F	4	H, I
G	1	J
H	5	L
I	3	L
J	1	L
K	3	L
L	0	–

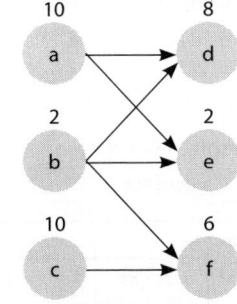

AON network

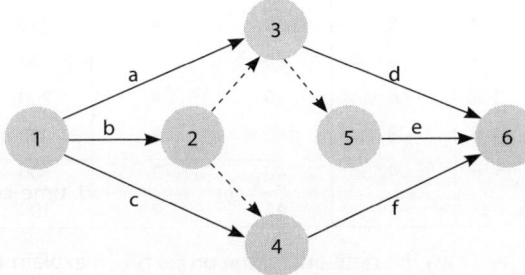

AOA network

3. Refer to the following CPM network as shown in the figure below. The durations of activity are indicated on the activity arrows. Estimated time is 2 days in event 7 to 8.

Find out the following:

(a) different paths in the network and their time duration

(b) critical path and the critical activities

(c) total free and independent floats for the activities

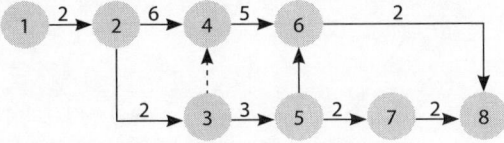

4. Consider the network for a small maintenance project in the following table. All given times are in days.

(a) Draw an arrow diagram representing the project.

(b) What is the critical path and what is the total slack time in the network?

(c) What is the expected time for 68%, 95%, and 99% completion limits?

Job	Initial node	Final node	Optimistic time	Pessimistic time	Most likely time
A	1	2	1	3	2
B	1	4	4	6	5
C	1	3	4	5	3
D	2	6	2	4	3
E	2	4	1	3	2
F	3	4	2	4	3
G	3	5	6	15	7
H	4	6	4	6	5
I	4	7	5	15	8
J	4	5	1	3	2
K	5	7	2	4	3
L	6	7	6	15	10

5. Consider the network for a small MIS project in the table below. All times are in days; network proceeds from node 1 to node 10.

Job (activity)	Initial node	Final node	Estimated Time
A	1	2	3
B	1	3	2
C	1	4	3
D	2	5	3
E	2	9	2
F	3	5	2
G	3	6	2
H	3	7	3
I	4	7	6
J	4	8	2
K	5	6	3
L	6	9	3
M	7	9	5
N	8	9	3
O	9	10	2

(a) Identify the critical path

(b) Calculate the total network slack time

(c) Suppose that activities A, B, C all utilize the same manpower base, and shortening any one of these three activities causes one of the other two to increase by the same amount. Can network re-planning, only for these three activities shorten and lengthen the critical path?

6. The figure below shows the network for a construction project, with three times estimates of each activity marked. Find out the following:

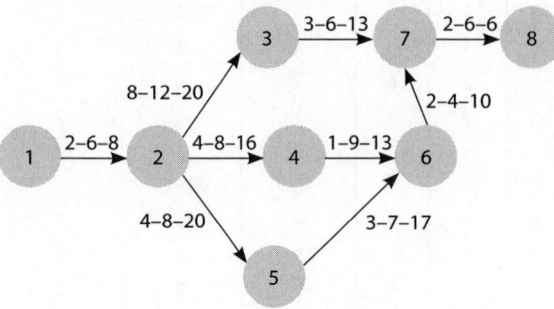

(a) Critical path and its standard deviation.
(b) Probability of completion of project in 42 days.
(c) Time duration that will provide 90 per cent probability of its completion in time.

7. Ms Rebecca sent a memo to her boss, the director of the project management, stating that the MS project would require 13 weeks for completion, as shown in the figure below.

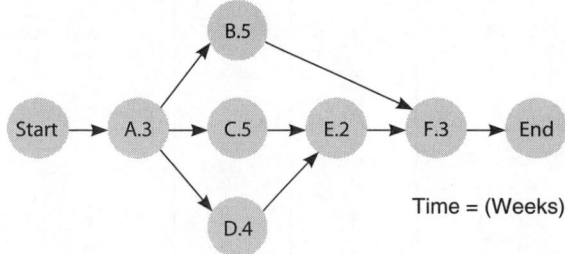

Time = (Weeks)

Ms Rebecca realized that the customer wanted the job completed in less time. After discussions with the functional managers, Rebecca developed the schedule shown in the table below.

Activity	Normal		Crash		
	Time (week)	Cost (Rs)	Time (week)	Cost (Rs)	Additional (crash) cost/week
A	3	5,000	2	7,000	2,000
B	5	10,000	4	13,000	1,000
C	5	15,000	3	21,000	2,000
D	4	6,000	2	9,000	1,000
E	2	5,000	1	6,000	1,000
F	3	12,000	1	18,000	3,000
		53,000			

According to the contract, there is a penalty payment of Rs 4,500 per week over 6 week. What is the minimum amount additional funding that Rebecca should request?

8. The following table gives data on normal and crash time and cost for a project.

Activity	Normal		Crash	
	Time (days)	Cost (Rs)	Time (days)	Cost (Rs)
1–2	5	50	4	100
1–3	4	60	2	200
2–4	5	50	4	140
2–5	4	50	1	65
3–4	6	90	4	200
4–6	8	80	3	280
5–6	4	40	2	100
6–7	3	45	3	100

(a) Draw the network for the project.
(b) Find the minimum total time of the project after crash and the corresponding cost. Taking into consideration the minimum crash cost.

9. A network for a project is shown in the figure below. The network is to be updated after 10 days of its execution. Estimated time between event 4 to 6 and 4 to 7 is both 8 days. The following conditions exist at the end of the 10 days:

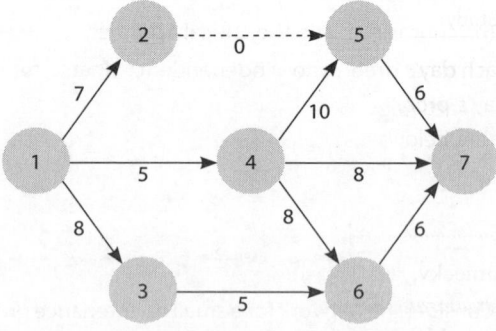

(a) Activity 1–2, 1–3 and 1–4 has been completed as per original schedule.
(b) Activity 4–5 is in progress and will require 5 more days for its completion.
(c) Activity 4–6 in progress and will require 5 more days for its completion.

(d) Activity 3–6 is in progress and will be completed in 1 day.

(e) Other activities have not been commenced and their original predicted durations will hold good except for activity 5–7 which will require only three days instead of 6 days originally planned.

Update the network and determine the critical path of the updated network. What is the total increase in the project duration?

ASSIGNMENTS

1. Suppose you want to develop your own website. Define the scope of the project and identify the deliverables. Develop a work breakdown structure for the project.

2. You have to get the internal walls of your flat plastered in 5 days. You will have to track progress and cost for each of the 5 days. The total job is for 5 days and it has estimated that the job will take 50 hours and 20 bags of cement. The requirement of each unit of the flat is shown in the table below. The work schedule is such that each room must be finished before the other can start. The sequence is bedroom, toilet, drawing cum dinning room, kitchen, and study.

Unit of flat	No. of hours	No. of bags
Bedroom	10	3.6
Toilet	5	2.4
Drawing cum dinning room	15	7.3
Kitchen	10	3.2
Study	10	3.6

Each day's progress will be given to you. Record each day's progress on a progress chart (as shown in the table below) and calculate the BCWS and BCWP for each day. Also, find out an estimate of the over all cost and time to complete the project.

Day	BCWS	ACWP	Progress	Remarks
1	3.6 bags	4 bags	+15%	
2	8.4 bags	2.8 bags	+36%	Finished the bedroom during the day (20% completion) and started the toilet
3	13.2 bags	13.6 bags	+5%	You had a full way plastering your way around the dinning room
4	16.4 bags	8 bags	35%	You finish the living room in the morning (30%) and start the kitchen
5	20 bags	8 bags	45%	You finish the kitchen (20%) and work more or less continuously to try and finish the study

If you reach 100% or more of physical progress, then the work was finished within the 50 hours. If not, then you had to return on the sixth day in order to round things off and to tidy up your materials.

SELECT REFERENCES

Adamiecky, K., 'Harmony graph', *Polish Journal of Organizational Review*, 1931.

Brown, J.W., 'Evaluation of Projects Using Critical Path Analysis and Earned Value in Combination', *Project Management Journal*, August 1985, pp. 59–63.

Clark, W., *The Gantt Chart*, Pitman, New York, 1954.

Clough, R.H. and G.A. Sears, *Construction Project Management*, John Willey and Sons, New York, 1991.

Corneil, D.G., C.C. Gotlieb, and Y.M. Lee, 'Minimal Event Node Network of Project Precedence Relation', *Communications of ACM*, vol. 16, 1973, pp. 296–98.

Demeulemeester, E. and W. Herroelen, *Project Scheduling: A Research Handbook*, Kluwer Academic Publishers, Massachusetts, 2002.

Elmaghraby, S.E.E., *Activity Networks-Project planning and Controls by Network Models*, John Wiley and Sons New York, 1997.

Elmaghraby, S.E.E. and J. Kamburowski, 'The Analysis of Activity Networks Under Generalized Precedence Relations (GPRs)', *Management Science*, vol. 38, no. 9, 1992, pp. 1245–63.

Goldratt, E.M., *Critical Chain*, The North River Press, US, 1997.

Gutierrez, G.J. and P. Kouvelis, 'Parkinsons Law and Its Implication For Project Management', *Management Science*, vol. 37, no. 8, 1991, pp. 990–1001.

Herroelen, W., E. Demeulemeester, and B.D. Reyck, 'A Classification Scheme for Project Scheduling', Proceedings of the sixth International Workshop on Project Management Scheduling, Bogazici University, 1998, pp. 67–70

Herroelen, W., R. Leus, and E. Demeulemeester, 'Critical Chain Scheduling: Do not over simplify', *Project Management Journal*, 2001.

Kelley, J.F., 'Critical Path Planning and Scheduling: Mathematical Basics', *Operations Research*, vol. 9, no. 3, 1961, pp. 296–320.

Kelley, J.F. and M., Walker, 'Critical Path Planning and Scheduling', proceedings of The Eastern Joints Computer Conference, 1959.

Kerzner, H., *Project Management: A Systems Approach to Planning Scheduling and Controlling*, 4th edn, Van Nostrand Reinhold, New York, 1992.

Kerzner, H. and H. Thamhain, *Project Management Operating Guidelines: Policies, Procedures and Forms*, New York, 1986, pp. 475–83.

Lumsden, P., *Line of Balance Method*, Pergamon Press, Exeter, 1968.

Meredith, J.R. and S.J. Mantel, Project *Management: A Managerial Approach*, 2nd edn, 1999.

Moder, J.J., C.R. Philips and Davis, *Project Management with CPM, PERT and Precedence Diagramming*, 3rd edn., Van Nostrand Reinhold Co., 1983.

Neumann, K., Scheduling of Projects with Stochastic Evolution Structure', *Handbook of Recent Advances in Project Scheduling*, Kluwer Academic Publishers, 1998, pp. 309–32.

Neumann, K. and U. Steinhardt, 'GERT Networks and the Time Oriented Evaluation of Projects', *Lecture notes in Economics and Mathematical Systems*, Springer, Berlin, 1979, p. 172.

Parkinson, C.N., *Parkinson's Law*, The Riverside Press, Cambridge, 1957.

Schonberger, R.J., 'Why Projects Are Always Late: A Rationale based on Manual Simulation of a PERT/CPM Network', *Interfaces*, vol. 11, no. 5, 1981, pp. 66–70.

Other resources

www.cheltehamcourseware.com, accessed 2 July 2010.

CASE STUDY

An Improved MIS at DCF Corporation

DCF Corporation is a Rs 70-crore consultancy firm specializing in electrical components required for large manufacturing plants. The CEO, Mr T.S. Kundan, being a man of vision, has set an eye on large government contracts to increase the business volume. Last year, he reorganized the 500 employees into a modified matrix structure to provide the customer focal point policy that is preferred by government agencies. Now he has set the ball rolling in the second phase and improved the MIS system for better processing of data and generation of reports in various forms.

Kundan called a meeting with the departmental managers from projects, cost accounting, MIS, IT, planning, and operations departments.

KUNDAN: We have to strengthen our computer department with new advanced computers and state-of-the-art systems to update our MIS reporting procedures. We shall need weekly, or even daily, cost data in order to control our projects better. This will not only impress our government customers, but also help us increase our business base and grow.

MIS MANAGER: I feel the first step required in the design, development and implementation process is to do a feasibility study. Here is a list of topics which I have prepared for the feasibility study (see Exhibit 2.1).

EXHIBIT 2.1 Feasibility study

- Objectives of the study
- Costs
- Benefits
- Manual or computer-based solution
- Objectives of the system
- Input requirements
- Output requirements
- Processing requirements
- Preliminary system description
- Evaluation of bids from the vendors
- Financial analysis
- Conclusion

KUNDAN: What kind of costs are you considering in the feasibility study?

MIS MANAGER: The major cost items include input/output demands, processing, storage capacity, rental, purchase or lease of a system, recurring and non-recurring expenditure, cost of supplies, facility and training requirements. We'll have to get a lot of this information from the IT department.

IT MANAGER: For a short period of time we shall have two systems working simultaneously. This cannot be helped at all. However, I have prepared a schedule of my own. (See Exhibit 2.2.) You will see from this schedule that I am quite optimistic as to how long it would take.

EXHIBIT 2.2 Typical schedule (in months)

Activity	Normal time to complete	Crash time to complete
Management go-ahead	0	0
Release of preliminary system specs.	5	2
Receipt of bids on specs.	2	1
Order hardware and systems software	2	1
Flow charts completed	2	2
Applications programs completed	3	4
Receipt of hardware and systems software	3	1
Testing and debugging done	2	2
Documentation, if required	2	2
Changeover completed	21	15*

* This assumes that some of the activities can be run in parallel, instead of series.

KUNDAN: Have we prepared a check-list on how to evaluate a vendor?

IT Manager: Besides the benchmark test, I have also prepared a list of topics that we must include in evaluation of any vendor (see Exhibit 2.3). We shall have to visit other organizations that have purchased the same system and see the system in action. We shall have to start developing the software packages simultaneously, and I think we should start right now.

EXHIBIT 2.3 Vendor support evaluation factors

- Availability of hardware and software packages
- Hardware performance, delivery, and past track record
- Vendor proximity and service and support record
- Emergency backup procedure
- Availability of applications programs and their compatibility with our other systems
- Capacity for expansion
- Documentation
- Availability of consultants for systems programming and general training
- Who burdens training cost?
- Risk of obsolescence
- Ease of use

KUNDAN: I appoint Rajiv Jain from planning department as the project leader for this entire programme. Though he is not as knowledgeable as you people as far as the computers are concerned, he is very good at laying out a schedule and getting the job done. I'm sure you all will give him the required support. Seeing the importance of the project, I'll be behind it all the way. We shall meet every week from now on to discuss the pros and cons. Next week I expect to see a detailed schedule covering all major activities identified. I'd like this project to be complete in 16 months. If there are any risks involved, identify them. Any questions?

Discussion questions

1. Prepare a list of questions to ask Kundan. According to you, what are the possible risks involved in this project?

2. Prepare a detailed scheduled network of this project.

PART II
PROJECT APPRAISAL

GENERATION OF PROJECT IDEAS

Ideas are like stars: you will not succeed in touching them with your hands, but like the seafaring man on the ocean desert of waters, you choose them as your guides, and following them, you reach your destiny.

— CARL SCHURZ

LEARNING OBJECTIVES

After studying this chapter, you will be able to

- Know how to search for project opportunities and ideas
- Understand how resources are allocated at both corporate and business unit level
- Conceptualize various strategic analyses such as PEST, Porter's five force model, value chain analysis, BCG growth matrix, and flexibility analysis
- Understand how creativity and idea generation can be achieved by individual and group effort

A popular saying, taken from the writings of Tagore, goes: 'Wherever you find some ash, blow it off, and you may get the invaluable gem.'

It is not that a gem is always wrapped in cotton wool, kept in a precious case, and can be easily obtained. The gem may lie around us, ignored, in a heap of mud or a pile of ash. He, who has the perseverance, the urge, and the will to achieve it must leave no stone unturned. He should explore every available alternative, however impossible or irrelevant it may appear. On trying out various ideas and opportunities, the most feasible or most rewarding idea is arrived at.

For instance, before 2000, road connectivity and infrastructure networking was not considered as important as it is today. Under the initiative of the Government of India, the Golden Quadrilateral project was conceived. It converted the single- or double-lane national highways into a four-lane road connecting the four major metros in India. The total length of the road is 5846 km. This project was completed in 2004. Prior to its inception, it was thought of as an impossible task. The road is a significant addition to the infrastructure of the country with regard to its growing economy.

To transform an idea into an active ongoing project, it is important to check on some areas. One of the important areas to be considered is resource allocation, which is discussed in the following paragraphs.

3.1 RESOURCE ALLOCATION AT THE CORPORATE LEVEL

Efficient resource allocation refers to the judicious and timely use of various resources so that a project is completed as per schedule.

Efficient project scheduling is a useful tool for the effective allocation of resources. The matter or issue of resource allocation by a company can be dealt in different ways. It may depend on the business function of the company, the demographical location of the company, or the type of service provided by them. While allocating resources, a company always keeps the optimal utility of resources. The optimal utilization of resources depends on how the firm is divided so that each division can contribute to the achievement of the firm's ultimate goal. The resource allocation pattern depends on the need for a change in the existing pattern of allocation and the need to make the decision-making process more centralized. It is also influenced by the decline of resources allocated in the existing pattern.

With the growth in the existing resources, it is easier for a firm to bring about a change in the way resource allocation was previously planned. This can be done by simply channelizing the fresh inflows to the areas where they are most required. Another way to keep a check on this is to create a central inflow of funds and make allocations from there. This refers to monitoring. In case of a strong central control, the company can hold competitive bidding among its divisions and the division with higher returns would get the fund first. In case of a weak central control, the allocation of the funds will be done through open negotiation between central and other divisions. If the need for a change in pattern is not felt strongly, then the allocation is made according to the existing pattern.

So, in short, it can be said that efficient project scheduling along with proper monitoring of the uses of resources and funds at the right time and right place results in optimum output (see Figure 3.1). All of them together are useful for effective allocation of resources.

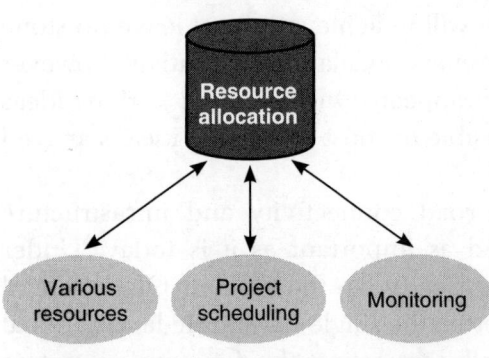

FIGURE 3.1 Resource allocation

3.2 RESOURCE ALLOCATION AT THE BUSINESS UNIT LEVEL

After the resources are allocated to the divisions or the business units of the firm, it is time for the units to think over the deployment of the allocated resources. A business unit level of a firm must identify the available opportunities for investing its resources. This identification can be done in two ways—by analysing its environment and by analysing its strategic capabilities.

Ideas that are new and beyond the framework are always subjected to these two types of analysis, as a company cannot invest its resources in a venture beyond its capabilities. Let us now discuss these methods in detail.

3.3 ENVIRONMENTAL ANALYSIS

Environment analysis can be done using various models such as PEST analysis and Porter's five force model.

3.3.1 PEST Analysis

To analyse the macro economy, it is important to find out factors that affect the most vital variables of organizations such as its supply and demand levels and its costs (Johnson and Scholes 1993). Tsiakkiros (2002) said, 'The radical and ongoing changes occurring in society create an uncertain environment and have an impact on the function of the whole organization.' To figure out issues that affect an industry, various analyses are used. PEST analysis is one of them. It factorizes environmental impacts such as political, economical, social, and technological forces (see Figure 3.2). If it considers additional forces, such as environmental and legal forces, then the analysis will be a PESTEL analysis.

Kotler (1998) opines that this analysis can be an effective strategic instrument for realizing market growth, decline, and the potential of the business. In addition to PEST, SWOT (strength, weakness, opportunities and threat) and Porter's five force

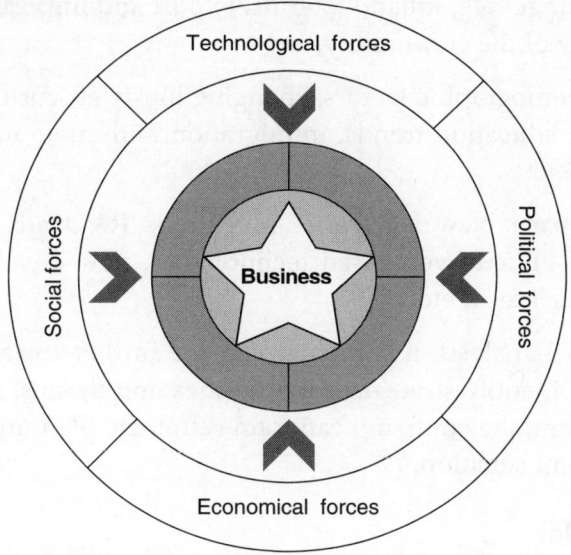

Source: http://thechangemanagementgroup.com, accessed 30 March 2010.

FIGURE 3.2   PEST analysis

models can also be applied by companies to analyse and frame strategic directions. PEST analysis also assures that the company's growth is positively inclined with the changes that are affecting the business environment (Porter 1985).

How political conditions affect the strategic decisions of a company can be easily experienced by the change in government policies, fluctuation of foreign currencies, etc. Economic conditions affect the success rate of a firm as they affect the availability of capital and the demand for a firm's product (Thompson 2002). The socio-cultural environment affects demand, tastes, cultures, customs (which vary with fashion), and these can provide both opportunities and threat for a particular company (Pearce and Robinson 2005). Technology is also an important instrument used as competitive advantage by a firm. Many a times, researchers have recognized the need for technological advantage and have mentioned it in various literatures on strategic management (Johnson and Scholes 1993; Jan 2002).

In conducting PEST analysis, each PEST factor, which has a significant role in affecting the overall business environment, needs to be considered. Examples of important factors are as follows.

Political   Elections, labour law, consumer protection, industry-specific regulations, environmental regulations, war, terrorism, world political trends, stability of the government, government policies, tax structure, relationship with neighbouring countries, etc. (including legal and regulatory).

Economic   Economic trends (both for the respective country as well as other countries), government economic policies, disposable income, unemployment rate, exchange rate, inflation, tariffs, export and import, production level, demand and supply of the commodity, etc.

Social   Demographic factors, changing lifestyles, customs, culture, fashion, living standards, education trends, immigration and emigration, family size, attitude of the people, etc.

Technological   New discoveries, inventions, R&D, advancement in manufacturing processes, IT and web-based technologies, new developments such as bio-tech, genetics, agri-tech, etc.

With PEST analysis, a company can see further towards the horizon of time. It can better identify strategic opportunities and threats. By looking into the outside environment, the company can frame strategic planning process for the future out of its present situation.

3.3.2 Porter's Model

Porter's analysis deals with factors outside an industry that affects the competition within it. A firm has to understand the dynamics of its industries and markets to compete efficiently. The original competitive forces model, as proposed by Porter, suggested five forces (Figure 3.3).

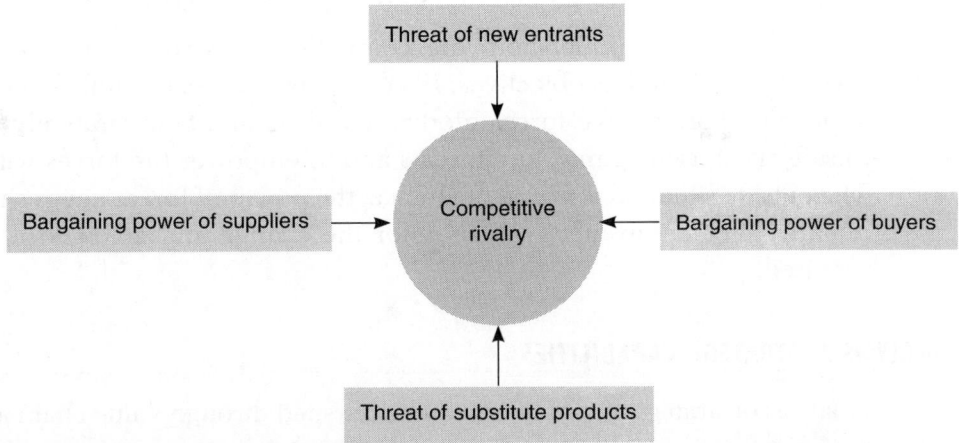

Source: Adapted from Porter M.E., *Competitive Strategy*, Free Press, 1980.

FIGURE 3.3   Five forces analysis

Degree of rivalry   This occurs between existing sellers in the market. It helps in determining the extent to which 'value' is created by an industry through head-to-head competition with other sellers. It is the most obvious out of the five forces, which is why it is located at the centre of the diagram. It is expected to be high where there is a threat of substitutes and from existing power of suppliers as well as customers in the market.

Threat of entry   There is always a threat of potential entry by new sellers in the existing market. The threat of new entrants is generally based on the entry barriers of the market. Cost of entry (investment in technology) and scale of economy (benefits associated with bulk purchasing) are examples of entry barriers. Both potential and existing competitors have an impact on the profitability of an industry. The existing competitors enjoy maximum market share and profit and also create an entry barrier for the new players in the market.

Threat of substitutes   The threat of availability of substitutes influences an industry's profitability. The degree of threat depends on the relative price and performance ratios of different types of products or services. For example, after laptops were launched in the computer peripheral market, sales of PCs reduced drastically.

Buyer power   In today's market, the customer is the king. Out of the two horizontal forces that influence the value creation of an industry, buyer power is more important. Buyer power determines the size and concentration of the customers.

Supplier power It is the mirror image of buyer power. It emphasizes first on the relative size and concentration of the suppliers with respect to the industry and second on the degree of differentiation in the input supplied.

A company must understand the competitive environment if it is to become successful and fulfil its objectives. If a company can successfully conceptualize and appreciate Porter's five forces model, it will be in a comparatively safer position to safeguard itself against any threats and to empower the forces with its strategy. The outside situation is not static; hence, the power of forces keeps shifting. Consequently, a company needs to monitor the change and adapt to it as and when required.

3.4 ANALYSIS OF STRATEGIC CAPABILITIES

Analysis of strategic capabilities can be pursued through value chain analysis, BCG matrix, etc.

3.4.1 Value Chain Analysis

The approach of value chain analysis was first pioneered by Michael Porter in his 1985 book *Competitive Advantage: Creating and Sustaining Superior Performance.* Value chain analysis is a concept of value addition and is utilized to develop a firm's competitive advantage. It is a useful tool for managers to identify the key activities within the firm that form its the value chain. It shows activities that have potential, sustainability, and competitive advantage for a firm. Figure 3.4 shows how, in order to pursue the value chain analysis, a firm can separate its activities into primary and support activities.

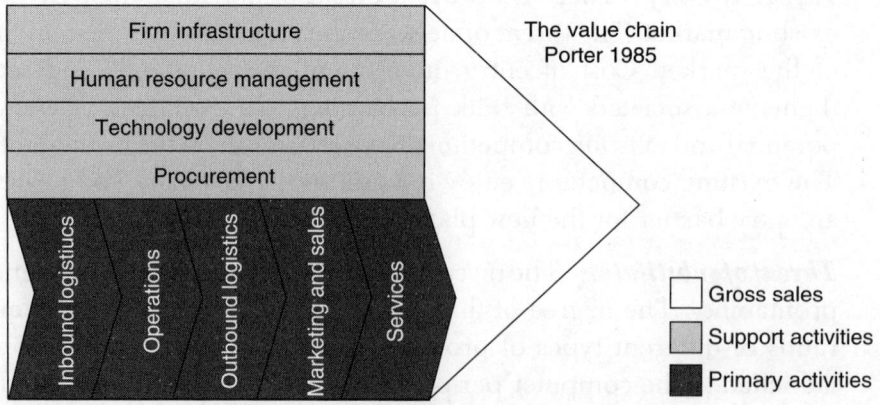

Source: http://www.kbrconsulting.com/methods/value_chain, accessed 30 March 2010.

FIGURE 3.4 Porter's value chain analysis

Activities that are directly associated with the core processes, such as inbound logistics, operations, outbound logistics, marketing and sales, and after-sales services, are called primary activities. Inbound logistics may involve processes such as transportation and storage of raw material. Outbound logistics include networking and distribution channels. Market research and promotion activities comprise the marketing process. After-sales process may include repair and replacement activities. Apart from these primary activities, a firm also requires certain support processes in order to function effectively. They are referred to as support activities. Infrastructure maintenance, raw material procurement, and human resource management are various kinds of support activities.

Wal-Mart adopted creative and pioneering ideas to strengthen its market position. It could make its motto Everyday Low Prices possible by optimum utilization of logistics, IT, and other processes. In case of IBM, its global network gives it a clear edge over its competitors. Also, it has put particular emphasis on customer care in order to maintain the reputation of the brand.

The interrelationship between different value chain activities are depicted by the value chain model. These relationships yield value to customers. The model consists of five primary activities and four support activities connected to each other by linkages. The potential of these activities to create value is computed by reducing them to micro activities. Cost differentiation (or cost advantage) method is used to calculate the value.

3.4.2 Portfolio Analysis/BCG Matrix

BCG is the abbreviation for Boston Consulting Group—the world's leading strategic consulting firm based in the US. BCG growth share matrix (Figure 3.5) is one of the popular BCG strategic concept evolved in the late 1970s.

There are two variables in this matrix structure. The vertical axis measures the market growth and the horizontal axis depicts the corresponding market share of the firm in a particular industry. Products with high market share growing rapidly in a market are expected to earn high profit margins, and vice versa (McDonald 2003, www.bcg.com).

The basic concept of BCG matrix says that by performing a task repeatedly, a firm tends to develop different optimistic ways that result in lowering costs and also scale economics (www.mindtools.com). The accompanying dominant market share invariably has a cost advantage for the firm over its competitors. Therefore, there is a positive correlation between market share and experience. Apple's blue-chip product called the iPod has 73 per cent market share in the portable music player market (Cantrell 2006). It is the iPod that has resurrected Apple, as its sales have increased by 40 per cent. Dell's PC lines also share the same market dominance theory as the iPod market. Dell occupies a world-wide market share of 18.1 per cent,

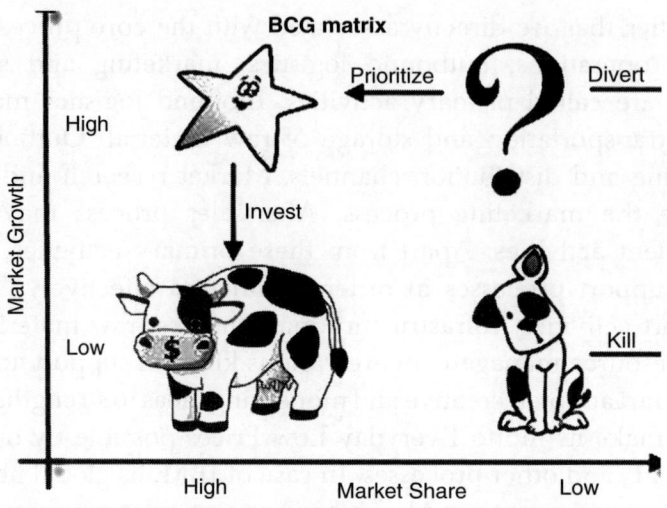

Source: http://share.sweska.net, accessed 30 March 2010.

FIGURE 3.5 BCG matrix

which is contributing towards its maximum market revenue in the PC market (Table 3.1).

TABLE 3.1 Company rankings as per revenue

	Name	Revenue
1	Dell Inc.	57,404.0
2	Ingram Micro Inc.	29,010.2
3	Tech Data Corporation	20,492.7
4	Apple Computer, Inc.	18,156.0
5	Sun Microsystem, Inc.	13,068.0
6	Gateway, Inc.	4,140.3
7	Agilysys, Inc.	1,720.9
8	Palm, Inc.	1,562.1
9	GTSI Corp.	879.1
10	Pomeroy IT Solutions. Inc.	671.7

Note: Figures in millions of dollars, as on 27 September 2006.

Source: http://university-essays.tripod.com/bcg_growth_share_matrix_boston_consulting_group.html, accessed 4 April 2010.

There is a definite role for market share and market growth in the decision-making of a product life-cycle paradigm. A product can be identified by one of the following characteristics.

Cash cows These products are highly profitable but require less investment because they play in a low-growth market. According to Drummond and Ensor (2004), excess cash from cash cow products should be channelized into stars and questions for creating future cash cows. Cash cows generate investment for their own growth. They also pay to their shareholders and debtholders. They pump their excess resources or funds to other products. According to Henderson (1976), they protect other weaker products. A good example would include steel factories of any manufacturing giant.

Stars They are the leaders in a high-growth market. They generate a large amount of cash but also require greater spending because of being in a high-growth market. For example, Apple Computers, which has a large share in the rapidly growing market for portable music players (Figure 3.6).

Problem children Also known as question marks they are unable to achieve a dominant market position and hence cannot generate much cash. At the same time, they tend to use a lot of cash because of high growth. Consider the Mac product range in the laptop and PC markets. They consist of a small share in a rapidly growing market (Figure 3.6).

Dogs They have both low market share and low growth rate hence they generate very little cash and have very bleak future prospects.

Once products have been positioned, the marketing analyst has to decide on the future business strategy. At this juncture, cash generated from cash cows should be invested in stars and question marks or problem children in an effort to create the future cash cows. Dogs should be liquidated. There are four available strategies that can be pursued at this stage.

1. *To build*—The market share of the product needs to be increased to strengthen position. Short-term gains can be foregone in consideration of long-term benefits. This is particularly applicable to question marks if they are to become stars.
2. *To hold*—To maintain the current status of market share (e.g., cash cows).
3. *To harvest*—Here management is willing to increase short-term cash flows as much as possible. This is used for question marks when there is no possibility of turning them into stars.
4. *To divest*—This strategy is used to drain out profits and use them for other purposes in order to have greater benefits. It is typically used for dogs.

Source: http://university-essays.tripod.com/bcg_growth_share_matrix_boston_consulting_group.html, accessed 4 April 2010.

FIGURE 3.6   Boston matrix

3.4.3 Flexibility Analysis

The flexibility of resources at the company's disposal is determined by flexibility analysis. In case of some unforeseen occurrence, the company should not be too rigid to modify its strategies. Identification of vague areas at work helps in the assessment of the company's ability to deal with actual instances of uncertainty that may occur in the future. After identification, it is important to understand the potential strength of the uncertain areas and the impact that they can have on the company. The company can make required preparations, in advance, to shield itself against the worst. Also, flexibility analyses take into account the way in which the company's resources would respond in case of an adverse situation, where the initial strategy may undergo considerable change.

For instance, in the case of a food processing company, sudden inflation in the cost of raw materials would immediately impact the prices of its finished products. Flexibility analysis can enable the company to decide on a feasible solution to this unforeseen problem. It could replace the raw materials it uses, provided its existing infrastructure allows so. It could also look for an alternative supplier of the raw materials. Thus, flexibility analysis helps in dealing with such uncertain situations at work.

3.5 CREATIVITY AND IDEA GENERATION

Initiation of a new project, review and renewal of an existing one, and introduction of a new customer care strategy are various activities that refer to a project lifecycle. In order to initiate this process, a request for proposal (RFP) is required. The RFP can be about introduction, upgradation, design, etc. of a new or older product. It is critical for a firm that wants to create and maintain a standing in the market. It demands a genuine inflow of creative ideas (Figure 3.7). The nature of the project determines the level of creativity required. It needs to be seen whether the product already has a market (and therefore also competition) or is it a pioneering initiative.

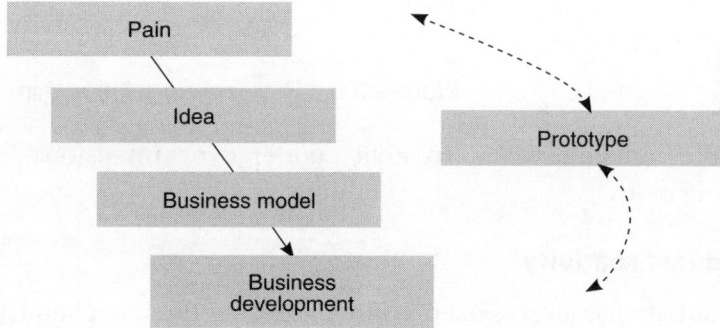

FIGURE 3.7   New idea generation

For example, Apple's I-Pod is a first-of-its-kind product in the market. It has more unique features than the I-Phone, which despite its path-breaking design and technology had to compete with other touchscreen phones. Both products required creative attention. In order to survive in an existing market and grow, a product such as the I-Phone has to go through a continuous process of creativity and innovation.

Creativity is an essential component of a project lifecycle. The management must be able to channelize creative ideas appropriately. It must know when to encourage creativity and when to avoid it. Depending on the nature of the task at hand, innovative ideas can come from groups as well as individuals. Not just project management, but all management processes today seek creative potential in the workforce.

Innovation may not always yield success. A new idea is like a new risk. It may backfire. Today, managers are trained to avoid unnecessary risks. But such an attitude also limits the free flow of creative ideas. According to Hayes and Abernathy in *Managing Our Way to Economic Decline* (1980), the apprehension among firms to take up risky initiatives is so high that it often leads them to ignore and miss out on the considerable benefits that they may be capable of yielding (Figure 3.8).

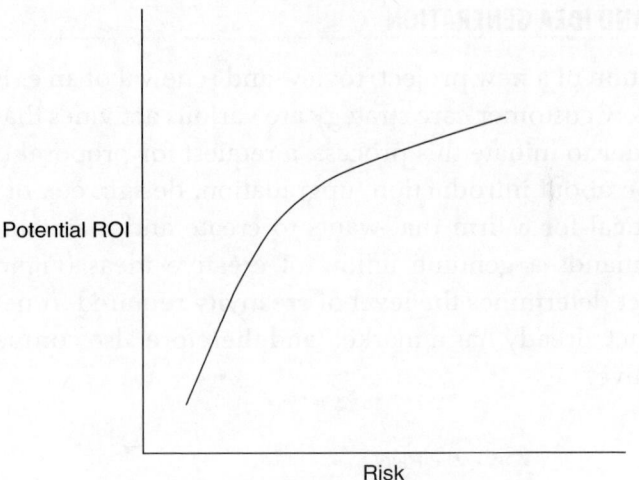

FIGURE 3.8   Risk–return relationship

We can understand creativity under two dimensions—individual and group-level creativity.

3.5.1 Individual Creativity

Creativity has always been instinctive rather than mechanical. The institutional and disciplined prototype approaches for creativity do not help in producing unique ideas. However, they help people to produce more generalized ideas from which they can choose the most suitable one. People generate more and more creative ideas as they start thinking out of the box and diverging beyond the borders.

Some methods to encourage individual creativity are given below:

1. *Attribute listing*—This method was developed by Zwicky (1969). In this method, attributes of a new product become new qualities. An attribute list can be constructed by separating all major characteristics of the desired capabilities with no boundaries. After the modifications are envisaged, they go through a feasibility check.

2. *Checklist*—This consists of a set of conditions that fit in the situation to envision new solutions (as depicted in Figure 3.9).

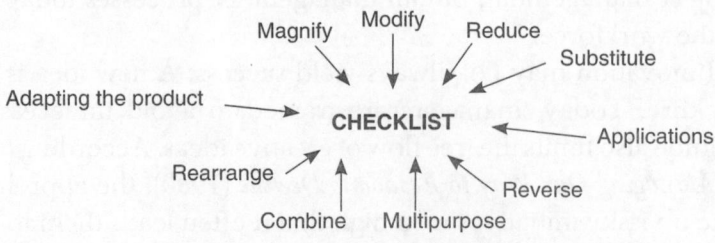

FIGURE 3.9   Checklist points

3. *Working backwards*—Here, the perfect solution is postulated and technical capabilities of the solution are considered through working backwards.

4. *Black box*—In this approach, available inputs and desired outputs are listed, after which all possible transformation solutions based on general ideas from inputs to the desired output are formatted.

5. *Directed dreaming*—This is an attempt to reach the best possible solution of a problem through deep dreaming using the subconscious mind.

3.5.2 Group Creativity

Group creativity is needed when the problem faced is not well understood. Group creativity is more effective than individual creativity when the nature of the problem is ambiguous and not well defined. The argument is also supported by the effect of synergy, i.e., the whole is greater than the sum of its parts.

Following are some commonly used techniques for group creativity.

Brainstorming This technique was developed by Alex Osborn in 1953 and since then has been used most widely in the generation of ideas in groups. It is a method of sharing new ideas and opinions in a group through an exhaustive thinking process.

Morphology This method was invented by Zwicky in 1947. In this process, the problem is stated by capabilities most likely to be in the solution and then cross-checked for feasibility. All factors affecting the solution are structured into categories and then the intersections of all the categories are analysed. Each point of intersection is then cultivated in favour of the solution.

Storyboarding This is a method of finding out a solution to the problem, where in all the attributes of a problem are listed. All possible variations and combinations of such attributes are made in such a way that the maximum number of feasible solutions are obtained for a single problem.

Delphi Though Delphi is one of the popular methods of forecasting, it is also used as a type of group creativity method. In this method, the collective knowledge of a group is used for identifying, forecasting, and solving the problem. It is a method in which individual biases in a formal group can be avoided.

Nominal group techniques It is a structured and organized method that involves both group and individual contribution to the solution of the problem. Generally it is headed by a coordinator. It is done through steps such as silent idea generation, idea presentation, idea clarification, prioritization, selection, and discussion of results.

Thus, individual and group creativity contributes towards generating unique ideas for projects as per their suitability. But innovation is not an easy task. It demands a lot of initiative and involvement at all the levels of the project team.

SUMMARY

Generating project ideas calls for scouting for opportunities after which the resources are allocated at both the corporate and business level. PEST analysis is carried out to figure out the political, economical, social, and technological factors affecting an organization. Porter's five forces analysis deals with factors outside an industry that affects the competition within it. The original competitive forces model, as proposed by Porter, suggested five forces namely, the degree of rivalry, the threat of entry, the threat of substitutes, buyer power, and supplier power. Some other methods used are value chain analysis, BCG growth matrix, and flexibility analysis. Certain individual and group creativity techniques are used to solve problems that are faced by organizations.

KEY TERMS

BCG matrix   BCG (Boston Consulting Group) matrix is a popular strategic concept which states that market share and its growth play a role of in the decision-making of a product lifecycle paradigm.

PEST analysis   An analysis of the factors that play a significant role in shaping the overall business environment, that is political, economic, social, and technological factors.

Value chain analysis   It is a useful instrument for managers to identify the key activities within the firm. These activities form the value chain for that firm and create potential and sustainable competitive advantage. In order to pursue the value chain analysis, the company separates its activities into primary and support activities.

CONCEPT REVIEW QUESTIONS

1. Describe with an example how resource allocation can be pursued both at corporate and business unit level.
2. What are Porter's 'five forces'? Describe how they are significant for strategizing a company's goal.
3. What are the primary and support activities in case of Porter's value chain analysis?
4. What can a firm do to augment the generation of project ideas and creativity? Explain how it can be possible through individual and group effort.

CRITICAL THINKING QUESTION

Sriram Enterprises Limited is a diversified group targeting different types of consumer products. The Sriram Soap division is performing extremely well but consumes excess financial resources. Sriram Cosmetics Limited targets various cosmetics used by men and women. Both these units demand not only funds but also creative talent. The company wants to perform a portfolio analysis using the BCG matrix. Explain how the analysis can be performed.

ASSIGNMENT

Perform the PEST analysis and value chain analysis of any upcoming project in your state or country.

SELECT REFERENCES

Cantrell, A., 'Apple's Remarkable Comeback Story', CNNMoney.com, 2006, accessed 13 September 2010.

Drummond, G. and J. Ensor, '*Strategic Marketing: Planning and Control*', 2nd ed. Butterworth-Heinemann, MA, 2004, pp. 96–100.

Heyes, R., and W. J. Abernathy, 'Managing our way to economic decline', *Harvard Business Review*, July-Aug, 1980.

Jan, Y., 'A three-step matrix method for strategic marketing management', *Marketing Intelligence and Planning*, vol. 20, issue 5, 2002, pp. 269–72.

Johnson, G. and K. Scholes, '*Exploring Corporate Strategy—Text and Cases*', Hemel Hempstead, Prentice-Hall, 1993.

Kotler, Philip, '*Marketing Management—Analysis, Planning, Implementation, and Control*', 9th edn, Englewood Cliffs, Prentice-Hall, 1998.

Lynch, R., '*Corporate Strategy*', 3rd edn, Prentice Hall Financial Times, 2003.

McDonald, M., '*Marketing Plans: How To Prepare Them, How To Use Them*', MA: Butterworth-Heinemann, 2003, pp. 175–245.

Magretta, J., '*Why business models matter*', *Harvard Business Review*, 2002.

Pearce, J. and R. Robinson, '*Strategic Management*', 9th edn., McGraw-Hill, New York, 2005.

Porter, M., '*Competitive Strategy*', Free Press, New York, 1980.

Porter, M., '*Competitive Advantage: Creating and Sustaining Superior Performance*', Free Press, New York, 1985.

Rai, S., '*India becoming a crucial cog in the machine at IBM*', *The New York Times*, 2006.

Thompson, J., '*Strategic Management*', 4th edn., Thomson, London, 2002.

Tsiakkiros, A., 'Strategic planning and education: The case of Cyprus', *The International Journal of Educational Management*, Bradford, 2002.

Zwicky, F., '*Discovery, invention, research through the morphological approach*'. NYC: Macmillian, 1969.

Other resources

www.bcg.com, accessed 4 April 2010.

www.mindtools.com/pages/article/newTED_97.htm, accessed 4 April 2010.

VARIOUS APPRAISAL METHODS IN PROJECT SCANNING AND SELECTION

On project selection my personal philosophy is not to undertake a project unless it is manifestly important and nearly impossible.

— EDWIN LAND

LEARNING OBJECTIVES

After studying this chapter, you will be able to

- Know how to identify a target market
- Discuss how to conduct a market survey and forecast market demand
- Understand project purchase, vendor selection, and contract administration
- Conceptualize plant capacity, importance plant location, etc.
- Understand pollution prevention and environmental regulations
- Analyze various social appraisal approaches such as UNIDO, LM, etc.
- Understand the linkages between CSR and project management

Chemical Hub on West Bengal–Nayachar Island—Will Damage Environment

A citizen's expert committee has slammed the West Bengal government's dream chemical hub project on the Nayachar Island on Hooghly River saying that it would cause serious ecological damage. Nayachar, a 47-sq. km island on Hooghly River in East Midnapore district, has been selected as the likely place for the proposed chemical hub in West Bengal. The state government settled for Nayachar after being forced to move from Nandigram, the first site chosen for the chemical hub.

The committee, formed by city-based environmental activists, said that Nayachar is an estuarine shoal and any structural intervention on the land would imperil its delicate ecology. They also commented that the newly selected location for the chemical hub at Nayachar cannot be termed an island. It is better to call it a land of alluvial deposit which emerged above water level in 1930 and continues to evolve by the process of erosion and accretion. This vast area has been a major source of nutrients to various aquatic life forms. Setting up of any type of petrochemical industry could cause serious contamination in the river water by its toxic discharge.

Further, more than 2,50,000 people earn their livelihood by fishing at Nayachar. West Bengal contributes 2,00,000 tonnes of fish every year, which generates an export revenue of about Rs 10 billon (Rs 1,000 crore) annually. The fishing community would stand to lose their livelihoods if the project came up.

That is why the committee was questioned about not only environmental appraisal but also the socio-economic viability of the upcoming 'chemical hub' project at Nayachar.

Source: Indo-Asian News Service (IANS), 18 March 2008, at www.ians.in, http://www.thaindian.com, accessed 1 April 2010.

4.1 MARKET APPRAISAL

The success of any project depends on the demand for the output produced by it. The firm should identify the demand for a product in the market as well as the needs of customers. Different features of a market should be tested before launching any new product or brand in the market. This is termed as 'market appraisal of a project'.

When analysing the markets, a marketing analyst is interested in knowing the market demand of the proposed product which will be manufactured after the successful completion of the project. To answer this question, following information is required:

1. Consumer behaviour trend
2. Past and present demand and supply
3. Nature of competition in the market
4. Pattern of demand
5. Size of the market and market share
6. Channels of distribution
7. Market segmentation
8. Pricing policies
9. Administrative and legal issues
10. Government tax, excise duty, and other regulations

4.1.1 Target Market Identification

Though there are many opportunities in the world, identifying the right project at the right time is very difficult. Though there are no clear-cut methods for project identification, the basic factors guiding identification are more or less the same for all projects. Identification is the process of hitting upon the right project. But how does one chose the right project or get a perfect business idea? How did JRD Tata think of a steel plant and set up a steel city called Tata Nagar? How did Dr Kurien get the idea of launching Amul? How did Dhirubai Ambani hit upon the idea of starting a textile unit and building the Reliance empire?

The potential of a project idea lies in its ability to transform into a profit-making venture. Long-term government policies and its development strategies are critical to determine the feasibility of a project idea. A project, whether government or private, must take into account and be responsible towards the socio-economic situation and culture of its immediate society, as well as the whole country. A new project usually caters to either the manufacturing or services segment.

In India, a new venture requires the approval of the central government's Planning Commission and Departments of Economic Affairs and the Industrial Development Organizations. The state governments also have their respective industrial development organizations for this process.

A manufacturing or services enterprise can be successful only if there is a market for their output. Target market identification helps in this regard. Once the target market is determined, the available resources and means of production can be utilized to their optimum potential to achieve the desired output. Such an enterprise can be called a success as it not only makes profit for itself, but fulfils the requirement of it customers as well.

Pre-feasibility (PF), techno-economic feasibility report (TEFR), and detailed project report (DPR) (refer to Appendix 3) are the three essential stages in which a project proposal is analysed and, eventually, rejected or cleared (Figure 4.1). After a project proposal is scrutinized by the government and the governing body of the enterprise, a preliminary sanction is given to the project feasibility report (PFR). Exhibit 4.1 shows the list of data required in a PFR.

The objective of appraisals in all the three stages of evaluation and project decision is to ensure that the project is viable from the following angles:

- Market share for the project's end product and plant capacity (Section 4.2).
- Raw materials and other inputs—Details of raw materials, other inputs and utilities according to different specifications, their selection, description, location, and estimation of costs.
- Demographic location and project site—Final selection of site depends on many local considerations and clearances. There are a few industries whose survival has much to do with the local political and communal sentiments. Other aspects to be considered are the availability of land (Tata's Singur Nano car project), environmental clearance (Nayachar's Chemical Hub), law and order situation (the recent Vedantya case in Orissa), and labour productivity influenced by the local political environment (the Koel Karo project in Bihar).
- Technology used in the project (details in the discussion on technical appraisal in Section 4.2).
- Project costs—This represents the total cost of all the items of outlay associated with a project, which are supported by long-term funds.
- Human resources—No project can become successful without the required manpower and their effective participation.
- Network scheduling—Identification of project activities and events and scheduling them in the correct sequence is a key requirement for the success of a project.
- Financial appraisal—A company can undertake a project if it is financially feasible, i.e., if the project creates wealth for its shareholders.
- Statutory clearances—Before starting a project it should get various statutory clearances. Its PFR should receive a green signal from concerned administrative ministry (AM) and the committee of public investment board (CPIB). After that, the TEFR must get a clearance from the Public Investment Board (PIBF). Then

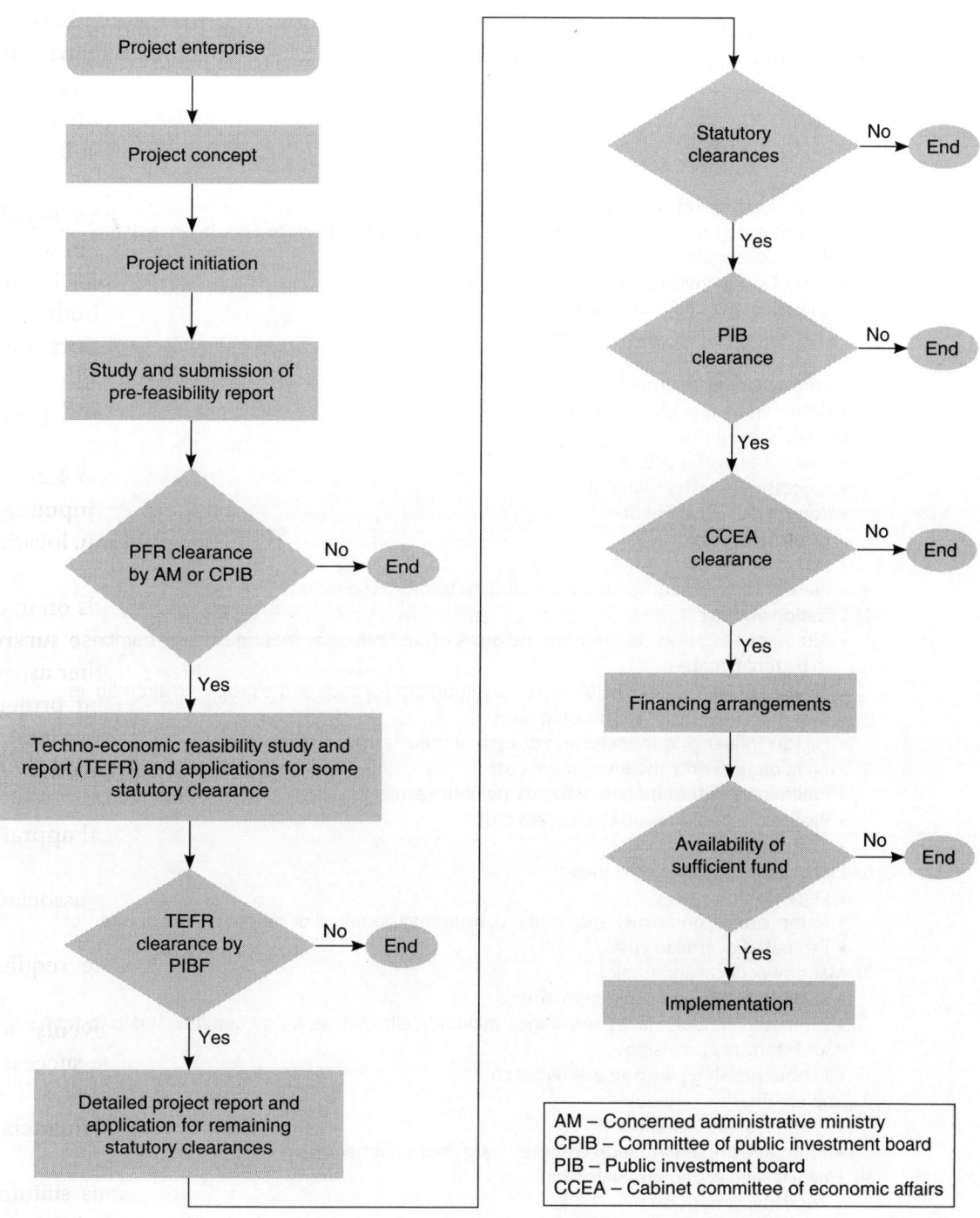

Source: Manual for the Preparation of Industrial Feasibility Studies, IDBI edition, UNIDO, 1997.

FIGURE 4.1   Project clearance cycle

a DPR should be prepared and it must be cleared by the PIB and the cabinet committee of economic affairs (CCEA). Finally, it has to be checked whether the required fund is available.

EXHIBIT 4.1   Information to be contained in a PFR

1. Project background and description
   • Project enterprise's name and profile, its experience and performance in project implementation
   • Project description
   • Cost of study/investigation already carried out
2. Market demand and plant capacity
   • Demand pattern, size, and market
   • Sales forecast and marketing plan
   • Production programme
   • Determination of plant capacity
3. Materials and inputs
   • Raw materials/feedstock
   • Processed industry material
   • Bought-out components
   • Auxiliary materials
   • Factory supplies
   • Power, water, and other utilities, including transport services
4. Location and site
   • Alternative location, description, and areas of land pre-selected (indicate the number of families to be rehabilitated)
   • Estimated cost of land including its development for each of the proposed alternatives
   • Schedule and cost of soil investigation
   • Factors influencing the selection of each of the alternatives proposed
5. Project engineering and investment cost
   • Preliminary determination of the scope of the project
   • Process technology and equipment cost
   • Civil engineering works
6. Plant organization and overheads
   • Organization layout
   • Name, profile, and experience of the consultant appointed or proposed for appointment
   • Estimated overhead costs
7. Manpower (local and foreign)
   • Estimated manpower requirements
   • Estimated annual salaries and wages, including allowances, fringe benefits, and long-term social and statutory provisions
   • Labour housing plan and estimated cost
8. Implementation schedule
   • Proposed time schedule
   • Estimated implementation cost matching the implementation programme
9. Financial and economic evaluation
   • Total investment cost
   • Project financing arrangement proposed
   • Operating costs
   • National economic evaluation

10. Status of clearance and approvals from various central and state government bodies mentioned below (as per Industrial Policy Act, 1991):
    - Soil investigation report
    - Industrial license/letter of intent
    - Automatic permission of specific approval, as the case may be, for foreign technical collaboration
    - Automatic permission of specific approval, as the case may be, for foreign investment
    - Approval for appointment of foreign consultant
    - Foreign exchange permission
    - Import license or automatic permission for import of capital goods and raw materials, as per Press Note No. 13 of 1991
    - Vetting of the draft prospectus for capital issues by the Securities and Exchange Board of India (SEBI)
    - Clearance from the Pollution Control Board
    - International Airport Authority's clearance
    - Clearance from the Ministry of Railways
    - Electricity authority/board clearance
    - Clearance from the chief controller of explosives
    - Clearance from the chief conservator of forest
    - Clearance from the state industries department

Source: Manual for the Preparation of Industrial Feasibility Studies, IDBI edition, UNIDO, 1997.

4.1.2 Market Survey

Before the finalization of the project report, the capability of the product to penetrate the market should be analysed. The demand for the product and the revenue that the product can possibly generate should be analysed considering factors such as the technology used, plant capacity, production programme, and marketing strategy. The marketing strategy must be projected for at least 10 years from the year of inception. Competitors' strategising of price, ad-campaigns, and the distribution channel networking should also be analysed. While preparing the project revenue statement, the most important thing that should be taken into account is the cost associated with the above mentioned factors.

The following parameters and factors should be kept in mind before marketing decisions are taken:

- What is the current market or the customer base of the product? On the basis of a proper survey, the market demand and supply of the product should be projected. It can be applicable for a single product or the product mix. Demand has to be analysed in both domestic and foreign markets.
- The next thing to do is to analyse the competitor's marketing and product strategy.
- Decision has to be taken regarding the external marketing assistance or agencies, existing marketing channel and distribution networking system, and the possibility for improvement.

- Whether any tax concession financing scheme/subsidiary incentives are offered by governments/banks to enhance the sale or export of a particular product/ service. For example, special economic zones (SEZs), export processing zones (EPZs) or free trade zones, etc.
- Selling price movement of the last few years and its relationship with the wholesale price index or consumer price index and also the prices of raw material and other overheads. In this regard, a detailed sensitivity analysis (discussed in Chapter 7) would be helpful in developing a pricing mechanism.

However, the above market information is not sufficient for the survival of a firm in a competitive market. A strong interconnection between the marketing plan and production schedule (Figure 4.2) must be established. That is why plant capacity, scale of economy, and capacity utilization according to the demand should also be taken care of. For these, following issues should be considered:

1. Scale of economy—If there is a large demand for a product in the market, then producing on a large scale ultimately decreases the per unit cost of production.
2. Latest research and development feedback available from known sources— These are to be assessed over product improvement and future demand curve. It should be noted that penetrating time for a more sophisticated product, such as an ERP package, IT product, or any other technology-driven product, is longer than that for others because customers might hesitate to use a complex product. It takes more time to make them comfortable with such a product.
3. Examine market stability aspects, i.e., whether the present demand pattern is durable or not? Is the expansion and growth projection linked with some temporary boom or depression, and if so, then how long is it expected to last on a reasonable assessment?
4. What percentage of the demand projection is supported by a captive market?
5. What are the company's strengths for succeeding in a competing market? Is the product or the process unique? Does the firm have a history of success? Up to what extent does the project assure quality of the product with respect to its targeted price? Are the assumptions of input cost, financing, and overhead expenses that form the base of the estimated selling price error-free?
6. Effective output of the plant—This should be decided with reference to the designed capacity, number of working days, number of shifts, number of hours per shift, percentage utilization of capacity taking into account the plant shutdown for maintenance and overhauling, possible breakdown or any other downtime, efficiency factors of labour and machines, and other operating norms.

Figure 4.2 shows the relationship between production programme and marketing programme.

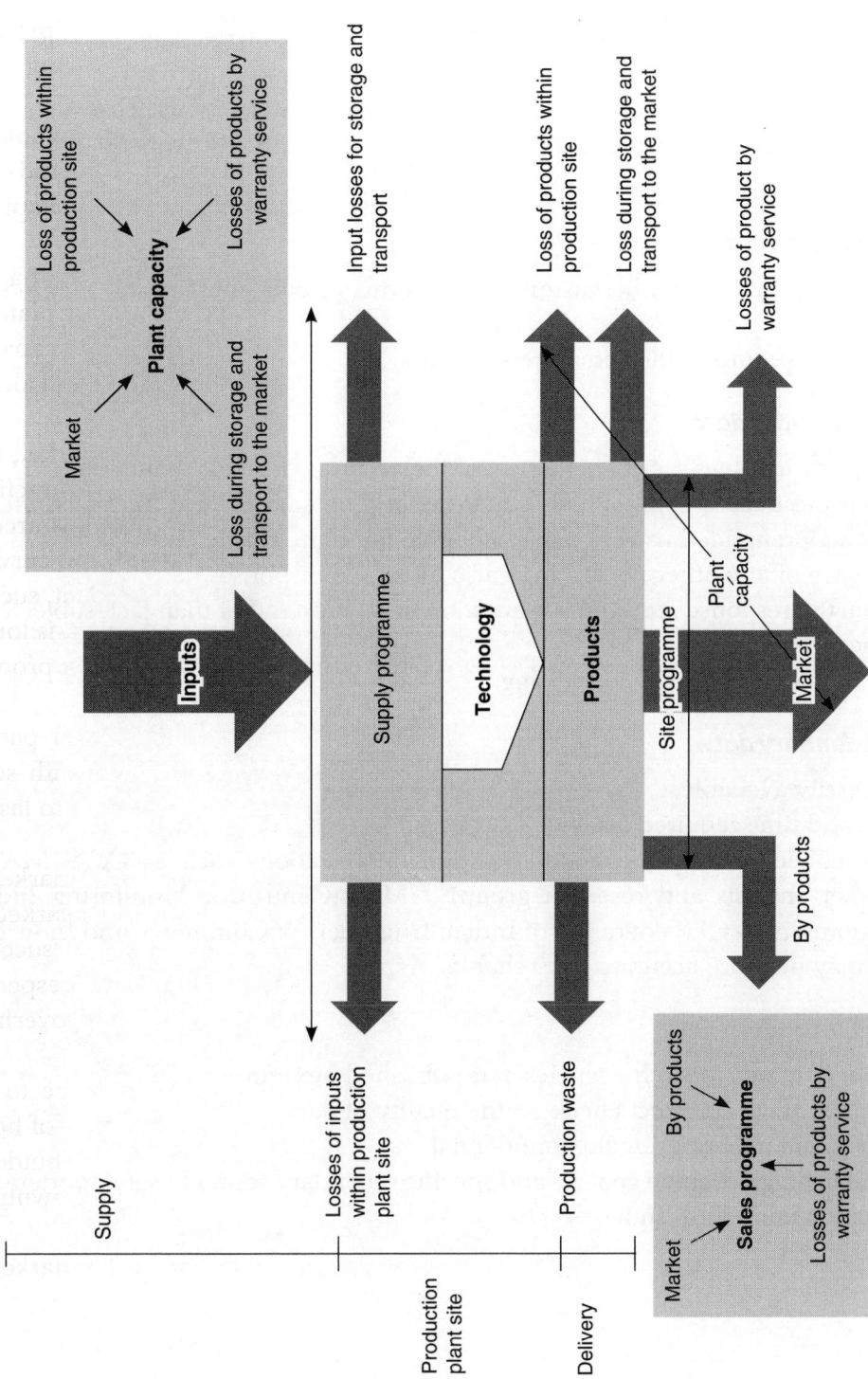

FIGURE 4.2   Plant input and output

Source: Manual for the Preparation of Industrial Feasibility Studies, IDBI edition, UNIDO, 1997.

4.1.3 Demand Forecasting using Primary and Secondary Data

The base of the market and demand analysis depends upon the data sources. These data can be from primary or secondary sources. Primary information represents data that is collected for the first time to meet a specific purpose whereas secondary data has been gathered in some other context and it is already available in the data source.

Advantages of primary data

1. The study/survey can be customized in terms of data sources and methods of analysis.
2. Higher exposure to the actual trends of market.

Disadvantages of primary data

1. Sampling involves sacrificing a part of the accuracy for cost reduction.
2. When the data is confidential, embarrassing, or unknown to the respondents, they may refuse to answer or may not give the right answer.
3. Presence of any other person may also affect the responses.
4. When the response required is a question of opinion rather than fact, subjectivity comes into play.
5. It is both cost and time consuming.

Advantages of secondary data

1. It is easily available.
2. Cost and time required are less.
3. Data collected by professional research organizations such as ORG MARG (market analysis and research group), CMIE (Centre for Monitoring Indian Economy), FICCI (Federation of Indian Chambers of Commerce and Industry), etc. may be more accurate and reliable.

Disadvantages of secondary data

1. Dependent on research agencies and published literature.
2. User can have no direct check on the quality of data.
3. User's plan may not remain confidential.

Exhibit 4.2 gives some general and specific secondary sources useful for demand and market analysis in India.

Exhibit 4.2 Sources of secondary information

General sources
Reserve Bank of India—www.rbi.org.in
National Stock Exchange of India—www.nseindia.com
Bombay Stock Exchange—www.bseindia.com
Annual Survey of Industries—www.mospi.nic.in/stat_act_t3.htm
Economic Survey—www.indiabudget.nic.in
Indian Year Book—www.rrtd.nic.in
Central Statistical Organization India—www.mospi.gov.in
Census of India—www.censusindia.net

Industry-specific secondary sources
Automobile Association of India—www.automobileindia.com, www.siamindia.com
Fertilizers Association of India—www.faidelhi.org
Organization of Pharmaceutical Producers of India—www.indiaoppi.com
Central Electricity Authority of India—www.cea.nic.in
All India Radio and Electronics Association—www.airea.org
Indian Electrical Manufacturers Association—www.ieema.org
Indian Machine Tool Manufacturers Association—www.imtma.in
Steel Wire Manufacturers Association of India—www.swmai.org/steel.htm
Bombay Silk and Art Silk Mills Research Association—www.sasmira.org
Indian Jute Mills Association—www.ijma.org
Cement Manufacturers Association of India—www.cmaindia.org
Federation of Hotel and Restaurant Association of India—www.fhrai.com
Indian Institute of Packaging—http://iip-in.com
Marine Product Export Development Authority—www.mpeda.com

4.1.4 Projection of Demand Using Qualitative and Quantitative Model

Demand forecasting of a particular product in a market is possible through using various qualitative or quantitative models.

Quantitative approach (time series)   In forecasting techniques, instead of using qualitative approach, a statistical-based quantitative approach is adapted. This approach is more accurate and methodical and obviously less biased. However, it is more complex and tedious to compute. Forecasting can be done by moving average, exponential smoothing, method of least squares, etc. Detailed discussions of each are given in Chapter 8. Numerical examples of each method are explained below.

Example 4.1 The information given in Table E4.1 is related to the sales of a particular commodity of ABC Limited. Find out three yearly moving averages and give the forecast for the year 2011.

TABLE E4.1

Sl No.	Year	Sales in Rs
1	1998	2,00,000
2	1999	1,89,000
3	2000	1,86,000
4	2001	1,78,000
5	2002	1,67,000
6	2003	1,56,000
7	2004	1,54,000
8	2005	1,83,000
9	2006	1,57,000
10	2007	1,60,000
11	2008	1,70,000
12	2009	1,63,000
13	2010	1,51,000

Solution

Moving averages are given in Table E4.2.

TABLE E4.2

Sl No.	Year	Sales in Rs	Three-year moving total	Three-year moving average
1	1998	200,000	–	–
2	1999	1,89,000	5,64,000	1,88,000
3	2000	1,86,000	5,53,000	1,84,333.34
4	2001	1,78,000	5,31,000	1,77,000
5	2002	1,67,000	5,01,000	1,67,000
6	2003	1,56,000	4,77,000	1,59,000
7	2004	1,54,000	4,93,000	1,64,333.33
8	2005	1,83,000	4,94,000	1,64,666.66
9	2006	1,57,000	5,00,000	1,66,666.66
10	2007	1,60,000	4,87,000	1,62,333.33
11	2008	1,70,000	4,93,000	1,64,333.33
12	2009	1,63,000	4,84,000	1,61,333.33
13	2010	1,51,000	–	–
14	2011	1,50,000		

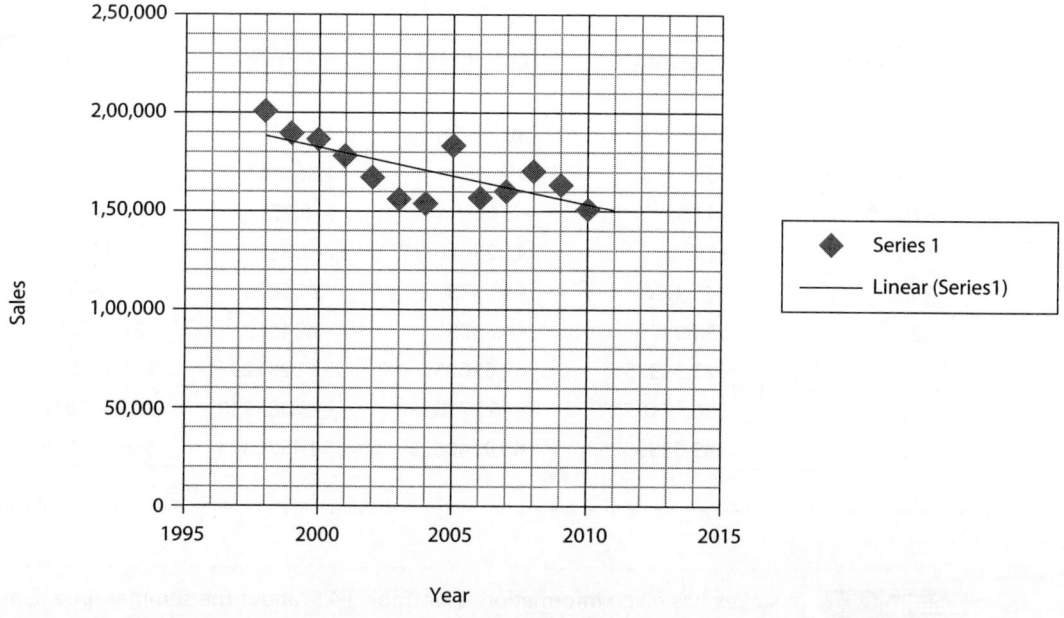

FIGURE E4.1

The forecasted sales of the company for the year 2011 is Rs 1,50,000 (as can be determined from Table E4.2 and Figure E4.1).

....

....

Example 4.2 If the initial forecast for a product is 320 units, find out and compare the forecast for $\alpha = 0.5$ by exponential smoothing method based on information given in Table E4.3.

TABLE E4.3

Sl No.	1	2	3	4	5	6	7	8	9
Forecasted units in numbers	350	360	310	370	300	320	390	310	400

Solution

Old forecast = F_1 = 320 units

Actual observation = D_1 = 350 units

For $\alpha = 0.5$,

$$F_0 = F_1 + \alpha(D_1 - F_1)$$

$$= 320 + 0.5 \,(350 - 320)$$

$$= 320 + 15$$

$$= 335$$

Similarly, we can calculate for all the observations as is shown in Table E4.4.

TABLE E4.4

Observation D1	Forecast (F_1)	Error (D1–F1)	$\alpha \times$ Error	New forecast in units ($F_1 + (\alpha \times$ error))
350	320	30	15	335
360	335	25	12.5	347.5
310	347.5	–37.5	–18.75	328.75
370	328.75	41.25	20.625	349.375
300	349.375	–49.375	–24.6875	324.6875
320	324.6875	–4.6875	–2.34375	322.34375
390	322.34375	67.65625	33.828125	356.171875
310	356.171875	–46.171875	–23.085938	333.0859375
400	333.0859375	66.9140625	33.4570313	366.5429688

Example 4.3 A survey has given information, as in Table E4.5, about the summer time demand for air conditioners in nine cities across India.

TABLE E4.5

Population in city in 10^6 (X)	5	7	8	11	14	16	18	22	23
Number of ACs demanded (Y)	45	65	55	75	95	98	100	106	107

Fit a linear regression of Y on X and estimate the demand for ACs of a city whose population is 21×10^6.

Solution

Regression equation $= Y = a + bX$

$\Sigma Y = na + b\Sigma X$

$\Sigma XY = a\Sigma X + b\Sigma X^2$

TABLE E4.6

Population of the town (X)	No. of coolers demanded (Y)	Size of population sq. of X	Product of X and Y
5	45	25	225
7	65	49	455
8	55	64	440
11	75	121	825
14	95	196	1330
16	98	256	1568
18	100	324	1800
22	106	484	2332
23	107	529	2461
$\Sigma X = 124$	$\Sigma Y = 746$	$\Sigma X^2 = 2048$	$\Sigma XY = 11436$

Substituting the values from Table E4.6, we get

$$746 = 9 \times a + b \times 124 \qquad (1)$$

$$11436 = a \times 124 + b \times 2048 \qquad (2)$$

Solving Eqn (1) and (2), we get

$a = 35.91$ and $b = 5.58$

Now the required equation is $Y = 35.91 + 5.58X$

The demand for ACs for a town whose population is 21×10^6 is $Y = 35.91 + 5.58 \times 21 = 153.09$ (nearly 154 ACs).

Subjective or qualitative or judgmental techniques   Quantitative methods generally produce a more reliable forecast than qualitative techniques. But it is not always possible to apply quantitative methods due to time shortage, data insufficiency, and cost curtailment. A few qualitative approaches used for forecasting demand of an existing or new product are jury of executive opinion, Delphi technique, sales force opinion, and market survey (detailed discussions of each in Chapter 8).

4.2 TECHNICAL APPRAISAL

Technical appraisal means the identification and scanning of the engineering aspects of a project. It seeks to determine whether all the features or attributes required for the successful commissioning of the project have been considered or not. Analysis also happens with respect to its location, size, and process. Accordingly, the entire layout plan and the work schedule are prepared.

4.2.1 Project Purchase Management

Project purchasing is one of the fundamental functions that is performed by all types of business organizations. It is impossible for any project to achieve its final target without a successful purchasing activity.

The primary objective of project purchasing is to buy materials as well as services of the optimum quality in right quantity from the best possible sources at the right place and time. In case of project procurement, basic objectives must be satisfied. An efficient manufacturing process requires an uninterrupted supply of input material. The inventory needs careful management in order to avoid any shortage or excess of material. Vendors play an important role in this regard. Therefore, multiple vendor-sourcing is vital, as a single vendor may not be equipped to supply the required quantity of raw material at all times. A good rapport with vendors and indenters is important to deal with any conflict regarding material supply. Finally, the best quality of raw material supply should be opted for within the budget.

4.2.2 Vendor Selection

After the need has been identified, the next step is to search for an appropriate vendor. If the project involves items of regular nature for which sources are known, search for a good vendor does not require much time. However, if the requirement list consists of high value or rare items, then a lengthy investigation procedure may be involved in finding a potential supplier. After a potential supplier has been identified, the project manager may use the technique of competitive bidding or negotiation to get the best rate.

Documenting of the purchasing process is a very important part of this job. Since the purchase order is a legal document, the company must specify the price, quantity, and delivery requirement and the provisions that are unique for the particular contract. The contract detail containing the terms and conditions of the contract in a clear-cut manner is popularly known as boiler plate.

4.2.3 Contract Administration

A project manager stays responsible for governing all the contracts associated with the project. It could be fixing of rules and regulations, exercising rights and obligations, or issuing amendments to orders.

Companies often use a project summary to keep persons associated with the project informed about the critical deadlines of the project. It is a kind of desktop reminder containing a brief description of the project, critical deadlines, and important clauses of the project.

4.2.4 Procurement of Equipment and Materials

Project purchasing is little different from regular day-to-day production purchasing. Project purchase is mainly concerned with the procurement of equipment or machinery and project materials. Capital equipment procurement is pursued step by step as discussed below:

1. For more than 75 per cent of the capital equipment purchased, the user department's need is to be recognized first.
2. As capital equipment procurement is a very costly affair, it can usually be postponed until the conditions for purchase become favourable. The initial inquiry may come to the purchase department in the form of a requisition. After which, the purchasing department consequently obtains general sales and operating literature, together with the approximate price and delivery information.
3. The user department studies the preliminary information obtained by the purchasing department and determines the feasibility of pursuing the matter further.
4. If the joint decision is favourable, then detailed specifications should be drawn up both by the user and purchase departments.

5. When the investigation is complete and the specifications are firmed, the purchasing department formally requests for proposals from selected vendors. If one or two vendors produce an acceptable machine, the buyer might very well choose to negotiate rather than purchase at that very instance.

6. An economic analysis of the various feasible alternatives is made at this point. The finance department typically makes this analysis, based on operating and technical information provided by the purchasing, engineering, and user departments.

7. The necessary facts are now ready for evaluation by the departments participating in the decision. In a small company, evaluation is frequently an informal affair; in large organizations, a formal committee meeting is the typical method of operation.

8. The written report is submitted to the top management for decision-making purposes.

4.2.5 Plant Capacity and Location

The location of a plant is finalized depending on its capacity requirements. For example, if a plant operates at 80 per cent capacity utilization, it should be located in such a place where the required amount of raw material, labour, etc. is available in nearby places. Hence, both the plant and the place are interdependent.

Plant capacity

It is defined as the number of units produced by a plant per unit time. Machinery, workforce, raw material, etc. comprise the productive resources for a manufacturing unit unlike the service-oriented units, where customers are the most important resource. For instance, in a production unit, maximum capacity is recorded when it is operating at its full capacity utilization. When the unit tries to just achieve the breakeven point in production, it is said to be operating at its minimum capacity. Similarly, a consultancy firm, at an average, attends to 4 customers in an hour. In 8 working hours, it is able to serve about 32 customers. Hence, 32 is the capacity per day of the given service industry firm.

Capacity is a rate that can be measured during the input or the output of a production system, as shown in Figure 4.3.

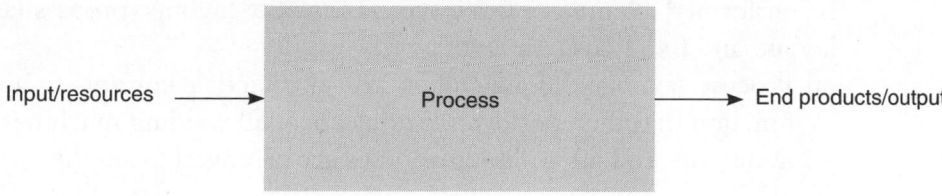

FIGURE 4.3 Production systems

System can be defined as a repetitive work that involves certain inputs or resources and produces specific outputs. In multi-product manufacturing firms, capacity is measured in terms of aggregate units per time period, notwithstanding the combination of the output produced. This method is adopted because it is difficult to compute individual capacities of different products, as their resource base is common.

Location

A plant refers to a place where the workforce, raw material, capital, and machine equipment are combined to produce goods. The efficient functioning of a plant greatly depends on its location. The plant should accommodate alterations that may have to be introduced due to changes or upgradations in the product type. A plant may have to be terminated, expanded, or diversified in the future, depending upon its performance. The firm should consider these factors while deciding upon the appropriate location for the plant. Availability of labour, raw material, and changing market conditions also influence the location of plant site.

Factors of location A plant location is finalized after considering certain important factors. They can be divided into primary and secondary factors. Availability of raw material, skilled workforce, local market for finished products, etc. are the primary factors. Topographic and climatic site conditions of environment, stable socio-economic availability of funds and aids, and support facility for the workforce such as hospital, housing, school, etc. form the secondary factors.

4.2.6 Project Layouts and Work Schedule

Project layouts Layout decisions are concerned with the arrangement of production, customer service, uninterrupted flow of materials and other resources, efficient use of materials and workers, communication systems, etc. The word layout is used to define the physical arrangement of machinery and other equipment in various parts of the project. In the case of a project, the most important layouts, other than the plant layout, are discussed below.

1. *Facility or utility layout*—The arrangement of various machines and equipment on the shopfloor is called facility layout. The layout should be designed keeping in mind the type of manufacturing process and the extent of each process to be performed. There are three types of facility layouts: process layout, product layout, and fixed position layout.
   (a) Process layout—All machines are arranged according to the process or function that they perform. For instance, all welding machines are arranged at one site and all drilling machines are arranged at another site.

(b) Product layout—All the machines are arranged in a line and also in a sequence according to the order of operations to be performed. Such layouts are also known as assembly lines.

(c) Fixed position layout—It is used when the item to be manufactured is huge in size and too bulky to be moved around. For example, shipbuilding, aircraft building, boiler manufacturing, etc. need a fixed position layout.

2. *Functional layout*—In this layout, the relationship of the building and the equipment is considered. It is designed in such a way that from the receiving of raw material to the processing and the outgoing, the movement of finished stock happens without interruption and hazard.

3. *Transport layout*—Here, the distance between various facilities outside the production line and the modes of transport is considered.

4. *Communication layout*—It shows the networking directions between various divisions such as telephone lines, IT network, etc.

5. *Organizational layout*—It is concerned with the number of people required for a particular project site in each stage and their hierarchical relationship.

Work schedule

Work schedule can be defined as the schedule of construction of the entire project, installation of the plant, making the facilities ready for their services, or making commercial production. Work schedule tells the project manager that all tasks are synchronized and coordinated. It also assures the supply or availability of power, fuel, raw material, etc. A good work schedule is responsible for making the construction, installation, and the commissioning of the project smooth and successful.

4.3 ENVIRONMENTAL APPRAISAL

Like market, technical, and financial appraisal, environmental appraisal is another criterion for the selection of a project. A project may cause environmental pollution in several ways. It may pollute air by hazardous gaseous emission. It may produce liquid and solid discharges that get mixed in nearby water bodies and lead to several diseases. Industries may also create noise, heat, and vibrations that are above the safety limits, resulting in various types of discomforts and disorders to the general population.

While selecting a project, the following environmental aspects need to be considered:

• The types of effluents and emissions produced by the proposed project
• Proper prevention mechanism for their disposal
• Whether projects can get the necessary environmental clearance and fulfil all statutory requirements

Exhibit 4.3 gives an insight into the Environment Protection Rules (1986).

EXHIBIT 4.3   Environment and pollution

The Environment (Protection) Rules, 1986, defines environmental pollution as the build-up and concentration of toxic levels of chemicals in the air, water, and land, which reduce the ability of the affected area to support life. Pollutants may be gaseous such as ozone and carbon monoxide, liquid discharge from industrial plants and sewage systems, or solid-landfills and junkyards.

Pollution is the presence of any extraneous substances in any of the components of the environment in amounts that cause harm to life, directly or indirectly. The definition given to the term 'air pollution' by the Air (Prevention and Control of Pollution) Act 1981 is more specific and also considers excessive noise as a pollutant. The Water (Prevention and Control of Pollution) Act, 1974, has a more stringent definition: 'Pollution means such contamination of water or such alteration of the physical, chemical or biological properties of water or such discharge of any sewage or trade effluent or of any other liquid, gaseous or solid substance into water, harmful or injurious to public health or safety, or to the life and health of plants or animals or aquatic organisms.'

Source: http://www.moef.gov.in accessed 17 April 2010.

4.3.1 Pollution Prevention

Pollution prevention is a set of activities/methods carried out to decrease the amount of pollution generated at the source. We will be discussing some of these methods for preventing pollution in air and water separately.

Air pollution treatment   Air pollutants can be separated by using different separation methods. These are as follows:

1. *Mechanical separation*—Air containing particles of the pollutants is passed slowly through chambers called collectors. Particulate matter being heavier than air settles down at the bottom of the chambers.
2. *Electrostatic precipitation*—In this method, an electrostatic precipitator imparts electric charge to the particulate matter. Then the air containing the particulate matter is passed over an electric plate with an electric charge opposite to the particles. The particles get attracted towards the plate and are collected.
3. *Filtering*—Air containing pollutants is passed through porous media such as felt or fibrous materials. This method is considered to be very effective and very popular too.
4. *Scrubbing*—In this method, generally, minute drops of water are used to trap the particulate matter. As some gases react with water, some gaseous pollutants can be eliminated.

Water pollution treatment   The main challenge in preventing water pollution is how to treat effluents. Processing of the industrial effluence before releasing into the rivers is called effluent treatment. It is done in the following three phases:

1. *Primary treatment*—Primary treatment is aimed at removing the undesirable chemicals, particles, suspended matters, or organic matters through mechanical means. Mechanical devices such as screens and filters are used for removing

particles. Water containing particulate matter is allowed to stand for sufficient time in the tanks (grit chambers), so that the particles settle down to the bottom of the tank.

2. *Secondary treatment*—It is carried out to eliminate pollutants, such as proteins, carbohydrates, and fats, which cannot be separated and are carried over from the primary treatment. Secondary treatment is done by generally using suitable micro-organisms. The mechanisms commonly used are trickling filters, activated sludge, oxidation ponds, and biological disc.

3. *Tertiary treatment*—There are many chemicals that cannot be degraded using the above mentioned procedures. They are dealt with during the tertiary treatment. Chemicals such as detergents, pesticides, and petro-chemicals call for modern treatment methods. In chemical precipitations, certain chemicals are added to the effluents to precipitate the polluting substances. This is known as the method of oxidation. Pollutants are converted to other harmless substances through oxidation. Oxygen, potassium permanganate, and hydrogen peroxide are commonly used as oxidation agents.

4.3.2 Environmental Regulation Regarding Project

Dabhol Power Project

Nayachar Chemical Hub

Larson and Gray (1999) pointed out correctly the importance of environment factors in project execution referring to the Enron Dabhol power project. They opined that change of site layout would involve very difficult tanker manoeuvring, relocation of about 2000 families, and possible adverse effects on river estuary ecology.

Another example is that of the Nayachar chemical hub. Nayachar is an island in Hooghly River (East Midnapore, India). The West Bengal government started the project of developing a mega chemical hub with more than 5000 acres of land to be given to chemical industries. Fifty-four sq. km land was allotted to PC Roy Chemicals Pvt. Ltd in February 2009. However, the vast area of Nayachar has been a major source of nutrients to the various aquatic life forms. Environmental experts have commented that setting up of any type of petrochemical industry could cause serious contamination in the river water by its toxic discharge. They strongly feel that Nayachar is not environmentally viable for setting up of a chemical hub.

According to the Indian constitution, the responsibility of safeguarding the environment, the forests, and the wildlife lies with the government. The ministry of environment and forest looks after these issues. Several acts and regulations have been passed by the parliament in the interest of the environment. Some of them are as follows:

1. The Environment (Protection) Act, 1986 (see Appendix 4.1)
2. The Water (Prevention and Control of Pollution) Act, 1974
3. The Air (Prevention and Control of Pollution) Act, 1981
4. The Indian Forest Act, 1927.
5. The Wild Life (Protection) Amendment Acts, 2002
6. The Air (Prevention and Control of Pollution) Rules, 1982
7. The Water (Prevention and Control of Pollution) Rules, 1975
8. The Environment (Protection) Third Amendment Rules, 2002
9. The Environment (Siting for Industrial projects) Rules, 1999 (see Appendix 4.2)

Source: http://www.moef.gov.in, accessed 14 April 2010.

4.4 SOCIAL APPRAISAL

Besides financial appraisal (which is discussed in detail in Chapter 5), demand appraisal, technical appraisal, and environmental appraisal of a project, social appraisal is also becoming a key factor in the final selection, execution, and success of a project. In Exhibit 4.4, the story of Tata's small car project in Singur explains how socio-economic impact is important for a project's implementation.

EXHIBIT 4.4 Pull out of Singur

It may be recalled that in March 2006, Tata Motors had announced their intention of establishing an automobile plant at Singur, West Bengal, and the company decided to roll out by 2008 a small and cheap car called Nano priced at US$2000 with a capacity of 2,50,000 vehicles per annum with a flexibility to raise it to 3,50,000 vehicles per annum targeting both the foreign and domestic market.

In March 2007, the West Bengal government entered into an agreement with Tata Motors on the proposed plant. It has been alleged that Tata was offered several concessions by the government, which both parties felt shy of disclosing to the public. A total of 997.11 acres of land spread across Singur, a town in district Hooghly, had been acquired by WBIDC and handed over to Tata. However, in the face of serious socio-political protests, Mr Ratan Tata, the chairman of the Tata Group of Companies, made a press statement on 22 August 2008 expressing his willingness to 'pull out' of

Singur. In response to such an unwarranted statement, it has been pointed out by Mr Ravindra Kumar that the Tata project management team had done little to address the social impact of the investment.

On 2 September 2008, Tata Motors communicated through an official release that the company is evaluating alternative sites for manufacturing Nano car and came up with the detailed plan to relocate the plant and machinery to an alternative site. This pull-out threat was a strategic move to negotiate further with other competing states. In case of Ford's Amazon project in Brazil (1999), crisis took place in the same way. Hanson Gordon's analysis (2001) explains the political motives of the government as well as the firm. From day one, the Singur-Nano project became controversial mainly due to land issues. IBS research centre, Kolkata (2008) had prepared a survey report for the feasibility of Tata's small-car project at Singur. They raised questions about setting up plant on heavily fertile land and the compensation package offered to landowners.

Source: 'Strategic Evaluation by Using Real Options', an article written by the author and presented as a paper at the International Finance Conference 2009 at IIM, Calcutta (3–5 December 2009).

4.4.1 Social Cost-Benefit Analysis

Social cost-benefit analysis (SCBA) refers to the assessment of a proposed project on the basis of its social advantages and disadvantages in financial terms. The advantages can be direct or indirect, visible or invisible, real or nominal. SCBA is conducted keeping in mind the socio-economic conditions of the country.

According to Scidler and Ramanathan (1989), social accounting analyses the social relevance and contribution of a firm, both from within and outside its business interests. Financial viability alone cannot ensure selection of any project. It must also perform well in the analysis of its socio-economic role. In case of the Delhi Metro Rail, the project was implemented more for its social role of providing an advanced and yet affordable means of transport to the masses as opposed to the pure financial benefits.

Differences between the financial analysis and economic analysis are due to the following reasons:

1. *Imperfect market*—Market prices depict the exact social values clearly only in the case of perfect competition, which is a rare phenomenon in real life.
2. *External benefits or cost*—There might be some externalities, which may not be relevant in the case of financial evaluation of a project. But they are included in the case of SCBA. For example, in the case of Delhi Metro, the social benefit obtained is reduction in pollution, which is not considered or reflected in the financial evaluation.
3. *Taxes and subsidies*—In case of SCBA, taxes and subsidies are considered as transfer payments and receipts and hence they are irrelevant.
4. *Concern for savings*—The parts of benefits saved is considered to be more important than the parts of benefits consumed. In SCBA, savings are given more priority than consumption, whereas in financial appraisal it is not.
5. *Concern for redistribution*—A single rupee going to the poor or needy is considered to be more important and significant than huge benefits to the affluent.

4.4.2 UNIDO Approaches

The UNIDO approach (named after United Nations Industrial Development Organization) is an inclusive process of conducting social cost-benefit analyses (see Exhibit 4.5). This approach is a result of several important conferences organized by UNIDO in the 1960s. The final compilation of the approach was published in the early 1970s.

EXHIBIT 4.5 The UNIDO method

UNIDO method involves five stages:

Stage I: *Calculation of financial profitability measured at market prices*—In this stage financial profitability of a project is analysed.

Stage II: *Obtaining the net benefit of the project measured in terms of economic (efficiency) prices*—The next stage is to obtain the cost and benefit, of the project at current market price and find out the net economic benefit which is the difference between these two at current market price in an imperfect market.

Stage III: *Adjustment for the impact of the project on savings and investment*—This is important for a project since it generates benefits to groups who save very little out of additional income. In case of developing countries where there is a shortage of capital as well as the required amount of savings and investment, this stage must be carried out.

Stage IV: *Adjustment for the impact of the project on income distribution*—Every project has to be analysed on the basis of whether it will make poor people poorer and rich people richer.

Stage V: *Adjustment for the impact of the project on merit goods and demerit goods*—If the project produces a product whose social and economic values are different, adjustment for this impact should be analysed. Though in reality, this case is very rare.

Source: www.unido.org, accessed 16 April 2010.

To obtain the net benefit of the project measured in terms of socio-economic parameter, the concept of shadow pricing needs to be understood.

Shadow pricing

Financial profit or the net present values of a project are measured at market prices and a detailed analysis of this will be covered in the next chapter. According to SCBA and UNIDO approaches, shadow price or economic price represents the market price under perfect market condition. Net socio-economic benefit is measured with respect to shadow price.

Basics of shadow pricing Shadow pricing is based on the basic items of shadow pricing, concept of tradability, sources of shadow prices, tax treatment, and determination of numeraire.

Basic items of shadow pricing The thee basic items of shadow pricing are main outputs (the series of benefit if there are no externalities and they are sold at protected prices), material inputs—both imported and non-imported—and unskilled labour.

(a) Concept of tradability—A commodity is said to be tradable if it is importable instead of being domestically produced and can be exported instead of being domestically consumed. The economic opportunity cost or its real value to the country in terms of pure efficiency is the international price. The major categories related to tradability of goods are tradable, traded, non-tradable, and non-traded. A good is tradable if it can be imported or exported in the absence of trade barriers. A good is said to be non-tradable when its real domestic cost of production together with its international transport cost is too high to permit export and too low to make import attractive.

(b) Sources of shadow prices—UNIDO approach suggests three sources of shadow pricing (Figure 4.4):
   (i) Increase or decrease the total consumption in the economy (consumer willingness to pay)
   (ii) Decrease or increase production in the economy (cost of production)
   (iii) Increase or decrease export or import (foreign exchange value)
   where, DD' = Demand schedule
   SS' = Supply schedule
   OQ = Quantity bought
   OP = Price per unit
   ODEQ = Total willingness
   OPEQ = Price paid
   DEP = Consumer surplus

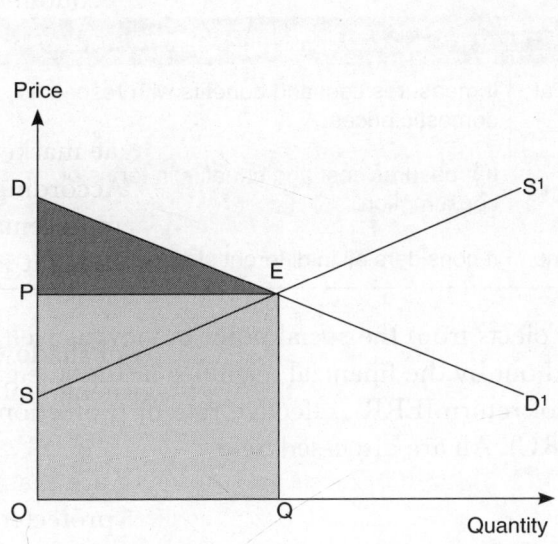

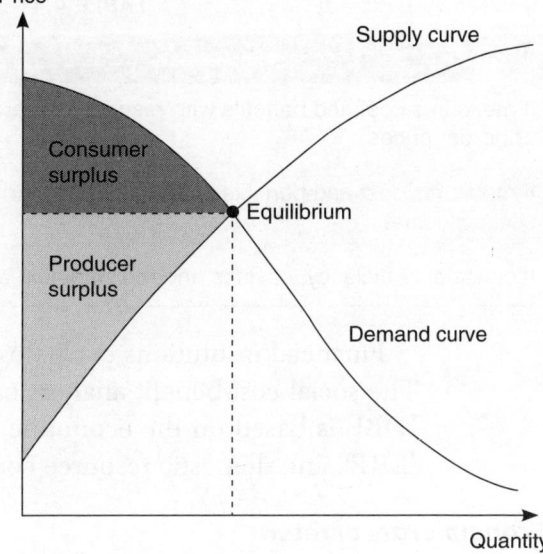

Source: www.unido.org, accessed 17 April 2010.

FIGURE 4.4 Shadow pricing

(c) Tax treatment—The general rule of tax treatment is that when a project uses non-traded goods in fixed amount, taxes should be implemented as a part of the customer's willingness to pay the marginal shadow price. There will be no tax burden for fully traded goods.

(d) Determination of numéraire—In this case, unit of accounts for the evaluation of inputs and outputs are considered. For instance, what unit and how much amount of currency should be taken care of for a particular—present or future—consumption or investment?

UNIDO numéraire According to UNIDO approach, 'UNIDO numéraire is the net present consumption benefits in the hands of people at the base level of consumption in the private sector in terms of constant price in domestic accounting unit.'

4.4.3 Little and Mirrlees Approaches

Little and Mirrlees (LM) approach is a method of measuring a project with respect to its socio-economic costs and benefits. It calculates cost and benefit in terms of international prices. Hence, it is applicable only to foreign projects.

The similarities with UNIDO and LM for social cost-benefit analysis are as follows:
- In both cases, discounted cash flow analysis is used.
- Forex savings and unskilled labour calculation of shadow prices is done in both cases.

Dissimilarities between these two approaches are listed in Table 4.1.

TABLE 4.1   LM versus UNIDO

LM approach	UNIDO approach
It measures cost and benefits with respect to international or border prices.	It measures cost and benefits with respect to domestic prices.
It measures cost and benefits in terms of uncommitted social income.	It measures cost and benefits in terms of consumption.
It considers efficiency, savings and redistribution at a time.	It considers all in different stages.

Financial institutions evaluate all projects from the social point of view as well. The social cost-benefit analysis carried out by the financial institutes in India (e.g. IDBI) is based on the economic rate of return (ERR), effective rate of protection (ERP), and domestic resource cost (DRC). All are discussed below.

Economic rate of return

ERR is the rate of return of a project in terms of social cost and benefit. It can be calculated in the following ways:

- All non-labour inputs are evaluated at border prices, which perfectly reflect the true economic value.
- For tradable items whose international or border prices are directly available, CIF prices are considered for input and FOB prices are considered for output.
- For tradable items whose international or border prices are directly available, social conversion factors (SCF) are used. The SCF and weightage for different components like tradable (T), labour (L), and residual (R) used by the IDBI are shown in Table 4.2.

TABLE 4.2   SCF values and weightages used by IDBI

Item	SCF or proportion
Land	SCF = 1/1.5
Building and construction	Proportion: T = 0.5, L = 0.25, R = 0.25
Indigenous equipment	SCF = 0.70
Transportation	Proportion: T = 0.65, L = 0.25, R = 0.10
Engineering and know-how fees	SCF = 1.50
Bank charges	SCF = 0.02
Preoperative expenses	SCF = 1.00
Labour	SCF = 0.50
Salaries	SCF = 0.80
Repairs and maintenance	SCF = 1/1.5
Water, fuel, etc.	Proportion: T = 0.50, L = 0.25, R = 0.25
Electricity	Proportion: T = 0.50, L = 0.13, R = 0.16
Domestic stores	SCF = 0.80
Other overheads	SCF = 1/1.5
The social conversion factors for various components (tradable, non-tradable, and residual)	
Tradable component	1/1.5
Non-tradable component	0.5
Residual component	0.5

Source: www.idbi.com, accessed 17 April 2010.

Example 4.4   ABC limited is evaluating a project to produce a particular raw material, which is being imported. The capital expenditure estimation for the project is shown in Table E4.3.

TABLE E4.3

Capital expenditure	(Rs in lakhs)
Land	50
Building	120
Plant and machinery (imported) (CIF value = Rs 100 lakh)	80
Plant and machinery (indigenous) (CIF value = Rs 600 lakh)	700
Transportation cost	20
Technical know-how fees	50
Preoperative expenses	50
Bank charges	10
Total	1,080

Projected annual income statement of the company is as follows in Table E4.4.

TABLE E4.4

Income	(Rs in lakhs)
Net sales (18,000 tonnes @ Rs 80,000 per tonne, CIF value Rs 70,000 per tonne)	1,440
Expenditure	
Imported raw material (CIF value Rs 80 lakh)	100
Indigenous raw materials	800
Labour	80
Salaries	50
Repairs and maintenance	20
Water, fuel, etc.	80
Electricity (Rate = 40, Duty = 20)	60
Other overheads	70
Profit before tax	180

If the life of the project is 10 years and working capital requirement is Rs 200 lakh (CIF value is Rs 175 lakh) estimate the social value of the proposed project as per LM approach.

Solution

To find out the value of the social cost of the project, first the social cost of the initial investment has to be calculated. It is done in two steps:

Step 1: Dividing all capital inputs into tradable and residual components

Step 2: Calculation of social values of various components

Step 1. Splitting of capital inputs (items from capital expenditure statement) Table E4.5

TABLE E4.5

Item	Financial cost	Basis of conversion	Tradable value	Tradable (T)	Labour (L)	Residual (R)
Land	50	SCF = 1 / 1.15	43.47			
Building	120	T = 0.5, L = 0.25, R = 0.25		60	30	30
Plant and machinery (imported) (CIF value = Rs 100 lakh)	80	CIF value	100			
Plant and machinery (indigenous) (CIF value = Rs 600 lakh)	700	CIF value	600			
Transportation cost	20	T = 0.65, L = 0.25, R = 0.1	–	13	5	2
Technical know-how fees	50	SCF = 1.5	75			
Pre-operative expenses	50	SCF = 1	50			
Bank charges	10	SCF = 0.02	0.2			
Working capital	200	CIF value	175			
Total	1,280		1,043.67	73	35	32

Step 2. Calculation of social value (items from capital expenditure statement): Table E4.6

TABLE E4.6

	Rs in lakhs
Total tradable value	1,043.67 (taken from the above table)
Social cost of tradable component (73 / 1.5)	48.67
Social cost of labour component (35 * 0.5)	17.5
Social cost of residual component (32 * 0.5)	16
Total social value	1,125.8

Similarly, the social value of various inputs used in the production process can also be estimated. It is done in two similar steps.

Step 1. Splitting of capital inputs (items from income statement) Table E4.7

TABLE E4.7

Item	Financial cost	Basis of conversion	Tradable value	Tradable (T)	Labour (L)	Residual (R)
Imported raw material (CIF value Rs 80 lakh)	100	CIF value	80			
Indigenous raw materials	800	SCF = 0.8	640			
Labour	80	SCF = 0.5	40			
Salaries	50	SCF = 0.8	40			
Repairs and maintenance	20	SCF = 1 / 1.5	13.33			
Water, fuel, etc.	80	T = 0.5, L = 0.25, R = 0.25	–	40	20	20
Electricity (Rate = 40, Duty = 20)	60	T = 0.71, L = 0.13, R = 0.16	–	42.6	7.8	9.6
Other overheads	70	SCF = 1 / 1.5	46.67			
Total	1,260		860	82.6	27.8	29.6

Step 2. Calculation of Social value (items from income statement) shown in Table E4.8

TABLE E4.8

	Rs In lakhs
Total tradable value	860 (taken from above table)
Social cost of tradable component (82.6 / 1.5)	55.07
Social cost of labour component (27.8 * 0.5)	13.9
Social cost of residual component (29.6 * 0.5)	14.8
Total social value	943.77

Given: Net sales is Rs 144 crore (18,000 tonnes @ Rs 80,000 per tonne, CIF value Rs 70,000 per tonne)

Hence,

CIF value of output = 18,000 × 70,000 = Rs 1,260 lakh

Therefore,

Social net benefit per annum = CIF value of output – social value of input = 1,260 – 943.77 = Rs 31,6.23 lakh

Source: 'Project management' of the ICFAI University Press, 2006

Effective rate of protection

Effective rate of protection (ERP) = (Value added at domestic price – Value added at world prices) / Value added at world prices

Value added = Selling price – Input costs

The selling price used is the price, net of taxes and excise duties, but including the selling commission. The world prices for exported goods are FOB prices and CIF prices for imported goods.

Domestic resource cost

DRC is the expenditure required in terms of domestic currency to generate a saving of one unit of a foreign currency. The commonly used foreign currency for estimating DRC is the US dollar.

Domestic resource cost = (Value added at domestic prices / Value added at world prices) × Exchange rate

4.4.4 CSR in Project Management

According to Fonteneau (2003), corporate social responsibility (CSR) means moral and ethical concerns, good governance in the form of codes of conduct, self-proclaimed charters, social and ethical levels, and socially responsible investments. Today, CSR is a must for successful business in all business organizations and institutions.

We have experienced with the Satyam issue, global financial fraud, and many more socially and ethically irresponsible practices such as bankruptcies, high level of window dressing, very high manager salaries, disrespect of moral values, and no linkage between financial and socio-economic activities.

Society is the entire backdrop against which a company should do business and generate wealth for its shareholders. At the same time, the company's contribution towards society in terms of some tangible works described in Figure 4.5 should not be forgotten.

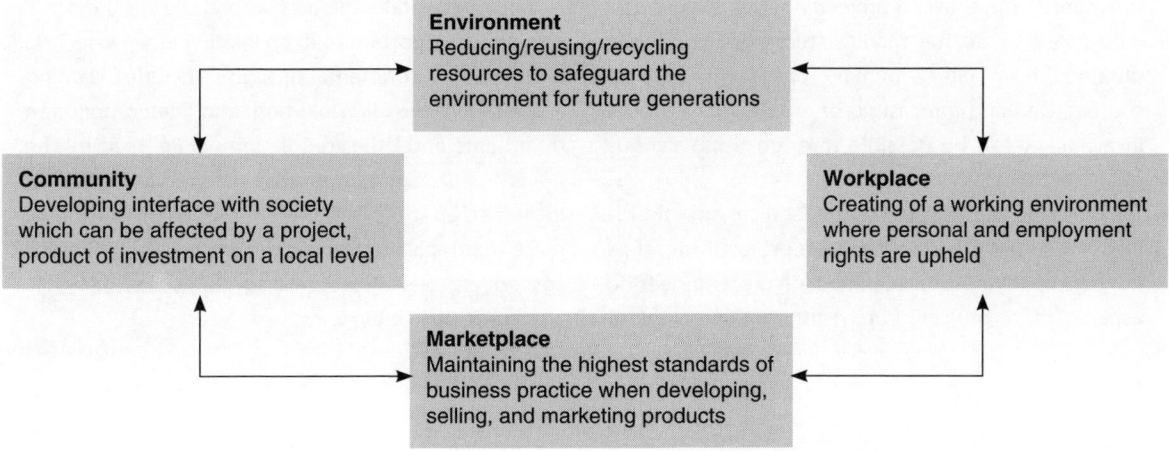

FIGURE 4.5   Need for CSR

CSR is not a new bit of jargon in management studies. With the evolution of market economy, malpractices, misconduct, anti-social, and inhumane incidents are coming to light at an increasing rate. According to the neo-liberal ideology, the ultimate objective of a company is how to increase shareholder's value to the maximum possible without hampering social and ethical mandates.

4.4.5 PSU investments

SCBA is obviously more relevant and useful in public sector than in private sector. In case of PSU investments, public money is involved. That is why it is expected that these projects will give the highest consideration to the entire society. PSU projects are rooted through the central or state government and are appraised by the project appraisal division of the planning commission. While appraising projects, the department considers some basic principles. To evaluate tradable inputs, international prices are always used. Power transports and other non-tradable items are evaluated at marginal cost and forex valued at predetermined rate. On the other hand, semi-skilled and unskilled labour is valued at shadow wage rates. Taxes and other duties are not taken into consideration during evaluation.

SUMMARY

The success of any project depends on the demand for the output produced by it. The firm should identify, realize, or generate a need for a product among its customers. There are different features of a market that should be tested before launching any new product or brand in the market. This is termed as the market appraisal of a project. A lot of information is required to do the market study, which can be obtained from either primary or secondary data sources. Demand forecasting of a particular product in a market can be possible through using various qualitative or quantitative models.

Similar to market appraisal, technical appraisal is also carried out prior to selecting a project. This refers to the identifying and scanning of the engineering aspects of a project. Purchasing activity, vendor selection, and plant location decisions are important for the overall success of the business. Relocation opportunity arises as firms alter their product lines, and as labour, material requirements, or market conditions change. Project layouts also define the physical arrangement of all the machinery used.

Environmental and social appraisals are the other key factors important to keep in mind while selecting a project. Environmental appraisal includes keeping a check on the air pollution and water pollution treatments and other regulation acts passed by the government. Social appraisal, on the other hand, includes SCBA, UNIDO, the LM approach, and many more that measure the socio-economic benefits and costs of a project. Corporate social responsibility has also come up in a big way.

KEY TERMS

Domestic resource cost (DRC) It is the spending required in terms of domestic currency to generate a saving of one unit of a foreign currency. DRC = (Value added at domestic prices / Value added at world prices) × Exchange rate

Economic rate of return (ERR) It will be calculated by evaluating all non-labour inputs at border prices, which perfectly reflect the true economic value.

Effective rate of protection (ERP) Effective rate of protection = (Value added at domestic price – Value added at world prices) / Value added at world prices.

LM approach LM (Little and Mirrlees) approach is a method of measuring a project with respect to its socio-economic costs and benefits. It calculates cost and benefit in terms of international prices. Hence, it is applicable only for foreign projects.

Project layout It is defined as the physical arrangement of the machinery and other equipments in the various parts of the project.

Shadow pricing Financial profit or the NPVs of a project are measured at market prices. It is the market price represented under perfect market conditions.

UNIDO approach The United Nations Industrial Development Organization has developed a comprehensive approach to social cost-benefit analysis.

CONCEPT REVIEW QUESTIONS

1. Between primary and secondary data source, which do you think is more relevant and useful for conducting research?
2. What are the different types of demand forecasting methods known to you? Describe each of them.
3. Which factors are to be considered for plant capacity and plant location?
4. Define work schedule. What purpose does it serve?
5. Using a real-life example, state how environment factor is the key deciding factor for project appraisal.
6. Enumerate the similarities and dissimilarities between the UNIDO and LM approaches.
7. Define shadow pricing, effective rate of protection, and domestic resource cost.
8. Explain the CSR concept with the background of the Singur Nano factory.

NUMERICAL PROBLEMS

1. The following data is available regarding sales of a certain product. Find the trend of sales by using (a) 3-yearly moving average and (b) 4-yearly moving average. Refer to Table E4.9.

TABLE E4.9

Year	–	2001	2002	2003	2004	2005	2006	2007
Sales in '000	30	31	34	36	29	37	39	32

2. Time demand sales of Super Tech Private Limited for the past 6 years have been given in Table E4.10. Initial sales forecast is 40,000 and α = 0.5 for the year 2000.

TABLE E4.10

Year	2000	2001	2002	2003	2004	2005
Sales in '000	51.00	52.00	54.00	57.00	58.00	59.00

(a) Find the forecasted sales using exponential smoothing method.
(b) What is the demand for the forecasted sales for 2006 under least square method? What is the forecasted sale for 2007?

3. Tri-Star limited uses a simple exponential smoothing with a smoothing constant α = 0.1 to forecast demand. The forecast for the year 2001 was 800 units.

The actual demand for the following year is given in Table E4.11.

TABLE E4.11

Year	2001	2002	2003	2004	2005	2006	2007	2008
Demand	967	1,020	1,300	1,560	1,200	998	1,114	1,087

Derive the forecast for period 2001 to 2008 based on the above data.

4. A new project for manufacturing a product which is currently imported into the country is being appraised. The capital outlay of the project would be as in Table E4.12.

TABLE E4.12

Item	Rs in lakhs
Land	70
Building	180
Imported equipment (CIF value: Rs 120 lakh)	160
Indigenous equipment (CIF value: Rs 600 lakh)	850
Transport	20
Technical know-how	100
Pre-operative expenses	90
Bank charges	30

The working capital requirement of the project will be Rs 600 lakh (CIF: Rs 400 lakh).

What is the social cost associated with the initial outlay of this project? Calculate the social conversion factor (SCF) or proportion of three components – tradable (T), labour (L), and residual (R) using data from the following Table E4.13.

TABLE E4.13

Items	SCF or proportions
Land	SCF = 1 / 1.5
Buildings and construction	Proportion: T = 0.65, L = 0.25, R = 0.10
Engineering and know-how fees	SCF = 1.50
Bank charges	SCF = 0.02
Pre-operative expenses	SCF = 1.00
Labour	SCF = 0.50
Salaries	SCF = 0.80
Repairs and maintenance	SCF = 1 / 1.5
Water, Fuel, etc.	Proportions: T = 0.5, L = 0.25, R = 0.25
Electricity	Proportions: T = 0.71, L = 0.13, R = 0.16
Domestic stores	SCF = 0.80
Other overheads	SCF = 1 / 1.5

5. The details in Table E4.14 are available in respect to a project.

TABLE E4.14

Particulars	Rs Crores
Value of tradable inputs in domestic prices	600
Value of non-tradable inputs in tradable inputs in domestic prices	200
Value of tradable inputs at world prices	750
Sales realization at domestic prices	1,200
Sales realization at world prices	900

Find out the ERP and DRC of the project if the exchange rate is 46.50 per USD.

ASSIGNMENT

Apart from marketing, technical, and financial appraisal of a project, a financial institution evaluates it from economic and managerial angles too. Enumerate factors that would be considered by any commercial bank in appraising the project from economic and managerial angles. State assumptions if any.

SELECT REFERENCES

Freidman, M., *Capitalism and Freedom*, University of Chicago press, Chicago, 1962.

Fonteneau, G., 'Corporate Social Responsibility: Envisioning its social implications', *Tjsga-Tlwnsi-essay*, October 2003.

Gordon, H.H., 'Should Countries Promote FDI?', *G-24 Discussion Paper Series*, 9, UNCTD and Centre for Industrial Development, Harvard University, United Nation, Sept–Oct, 2001

Larson, E.L., R.J. Gray, and R. Gopalarathinam, 'Dabhol Phase I: Project Management Issues', *Modern Power Systems*, July 1999, pp. 37–39.

Murty, M.N., K.K. Dhavala, M. Ghosh, and R. Singh, 'Social Cost Benefit Analysis of Delhi Metro', *Institute of Economic Growth,* Delhi University, October 2006.

Yaziji, M., 'Turning Gadflies into Allies', *Harvard Business Review,* July–August 2004.

Other resources

http://www.envfor.nic.in/legis/eia/sitnot99.html, accessed 15 April 2010.

http://www.moef.gov.in, accessed 17 April 2010.

www.unido.org, accessed 17 April 2010.

www.idbi.com, accessed 17 April 2010.

CASE STUDY
Diversification of a Pharmaceutical Company

XYZ Corporation, incorporated in 2004, is a profit-making, dividend-paying, pharmaceutical company in the western part of Gujarat. The company's promoters have earlier been employed with a leading Mumbai-based pharmaceutical company. Their entrepreneurial bent of mind inspired them to take off from the service and set up their own drug manufacturing unit. The unit became operational by the end of 2004. To start with, the company began to work as a supplier of formulations to be marketed by their earlier company. With steady growth, the project began to earn profit and gradually turned into a success. This ignited the promoters to grow further and faster. The Government of India has been encouraging the production of life-saving drugs to curb imports. The company is looking at a bright future ahead and also deciding to enter and expand in other division of drugs. They have appointed an expert to prepare a project feasibility report, market surveys and technical requirements.

Discussion question

What factors should be taken into consideration for the market survey while deciding on the size of the plant and the type of technology for the project?

ANNEXURE 4.1

The Environment (Protection) Rules 1986

Emission standards for diesel engines (engine rating more than 0.8 MW (800 KW)) for power plant, generator set applications and other requirements.

Parameter		Area category	Total engine rating	Generator sets commissioning date		
				Before 1.7.2003	Between 1.7.2003 and 1.7.2005	On or after 1.7.2005
No_x at No_2 at 15% O_2, dry basis in ppm		A	Up to 75 MW	1100	970	710
		B	Up to150 MW			
		A	more than 75 MW	1100	710	360
		B	more than 150 MW			
NMHC (as C) at (15 % O_2), mg/Nm_3		both A and B		150	100	
PM (at 15 % O_2), mg/Nm_3	Diesel fuel – HSD and LDO	both A and B		75	75	
	Furnace oils – LSHS and FO	both A and B		150	100	
CO (at 15 % O2), mg/Nm_3		both A and B		150	150	
Sulphur content in fuel		A			< 2%	
		B			< 4%	
Fuel specification		For A only	Upto 5 MW		Only diesel fuels (HSD, LDO)	
Stack height (for generator sets commissioned after 1.7.2003)		Stack height shall be maximum for the following: 1. $14Q^{0.3}$, Q = total SO^2 emission from the plant in kg/hr 2. Minimum 6 m above the building where the generator set is installed 3. 30 m				

(a) Area categories A an B are defined as follows

Category A Area within the municipal limits of towns/cities having population more than 10 lakh and also up to 5 km beyond the municipal limits of such towns/cities.

Category B Areas not covered by category A.

(b) The standard shall be regulated by the State Pollution Control Board or Pollution Control Committees, as the case maybe.

(c) Individual units with engine ratings less than 800 kw or equal to 800 KW are not covered by this notification.

(d) Only following liquid fuels, viz, High Speed Diesel, Light Diesel Oil, Low Sulphur Heavy Stock and Furnace Oil or liquid fuels with equivalent specifications shall be used in these power plants and generator sets.

(e) For expansion project, stack height of new generation sets shall be as per total sulphur dioxide emission (including existing as well as additional load).

(f) For multi-engine plants, fuels shall be grouped in cluster to get better plume rise and dispersion. Provision for any future expansion should be made in planning stage itself.

(g) Particulate matter None. Methane Hydrocarbon and Carbon Monoxide results are to be normalized to 25 C, 1.01 kilo Pascal (760 mm of mercury) pressure and zero percentage moisture (dry basis).

(h) Measurement shall be performed at steady load conditions of more than 85% of the rated load.

(i) Continuous monitoring of nitrogen oxide shall be done by the plants whose total engine capacity is more than 50 Mega Watt. However, minimum once in six month monitoring of other parameters shall be adopted by the plants.

(j) Following methods may be adapted from the measurement of emission parameters:

Sl No.	Emission parameters	Measurement methods
1.	Particulates	Gravimetric
2.	SO_2	Barium perchlorate–thorin indicator method
3.	NO_x	Chemiluminescence, non-dispersive infra red, non-dispersive ultra-violet (for continuous measurement), phenol disulphonic method
4.	CO	Non-dispersive infra red
5.		Paramagnetic, electrochemical sensor
6.	NMHC	Gas chromatograph – flame ionisation detector

Source: http://www.envfor.nic.in/legis/eia/sitnot99.html, accessed 15 April 2010.

ANNEXURE 4.2

The Environment (Siting for Industrial projects) Rules 1999

1. **Prohibition for setting up of certain industries** No new unit of the industries listed in list 1 shall be allowed to be set up in the following areas:

   (i) The entire area within the municipal limits of all municipal corporations, municipal councils and nagar panchayats (by whatever name these are known in each state) and a 25 km belt around the cities having population of more than 1 million;

   (ii) 7 km belt around the periphery of the wetlands listed in list 2;

   (iii) 25 km belt around the periphery of national parks, sanctuaries and core zones of biosphere reserves;

   (iv) 0.5 km wide strip on either side of national highways and rail lines.

2. **Establishment of new units with certain conditions** Establishment of new units of the industries listed in list 1 shall be allowed in 7 km to 25 km belt around the periphery of the wetlands listed in list 2 only after careful assessment of their adverse ecological and environmental impacts.

3. **Restrictions on the units in Taj Trapezium** Establishment of new units and expansion or modernization of existing units of the industries listed in list 1 in the 10,400 sq. km. (Approx) area between 26°45′N and 77°15′E to 27°45′N and 77°15′E to the West of Taj Mahal and between 27°00′N and 78°30′N and 78°30′E to the East of Taj Mahal, known as the Taj Trapezium, shall be regulated as per the guidelines laid down specifically for this area by the Central Pollution Control Board (CPCB), entitled 'Inventory and Assessment of Pollution Emission in and around Agra–Mathura Region (Abridged)'.

4. **Establishment of new units around Archaeological Monuments** New units of industries mentioned in list 3 shall not be allowed to be set up within 7 km periphery of the important archaeological monuments.

5. **Application of other Acts and Rules not barred** The provisions of this rule shall be in addition to and not in derogation of, the Forest (Conservation) Act, 1980, and the rules made there under, the areas covered by the Notifications S.O.No. 102 (E) dated 1 February 1989; S.O. 114 (E) dated 20 February 1991; S.O. No. 416 (E) dated 20 June 1991, S.O.No. 319 (E) dated 7 May 1992. [No. J-11013/3/96 IA.II(I)].

List 1

1. Petroleum refineries
2. Chemical fertilizers
3. Petro-chemical complex (both olefinic and aromatic) and Petrochemical intermediates such as DMT, Caprolactam LAB, etc. and production of basic plastics such as LLDPE, HDPE, PP, PVC
4. Hydrocyanic acid and its derivatives
5. Primary metallurgical industries (such as production of iron and steel, aluminium, copper zinc, lead and ferro alloys)
6. Viscose staple fibre and filament yarn
7. Storage batteries integrated with manufacture of oxides of lead and antimony alloys
8. Distilleries
9. Raw skins and hides, and tanneries
10. Dyes and dye intermediates
11. Pesticides
12. Bulk drugs and pharmaceuticals
13. Caustic soda/chlorine
14. Pulp and paper
15. Cement

List 2

1. Chilka, Orissa
2. Keoladeo Ghana National Park, Rajasthan
3. Sambhar, Rajasthan
4. Wullar, Jammu and Kashmir
5. Loktak, Manipur
6. Harike, Punjab

List 3

1. Petroleum refineries
2. Chemical fertilizers

3. Petro-chemical complex (both olefinic and aromatic) and petro-chemical intermediates such as DMT, caprolactam LAB, etc., and production of basic plastics such as LLDPE, HDPE, PP, PVC
4. Hydrocyanic acid and its derivatives
5. Primary metallurgical industries (such as production of iron and steel, aluminium, copper zinc, lead and ferro alloys)
6. Viscose staple fibre and filament yarn
7. Storage batteries integrated with manufacture of oxides of lead and antimony alloys
8. Distilleries
9. Raw skins and hides and tanneries
10. Pulp and paper

Source: http://www.envfor.nic.in/legis/eia/sitnot99.html, accessed 15 April 2010.

FINANCIAL APPRAISAL IN PROJECT SCANNING AND SELECTION

Money is an arm or leg. You either use it or lose it.

— HENRY FORD

LEARNING
OBJECTIVES

After studying this
chapter, you will be
able to
• Understand the concept
  of time value of money
• Understand cost of
  capital, the opportunity
  cost of capital, and cost
  of equity along with
  DCF, CAPM, WACC, etc.
• Explain capital
  budgeting and the types
  of capital budgeting
  proposals
• Understand the various
  evaluation techniques of
  investment proposal
• Compute ARR method,
  payback period method,
  NPV method, IRR
  method, and MIRR
• Understand various
  methods of capital
  budgeting and know
  their respective merits
  and demerits

Arjun's Predicament

A miner on his deathbed handed over his lifetime savings of Rs 5,000 to his 10-year-old son Arjun. Instead of spending his entire savings on the treatment of his respiratory disease, he decided to give up his life. Arjun kept the money safely and grew up in his uncle's house. When Arjun was 20 years old, his uncle fell prey to the same disease and wanted to follow the route of his elder brother. But Arjun, remembering his father's pain and being more mature, protested his decision. He wanted his uncle to get treatment with his father's lifelong savings but he could not. This was because at this point of time by spending Rs 5,000 one could only survive from a fever but not from a critical disease. Within ten years, the money value or purchasing power of Rs 5,000 has gone down.

That means, money value can be increased if it keeps on rolling.

The above story vividly explains the changing value of money with time. This is what is termed as the time value of money.

5.1 TIME VALUE OF MONEY

5.1.1 Basis of Time Value

An important concept in financial management is that 'cash flow' is a more important term than 'profit' in understanding business. 'Cash flow is king' seems to be the slogan for current businesses. The cash inflow or outflow usually occurs over a period of times. This leads us to consider the time value of money.

The value of money depends on when the cash flow occurs, i.e., Rs 100 at present is worth more than Rs 100 at a future date. Thus, the earlier value of money is greater than the latter one. The reasons for this are as follows.

Interest or rent   Money, like any other commodity, has a price. If you own it, you can rent it or deposit it in your bank and earn some money or interest on that. The rent or interest on money is the investor's return, which reflects the time value of money. It comprises

(a) Risk-free rate of return rewarding investors for forgoing immediate consumption

(b) Compensation for risk and loss of purchasing power

Money can be invested productively to generate real returns. For example, if a sum of Rs 100 is invested in raw material, and the finished goods are worth Rs 107, we can say that the investment of Rs 100 has earned a rate of return of 7%.

Uncertainty   Rs 100 now is more certain than Rs 100 at a future date. This 'bird-in-the-hand' principle affects many aspects of financial management. That is why individuals prefer current consumption to future consumption.

Inflation   Under inflationary conditions, the value of money, expressed in terms of its purchasing power over goods and services, declines.

Nominal or Market interest rate = Real rate of interest or return + Risk premiums + Expected rate of inflation

The basis of finding time value of money is normally specified by the rate per period, denoted in percentage terms. Usually the chosen period is one year more by convention than by rule.

Basically, there are two methods by which the time value of money can be estimated—process of compounding and process of discounting. To understand the basic idea of time value of money, let us consider a venture that requires an immediate outlay of Rs 1,000 and the subsequent inflows of Rs 250 in each of the next 4 years. The timeline of the above cash flows is shown in Table 5.1.

TABLE 5.1   Line of above cash flows

Year	0	1	2	3	4
Rs	−1,000	250	250	250	250

Compounding and discounting   Cash flows occur at different points of time. For meaningful comparison, all these cash flows should be assessed at the same point of time. Either the cash flow occurring today has to be converted into its equivalent at a future date or the cash flow occurring later has to be converted back to today's value.

The future value of money that is available today can be calculated using the concept of compounding and that value is known as future value (FV) or compounded value (CV), as shown in Table 5.2.

TABLE 5.2   Process of compounding

Cash outflow in the beginning	Cash inflow in year 1	Cash inflow in year 2	Cash inflow in year 3	Cash inflow in year 4
−1000	250	250	250	250
				+FV(250)
				+FV(250)
				+FV(250)
				+FV(−1000)

The present value of money accruing later is estimated by the process of discounting and the value is known as present value (PV) or discounted value (DV), as shown in Table 5.3.

TABLE 5.3   Process of discounting

Cash outflow in the beginning	Cash inflow in year 1	Cash inflow in year 2	Cash inflow in year 3	Cash inflow in year 4
−1000	250	250	250	250
+PV(250)				
+PV(250)				
+PV(250)				
+PV(250)				

5.1.2 Compounded or Future Value/Simple and Compound Interest

The FV of a sum of money invested at a given annual rate of interest will depend on whether the interest is paid only on the original investment (called simple interest), or whether it is calculated on the original investment plus accrued interest (called compound interest). In the case of compound interest, there is a further factor affecting the future value, namely the frequency with which interest is paid (e.g., monthly, quarterly, or annually).

With simple interest, the future value is determined by

$$FV_n = V_0(1 + i \cdot n)$$

where, FV_n = future value at time n

V_0 = original sum invested or the principal value

i = annual rate of simple interest

Suppose, you win Rs 1,00,000 on a reality television show and decide to invest in fixed deposit of a commercial bank at the simple interest rate of 10% for 5 years. The future value will be the original of Rs 1,00,000 plus 5 years interest, giving a total of Rs 1,50,000.

$$FV_5 = \text{Rs } 1,00,000\,[1 + (0.10)(5)] = \text{Rs } 1,50,000$$

If i is the compound interest, in subsequent years the interest is paid on the original capital plus accrued interest. The process of compounding provides a convenient way of adjusting for the time value of money. An investment made now in the capital market of V_0 gives rise to a cash flow of $V_0(1 + i)^2$ after 2 years, and so on. In general, FV of V_0 invested today at a compound rate of interest $i\%$ for n years will be.

$$FV_{(i,n)} = V_0(1 + i)^n$$

Suppose, an investment of Rs 1,00,000 was put into building a society, paying a fixed 10% compound interest yearly. What will your investment be worth after 5 years? In a year's time, the investment will be worth

1,00,000 $(1 + 0.10) = \text{Rs } 1,10,000$

After 2 years, it will be worth 1,00,000 $(1 + 0.10)^2 = 1,21,000$

After 5 years, it will be worth $FV_5 = 1,00,000\ (1 + 0.10)^5 = 1,61,000$

Hence, the effect of compound interest yields a much higher value than simple interest, which yielded 1,50,000.

This is why fixed deposits in banks follow a compounded interest rate and hence yield a higher return as compared to any investment that follows a simple interest rate.

Effect of change on interest rate

The value of money broadly depends on two things: interest rate and time period. Hence, if interest rate changes, the money value will change as well. The following example explains the effect of change of interest rate.

Banks usually offer variable, rather than fixed rates of interest. Assume the rate to be 10% for the first 2 years, but it falls to 8% for the years 3 to 5. The calculation now has two elements:

$$FV_5 = \text{Rs } 1,00,000\ (1 + 0.10)^2(1 + 0.08)^3 = \text{Rs } 1,52,400$$

If interest rate remains 10% throughout 5 years, $FV_5 =$ Rs 1,00,000 $(1 + 0.10)^5 =$ Rs 1,61,051. See, how future value of money changes with change in interest rate!

Effect of more frequent compounding

Unless otherwise stated, it is always assumed that compounding or discounting is an annual process; cash payments of benefits arise either at the start or at the end of the year. But government bonds pay interest semi-annually or quarterly. Interest charged on credit cards is applied monthly. To compare the true costs or benefits of such financial contracts, it is necessary to determine the effective rate of interest, termed annual percentage rate (APR) or effective interest rate.

Returning to our earlier example of Rs 1,00,000 invested for 5 years at 10% compound interest, we now assume 5% payable every 6 months. After the first 6 months, the interest is Rs 5,000, which is reinvested to give interest for the second half year of Rs 5,200 (Rs 1,05,000 $*$ 10/2%). The end-of-year value is therefore Rs 1,10,200 (1,05,000 + 5,200).

We can still use the compound interest formula but with i as the six-monthly interest rate and n as the six-monthly, rather than annual, interval. In converting the annual compounding formula to another interest payment frequency, the trick is simply to divide the annual rate of interest i and multiply the time period n by the number of payments each year.

The generalized formula for this shorter compounding period is

$$FV_n = V_0 (1 + k/m)^{m*n}$$

where, m is number of years compounding is done and k is the nominal interest rate.

....

Example 5.1 Suppose you deposit Rs 20,000 with an investment company that pays 12% interest with quarterly compounding. How much will this deposit grow in 5 years?

Solution

$FV = 20,000 * (1 + .12/4)^{4*5} = 20,000 (1 + .03)^{20} =$ Rs 36,120

Table E5.1 calculates the APRs based on a range of interest payment frequencies for a 22% per annum loan. It can be seen that by charging compound interest on a daily basis, the effective annual rate is 24.6%, some 2.6% higher than on an annual basis.

TABLE E5.1

Annually	$(1 + 0.22) - 1$	0.22 or 22%
Semi-annually	$(1 + 0.22/2)2 - 1$	0.232 or 23.2%
Quarterly	$(1 + 0.22/4)4 - 1$	0.239 or 23.9%
Monthly	$(1 + 0.22/12)12 - 1$	0.244 or 24.4%
Daily	$(1 + 0.22/365)365 - 1$	0.246 or 24.6%

Hence, for more frequent compounding, we have to calculate effective interest rate from nominal interest rate with corresponding frequency per year. The general relationship between the effective and nominal interest rate is as follows:

$r = (1 + k/m)^m - 1$, where r = effective interest rate

k = nominal interest rate

m = frequency of compounding per year

To understand the concept better, refer to the following example.

If the nominal interest rate is 10% and frequency of compounding is half yearly, the effective interest rate is

$r = (1 + k/m)^m - 1 = (1 + .10/2)^2 - 1 = .1025$ or 10.25%

Doubling Period (DP)

A question frequently asked by investors is, 'How long will it take to double an amount at a certain rate of interest?' This question can be answered by a thumb rule known as 'rule of 72' or 'rule of 69'.

By rule of 72, DP = 72 / i for an interest rate = i %.

By rule of 69, DP = 0.35 + 69 / i for an interest rate = i %.

Example 5.2   Find out the doubling period for an interest rate of 10% by applying the two rules.

Solution

By rule of 72 , DP = 72 / i = 72 / 10 = 7.2 years.

By rule of 69, DP = 0.35 + (69 / i) = 0.35 + (69 / 10) = 0.35 + 6.9 = 7.25 years.

(Refer to Figure E5.1.)

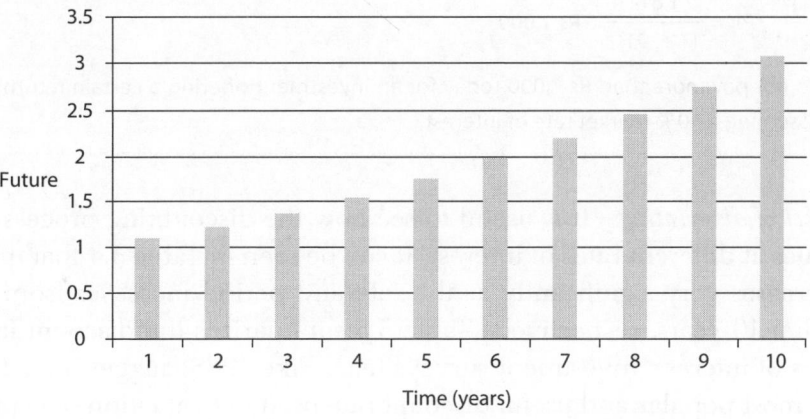

FIGURE E5.1

5.1.3 Discounted or Present Value

An alternative way of assessing the worth of an investment is to invert the compounding process to give the present value of the future cash flows. This process is called discounting. Today's value of any future cash flow is known as discounted or present value.

When the choice is between Rs 100 now and the same amount in one year's time, it is always preferable to take the Rs 100 now because it could be invested over the next year at, say, a 10% interest rate to produce Rs 110 at the end of the year. If 10% is the best available annual rate of interest, then one would be indifferent to receive Rs 100 now or Rs 110 after one year. Hence, the present value of Rs 110 received after one year is Rs 100.

We can obtain present value simply by dividing the future cash flow by 1 plus the rate of interest i, i.e.,

$$FV = \frac{Rs\ 110}{(1 + 0.10)} = \frac{Rs\ 110}{(1.1)} = Rs\ 100$$

Discounting is the process of adjusting future cash flows to their present values. It is, in effect, compounding in reverse.

Recall that earlier we specified the future value as

$$FV_n = V_0(1 + i)^n$$

Dividing both sides by $(1 + i)^n$

$$\text{Present value} = \frac{FV_n}{(1 + i)^n} = PV_n$$

Example 5.3   Compute the present value of Rs 1,611 receivable after 5 years at the rate of 10%.

Solution

$$PV = \frac{1,611}{(1 + .01)^5} = Rs\ 1,000$$

Note: Do not pay more than Rs 1,000 today for an investment offering a certain return of Rs 1,611 after 5 years, assuming a 10% market rate of interest.

Effect of discounting   It is useful to see how the discounting process affects present values at different rates of interest. It can be seen in Table 5.4 that the value of Re 1 decreases very significantly as the rate and period increases from 0 to 20% and within 10 years, respectively. Table 5.5 summarizes the discount factors for three rates of interest. Investment surveys (e.g., Pike 1988) suggest that 15% discount is the most popular and useful discount rate used in evaluation of capital projects. In this case, the discounted value approximately halves every 5 years. Thus, the value of Re 1 is 50 paise after 5 years, 25 paise after 10 years, and so on.

TABLE 5.4 Effect of the rate of interest and period

Year	10%	15%	20%
0	1.0	1.0	1.0
5	0.6	0.5	0.4
10	0.4	0.25	0.16
15	0.24	0.12	0.06
20	0.15	0.06	0.03
25	0.19	0.03	0.01

Present value of a single future sum Re 1

TABLE 5.5 Discount factors

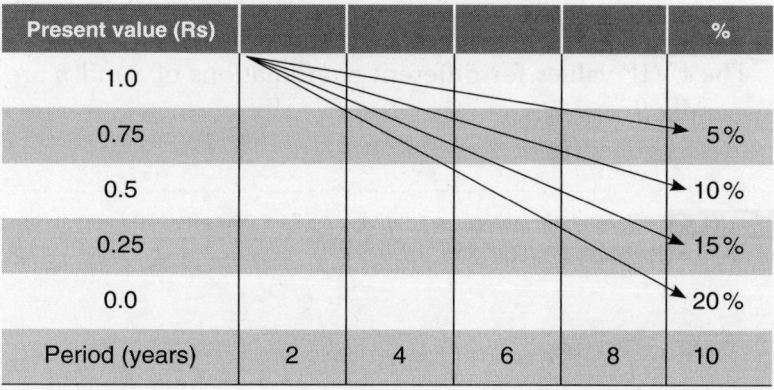

Present value (Rs)					%
1.0					
0.75					5%
0.5					10%
0.25					15%
0.0					20%
Period (years)	2	4	6	8	10

The relationship between present value of Re 1 and interest over a period of time

Discount table and present value formula Much of the medium of using formulae and power functions can be eased by using discount tables or computer-based spreadsheet packages. The discount factor or interest factor Re 1 for a 10% discount rate in 3 years time is

$$1 / (1.10)^3 = 1 / 1.33 = 0.751$$

This can be found in Table X of Appendix 2 by locating the 10% column and the 3 years row. We call this the present value interest factor (PVIF) and express it as $PVIF_{(10\%,3yrs)}$ or $PVIF_{(10,3)}$.

$$PV_n = \text{Present value} = \frac{FV_n}{(1 + i)^n} = FV_n * PVIF_{(i,n)}$$

$$PVIF_{(i,n)} = 1 / (1 + i)^n$$

Hence, the present value of a future sum can be estimated by determining the PVIF factor for the given values of i and n. The factor value needs to be multiplied by the given sum. The PVIF values cannot be greater than one as PVIF (i, n) is the present value of Re 1 that will be received after n years at a rate of interest i%. The PVIF values for different combinations of i and n are given in Table X of Appendix 2.

Compounded table and future value formulae   The inverse of PVIF is future value interest factor (FVIF). The above equation can be written as follows:

$$PV_n = \text{Present value} = \frac{FV_n}{(1 + i)^n} = FV_n * PVIF_{(i,n)}$$

Therefore, compounded value or future value $= FV_n = PV_n * (1 + i)^n$

$$= PV_n * FVIF_{(i,n)}$$

$$FVIF_{(i,n)} = (1 + i)^n$$

Therefore, $PVIF_{(i,n)} = 1 \, / \, FVIF_{(i,n)}$

The FVIF values for different combinations of i and n are given in Table Y of Appendix 2.

Example 5.4   Rama Raju promises to give you Rs 5,000 after 10 years in exchange for Rs 1,000 today. What interest is implicit in his offer?

Solution

Let i be the rate of interest.

It is given that Rs 1000 $* FVIF_{(i,10)} = 5000$, $FVIF_{(i,10)} = 5$

From the values given in Table Y of Appendix 2 we find $FVIF_{(16,10)} = 4.411$

And $FVIF_{(18,10)} = 5.234$

Applying a linear approximation in the interval, we get

$$i = 16\% + 2\% * \frac{(5.0 - 4.4111)}{(5.234 - 4.411)} = 16\% + 2\% \frac{(0.5889)}{(0.823)}$$

$$= 16\% + 0.0143 = 17.4\%$$

Refer to Figure E5.2.

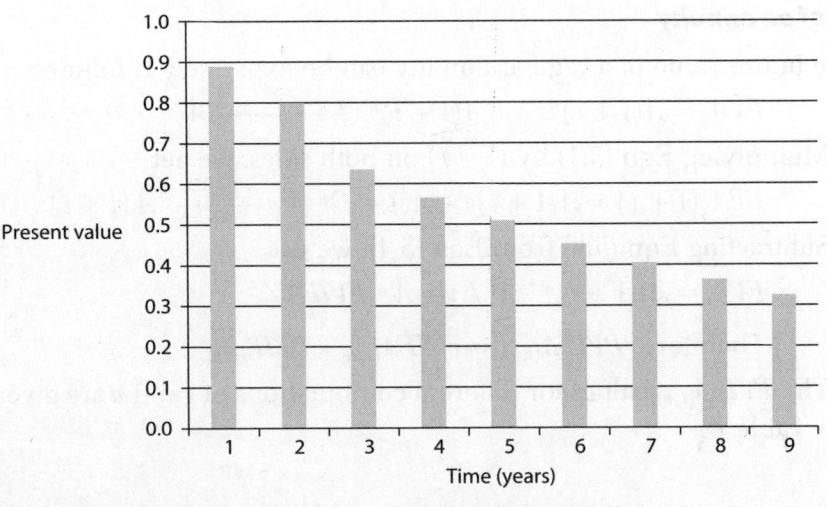

FIGURE E5.2

5.1.4 Annuity

Annuity is an investment paying a fixed sum A each year for a specified period of time n at the rate of interest k. It is applicable in the case of a series of periodic receipt or payment. The equal amount of payment or receipt is known as annuity. Examples of annuities include many credit agreements and house mortgages.

5.1.4.1 Present value of an annuity

The present value of a regular annuity can be represented in terms of the symbols defined in Table E5.3 as follows:

$$PVA_n = A / (1 + i) + A / (1 + i)^2 + A / (1 + i)^3 + \text{----------} + A / (1 + i)^n \quad (5.1)$$

Multiplying both sides by $(1 + i)$, we get,

$$PVA_n(1 + i) = A + A / (1 + i) + A / (1 + i)^2 + \text{----------} + A(1 + i)^{n-1} \quad (5.2)$$

Subtracting Eqn (5.1) from Eqn (5.2), we get

$$PVA_n i = A - A / (1 + i)^n = A[1 - 1 / (1 + i)^n]$$

$$PVA_n = \frac{A[(1 + i)^n - 1]}{i*(1 + i)^n} = A * PVIFA_{(i,n)}$$

The $PVIFA_{(i, n)}$ values for different combinations of k and n are given in Table Z_1 of Appendix 2.

To understand it better, look at the following example.

Suppose an annuity of Rs 1000 is issued for 20 years at 10%. Using Table Z_1 in Appendix 2, we can find the present value as follows:

$$\text{PVA}_{(10, 20)} = \text{Rs } 1,000 * \text{PVIFA}_{(10, 20)} = \text{Rs } 1,000 * 8.5136 = \text{Rs } 8,513.60$$

Future value of an annuity

The future value of a regular annuity can be expressed as follows:

$$FVA_n = A(1 + i)^{n-1} + A(1 + i)^{n-2} + \text{----------} A \tag{5.3}$$

Multiplying Eqn (5.1) by $(1 + i)$ on both sides, we get

$$FVA_n(1 + i) = A(1 + i)^n + A(1 + i)^{n-1} + \text{----------} A(1 + i) \tag{5.4}$$

Subtracting Eqn (5.3) from Eqn (5.4), we get

$$FVA_n = A[(1 + i)^n - 1] / i = A * FVIFA_{(i,n)}$$

Therefore, $PVIFA_{(i, n)} = FVIFA_{(i, n)} * PVIF_{(i, n)}$

The $FVIFA_{(i, n)}$ values for different combinations of i and n are given in Appendix 2 in Table Z_2.

Example 5.5   You can save Rs 6,000 a year for 5 years. What will these savings cumulate to at the end of 10 years, if the rate of interest is 10%?

Solution

The accumulated value after 10 years will be as follows:

= Rs [6,000 * FVIFA$_{(10,5)}$ * FVIF$_{(10,5)}$] = Rs [6,000 * 6.105 * 1.611] = Rs 59,010.93

Refer to Tables E5.2 and E5.3.

TABLE E5.2

Time (in years)	Amount	Amount	Amount	Amount	Amount
1	1,000				
2		1,000			
3			1,000		
4				1,000	
5					1,000
MV	$1,000(1.1)^5$	$+ 1,000(1.1)^4$	$+ 1,000(1.1)^3$	$+ 1,000(1.1)2$	$+ 1,000(1.1)$

TABLE E5.3

Time (in years)	Amount	Amount	Amount	Amount	Amount
1	1,000				
2		1,000			
3			1,000		
4				1,000	
5					1,000
MV	1,000	$+ 1,000(1.1)^{-1}$	$+ 1,000(1.1)^{-2}$	$+ 1,000(1.1)^{-3}$	$+ 1,000(1.1)^{-4}$

Annuity due

In case of annuity, it is generally assumed that payment has been made at the end of each year. If payment is made at the beginning of each year, then this is called annuity due and its value is found by the product of the value (either present or future) of a regular annuity and the factor $(1 + i)$.

$$FVA_n(\text{due}) = A * FVIFA_{(i,n)} * (1 + i)$$

$$PVA_n(\text{due}) = A * PVIFA_{(i,n)} * (1 + i)$$

For instance, the present value of a 5 year annuity due of Rs 5,000 at 10% will be:

$$PVA_n(\text{due}) = A * PVIFA_{(i,n)} * (1 + i) = \text{Rs } 5,000 * PVIFA_{(10,5)} * (1 + 0.1) = \text{Rs } 20,850.5$$

Perpetuity

Frequently, an investment pays a fixed sum each year for a specified number of years. A series of annual receipts or payments is termed an annuity. The simplest form of an annuity for an infinite series is called perpetuity.

For example, certain government stocks offer a fixed annual income, but there is no obligation to repay the capital. The present value of such stocks (called irredeemable) is found by dividing the annual sum received by the annual rate of interest.

$$PV_{\text{perpetuity}} = A / i$$

....

Example 5.6 Uncle Shyam in his will wishes to leave you an annual sum of Rs 10,000 a year, starting next year. Assuming an interest rate of 10%, how much of his estate must be set aside for this purpose?

Solution

$PV_{\text{perpetuity}} = A / i$

$PV = \text{Rs } 10,000 / 0.1 = \text{Rs } 1,00,000$

Let's suppose that your benevolent uncle wishes to compensate for inflation estimated to be at 6% per annum.

Then, $PV = A / (i - g) = \text{Rs } 10,000 / (0.1 - 0.06) = 2,50,000$

Similarly, present value of growing perpetuity $= A / (i - g)$, where $g =$ growth rate.

....

Calculating interest rates

We know that $PV = FV * PVIF_{(i,n)}$

Therefore, $PVIF_{(i,n)} = PV / FV = 1 / (1 + i)^n$

Or, $(1 + i)^n = FV / PV$

$i = (FV / PV)^{1/n} - 1$

For instance, if a credit company offers to lend you Rs 1,000 today on a condition that you repay Rs 1,643 at the end of 3 years, then the compound interest rate for this offer would be

$i = (1643 / 1000)^{1/3} - 1 = 18\%$

5.2 COST OF CAPITAL—OVERVIEW

Each company has to spend a certain amount of money either to generate capital from the market or to hold capital within it. This is known as the cost of capital.

The cost of capital concept has a very important role to play within corporate finance. It is the company's cost of capital that is used as the discount rate in the investment appraisal process. We assume that a company is a rational agent and so it will seek to raise capital by the cheapest and most efficient methods, hence minimizing its cost of capital. It first requires information on costs associated with the different ways of raising finance. Second, it needs to know how to combine the different sources of finance in order to reach its optimal capital structure.

The cost of source of finance is defined as the rate of discount that equates the present value of the expected payments of a source of finance with the net proceeds received from the same source.

5.2.1 Opportunity Cost of Capital

A firm can have different sources of funding and each consumes different cost. Therefore, if a firm selects a particular type of capital and foregoes the other, the income so foregone is known as opportunity cost of capital.

The first step in calculating a company's weighted average cost of capital (WACC) is to calculate the cost of the individual components of its capital. Here, we consider the different sources of long-term finance available to a company and how to calculate the cost of using the source.

5.2.2 Cost of Equity

Though equity is the owner's capital, a significant amount is required to generate equity capital and to hold it over a period of time, by way of cost of issuing equity, administrative cost, agency cost, dividend distribution cost, and other related costs. These costs collectively constitute the cost of equity.

Discounted cash flow (DCF) approach

Equity finance can be raised either through issuing new securities or through the utilization of retained earnings. To find out the cost of equity (k_e), we can adapt the Gordon growth model for the valuation of equity capital as follows.

According to the dividend forecast approach, the intrinsic value of an equity stock is equal to the sum of the present values of the dividends associated with it, i.e.,

$$P_e = \sum D_t / (1 + k_e)^t \text{ for } t = 1 \text{ to } n$$

where, P_e = price per equity share

D_t = expected dividend per share at the end of year t

k_e = rate of return required by the equity shareholders

The cost of equity, from the company's point of view, is the rate at which the intrinsic value or the market price of the share is equal to the discounted value of the dividends. Assuming the constant growth rate in dividends, the above equation can be written as

$$P_e = D_1 / (k_e - g)$$

$$\text{Or, } k_e = (D_1 / P_e) + g = \{D_0(1 + g) / P_0\} + g$$

where, P_0 = ex-dividend current share price, g = expected annual increase in dividends, D_0 = dividend to be paid shortly, D_1 = dividend to be paid after one year

Capital asset pricing model

An alternative and arguably more reliable method of calculating the cost of equity finance is to use the capital asset pricing model (CAPM). This model allows investors to work out their required return on the equity finance of a company, based on the rate of return earned on risk-free investments plus a risk premium. The risk premium reflects both the systematic risk of the company and the excess generated by the market relative to the risk-free rate.

Using the CAPM, the cost of equity finance is given by the following linear relationship:

$$k_j = R_f + \beta_j * (R_m - R_f)$$

where, k_j = the rate of return of security j predicted by the model

R_f = the risk-free rate of return

β_j = the beta coefficient of security j

R_m = the return of the market

Bond-yield-plus-risk-premium approach

Sometimes a company's cost of common equity is calculated using a subjective process. It is done by adding a judgmental risk premium (about 3% to 5%) to the interest rate on the company's long-term debt. It is appropriate to say that a company with a debt that is low rated, risky, and therefore at high interest rate will have risky high cost equity. This logic is considered for basing the cost of equity on debt cost. This debt cost should be easily observable. For example, if an extremely strong firm X and Co. had a bond that yielded 9%, its cost of equity might be estimated as follows:

$$k_x = \text{Bond yield} + \text{Risk premium} = 9\% + 4\% = 13\%$$

The 4% risk premium is a judgmental estimate, and the estimated value of k_x is also judgemental. Empirical work in recent years suggests that the risk premium over a firm's own bond yield has generally ranged from 3% to 5%. So this method is not likely to produce a precise cost of equity.

Almost all research reports and survey results show that the CAPM approach is more widely used than DCF. The bond-yield-plus-risk-premium is primarily used by companies that are not publicly traded (Graham and Harvey 1982).

Cost of retained earnings and cost of external equity

A common misconception is that retained earnings are a costless source of finance. Although retained earnings do not have any servicing costs, they have an opportunity cost equivalent to the ongoing cost of equity. This is because had these funds been returned to investors, they could have achieved an equivalent return through reinvestment at a personal level.

The cost of retained earnings or internal accruals is generally taken to be the same as the cost of equity, i.e., k_r (representing cost of retained earnings) $= k_e$.

There are times when for raising external equity the company has to incur certain floatation costs (costs incurred during public issue, like brokerage, underwriting commission, fees to managers of issue, legal charges, advertisement and printing expenses, etc.). The formula for k_e in this case will be as follows:

$$k_e = k_r / (1 - f) \text{ where, } f = \text{floatation costs}$$

Example 5.7   Gorky Ltd has issued 5,00,000 Re 1 ordinary shares whose current ex-dividend market price is Rs 1.5 per share. The company has just paid a dividend of 27 paise per share, and dividends are expected to continue at the same level for some time. If the company has no debt capital, what is the cost of capital?

Solution

Cost of equity $= k_e =$ dividend / market price per share $= 0.27 / 1.5 = 0.18$ or 18% (growth rate of dividend $= g = 0$)

Since there is no debt capital, cost of capital $= 18\%$.

Example 5.8   Gorky Ltd has got Rs 5 lakh of retained earnings and Rs 5 lakh of external equity through a fresh issue in its capital structure. The equity investors expect a rate of return of 18%. The cost of issuing external equity is 3%. What is the cost of retained earnings and the cost of external equity?

Solution

Cost of retained earnings $= k_r = k_e = 18\%$

Cost of external equity $= k_e = k_r / (1 - f) = 0.18 / (1 - 0.03) = 18.56\%$

5.2.3 Cost of Debt

Like the cost of equity, the company has to spend a certain amount on debt capital also in the form of interest payment and principal repayment. This is known as the cost of debt.

There are two major types of securitized debt: redeemable bonds and irredeemable bonds. To find the cost of redeemable bonds, we need to find the overall required return of the providers of debt finance, which combines both revenue (interest) and capital (principal) returns. This is equivalent to the internal rate of return (k_d) of the following valuation model:

$$P = \sum I(1 - t) / (1 + k_d)^t + RV / (1 + k_d)^n$$

Time $= 1$ to n

where, $k_d =$ post-tax cost of debt

$I =$ annual interest payment

$t =$ corporate tax rate

$RV =$ redemption value

$n =$ number of years to redemption

$P =$ current market price of bond

An approximation formula, to save the trouble of doing an interpolation calculation, can also be used.

$$k_d = \frac{I(1 - t) + (RV - P) / n}{(RV + P) / 2}$$

Alternatively, k_d can be estimated using the yield approximation method developed by Hawanini and Vora (1982). This is given by the following equation:

$$k_d = \frac{I(1 - t) + (P - NPD) / n}{P + 0.6\,(NPD - P)}$$

where, $P =$ face value or per value

$NPD =$ net proceed from sale or market value

$I, t, n =$ as above

Example 5.9 Apeejay Limited has recently made an issue of non-convertible debentures for Rs 500 lakh. The terms of the issue are as follows. Each debenture has a face value of Rs 100 and carries a rate of interest of 15%. The interest is payable annually and the debenture is redeemable at a premium of 7% after

7 years. If Apeejay Limited realizes Rs 90 per debenture and the corporate tax rate is 50%, what is the cost of the debenture to the company?

Solution

Using the formula from above

$$k_d = \frac{15(1 - 0.5) + (107 - 90) / 7}{(107 + 90) / 2} = 9.93 / 98.5 = 10.08\%$$

The cost of irredeemable bonds is calculated in a manner similar to that of irredeemable preference shares. In both the cases, the model being used is one that values a perpetual stream of cash flows. Since the interest payments made on irredeemable bonds are tax deductible, it will have both before and after tax cost of debt. The before-tax cost of irredeemable debt (k_{id}) can be calculated as follows:

k_{id} = interest rate payable / market value of bond

The after-tax cost of debt is then easily obtained if the company taxation rate (t) is assumed to be constant:

k_{id} (after-tax) = $k_{id}(1 - t)$

Cost of term loans The cost of term loans will be simply equal to the interest rate multiplied by $(1 -$ tax rate$)$. The interest rate to be used here will be the interest rate applicable to the new term loan. The interest is multiplied by $(1 -$ tax rate$)$ as interest on term loans is also tax deductible.

5.2.4 Cost of Preference Capital

The cost of irredeemable preference share is equal to the cost of irredeemable bond or debenture (as discussed above).

The cost of redeemable preference share (k_p) is defined as that discount rate which equates the proceeds from preference capital issue to the payments associated with the same, i.e., dividend payments and principal payments.

$$P = \sum D / (1 + k_p)^t + F / (1 + k_p)^n$$

$t = 1$ to n

where, k_p = cost of preference capital

D = annual preference dividend per share

F = redemption value

n = maturity period

P = net amount realized per share

An approximation formula, to save the trouble of doing an interpolation calculation, can also be used.

$$K_p = \frac{D + (F - P) / n}{(F + P) / 2}$$

Example 5.10 The terms of preference share issue made by Arjun Co. Ltd are as follows. Each preference share has a face value of Rs 100 and carries a rate of dividend of Rs 15% payable annually. The share is redeemable after 10 years at par. If the net amount realized per share is Rs 105, what is the cost of preference share capital?

Solution

Given, $D = 15, F = 100, P = 105, n = 10$

$$K_p = \frac{D+(F-P)/n}{(F+P)/2} = \frac{15+(100-105)/10}{(100+105)/2} = 14.14\%$$

Relationship between costs of different sources of capital

While estimating the cost of various sources of finance utilized by a firm, a certain logical link should occur between different sources of cost and the risk that the funds supplier has to deal with. The highest risk category of finance to investors is characterized by equity finance as a result of the capital gains and risk and improbability involved in dividend payments. Therefore, when a firm opts for liquidation, equity finance represents the lowest level of the creditor hierarchy. Hence, new equity will be the most expensive capital for the company, and retained earnings will be slightly cheaper because it saves issue cost.

The cost of preference shares will be less than the cost of equity for two reasons. First, preference dividends must be paid before those of ordinary equity shares and, second, preference shares rank higher up the creditor hierarchy than equity shares. There are no risks regarding interest payments unless a company is likely to be declared bankrupt. Debt capital is a cheaper source of finance than equity and preference share. Whether bank borrowings are cheaper than bonds will depend upon the relative costs associated with issuing bonds and obtaining a bank loan. Generally, the longer the period, the higher the cost. The cost of debt will also be lowered for a company if it is secured rather than unsecured.

5.2.5 Weighted Average Cost of Capital

Most companies utilize capital components; these are basically various types of capital. Some of the most popular types include debt and common and preferred stock. The common characteristic among all capital components is that the concerned investor expects a return on his/her invested funds. Companies prefer different types of capital due to difference in risk associated with them. The required rate of return varies with the different securities. Component cost represents the required rate of return on each capital component. The weighted average of the various components' costs determines the cost of capital, which in turn influences the capital budgeting decisions. This is referred to as weighted average cost of capital (WACC).

The overall WACC can be estimated after calculating the cost of firm's individual sources of finance. WACC is determined by weighing the costs of the individual sources of finance as per their relative importance as a source of finance. WACC can be estimated either on average basis (for existing capital structure) or marginal basis (for additional incremental finance packages).

Therefore, the WACC equation can be written as

WACC = Cost of equity * Weight of equity + (1 − tax rate) * Cost of debt * Weight of debt (considering only equity and debt)

Suppose that X and Co. Ltd has a total capital structure C.

Let E = value of equity share capital, R = value of retained earnings, P = value of preference capital, D = value of debenture, T = value of term loan, t = corporate tax rate, k_e = cost of equity, k_r = cost of retained earnings = k_e, k_p = cost of preference capital, k_d = cost of debenture, and k_i = cost of term loan.

Therefore, $C = E + R + P + D + T$

$$\text{WACC} = k_e \times E / C + k_r \times R / C + k_p \times P / C + k_d \times D(1 - t) / C + k_t \times T / C$$

$$= k_e \times W_e + k_r \times W_r + k_p W_p + k_d (1 - t) W_d + k_t \times W_t$$

$$= \sum k_i W_i \text{ for } i = 1 \text{ to } n, \ W_i = (\text{value of capital } i) / (\text{value of total capital})$$

Market value or book value weights

The next challenge is which value of the capital should be considered in the WACC calculation—book value weights or market value weights? Though book values are easy to access, their use to determine the WACC cannot be recommended. Book values do not usually represent the current required rate of return (equity or debt). These values are estimated on the basis of historic costs. The effect of the cost of equity finance on the average cost of capital will be devalued by the use of book value. Also, the WACC would also be devalued as the cost of equity is always higher than the cost of debt. If that happens, unprofitable projects would be taken up.

Hence, market value weights will be more recommended in case of WACC calculations.

Example 5.11   DLPC Ltd is currently trying to work out its weighted average cost of capital (WACC). As a finance manager of the company, find out the WACC and show the necessary calculations. The balance sheet of the company is shown in Table E5.4.

TABLE E5.4

Balance sheet as on 31 March 2009

Item	In Rs crores
Fixed asset	545
Current asset	135
Current liabilities	(210)
Total asset	470
Ordinary share capital (Re 1 per share)	90
10% preference shares (Re 1 per share) (redeemable after 5 years)	40
Reserves	130
12%, 5-year redeemable debenture (15 crores)	150
Bank loans	60
Total liability	470

Solution

1. The current dividend, shortly to be paid, is 25 paise per share. Dividends in future are expected to grow at a rate of 6% per year.

2. Corporate tax is currently 40%.

3. The interest rate on bank borrowings is 11.55%.

4. Stock market prices as on 31 March 2009

   • Ordinary shares: Rs 5.6 per share

   • Preference shares: Rs 0.89 per share

   • For 12% redeemable debenture, current market rate: Rs 9.5 per share

Cost of each source of finance

1. Cost of equity, using the Gordon model and ignoring issue cost

$$ke = D_o(1 + g) / P_o + g = 0.25(1 + 0.06) / 5.6 + 0.06 = 10.73\%$$

2. Cost of retained earnings $= k_r = 10.73\%$

3. Cost of preference shares

$$K_p = \frac{D + (F - P)/n}{(F + P)/2} = \frac{1 + (1 - 0.89)/5}{(1 + 0.89)/2} = 10.82\%$$

4. Cost of debenture

$$K_d = \frac{I(1 - t) + (RV - P)/n}{(RV + P)/2} = \frac{1.2(1 - 0.4) + (10 - 9.5)/5}{(10 + 9.5)/2} = 8.41\%$$

5. Cost of bank loan (after tax): $k_i = 11.55(1 - 0.4) = 6.93\%$

TABLE E5.5

Source of finance	Book value (Rs crores)	Market value (Rs crores)
Equity	90 + 130 = 220	90 * 5.6 = 504
Preference shares	40	40 * 0.89 = 35.6
Redeemable debenture	150	15 * 9.5 = 142.5
Bank loan	60	60
Total	470	742.1

WACC (book value)

$= 10.73\% * 220 / 470 + 10.82 * 40 / 470 + 8.41\% * 150 / 470 + 6.93\% * 60 / 470 = 9.51\%$

WACC (market value)

$= 10.73\% * 504 / 742.1 + 10.82\% * 35.6 / 742.1 + 8.41\% * 142.5 / 742.1 + 6.93\% * 60 / 742.1$

$= 9.98\%$

5.2.6 Marginal and Average Cost of Capital

The cost of capital is calculated in two ways. If it is calculated using a company's balance sheet, as in the above example, it represents the cost of the capital currently employed. This represents financial decisions taken in previous periods. Alternatively, the cost of raising the next increment of capital can be determined, which is known as the marginal cost of capital.

The relationship between the marginal cost (MC) and average cost (AC) curves can be explained as follows. While the marginal cost is less than the average cost of capital, the average cost of capital will fall. However, once the marginal cost rises above the average cost of capital, the marginal cost of capital will pull up the average cost of capital (Figure 5.1).

Now the question is, which cost of capital should be considered when appraising investment projects? The costs associated with raising the marginal capital to finance a project should be used rather than an average cost of capital. The problem with calculating the marginal cost of capital, though, is that it is difficult to allocate particular funding to a specific project. Furthermore, companies which have a specific targeted capital structure will often raise marginal finance by utilizing only one source of finance at a time. The problem is that the marginal cost of capital will fluctuate at low levels when debt finance is used and at the margin to high levels when equity financing is used. Therefore, it could be argued that a rolling average cost of capital is more appropriate than a straight marginal cost of capital.

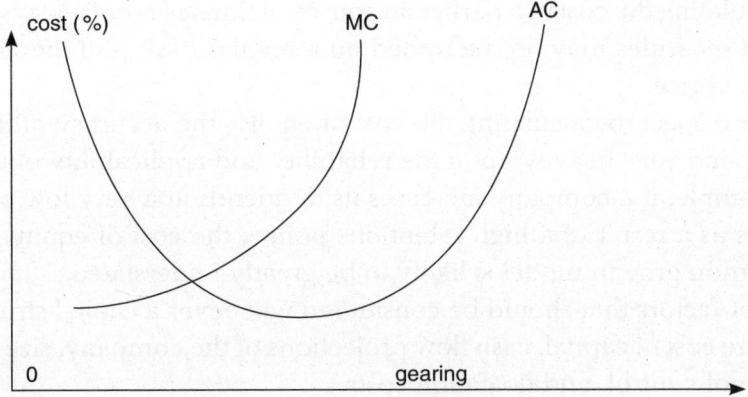

FIGURE 5.1 The MC and AC of capital

5.2.7 Factors affecting Cost of Capital

A number of factors influence the cost of capital. The company can control some of these factors by its financing and investment policies.

Factors beyond firm's direct control However, the following depend totally on the market.

(a) *Interest rates*—The cost of debt rises with the increase in the interest rate in the economy as the companies will need to pay a greater interest rate to its bondholders, in order to acquire debt capital. The cost of common and preferred equity is also increased by high interest rates, according to CAPM.

(b) *Market risk premium*—The perceived risks inherent in stocks, along with investors' aversion to risk, determine the market risk premium. This factor can not be controlled by companies. It influences the cost of equity. Next, the cost of debt is affected through a substitution effect. Finally, WACC is also influenced.

(c) *Tax rates*—Although, usually this factor cannot be controlled by companies, it has a significant influence over the cost of capital. The estimation of the cost of debt, as utilized in WACC, requires these tax rates. Tax policy influences the cost of capital in other ways as well, which are not as apparent. For example, interest tax shield, depreciation tax shield, etc., are influenced by the change in the tax rate. As a result, the cost of capital is affected.

Factors under firm's control A company's cost of capital can be influenced by its capital structure policy, dividend policy, and investment or capital budgeting policy. A stock's required rate of return may be influenced by the percentage of earnings paid out in dividends. Moreover, if a company has to issue new stock to fund its capital budget, due to very high payout ratio, then the company would have to deal with floatation costs. Besides, its cost of capital would also be influenced.

Calculating the cost of a particular source of finance is not always straightforward. Certain securities may not be traded on a regular basis and therefore do not have a market price.

With respect to calculating the cost of equity, the accuracy of the cost obtained will depend very heavily upon the reliability and applicability of the models used. For example, if a company increases its dividends at a very low but constant rate, perhaps as a result of a high retentions policy, the cost of equity calculated using the Gordon growth model is likely to be greatly understated.

Other factors that should be considered whenever a capital structure decision is taken are cost of capital, cash flow projections of the company, size of the company, dilution of control, and floatation costs.

5.3 FUNDAMENTALS OF CAPITAL BUDGETING DECISIONS

A firm may have various opportunities for investing its capital in the upcoming year. Simultaneously, it has to explore the feasibility and the expected return on each opportunity. Capital budgeting deals with the investment decisions that a company may undertake for the long-term profitability. This investment may involve purchase of stocks as well as new equipment, or even introduction of new products in the market. Based on this, the firm has to take a judicious decision as to which CAPEX (capital expenditure) proposal will it undertake in near future. Accordingly, the firm prepares a CAPEX budget for the current fiscal.

5.3.1 Need for Capital Budgeting Decisions

Capital expenditure decisions are deemed to be very important for three inter-related reasons. First of all, they all have very long-term consequences. Secondly, such decisions usually involve substantial outlays of funds. Lastly, it is usually difficult to reverse capital expenditure decisions at a later date because the market for used capital equipment is often imperfect.

In view of the crucial significance of capital expenditure decisions, it is not surprising that firms devote considerable time, energy, and effort in planning and executing these decisions. Their efforts are usually categorized as follows:
1. Identification of potential investment opportunities
2. Assembly of proposed investments
3. Decision-making
4. Implementation
5. Performance review

5.3.2 Value Creation and Corporate Investment

Stakeholders supply funds to a firm for one simple reason. The aim is to earn appropriate return on their resources. Estimated resources are invested in capital assets by the management of the company to create return. In order to evaluate the potential investment opportunity to generate best returns, the management must carefully select the most suitable technique avai able. This would ensure economic well-being of the firm as well as the finance providers.

The purpose of investment within a firm is driven by the need to generate value for its owners, as well as its shareholders. Funds are supplied to a particular project in order to produce cash inflow in future that is appreciably higher than the invested amount. Thus, the project appraisal decision is one involving the comparison of the amount of cash put into an investment with the amount of cash finally returned. Figure 5.2 explains the cash flow through a schematic diagram.

It may be considered that if investors put their funds in a capital project, they have an opportunity cost, as there are other uses of their funds as well. The opportunity cost represents the forgone possibilities of return that would have been generated from other investment options. Investments should at least be able to insure that the required returns of all investors are achieved. The wealth of the shareholders would register a decline if the cash generated is less than the investors' opportunity cost.

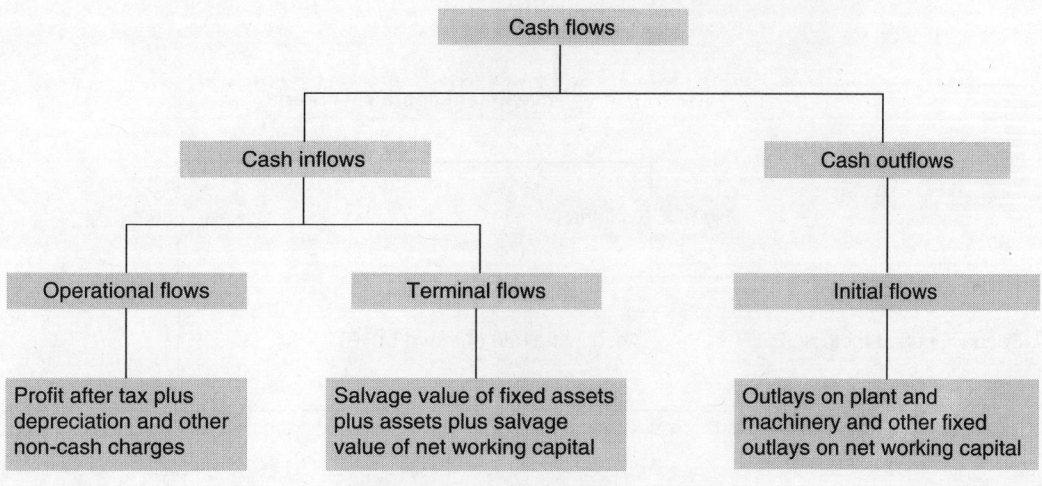

FIGURE 5.2 Cash-flow table

5.3.3 Investment Appraisal Techniques

For financial appraisal in capital budgeting decision, all decision alternatives have to be evaluated with a key question—will it create shareholders wealth? Various appraisal techniques are broadly classified under these two heads—discounted cash-flow techniques (DCF) and non-discounted cash-flow techniques (non-DCF). In DCF, time value of money is taken care of, whereas in non-DCF, time value is not considered. Figures 5.3 and 5.4 outline these techniques.

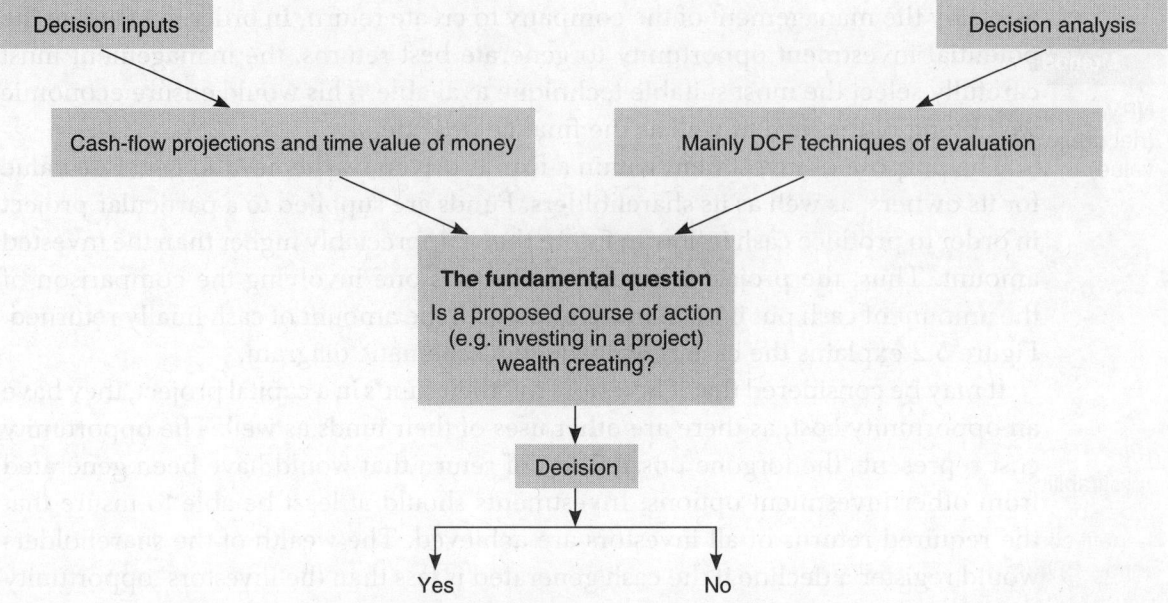

FIGURE 5.3 Investment appraisal techniques

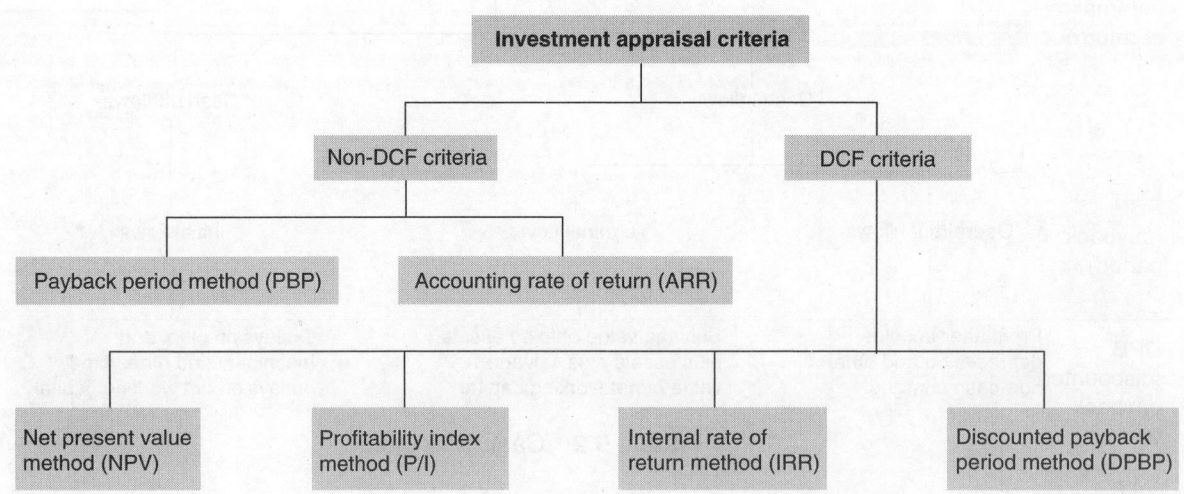

FIGURE 5.4 Investment appraisal criteria

Table 5.6 highlights key features and rules pertaining to each technique mentioned earlier.

TABLE 5.6 Various methods of investment appraisal techniques

Method	Techniques	Rule
NPV (net present value)	Decide on the discounting rate applicable for the project under review, keeping the risk exposure of the project in consideration. Compute the discount factors for each year over which the project is spread out. Estimate the future cash flows of the project over its useful life. Find out the present values of cash outflows and cash inflows. Compute NPV as follows: NPV = PV of cash inflows − PV of cash outflows	(a) Accept projects with positive NPV. (b) Reject projects with negative NPV. (c) When comparison is made between two or more projects, the project with the highest positive NPV is undertaken.
P/I (profitability index or benefit cost ratio—BCR)	The P/I is alternatively known as desirability factor (D/F) or benefit cost ratio (BCR). It may be noted that, although, sometimes BCR is defined in a different manner, here both the terms P/I and BCR will be used synonymously. P/I = PV of cash inflows/PV of cash outflows	(a) Accept projects where P/I is greater than one. (b) Reject projects where P/I is less than one. (c) When comparison is made between two or more projects, the project with the highest P/I is selected provided it is greater than one.
IRR (internal rate of return)	The IRR of a project is defined as that discount rate for which its NPV is equal to zero. In other words while applying the NPV technique, the discount rate is assumed and the NPV is assumed as zero and the corresponding discount rate is discovered (say by applying trial and error approach).	The project with the highest IRR is considered better and safer.
PBP (payback period)	The PBP, defined as the expected number of years required to recover the original investment, was the first method used to evaluate capital budgeting projects.	The shorter the payback period, the better.
DPB (discounted payback period)	Under this system, the future cash flows are discounted prior to payback calculations.	Same as above.
ARR (accounting rate of return)	ARR = Average profit after tax/Average book value of the investment	To use it as an appraisal criterion, the ARR of a project is compared with the ARR of the firm as a whole or against some external yardstick like the average rate of return for the industry as a whole.

We can now discuss a few key issues related to NPV and IRR methods as outlined in Table 5.6.

5.3.4 Net Present Value

The ultimate objective of a firm is how to maximize shareholders wealth. Under DCF mechanism, the NPV or net present value method of capital budgeting is fundamentally stronger in nature because it exactly talks about shareholders wealth. NPV is the difference between present value of cash inflows and present value of cash outflows. If the difference is positive, it means that the project is generating wealth for its shareholders. The detailed techniques and rules are discussed in Table 5.6.

5.3.5 Internal Rate of Return

It is not advisable to use the typical internal rate of return (IRR) to assess capital projects. IRR calculations often produce exaggerated reinvestment assumptions. They make bad projects appear better and promising ones excellent. However, despite the discouragement of this practice by academicians, nearly three-fourths of CFOs use IRR while analysing capital projects (Graham and Harvey 2001).

An informal survey conducted by Kelleher and MacCormach (2004) at venture capital firms, corporations, etc. revealed a serious lack of knowledge among executives regarding important shortcomings of IRR. About 24 to 30 executives were not fully aware of IRR's deficiencies. Around two dozen actual investments that a firm made on the basis of attractive IRR were reevaluated. It was found that if the deficiencies of IRR were considered by the firm, there would have been a significant change in the way certain projects were given importance by the management and the overall attractive picture presented by the calculated IRR.

Setting aside the shortcomings, IRR does make certain simple assumptions possible. For example, one can compare the 30 per cent annual return of a certain project with 12 per cent to 36 per cent rate that most people pay on their credit cards, loans, etc. This possibility of an easy comparison dominates the technical shortcomings that lead to misrepresentations in relatively isolated situations.

It is noted that some of these shortcomings are technical. They may even be arcane. In a project, if the future cash flows change from positive to negative or vice-versa, IRR can produce two distinct values. Also, in terms of IRR, big projects appear less attractive than small ones as the rate is expressed in percentage. However, if the comparison is done on NPV basis, the same may not hold true. The deficiencies of IRR can have serious consequences for capital budget managers. Finance decisions based on highest often overlook the distorted calculations involved and in the process may opt for an unsuitable project. This finally leads to risking of shareholders' value. It also leads to the creation of impractical expectations from the project. The belief that the interim cash flows will be reinvested at the same high rates of return is the most serious drawback while dealing with IRR.

In case of a given investment, the IRR is often understood by professionals as the annual equivalent return. The attractiveness of IRR is highlighted by this simple interpretation. It, however, may not be applicable in all cases. Only under the following conditions can IRR be seen as a valid representation of a project when no interim cash flows is generated by the projector, and if the cash flow is generated, the company should be able to invest them at the actual IRR.

The annual equivalent return from the project would be greatly overestimated if the value of IRR exceeds the real reinvestment rate for interim cash flows. The formula for calculation is such that it takes for granted that the firm has more similarly attractive projects in which the interim cash flows can be invested. The formula assumes the presence of these additional projects. Contrary to this, the estimation of net present value (NPV) only presupposes that the cost of capital is earned by a firm on its interim cash flow. All future incremental project values are left to be considered with those future values. In case of IRR, the assumption regarding the reinvestment rate can cause serious misinterpretation in the capital budget.

Let there be a situation where an organization is having two options (option 1 and 2), and both the options will be able to generate the same amount of cash flows. Both the ventures will be discounted at the same rate and have a similar life span. Therefore, according to the traditional mechanism of IRR, both the options will have the same IRR (36%). A manager may use the IRR method as the benchmark for choosing any of the options. In that case, the manager might make a mistake as the impact of the reinvestment rate assumptions for the interim cash flows is not considered. In the given case, obviously, option 1 will be more attractive because of more IRR (36%) as per the traditional method.

But it will be unrealistically optimistic for any company operating in any country or economy to come up with an equally attractive project year after year. Because then the firm can only reinvest the interim cash flows at the same rate (IRR) in intermittent years. In that case, it will be a more realistic approach if we can consider the opportunity cost of capital of the firm or the minimum expected rate of return of the investors as the reinvestment rate for the interim cash flows instead of the same IRR. This particular approach is followed in the case of option 2, where the reinvestment rate is considered as the WACC of the firm (7%). For this reason, the compounded annual growth rate (CAGR) becomes 24.46 per cent instead of 36 per cent of option 1. Considering the practicality, the CAGR of option 2 will be more realistic and logical. This is discussed in Tables 5.7 and 5.8.

TABLE 5.7 Cash-flow projection in option 1 and 2

Option 1					Option 2				
Year	0	1	2	3	Year	0	1	2	3
CF in Rs (millions)	−5	3	3	3	CF in Rs (millions)	−5	3	3	3
IRR	36%				IRR	36%			

TABLE 5.8 CAGR calculation in case of option 1 and 2

Key assumption: Reinvestment rate = IRR for Option 1					
Year	0	1	2	3	CAGR
CF at Year 3 if reinvested at 36%		3		5.54	36%
			3	4.08	36%
				3	36%
Year 3 value of Rs 5 million investment				12.62	36%

Key assumption: Reinvestment rate = Weighted average cost of capital for Option 2					
Year	0	1	2	3	CAGR
CF at Year 3 if reinvested at 7%		3		3.43	7%
			3	3.21	7%
				3	7%
Year 3 value of Rs 5 million investment				9.64	24.46%

However, interim cash flows are reinvested at different rates.

Hence, the real return of this venture will be 24.46% of the return, whereas traditional methods claim 36%, which is 1.47 times more than actual. In this way, the conventional way of calculating IRR will give hyperbolic or exaggerated rate of return for a particular project. Due to this amplification, ultimately it will be misleading for all stakeholders like investors, bankers, managers, and end users. From their research Kelleher and MacCormack also commented in 2004, 'the company's highest rated projects—showing IRRs of 800%, 150%, 130%—dropped to just 15%, 23%, and 22%, respectively, once a realistic decision had already been made.'

If the interim cash flows happen before time, the IRR variations would be higher. However, this situation does not arise if the interim reinvestment rate is correct. This problem occurs because there is a certain time difference between assumed IRR and actual reinvestment rate. In this time gap, the influence of the distortion adds up.

In a situation where two projects have identical IRRs, the project with interim cash flows will not be given preference. Instead the one that at the end of the investment period has single bullet cash flow would be chosen. The preference is made by looking at the two projects in real circumstances, keeping aside the misrepresentation caused by the IRR method of investigation.

Following are two survey evidences for proof of the above statement shown through Tables 5.9 and 5.10.

TABLE 5.9   Percentage of CFOs using different financial appraisal techniques

Techniques	Percentage of CFO
Profitability index	12
Book rate of return	20
Payback	57
IRR	76
NPV	75

Source: Graham and Harvey 2001.

TABLE 5.10   Percentage of CFOs using different financial appraisal techniques in India

Techniques	Percentage of CFO
Profitability index	35.1
Book rate of return	34.6
Payback	67.5
IRR	85
NPV	65
Break-even analysis	58.2

Source: Anand 2002.

Hence, though IRR has major shortcomings, it has been very popular in India and other countries through the years (Ryan and Ryan 2002; Block 2005; Dedi and Orsag 2007). It has various demerits and other alternatives are also available, but it is widely accepted by firms.

Literature review

The evaluation of NPV and IRR is well documented in many publications, some representative ones of which are Muro (1998) and Lang and Merino (1993). IRR and NPV are the most common and important indicators in investment decisions. ARR (accounting rate of return), as reported by Lefley (1996), is also a common indicator whose role is fully discussed by Brief and Lawson (1992). However, Muro (1998) and Lefley and Morgan (1998) opined that ARR has shortcomings and that the discounted cash-flow methods, such as IRR and NPV, should be preferred in capital investment appraisals.

Although, both IRR and NPV are discounted cash-flow methods, they have intrinsic differences. Tang (1991, 2003) and Robinson and Cook (1996) illustrated that the ranking of investment alternatives is not necessarily the same when obtained by the two methods. Differences in rankings between NPV and IRR are further exhibited in Asquith and Bethel (1995), who reported that IRR might be preferred to NPV under certain circumstances.

Evans and Forbes (1993) also reckoned that IRR is more cognitively efficient than NPV because IRR is expressed as a percentage or a rate of return, while NPV was just a monetary value cognitively inefficient to decision-makers, and hence, the use of IRR should be promoted. Other researchers, such as Lefley and Morgan (1998), took the view that NPV is more conceptually correct despite the fact that IRR is more popular than NPV, and that NPV is more theoretically sound as IRR may be too capricious or fickle and may not rank some projects in the same order as NPV. It has been pointed out in the paper by Battaglio et al. (1996) that IRR is meant for a consumer's point of view and NPV for a banker's point of view. This is close to the true definition as usually consumers have relatively limited money and banks have relatively unlimited money. As Tang and Tang (2003) had correctly defined that IRR gives the private investor's point of view and NPV the society's point of view. In other words, IRR is a financial indicator and NPV an economic indicator.

Tang and Tang (2003) also look into the advantages of IRR as a usable option in place of NPV. They are of the opinion that the shortcomings of IRR are particularly highlighted in the academic circles (Brigham et al. 1994; Hirshleifer 1958; Rapp 1980; Solomon 1963). According to them, if understood in the correct manner, the IRR method can be effective and usable. In order to provide a solution to the problem of inaccurate definitions of IRR and NPV, Tang and Tang put forth their own version for the same.

However, regardless of the point of view, mathematics of NPV/IRR relationships remain the same (Fisher 1930; Fleischer 1966; Hirshleifer 1958; Mao 1996). In what follows, it is demonstrated using Tang and Tang and other numerical examples that direct comparison of IRRs of various project-financing alternatives for the purpose of ranking is not a recommended approach. The proper approach will be revisited, and the limitations of IRR applicability will again be emphasized.

The major drawback of IRR method of investment appraisal

It needs to be admitted that IRR suffers from some inherent computational problems, which goes against its acceptability under certain circumstances. In spite of the above drawback, its greatest demerit lies in the concept of reinvestment rate assumption, which is an implicit factor in IRR computation vis-à-vis decisions applying IRR method.

Mini case The life of both projects A and B is two years and the appropriate rate of discount for both projects can be taken as 10%. Other information, i.e., initial investment, cash inflows, NPV, and IRR are given in Table 5.11.

TABLE 5.11 Conflict between NPV and IRR

Projects	Initial investment (Rs lakhs)	Cash inflows (Rs lakhs)		NPV	IRR
		Year 1	Year 2		
A	100	200	0	81.82	100%
B	100	0	400	230.58	100%

As per NPV, B is better, and as per IRR, both projects have equal weightage.

Conclusion

Ranking by the NPV decision criteria would theoretically be more accurate as it is consistent with the goal of maximization of shareholders' wealth in absolute terms. Further, the reinvestment rate of funds released by the project is based on certain assumptions, which are more logical compared to the implicit assumptions in case of IRR calculations. In certain cases of conflict between NPV and IRR, the modified IRR technique can prove to be quite handy, but, as explained earlier, it involves additional computation and finally it is bound to give the same results as NPV.

Thus, in view of the above, NPV emerges as a superior tool.

Reasons for continued popularity of IRR

Firms use IRR as much as they use the theoretically superior NPV model. In view of the above discussions, it is indeed strange why certain firms adopt this technique in preference to NPV. It is probably due to the following reasons:

1. *Knowledge of required rate of return is not required*—In case of NPV calculations, it is necessary to project future cash flows along with estimation of the required rate of return, namely the cost of capital, which is applied as the discounting factor in NPV computation. It is needless to say that cost of capital estimation is a very complicated and tedious exercise and none of the accepted techniques for the same are free from assumptions. Alternatively, in IRR calculation estimation of discount rate or cost of capital is not required. It is simply vetted against a pre specified cut off rate and if the estimated IRR is more than the cut off rate then that specific project will be accepted.

2. *Lack of knowledge*—Some of the managers may not be fully aware or familiar with the inherent limitations of the IRR method and may be of the opinion that ranking can be accurately done with the aid of this method.

3. *Psychological*—Usually managers are comfortable in expressing financial data in percentage form.

5.3.6 NPV vs IRR

In certain situations, NPV and IRR may produce contradictory results. This means that in certain situations the NPV method may rank one project as superior to another whereas under the IRR criterion the result may just be the opposite. These different rankings may occur under the following circumstances:

Projects with unequal life If the projects have different useful lives, it is possible that rankings may vary under NPV and IRR methods.

Mini Case Let there be two projects X and Y of unequal life but equal initial investment. Project X's life span is 1 year and project Y's life span is 3 years. The initial cash outlay for both the projects is Rs 1,00,000. The cash proceeds for project X at the end of first year is Rs 1,50,000 and for project Y one-time cash generated at the end of third year is Rs 2,00,000. Assumed that the appropriate discount rate for both the projects is 12% (Table 5.12).

TABLE 5.12 Projects with unequal life

Project	Life (years)	Initial outlay (Rs)	Cash proceeds in year 1 (Rs)	Cash proceeds in year 2 (Rs)	Cash proceeds in year 3 (Rs)	Present value of cash proceeds (discount rate 12%) (Rs)	NPV (Rs)	IRR
X	1	1,00,000	1,50,000			1,33,930	33,930	50%
Y	3	1,00,000			2,00,000	1,42,356	42,356	26%
Decision							Y is better	X is better

Hence, as per NPV rule project Y is better whereas, as per IRR rule project X is better.

Time disparity problem Mutually exclusive proposals may differ on the basis of the pattern of cash flows generated although their initial investments are identical. This is known as time disparity problem. In other words, time disparity problem may be defined as the conflict in ranking of proposals by the NPV and IRR methods, which have different patterns of cash flows.

Mini Case The initial investment of both projects A and B is Rs 1,05,000. Useful lives in both cases is 4 years and appropriate discounting rate in both cases can be taken as 8%. The expected cash flows of the above projects for those 4 years are shown in Table 5.13.

TABLE 5.13 Time disparity problem

Project	Initial investments (Rs)	End of year 1 (Rs)	End of year 2 (Rs)	End of year 3 (Rs)	End of year 4 (Rs)
A	1,05,000	60,000	45,000	30,000	15,000
B	1,05,000	15,000	30,000	45,000	75,000

NPV of project A $= -1,05,000 + (60,000 \times 0.9259) + (45,000 \times 0.8573) + (30,000 \times 0.7938) + (15,000 \times 0.7350) = 23,971.5$

NPV of project B $= -1,05,000 + (15,000 \times 0.9259) + (30,000 \times 0.8573) + (45,000 \times 0.7938) + (75,000 \times 0.7350) = 25,453.5$

Hence, project B is better as per the NPV rule, but the IRR of project A is higher than that of project B.

Size disparity problem This arises when initial investments in projects under consideration are different. In such situations, NPV and IRR may give different rankings. The conflict can be resolved by computation of the investment IRR based on an incremental approach. According to this approach, if the investment IRR exceeds the required rate of return expected by the investors, then the project with greater initial investment outlay should be selected, otherwise rejected. It is interesting to note that the investment IRR will give identical results as in the case of NPV calculation.

Mini Case A and B are two mutually exclusive projects with a life of 1 year each involving different outlays. The effective rate of discount for both the projects can be taken as 10%. The relevant details of the projects are as follows:

A: Initial investment	Rs 5,000	Cash inflow	Rs 6,250
B: Initial investment	Rs 7,500	Cash inflow	Rs 9,150

NPV of project A $= -5000 + 6250 / 1.1 = 681.82$

NPV of project B $= -7500 + 9150 / 1.1 = 818.20$

IRR of project A $= 6250 / 5000 - 1 = 0.25$, i.e., 25%

IRR of project B $= 9150 / 7500 - 1 = 0.22$, i.e., 22%

Hence, as per NPV, project B is better, whereas as per IRR project A is better.

Ranking Problem (IRR vis-à-vis NPV—a conceptual clarification)
The IRR decision rule does not always rank projects in the same way as the NPV method. Sometimes it is important to find out not only which project gives a positive return, but which one gives the greater positive return as well. For instance, projects may be mutually exclusive and a choice needs to be made because only one such project needs to be undertaken due to, say, some managerial constraints. Now, in such cases the use of IRR alone sometimes leads to poor choice. The concept is being explained through the help of Tables 5.14 and 5.15, which is accompanied by a graph in Figure 5.5.

TABLE 5.14   NPV vs IRR

Projects	Cash flows (Rs in lakhs)		IRR (%)	NPV (15% discount rate)
(1 year life)	Year 0	Year 1		
A	(20)	40	100%	14.78
B	(40)	70	75%	20.87

TABLE 5.15   Computation of NPV applying different discount rates

Discount rate (%)	Project A	Project B
0	20	30
20	13.33	18.33
50	6.67	6.67
75	2.86	0
100	0	(5)
125	(2.22)	(8.89)

Analytical comments   Table 5.15 and Figure 5.5 clearly show that the NPV ranking depends on the discount rate applied. Thus, if the discount rate used in the NPV calculation was higher than 50%, the ranking under both IRR and NPV would be the same, i.e., project A is superior. Now, if the discount rate falls below 50%, project B is invariably a better choice as per the NPV criterion.

One of the major elements leading to the theoretical dominance of NPV is that it takes into account the scale of investment as well. NPVs are measured in absolute terms.

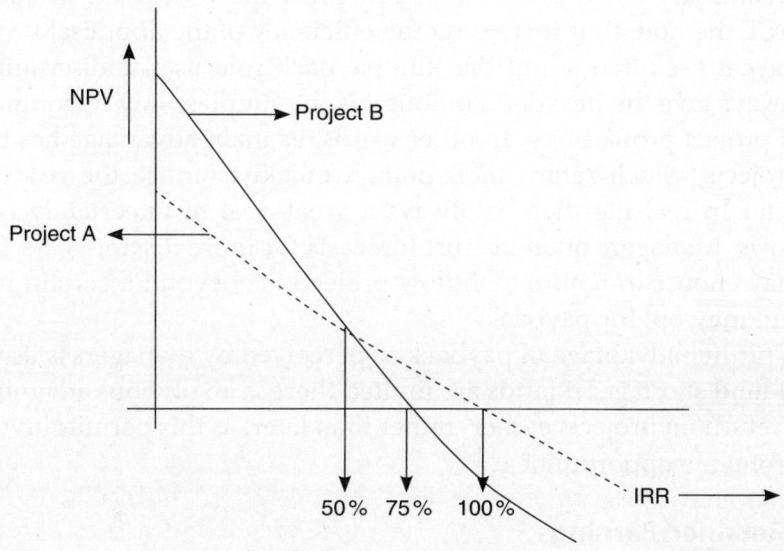

FIGURE 5.5   NPV graph

5.3.7 Payback/Discounted Payback

Payback is the simplest and most widely used method. It is the period within which initial investment will be accumulated from cash inflows of the project. If time value is considered in cash-flow calculation, it is known as discounted payback.

Major drawbacks of the payback/discounted payback criteria

1. It does not acknowledge the time value of money. Cash flows are not discounted in an appropriate manner before being added in the payback calculations. As per the basic principal of financial management analysis, cash flows that take place at various points in time must be properly compounded/discounted before being added or subtracted. The discounted payback computation manages this drawback and is a better choice over simple payback computations.

2. Payback method of investment appraisal does not acknowledge the cash flows beyond the payback period. This is another shortcoming in this method. It devalues the projects that produce significant cash flows in the later years. Even the discounted payback method of investment appraisal does not provide a solution to this problem.

Reasons for continued popularity of payback method

Payback remains a widely-used project appraisal technique despite its drawbacks. Some of the reasons for the same are as follows:

1. Payback may be used at an early stage to filter out projects which have clearly acceptable risk and return characteristics. Identifying those projects at a preliminary stage avoids the need for a more detailed evaluation through a DCF method, thus increasing the efficiency of the appraisal process.

2. Executives often admit that the payback rule used indiscriminately does not always give the best decision but it is the simplest way to communicate an idea of project profitability. In other words, its main advantage lies in its simplicity.

3. Projects, which return their outlays quickly, reduce the risk exposure of the firm. In real life there is always a great deal of uncertainly over future cash flows. Managers often distrust forecasts for more distant years. Thus, managers may choose to ignore cash-flow projections beyond a certain number of years and may opt for payback.

4. A further advantage of payback as perceived by managers is its use in situations of fund shortage. If funds are limited there is an obvious advantage in receiving a return on projects earlier, rather than later, as this permits investment in other profitable opportunities.

5.3.8 Cost of Retained Earnings

When a company expands its businesses by utilizing the saved profits, it also involves cost. The notion that retained earnings do not cost is incorrect. A cost is incurred on the retained earnings by virtue of not giving out the shareholders' part in the earnings. It is also known as opportunity cost of retained earnings. In a situation where the earnings are given out to the respective shareholders who in turn put the funds in new ordinary shares, opportunity cost of retained earnings would represent the expectation of the investor from the new ordinary share.

In the above example, an adjustment will be required on account of the fact that the dividends actually received by shareholders are not the amount of gross dividend since income tax is levied on them. Hence, the shareholders can only invest the net amount of the dividend received. Taxation adjustment in working out the cost of retained earnings poses a number of problems because all shareholders do not have the same rate of personal taxation.

Thus, due to this reason it becomes quite a tedious exercise to compute the cost of retained earnings. Hence in practical situations the cost of retained earnings is assumed identical to that of equity shares.

5.3.9 Modified Internal Rate of Return

One problem of IRR centres on the reinvestment assumption (as mentioned earlier). With NPV it is assumed that cash inflows arising during the life of the project are reinvested at the opportunity cost of capital. Whereas the central issue with IRR is that it makes an impractical assumption that until the project is over, the cash inflows can be reinvested somewhere else at the same rate as the IRR. For example, if a company invests in a very lucrative project and a certain cash inflow is registered after a short while, now it may not be possible for the company to obtain similar high yield by investing the cash elsewhere until the end of the project. Yet this is what the IRR implicitly assumes. The more likely eventuality is that the intra-project cash flows will be invested at the 'going rate' or the opportunity cost of capital. In other words, that is to say, a more appropriate means to calculate the reinvestment rate for a company is by referring to its normal discount rate. Such an assumption regarding the reinvestment makes the IRR of the project under analysis highly attractive. In case a need arises, for practical purposes, modified internal rate of return (MIRR) must be utilized to determine project appraisal in percentage.

This takes, as its starting point, the notion that for the sake of consistency with NPV, any cash flows arising during the project are reinvested at the opportunity cost of funds. That is at the rate of return available on the next best alternative use of the funds in either financial or real assets. The MIRR is the rate of return m, which if used to compound the initial investment amount (i.e. the original cash outlay) produces the same terminal value as the project cash inflows.

Here we will try to find the rate of compounding, which will equate the terminal value of the intra-project cash flows with the terminal value of the initial investment.

The following examples would clarify the concept.

Example 5.12 The business development team of M/s A Limited has been working to find uses for a vacated factory premise. Its senior management has selected two projects for further consideration but both have a life of only 3 years as the site will be flattened in this duration when a new motorway would be constructed. On the basis of the IRR, the business development team is leaning towards acceptance of project B, but it is aware that the key senior manager believes in MIRR and therefore feels the necessity to present the data calculated through the available techniques. The opportunity cost of capital is 10%.

Table E5.6 shows cash flow and IRR of both the projects.

(Rs in lakhs)

TABLE E5.6

Time	0	1	2	3	IRR%
Project A	− 1	0.5	0.5	0.5	23.4
Project B	− 1	1.1	0.1	0.16	27.7

You are required to complete the MIRR and NPV of both projects and show their ranking as per these criteria.

Solution

TABLE E5.7

Project	IRR%	NPV	MIRR
A	23.4	0.2	19%
B	27.7	0.175	18%
Decision	B is better	A is better	A is better

MIRR calculations:

$0.5 (1 + r)^2 + 0.5 (1 + r)^1 + 0.5 (1 + r)^0 = (1) (1 + mirr)^3$, mirr = 19% for project A

$1.1 (1 + r)^2 + 0.1 (1 + r)^1 + 0.16 (1 + r)^0 = (1) (1 + mirr)^3$, mirr = 18% for project B

For both the cases, r = opportunity cost of capital = 12%.

Therefore, MIRR and NPV have given the same solution.

....

....

Example 5.13   Case study on simple CAPEX decision

A company is planning to set up a project at a cost of Rs 3,00,00,000. It has to decide whether to locate the plant in Bengaluru or Baharampur (which is a backward district). Locating the plant in Baharampur would mean a cash subsidy of Rs 15,00,000 from the central government. In addition to this, the taxable profit to the extent of 20% would be exempted from taxes for a period of 10 years if the plant were to be located at Baharampur.

The above project envisages a borrowing of Rs 2,00,00,000 in either case. The cost of borrowing will be 12% for Bengaluru and 10% in case of Baharampur. However, the revenue costs are likely to be higher in Baharampur as compared to Bengaluru. The borrowings have to be repaid in four equal annual instalments beginning from the end of the fourth year.

With the help of information given in Table E5.8, please advise the management of the company as to where the project should be set up.

Note:

(a)   A discount rate of 15% can be assumed for computational purposes.

(b)   Income tax rate applicable to the company is 50% of their profits.

(c)   Please apply the NPV criteria.

TABLE E5.8

Year	Profit (or loss) before interest/depreciation and taxes (Rs in lakhs) Bengaluru	Profit (or loss) before interest/depreciation and taxes (Rs in lakhs) Baharampur	Discounting factors applying a rate of 15%
1	(6)	(50)	0.87
2	34	(20)	0.76
3	54	10	0.66
4	75	20	0.57
5	110	50	0.50
6	140	100	0.43
7	150	150	0.38
8	250	200	0.33
9	350	225	0.28
10	450	350	0.25

Solution

Option in Bengaluru: Refer to Table E5.9 (all figures are in Rs lakhs).

TABLE E5.9

Year	EBDIT (Rs in lakhs)	Depreciation 10% straight line	Interest (12% of 200 lakhs or 2 crores)	PBT	Tax (50%)	PAT	NCF Net cash flow = (PAT + Dep.— cash out flow)	PV Present value 15% discount factor
1	(6)	(30)	(24)	(60)	0	(60)	– 100 – 30 = – 130	– 113.1
2	34	(30)	(24)	(20)	0	(20)	– 20 + 30 = 10	7.6
3	54	(30)	(24)	0	0	0	30	19.8
4	75	(30)	(24)	21	0	21	– 50 + 51 = 1	0.57
5	110	(30)	(18)	62	1.5	60.5	– 50 + 90.5 = 40.5	20.25
6	140	(30)	(12)	98	49	49	– 50 + 79 = 29	12.47
7	150	(30)	(6)	114	57	57	– 50 + 87 = 37	14.06
8	250	(30)	0	220	110	110	140	46.2
9	350	(30)	0	320	160	160	190	53.2
10	450	(30)	0	420	210	210	240	60
								Total = 121.05

Tax rule: Previous years losses will be compensated from future profit.

NPV for Bengaluru = Rs 1,21,05,000 (positive), hence accept the project.

Taking into consideration the cash subsidy of Baharampur.

Cash outflow at the initial year = 1,00,00,000 – 15,00,000 = Rs 85,00,000.

After 20% exemption, effective tax rate = 50% of (80% of profit) = 40%.

By applying the similar methods, NPV for Baharampur projects.

NPV = –Rs 17 lakh.

Hence, the project should be rejected.

Example 5.14 Exe Limited is considering three financing plans. The key information is as follows. Total funds to be raised = Rs 2,00,000 and plans of financing proportions are given in Table E5.10.

TABLE E5.10

Plans	Equity (%)	Debt (%)	Preference Shares (%)
A	100	–	–
B	50	50	–
C	50	–	50

Pre-tax cost of debt and cost of preference share can be taken as 8% each and the effective tax rate of the organization is 50%. It may also be noted that the company will be in a position to issue equity shares (face value Rs 10) at a premium of Rs 10 per share. The expected Earnings Before Interest and Tax (EBIT) under all the financing plans can be taken as Rs 80,000.

For each plan

(a) Determine earnings per equity share.

(b) Compute the EBIT range among the plans for indifference.

(c) Indicate whether any of the plans dominate, supported by adequate reasons.

Solution

(a) Required fund = Rs 2,00,000 (refer to Table E5.11)

TABLE E5.11

Plans	A	B	C
	100% equity	50% equity 50% debt	50% equity 50% preference share
No. of equity shares	10,000 @Rs 10	5,000 @Rs 10	5,000 @Rs 10
Equity	Rs 1,00,000	Rs 50,000	Rs 50,000
Share premium @ Rs 10	Rs 1,00,000	Rs 50,000	Rs 50,000
Total equity	Rs 2,00,000	Rs 1,00,000	Rs 1,00,000
Preference share @ 8%			Rs 1,00,000
Debt @ 8%		Rs 1,00,000	
Total capital	Rs 2,00,000	Rs 2,00,000	Rs 2,00,000
EBIT	80,000	80,000	80,000
Less interest @ 8%	–	–8000	–
PBT	80,000	72,000	80,000
Tax @ 50%	40,000	36,000	40,000
PAT	40,000	36,000	40,000
Preference dividend @ 8%	–	–	–8,000
Earnings available to equity shareholders	40,000	36,000	32,000
EPS	4	7.2	6.4

(b)   EPS = [(EBIT – Interest)(1 – t) – D_p] / No. of shares

Say EPS for Plan A and B is equal, for EBIT = x

where, t = tax rate, D_p = Preference dividend

For Plan A and B

[(x – 0) 0.5 – 0] / 10,000 = [(x – 8000) 0.5 – 0] / 5000

EBIT = x = 16,000, indifferent of A and B

If x > 16,000, plan B is better and if x < 16000, plan A is better

For Plan A and C

[(x – 0) 0.5 – 0] / 10,000 = [(x – 0)0.5 – 8000] / 5000

EBIT = x = 32,000, indifferent of A and C

If x > 32,000, plan C is better and if x < 32,000, plan A is better

For Plan B and C

[(x – 8000) 0.5 – 0] / 5000 = [(x – 0) 0.5 – 8000] / 5000

0.5x – 4000 = 0.5x – 8.000

For same amount of EBIT, EPS of B is more than C at every level of EPS.

B would dominate C due to tax implication (tax shelter).

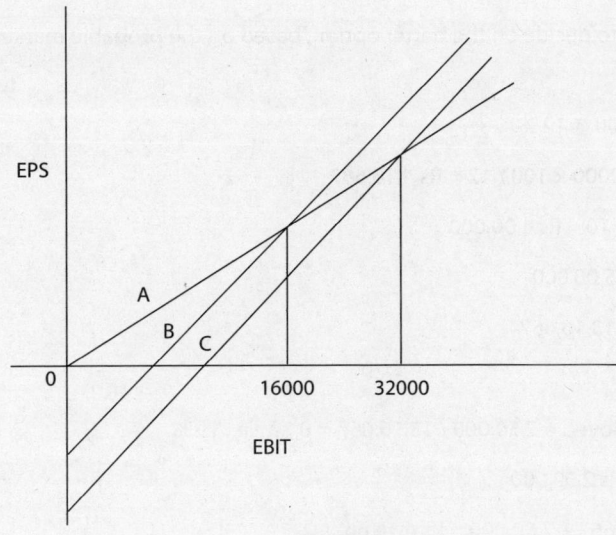

FIGURE E5.3

Finally, for up to EBIT = 16,000, option A will dominate (because of more EPS) and beyond EBIT > 16,000, option B will predominate.

Example 5.15

TABLE E5.12

EBIT (Rs)	2,50,000
Interest on debentures @ 12% (Rs)	50,000
PBT (Rs)	2,00,000
Income tax @ 50% (Rs)	1,00,000
PAT (Rs)	1,00,000
Number of equity shares @ 10 each	40,000
Earnings per share (Rs)	3.00
Ruling price of each share in the market (Rs)	30.00
Price earnings ratio	10
Free reserves and surplus	5,00,000
Additional fund required for diversification	2,00,000

For the diversification plan company anticipates the ratio of EBIT to capital employed to be same. If debt equity ratio is more than 45% then corresponding *P/E* ratio decreases to 9 and the interest rate increases to 15% for additional loan. The company is considering the following options in respect of raising the additional funds:

(a) Through debt.

(b) Issuing equity shares at a premium of Rs 20 per share.

You are required to decide on the better option, based on the probable market price of share.

Solution

Interest = Rs 50,000 @ 12%

Existing debt = 50000 × 100 / 12 = Rs 4,16,667

Equity = 40,000 × 10 = Rs 4,00,000

Free reserve = Rs 5,00,000

Total capital = Rs 13,16,667

EBIT = Rs 2,50,000

EBIT/Capital employed = 2,50,000 / 13,16,667 = 0.19, i.e., 19%

Required debt = Rs 2,00,000

Total debt = 4,16,667 + 2,00,000 = Rs 6,16,667

Equity + Free reserve = Rs 9,00,000

Total capital = Rs 15,16,667

D/E ratio = 6,16,667 / 9,00,000 = 68.52% > 45%

P/E ratio = 9, Interest Rate = 15% (of Rs 2,00,000)

New EBIT = 19% of 15,16,667 = Rs 2,88,167

Option 1: EBIT = Rs 2,88,167

Interest (earlier) = Rs 50,000

Interest (new) = 15% of 2,00,000 = Rs 30,000

PBT = Rs 2,08,167

Tax (50%) = Rs 1,04,083.5

PAT = Rs 1,04,083.5

Number of equity shares @Rs 10 = 40,000

EPS = 1,04,083.5 / 40,000 = 2.6

P/E ratio = MPS / EPS = 9

MPS = 9 × 2.6 = 23.42

Option 2: Equity @ premium of Rs 20 per share

Debt = Rs 4,16,667

Equity + new issue + Free reserve = 4,00,000 + 2,00,000 + 5,00,000 = Rs 11,00,000

D/E ratio = 4,16,667 / 11,00,000 = 37.8%% < 45%.

EBIT = Rs 2,88,167

Interest (earlier) = Rs 50,000

PBT = Rs 2,38,167

Tax (50%) = Rs 1,19,083.5

PAT = Rs 1,19,083.5

Number of equity shares @Rs 10 = 46,667 (40,000 + 2,00,000 / 30 = 40,000 + 6,667)

EPS = 1,19,083.5 / 46,667 = 2.55

MPS = 30

P/E ratio = 30 / 2.55 = 11.77

Therefore, option 2 is better for better *P/E* ratio, not the EPS.

Example 5.16   One poultry firm has produced presently 45,000 eggs per week on an average. Recently it is operating with 150 employees. Its total weekly turn over is Rs 6,00,000 and total weekly contribution Rs 2,50,000. The firm is planning to implement more developed mechanism of production. For this modernization plan firm has to invest Rs 1,50,000 and then onwards it can operate with 118 employees. But modernization increases the individual productivity by 50%. Firm owners decide to motivate their employees by providing an incentive of 1% increase in piece work rate of Re. 1 per unit for every 2% increase in average individual output achieved.

In order to sell such increased output, it would be necessary to decrease the selling price of the product by 4%.

Evaluate the firm's proposal from the above mentioned information.

Solution

Average output per week = 45,000 units from 150 employees

Average weekly output per employee = 300 units

50% productivity increased, average weekly output per employee = $300 \times 1.5 = 450$

New number of employees (after reduction) = 118

Therefore total average weekly production = $450 \times 118 = 53,100$

Earlier selling price per unit = 6,00,000 / 45,000 = Rs 13.33

New selling price per unit after reduction of 4% = $13.33 \times 0.96 = $ Rs 12.8

Earlier variable cost per unit = (6,00,000 – 2,50,000) / 45,000 = 3,50,000 / 45,000 = 7.78 = 1 + 6.78

New variable cost per unit = $1 \times (1 + 0.25) + 6.78 = $ Rs 8.03 (There is 1% increase for every 2% increase, therefore 25% increase in case of 50% increase of productivity.)

New contribution per unit = New selling price per unit – New variable cost per unit = 12.8 – 8.03 = Rs 4.77

Contribution per week = $4.77 \times 53,100 = $ Rs 2,53,287

Earlier contribution per week = Rs 2,50,000

Increment in weekly contribution = Rs 3,287 (positive)

Yearly increment in contribution = $3,287 \times 52 = 1,70,924$

ROI = 1,70,924 / 1,50,000 = 113.95%

Payback period is less than 1 year.

Therefore, the firm owners should implement this modernization plan.

Example 5.17 Cash flows associates with initial investment are shown in Table E5.13. Calculate BCR.

TABLE E5.13

Year	Cash flow (Rs)	BCR
0	(1,00,000)	
1	25,000	
2	40,000	
3	50,000	
4	40,000	
5	30,000	

Solution

BCR = [25,000 / 1.12 + 40,000 / 1.12^2 + 50,000 / 1.12^3 + 40,000 / 1.12^4 + 30,000 / 1.12^5] / 100000

= 1.32 > 1, Accept the project.

NBCR = Net benefit cost ratio = BCR – 1 = 0.32, Positive, Accept the project.

Payback period = 2 years 9 months

Example 5.18 What is IRR of the following cash-flow stream as shown in Table E5.14?

TABLE E5.14

Year	Cash Flow (Rs)
0	(3,000)
1	9,000
2	(3,000)

Solution

$-3000 / (1 + r) + 9000 / (1 + r)^2 - 3000 / (1 + r)^3 = 0$

IRR = r = 162% or – 62%

Example 5.19 If equipment costs Rs 5 lakh and lasts for 8 years, what should be the minimum annual cash inflow before it is worthwhile to purchase the equipment? Assume cost of capital = 10%.

Solution

Let C be the minimum annual cash inflow for using the machine.

$\sum C / (1.1)^t = 5,00,000$ for t = 1 to 8 years

$C.\text{PVIFA}_{10,8} = 5,00,000$

$C = 500,000 / 5.335 = 93721$

5.3.10 Alternative Project Evaluation Approach

One cannot clearly predict the future outcome of conventional investment decision. One can choose the amount invested in a project but the return generated cannot be fully controlled. Such investment decisions are primarily made on the basis of certain assumptions regarding the future scenario, along with the understanding of the management's business strategy.

Despite best estimations, it is possible that the real cash flows would vary from what the management had foreseen as a result of competition and other unpredictable events in the real world. Management can revise its strategy from time to time by observing the market and thereby, it can to a great extent remove the uncertainty involved in future cash flows. This revision and updating of strategy improves the upside potential of the investment opportunity's value. It also controls the downside losses that occur as a result of initial estimation of the future performance under passive management.

Real option analysis

Using the analogy with options on financial assets, investment flexibility is often called a real option (Dixit and Pindyck 1994; Trigeorgis 1996; Huchzermeier and Loch 2001). Real options elaborately discussed in Chapter 10 are options on real assets that can be defined as opportunities to make a choice. It gives rights but not obligations to take some action in the future (Dixit and Pindyck 1995). Many of these real options occur naturally, while others may be planned and built-in at some extra cost. The role of real options analysis is to quantify how much future opportunities are worth today. Using option pricing models, it is possible to quantify these opportunities and to indicate when these options should be optimally exercised (Botteron 2001).

Similar to financial options, real options can be divided into call options and put options. Under call options, the holder gets to pay the investment price/exercise price in a particular duration of time. He/she receives certain asset or project with some value in return. The difference between the value of underlying asset and exercise price determines the project option at the time of exercise. For instance, in case of deferral option, the starting of a project can be postponed until adequate information is available. The reverse of this is true in case of put option. Under this, the holder can see the underlying asset or a project to get the exercise price. For instance, a holder has a choice of withdrawing from an unsuitable project and receives a fixed salvage value for the same.

This section discusses consecutively the NPV method, decision tree analysis (DTA), real options analysis, and adjusted present value (APV) methods. The following example shows how deferral option mechanism can produce better worth in execution of a project, specially when it generates a negative NPV. In the following situation for an initial outlay of Rs 120, there will be 50% equal chance of generating cash flow of Rs 120 and Rs 60 in the next year. This venture produces NPV of –Rs 18.31.

Option I Conventional NPV

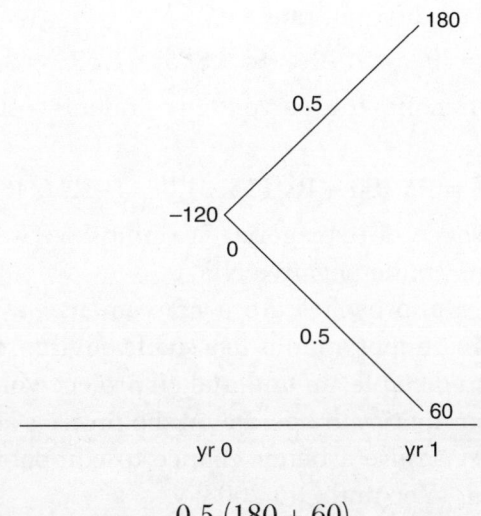

$$\text{NPV}_\text{I} = -120 + \frac{0.5\,(180 + 60)}{1.18} = -18.31$$

Option II Using deferral option

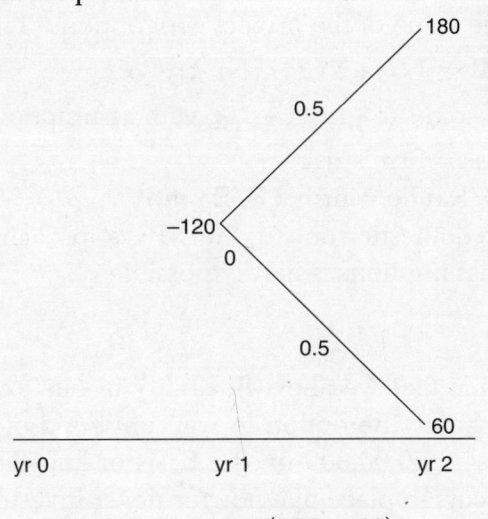

$$\text{NPV}_\text{II} = \frac{1}{1.07}\left\{ -120 + \frac{0.5\,(180 + 60)}{1.18} \right\} = -17.12$$

If this particular venture can be delayed for one year without any risk, negativity of NPV can be reduced up to the extent of Rs 1.19. We assume risk free interest rate is 7% and cost of capital is 18% (Copeland and Antikarov 2001).

NPV analysis

Consider first the case without flexibility. We can only use the information that is available today and we have to decide now whether or not to invest. The current gross project value is obtained by discounting the project's end-of-period values at the appropriate discount rate, i.e.,

$$P(c) = (0.5 * \$170 + 0.5 * \$65) / 1.175 = \$100$$

After subtracting the current investment costs, the project's NPV is finally given by

$$NPV = Rs\ 100 - Rs\ 115 / 1.08 = -Rs\ 6.48$$

In the absence of managerial flexibility, we would decide not to invest in this project, based on the negative NPV.

NPV-based approaches are a convenient way to understand the decision to select new investment options in a stable environment. It ensures that although the future is unpredictable, an undertaken project would be analysed and modified till its end. Opportunities to operate on the projects as per the changing requirements of the market ensure a better chance to companies to minimize losses and earn higher returns (Yeo and Qiu 2003).

This should not undermine the importance of traditional NPV calculations. They are vital input for option based analyses. The option value of operating and strategic flexibility and the traditional (static or passive) NPV are the two parts that comprise the value of the project with options (Trigeoris 1993).

$$NPV = - C_0 + \Sigma CF_t / (1 + k_w)^t$$

$$K_w = \sigma k_e + (1 - \sigma)(1 - t)k_d \text{ with assumption}$$

1. Project risk = firm's risk
2. Project D/E ratio = firm's D/E ratio

Even in a domestic context, the NPV approach has limitations and fulfilling the above two assumptions is hardly possible.

Decision tree analysis

Let us assume that we allow flexibility in our example. We have an impractical situation at hand, the option to wait until end of the period and decide whether to spend Rs 11,50,00,000 on the basis of knowledge of the state of nature. This situation occurs in place of a now-or-never investment circumstance.

Only in case cash flows is Rs 17,00,00,000, we decide to invest. When cash flows turn out to be only Rs 6,50,00,000, we decide not to invest instead of incurring a loss of Rs 5,00,00,000. A particular price needs to be paid in order to defer the decision. In the process, unpredictability and the risk involved in the investment are dealt with. Decision tree analysis (DTA) is often utilized to determine the value of flexibility. The flexibility is introduced with the help of decision nodes. These decision nodes make future decision by the management possible, and alterations are made to tackle uncertainty and gather more relevant information:

Rs 170 – Rs 115 = Rs 55 (invest)

Rs 65 – Rs 115 = –Rs 50 (do not invest)

The expected return is estimated by discounting the expected cash flows of the project. With the option to defer at the cost of capital of 17.5%. NPV of the project becomes:

NPV = (0.5 × 55,00,000 + 0.5 × 0) / 1.175 = Rs 2,34,00,000

In initial case: NPV = –1,15,00,000 + 0.5 × 1,70,00,000 + 0.5 × 65,00,000

Since the flexibility to defer increases the NPV of the project from Rs 25,00,000 to Rs 2,34,00,000, the deferral option would be Rs 2,34,00,000 – Rs 25,00,000 = Rs 2,09,00,000.

Initially, this method seems fine but in the given case, the use of the DTA method may not be appropriate as a result of the flexibility present in the future decision nodes. It leads to a change in the payoff structure and thereby in the risk features. Therefore, the use of same constant discount rate is not applicable here. As the variation in the cash-flow pattern of the project causes changes in its profile, risk adjustment needs to be done accordingly. The real option analysis is useful here. In the decision tree context, the option approach can be understood as modifying the discount rate to reflect the actual risk involved in the cash flows (Copeland and Keenan 1998).

Adjusted present value

All discounted cash-flow methodologies involve forecasting future cash flows and then discounting them to their present value at a rate that reflects their riskiness. But the methodologies differ in the details of their execution, most particularly in how they account for the value created or destroyed by financial manoeuvres, as opposed to operations. The adjusted present value (APV) approach analyses financial manoeuvres separately, and then adds their value to that of the business (Luehrman 1997).

The weighted average cost of capital (WACC) approach helps in reflecting financial enhancements by adjusting the discount rate. This adjusted discount rate is directly applied to the business cash flows. Without the need for any later addition, all financial side effects are to be managed by WACC automatically.

In practical processes, WACC is not that effective in tackling financial side effects. With exception of simple capital structures, WACC is not very useful as it addresses only the tax effects. However, its most important advantage is that it needs just one discounting operation. It was a significant feature in the past to the users of calculators and slide rulers. In today's times that significance does not hold much ground. With the advancement of technology (such as high-speed spreadsheets), extra discounting need in APV is not a problem. Today, APV along with being highly informative is also very inexpensive.

One of the important characteristics of APV is that it is flexible. Depending upon the requirements of the people managing the different parts of a valuation, a trained analyst can determine the valuation accordingly. As APV needs fewer restrictive assumptions, it works in most situations where WACC does or does not work. WACC is subject to more serious errors than APV. Most importantly, APV can provide a gamut of relevant information to the management. Through APV, managers can know about an asset's worth along with the source of its value. The parts contributing to the value are distinguished and observed separately. In contrast, all financing side effects are clubbed into the discount rate by WACC.

APV works on value additivity principle and separates cash flows into different segments with different discounting factors.

APV = Base-case NPV + Value of all financing side effects

= Value of the project as if it were financed entirely with equity + Interest tax shield, subsidies, cost of financial distress, hedges, issue cost, and other costs

APV is a step-by-step project evaluation approach. There are five steps that are categorised under three broad headings:

Prepare performance forecast for the target business.

Step 1: Prepare performance forecasts (income statements and balance sheet) and base-case incremental cash flows for the business.

(Here the components of values are bundled together.)

Prepare a valuation spreadsheet for each component of value.

Step 2: Discount base-case cash flows and terminal value to present value.

Step 3: Evaluate financing side effects. For example, interest tax shield.

Prepare present value of estimated interest tax shields from borrowing.

(Here they are unbundled.)

Add the components of value.

Step 4: Add the pieces together to get an initial APV.

APV = Base-case value + Value of financing side effects

Step 5: Tailor the analysis to fit managers' needs.

(Finally, they are re-bundled.)

5.3.11 Replacement Decisions

The decision to replace an existing machine which has yet to reach the end of its useful life is often necessary because of developments in technology and generous trade-in values offered by manufacturers. In analysing replacement decisions, it is important to recognize that we assess the additional costs and benefits arising from the replacement, rather than the attractiveness of the new machine in isolation. Exhibit 5.1 elaborates an example to make the concept clearer.

EXHIBIT 5.1   Prohibiting of S and S project

S and S Company manufactures components for the car industry. It is considering automating its line for producing crankshaft bearings. The automated equipment will cost Rs 7,50,000. It will replace equipment with a residual value of Rs 80,000 and a written-down book value of Rs 2,00,000. It is anticipated that the existing machine has a further 5 years to run, when its scrap value would be Rs 5,000.

At present, the line has a capacity of 1.25 million units per annum but, typically, it has only been run at 80% of capacity because of the lack of demand for its output. The new line has a capacity of 1.4 million units per annum. Its life is expected to be 5 years and its scrap value at that time Rs1,05,000. The main benefits of the new proposal are reduction in manpower and an improvement in price due to its superior quality.

The accountant has prepared the cost estimates shown in Table A based on output of 10,00,000 units p.a. Fixed overheads include depreciation on the old machine of Rs 40,000 p.a. and Rs 1,30,000 for the new machine. It is considered that overall for the company other fixed overheads are unlikely to change.

The introduction of the new machine will enable the average value of stocks held to be reduced by Rs 1,60,000. After 5 years, the machine will probably be replaced by a similar one.

The company uses 10% as its discount rate. We shall ignore taxation.

The solution is given in Table E5.17. Several comments are worthy of note:

1. It has been assumed that no benefits can be obtained from the additional capacity due to sales constraints. In reality, it would be useful to explore whether, for example by investing in advertising, demand could be increased.

2. Fixed costs are not relevant. Depreciation is not a cash flow, and we are told that other fixed costs will not alter with the decision. The incremental cash flow per unit is therefore 16 p, given Rs 1,60,000 (i.e., 1 million units at 16 p) additional cash each year on the expected sales.

3. In addition to the scrap values of Rs 80,000 in year 0 and Rs 1,05,000 in year 5 on the old and new machines, respectively, there is a Rs 5,000 opportunity cost in year 5. This is the scrap value no longer available as a consequence of the replacement decision.

TABLE E5.16

Items	Old line (paise per unit)	New line (paise per unit)
Materials	40	36
Labour	22	15
Variable overheads	14	14
Fixed overheads	34	40
	110	**105**
Selling price	**150**	**155**
Profit per unit	40	50

Solution

TABLE E5.17

	Old line (paise per unit)	New line (paise per unit)
Selling price	150	155
Less:		
Materials	(40)	(36)
Labour	(22)	(15)

Contd

Table E5.17   *Contd*

	Old line (paise per unit)	New line (paise per unit)
Variable overheads	(14)	(14)
Variable costs	(76)	(65)
Cash contribution	74	90
Incremental cash flow per unit (90–74)		16p
Total incremental cash flow on 1 million unit sales		Rs 160,000

					(Rs in thousands)	
Year	0	1	2	3	4	5
Cost savings		160	160	160	160	160
New machine	(750)					105
Scrap old machine	80					(5)
Working capital	160					
New cash flow	(510)	160	160	160	160	160
Net present value						
10% discount factor	1.000	0.909	0.826	0.751	0.683	0.621
Present value	(510)	145	132	120	109	161
Cumulative present value	(510)	(365)	(233)	(113)	(4)	157
NPV	157					

4. Working capital will be reduced by Rs 1,60,000 for the period of the project and it therefore appears as a benefit in year 0. Because the project will be replaced after 5 years with a similar machine, this benefit will continue indefinitely.
5. The book value of the existing machine represents the undepreciated element of the original cost, a sunk cost which is not relevant to the decision. Book value of assets, however, may be important in practice, as it can sometimes mean a heavy accounting loss in the year of acquisition. In this case, the loss would be Rs 120,000 (i.e., book value of Rs 2,00,000 less Rs 80,000 residual value). This is not a cash flow, but in practice, it may still be regarded as undesirable to depress reported profit figures in this way. This, of course, raises issues of market efficiency—will the market see through the accounting adjustment?

The replacement decision is a wealth-creating opportunity offering an NPV of Rs 1,57,000, although the cumulative present value calculation in Table E5.16 shows that the project does not come into surplus, in net present value terms, until the final year.

5.3.12 Optimal Capital Budget

A group of projects that optimize the value of the firm constitute the optimal capital budget. This budget includes positive NPV projects. Theoretically, all projects with positive NPVs should be accepted. However, optimal capital budget involves the following problems:

1. An increasing marginal cost of capital
2. Capital rationing

Increasing marginal cost of capital

The capital budget may determine the cost of capital. As mentioned before, the issuing of new equity or public debt involves high floatation cost. It implies that the cost of capital rises after the internally generated cash of a firm is invested by it. It then needs to sell new common stock. Also, very large capital investment appear riskier to investors. As a result, the cost of capital increases with the increase in the size of capital budget. Therefore, a project may have a positive or negative NPV depending upon whether it is a part of a 'normal size' capital budget, or whether, it involves a very large capital budget. However, this problem is very rare in case of most firms, and besides an established firm does not usually require new external equity.

Capital rationing

Amritsor Pyrotechniques, a manufacturer of fireworks and lasers for light shows, has identified 40 potential independent projects, with 15 having a positive NPV based on the firm's 12% cost of capital. The total cost of implementing these 15 projects is Rs 75,00,000. Based on finance theory, the optimal capital budget is Rs 75,00,000, and Amritsor should accept the 15 projects with positive NPVs. However, Amritsor's management has imposed a limit of Rs 50,00,000 for capital expenditures during the upcoming year. Due to this restriction, the company must forego a number of value-adding projects. This is an example of *capital rationing,* defined as a situation in which a firm limits its capital expenditures to less than the amount required to fund the optimal capital budget. Despite being at odds with finance theory, this practice is quite common.

Why would any company forego value-adding projects? Here are some potential explanations, along with some suggestions for better ways to handle these situations.

1. *Reluctance to issue new stock*—Many firms are extremely reluctant to issue new stock, so all of their capital expenditures must be funded out of debt and internally generated cash. Also, most firms try to stay near their target capital structure and combined with the limit on equity, this limits the amount of debt that can be added during any one year. The result can be a serious constraint on the amount of funds available for investment in new projects.

   This reluctance to issue new stock could be based on some sound reasons: (a) flotation costs can be very expensive; (b) investors might perceive new stock offerings as a signal that the company's equity is overvalued; and (c) the company might have to reveal sensitive strategic information to investors, thereby reducing some of its competitive advantages. To avoid these costs, many companies simply limit their capital expenditures.

However, rather than placing a somewhat artificial limit on capital expenditures, a company might be better off explicitly incorporating the costs of raising external capital into its cost of capital. If there still are positive NPV projects even using this higher cost of capital, then the company should go ahead and raise external equity and accept the projects.

2. *Constraints on non-monetary resources*—Sometimes a firm simply does not have the necessary managerial, marketing, or engineering talent to immediately accept all positive NPV projects. In other words, the potential projects are not really independent, because the firm cannot accept them all. To avoid potential problems due to spreading existing talent within a few projects, many firms simply limit the capital budget to a size that can be accommodated by their current personnel.

A better solution might be to employ a technique called linear programming. Each potential project has an expected NPV, and each potential project requires a certain level of support by different types of employees. A linear programme can identify the set of projects that maximizes NPV, subject to the constraint that the total amount of support required for these projects does not exceed the available resources.

3. *Controlling estimation bias*—Many managers become overtly optimistic when estimating the cash flows for a project. Some firms try to control this estimation bias by requiring managers to use an unrealistically high cost of capital. Others try to control the bias by limiting the size of the capital budget. Neither solution is generally effective since managers quickly learn the rules of the game and then increase their own estimates of project cash flows, which might have been biased upward to begin with.

A better solution is to implement a post-audit programme and to link the accuracy of forecasts to the compensation of the managers who initiated the projects.

SUMMARY

The basis of finding the time value of money is normally specified by the rate per period, usually denoted in percentage terms. Normally, the chosen period is a year more by convention than by rule. There are two methods by which the time value of money can be taken care of—the process of compounding and the process of discounting. The future value of money that is available today can be calculated using the concept of compounding and that value is known as FV or CV. The present value of money accruing later is estimated by the process of discounting and the value is known as PV or DV.

The cost of source of finance is defined as the rate of discount that equates the present value of expected payments to the source of finance with the net proceeds received from that source. The cost of equity from the company's point of view is the rate at which the intrinsic value or the market price of the share is equal to the discounted value of dividends. An alternative, and arguably more reliable, method of calculating the cost of equity finance is to use the CAPM. There are two major types of securitized debt: redeemable bonds and irredeemable bonds. In order to calculate the WACC, costs of individual sources of finance are weighted according to their relative importance as a source of finance. WACC can be calculated either for the existing capital structure (average basis) or for additional incremental finance packages (marginal basis).

The IRR of a project is defined as that discount rate for which its NPV is equal to zero. The project with the highest IRR i; considered better and safer.

In certain situations, NPV and IRR may produce contradictory results. This means that in certain situations, the NPV method may rank one project as superior, whereas under the IRR criterion, the decision may be just the opposite. Optimal capital budget is the set of projects that maximizes the value of the firm. Finance theory states that all projects with positive NPVs should be accepted, and the optimal capital budget consists of these positive NPV projects. However, two complications arise in practice: an increasing marginal cost of capital and capital rationing.

KEY TERMS

Accounting rate of return Rate of return on an investment is defined as profit after tax divided by book value of investment. It is also referred to as the average rate of return.

Annuity A fixed and equal amount of money receivable or payable at periodic intervals evenly spaced over time, usually a year, is referred to as annuity.

$$PVA_n = \frac{A\,[(1+i)^n - 1]}{i \times (1+i)^n} = A \times PVIFA_{(i,n)}$$

$$FVA_n = A[(1+i)^n - 1]\,/\,i = A \times FVIFA_{(i,n)}$$

Annuity due If the payment is made at the beginning of each year, then this is called annuity due and its value is the product of value (either present or future) of a regular annuity and $(1 + i)$.

Book value weights Proportions of different sources of cost of capital based on the value as recorded in the books of the firm are book value weights.

Book value Value of an asset given in the financial statement is called the book value. The acquired price of an asset can also be considered its Book value.

Compounding The process of application of interest over a period of time for a given sum at a specified rate to know the worth of the money at a future date is called compounding.

Depreciation tax shield Amount of tax saved on depreciation is referred to as the depreciation tax shield.

Discounted payback period Under discounted payback period system, future cash flows are discounted prior to payback calculations.

Discounting The process of removal of interest for a period of time on the given money at a future date to find out its worth in today's date is discounting.

Dividend capitalization model Dividend capitalization model states that the present value of dividend would be equal to the price of the share.

External equity External equity refers to the issue of fresh capital by the firm.

Flotation cost Flotation costs are expenses incurred in mobilizing any kind of capital from the market.

Future value   The value of money at a future date with the given interest rate is called future value.

$$FV_{(i,n)} = V_0 (1 + i)^n$$

Internal equity   Internal equity refers to retained earnings that are not distributed to shareholders and are deployed in the business for its needs.

Internal rate of return (IRR)   Rate of discount at which the net present value of an investment is zero is the internal rate of return.

Marginal cost of capital   Cost of raising incremental cost is called the marginal cost of capital.

Marginal proportions   Proportions of different sources of capital in raising incremental finance are marginal proportions.

Market value weights   Proportions of different sources of cost of capital based on their market value are market value weights.

Modified IRR (MIRR)   It is that rate of compounding, which will equate terminal value of intra-project cash flows with terminal value of initial investment.

Net present value (NPV)   A method for evaluating investment proposals. NPV is defined as present value of benefits minus present value of costs.

Opportunity cost   The returns foregone in the next best investment option is called opportunity cost.

P/E ratio   Price of the share divided by the earnings per share is called P/E ratio, and it is often used as benchmark for valuation.

Payback period   The length of time required for an asset to generate cash flows just enough to cover the initial outlay.

Preference capital   Preference capital is the capital where the fixed amount of dividend is paid with prior claim to that of shareholders. No dividend to equity shareholders can be paid unless the claims of preference shareholders are satisfied.

Present value   The worth of money today that is receivable or payable at a future date is called present value.

$$\text{Present value} = PV_n = \frac{FV_n}{(1+i)^n}$$

Reinvestment rate   Rate at which interim cash flows are reinvested is called reinvested rate.

Salvage value   Salvage value is the expected realizable value at the time of disposal of the asset.

Sunk costs   It is the difference between the current market price and the salvage value of an equipment or machine.

Weighted average cost of capital (WACC)   Weighted average cost of capital is calculated by multiplying each component of capital by its proportion in the capital structure.

CONCEPT REVIEW QUESTIONS

1. Define the following terms:
    (a) PV_n, FV_n, PVA_n, FVA_n
    (b) $FVIF_{i,n}$, $PVIF_{i,n}$, $FVIFA_{i,n}$, $PVIFA_{i,n}$
    (c) Annuity and annuity due
    (d) Lump sum payment; cash flow; and uneven cash-flow stream
    (e) Perpetuity
    (f) Compounding and discounting
    (g) Annual; semi-annual; quarterly; monthly, and daily compounding

    (h) Effective annual rate and nominal interest rate
    (i) Terminal value

2. What is an opportunity cost rate? How is this rate used in DCF analysis? Is the opportunity rate a single number that is used in all situations?

3. As per the definition of annuity, Rs 100 a year for 10 years is an annuity, but Rs 100 in year 1, Rs 200 in year 2, Rs 400 in year 3 through 10 does not constitute an annuity. However, the second series contains an annuity. Is this statement true or false? Explain.

4. If a firm's EPS grew from Re 1 to Rs 2 over a 10-year period, the total growth would be 100%, but the annual growth rate would be less than 10%. Is this statement true or false? Explain.

5. Would you rather have a savings account that pays 6% interest compounded semi-annually or one that pays 6% interest compounded daily? Explain.

6. The present value of a perpetuity is equal to the payment on the annuity A divided by the interest rate i; ($PV = A/i$). What is the sum, or future value, of perpetuity of Rs A per year? (Hint: The answer is infinity, but explain why.)

7. What is the cost of capital and WACC?

8. What are the DCF and CAPM approaches to the determination of cost of equity?

9. Differentiate between internal equity and external equity. Which one is costlier and why?

10. What is marginal cost of capital? How is it different from WACC? Can WACC ever exceed marginal cost of capital?

11. If the cost of debt is far less than cost of equity, why do firms not finance the entire funding requirement by way of debt?

12. While using CAPM approach to find the cost of equity, one is required to use a risk-free rate. There are two options of short term T-bills or long term dated securities the yield on which may be used as a reasonable substitute. Which of the two yields—on the T-bills or on the long term dated securities—is a better substitute?

13. Explain why the payback period method cannot be recommended as the main method used by a company to assess potential capital investment projects.

14. Explain the shortcomings of IRR as an investment appraisal method and reasons for its popularity.

15. List advantages of the NPV method of investment appraisal.

16. Explain how NPV and IRR deal with non-conventional cash flows.

17. Discuss the problem of selecting between mutually exclusive projects with respect to their NPVs and IRRs.

18. What techniques can be used to determine the optimum investment schedule for a company under conditions of capital rationing?

NUMERICAL PROBLEMS

1. Assume that it is now 1 January 2003. On 1 January 2004, you will deposit Rs 1,000 in a savings account that pays 9%.
   (i) If the bank compounds interest annually, how much will you have in your account on 1 January 2007?
   (ii) Suppose you deposited four equal payments in your account on the 1 January of 2004, 2005, 2006, and 2007. Assuming a 9% interest rate, how much would each of your payments have to be for you to obtain the same ending balance as you calculated in part (i)?

2. Assume that it is now 1 January 2009 and you will need Rs 1 lakh on 1 January 2013. Your bank compounds interest at a 9% annual rate.
   (i) How much must you deposit on 1 January 2010 to have a balance of Rs 1 lakh on 1 January 2013?
   (ii) If you want to make equal payments on every January 1 from 2010 to 2013 to accumulate Rs 1 lakh, how much must each of the four payments be?

3. Bank MBI pays 6% interest, compounded quarterly, on its money market account. The managers of the bank NBI want its money market account to equal bank MBI's effective annual rate, but interest is to be compounded on a monthly basis. What nominal interest rate must bank NBI set?

4. Use equations and a financial calculator to find the following values:
   (i) An initial Rs 1000 compounded for 10 years at 9%.
   (ii) The present value of Rs 1000 due in 10 years at a 9% discount rate.

5. To the closest year, how long will it take Rs 4000 to double if it is deposited and earns following interest rates?
   (i) 9%   (ii) 10%   (iii) 100%

6. While Nagarjuna was a student at the University of Chennai, he borrowed Rs 1,20,000 in student loans at an annual interest rate of 9.5%. If he repays Rs 15,000 per annum, how long to the nearest year will it take him to repay the loan?

7. Which amount is worth more at 14%—Rs 1,000 in hand today or Rs 2,000 due in 6 years?

8. X Ltd invests Rs 8 lakh to clear a tract of land and to plant some young mahogany trees. The trees will mature in 10 years, at which time X Ltd plans to sell the forest at an expected price of Rs 80 lakh. What is X Ltd's expected rate of return?

9. (i)   Find the present values of the following cash-flow streams as shown in Table E5.18. The appropriate interest rate is 9%.

TABLE E5.18

Year	Cash stream A(Rs)	Cash stream B (Rs)
1	1,000	3,000
2	4,000	4,000
3	4,000	4,000
4	4,000	4,000
5	3,000	1,000

(ii) What is the value of each cash-flow stream at 0% interest rate?

10. The market price of a share is Rs 90, the growth rate of dividend is 12% and the earnings per share is Rs 18. Find the cost of retained earnings.

11. A company has the following capital structure as shown in Table E5.19.

TABLE E5.19

Securities	Book value (Rs)	After tax cost (%)
Equity capital	8,50,000	15
Retained earnings	2,25,000	10
Preferred capital	1,50,000	18
Debentures	10,00,000	6
Total capital	22,25,000	

From the above information, find the WACC of the company.

12. Shares of a company are selling at Rs 30 per share. The firm had paid dividend at the rate of Rs 3 per share last year. The estimated growth of the company is 6% per year. Determine the cost of equity capital of the company and the estimated market price of the share if the anticipated growth rate of the company (a) rises to 9% and (b) falls to 3%.

13. A company wishes to raise additional finance of Rs 10,00,000 for meeting its investment plans. It has Rs 2,10,000 in the form of earnings available for investment purposes. The following are the further details:

(i)	Debt equity ratio	2 : 3
(ii)	Cost of debt up to Rs 2,00,000	11% (before tax)
(iii)	Cost of debt beyond Rs 2,00,000	15% (before tax)
(iv)	Earnings per share	Rs 3
(v)	Dividend pay out	60%
(vi)	Expected growth rate in dividend	9%
(vii)	Current market price	Rs 40
(viii)	Tax rate	50%

Find the pattern for raising additional funds, post-tax average cost of additional funds, cost of retained earnings, cost of equity, and overall WACC (after tax).

14. S limited has the following capital structure:

Common shares (25,000 shares)	Rs 50,00,000
11% preference shares	Rs 10,00,000
13% debentures	Rs 20,00,000
	Rs 80,00,000

One share of the company sells for Rs 35. It is expected that in the following year the company will pay a dividend of Rs 3 per share which will grow at 6% forever. Assuming 50% tax rate, compute the weighted average cost of capital based on the existing capital structure. If the company raises additional Rs 20,00,000 debt by issuing 14% debentures, expected dividend increases to Rs 4 and the growth rate is left unchanged. However, if the price per share falls to Rs 30, then what will be the new WACC?

15. Given below is the summary of balance sheet of A limited as on 1 January 2009 in Table E5.20.

TABLE E5.20

Liabilities	Amount (Rs)	Assets		Amount (Rs)
Share capital (25,000 equity shares @ Rs 10 fully paid up)	2,50,000	Land		23,00,000
Reserves and surplus	80,000	Plant	1,20,000	
8% redeemable debentures	50,000	Less depreciation	50,000	70,000
Current liabilities		Investment		1,00,000
Short-term loan	30,000	Stock		10,000
Accounts payables	15,000	Cash		15,000
	4,25,000			4,25,000

You are required to calculate the firm's WACC using balance sheet valuation. The following additional information is provided.

(i) 8% debentures were issued and are redeemable at par after 5 years.

(ii) Short-term loan carries interest @ 15% p.a.

(iii) All interest payments are up-to-date and equity dividend is currently 10%.

(iv) Tax rate may be assumed at 50%.

16. Calculate ARR for the following projects based on average investment, and show which one would be selected if the target rate of return is 12%. Assume straight-line depreciation over life of the project, with zero salvage value. Refer to Table E5.21.

TABLE E5.21

	Project A (Rs)	Project B (Rs)	Project C (Rs)
Initial outlay	15,00,000	15,00,000	20,00,000
Net cash inflow			
Year 1	5,00,000	4,00,000	10,00,000
Year 2	5,00,000	5,00,000	8,00,000
Year 3	2,00,000	5,00,000	4,00,000
Year 4	1,00,000	7,00,000	1,00,000
Year 5		1,00,000	

17. Expected cash flows of three projects are given in Table E5.22. The cost of capital is 10%.

(a) Calculate payback period, accounting rate of return, IRR, and NPV of each project.

(b) Show the ranking of projects by each of the four methods.

TABLE E5.22

Expected cash flows of projects A, B, and C

Period	Project A (Rs)	Project B (Rs)	Project C (Rs)
0	(5,00,000)	(5,00,000)	(5,00,000)
1	90,000	70,000	2,00,000
2	90,000	80,000	2,00,000
3	90,000	90,000	2,00,000
4	90,000	1,00,000	1,00,000
5	90,000	1,10,000	
6	90,000	1,20,000	
7	90,000	1,30,000	
8	90,000	1,40,000	
9	90,000	1,50,000	
10	90,000	1,60,000	

18. M limited is considering buying a new machine that would have a life of 5 years, a cost of Rs 1,00,000, and a scrap value of Rs 5,000. The machine would produce 40,000 units per annum of a new product with an estimated selling price of Rs 2.5 per unit. Direct costs would be Rs 1.75 per unit and annual fixed cost, including depreciation, would be Rs 50,000 per annum.

In years 1 and 2, sales promotion expenditure amounting to Rs 15,000 and 10,000 respectively would be incurred. These are not included in the above costs. As a consequence of this particular project, investment by the company in debtors and stocks would increase, during year 1 and 2, by Rs 15,000 and 10,000, respectively, and creditors would also increase by Rs 10,000. At the end of machine life, debtors, stocks, and creditors would revert to their previous levels.

Evaluate the project using the NPV method of investment appraisal, assuming the company's cost of capital is 10%.

19. A company has a cost of capital of 10% as investment opportunity and the estimated cash flows are shown in Table E5.23.

TABLE E5.23

Estimated cash flows

Year	Project A (Rs)	Project B (Rs)	Project C (Rs)	Project D (Rs)	Project E (Rs)
0	(1,00,000)	(80,000)	(75,000)	(50,000)	(80,000)
1		20,000	30,000	15,000	
2		30,000	30,000	15,000	35,000
3		40,000	30,000	15,000	35,000
4		30,000	30,000	15,000	35,000
5		20,000	30,000	15,000	35,000
6		(10,000)		15,000	35,000
7				15,000	35,000
8	3,00,000			15,000	35,000

Decide which projects are accepted in the following circumstances:

(i) The company is not in a capital rationing situation.

(ii) The company is in a capital rationing position, the projects are divisible, and only Rs 2,50,000 is available.

(iii) The company is in a capital rationing position, the projects are not divisible, and only Rs 2,50,000 is available.

20. A firm is considering purchase of a machine that costs Rs 2,00,000. It is estimated that an annual savings of Rs 50,000 will result from the machine's installation, that the life of the machine will be 5 years, and that its residual value will be Rs 10,000. Assuming the required rate of return is 10%, what action would you recommend?

21. The finance director of Nagarjuna Fertilizers Plc is considering several investment projects and has collected the following information about them as in Table E5.24.

TABLE E5.24

Project	Estimated initial outlay (Rs)	Cash inflow Year 1 (Rs)	Cash inflow Year 2 (Rs)	Cash inflow Year 3 (Rs)
A	2,00,000	1,50,000	1,50,000	1,50,000
B	4,00,000	3,50,000	3,50,000	3,00,000
C	5,00,000	8,50,000	8,50,000	8,50,000
D	2,00,000	2,75,000	2,00,000	
E	2,00,000	2,50,000	2,50,000	2,50,000
F	3,00,000	3,30,000	3,00,000	

Projects D and E are mutually exclusive. Capital available for investment in these new projects is limited to Rs 10,00,000 in the first year. All projects are divisible and none may be postponed or repeated. The cost of capital of Nagarjuna Fertilizers is 15%.

(a) Discuss possible reasons as to why Nagarjuna Fertilizers may limit the amount of capital available for investment in its projects.

(b) Determine which investment projects the finance director of Nagarjuna Fertilizers should choose in order to maximize the return on capital available for investment. If the projects were not divisible, would you change your advice to the finance director?

(c) Critically discuss reasons why NPV is the method of investment appraisal preferred by academics. Has the IRR method now been made redundant?

22. You are a financial analyst for the Brigadier Company. The director of capital budgeting has asked you to analyse two proposed capital investments, projects X and Y. Each project has a cost of Rs 10,000 and the cost of capital for each project is 12%. The projects' expected net cash flows are as follows:

Year	Expected net cash flows	
	Project X	Project Y
0	(Rs 10,000)	(Rs 10,000)
1	6,500	3,500
2	3,000	3,500
3	3,000	3,500
4	1,000	3,500

(i) Calculate each project's payback period, NPV, IRR, and MIRR.

(ii) Which project or projects should be accepted if they are independent?

(iii) Which project should be accepted if the projects are mutually exclusive?

(iv) How would a change in the cost of capital produce a conflict between NPV and IRR rankings of the two projects? Would this conflict exist if the cost of capital were 5%? (Hint: Plot the NPV profile.)

(v) Why does the conflict exist?

23. Virginia Tech is negotiating with the mayor of Kolkata to start a manufacturing plant in an abandoned building. The cash flows for Virginia's proposed plant are shown in Table E5.25:

TABLE E5.25

Year 0	Year 1	Year 2	Year 3	Year 4
–Rs 10,00,000	Rs 3,70,000	Rs 3,65,000	Rs 3,70,000	Rs 3,75,000

The city has agreed to subsidize Virginia. In preliminary discussions, Virginia suggested four alternatives:
(i) Subsidize the project to bring its IRR to 24%.
(ii) Subsidize the project to provide a 2-year payback.
(iii) Subsidize the project to provide NPV of Rs 70,000 when cash flows are discounted at 18%.
(iv) Subsidize the project to provide ARR of 40%.
You have been hired by Kolkata city to recommend a subsidy that minimizes costs to the city. Please indicate how much of a subsidy you would recommend for each year under each alternative suggested by Virginia. Which of the four subsidized plants would you recommend to the city if the appropriate discount rate is 18%?

24. Ari Airlines is considering two alternative planes. Plane A has an expected life of 5 years, will cost Rs 100 crore, and will produce net cash flows of Rs 30 crore per year. Plane B has a life of 10 years, will cost Rs 130 crore, and will produce net cash flows of Rs 24 crore per year. Inflation in operating costs, airplane costs, and fares is expected to be zero and the company's cost of capital is 12%. By how much would the value of the company increase if it accepted the better project (plane)?

Following are the data evaluated by management of X Limited in case it purchases machine (M).

TABLE E5. 26

Particulars	Machine (M)
Annual cash cost saving	Rs 40,000
Useful life	4 years
IRR	15%
Profitability index	1.064
NPV	?
Opportunity cost of capital	?
Machine purchase cost	?
Payback period	?
Salvage value	Zero

You are required to supply the missing values considering Table E5.27 of discount factors only.

TABLE E5.27

Disc. factors (%)	Year 1	Year 2	Year 3	Year 4	Total
15	0.869	0.756	0.658	0.572	2.855
14	0.877	0.769	0.675	0.592	2.913
13	0.885	0.783	0.693	0.613	2.974
12	0.893	0.797	0.712	0.636	3.038

ASSIGNMENTS

1. Visit a car dealer and find out the EMIs for a car loan of Rs 3 lakh repayable over a period of 3 years, 5 years, and 7 years. Find out the effective rate of interest from the amounts of EMIs.
2. Visit a housing finance company and find out the EMIs for a housing loan of Rs 10 lakh repayable over a period of 10 years, 15 years, and 20 years. Find the effective rate of interest from the amounts of EMIs.
3. What difference do you find in the effective rate of interest in case of A and B?

4. Collect the balance sheet of a large company like Infosys Limited of the current fiscal and calculate its WACC using book value weights and market value weights.
5. Analyse 3 public issues of equity of less than Rs 100 crore, from Rs 100 to 500 crore and more than Rs 500 crore and identify the expenses of floatation and the costs for each of them.

6. What are the primary investment appraisal techniques employed in your organization or any other organization known to you? How well does that organization handle the problems of evaluating mutually exclusive projects and capital rationing?

SELECT REFERENCES

Anand, M., 'Corporate Finance Practices in India: A survey', *Vikalpa*, vol.27, no.4, 2002, pp. 29–56.

Asquith, D., and J.E. Bethel, 'Using Heuristics to evaluate projects: The case of ranking projects by IRR', *The Engineering Economist*, vol.40, no.3, 1995, pp. 287–94.

Battaglio, C., G. Longo, and L. Peccati, 'Restyling of fees in consumers credit and their optimization', *European Journal of Operational Research*, vol.91, no.2, 1996, pp. 330–37.

Block, S., 'Are there differences in capital budgeting procedures between industries?—An empirical study', *The Engineering Economist*, vol.50, 2005, pp. 55–67.

Botteron, P. 'On the practical application of the real options theory,' *Thunderbird International Business Review*, vol. 43, 2001, pp. 469–79.

Bradley, S.P. and S.C. Jr. Frey, 'Equivalent Mathematical Programming Models of Pure Capital Rationing,' *Journal of Financial and Quantitative Analysis*, June 1978.

Brealey, R.A. and S.C. Myers, *Principles of Corporate Finance*, 9th ed., Tata McGraw Hill, 2003.

Brief, R.P., and R.A. Lawson, 'The role of the Accounting rate of return in Financial Statement', *The Accounting Review*, vol.67, no.2, 1992, pp. 411–26.

Brigham, E.F., A.L. Kahl, W.F. Rentz, and L.C. Gapenski, *Canadian Financial Management*, 4th ed., Toronto: Harcourt Brace and Co., 1994.

BT 500 Companies, *Business Today*, October edition, 2006, pp. 7–19.

Copeland, T. and V. Antikarov, *Real Options—A Practitioner's Guide*, New York: Texere, 2001.

Copeland, T.E. and P.T. Keenan, 'How much is flexibility worth?' *Mckinsey Quarterly*, vol.2, 1998, pp. 38–49.

Dedi, L. and S. Orsag, 'Capital Budgeting Practices: A Survey of Croatian Firms' *South East European Journal of Economics and Business*, vol.2, no.1, 2007, pp. 59–67.

Dixit, A.K. and R.S. Pindyck, 'The options approach to Capital Investment', *Harvard Business Review*, May–June, 1995, pp. 105–115.

Dixit, A.K. and R.S. Pindyck, *Investment under uncertainty*, Princeton University Press, Princeton, 1994.

Evans D.A. and S.M. Forbes, 'Decision making and display methods: The case of prescription and practice in capital budgeting', *The Engineering Economist*, vol.39, no.1, 1993, pp. 87–92.

Fisher, I., *The Theory of Interest*, Macmillan, New York, 1930.

Fleischer, G.A., 'Two major issues associated with the rate of return method for Capital Allocation: The Ranking Error and Preliminary Selection', *The Journal of Industrial Engineering*, vol. 17, no. 4, 1966, pp. 202–08.

Gitman, L.J. and V. Mecurio, 'Cost of capital techniques used by major U.S. firms: Survey analysis of Fortune's 1000', *Financial Management*, vol. 14, 1982, pp. 21–29.

Graham, H. and N. Harvey, 'The Theory and Practice of Finance: Evidence from the Field', *Journal of Financial Economics*, vol. 2, 2001, pp. 154–67.

Graham, J.R. and C. Harvey, 'The Theory and practice of Corporate Finance: Evidence from the field', *Journal of Financial Economics*, vol. 60, no. 1, 2001.

Hajdasinski, M.M., 'Technical note—The Internal Rate of Return (IRR) as a financial Indicator', *The Engineering Economist*, vol. 49, 2004, pp. 185–97.

Hirshleifer, J., 'On the Theory of Optimal Investment Decisions', *The Journal of Political Economy*, vol. 66, no. 4, 1958, pp. 329–52.

Huchzermeier, A., and C.H. Loch, 'Project Management Under Risk: Using the Real Options approach to evaluate flexibility in R and D', *Management Science*, vol. 47, 2001, pp. 85–101.

Kelleher, J.C. and J.J. MacCormack, 'Internal Rate of Return: A cautionary tale', *The Mckinsey Quarterly*, August, 2004, pp. 124.

Lang, H.J. and D.N. Merino, *The Selection Process for Capital Projects*, Wiley, 1993, Chapters 6 and 7.

Lefley, F. 'The payback method of Investment appraisal: A Review and Synthesis', *International Journal of Production Economics*, vol. 44, no. 3, 1996, pp. 207–44.

Lefley, F. and M. Morgan, 'A New pragmatic approach to Capital investment appraisal', *International Journal of Production Economics*, vol. 55, no. 3, 1998, pp. 321–41.

Luehrman, T.A., 'Investment opportunities as real options: Getting started on the numbers', *Harvard Business Review,* July–August, 1998, pp. 51–67.

Luehrman, T.A., 'Using APV: A better tool for valuing operations', *Harvard Business Review,* May–June, 1997, pp. 145–54.

Luehrman, T.A., 'What's it worth? A General Manager's guide to valuation', *Harvard Business Review,* May–June, 1997, pp. 132–42.

Mao, J.C.T., 'The Internal rate of Return as a ranking criterion', *The Engineering Economist*, vol. 11, no. 1, 1996, pp. 1–13.

Muro, V., *Handbook of Financial Analysis for Corporate Managers* (Revised Edition), Prentice Hall, 1998, Chapters 4 and 5.

Rapp., B., 'The internal rate of return–A critical study', *Engineering Costs ad Production Economics,* vol. 5, 1980, pp. 43–52.

Robinson, D., and Cook, W.R., 'Optimal Termination and the IRR revisited', *The Engineering Economist*, vol. 41, no. 3, 1996, pp. 271–81.

Ryan, P.A. and G.P. Ryan, 'Capital Budgeting Practices of the Fortune 1000: How have things changed?' *Journal of Business and Management*, vol. 8, no. 4, 2002, pp. 355–64.

Solomon, E., *The Theory of Financial Management,* New York: Columbia University Press, 1963.

Tang, S.L. and H.J. Tang, 'Technical note—The variable financial indicator IRR and the constant economic indicator NPV', *The Engineering Economist*, vol. 48, no. 1, 2003, pp. 69–78.

Tang, S.L., *Economic Feasibility of Projects: Managerial and Engineering Practice*, McGraw Hill, 1991.

Tang, S.L., *Economic Feasibility of Projects: Managerial and Engineering Practice*, McGraw Hill, 2003.

Trigeorgis, L., 'Real options and interactions with financial flexibility', *Financial Management,* vol. 22, 1993, pp. 202–24.

Trigeorgis, L., *Real Options: Managerial flexibility and Strategy in resource allocation*, MIT Press, Cambridge, MA, 1996.

Weingarten H.M., 'Capital Rationing: An Author in Search of a Plot,' *Journal of Finance*, December, 1977, pp. 1403–31.

Yeo, K.T. and F. Qiu, 'The value of management flexibility—A real option approach to investment evaluation', *International Journal of Project Management*, vol. 21, 2003, pp. 243–50.

Other resources

http://www.mca.gov.in/.

CASE STUDY

A Real-life CAPEX Proposal for Consideration

M/s V Limited, which wishes to improve its competitive position in the market, is considering expediting its delivery time to customers by increasing the levels of finished stocks held. Dependant upon the degree of increase in finished stocks, it estimates that its existing sales of 3,00,000 units per annum would change as shown in Table E5.28.

Other changes resulting from increase in finished stock would be as follows.

(a) Extra storage accommodation would be required. If the stocks increase up to 10%, construction costs of Rs 1,80,000 and annual maintenance costs of Rs 22,500 would be required. If stocks increase above 10%, the construction costs would be Rs 4,12,500 and annual maintenance costs Rs 67,500. The company treats investments of this kind as having a life of 7 years requiring a 15% DCF yield.

TABLE E5.28

Finished stock increase by (%)	New sales equal to 3,10,000 units (probabilities)	New sales equal to 3,20,000 units (probabilities)	New sales equal to 3,30,000 units (probabilities)	New sales equal to 3,40,000 units (probabilities)
10%	0.45	0.40	0.15	–
15%	0.30	0.45	0.25	–
20%	0.15	0.50	0.30	0.05
25%	–	0.40	0.40	0.20

(b) Extra handling equipment would be required as well. If the stocks increase is up to 15%, new equipment costing Rs 60,000, with additional running costs of Rs 8,250 per annum would be required. If the finished stock increase were above 15%, new equipment of Rs 1,42,500 with annual running costs of Rs 11,250 would be required. For this type of investment, the company's criterion is 20% DCF with a life of 4 years.

(c) The present value of an annuity of Re 1 for 7 years at 15% is Rs 4.16 and for 4 years at 20% is Rs 2.59.

(d) Additional raw material and work in process (WIP) inventory needs to be held as well. If finished stock level increased by less than 20%, both raw materials and WIP inventory would go up by 15% each. However, if increase in finished stock is 20% or more, both raw material and WIP inventory would increase by 25% each.

(e) The present levels of stocks held are finished stock Rs 1,20,000, raw materials Rs 20,000, and WIP Rs 40,000.

(f) Extra warehouse staff would also be required. Extra staff costs per annum would be Rs 4,500, Rs 4,750, Rs 5,000, and Rs 5,250 for finished stock increase by 10%, 15%, 20% and 25%, respectively.

(g) Other relevant information: The average selling price of products is Rs 45 per unit, variable cost is Rs 27 per unit, and the company finances its entire inventories through bank overdraft and interest on bank overdraft is 12%. Currently stocks are insured at an annual premium of Rs 15,000 and such premium would increase proportionately for all additional inventories.

Discussion question

What would be your recommendation to the concerned company if we assume an effective corporate income tax rate of 40% for our calculations.

A probable solution to the CAPEX case

Anticipated increase in sales (units) with respect to percentage increase in finished stock is shown in Table E5.29.

TABLE E5.29

(Figures in Rs)

Sales (units)	10%	15%	20%	25%
3,10,000	1,39,500	93,000	46,500	–
3,20,000	1,28,000	1,44,000	1,60,000	1,28,000
3,30,000	49,500	82,500	99,000	1,32,000
3,40,000	–	–	17,000	68,000
Total	3,17,000	3,19,500	3,22,500	3,28,000
Total contribution	57,06,000	57,51,000	58,05,000	59,04,000
Existing contribution	54,00,000	54,00,000	54,00,000	54,00,000
Inc. in contribution	3,06,000	3,51,000	4,05,000	5,04,000

Contribution per unit = 45 − 27 = 18

Anticipated increase in working capital investments with respect to percentage increase in finished stock.

TABLE E5.30

(Figures in Rs)

Sales increase in % (additional WC)	10 %	15 %	20 %	25 %
Finished	12,000	18,000	24,000	30,000
Raw material	3,000	3,000	5,000	5,000
WIP	6,000	6,000	10,000	10,000
Total	21,000	27,000	39,000	45,000
WC financing change	2,520	3,240	4,680	5,400
Staff cost	4,500	4,750	5,000	5,250
Insurance premium	1,750	2,250	3,250	3,750
Storage cost	22,500	67,500	67,500	67,500
Handling cost	8,250	8,250	11,250	11,250

Note: Insurance premium charge considered to increase in proportion to total inventory holding (in line with available case information).

Problems encountered while developing the probable solution.

(a) Criticism of the approach adopted.

- The salvage value of fixed assets and working capital has been assumed to be zero in absence of relevant information.
- It has been assumed that straight line depreciation is allowed for IT purposes, which is not the case in reality.
- It has been effectively assumed that fresh investment in handling equipment is not required at the beginning of the fifth year, which contradicts the case facts.
- The calculation of additional working capital investment is questionable because the impact on other working capital items, namely debtors and creditors, has not been taken into consideration due to the absence of relevant case data.

- The same exercise of Excel sheet calculation needs to be undertaken for all four scenarios, i.e., when finished goods holding increases by 15 %, 20 %, and 25 %, respectively. As of now, we have done it for increase of 10 % finished stock.

(b) Conceptual difficulties.

- What would be the appropriate discount factor while evaluating this proposal?
- Should we compute APV in this case?
- The incremental cash flows generated may be segregated into few components, namely tax shield provided by depreciation on storage equipment (discounted it by 15 % rate), tax shield provided by depreciation of handling working capital finance charges (discounted at after-tax borrowing rate of 12 %), and the residual incremental cash flows (discounted at a different rate).
- This last rate as mentioned may be the company cost of capital rate if we assume that the risk of this project is same as company's existing business.
- This is not a bold assumption simply because this project is in the nature of expansion of the existing business activity.
- However, the so-called company cost of capital information is not provided in the case under review.
- Will we indulge in all these tedious computational exercises in a real-life scenario where the management requires the finance team to arrive at a quick decision?
- Or will we simply compute a project IRR (in spite of all its limitations) and compare the same with the company benchmark IRR rate and arrive at a quick decision?

TABLE E5.31

(Figure in Rs)

Details	10%	15%	20%	25%
Additional contribution	3,06,000	3,51,000	4,05,000	5,04,000
WC financing charges	2,520	3,240	4,680	5,400
Addn staff costs	4,500	4,750	5,000	5,250
Addn insurance premium	1,750	2,250	3,250	3,750
Storage cost	2,2500	67,500	67,500	67,500
Handling charges	8,250	8,250	11,250	11,250
Share of capital cost (S)				
180000 / 4.16	43,269			
412500 / 4.16		99,159	99,159	99,159
Share capital cost (H)				
60000 / 2.59	23,166	23,166		
142500 / 2.59			55,019	55,019
Total addn cost	1,05,955	2,08,315	2,45,858	2,47,328
Net gain	2,00,045	1,42,685	1,59,142	2,56,672

Hence, 25% case will be given the maximum net gain that is Rs 2,56,672 out of 4.

Cash-flow approach to the case (incremental cash flows)

TABLE E5.32

(Figures in Rs)

Finished goods increases by 10% (Case I)	Year 0	Year 1	Year 2	Year 3	Year 4	Year 5	Year 6	Year 7
Storage construction cost	180,000							
Handling equipment CAPEX	60,000							
Working capital investment	21,000							
Incremental cash flows generated								
Increase in contribution		3,06,000	3,06,000	3,06,000	3,06,000	3,06,000	3,06,000	3,06,000
Additional working capital financing charges		−2,520	−2,520	−2,520	−2,520	−2,520	−2,520	−2,520
Additional insurance premium payment		−1,750	−1,750	−1,750	−1,750	−1,750	−1,750	−1,750
Additional staff costs		−4,500	−4,500	−4,500	−4,500	−4,500	−4,500	−4,500
Additional annual storage cost		−22,500	−22,500	−22,500	−22,500	−22,500	−22,500	−22,500

Contd

Table E5.32   *Contd*

Finished goods increases by 10% (Case I)	Year 0	Year 1	Year 2	Year 3	Year 4	Year 5	Year 6	Year 7
Additional annual handling cost		− 8,250	− 8,250	− 8,250	− 8,250	− 8,250	− 8,250	− 8,250
Depreciation on storage equipment		− 25,714	− 25,714	− 25,714	− 25,714	− 25,714	− 25,714	− 25,714
Depreciation on handling equipment		−15,000	−15,000	−15,000	−15,000	0	0	0
Incremental profit before tax		2,25,766	2,25,766	2,25,766	2,25,766	240,766	240,766	240,766
Taxation (effective tax rate 40%)		96,306	96,306	96,306	96,306	96,306	96,306	96,306
Incremental profit after tax		1,35,460	1,35,460	1,35,460	1,35,460	1,44,460	1,44,460	144,460
Add back depreciation (storage equipment)		25,714	25,714	25,714	25,714	25,714	25,714	25,714
Add back depreciation (storage equipment)		15,000	15,000	15,000	15,000	0	0	0
Net operating cash flows		1,76,174	1,76,174	1,76,174	1,76,174	1,70,174	1,70,174	1,70,174

SELECTION OF EXACT DISCOUNT FACTOR

The real challenge in project evaluation is how you discount your expected cash flows throughout the project life.

— ANONYMOUS

LEARNING OBJECTIVES

After studying this chapter, you will be able to

- Understand the concept of discount factor
- Explain the relationships between cost of capital and discounting factor and between IRR and cost of capital
- Know the most appropriate discounting rate for the different types of cash flows
- Know the impact of inflation and taxation on capital budgeting decisions
- Understand the relevance of cash-flow estimation
- Understand concepts of adjusted present value method, depreciation tax shield, and interest tax shield

Srini's Dilemma

It is 7.30 a.m., Monday, 29 of November. Mr Srinivasan (VP – Finance) of AZR Ltd is sitting with his first cup of coffee and newspaper in hand. The phone rings.

SRINIVASAN: Hello, Srini here. Who's calling?

MUKESH (VP – Marketing): Good morning. Mukesh speaking. How's everything? All set for today's meeting?

SRINI: Yeah! So-so, err … I think I'll manage something.

MUKESH: I hope you have the blueprint ready. You know, the capital budgeting matter is the main agenda of today's meeting. And you know how particular big boss is. Well, see you at 10.

At 10.00 a.m. sharp, the door of the conference room opens and Mr Sasikumar (MD of AZR Ltd) enters. Mukesh, Srinivasan, Dass (GM Projects), Pathak (GM Business Planning), and Ali (GM Finance) are seated among other senior officials.

SASIKUMAR: Hello! Good morning everybody and welcome to the meeting. I thank you all for our brilliant performance in the last fiscal. Our capital budgeting decisions have worked marvellously, and the results have reflected the same. I hope this year too we shall continue with this trend. We have generated some surplus funds and we shall recycle it into the business. I want your suggestions on it. We shall discuss and arrive at some decision to gainfully utilize the situation. Mukesh, have you thought of something?

MUKESH: Sir, I think it will be wise to increase our production capacity so that we can capture higher market share. As we have been in this business for so many years now, we shall have no problem in managing the show, and the surplus fund can be utilized too.

PATHAK: But I don't think this is a good proposition. We are already market leaders in our segment, and the market for our product is saturated both in domestic and overseas markets. Further investment in the same product will not increase our gains proportionately. I think we can go for diversification. If we diversify judiciously, we shall reap good profits.

The entire house agrees and a unanimous decision is taken in favour of diversification.

DASS: All right then. For this new diversification project, at what rate should we discount for making the financial appraisal decision? Shall we continue to discount at the same rate as our existing capital intensive project?

ALI: No, that would be absurd. This project belongs to a different risk class than our existing one. It is a completely new business, and the discounting factor will be different. I think the cost of capital can be the proxy discount factor.

SASIKUMAR: But then, why should we go for this new venture at all? If the cost of generating the fund is same as the discount factor or return on the project, why should we take the extra pain?

SRINI: Sir, you are absolutely right. I suggest that we use the risk class of the new project as the discounting factor. It will give us the most relevant present value of the forecasted cash flow.

ALI (astonished with his boss's ignorance): I beg to differ, Sir. I think it contradicts the basic concept of CAPEX, because as per the NPV equation, a firm's risk class and project risk class must be the same.

A heated argument follows, and the house is in confusion.

SASIKUMAR: Enough! No more deliberation on this. Srini, this part of the decision is in your jurisdiction. I give you 48 hours. Sit with your team and come out with a concrete proposal on what discounting factor shall be used for the new project. So, what is our next agenda?

The house starts discussing the next issue. Srini sits with a blank face, lost in his thoughts. What can he come up with in the next 48 hours?

6.1 COST OF CAPITAL AS A DISCOUNT FACTOR

The objective of investment within a firm is to create value for its owner, i.e., stakeholders. The investment of capital in a particular assignment or department is done in order to create higher returns. The key phrase and tricky issue is the phrase 'higher returns'.

For instance, would you, as part of a firm, be content if the firm asks you to swap Rs 10,000 of your hard-earned money for some of their new shares? What if it came with an assurance that the management would hand back to you the Rs 10,000 plus another Rs 1000 in five years time? Is this a significant return? Would you feel that your wealth had been enhanced if you, for instance, were aware that by investing Rs 10,000 in government plans/bonds, you could receive a 6% return per year, or that you could obtain a return of 15–20% per annum by investing in other shares in the stock market?

In presence of other viable options, an offer of less than 2% return from the management team would appear unfair and unacceptable. Here, we are dealing with the time value of money, which is the key concept in business, in general, and finance, in particular.

Opportunity cost for an investor is the ROI that would have been generated in the next-test alternative forgone. Investment returns must cater to the expectations of the investors. The investors' wealth would register a decline if the investment returns are less than their opportunity cost. Therefore, the net present value (NPV) of an investment proposal is computed by marking down the future net cash receipts by a certain rate. This rate takes into consideration the cost of alternative use of funds and putting them down together over the life of the proposal, while subtracting the initial expenditure.

Herein lies the rationale for applying the cost of capital as discount rate in NPV calculations.

— Glen Arnold

IRR and opportunity cost of capital—The confusion Here is a word of caution. Some people confuse internal rate of return (IRR) and opportunity cost of capital (OCC) because both appear as discount rates in the NPV formula. The IRR is a profitability measure, which depends solely on the amount and timing of the project cash flows. OCC is a standard of profitability for the project, which we use to calculate how much the project is worth. OCC is generally established in the capital markets. It is the expected rate of return offered by other assets equivalent in risk to the project that is being evaluated (Brealey and Myers 2006).

6.2 PROBLEMS IN DISCOUNTING FACTOR

Allocating the most appropriate discounting factor of a project is a major challenge for any firm. It could either be the cost of capital of the firm or the risk class of the firm. Now a project's risk class can be different from the firm's risk class. Then, what should be the exact discounting factor for a specific project?

Let's get the concept right. The existing business of a company and the new project taken up by it should be in the same risk class. In such an event, the company would be in a safer position vis-à-vis its cost of capital rule. However, in case of dissimilarities in the risk classes, the cost of capital rule would become a serious concern for the company.

OCC is the key factor for the evaluation of any project.

Consider two projects X and Y. The probable investors would judge their viability by discounting the forecasted cash flows of project X and project Y, at a rate pertaining to their respective risks. In most cases, it would result in different discount rates. Now, if there is another project, project Z, its discount cash flow would also take into consideration the expected rate of return, keeping in mind the investors requirements. Hence, the utility of capital is the determining factor of its true cost.

For example, the discount rate might be structured as in Table 6.1.

TABLE 6.1   Discount rate of the project

Category of the project under consideration	Discount rate (%)
Speculative ventures	28
Projects pertaining to the manufacture of new products	24
Expansion of existing business	13

CAPM is widely used by large corporations to estimate the discount rates. As per CAPM, the most appropriate discount rate for appraising CAPEX decisions should be computed as:

Expected project return (the appropriate discount factor) = risk-free return + project beta × (market return – risk free return)

$$r = r_f + \beta(r_m - r_f) \tag{6.1}$$

To calculate this, you have to figure out the project beta. The company cost of a capital is the correct discount rate for projects that have the same risks as the company's existing business. However, the same does not hold true for those projects that are safer or riskier than the company's average assets. The challenge is to judge the relative risks of the projects available with the firm. Another complication is that project beta can shift over a period of time. There may be separate betas for each year of the project's life as well.

Before investing in a capital project, a lot of time is invariably spent in estimating the company cost of capital and, sometimes, even the cost of the capital of industry sector to which that particular company belongs. Is it worth that effort?

The efforts must be put for two reasons. First, it is important to consider the company's cost of capital to initiate projects (and set their respective discount rates) that greatly vary in their risk class vis-à-vis the company's resources. Instead of calculating the project cost of capital from the scratch, it is more convenient to make necessary changes in the company's cost of capital.

Second, projects that belong to the same risk class as the other resources of the company can be termed as average risk projects, and be dealt with accordingly. It is important to note that it is the project risk that governs the true discounting factor (associated with a certain capital expenditure decisions), instead of the company that takes on the project.

It may be appreciated that businesses all over the world have institutions about relative risks, at least in the industries that they are comfortable with. Therefore, they set a company-wide or industry-wide cost as a benchmark. It goes without saying that this is not the right hurdle rate for any capital project. However, necessary adjustment can always be made with this rate depending on the relative risk exposure of the project under consideration. But in practice, to find out the exact discount factor of a project is really difficult (Exhibit 6.1).

Exhibit 6.1 Mr Shyam's confusion

Mr Shyam has won a Rs 1,00,000 lottery. Now he is wondering where he should invest the money so that he can earn maximum return. He has been offered the following alternatives:

Economic conditions	Slump	Normal	Boom
Pay off (Rs)	70,000	1,15,000	1,50,000

The probability of any economic condition occurring at the end of one year is equal. Now suppose Shyam has found out that the shares of a certain company, X & Co., have equally uncertain prospects considering the outcome one year down the line. The current market price per share of X & Co. is Rs 97 and, depending on the three states of the economy, the price per share at the end of one year is expected to be as follows: slump—Rs 70, normal—Rs 115, and boom—Rs 150.

If Shyam invests in company X & Co., for say 1000 shares, then there will be an initial investment of Rs 97,000 and it would fetch an expected pay off of Rs 1,11,667 [after recognizing the impact of various probable economic conditions: (Rs 70,000 + Rs 1,15,000 + Rs 1,50,000) × 33.33% probability] one year down the line resulting in a return of 15.12% [(Rs 1,11,667 – Rs 97,000) / Rs 97,000].

Now, conceptually, the OCC for an investment proposal is the expected rate of return demanded by investors from alternative investment opportunities. They are subject to the same risk exposure as a project under review. When we discount the cash flow pertaining to the project under consideration, the resultant present value (PV) effectively represents the amount investors would be willing to invest in the said project. In fact, herein lies the basic rationale of the NPV rule.

Analogy of Shyam's confusion

Going by the facts of the case discussed above, it distinctly appears that capital investment under consideration has got identical risk exposure as the investments in 1000 shares of company X & Co. Hence, going by the conceptual understanding and implications of the OCC, 15.12% should be treated as the appropriate discounting factor for evaluating the said CAPEX proposal. It may also be observed that this 15.12% is the expected rate of return that investors are foregoing by investing in the proposal. Therefore, it makes sense to treat this rate as an OCC, namely the appropriate discounting factor. At this rate, the proposal would fetch a negative NPV and hence, the same needs to be rejected.

Practical difficulties encountered while evaluating such proposals

The case under review appears to be an oversimplified example due to the following reasons:

In a real life situation, it is impossible to restrict the future states of economy into three categories alone (namely slump, normal, and boom), as was the case in the aforementioned hypothetical example.

Moreover, assigning probabilities to these different scenarios is another area of concern while evaluating such proposals.

6.3 INFLATION AND CAPITAL BUDGETING

Inflation can have a major impact on the ultimate success or failure of capital projects and, therefore, it should be treated wisely in discounted cash-flow analysis (Van Horne 1971; Cooley and Roenfeldt 1975).

Two problems that arise in this regard are, first, how inflation affects the estimated cash flows from the project and second, how it affects the discount rate.

Let us consider an example. A machine costs Rs 18,00,000 and is projected to produce cash flows of Rs 6,00,000, Rs 10,00,000, and Rs 7,00,000, respectively, over the next three years. The rate of inflation is expected to be 6% and the firm's cost of capital is 16.6%.

In this case, inflation can be adjusted in the following ways.

Like interest rate, discounting rate can be taken as real rate (k_r) and nominal rate (k_n) and similarly expected cash flows will be real cash flow (RCF_t) and nominal cash flow (NCF_t). Let i be the rate of inflation, then

NPV (no inflation) =

$$\sum_{t=0}^{n} \frac{RCF_t}{(1 + k_n)^t} = \sum_{t=0}^{n} \frac{NCF}{(1 + k_n)^t} \tag{6.2}$$

$$\text{NPV (with inflation)} = \sum_{t=0}^{n} \frac{NCF}{(1 + k_n)^t} = \sum_{t=0}^{n} \frac{RCF_t\,((1 + i)^t)}{\langle(1 + k_r)^t \mid (1 + i)^t\rangle} \tag{6.3}$$

Real cost of capital (k_r) is obtained from the nominal (or money) cost of capital (k_n) by making an adjustment to the nominal cost of capital to allow for inflation (i). Rearranging the expression for the Fisher effect:

$$(1 + k_n) = (1 + k_r) \times (1 + i)$$

Therefore, $(1 + k_r) = (1 + k_n)/(1 + i)$ \hfill (6.4)

For example, if nominal cost of capital is 12% and inflation rate is 8%, then the real cost of capital will be 3.7% [since $(1 + 0.12)/(1 + 0.08) = 1.037$].

Example 6.1   Geo Limited is planning to sell a new toy. This new venture would require fixed assets investments of Rs 7,50,000 with two-thirds payable at once and balance Rs 2,50,000 payable after one year. An investment of Rs 3,30,000 would be the working capital requirement and that would be made at the start of the project.

Geo anticipates that the new toy will be obsolete within four years with a zero-salvage value. The project would incur Rs 6,00,000 per year at current price, including annual depreciation of Rs 1,90,000. The company predicts sales of 1,20,000 per year, at a selling price of Rs 25 per unit and variable cost of Rs 18 per unit, both in current price terms. It expects the following annual increases because of inflation:

Fixed costs: 4%

Selling price: 5%

Variable costs: 7.5%

General prices: 5%

If Geo's real cost of capital is 7.5% then what would be your suggestion regarding the viability of the project (ignore impact of taxation)?

Solution

Fixed cost per year (minus depreciation) = Rs 6,00,000 – Rs 1,90,000 = Rs 4,10,000

Inflating by 4% per year:

Impact of inflation (4%) in fixed cost is given in Table E6.1.

TABLE E6.1

Fixed cost of years	Amount × Inflation factor	Final amount in Rs
Year 1 fixed costs	4,10,000 × 1.04	4,26,400
Year 2 fixed costs	4,26,400 × 1.04	4,43,456
Year 3 fixed costs	4,43,456 × 1.04	4,61,194
Year 4 fixed costs	4,61,194 × 1.04	4,79,642

Contribution per unit is the difference between sales price and variable cost per unit, inflated by their respective inflation rates. The nominal rate of operating cash flow for each year is the difference between the total contribution and the inflated fixed cost for that year, as shown in Table E6.2.

TABLE E6.2

Year	1	2	3	4
Selling price per unit (Rs)	26.25	27.56	28.94	30.39
Variable cost per unit (Rs)	19.35	20.80	22.36	24.04
Contribution per unit (Rs)	6.9	6.76	6.58	6.35
Contribution per year (Rs)	8,28,000	8,11,200	7,89,600	7,62,000
Fixed costs per year (Rs)	4,26,400	4,43,456	4,61,194	4,79,642
Net operating cash flow (Rs)	4,01,600	3,67,744	3,28,406	2,82,358

Investment in fixed assets in year 0 is 7,50,000 × 2 / 3 = Rs 5,00,000.

Investment in fixed assets in year 1 is 7,50,000 × 1 / 3 = Rs 2,50,000.

Investment in working capital in year 0 is Rs 3,30,000.

Investment in working capital is recovered at the end of year 4.

We could deflate the nominal cash flows by the general rate of inflation to obtain real cash flows and then discount them by Geo's real cost of capital. It is simpler and quicker to inflate Geo's real cost of capital into nominal or money terms and use it to discount the nominal cash flows that we have calculated. Geo's nominal cost of capital is $1.075 \times 1.05 = 1.12875 = 13\%$ (approx.).

Calculation of NPV, using a nominal (money terms) approach is given in Table E6.3.

TABLE E6.3

Year	0	1	2	3	4
Capital (Rs)	(5,00,000)	(2,50,000)			
Working capital (Rs)	(3,30,000)				3,30,000
Net operating cash flow (Rs)		4,01,600	3,67,744	3,28,406	2,82,358
Net cash flow (Rs)	(8,30,000)	1,51,600	3,67,744	3,28,406	6,12,358
13% discount factor	1.0000	0.8850	0.7831	0.6931	0.6133
Present value (Rs)	(8,30,000)	1,34,166	2,87,980.33	2,27,618.20	3,75,559.16

NPV = (1,34,166 + 2,87,980.33 + 2,27,618.20 + 3,75,559.16) − 8,30,000 = Rs 1,95,323.6

Since NPV is positive, the project can be recommended on financial grounds. But at the same time NPV is not so large, hence care must be taken for proper estimation of cash flow, as well as, the rate of inflation. Any minute change in inflation can make the project financially uneconomical.

That is why the impact of inflation cannot be ignored in case of capital investment decisions.

6.4 SIGNIFICANCE OF TAXATION IN CAPITAL BUDGETING

The influence of taxation on capital investment decisions cannot be overruled. An estimate must be made of the benefits or burdens that arise as a result of the corporate taxation system during cash flow estimations. There are a number of factors allied with taxations that have to be considered while estimating cash flows. Some of these are as follows.

1. *Capital allowance*—Tax relief can be received on the capital expenditure undertaken for various kinds of capital investments. Capital allowances are usually decided by government policies. The internal corporate taxations and capital allowance policies of different countries influence the rate of allowance at a given point in time.

An organization, according to the relevant accounting standards, decides the annual depreciation charges for financial accounting. The capital expenditure, in the form of these depreciation charges, is then processed through the profit and loss account. The governmental tax policies decide the way in which capital expenditure is calculated vis-à-vis the taxable profits.

Calculating taxable profit and tax liabilities, at the same time, can result in confusion. Therefore, it is beneficial to calculate the two separately, before the NPV of a project is estimated.

2. *Tax allowable deductions and relevant costs*—Tax liability will arise on the taxable profit generated by an investment project. However, liability to taxation is reduced to the extent that expenses are allowed to be deducted from annual revenue in the calculation of taxable profit in a given year.

3. *Tax relief on interest payments*—While interest payments on debt are an allowable deduction for the purpose of determining taxable profit, they should not be included as a relevant cash flow while making an appraisal of the capital investment project. The reason is that on any debt, the finance used in the investment project is already accounted for as a part of the cost of capital used to discount the project cash flows.

Scarlet (1993 and 1995) shows that if a simple project is determined to be viable using the NPV method, introduction of corporate taxation is unlikely to change the capital budgeting decisions. Taxation can make a difference to project viability as the profit changes due to tax liability. This is different from the cash flow generated by an investment project. Even when the effects of capital allowances are introduced into the evaluation, the impact is still a small one. It can be amplified only under conditions of inflation, since capital allowances are based on the historical cost of investment and their real value declines over the line of the project.

We may conclude that while introduction of the effects of taxation in investment appraisal calculations makes them more accurate and more complex, they may not lead to better investment decisions.

Example 6.2 ABC Bearing is considering buying a new machine costing Rs 2,00,000 which would generate the following pre-tax profits from the sale of goods produced.

TABLE E6.4

Year	PBT in Rs
1	55,000
2	65,000
3	75,000
4	65,000

ABC pays corporate tax of 45% one year in arrears and also receives capital allowances on a 25% reducing balance basis. The machine will be sold after 4 years for Rs 60,000. If ABC's post-tax cost of capital is 10%, should the company buy the machine in the first place?

Solution

Calculation of capital allowances:

Year 1: Rs 2,00,000 × 0.25 = Rs 50,000

Year 2: Rs (2,00,000 − 50,000) × 0.25 = Rs 37,500

Year 3: Rs (2,00,000 − 50,000 − 37,500) × 0.25 = Rs 28,125

Year 4: Rs (2,00,000 − 50,000 − 37,500 − 28,125) × 0.25 = Rs 21,094

Sum of capital allowances at the end of Year 4 = Rs 1,36,719

Initial value of the machine is Rs 2,00,000

Salvage value: Rs 60,000

Value consumed by the business over 4 years = Rs (2,00,000 − 60,000) = Rs 1,40,000.

Sum of capital allowances at the end of Year 4 = Rs 1,36,719

Therefore year 4 allowance = Rs (1,40,000 − 1,36,719) = Rs 3,281

Total Capital allowances over 4 years = Rs (50,000 + 37,500 + 28,125 + 21,094 + 3,281) = Rs 1,40,000

Taxation benefits

Year 1 (taken in year 2): (50,000 × 0.45) = Rs 22,500

Year 2 (taken in year 3): (22,500 × 0.45) = Rs 10,125

Year 3 (taken in year 4): (10,125 × 0.45) = Rs 4,556.25

Year 4 (taken in year 5): (4,556.25 + 3281) × 0.45 = Rs 3,526.75

Total benefits = Rs 1,40,000 × 0.45 = Rs 63,000

Tax liabilities arising from taxable profits, which are found by subtracting capital allowances from pre-tax profits, are as follows.

Year 1 (taken in year 2): (55,000 − 50,000) × 0.45 = Rs 2,250

Year 2 (taken in year 3): (65,000 − 37,500) × 0.45 = Rs 12,375

Year 3 (taken in year 4): (75,000 − 28,125) × 0.45 = Rs 21,093.75

Year 4 (taken in year 5): (65,000 − 24,375) × 0.45 = Rs 18,281.25

The calculation of net cash flows and NPV is shown in Table E6.5.

TABLE E6.5

Year	Capital (Rs)	Operating cash flows / PBT (Rs)	Tax (Rs)	Net cash flows (Rs)	10% discount factor	Present value (Rs)
0	(2,00,000)			(2,00,000)	1.000	(2,00,000)
1		55,000		55,000	0.909	49,995
2		65,000	(2,250)	62,750	0.826	51,831.5
3		75,000	(12,375)	62,625	0.751	47,031.4
4	60,000	1,25,000	(21,093.75)	1,63,906.25	0.683	1,11,947.97
5			(18,281.25)	(18,281.25)	0.621	(11,352.7)

NPV = −2,00,000 + 49,995 + 51,831.5 + 47,031.4 + 1,11,947.97 − 11,352.7 = Rs 49,453.17

Since NPV is a positive value of Rs 49,453.17, the purchase of the machine by ABC can be recommended on financial grounds.

Finding out the exact discounting factor in any capital budgeting project is really a tricky job for a finance manager or an analyst. The practical implication of the concepts are discussed in the following queries and their respective answers.

Query

Consider a situation in which a bank is ready to lend you Rs 1,00,000, which you need for a project, at 8% interest rate. Would you assume 8% as the suitable discounting factor for NPV estimation while analysing the project?

Answer

First, interest rate on the loan has got nothing to do with the risk of the project. It simply reflects your existing business. Second, whether you take the loan or not, you still face a choice between the two alternatives—one which fetches 10% return and another equally risky option fetching 15% return. So a finance manager who borrows at 8% and invests at 15% is not smart if another option, which is readily available, entails identical risks but fetches much higher returns, i.e., 15% in this case.

6.5 RELEVANT CASH FLOWS

A relevant cash flow occurs when the undertaken project is directly responsible for the cash flow. Obviously, an increasing relevant cash flow adds to the viability of the project in hand. These are the only cash flows that should be included in investment appraisal. There are several cash flows, however, that are worthy of careful consideration.

Query

It is said that uncertainties can be tackled by overt identification of upside and downside possibilities. In such a situation one can argue that the expected cash flows can be discounted at a risk-free rate. What do you think?

Answer

The argument is faulty. If you can get an expected pay off of Rs 1,10,000 for Rs 95,650 in the stock market, why would somebody pay Rs 1,00,000 for the project? The stock of Company X is not a government security and hence it is risky. Now capital investment is also risky. No investor would accept less than 15% from the project when the stock of Company X is a freely available alternative in the market. Hence, 15% should be treated as the appropriate discounting factor.

Exhibit 6.2 depicts the relevance of cash flows in project evaluation and selection.

EXHIBIT 6.2   Need for relevant information

To Invest or Not to Invest?

Ms Sevika, the Marketing Manager of a sports equipment manufacturer, has recently submitted a proposal for production of a range of clubs for beginners. She has just received the following response from the Managing Director.

Memorandum

To: Ms Sevika

From: Mr B Singhania   9 August 2009

Proposal I–09

I have examined your proposal for the new product in which you promise three-year payback and a 28% DCF return. Great idea! But you seem to have forgotten the following relevant points:

1. We have a policy that all investments are subject to a depreciation charge of 25% on the reducing balance.
2. Factory fixed overheads on the new machine will need to be recovered.
3. We need to charge against the project a huge cost on conducting marketing research to assess the size of the market for the new product.
4. What will be the financing cost? I believe it would be not less than 17–18%.

  I suggest that your 28% return is more like 4%, considering the above. Should we proceed with a project with that level of return?

  What can be Ms Sevika's reply be to this correspondence? Is Mr Singhania correct regarding the four points raised above?

  (Ms Sevika's answer is discussed later in Exhibit 6.4.)

Relevant information for investment decision-making reduces the uncertainty about the project. Thus, information on the likely costs and benefits of a investment proposal, its expected economic life, appropriate inflation rates, and discount rates are gathered to provide a clear picture of the project's economic feasibility. Hence, investment decision analysis should be based on the incremental cash flows arising as a consequence of these decisions. Here, we consider how investment analysis handles opportunity costs, sunk costs, interest costs, apportioned fixed costs, incremental working capital, associated costs, etc.

6.5.1 Opportunity Costs

An opportunity cost is the benefit foregone by using an asset for one purpose rather than another. If an asset is used for an investment project, then it is important to ask what benefit has thereby been lost? This is because, this lost benefit or opportunity cost is a relevant cost as far as the project is concerned. Exhibit 6.3 explains the concept of opportunity cost in a different way.

EXHIBIT 6.3   Opportunity cost example—ABC Bearing

We often see opportunity costs in replacement decisions. For example, in ABC Bearing an existing machine can be replaced by an improved model costing Rs 50,000, which generates cash savings of Rs 20,000 each year for 5 years, at the end of which it will have a scrap value of Rs 5,000. The equipment manufacturers are prepared to give an allowance of Rs 10,000 on the existing machine, making a net initial cash outlay of Rs 35,000. But, in pursuing this course of action, we terminate the existing machine's life, preventing it from yielding Rs 3,000 scrap value in 3 years. The prospective scrap value denied is the opportunity cost of replacing the existing machine. The cash flows associated with the replacement decision are therefore:

Year 0	Net cost	Rs 35,000
Year 1–5	Annual cash savings	Rs 20,000
Year 3	Opportunity cost	Rs 3,000
Year 5	Scrap value on new machine	Rs 5,000

6.5.2 Sunk Costs

An outlay that has already taken place is referred to as a sunk cost. It is not influenced by decision under evaluation. Sunk costs should not be considered while evaluating investment as they are not incremental costs. For instance, in 2008, the Bank of Rajasthan was considering the establishment of a branch office in a newly developed section in Kolkata. To help with its evaluation, in 2007, the bank had hired a consulting firm to perform a site analysis at a cost of Rs 1,00,000 and this amount was expensed for tax purposes in 2007. Was this expenditure (in 2007) a relevant cost with respect to the 2008 capital budgeting decision? The answer is no. The cost of Rs 100,000 is a sunk cost and it will not affect the bank's future cash flows regardless of whether or not the new branch is established. It often turns out that a particular project has a negative NPV if all the associated costs, including sunk costs, are considered. The project, however, appears attractive from the perspective of incremental cash flows. A positive NPV can be obtained on the incremental investment as the future incremental cash flows are sufficiently high.

6.5.3 Interest Costs

Capital project must be financed either through equity or debt route. Commonly, this involves borrowing, which requires a series of cash flows in the form of interest payments. Should these interest charges be considered as relevant for estimating expected future cash flows in the case of capital investment decisions? The answer is a resounding no. Interest charges should not be included because they relate to financing decisions rather than investment decisions. Both are separate as far as investment appraisal decisions are concerned. If interest payments were to be deducted from cash flows, it would amount to double-counting since the discounting process already considers the cost of capital in the form of discount rate. To include interest charges as a cash outflow could, therefore, result in serious understating of the true NPV.

6.5.4 Apportioned Fixed Costs

Certain costs are incurred over the life of a project regardless of whether it is undertaken or not. Such costs, such as the apportioned fixed cost (e.g., rent and building insurance) or apportioned head office charges or R&D costs, are not relevant to the evaluation of the project and should be excluded. Only incremental fixed costs, which arise as a result of a project, should be included as a relevant project cash flow.

6.5.5 Incremental Working Capital

Normally, additional inventories are required to support a new operation or an expansion and enhancement of sales. However, payables and accruals also increase simultaneously and this reduces the cash required to finance inventories and receivables. The difference between the required increase in current operating assets and liabilities is the change in net working capital or incremental working capital. If this change is positive then working capital finance will be needed.

Towards the end of a project's life, inventories would be used but not replaced, and receivables will be collected. Hence, investment in net working capital will be returned by the end of the project's life.

6.5.6 Associated Costs

Investments in capital projects may have company-wise cash-flow implications. There is always a danger that those involved in forecasting cash flows may not realize how the project affects the other parts of the business. Management should, therefore, carefully consider if there are any additional cash flows associated with the investment decisions. The decision to produce and launch a new product may influence the demand for other products within the product range. While making a capital budgeting decision and estimating relevant cash flows in capital investment, these things have to be considered.

6.5.7 Non-cash Charges

As per the usual method followed by accountants, the depreciation is subtracted from the revenues in order to eliminate net income. Although the purchase price of fixed assets is not subtracted during the estimation of accounting income, the charge is subtracted as each year's depreciation. The income is protected from taxation due to depreciation, which in turn influences the cash flows. However, depreciation cannot be termed as cash flow. It is added to NOPAT (net operating profit after tax) to calculate the cash flow of the project.

In Exhibit 6.2, we have discussed the relevance of cash flows in project selection through an example. Exhibit 6.4 helps us understand the various types of costs through a response in continuation of the queries generated in Exhibit 6.2.

EXHIBIT 6.4   Analysis of the need for relevant information

Memorandum

To: Mr B. Singhania
From: Ms Sevika   12 August 2009

Proposal I–09

I have re-examined the points raised in the memorandum dated 9 August and discussed them with our VP – Finance. In analysing capital projects, only future investment cash flows implemented in the business are relevant to the decisions.

1. Depreciation is not a cash flow. It is a charge against profits by comparing operating cash flow against initial outlay. Thus, the need for depreciation becomes unnecessary.
2. Only additional fixed costs, resulting from introduction of the new project, should be charged. I have checked that there are no extra overheads.
3. The marketing research is a passed cost. Its existence is not dependent upon outcome of the decision, so it should not be included.
4. I agree that finance costs are important, but the cost of finance has already been accounted for within the discount rate.

My new proposal is an attractive one from which the business would benefit.

6.6 PROJECT EVALUATION VIS-À-VIS PROJECT FINANCING DECISION

Let us assume that a project is financed through equity only (i.e., a hundred per cent equity financed object). What happens if the financing structure changes and a certain portion of the project is now financed through debts? In other words, here we are planning to reconsider the capital structure decision. Hence, investment and financing decisions interact and cannot be wholly separated. There are essentially no different ways of handling such issues.

Adjust the discount rate   It is a very common practice. In order to accommodate the positive influence of interest of tax shields, the adjustment is particularly downwards. It is generally put to use through the estimation of after-tax WACC (weighted average cost of capital).

Adjust the present value   To begin with, the base-case NPV is calculated as an all-equity financed project. The base-case NPV is analysed to accommodate the influence change to capital structure.

Once the value and side effects of financing a project are identified, calculating NPV for such changes in financing strategies is no more than addition or subtraction.

6.7 ADJUSTED PRESENT VALUE

According to the process of adjusted present value (APV), cash flows and present values (PV) are clearly adjusted for costs or benefits of financing strategies. The APV method is most comprehensible in case of simple numerical examples. One starts by evaluating a project under base-case assumption and, thereafter, analyses the probable financing side effects of accepting the project.

Consider a project to produce solar water heaters. It requires an investment of Rs 1,00,00,000 and offers after-tax cash flows of Rs 18,00,000 per annum for 10 years. The project is 100% financed through equity, and the opportunity cost of capital (equity) is 12%, which represents the business risk of the project. Based on the available data, the base-case NPV can easily be calculated, and it is Rs 1,70,000 in this case. Thus, we should accept the project under the 'all-equity financing' scenario.

Now consider a different financing scenario. Suppose the firm has a 50% target D/E ratio. Its policy is to limit its debts to 50% of the assets. Thus, if it invests more, it borrows more. In this sense, it can be said that the additional investment adds to the firm's debt capacity. Now, is debt capacity worth anything? The most accepted answer is yes, because of the tax shields generated by interest payments on corporate borrowings. Now this theory automatically tells us to compute the value of the firm in the following two steps:

First: Compute base-case NPV under all-equity financing.

Second: Add the PV of tax savings due to departure from all-equity financing.

For example, the solar heater project increases the firm's assets by Rs 1,00,00,000 and, therefore, prompts it to borrow Rs 50,00,000 more. Suppose this Rs 50,00,000 is repayable in equal installments so that the outstanding loan amount declines with the depreciating book value of the solar heater project. We assume that the said loan carries an interest rate of 8%. Given this data, PV of interest tax shield may be computed as shown in Table 6.2. As per our computation, PV of such interest tax shield is Rs 5,76,000.

Thus, APV = Rs 1,70,000 + Rs 5,76,000 = Rs 7,46,000

TABLE 6.2 Present value of interest tax shield computation

(Figures in '000 Rs) (Tax rate assumed as 35%)

Year	Outstanding	Interest @ 8%	Interest tax shield	Present value of tax shield
1	5,000	400	140	129.60
2	4,500	360	126	108.00
3	4,000	320	112	88.90
4	3,500	280	98	72.00
5	3,000	240	84	57.20
6	2,500	200	70	44.10
7	2,000	160	56	32.60
8	1,500	120	42	22.70

Contd

Table 6.2 *Contd*

Year	Outstanding	Interest @ 8%	Interest tax shield	Present value of tax shield
9	1,000	80	28	14.00
10	500	40	14	6.50
			Total	576.00

Significant assumptions:

- Principal of borrowed amount is repaid in 10 equal installments.
- Interest rate on loan is taken as 8%.
- PV is calculated at 8% borrowing rate.
- As interest rate and discount rate are same, it can be assumed that tax shields are just as risky as interest payment.

Query

Why is the APV format more suitable for evaluating foreign projects than the conventional NPV format of investment proposals?

Answer

The APV format is more suitable for evaluating foreign projects because it allows different formats of the project's cash flows to be discounted separately. This provides the needed flexibility for treating each variable as mentioned above. In addition, the AVP format also makes it feasible to use different discount rates for different segments of total cash flows, depending on the degree of certainty attached with each variety of cash flow.

6.8 WEIGHTED AVERAGE COST OF CAPITAL

Business acquisition or processes are funded by debt and equity capital. The net cost of these sources of finance, as per their relative share in the deal composition, is referred to as weighted average cost of capital (WACC). That is, if the share of equity and debt in the company's net capital is 70% and 30%, respectively, the WACC would have to be calculated keeping in mind the given proportions. It is the calculation of a company's cost of capital in which every source of capital is weighted in proportion to how much capital it contributes to the company (*Farlex Financial Dictionary*). When a company takes a risk and spends relatively higher amount of money to acquire capital, it will register a high WACC. Whereas, the company that spends less to raise capital will have a lower WACC.

Exhibit 6.5 demonstrates the use and relation among WACC, NPV, and discounting factor.

EXHIBIT 6.5 Relation between WACC, NPV, and discounting factor

Let's calculate WACC for S & Co. Its book value and market value balance sheets are as follows.

Book value balance sheet (in Rs '0,00,000)			
Asset		Liability	
Asset value	– Rs 100	Debt	– Rs 50
		Equity	– Rs 50
Total	– Rs 100	Total	– Rs 100

Market Value Balance Sheet (in Rs '0,00,000)			
Asset		Liability	
Asset value	– Rs 125	Debt	– Rs 50
		Equity	– Rs 75
Total	– Rs 125	Total	– Rs 125

The market value of S & Co.'s equity had been computed as follows:
No. of shares (1,00,00,000) × current stock price (Rs 7.50 / share)
= Rs 7,50,00,000

The company has done well and its future prospects are good, so the stocks are trading above book value of Rs 5.00 per share. However, it has been assumed that book value and market value of debt is identical in the above case. Let's suppose, S & Co's cost of debt (pre-tax) is 8% and its cost of equity is 14.6%.

Also, the market value balance sheet shows assets worth Rs 12,50,00,000, which is effectively the market value of debt plus market value of equity put together.

As seen, we do not need to look at the book balance sheet to estimate WACC. This is because when calculating WACC one is more interested in current values and expectations for the future, than past experiences. The company's true debt/equity ratio is actually 40:60 because its assets are worth Rs 12,50,00,000. Cost of equity of 14.6% is basically the expected rate of return from purchase of the company's stocks @ Rs 7.50 per share. Now, let us assume that, S & Co. is a 'consistently profitable firm' and pays taxes at a marginal rate of 35%.

Thus, WACC of S & Co. can be computed as follows:
0.08 (1 – 0.35) (0.40) + 0.146 (0.60) = 0.1084 = 10.84%

Now let's assume that S & Co.'s executives are planning to invest Rs 1,25,00,000 in the construction of a perpetual crushing machine, which (for our convenience) never depreciates and generates a perpetual stream of cash flow of Rs 20,85,000 per annum pre-tax.

After-tax cash flow is Rs 20,85,000 × (0.65) = Rs 13,55,000 per annum on perpetual basis. Interest payment, if any, has not been considered in the above cash-flow estimates.

Please note that the after-tax cash flow takes no account of tax shields on debts. Under standard capital budgeting practice, we invariably calculate after-tax cash flows as if the projects were all-equity financed. However, the interest shield will not be ignored. We are about to discount project cash flows by S & Co.'s WACC, in which the cost of debt after-tax had been included. The value of interest tax shield is picked up, not in the form of the higher after-tax cash flows, but through a lower discount rate.

Thus, $NPV = -12.50 + 1.355 / 0.1084 = 0$

Now, if NPV equals zero, the return to equity investors must exactly equal the cost of equity, i.e., 14.6%. Let's suppose that S & Co.'s shareholders could actually forecast a 14.6% return on their investment in the perpetual crusher project as a mini firm. Its market value balance sheet would look like this.

Market Value Balance Sheet (in Rs '000,000)			
Asset		*Liability*	
Project value	– Rs 12.50	Debt	– Rs 5
		Equity	– Rs 7.50
Total	– Rs 12.50	Total	– Rs 12.50

After-tax interest = $0.80 \times 5.00 \times 0.65$ = Rs 0.26 lakh

Expected equity income = $1.355 - 0.26$ = Rs 1.095 lakh

Thus, expected equity returns = $1.095 / 7.50$ = 14.6%

Thus, the expected return to equity shareholders equals the cost of equity. Therefore, it makes sense that the project's NPV is equal to zero.

Assumptions

By discounting that the perpetual crusher project's business risks are identical to S & Co.'s WACC, we assume that.

- The project's business risks are identical to S & Co.'s other assets.
- The project supports same fraction of debt to equity as in S & Co.'s overall capital structure.

The importance of these assumptions can easily be observed. If the project had greater business risks than S & Co.'s other assets, or if the acceptance of the project would lead to a permanent and material change in S & Co.'s, shareholders would not be content with a 14.6% expected return on their equity investment in the project.

In the following condition, a small variation in the perpetual crusher project is done in order to explain another vital concept:

Initial investment (say) = Rs 1,00,00,000

(i.e., the adjusted cost of capital) = 0.1084 = 10.84%

Opportunity cost of capital attributed to the project = 12% (in case of all equity financing)

In the above example = NPV (discounting at WACC) = Rs 25,00,000.

The base-case NPV (discounting at the opportunity cost of capital) for the purpose of computation of APV,

= $-10 + 1.355 / 0.12$ = Rs 12,90,000 (positive)

Thus, the project will be worthwhile even with all equity financing. We are now planning to study and analyse the financing side effects in this deal through the concept of computation of APV.

APV for the perpetual crusher project

As the base-case NPV is equal to Rs 12,90,000 (positive), the interpretations is that the project would be worthwhile even with all equity financing. However, as the targeted D/E ratio of the company is 40%, its debt will be Rs 40,00,000. At 8% borrowing rate, the annual interest tax shield will be $0.35 \times 0.08 \times 4$ = Rs 1,12,000 (considering a tax rate of 35%).

In the current case, under financing rule 1, debt stays at Rs 40,00,000, and interest tax shield at Rs 1,12,000 per annum. The tax shields are tied to the fixed interest payments and hence 8% cost of debt (pre tax) is a reasonable discount rate. Thus, as per financing rule 1, *PV* of interest tax shields = $1,12,000 / 0.08$ = Rs 14,00,000 (based on perpetuity concept).

Therefore, APV under this case is base-case *NPV* + *PV* of interest tax shields =

Rs 12,90,000 + Rs 14,00,000 = Rs 26,90,000.

Now under financing rule 2, debt is rebalanced to 40% of actual project value. That means future debt levels are not known at the start of the project, and they keep shifting up and down depending on the success or failure of the project. In case of interest tax shields, discount factor should therefore be considered as the project's business risk. If the interest tax shields are just as risky as the project, they should be discounted at the opportunity cost of capital, i.e., 12% in this case. Thus, as per financing rule 2, *PV* (interest tax shields) = $1,12,000 / 0.12$ = Rs 9,34,000, based on the concept of perpetuity.

Thus, APV in this case is base-case *NPV* + *PV* of interest tax shields = Rs (12,90,000 + 9,34,000) = Rs 22,24,000.

After reading the exhibit above, the question of the worth of those tax shields arises. It depends on the financing rule that the company follows. As per f nancing rule 1, debt is fixed, i.e., borrow a fraction of initial project investment and make debt repayment as per a pre-determined schedule. As per financing rule 2, debt is rebalanced, i.e., it is adjusted in each future period to keep it at a constant fraction of future project value.

Query

Which financing rule is better—debt fixed or debt rebalanced?

Answer

As a general rule, we vote for the assumption of rebalancing of debt, i.e. financing rule 2. Any capital budgeting procedure of a project that assumes debt levels are always fixed and is grossly oversimplified. The financing rule effectively says that always borrow 40% of the value of perpetual crusher. If the project value increases, the firm borrows more. If the project value decreases, the firm borrows less. Under this policy, one can no longer discount future interest tax shields at the borrowing rate because they are not certain. Thus, financing rule 2 is based on feasible assumption and hence it is conceptually sound.

6.9 IMPACT OF DEPRECIATION TREATMENT

In general, an inflationary economy distorts capital budgeting decisions. For one thing, depreciation charges are based on original rather than replacement costs. As income grows with inflation, an increasing portion is taxed, with the result that the real cash flows do not keep up with inflation. Consider an investment proposal costing Rs 24,000 under the assumption that no inflation is expected. That depreciation is a straight line over 4 years and tax rate is 40%. The following cash flows (Table 6.3) are expected to occur.

TABLE 6.3 Expected cash flows after tax without considering inflation

Years	Cash savings (Rs)	Depreciation (Rs)	Taxes (Rs)	Cash flow after taxes (CFAT) (Rs)
1	10,000	6,000	1,600	8,400
2	10,000	6,000	1,600	8,400
3	10,000	6,000	1,600	8,400
4	10,000	6,000	1,600	8,400

Without inflation, depreciation charges represent cost of replacing the investment as it wears out. The IRR that equates value of cash inflows with the cost of the project is 14.96%.

Now, consider a situation in which inflation is at a rate of 7% per annum and cash savings are expected to grow at the given rate of inflation. CFAT will be as shown in Table 6.4.

TABLE 6.4 Expected cash flows after tax after considering inflation

Years	Cash savings (Rs)	Depreciation (Rs)	Taxes (Rs)	CFAT (Rs)
1	10,700	6,000	1,880	8,820
2	11,449	6,000	2,180	9,269
3	12,250	6,000	2,500	9,750
4	13,108	6,000	2,843	10,265

TABLE 6.5 CFAT values

Real CFAT	Year 1	Year 2	Year 2	Year 3
	8,243	8,096	7,959	7,831

Although, these cash flows are larger than before, they must be deflated by the inflation rate. Therefore, the last column becomes as is shown in Table 6.5.

As we see, the real CFAT are less than before and decline over a period of time. The reason is that depreciation charges do not change in keeping with inflation, so that an increasing portion of cash savings is subject to taxation. The IRR based on real CFAT is 12.91%.

The presence of inflation, therefore, results in lower real rates of return and less incentive for companies to undertake capital investments. Cash-flow situation is improved with accelerated depreciation but the same may not be allowable under income tax act in various countries, including India. This is a disincentive for companies to undertake capital expenditure, so they typically invest less capital incentives during periods of inflation. In fact, this may be treated as one good reason for the popularity of payback for investment appraisal criterion.

6.10 VALUE OF INTEREST TAX SHIELDS

In the perpetual crusher project example (mentioned in Exhibit 6.5), we assume that the firm can fully capture interest tax shields of Rs 0.35 on every rupee of interest payment. We also treat interest tax shields as safe cash inflows (effectively) and hence, discount them by applying a low discount rate of 8%. Is our treatment correct? Let us look at the following points.

- You cannot use tax shields unless you pay taxes and you do not pay taxes unless you make taxable profits. Few firms can be sure that future profitability will be sufficient to use up the interest tax shields.

- A project's debt capacity depends on how well it performs. When profits exceed expectations, the firm can borrow more but if the project fails, it will be difficult to support the debt. It may be appreciated that if the future amount of debt is tied to future project value, then interest tax shields, given in the perpetual crusher project example, are estimates only and not fixed amounts.

The present value of tax shield drops even further if the tax shields are treated as forecasts and are discounted at a higher rate. Let us suppose the firm ties the amount of debt to the actual future project cash flows. Then, the interest tax shield becomes just as risky as the project itself and should therefore be discounted at 12% opportunity cost of capital in the current case. This automatically reduces PV of interest tax shields and hence, the APV as well.

Cost capital—The financing side effects

Let us clarify the difference between the two concepts—opportunity cost of capital and adjusted cost of capital.

Opportunity cost of capital is the expected rate of return offered in capital markets by the assets of equivalent risks. This depends solely on timing, quantum, and possibilities of the project's cash flows. It may be noted that opportunity cost of capital is the correct discount rate for the project, if it is all equity financed.

Adjusted cost of capital is the adjusted opportunity cost, which reflects the financing side effects of an investment project (i.e., it captures the dual effects of equity plus debt financing as well).

Some people simply say cost of capital and, at times, their meaning is clear in the context. On other occasions, one does not know which concept they are referring to and that can cause a lot of confusion. When financing side effects are important, you should accept projects with a positive APV. But if you know the adjusted cost of capital, you do not need to calculate the APV. You just calculate the NPV, applying the adjusted cost of capital as the discount rate.

We must remember that the WACC formula is the most common way to calculate the adjusted cost of capital.

A practical view point In practice, it really does not matter whether interest tax shields are valued or discounted appropriately or not. In the context of the entire CAPEX decision-making process, it hardly matters whether interest tax shields have been discounted approximately or exactly. Your time will be much better spent in refining the forecasts of operating cash flows.

In real life, what matters the most is the cash flows and the cash flows only.

Discounting safe and nominal cash flows

Let us suppose that you are considering the purchase of a machine worth Rs 1,00,000. The manufacturer sweetens the deal by offering to finance the purchase by lending Rs 1,00,000 for 5 years with annual interest payments at 5%. You would have to pay 13% interest if you were to borrow from a bank and your applicable tax rate would be 35%. How much is this loan worth? If you accept the scheme offered by the manufacturer, the stream of cash flows would be in thousands of rupees, as given in Table 6.6.

TABLE 6.6   Cash-flow details

(in '000 Rs)

	Period					
	0	1	2	3	4	5
Cash flows	100	(5)	(5)	(5)	(5)	(105)
Tax shields		1.75	1.75	1.75	1.75	1.75
After-tax cash flows	100	(3.25)	(3.25)	(3.25)	(3.25)	(103.25)

Now the question is about the right rate to discount the above. Please note that here you are discounting safe, nominal cash flows. It is called safe as the company must commit to pay if it takes the loan and nominal because payment will be fixed regardless of future inflation. The correct discount rate for discounting safe, nominal rate cash flows is your company's 'after-tax subsidized borrowing', i.e., $0.13 (1 - 0.35) = 0.0845$ or 8.45% in the current case.

You might wonder why the after-tax subsidized borrowing rate should be considered as the appropriate discount rate while discounting safe and nominal cash flows. The subsidized borrowing rate is invariably taken because it is the investors' opportunity cost of capital, i.e., the rate they would demand for your company's debt. But why should this rate be converted to an after-tax rate?

Let us simplify the situation by taking one year's subsidized loan of Rs 1,00,000 at 5%. The cash flows are given in Table 6.7.

We can calculate the maximum amount X that can be borrowed for one year through regular channels. It would mean a borrowing at 13% pre-tax or 8.45% post-tax. Therefore, you will need 108.45% of the amount borrowed to payback principal plus after-tax interest charges. If $108.45 \times X = 103,250$, $X = 95,205$.

TABLE 6.7   After tax cash flows (in '000 Rs)

	Period	
	0	1
Cash flow	100	(105)
Tax shield		1.75
After-tax cash flow	100	(103.25)

Now, if you borrow Rs 1,00,000 through a subsidized loan and Rs 95,205 through normal channels, the difference of Rs 4,795 must be the money in the bank. Therefore, it must be NPV of this one-year period subsidized loan. When you discount a safe nominal cash flow at an after-tax borrowing rate, you are implicitly calculating the equivalent loan, i.e., the amount you could borrow through normal channels for debt servicing.

Equivalent loan = Present value of cash flow available for debt servicing (in this case, equivalent = 1,03,250 / 1.0845 = 95,205)

In some cases, it may be easier to think from the lender's perspective. For example, you could ask, 'How much my company has to invest today in order to cover next year's debt service on subsidized loan?' The answer is Rs 95,205. If you lend that amount at 13% you would earn 8.45% after tax and have Rs 1,03,250 (95205 × 1.0845), which is incidentally the amount required for servicing the subsidized loan. Herein lies the basic rationale behind applying the after-tax borrowing rate on subsidized loans as the appropriate discounting factor for discounting safe and nominal cash flows.

Therefore, regardless of whether it is easier or not to think of borrowing, the correct discount rate for safe and nominal cash flows is an after-tax interest on the subsidized loan. In some ways, it is quite obvious. Companies are free to borrow or lend money if they lend the after-tax interest (effectively) on their investments. If they borrow, they pay the after-tax interest (effectively).

6.11 DEPRECIATION TAX SHIELDS

Capital projects are expected to generate certain after-tax cash flows. Now the discounting of the total after-tax cash flows determines the value of the capital projects. Depreciation cash flows are not valued separately, although they add to project cash flows. They are folded into project cash flows along with other type of cash flows. The net average risk of the cash flows constitutes the project's opportunity cost of capital. However, we can ask what tax shield may surely be considered safe and nominal flows and hence it may be discounted at the firm's after-tax borrowing rate. Table 6.8 gives a summary statement showing the most appropriate discount rate for various types of cash flows.

TABLE 6.8 A brief summary of appropriate discount rate

The nature of cash flow	The most appropriate discounting rate
Safe and nominal cash flows	After-tax interest on subsidized loan
Cent per cent equity financed project cash flows (reflecting same degree of risk as other assets of the business under review)	OCC
Cash flows of projects characterized by 'financing side effects' (as explained)	WACC (alternatively APV may be computed as well)
Cash flows relating to projects that are riskier as compared to other business activities	Apply higher discount rates in order to capture such higher risks

SUMMARY

Investments must generate at least enough cash for all investors to obtain their required returns. If they produce less than the investor's opportunity cost, then the wealth of investors may be expected to decline. Hence, an investment proposal's NPV is derived by discounting future net cash receipts by a rate which reflects the value of the alternative use of funds, summing them over life of the proposal and deducting the initial outlay. IRR is a profitability measure, which depends solely on the amount and timing of the project cash flows.

The opportunity cost of capital is a standard of profitability for the project, which we use to calculate how much the project is worth. It is generally established in the capital markets. CAPM is widely used by large corporations to estimate discount rates. Interest rate discounting rate can be taken as real rate

(k_r) and nominal rate (k_n) and expected cash flows will be real cash flow (RCF_t) and nominal cash flow (NCF_t). Real cost of capital (k_r) is obtained from nominal (or money) cost of capital (k_n) by making an adjustment to the nominal cost of capital to allow for inflation (i).

The test of relevance of a cash flow is to check whether the cash flow comes about as a result of undertaking the project. If the answer is no, then the cash flow is not a relevant one. The APV rule is the easiest to understand in the context of simple numerical examples.

In general, an inflationary economy distorts capital budgeting decisions. For one thing, depreciation charges are based on original rather than replacement costs. As income grows with inflation, an increasing portion is taxed, with the result that real cash flows do not keep up with inflation.

KEY TERMS

Adjusted cost of capital   It is the adjusted opportunity cost, which reflects financing side effects of an investment project (i.e., it captures the dual effects of equity plus debt financing as well).

Adjusted present value (APV)   Adjusted NPV is equal to base-case NPV plus NPV for changes in financing strategy.

Appropriate discount factor   It is equal to risk-free return plus project beta multiplied by market risk premium. $r = r_f + \beta (r_m - r_f)$

Capital allowance   For many types of capital investments, tax relief is obtainable on capital expenditure incurred. Rate of allowance varies from time to time and country to country, depending on their internal corporate taxation and capital allowance policies.

Hence, capital allowances are a matter of government policy.

Internal rate of return (IRR)   It is a profitability measure, which depends solely on the amount and timing of the project cash flows.

Opportunity cost of capital   It is a standard of profitability for a project, which we use to calculate how much a project is worth. It is generally established in capital markets.

Real cost of capital   It is obtained from the nominal (or money) cost of capital (k_n) by making an adjustment to the nominal cost of capital to allow for inflation (i). Rearranging the expression for the Fisher effect:
$(1 + k_n) = (1 + k_r) \times (1 + i)$
$(1 + k_r) = (1 + k_n) / (1 + i)$

CONCEPT REVIEW QUESTIONS

1. Can cost of capital be a discount factor in investment appraisal techniques?
2. 'Inflation can have a major impact on the ultimate success or failure of capital projects.' Explain.
3. Discuss the significance of taxation in capital budgeting.
4. Which costs are relevant in capital budgeting decisions?
5. Differentiate between interest tax shields and depreciation tax shields.

CRITICAL THINKING QUESTION

A Swiss pharmaceutical company is considering construction of a new plant in the US. Assuming that we need to arrive at an appropriate discounting factor applying the CAPM model, what approach may be adopted in order to arrive at the desired goal.

NUMERICAL PROBLEMS

1. A machine is to be purchased by B Limited for Rs 1,20,000. The machine can work for four years and can be ended with a zero salvage value. B Limited pays 45% corporate tax and its discount rate for investment purposes is 10%. What are the present values of tax benefits arising to B Limited from the purchase of the machine in the following situations:
   (i) First year capital allowances of 100% are available.
   (ii) Capital allowances are available on the straight line basis over the asset's life.
   (iii) Capital allowances are available on a 30% reducing balance basis.

2. ABC Food Appliances is evaluating purchase of a milling machine, which will allow it to move from the supply of raw foods in local supermarkets to a more lucrative frozen foods market. Packets of frozen food would be sold in boxes of 8. The information in Table E6.6 applies to each box.

TABLE E6.6

	Rs per box
Selling price	10.7
Packaging and labour	3.2
Frozen food and processing	4.80

Selling price and cost of frozen food is expected to increase by 6% per year, while packaging and labour costs are expected to increase by 5% per year. Investment in working capital will increase by 1,00,000 during the first year. The freeze dryer will have a useful life of five years before being scrapped, and the net cost of disposal would be Rs 20,000. Sale in the first year is expected to be 80,000 boxes, but in the second and subsequent years it will be 1,10,000 boxes.

The manufacturer of the freeze dryer, in order to encourage ABC to go ahead with the deal, has offered to defer payment on part of the purchase price. The total cost of freeze dryer is Rs 10,00,000 and the offer is for the 50% that is to be paid initially, with remaining 50% to be paid one year later. The company's nominal cost of capital is 15%. Ignore taxation.
   (i) Assess whether ABC Food Appliances should invest in the freeze dryer.
   (ii) Explain your choice of discount rate in your answer to part I.

3. HMT Co. is increasing the level of automation in the production line dedicated to a single product. The options available are total automation and partial automation. The company works on a planning horizon of five years and either option will produce 10,000 units, which can be sold annually.

Total automation will involve a total capital cost of Rs 10,00,000. Material cost will be Rs 15 and labour and variable overheads cost will be Rs 18 per unit with this method.

Partial automation will result in higher material wastage and an average cost of Rs 15 per unit. Labour and variable overheads are expected to be Rs 45 per unit. The capital cost of this alternative is Rs 2,50,000. The products sell for Rs 80 each, whichever method of production is adopted.

Scrap value of the automated production line in five years' time will be Rs 1,00,000, while the line which is partially automated will be worthless. The management uses straight line depreciation and the required rate of return on the capital investment is 15% per annum. Depreciation is considered to be the only incremental fixed cost.

In analysing the investment opportunities of this type, the company calculates average total cost per unit, annual net profit, break even volume per year, and discounted net present value.

(i) Determine the figure that would be circulated to the management of ABC Food Appliances in order to assist their investment analysis.

(ii) Comment on figures produced in the question above and a make a recommendation with any qualifications you think appropriate.

ASSIGNMENT

Explain with a real-life example how net operating working capital is recovered at the end of a project's life, and why it is included in a capital budgeting analysis.

SELECT REFERENCES

Brealey, R.A. and S.C. Myers, *Principle of Corporate Finance*, Tata McGraw-Hill, 7e, 2006.

Cooley, Phillip J., Rodney L. Roenfeldt, and I.T. Keong Chew, 'Capital Budgeting Procedure under Inflation', *Financial Management*, Winter 1975, pp. 18–27.

Scarlett, R., 'The Further Aspects of Impact of Taxation on the Viability of Investments', *Management Accounting*, May 1995, p. 54.

Scarlett, R., 'The Impact of Corporate Taxation on the Viability of Investments', *Management Accounting*, May 1993, p. 54.

Van Horne, James C., 'A Note on the Biases in Capital Budgeting Introduced by Inflation', *Journal of Financial and Qualitative Analysis*, January 1971.

CASE STUDY
A Financial Analyst's Viewpoint

Rajib Sharma, the newly appointed financial analyst of Paharpur Metalix Ltd, shut his office door and walked over to his desk. He had only 24 hours to reexamine the accountant's profit projections and come up with a recommendation on the proposed new computer controlled milling machine.

At the meeting, the managing director was quite clear—if the project cannot pay in the first three years itself, it is not worth bothering with. He was then given a day's time by his MD to come up with a more realistic estimate, otherwise the Rs 24,00,000 capital project would be a non-starter. His first work was to reexamine the accountant's profitability forecast (given in Table E6.7) in light of the following facts that emerged from the meeting:

1. Given the rapid development in the market, it was unrealistic to assume that the product life span was more than 4 years. The machinery would have no other use and could not raise more than Rs 2,00,000 in scrap metal at the end of the project.

2. The opening stock of year 1 would be acquired at the same time as the machine. All other stock movement would occur at year ends.

3. This type of machine depreciated over a period of six years on a straight line basis.

4. Within the 'other production expenses', the apportioned fixed overheads equal 20% of the labour costs.

5. The administration charge was an apportionment over central fixed overheads.

TABLE E6.7

Profit projection for CNC milling machine (Rs in '0,000)				
Year	1	2	3	4
Sales	400	600	800	600
Less costs				
Material				
Opening stock	40	80	80	60
Purchases	260	300	360	240
Closing stock	(80)	(80)	(60)	–
Cost of sales	220	300	380	300
Labour	80	120	120	80
Other production expenses	80	90	92	100
Depreciation	40	40	40	40
Administrative overheads	54	76	74	74
Interest on loans to finance the project	22	22	22	22
Total cost	496	648	728	616
Profit (loss)	(96)	(48)	(72)	(16)

Later that day, Sharma met the production manager who explained to him that if the new machine is installed, it would have sufficient capacity to enable an existing machine to be sold immediately for Rs 2,00,000 and to create an annual operating savings of Rs 1,80,000. However, the accountant had told him that with the machine currently standing in the books for Rs 5,00,000, the company could not afford to write off the asset against this year's slender profit. 'We will do better to keep it for another four years, when its scrap value will be about Rs 80,000,' he said. Sharma then raised the proposal with the marketing director. It was not long before two new pieces of information emerged:

1. To stand a realistic chance of hitting sales forecast for the proposal, marketing would require Rs 4,00,000 for additional advertising and sales promotion at the start of the project and a further Rs 80,000 a year for remainder of the project life.

The sales forecast and advertising effort had been devised in consultation with marketing consultants, whose bill for Rs 1,80,000 had just arrived that morning.

2. The marketing director was very concerned about the impact on other products within the product range. If the investment went ahead, it would lead to a reduction of sales in value of a competing product of around Rs 6,00,000 a year. 'With net profit margin of 12%, gross profit margin of 30% on these sales, this is probably the "kiss of death" for the CNC proposal', Sharma reflected.

He went home that evening with a full briefcase and a number of unresolved questions. Even if the proposal were profitable, what was an acceptable return? The latest update for the division shows an 18% return on assets, but the MD talked about a three-year payback requirement. His phone call to the finance director at the head office, to whom this proposal would eventually be sent, was distinctly unhelpful. 'We have, in the past, found out that whenever we lay down a hurdle rate for divisional capital project, it merely encourages unduly optimistic estimates from divisional executives, eager to promote their pet proposals. So now we give no guidelines to the matter.'

Sharma figured that as an absolute minimum, the shareholders would be looking for a return of 15%, the current yield obtainable from risk-free government securities. Any risk associated with the project would be discussed separately. Paharpur Metalix Ltd pays corporate tax at 50%, and the annual writing down allowances of 30% on reducing balance may be claimed. The existing machine has a nil value for tax purposes.

Discussion question

Prepare the case to be presented by Sharma in tomorrow's meeting:

1. Ignoring taxation
2. With taxation

RISK ANALYSIS MODELS IN CAPITAL BUDGETING

It must be considered that there is nothing more difficult to carry out nor more doubtful of success nor more dangerous to handle than to initiate a new order of things.

— MACHIAVELLI

LEARNING OBJECTIVES

After studying this chapter, you will be able to

- Define risk and understand how risk is analysed by using probability theory
- Understand sensitivity analysis, scenario analysis, break-even analysis
- Understand certainty equivalent method, risk-adjusted discount rate method, Hiller model, simulation analysis, decision tree analysis
- Define capital rationing
- Differentiate between risk and utility
- Understand taxation (MAT and TDS, VAT, Cenvat, etc.)
- Understand depreciation and its treatment

Managing Risks—An Infrastructure (Finance) Project

Let's understand through the following case how an infrastructure finance project is set up and the steps taken to minimize risks.

A large oil-fired power station was set up in one of the Asian countries by New Age Power Corporation Ltd. First, a separate firm, Lab, was established to own the power station. The company, then, engaged a consortium of companies, headed by the Japanese XYZ & Co. to build the power station, while the British company EmPower became responsible for managing and running it. Lab agreed to buy the fuel from the Asian country's State Oil Corporation and also agreed to sell the output of the power station to another government body, namely PDA.

Lab's lawyers made a series of complex contracts to make sure that each of the parties involved is made accountable. In other words, the contracts were developed in a structured manner so as to ensure that all the parties involved in the deal would shoulder an appropriate quantum of the risks involved in this capital project. For example, the contractors (the Japanese company) would deliver the plant on time and it would operate as per specifications. The British firm agreed to maintain the plant and operate efficiently. The State Oil Corporation entered into a long-term contract for supplying oil to Lab, and PDA agreed to buy Lab's output for the next 30 years. In fact, it entered into a take-or-pay agreement with Lab, i.e., even if it does not take the electricity produced by Lab it would still continue paying for it.

Now, since PDA was going to pay for the electricity in rupees, Lab was concerned about the fall of the value of rupee. Therefore, the central bank of the country, agreed to provide Lab with foreign exchange at guaranteed exchange rates.

It may once again be noted that the sole purpose of these contracts was to ensure that each risk was borne by the party that was best able to measure and control it. For example, XYZ and Co. was the best participant to control on-time completion, so it made sense to ask them to bear the risk of construction delays. Similarly, EmPower was best placed to operate the plant and was to be penalized if it failed to do so. The contractor and the operator agreed to take the risk as the project involved established technologies and hence there were minimum chances of unpleasant surprises.

While these contracts sought to be as precise as possible as with each party's responsibilities, they could not cover every eventuality. Hence, both the Japanese and the British firms became major shareholders as well. This meant that they not only shared the profit but the losses as well.

The project finance in Lab was highly levered. Over 75 per cent of the Rs 10,00,000 investment of the project was financed through debt. A certain portion of the debt was provided by a fund that was set up by the World Bank and the US and the Japanese aid agencies. However, the bulk of the debt was provided by a group of major international banks. These banks were encouraged to invest because they knew that the World Bank and several governments were in the front line and would take the hit if the project were to fail. But they were still concerned that the government of the Asian country might prevent Lab from paying out in foreign currency. Or it might impose a special tax or might even prevent Lab from bringing in the specialist staff it requires.

Therefore, to prevent Lab from such political risks, the government of this Asian country promised to pay compensation if it interfered in such matters with the operation of the project. This was supposed to keep the government honest once the plant was built and started operating. Governments of developing countries can stay surprisingly relaxed in the face of the wrath of a private corporation but are usually reluctant to break an agreement that lands the World Bank in difficulties.

It is now evident that the arrangement of the Lab project was complex, costly, and time consuming. In spite of such efforts, not everything was plain sailing. The Gulf War suspended the project for over a year and it looked like it would be shelved forever because of the court ruling that the concept of interest on loans contravened the religious laws of that country.

However, the final reality was quite encouraging in the sense that ten years after the first initiation of discussions, the final agreement on project financing was signed and within a short period of time, the Lab was producing a fifth of the country's electricity.

Epilogue

This was not the end of the Lab story. After the fall of that particular government, the new government terminated the contract and announced a 30 per cent cut in electricity tariffs. This inevitably led to a dispute with the World Bank, which spelled out that, until the dispute could be resolved, nothing would move in the form of new loans.

7.1 WHAT IS RISK?

Risk can be understood as an exposure to potential danger or loss. Eating contaminated food can be a risk to health. A trapeze artist who performs stunts without a safety net risks her life. Similarly, investment in unplanned, dubious projects in order to derive higher returns is a form of financial risk.

A risk associated with an asset can be explained in two ways:
1. On a stand-alone basis
2. On a portfolio basis

The expected rate of return (discount factor) of a proposed project should be able to balance the probable risk of the investment. However, risky projects usually provide either more or less than the expected rates of return. It is unlikely that a risk prone venture would follow an expected pattern. The negative deviation from the expected path is in fact the 'risk' involved in the project. The perceived risk related to an investment decision is about having lower than expected returns. The magnitude of the risk depends upon the deviation of the output from the minimum expected rate of return.

Risk analysis In the business world, one cannot control nor confidently predict the turn around of events in the future. The outcome of investment decisions can be better or worse than expected. Therefore, it is vital to consider the diverse implications of plans and projects while undertaking an investment project.

However, a bigger failure would be to stay away from all risky propositions and, with it, lose newer opportunities to grow and diversify. Risks and losses are a part of exploring new business avenues. One cannot avoid risk. However, a proper strategy can go a long way in minimizing the negative impact of it. With the development of power techniques, risk analysis techniques are becoming better and more advanced. But at the same time, no risk management model can guarantee complete safety or success, as major and minor investment failures continue to occur along side development of risk analysis techniques.

In the context of project appraisal, the terms 'risk' and 'uncertainty' are usually used synonymously. Risk describes a situation where there is not just one possible outcome but there is a possibility of occurrence of an array of potential returns (Brealey and Myers 2006).

7.2 PROJECT RISK MANAGEMENT

A project is always appraised by making certain assumptions before proceeding with it. These appraisals always welcome or rather keep in mind various types of risk-yielding results that may deviate from reality. All projects are usually prone to some kind of risk or the other. In situations where one expects to receive certain additional benefits or returns, this seems to be inevitable. The various types of risks encountered in a project financing deal are given in Table 7.1.

TABLE 7.1 Risks encountered in project financing

Types of risks	Explaining the risk
Project risks	This threatens the operation of a specific project and thereby affects the repayment of the lender's loan.
Debtor's credit risk	It is a risk that a particular debtor company will default on its loan, for example, as a result of insolvency or other detoriation in its overall financial condition.
Sovereign credit risk	When the debtor is a country, the risk of such default is referred as a sovereign credit risk.
Commercial risk	It relates to technical, financial, and other concerns that would face a project, irrespective of its geographic location.
Political risk	Political or country risks relate to those risks presented by a particular country and its government. This is generally of importance when foreign investors are involved in the project.
Force majeure	These risks are outside the control of the participants.

How do the financiers address such risks? In a typical project finance structure, financiers look at the project and its revenue, rather than at the general assets of the sponsors. Consequently, any discrete risk that may interfere with the operation of the project and relate revenue flows to the financiers must be evaluated and addressed. In this context, project risks are critical and require significant attention from investors. In practice, sponsors are often required in project finance transactions to provide guarantees to specific financiers or other investors. Pursuant to these guarantees, financiers now also look at the sponsor for repayment and thus the sponsors' credit risk becomes significant. As a consequence, debtors' sovereign/credit risks are often important issues for financiers in project finance operations (Chandra 1975).

In view of the above, it would not be out of place to give a working definition of project financing as suggested by Peter Nevitt of Bank of America: 'Project financing may be defined as the financing of a particular unit in which a lender is satisfied to look initially to the cash flows and earnings of that economic unit as the source of funds from which a loan would be repaid and to the asset of that economic unit as collateral for the loan.'

Evaluation methodology From the view point of a financier, a project should essentially have the following features to be eligible for the financial assistance.
1. Managerial competence
2. Technical competence
3. Commercial viability
4. Economic justification
5. Financial soundness

A detailed discussion of the above features is available in Chapter 4 of this book.

7.3 SIMPLE PROBABILITY ANALYSIS

This is one of the most effective and conceptually sound tools of appraising projects in case of uncertainty. However, the basic underlying assumptions on which this model has been developed are as under.

(a) There is an array of potential future returns.

(b) Managers know the probabilities of each of such possible future returns.

Thus, the difficulties encountered by managers in assigning probabilities to such an array of potential future returns may be regarded as the potential limitation of this technique of risk analysis. However, if one goes with the assumption that such probabilities can be estimated with a reasonable degree of accuracy, it goes without saying that this model enjoys the inherent advantage of being based on a foundation that is conceptually extremely strong (Hertz 1964).

Major advantage of simple probability analysis The major advantage of the simple probability analysis is its simplicity in execution.

Major disadvantage of simple probability analysis Owing to the difficulty in assigning the exact probability under different options may be the main drawback.

Example 7.1 M/s A Limited has the option of investing in only one of several projects, the details of which are given in Table E7.1. With the aid of the available data and applying the systematic probabilistic approach of project appraisal in the given scenario of uncertainty, please advise the management on the selection criterion of the projects.

TABLE E7.1

Projects	NPV or future cash value	Probabilities
Project 1	16	1.00
Project 2	20	1.00
Project 3	(16)	0.25
	36	0.50
	48	0.25
Project 4	(8)	0.25
	16	0.50
	24	0.25
Project 5	(40)	0.10
	0	0.60
	100	0.30

Note: Figures in parentheses denote negative NPV

Solution

Refer to Table E7.2.

TABLE E7.2

Project	NPV with probability (*Xi pi*)	ENPV (mean / return) = (Σ *Xi pi*)	Standard deviation (risk) σ = √Σ *pi* (*Xi* − *ENPV*)2	Remarks
1	16 × 1	16	0	Zero-risk, lower return
2	20 × 1	20	0	Zero-risk, comparatively higher return
3	−16 × 0.25, 36 × 0.5, 48 × 0.25	26	28	Higher risk, maximum return
4	−8 × 0.25, 16 × 0.5, 24 × 0.25	12	14	Lower risk, lower return
5	−40 × 0.1, 0 × 0.6, 100 × 0.3	26	59	Too risky, maximum return

ENPV: Expect net present value

Analysing Table E7.1, project 3 will be accepted for maximum return with manageable risk. A graphical representation of risk versus return of all the five projects is shown in Figure E7.1

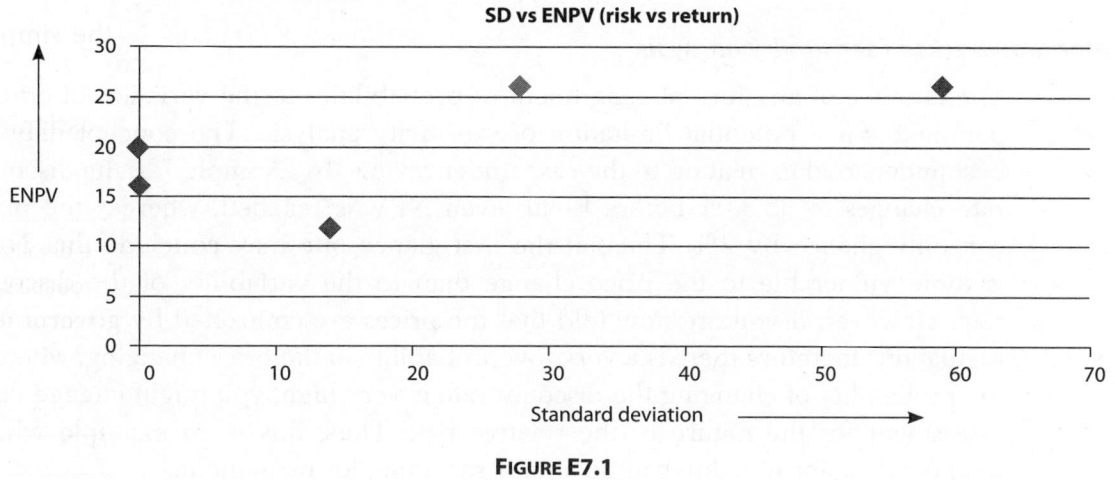

FIGURE E7.1

7.4 SENSITIVITY ANALYSIS

An approximate future outcome of an investment project is given by its NPV. To avoid conditions of improbability, a more comprehensive and practical value of NPV is required. The computation of NPV involves the analysis of some critical variables, such as the initial investment, cost of labour, hardware, etc. It would be interesting to note how NPV value (or the feasibility of a project) is influenced by the individual variables. It would be a measure of sensitivity of NPV to the changes in the variable values. For example, how would it be affected if the labour charges were to increase by 5%. This is what sensitivity analysis is concerned with.

By measuring the influence of individual variables on NPV, a comprehensive study of the nature and the extent of risks associated with the project can be derived. Sensitivity analysis helps in avoiding a negative NPV by monitoring the changes in it due to the change in the variables. Thus, it plays an important role in the success of a project.

Major advantages of sensitivity analysis

Sensitivity analysis allows decision-makers to be more informed about project sensitivities, or in other words, allows them to know the room they have for judgemental errors. Thus, they can decide whether they are in a position to accept risk. If sensitivity analysis points to some variables as more crucial than others, then the search time and the money can be concentrated with the objective of controlling and laying special emphasis on these variables. During the implementation phase of the investment process, sensitivity analysis may be used to highlight these factors, which makes a greater impact on NPV. Then these factors may be monitored more carefully in order to control major deviation from their project values.

Major drawbacks of sensitivity analysis

The absence of any formal assignment of probabilities to the variation of crucial parameters is a potential limitation of sensitivity analysis. The concept may be best understood in relation to the case under review. In Example 7.2, the discount rate changes to 33.33% before break even NPV is reached, whereas the price can only change by 2%. Thus, at the first glance one may conclude that NPV is more vulnerable to the price change than to the variability of the discount rate. However, if you are now told that the prices are controlled by government regulations therefore there is a very low probability of the price changing, whereas the probability of changing the discount rate is very high, you might change your assessment for the nature of the relative risk. Thus, this is an example where mathematical formulation can be a poor substitute for judgement.

Example 7.2   M/s X Limited is considering a capital project for selection, the relevant information about which are tabulated in Table E7.3.

Cash flow per unit = Sales price per unit – Cost per unit = Cash inflow – Cash outflow = 0.30

The finance department has estimated that the appropriate discount rate for a project of this risk class is 15%. The estimated life of the above project is 4 years. The estimated demand of the final product is about 10,00,000 units.

TABLE E7.3

Computation of cash flow per unit	Rs Cash outflow	Rs Cash inflow
Sales Price		1.0
Cost:		
Labour	0.20	
Material	0.40	
Relevant overhead	0.10	
Total cost	0.70	

TABLE E7.4

Year	Discount factor@15%
1	0.87
2	0.76
3	0.66
4	0.57
Total	2.86

The above company is a professionally managed company. With respect to project appraisal, it does not believe in simple NPV analysis and wishes to carry out a thorough sensitivity analysis before arriving at the final conclusion. Explain the approach that the company needs to follow under the given situation.

Solution

Refer to Table E7.4 for NPV computation (single point estimate).

Present value of cash in flow = $10,00,000 \times 0.3 \times 2.86 = 8,58,000$

Present value of cash out flow = Initial investment = (8,00,000)

Therefore, NPV = 58,000 (positive)

Hence the project is accepted. But here the risk exposure of the project is not considered. For that a sensitivity analysis is required to find out up to what extent various parameters like initial investment, sales price per unit, sales quantity, discount factor, etc. are sensitive with respect to NPV.

Sensitivity analysis

For initial investment (II)

$58,000 / 8,00,000 = 7.25\%$, and if initial investment increases by 7.25%, the project is not accepted.

Sales price per unit

Let cash flow per unit = x

For NPV = 0

$10,00,000 \times x \times 2.86 = 8,00,000$

Therefore, cash flow per unit = $x = 0.28$, and so the project is not accepted.

When contribution per unit is 0.3, the selling price per unit is 1.0.

Hence, when contribution per unit is 0.28 (x = cash flow per unit), then the selling price per unit will be 0.98, i.e., if the selling price is reduced by 2%, the project is not accepted.

Sales quantity

Let y = Sales quantity

$y \times 0.30 \times 2.86 = 8,00,000$

Therefore, $y = 9,32,400$

Therefore, negative NPV = $(10,00,000 - 9,32,400) / 10,00,000 = 67,600$

Hence, if demand falls by 6.67%, the project is not accepted.

Discount factor

Let z be the discount factor (annuity)

$10,00,000 \times 0.3 \times z = 8,00,000$

$z = 2.67 \rightarrow$ for 18.5%

Therefore, if discount factor increases by (18.5 − 15) / 15, i.e., 33.35%, then the project becomes unacceptable.

Sensitivity analysis of the above problem is given in Table E7.5.

TABLE E7.5

Parameter	Percentage (%)	(↑/↓)
Initial investment	7.25	↑
Selling price per unit	2	↓
Selling quantity	6.77	↓
Discount factor	33.35	↑

7.5 SCENARIO ANALYSIS

With sensitivity analysis, we change one variable at a time and look at the result. But in reality, there will hardly be any case where only one variable is changing at a time. Generally, it would be a combined effect of multiple variables and the end result would show different scenarios out of the effect of the changes of multiple variables at a time. Managers may be especially concerned about situations where a number of factors change at a time. They are often interested in establishing the worst case and the best case scenario. That is, the final NPV in situations when all the assumptions made turn out to be too optimistic, or, alternatively, when things go haywire on all fronts/assumptions. Scenario analysis basically works on similar principles as sensitivity analysis, keeping in mind that there would be more than one variable effecting the outcome of the project. Having carried out sensitivity and scenario analysis, the management has a more complete picture of the project under review. It then needs to apply the vital elements of the judgement in order to make a sound and appropriate decision.

The major advantages of scenario analysis   It has the same advantages as sensitivity analysis. It can give an idea of probable NPV of the project in three extreme phases such as boom, stable, and recession. Moreover, it is an improvement over sensitivity analysis because it considers variations in several variables together.

The major disadvantages of scenario analysis   Scenario analysis is based on the assumptions that there are only few well-defined scenarios such as (1) boom, (2) stable, and (3) recession in the case of defining economy. But this may not be true in many real-life cases as there can be a situation that is a combination of the extremes. This analysis expands the concept of estimating the expected values. Thus, in a case where there are twelve input variables, the analyst has to estimate thirty-six (3×12) expected values to do the scenario analysis (each twelve input variables for all three possible economic conditions—boom, stable, and recession). Example 7.3 illustrates this further.

Example 7.3 Unit sales price of a product would be Rs 4 per unit in good economic condition and it could sell 30,000 units in a year with a probability of 25%. For this scale of production, variable cost would be Rs 1.5 per unit. The same product would be sold at Rs 3 per unit in average economic condition and in that case it could be sold up to 25,000 units in a year with a probability of 50%. For this scale of production the variable cost would be Rs 2.5 per unit. In the case of poor economic condition, per unit sales price would be Rs 2 and the level of production would be up to 15,000 units in a year with a probability of 25%. In this case, the variable cost would be Rs 2.25 per unit. Fixed cost for all the cases would be Rs 22,000.

Find out the project's expected NPV and the project risk by analysing three possible scenarios (ignore depreciation, tax impact, and project's life in computation of risk and return).

Solution

Refer to Table E7.6.

TABLE E7.6

Scenario	Probability (p_i)	Unit sales price (Rs)	Unit sales	Variable cost per unit (Rs)	Fixed cost (Rs)	NPV_i (Rs)
Good	0.25	4.0	30,000	1.5	22,000	53,000
Average	0.5	3.0	25,000	2.5	22,000	3,000
Poor	0.25	2.5	15,000	2.25	22,000	(18,250)

Return = Expected NPV = $ENPV = \Sigma\ p_iNPV_i = (13{,}250 + 1{,}500 - 4{,}562.5) = $ Rs.10,187.5

Risk = Standard deviation = $\sigma = \sqrt{[0.25\,(53{,}000 - 10{,}187.5)^2 + 0.5\,(3{,}000 - 10{,}187.5)^2 + 0.25\,(-18{,}250 - 10{,}187.5)^2]} = $ Rs 26,196.00

Coefficient of variation = Standard deviation/Expected NPV = 2.57

The probability graph (Figure E7.2) shows the relationship of probability with the NPV and ENPV in several economic conditions given in Example 7.3.

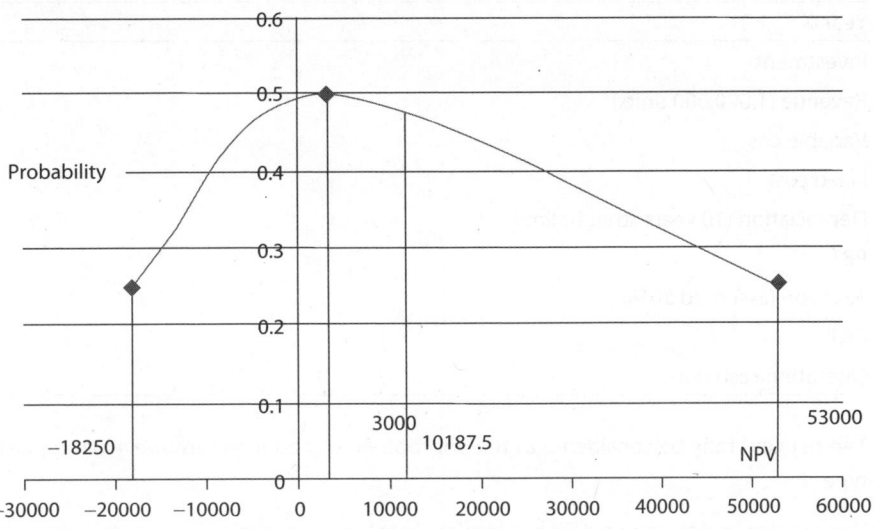

FIGURE E7.2

7.6 BREAK-EVEN ANALYSIS

It refers to the analysis of the worst state that a project can reach before it starts registering loss. Both sensitivity analysis and scenario analysis examine the situation where the worst costs and sales performance of a project is recorded. The point after which the project begins to record loss is referred to as break even point. It can be presented in both financial terms and accounting terms.

In case of financial break even point (financial BEP), the NPV of the project would be zero, as the present value of cash inflow would be equal to the present value of cash outflow. In accounting break even point (accounting BEP), the revenue earned by the project would be equal to the expenditure incurred, a situation of no profit no loss.

Advantages
1. It is logically very sound to understand and analyse the situation.
2. It is very useful for making judicious and cost-effective decision.
3. It considers the scale of economy.

Disadvantages
1. It is based on the forecasted market demand, which may differ from reality.
2. Fixed costs may change after a certain level of production.
3. Inflation factor is ignored.

Example 7.4   The relevant information pertaining to M/s Otbai's (a Japanese firm) electric scooter project is provided for your ready reference (all figures are in Rs '0,000,000).

Year 0	Year 1–10
Investment	15
Revenue (1,000,000 units)	37.5
Variable cost	30.0
Fixed cost	3.0
Depreciation (10 years straight line)	1.5
PBT	3.0
Taxation (assumed 50%)	1.5
PAT	1.5
Operating cash flow	3.0

Ten per cent may be considered as the appropriate discount factor for evaluating CAPEX proposal of this type.

You are required to carry out an appropriate break-even analysis based on the above information.

Solution

Refer to Table E7.7 and Figure E7.3.

TABLE E7.7

		Production unit	
	0	1,00,000	2,00,000
Revenue	**0**	**37.5**	**75**
Variable cost	0	30	60
Fixed cost	3	3	3
Depreciation	1.5	1.5	1.5
Profit before tax	(4.5)	3	10.5
Tax (50%)	(2.25)	1.5	5.25
Profit after tax	—	1.5	5.25
Total cost = (Tax + Variable cost + Fixed cost + Depreciation)	**2.25**	**36**	**69.75**

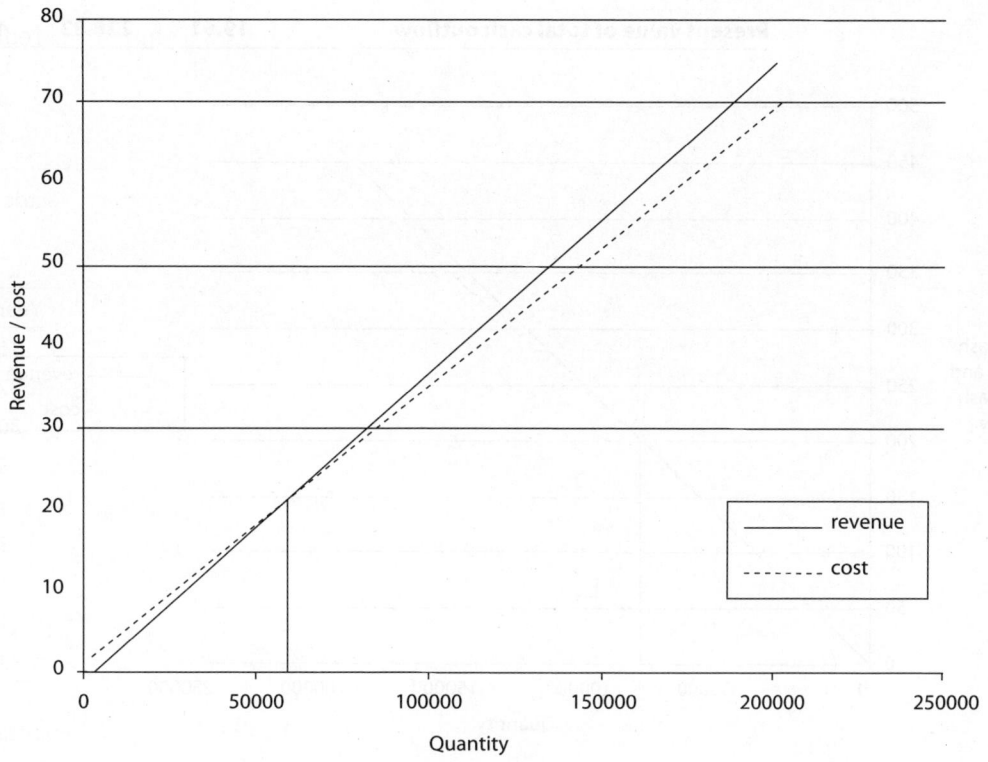

FIGURE E7.3

Financial break-even analysis has been done in Table E7.9 and Figure E7.4.

TABLE E7.8

Year	Discount factor @ 10%
1	0.91
2	0.83
3	0.75
4	0.68
5	0.12
6	0.56
7	0.51
8	0.41
9	0.42
10	0.39
Total	6.14

TABLE E7.9

	Production units		
	0	1,00,000	2,00,000
Cash inflow	0	37.5	75.0
Discount factor @10% (taken from Table E7.8)	6.14	6.14	6.14
Present value of cash inflow	**0**	**230.25**	**460.5**
Cost/cash out flow			
Variable cost	0	30	60
Fixed cost	3	3	3
Tax (50%)	(2.25)	1.5	5.25
Total cash outflow	0.75	34.5	68.25
Discount factor @10%	6.14	6.14	6.14
Present value of cash outflow	4.61	211.83	419.1
Initial investment	15	15	15
Present value of total cash outflow	**19.61**	**226.83**	**434.1**

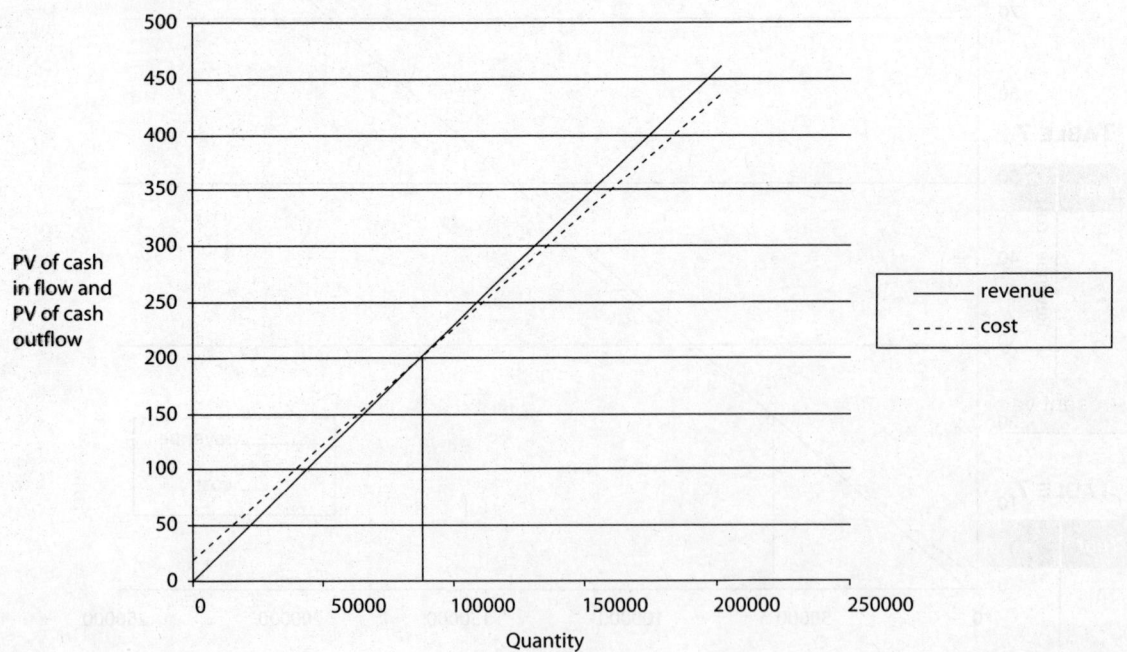

FIGURE E7.4

From Figures E7.3 and E7.4, it is clear that the financial BEP is greater than the accounting BEP mainly due to the opportunity cost of initial investment and considered depreciation as a non-cash cost element.

7.7 CERTAINTY EQUIVALENT METHOD

The certainty equivalent method says that certain cash flows that are equivalent to risky cash flows are equally attractive to investors. For example, a cash flow with an expected value of Rs 2,000 with a standard deviation of Rs 5,000 is equally valuable to a certain Rs 1,250 cash flow.

In this method, the first expected cash flows are adjusted and their certainty equivalents are evaluated after which they are discounted at the rate of risk-free rate of return. This method is based on risk and utility theory. It is the utility of the investor generated by taking one additional unit of risk. A certainty equivalent coefficient can range from 0–1. The higher the equivalent, the higher is the confidence about the expected return. On the other hand, if it is zero, it indicates that the managers are not sure about the projected cash flows.

Project A is expected to produce a cash flow of Rs 100 for each of three years (i.e., the life of the project), the risk-free interest rate is 6% and the market risk premium is 8%. The project beta is 0.75. Thus the opportunity cost of project A is $6 + 0.75(8) = 12\%$. Applying this 12% as the discount factor the NPV of project A can be computed as shown in Table 7.2.

Now, compare the figures with the cash flows of project B. Notice that B's cash flows are lower than A's. But B's flows are safe and therefore discounted applying the risk-free rate. The PV computation of project B is given in Table 7.3 and it is interesting to note that the PV of cash inflows is identical for both projects.

TABLE 7.2 Calculation of NPV of project A

Year	Cash inflow	PV @ 6%
1	94.6	89.3
2	89.6	79.7
3	84.8	71.2
Present value of cash inflows ⟶		240.2

TABLE 7.3 Calculation of NPV of project B

Year	Cash inflow	PV @ 6%
1	94.6	89.3
2	89.6	79.7
3	84.8	71.2
Present value of cash inflows ⟶		240.2

In year 1, project A has a risky cash flow of Rs 100. This has the same PV as the safe cash flow of Rs 94.6 from project B. Economists would describe Rs 94.6 as the certainty equivalent of Rs 100. Since the two cash flows have the same PV, it means that investors are willing to give up Rs 5.4, i.e., (100 – 94.6) in the form of the expected income in year 1 in order to get rid of the uncertainty.

In year 2, project A has a risky cash flow of Rs 100. B has a safe cash flow of Rs 89.6. Again both cash flows have the same PV. Thus, to eliminate the uncertainty in year 2, investors are prepared to give up Rs 10.4 (100 – 89.6) of future income. Similarly, to eliminate the uncertainty in case of the cash flows of year 3, investors are ready to sacrifice Rs 15.2 of future income (100 – 71.2).

Now, in order to value project A, we have discounted each cash flow at the same risk-adjusted discount rate of 12%. The implication is that we have effectively made a larger deduction for risk from the later cash flows. The second year cash flow is riskier than the first because it is exposed to two years of market risk. The third year cash flow is even more risky applying the same logic. This increased risk is automatically reflected in the steadily declining certainty equivalent.

Figure 7.1 depicts the relationship between the certainty equivalent method and the risk-adjusted discount rate.

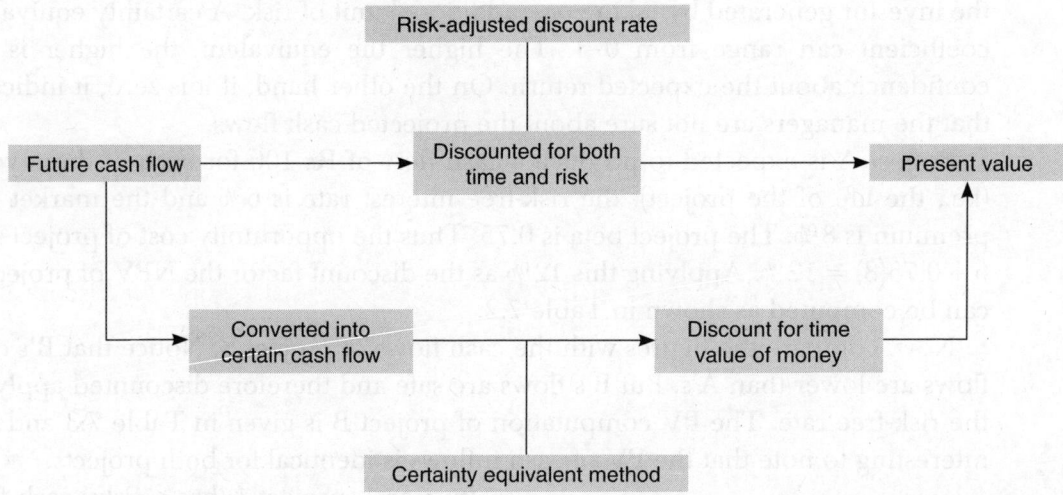

FIGURE 7.1 Relationship between certainty equivalent method and risk-adjusted discount rate

The major advantages of certainty equivalent method In this method, certainty equivalent coefficient of every individual year depends on the extent of risk vis-à-vis its cash flow. It is a more conceptually sound method than the risk-adjusted discount rate method (discussed next in this chapter), as it does not presuppose that risk increases at a constant rate with respect to time.

Major disadvantages of certainty equivalent method Although it is conceptually superior to the risk-adjusted discount rate method, the latter is more popular amongst professionals as it is easier to manage the discount rate. Also, specification of a series of certainty equivalent coefficient is a cumbersome process.

7.8 RISK-ADJUSTED DISCOUNT RATE METHOD

It is widely accepted that investors require a return in excess of the risk-free rate as compensation for taking on a risky investment. This concept is used in both portfolio theory and the capital asset pricing model (discussed in detail in section 7.14). The amount of risk premium expected by an investor increases with the increase in the risk factor. According to Grayson (1967), risk preference should be considered as one of the two parts of the discount rate (the other being time preference), while using discounted cash flow (DCF) investment analysis methods. Although this approach appears impressive, its major drawback lies in the computation of the amount of the risk premium that varies from one project to another.

One of the ways to deal with it is by first dividing the given projects into their respective risk class and then initiating the discounting process as per the different risk classes. However, determination of the project risk is a difficult process. Computing the discount rate for different risk classes is yet another problem. An alternative way of dealing with this situation would be to presuppose that the average risk of the current business is taken as the average risk of new investment projects. In this manner, all the investment projects can be discounted using a single overall rate, which would usually be the weighted average cost of capital (WACC).

According to the risk-adjusted discount rate method, the project risk increases with time at a constant rate. In some cases, these assumptions may be true and constant risk allowance would be applicable and the risk-adjusted discount rate should reduce with the passage of time. However, this assumption may not be true for risk profile of all investment projects. In such a situation, the risk-adjusted discount rate method would yield incorrect and misleading results. Since the risk is highest during the launch of a project, higher risk premium would be applicable. As the project nears its completion, the risk premium should decline at a constant rate.

Major advantage of risk-adjusted discount rate It is very popular and is commonly applied in practice due to its simplicity and convenience. It is easier to manage the discount rate that considers both risk and time.

Major disadvantages of risk-adjusted discount rate It is difficult to estimate the risk-adjusted discount rate for a project consistently—often it is determined in an ad hoc and arbitrary manner. This method wrongly assumes that risk increases at a constant rate with time.

7.9 HILLER MODEL

Hiller (1963) first introduced the difference between the expected NPV and the standard deviation of NPV with the help of deviation of standard deviation of NPV and expected NPV. This is possible when there is no correlation among cash flows as well as when there is a perfect correlation among them.

Hiller model can be used when a relationship can be established within expected cash flows. They can be either uncorrelated or they can be perfectly correlated with each other. When the expected NPV and the standard deviation of NPV may be obtained through analytical derivation, then this model can be used. Under certain circumstances, the expected NPV and the standard deviation of the NPV may be obtained through analytical derivation. Two cases of such analysis are discussed here:

1. Uncorrelated cash flows
2. Perfectly correlated cash flows

Let us now understand these two cases in detail.

Uncorrelated cash flows When there is no correlation between expected cash flows, expected NPV (ENPV) and standard deviation of NPV (σ_{NPV}) can be calculated as follows:

$$ENPV = \sum_{t=0}^{n} \frac{CF_t}{(1+i)^t} - 1 \qquad (7.1)$$

$$\sigma_{NPV} = \sum_{t=0}^{n} \left[\frac{\sigma_t^2}{(1+i)^{2t}} \right]^{1/2} \qquad (7.2)$$

where,

$ENPV$ = expected net present value

CF_t = expected cash flow for year t

I = initial outlay

i = discount rate

σ_t = standard deviation for the cash flow for year t

σ_{NPV} = standard deviation for the NPV

Note that in the above formulae, the discount rate is the risk-free interest rate because we try to separate the time value of money and the risk factor. The risk of the project reflected in σ_{NPV} is considered in conjunction with ENPV computed with the risk-free discount rate. If ENPV is computed with risk-adjusted discount rate and then if this is viewed along with σ_{NPV}, the risk factor would be counted twice.

Example 7.5 LIG Inc. is considering whether to invest Rs 1,25,000 in an investment proposal to add a new product to its existing product lines. The management forecasts that the new product will generate incremental net cash flows, each of which is assumed to be normally distributed random variables with the following parameters. The data is given in Table E7.10.

TABLE E7.10

Year	Expected cash inflows (Rs)	Standard deviation (Rs)
1	44,000	8,800
2	40,000	7,600
3	40,000	8,000
4	35,000	6,000
5	30,000	5,000

If discount rate applicable to the company is 10%, find out:

(I)   The mean of the present value distribution and its standard deviation

(II) The probability that the project would have a negative NPV

(III) The chances that the NPV would be at least Rs 18,000

(IV) Whether the project should be undertaken if the top management has laid down that no project would be under taken unless it has a 70% chance of giving an NPV of Rs 24,000

Solution

(i)   Expected NPV $= ENPV = \sum\limits_{t=0}^{n} \dfrac{CF_t}{(1+i)^t} - 1$

$= 44{,}000 / 1.10 + 40{,}000 / (1.10)^2 + 40{,}000 / (1.10)^3 + 35{,}000 / (1.10)^4 + 30{,}000 / (1.10)^5 - 125{,}000$

$=$ Rs 20,640

Standard deviation $= \sigma_{NPV} = \sum\limits_{t=0}^{n} \left[\dfrac{\sigma_t^2}{(1+i)^{2t}} \right]^{1/2}$

$= [7{,}74{,}40{,}000 / (1.10)^2 + 5{,}77{,}60{,}000 / (1.10)^4 + 6{,}40{,}00{,}000 / (1.10)^6 + 3{,}60{,}00{,}000 / (1.10)^8 +$
$25{,}00{,}00{,}000 / (1.10)^{10}]^{1/2}$

$=$ Rs 12,884.5

(ii) $Z = \dfrac{0 - 20{,}640}{12{,}884.5} = -1.602$

Probability that the project would have a negative NPV (based on standard normal distribution table or Z-value) $= 0.5 - 0.4474 = 0.0526$

(iii) $Z = \dfrac{18{,}000 - 20{,}640}{12{,}884.5} = -1.21$

Area corresponding to $Z = 0.0832$

Thus $p(NPV > $ Rs $18{,}000) = 0.0832 + 0.5 = 0.5832$ i.e. 58.32%

(iv) $Z = \dfrac{24{,}000 - 20{,}640}{12{,}884.5} = 0.2607$

Area corresponding to $Z = 0.1026$

Thus, $p(NPV > $ Rs $24{,}000) = 0.1026 + 0.5 = 0.6026$, i.e., 60.26%

Since this is only 60.36%, which is less than the required 70%, the project may not be acceptable to top management.

Perfectly correlated cash flows When the correlation between the expected cash flows of a project is hundred per cent perfect, the patterns of expected cash flows for the entire life of the project would be similar. It means that cash flows throughout the project life are linearly correlated to each other. The mean of NPV of the project and the standard deviation of the NPV in that case would be as follows:

$$ENPV = \sum_{t=0}^{n} \frac{CF_t}{(1+i)^t} - 1 \tag{7.3}$$

$$\sigma_{NPV} = \sum_{t=0}^{n} \left[\frac{\sigma_t}{(1+i)^t} \right] \tag{7.4}$$

All the terms in Eqns (7.3) and (7.4) are defined in this chapter.

Example 7.6 An investment project involves a current outlay of Rs 15,000. The mean and standard deviation of the cash flows, which are perfectly correlated, are given in Table E7.11. Calculate ENPV and σNPV, assuming a risk-free interest rate of 5%.

TABLE E7.11

Year	CFt (Rs)	σ_t (Rs)
1	6,000	1,500
2	4,000	1,000
3	5,000	2,000
4	3,000	1,500

Solution

$$ENPV = \sum_{t=1}^{n} \frac{CF_t}{(1+i)^t} - 1$$

$$= \frac{6000}{(1.05)} + \frac{4000}{(1.05)^2} + \frac{5000}{(1.05)^3} + \frac{3000}{(1.05)^4} - 15000 = Rs\ 1{,}132.03$$

$$\sigma_{NPV} = \sum_{t=1}^{n} \frac{\sigma_t^2}{(1+i)^t}$$

$$= \frac{1500}{(1.05)} + \frac{1000}{(1.05)^2} + \frac{2000}{(1.05)^3} + \frac{1500}{(1.05)^4} = Rs\ 5{,}298.75$$

7.10 SIMULATION ANALYSIS

We have studied the effect on NPV due to the change in one variable. Here, it is assumed that when one factor is variable, the others are constant. If one were to determine the value NPV for all the values of all the variable factors, then several NPV values would be derived. This makes the sensitivity analysis dysfunctional.

The simulation process (also known as Monte Carlo Simulation) helps in overcoming the difficulties faced by sensitivity analysis. This method requires that the structure and the logic of the problem associated with the investment be mentioned. This flexible operation research tool has been found effective in appraisal of risk-prone capital investments.

Simulation involves designing, creating, and using a model of the real system. It mirrors the real-world system in order to look into the random events in time that are faced by the investment projects under analysis. It puts to use a mathematical model that monitors the changing factors related to the project.

In the real world, events associated with risk do not follow a fixed pattern. The value of simulation analysis lies in its ability to deal with the random nature of events. Imitation of the random events affecting the output makes their study easier. A possible solution of a random event is arrived in some probability distribution. Say, there are the four variables associated with an investment project. Simulation analysis lists the range of values to which these variables can deviate, along with the probability of deviation.

While using simulation, the manager or decision-maker should

1. Define the problem.
2. Identify the fixed and variable factors.
3. Identify the various courses of action available.
4. Construct a mathematical model incorporating all the variables.
5. Decide on the best possible course of action.

Major advantages of simulation analysis   It is able to deal with the random nature of the factors associated with investment projects. It can handle endogenous variables, exogenous variables, and the complex interrelationship between them. It brings to light the uncertainties among various factors governing a project.

Major disadvantages of simulation analysis   The imitation of a real-world system is not an easy task. The probability distribution of exogenous variables is by nature imprecise. Creation of a realistic simulation model, which is both complex and difficult, requires scientific expertise. The management usually is not equipped to undertake this process themselves. And hence, this method often does not find favour with them.

To explain this better, we will use the following example. Suppose the McGraw Mount Manufacturing Company is evaluating an investment proposal that has uncertainty associated with all the three major aspects: the initial investment or the original cost; the useful life; and the annual cash flows. The probability distributions of all the three variables are given in Table 7.4.

The firm's cost of capital is 15% and the risk-free rate is 12%. The finance committee feels that these two values are likely to remain unchanged throughout the life of the projects, as given in Table 7.5.

The NPV of the investment using the step-by-step procedure would be as follows. Since, the definition of the problem and identification of the fixed and variable factors have already been done, we will start with the third step.

Step 3

The courses of action available are:

TABLE 7.4   Probability distributions

Original cost			Useful life			Annual net cash flow		
Value (Rs lakhs)	Probability	Cumulative probability	Values (years)	Probability	Cumulative probability	Value (Rs lakhs)	Probability	Cumulative probability
9.00	0.10	0.10	7.00	0.20	0.20	2.00	0.20	0.20
7.00	0.60	0.70	6.00	0.40	0.60	2.50	2.40	0.60
6.00	0.30	1.00	5.00	0.40	1.00	1.50	1.10	0.70
						1.00	0.30	1.00

TABLE 7.5   Probability distributions

Original cost			Useful life			Annual net cash flow		
Value (Rs lakhs)	Probability	Cumulative probability	Values (years)	Probability	Cumulative probability	Value (Rs lakhs)	Probability	Cumulative probability
9.00	0.10	0.10	7.00	0.20	0.20	2.00	0.20	0.20
7.00	0.60	0.70	6.00	0.40	0.60	2.50	2.40	0.60
6.00	0.30	1.00	5.00	0.40	1.00	1.50	1.10	0.70

(i) Go ahead if the expected NPV is positive.

(ii) Drop the investment plan if the expected NPV is less than or equal to zero.

Step 4

The mathematical model that suits this problem is the usual NPV formula:

$$ENPV = \sum_{t=1}^{n} \frac{CF_t}{(1+i)^t} - I \qquad (7.5)$$

where,

$ENPV$ = expected net present value

CF_t = expected cash flow for year t

I = initial outlay

i = discount rate

Step 5

This step in turn contains of five phases.

Phase I

In the first phase, the cumulative probability of each value that can be taken by the variables should be calculated. This makes the allocations of the random numbers easy.

Phase II

In the second phase, a range of random numbers are chosen, depending on how the simulation is proposed to be run. If it is proposed to run using two-digit random numbers, the range chosen should be 10 to 99, if three-digit numbers are to be chosen, the range should be 100 to 999, and so on. The random numbers may be chosen from tables, generated using a computer or simply by a lottery. For the example taken, we will use two-digit random numbers.

Phase III

In the third phase, the random numbers are distributed to each value of the variables. The allocation will be in proportion to the probability associated to each of the variables. In the example (Table 7.6), the range chosen is 10 to 99, should be allocated to each of the values of the variables. The number range allocated to each of the values of a variable depends on the value's cumulative probability. The number range for the first value starts at zero. If the probability is, say, 0.10, as is the case with the first value of original cost in the example, the numbers will be 0 to 9. For the second value of original cost, the cumulative probability is 0.70, which indicates that the number range ends at 69, and begins at the next number after it ended for the first value, i.e., at 10. The number range for the second value will therefore be 10 to 69. Similarly, the range for the third value is 70 to 99. The random numbers for the remaining two variables can also be decided on the same lines, starting with zero.

TABLE 7.6 Random number range

Original cost				Useful life				Annual net cash flow			
Value (Rs lakhs)	Original pro-bability	Cumu-lative pro-bability	Random no. range	Value (years)	Original pro-bability	Cumu-lative pro-bability	Random no. range	Value (Rs lakhs)	Original pro-bability	Cumu-lative pro-bability	Random no. range
9.00	0.10	0.10	0 to 9	7.00	0.20	0.20	0 to 9	2.00	0.20	0.20	0 to 19
7.00	0.60	0.60	10 to 69	6.00	0.40	0.60	20 to 59	2.50	0.60	0.60	20 to 59
6.00	0.30	0.30	70 to 99	5.00	0.40	1.00	60 to 99	1.50	0.70	0.70	60 to 69
								1.00	1.00	1.00	70 to 99

Phase IV

Running the model in the fourth phase, random numbers are generated. We use the following random number table for our simulation. Refer to Table 7.7.

A random number table can be read anyway that is convenient. We select the first three columns and read the values horizontally. The numbers in the first,

TABLE 7.7 Table of random numbers

52	06	50	88	53	30	10	47	99	37	66	91	35	32	00	84	57	07
37	63	28	02	74	35	24	03	29	60	74	85	90	73	59	55	17	60
82	57	68	28	05	94	03	11	27	79	90	87	92	41	09	25	36	77
69	02	36	49	71	99	32	10	75	21	95	90	94	38	97	71	72	49
98	94	90	36	06	78	23	76	89	85	29	21	25	73	69	34	85	76
96	52	62	87	49	56	59	23	78	71	72	90	57	01	98	57	31	95
33	69	27	21	11	60	95	89	68	48	17	89	34	09	93	50	44	51
50	33	50	95	13	44	34	62	64	39	55	29	30	64	49	44	30	16
88	32	18	5	62	57	34	56	62	31	15	40	90	34	51	95	26	14
90	30	36	24	69	82	51	74	30	35	36	85	01	55	92	64	09	85
50	48	61	18	85	23	08	54	17	12	80	69	24	84	92	15	49	59
27	88	21	62	69	64	48	31	12	73	02	68	00	16	16	46	13	85
45	14	46	32	13	49	66	62	74	41	86	98	92	98	84	54	33	40
81	02	01	78	82	74	97	37	45	31	94	99	42	49	27	64	89	42
66	83	14	74	27	76	03	33	11	97	59	81	72	00	64	61	13	52
74	05	81	82	93	09	96	33	52	78	13	06	28	30	94	23	37	39
30	74	87	01	74	11	46	82	59	94	25	34	32	23	17	01	58	73
59	55	72	33	62	13	74	68	22	44	42	09	32	46	71	79	45	89
67	09	80	98	99	25	77	50	03	32	36	63	65	75	94	19	95	88
60	77	46	63	71	69	44	22	03	85	14	48	69	13	30	500	33	24
60	08	19	29	36	72	30	27	50	64	85	72	75	29	87	05	75	01
80	45	86	99	02	34	87	08	86	84	49	76	24	08	01	86	29	11
53	84	49	63	26	65	72	84	85	63	26	02	75	26	92	62	40	67
69	84	12	94	51	36	17	02	15	29	16	52	56	43	26	22	08	62
37	77	13	10	02	18	31	19	32	85	31	94	81	43	31	58	33	51

Source: A Million Random Digits with 1,00,000 Normal Deviates, The Free Press, 1955, p. 7.

second, and the third columns from the left end will be used for original cost, useful life, and annual net cash flows, respectively.

The first value of the first column is 52. It falls in the range of 10 to 69 allocated for the value of Rs 7 lakh. So, in the first run, the value of original cost will be Rs 7 lakh. We now proceed to the right, i.e., to the first reading in the second column. The reading is 06, and falls in the range of 0 to 19, which indicates that the useful life for the first run is seven years. Moving further right, we read the first number in the third column, which, being in the range of 20 to 59, indicates that the annual net cash flow value for the first run to be Rs 2.5 lakh. This completes the first run. Once all the variables are known, the NPV for the first run is calculated using the mathematical model. It should be remembered that the discounting should be done using the risk-free rate.

For the second run, we have to start again from the first column, this time with the second value in the column (i.e., 37) and proceed to the right, on the same lines as in the first run. The model in the example has been run for ten times to get the output given in Table 7.8.

TABLE 7.8 Expected net present value

Run	Original cost		Useful life		Annual net cash flows (Rs lakhs)	Net present value (Rs lakhs)
	Random number	Corresponding value (Rs lakhs)	Random number	Corresponding value		
1	52	7	6	7	2.5	4.41
2	37	7	63	5	2.5	2.01
3	82	6	57	6	1.5	0.17
4	69	7	2	7	2.5	4.41
5	98	6	94	5	1.0	−2.4
6	96	6	52	6	1.5	0.17
7	33	7	69	5	2.5	2.01
8	50	7	33	6	2.5	3.28
9	88	6	32	6	2.0	2.22
10	90	6	30	6	2.5	4.28
Expected net present value						2.06

Phase V

The final phase is to interpret the output from the model. In this case, the output (expected NPV) is positive and hence the firm may proceed with the project.

7.11 DECISION TREE ANALYSIS

In this method, a decision tree is constituted to give a better presentation of related information connected with an investment proposal. Investment decisions in practice are quite complicated, especially because the outcomes are not certain. Further, the projections of the future are dependant upon the outcomes of the present. For example, the net risk flows arising in the future may be dependant on the net cash flows of the earlier years. To be more specific, the net cash out flows of the second year may be dependant on the net cash outflows of the first year. The net cash outflows of the first year itself are dependant on certain events and this makes all the future events as well as their expected consequences dependent on each other. A decision tree here helps to simplify the decision-making process.

Figure 7.2 depicts the various steps of decision tree analysis.

Major advantages of decision tree analysis To analyse situations where sequential decision-making in the face of risk is involved, the decision tree analysis is a useful tool. It is a step-by-step approach that helps the analyst understand what can be done at each point of the decision. It is a better presentation of information related to any investment proposal.

Major disadvantages of decision tree analysis It requires a huge amount of information before it can be applied. Therefore, it becomes difficult to apply the method to a new or a green project, where the firm has very little information on how the market will respond to it. When investments are gradually met over a period of time, instead of investing in well-defined stages, decision trees are also not easy to construct and apply.

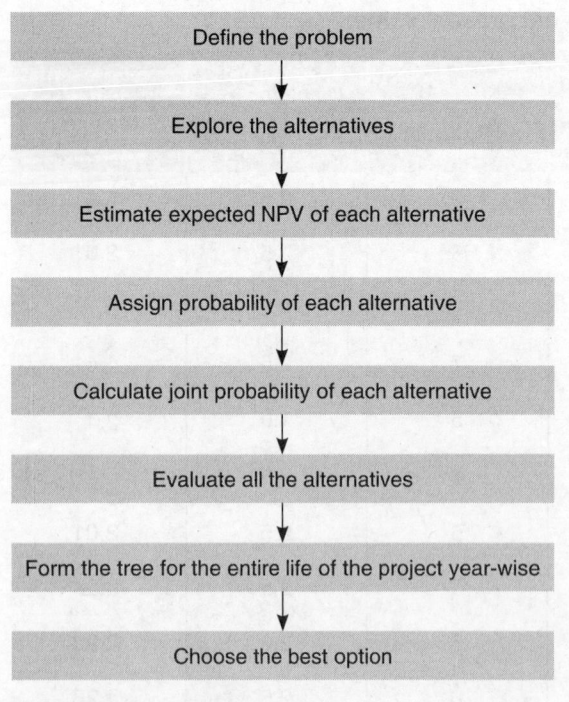

FIGURE 7.2   Steps of decision tree analysis

Example 7.7   M/s Horizon Ltd buys old pubs and invests a great deal of money in their renovation and publicity. It then sells the pub at the end of the two years in what it hopes is in a transformed and thriving state. The management is planning to buy a pub close to a university campus. The purchasing costs (at time zero) would be Rs 5,00,000. The cost of renovation is paid at the outset to the shop fitting firm, which is something that Horizon Ltd always does in order to obtain a discount, and this amounts to another Rs 2,00,000 at the end of the year zero.

Experience has taught the management team of Horizon that pub retailing is a very unpredictable game. Customers are fickle and the slightest change in the fashion would drastically bring down the level of customers. Through a mixture of objective historical data analysis and subjective expert judgement, the managers concluded that there is a 60% probability that the pub will become an attractive place for the targeted customers and there is 40% chance that the potential customers will shy away from the revamped pub. The following data is with respect to the first year operation. The net cash flow of year 1 is as in Table E7.12.

TABLE E7.12

	Probability	Net cash flow
Good customer response	0.6	100,000
Poor customer response	0.4	10,000

If the response of the customers is good in the first year then there are three possibilities for the second year. The customer flow will increase further and the pub can be sold at the end of the second year for a large sum of money. The total of the net operating cash flow of the second year and the sale proceeds will be as high as Rs 2,00,000. This has a probability of 10%.

(a) Customer levels will be the same as in the first year and at the end of the second year, total cash flow will be Rs 16,00,000. The probability stands at 70%.

(b) Many customers will abandon the pub. This may happen considering the competition factor, or perhaps due to the fashion changes. This will have a negative impact on the net cash flow at the end of the second year. It can come down to Rs 8,00,000 only. This outcome will have a 20% chance of occurring.

If however the response in the first year is poor then one of the following two eventualities may occur in the second year:

(a) Matters continue to deteriorate and sales fall further. At the end of the second year, the cash flow from trading and sale of the pub will total only Rs 7,00,000. This will have a 50% probability.

(b) In the second year, sales may rise resulting in a year 2 net cash flow of Rs 12,00,000. This will have a 50% probability.

You may consider appropriate discount factor of 10% for computational purposes.

Solution

Decision tree: Refer to Figure E7.5 and Table E7.13 (computation of ENPV).

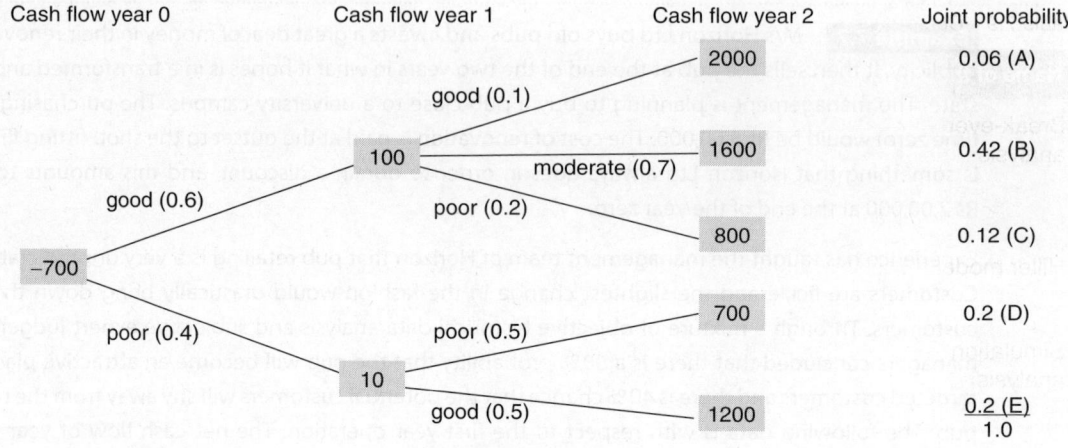

FIGURE E7.5

TABLE E7.13

Outcome	Calculation	NPV	Probability	ENPV
A	$-700 + (100 / 1.1) + (2000 / (1.1)^2) =$	1044	0.06	63
B	$-700 + (100 / 1.1) + (1600 / (1.1)^2) =$	713	0.42	300
C	$-700 + (100 / 1.1) + (800 / (1.1)^2) =$	52	0.12	6
D	$-700 + (10 / 1.1) + (700 / (1.1)^2) =$	−112	0.2	−23
E	$-700 + (10 / 1.1) + (1200 / (1.1)^2) =$	301	0.2	60
Total			1	406 (positive NPV)

Standard deviation of the project:

$$\sigma = \sqrt{[0.06\,(63 - 406)^2 + 0.42\,(300 - 406)^2 + 0.12\,(6 - 406)^2 + 0.2\,(-23 - 406)^2 + 0.2\,(60 - 406)^2]}$$

$$\sigma = 302.87$$

Table 7.9 gives a comparative analysis specifying the situation for which each model would be best suited.

TABLE 7.9   Risk analysis mode

Name of the model	Situation where applicable
Sensitivity analysis	Since the future is unknown, somebody wants to know what will be the feasibility or viability of the project, when some variable like sales or investment deviates from its expected value.
Scenario analysis	In the previous model, typically one variable is varied at a time. If variables are inter-related, i.e. there are more than one variable at a time, then it will be helpful to look at some plausible scenarios, wherein each scenario depicts a combination of variables.

Contd

Table 7.9   *Contd*

Name of the model	Situation where applicable
Break-even analysis	As a finance person, he or she might be interested in knowing how much should be manufactured and sold at a minimum to ensure that the project does not lose money. To know the answer to this basic question, one should have undergone this particular model.
Hiller model	When the expected NPV and the standard deviation of NPV may be obtained through analytical derivation, then this model can be used.
Simulation analysis	Sensitivity analysis is useful but may not be adequate for decision-making. If the decision-maker would also like to know the likelihood of different sensitive occurrences, then simulation can provide the best possible answer.
Decision tree analysis	To analyse situations where sequential decision-making in the face of risk is involved, decision tree analysis is a useful tool.
Risk-adjusted discount rate method	The risk-adjusted discount rate is commonly employed in practice. Firms use different discount rates for different types of investment projects. In that case, a risk-adjusted discount rate is the only solution.
Certainty equivalent method	When the risk-free rate is applied for discounting purposes and the expected cash flow of the project are converted into their certainty equivalent, then it will be useful.

7.12 CAPITAL RATIONING

If all the projects that a firm chooses to undertake have positive NPV, then the wealth of its shareholders would be maximum. This idea is central to capital budgeting. However, such a choice (of only positive NPV projects) appears hypothetical. In real situations, a company may have to accept projects that do not have the desired NPV. This is called capital rationing problem. As the capital is rationed, the company needs to select a combination of projects (not just positive NPV projects) in such a way that they are both within the budget of the company and yield the highest possible NPV. (Also refer to Chapter 5.)

Example 7.8   A company has opportunity cost of capital of 10% and it has the following options to evaluate where the life of all three projects are 2 years and each of such project is divisible in nature (this would mean that if only 50% of project B is undertaken, its NPV would be 80,00,000) (given in Table E7.14).

TABLE E7.14

Figures in Rs ('000,000)

Projects	Cash flow year 0	Cash flow year 1	Cash flow year 2	NPV@ 10% DF
A	−10	30	5	21 positive
B	−5	5	20	16 positive
C	−5	5	15	12 positive

Solution

All three projects are attractive but suppose the firm is capable of spending Rs 10,00,000 only. In that case it can invest in any one of the projects. Although individually B and C have lower NPV than A, when taken together they generate a higher NPV. Thus, in this case we cannot choose a project solely on the basis of NPV. When funds are limited, we need to get the maximum out of our investment. In other words, we need to choose the project that gives the highest NPV per rupee in the initial outlay, i.e., on the basis of profitability index.

Now, as per the computation, P/I are as follows. Project A = 3.1, Project B = 4.2, and Project C = 3.4 (as computed). Thus, project B has the highest P/I and Project C has the next higher P/I. Hence, these two projects are needed to be accepted under a situation of resource constraints in order to achieve a maximum possible NPV.

Limitations of capital rationing method   From Example 7.8, we can conclude that the ranking obtained suffers from certain deficiencies. For example, if the projects are not divisible by nature, the decision parameter is not P/I but NPV once again.

Moreover, the ranking methodology as mentioned above fails when more than one resource is rationed, which is a common phenomenon under real-life circumstances.

Example 7.9   Now, suppose the above mentioned firm can raise Rs 10,00,000 for years 0 and 1 and that the possible menu of project is as shown under. It is actually the identical example as shown earlier along with another additional project, namely D, which has a life of 1 year requiring an initial outlay in year 1 only. However, in this case, we are assuming that all the projects are of indivisible variety (given in Table E7.15).

TABLE E7.15

Projects	Cash flow year 0	Cash flow year 1	Cash flow year 2	NPV and P/I
A	−10	30	5	21 and 3.1
B	−5	5	20	16 and 4.2
C	−5	5	15	12 and 3.4
D	0	−40	60	13 and 1.4

Solution

Now, let us see the problem. One strategy is to accept project B and C in year 0 as we had done earlier. However, if we do this, we cannot accept D also, which costs more than our budget limit of year 1.

An alternative is to accept project A in year 0. Although this has a lower NPV than the combination of B and C, it provides a positive cash flow of Rs 30,00,000 in year 1. When this is added to the Rs 10,00,000 budget of year 1, then we can afford to take up project D.

Now A and D both have a lower P/I than B and C but have a higher NPV than B and C. The reason that P/I ranking fails in this example is because the resources are constrainted in the first two years.

In fact, the ranking of projects is inadequate whenever there is any other constraint on the choice of the project.

Linear programming in capital rationing problems Linear programming techniques (LPP) may be applied to handle capital rationing problems of this variety. Students should also note that divisional or fractional projects are quite uncommon in practical life and we generally deal with non-divisible capital investment in real life. Moreover, in real life, if we ever come across divisible propositions, the cash flow stream may not be exactly proportional to the size of the project and yet, this is what the P/I approach implicitly assumes.

Although LPP models seem to be tailor-made for solving capital budgeting problems when resources are in short supply, unfortunately, the technique is not very common in terms of industry applications. One reason is that these models are often not cheap to use. Moreover, as with any sophisticated long-range planning tool, there is the general problem of getting good data. It is just not worth applying expensive methods to poor quality data. Furthermore, these models are based on the assumption that the manager is aware of all the future investment opportunities. In reality, the discovery of investment ideas is an unfolding exercise.

Capital rationing can be possible in two ways: soft rationing and hard rationing.

Soft rationing Rationing can be done in the soft approach by taking lesser risk. Obviously it will generate lower expected NPV. It is a more traditional and comparatively safer approach. Here people can generate a decent amount of NPV by taking little risk.

Hard rationing Here rationing is done in a strict and calculative way, with the motive of higher expected NPV. It is needless to say that it creates more risk.

Hard rationing relates to capital from external source. Agencies external to the firm may not provide unlimited amount of investment capital even though positive NPV projects are identified. In a perfect capital market, hard rationing should never occur because if a firm has positive NPV projects, ideally it would be able to raise any amount of finance it needs. Hard rationing therefore implies market imperfections, which is predominant in India.

7.13 RISK AND UTILITY

Utility theory recognizes that money in itself is unimportant to human beings. What is important is the well-being, satisfaction, or utility that can be derived from money. For most people, doubling of annual income will not double annual well-being. Money is basically used to buy goods and services.

Let us take an example where the first Rs 10,000 of income will buy the most essential items (food, clothing, shelter, etc.). Thus, an individual going from an income zero to Rs 10,000 will experience a large increase in utility. If income is further increased by another Rs 10,000, then the utility will increase but the extent of increase would be less than the first Rs 10,000 because the goods and services bought with the second Rs 10,000 provide less additional satisfaction as compared to the first. Thus, if the process of adding incremental amounts to the annual income continues, the incremental utility from each of such process will decrease gradually.

In general for most people the additional utility from consumption diminishes as consumption increases. This concept is actually known as the concept of diminishing marginal utility (Newmann and Morgenstern 1944; Hammond 1967). The concept is explained further in the numerical example given in Table 7.10.

TABLE 7.10   Investment return with probabilities in various economic conditions

Conditions	Investment A		Investment A	
	Return (Rs)	Prob.	Return (Rs)	Prob.
Poor economic conditions	2,000	0.50	0.0	0.50
Good economic conditions	6,000	0.50	8,000	0.50
Expected return	4,000		4,000	

It may be noted that both investments give an expected return of Rs 4,000, but the outcome of investment B is more widely dispersed. In other words, B is riskier than A. An investor will receive Rs 2,000 less for investment in the year with poor economic conditions, whereas he will get Rs 2,000 more under good economic conditions. The question now is that for an investor, which investment is preferable? The answer hinges on the concept of diminishing marginal utility. While investment A and B have the same expected return, they do have different utility. The extra utility associated with B in the year with good economic conditions is small compared to the loss of utility in bad economic conditions with respect to the said investment. Thus, in this case, A may be preferred, because the utility is higher for the first Rs 2,000 in bad economic conditions as compared to the loss of the second Rs 2,000 under good economic conditions.

Risk-averse investors vs risk-loving investors   Risk-averse investors prefer to invest by diminishing marginal utility. A risk-lover investor prefers to choose risky investments. According to them, the marginal utility of every rupee rises with the passage of time. Despite their differences, both risk-averse investors and risk-lover investors are intelligent individuals who seek proper value and return for their investments. Therefore, in finance-related investments, most investors are risk averse.

This can be understood in relation to Example 7.1 (probability analysis).

The above concept may effectively be applied while taking a decision about selecting project 2 or project 3. In order to know which project would be chosen, knowledge of the specific utility characteristics of the decision-maker is useful. Some adventurous individuals may be willing to take a higher risk if rewards are high and hence accept project 3. Whereas, others will be risk-averse and accept project 2.

7.14 PORTFOLIO THEORY AND CAPITAL ASSET PRICING MODEL IN CAPITAL BUDGETING

A firm may have different types of projects. Generally, cash flows of all these projects held by a firm may be correlated, i.e., cash flow of a project may affect the cash flows of all or some of the projects of the firm. Therefore, it is essential to treat all the projects of the firm as a portfolio. A new project, though having a positive NPV, may have a perfect correlation with the firm's existing projects, thereby increasing the risk of the firm. Whereas, a project having a negative NPV may have a negative correlation with the cash flow of the existing project, thus reducing the overall risk of the firm. Thus, if a new project is evaluated as an addition to the existing portfolio of the projects, it may lead to a better decision. Therefore, the portfolio theory is an important tool in project management.

7.15 TAXATION INTERFACES IN CAPEX DECISION-MAKING PROCESS

Capital expenditure (CAPEX) involves huge amount of capital investment as well as returns in the name of profit. This ultimately boils down to the involvement of tax computations. The firm has to be pinched by the large amount of tax botheration; at the same time it cannot be ignored. Governments offer several policies by which a firm can enjoy various tax benefits. The following section deals with different tax interfaces related to the CAPEX decision-making process.

7.15.1 Interfaces with Existing Tax Provisions (Central Excise Duty)

Excise duty is the major source of revenue for the Government of India and it is in the nature of an indirect tax levy. An indirect tax (as distinguished from the direct tax) is a tax levied on the products or services, the incidence of which is borne by the consumer who ultimately consumes the products/services. Excise duty is a duty on the production of goods within India. The duty is levied on the manufacturer in respect of commodities produced or manufactured by him/her. Thus, it is a tax on the manufacture of goods and not upon sale.

7.15.2 The Concept of Value Added Tax and Cenvat

Before we discuss the concept of value added tax (VAT), it is important to consider the reasons for its introduction. Every stage in the processing of a raw material has certain characteristics. One level prepares the product for the next level. Many such levels eventually lead to the finished product. Now if a manufacturer

A, instead of undertaking all these stages himself, purchases the material (raw or processed to some level) from manufacturer B, then the output of manufacturer B becomes the input of manufacturer A. In real manufacturing processes, several such input–output relationships may be involved.

Now, if tax is levied on the selling price of a product, then as the raw material is processed at different levels and sold from one manufacturer to another, the overall tax budget would also rise. So the same raw material is taxed every time it is sold by one firm to another. This phenomenon is called the cascading effect of tax.

The shortcomings of the cascading effect are as follows:

(a) The tax burden on a product will not remain constant; it will vary as the product changes hands.

(b) Instead of focussing on less profitable yet important levels, the manufacturer would be interested in producing maximum raw material. It will not only increase the net cost of production, but also decelerate the growth of small-scale enterprises.

(c) It creates heterogeneous economic environment, wherein, the power is in the hands of the few.

The concept of VAT has been introduced to tackle this challenge. VAT removes the cascading effect of the indirect taxes. Under this tax system, instead of paying taxes on the selling price, the manufacturer pays for the 'value added' to the product.

One of the most popular methods of implementing VAT is the tax credit method. It is followed in India as the Cenvat (central value added tax). In this scheme, tax is computed on the full sales price, but credit is provided on the tax paid on purchases. Thereby, the tax is calculated on value added tax only.

Cenvat claim requires particular documents as proof of payment of duty on imports. Thus, the overall control is more effective in this method, as it helps in keeping cases of tax avoidance and tax evasion under check.

Cenvat guidelines for capital goods   In case of a company manufacturing the final product, the Cenvat guidelines provide a list of capital goods that come under Cenvat. Appliances and other equipment in the 'office' are not eligible for Cenvat. The term 'office', however, has not been clearly explained.

The essential condition for Cenvat is that the eligible capital goods should be utilized in the manufacturing process. The goods could be used in any manner, including quality check, packaging, processing, etc.; they would all come under Cenvat as per the guidelines. It is assumed that goods refers to the business/ commercial context that they are a part of.

The Cenvat credit can be received only when the manufacturing unit is registered and is in an active state. This is with particular reference to a situation in which the capital goods are present in a unit but not utilized for whatever reasons.

The duty-paying document is mandatory as proof in order to claim Cenvat on capital goods.

Excise duty portion, of capital goods on which Cenvat is claimed, is not eligible for income tax depreciation.

The Cenvat credit can be claimed in two years' time. The first half of the credit can be claimed when the goods are in possession and the rest in the following financial year. The said goods must be in possession of the manufacturer and should be in use in the corresponding year as well. This is mandatory to avail the 50 per cent credit. Moreover, if this condition is not met, the second half Cenvat is permanently lost.

Income tax redemptions available for newly established industrial undertakings
Profits and gains derived by a newly established industrial undertaking, from export of articles or computer software, qualifies for a deduction. Eligibility for this deduction is that the undertaking is located in a free trade zone, export processing zone, a special economic zone, an electronic hardware, or software technology park as notified by the central government (Section 10A of the Income Tax Act, 1961).

Profits and gains derived by a newly established industrial undertaking recognized as a 100 per cent export-oriented undertaking (EOU) from export of articles or computer software qualifies for deduction under section 10B of the Income Tax Act.

In other situations, such deduction is available for ten consecutive years, subject to the fulfilment of the following conditions.

(a) Splitting or reconstruction of an existing industrial undertaking does not form such industrial undertaking.
(b) The sale proceeds of such export should be brought into India in convertible foreign exchange within a period of six months of effective such collections.
(c) The assessee cannot claim any tax benefits in respect of depreciation or business losses pertaining to those ten years during which he/she claims such exemptions under the above clauses.

7.15.3 Tax Computation

Irrespective of the assessee, which can be an individual, a firm, or a company, etc., the pattern of computation to be adopted is somewhat similar. There are certain provisions which apply to a firm only or to a company only. If adjustments on the basis of those provisions are called for, such adjustments need to be carried out on a case-to-case basis. Generally, the computation is made in the following format. Refer to Table 7.11.

TABLE 7.11 Income tax computation for a business enterprise

Structure	Rs	Rs
Net profit as per profit and loss account		Xxx
Add Items debited to P / L but not deductible as per IT provisions Items chargeable as business income (as per IT) not considered	xxx xxx	xxx Xxx
Less Items credited to P / L but not taxable under this head Items allowable as deduction (as per IT) not considered	xxx xxx	Xxx
Taxable income from business		Xxx
Tax on the above as per applicable rates		Xxx

The above format is being ordered to improve the clarity of the thinking process with respect to income tax computation pertaining to business income.

Business income chargeable to tax should be computed on the basis of common principles of commercial understanding, subject to the express provision of the Act. It is not practical for lawmakers to specifically provide for allowances/ disallowances of each and every item. Thus, general commercial principles should also be borne in mind while taking a decision. However, when we talk about admissibility or disallowance of certain expenses (while computing taxable business profits), we definitely mean revenue expenses and revenue losses. In other words, capital expenses and capital losses shall not be allowed as deduction under any circumstances whatsoever while computing taxable business profits.

7.15.4 Carry Forward and Set off of Business Losses

The assessee is entitled to carry forward unabsorbed business loss and set it off in subsequent years subject to the following conditions.
(a) Such unabsorbed business losses carried forward can only be set off against business profits.
(b) Such carry forward is permissible up to eight assessment years counted the year of incurring such loss.
(c) Unabsorbed depreciation computed under the Income Tax Act can only be set off after setting off the brought forward business losses.
(d) Both unabsorbed business loss and unabsorbed depreciation can be set off against other business income of the assesse even if the assessee has discontinued the business in respect of which it was originally incurred and computed.

The legislature, having rightly envisaged the impracticability of listing out all the admissible expenses in the computation of the taxable business income, enacted subsection (1) of section 37 so as to accommodate all deductible expenses other than those specifically covered by other provisions. These provisions of section 37 read as follows.

Any expenditure shall be allowed as admissible expenditure for the purpose of computing business income, provided
(a) It is not in the nature of capital expenditure.
(b) It is not in the nature of personal expenditure of the assessee.
(c) It is an expenditure that has been incurred wholly and exclusively for the purpose of the business.
(d) It is not an expense that has been specifically disallowed under the Income Tax Act.
(e) It is not in the nature of an expenditure prohibited by the law.

7.15.5 Treatment of Depreciation

As per accounting norms, the value of every fixed asset reduces over a period of time and this reduced value is calculated on an yearly basis. This decrement of original cost of the fixed asset is known as depreciation as per accounting terms. Since depreciation is a non-cash type of expenditure, a company can avail a tax benefit due to depreciation.

The following basic conditions are required to be fulfilled for availing depreciation benefits:
(a) The assessee must be the owner of the asset. However, if the assessee is occupying any building as a tenant for the purpose of carrying out business, any capital expenditure incurred towards renovation, extension, etc. can be treated as the asset value belonging to the assessee and hence, depreciation may be claimed for the purpose of business income computation.
(b) The assessee must use the asset for the purpose of carrying on business and profession.
(c) The asset must be used during the relevant previous year during which depreciation is being claimed. However, if an asset acquired during the year is put to use for less than 180 days during the year under consideration, then only the 50 per cent of the normal depreciation may be claimed.
(d) The asset in respect of which depreciation is being claimed should fall within the eligible classification of assets.

7.15.6 Concept of Block of Assets

Block of assets means the group of assets falling within the class of assets (in respect of which the same percentage of depreciation is prescribed), comprising of
(a) Tangible assets (building, machinery, furniture)
(b) Intangible assets (know-how, patent, etc.)

Assets eligible for depreciation shall be classified into separate blocks. After such segregation, grouping needs to be done within each such classification on the basis of the rate of depreciation prescribed in the Income Tax Act. Each such group will be identified as a block of asset. It may also be noted that land is treated as a non-depreciable asset under the Income Tax Act. In Exhibit 7.1, the computation method of depreciation has been explained.

EXHIBIT 7.1   Depreciation computation

Computation of actual cost

Total cost price of the asset
Add
- Interest on loan (or borrowings) for acquiring the asset payable up to the date the asset is put to use
- Expenses incurred on acquiring such asset
- Expenses incurred in connection with installation, erection, etc.
Less
- Amount met by any other authority or other person by way of subsidy or grant in relation to the purchase of such assets
  Actual cost of the asset

Computation of written down value of the block

Opening value of the block
Add
- Actual cost of the asset required in the same block
Less
- Sum receivable with respect to any asset in the block, which is sold, demolished or discarded, etc.
- Written down value for the purpose of charging income tax depreciation
- Depreciation at the prescribed percentage
- Closing written down value of the block

Computation of capital gains in respect of depreciable assets

In case of block of assets, depreciation can be claimed on the WDV provided as on the last day of the concerned year, provided the following two requirements are satisfied.
(a) There must be one asset in the block.
(b) There must be some value for the block on which the prescribed percentage of depreciation can be applied.
   When any one or both of the above mentioned requirements are not satisfied on transfer of any asset from the block, the depreciation provision ceases to apply and automatically the capital gains provisions will apply resulting in short-term capital gains or losses as the case may be.
   The computation of short-term capital gain or loss is done in the following manner.

Full value of consideration

Less
(a) WDV of the block asset at the beginning of the year under consideration
(b) Asset acquired during the year and belonging to the same block

Short-term capital gains or losses

The capital gain provisions get attracted under the following circumstances:
(a) When one or some of the assets in the block is/are sold for the consideration, which is more than the value of the entire block.

(b) When all the assets are transferred for a consideration, which is more than the value of the entire block.

(c) When all the assets are transferred for a consideration, which is less than the value of the entire block.

It may be noted that while in the first two situations the net result of computation would result in short-term capital gains, in the third situation it boils down to short-term capital loss.

Carry forward or set off of the short-term capital loss

In the case of an assessee, where there is unabsorbed short-term capital loss, computed under the head 'capital gains' for any assessment year, such loss can be carried forward for a period of 8 assessment years to be set off against income under the head 'capital gains' in the subsequent year.

7.15.7 The Concept of Minimum Alternate Tax

The manufacturer can get benefit over the excise duty paid for the raw materials and components used in the process of manufacturing. This scheme of credit can be utilized towards payment of excise duty on the final product. This is known as modified VAT (MAT). It was introduced in March 1986. This type of scheme has been implemented for reducing multiple taxation.

(a) In the case of a company, the income tax payable on total business income (as computed) shall be compared with 7.5 per cent of its book profit and the higher of these two figures will be treated as the tax payable by the company. Surcharge shall be added to such payable amount.

(b) By the term 'book profit', we essentially refer to the profit computed in accordance with the specific provisions laid down in the Companies Act 1956. However, some minor adjustments are needed to such profits as per the provisions.

(c) It may please be noted that there is no tax credit available for the tax paid under the above mentioned section.

7.15.8 Interfaces with the Provision of the Service Taxes

Service tax is another indirect tax levy, which is similar to the levy of excise duty both in concept and in application (including the concept of VAT through tax credit method) except the fundamental difference between the two, namely, excise duty being tax on manufacture and service tax is attracted by the service that is being provided. It may be noted that on the CAPEX project, the students are expected to work on deal with providing services to the clients in one form or another. However, the services that would be provided through these activities may or may not attract service charges, depending on the nature of the services on offer and the impact of applicable regulation as framed by the authorities governing or monitoring the levy of these categories of taxes in India. CAPEX students are hereby advised to kindly go through the applicable regulations, in order to ascertain the impact of the service taxes as far as their CAPEX project is concerned.

7.15.9 Income Tax Deducted at Source

Any person who makes payment of a few varieties of specified incomes is liable to tax deductions at source (TDS) on such payments. In general, individuals are not liable to deduct tax at source on such payments, unless such individuals are running a business or profession whose gross annual turnover exceeds Rs 40,00,000 (www.finmin.nic.in). A particular provision, which is relevant for any CAPEX project would be as follows.

In a case where a person is making payment of fees for professional or technical services and the total of such fee payment attributable to various agencies during a year exceeds Rs 20,000 (so far the payee is concerned), a TDS of 5.25 per cent needs to be deducted from such payment. The TDS so deducted needs to be deposited with the tax authorities within a week from the last day of the month in which such tax was deducted. The party deducting and depositing such tax should file a return of Rs 26,000 with the tax authorities in form which is treated as a confide proof for such compliance to the rules.

Example 7.10 Treatment of depreciation and capital gains on depreciable assets

Mr X informs you that the opening WDV of the block of machinery in his factory is Rs 42 lakh as on 1 April 2008. The effective income tax depreciation rate is 25% on such assets. He has purchased a new machine worth Rs 14 lakh in February 2009 pertaining to the same block. Explain the tax consequences under each of the following cases:

Case I   One old machine in this block was sold for Rs 15 lakh before 31 March 2009.

Case II   The new machinery purchased for Rs 20 lakh before 31 March 2009.

Case III   All machinery in this block was sold for Rs 48 lakh before 31 March 2009.

Case IV   One asset was sold for Rs 60 lakh before 31 March 2009.

Solution

Case I

Opening WDV	Rs 42 lakh
Purchased new machine (February 2009)	Rs 14 lakh
Sold an old machine	−Rs 15 lakh
	Rs 41 lakh

Therefore, depreciation: $25\% (42 - 15) + 14 / 2 \times 25\% =$ Rs 8.5 lakh

Case II

Opening WDV	Rs 42 lakh
Purchased new machine (February 2009)	Rs 14 lakh
Sold a new machine	−Rs 20 lakh
	Rs 36 lakh

Therefore, depreciation: 25% of $36 =$ Rs 9 lakh

Case III

Opening WDV	Rs 42 lakh
Purchased new machine (February 2009)	Rs 14 lakh
	Rs 56 lakh
Sold all machinery	−Rs 48 lakh
Short-term capital loss (STCL)	Rs 8 lakh

Therefore, no depreciation.

Case IV

Opening WDV	Rs 42 lakh
Purchased new machine (February 2009)	Rs 14 lakh
	Rs 56 lakh
Sold one machine	−Rs 60 lakh
Short-term capital gain (STCG)	−Rs 4 lakh

Therefore, no depreciation.

SUMMARY

Risk refers to the chance that some unfavourable event might occur. No project should be undertaken unless the expected rate of return (discount factor) is high enough to compensate the investor for the perceived risk of the investment. In an environment of uncertainty, business operates and managers can never be sure about what might happen in the future. The various types of risks encountered during project financing are project risk, debtor's credit risk, sovereign credit risk, commercial risk, political risk, and force majeure.

Simple probability analysis is one of the most effective and conceptually sound tools of appraising projects in case of uncertainty. Sensitivity analysis, scenario analysis, break-even analysis are the other methods used to get a more complete picture of the project under review. Hiller model with uncorrelated and correlated cash flows and decision tree analysis are further used to get an in-depth understanding of the project.

KEY TERMS

Accounting breakeven point   The level of production, where revenue equals to cost, i.e., neither profit nor loss.

Certainty equivalent   A certain cash flow that is equal in desirability to an uncertain future cash flow.

Debtor's credit risk   It is a risk that a particular debtor company will default on its loan for some reason, for example, as a result of insolvency or other deterioration in its overall financial condition.

Default risk   The uncertainty of expected returns from a security attributable to possible changes in the financial capacity of the security issues to make future payments to the security owner. Treasury securities are considered to be default-free.

Financial break-even point   The level of production, where present value of cash in flow equals to present value of cash outflow, i.e., NPV equals zero.

Portfolio effect   The extent to which the variability of the returns on a portfolio is less than the sum of the variability of the individual assets in the portfolio.

Portfolio theory   Portfolio is a collection of assets and its theory. It is concerned with the delineation of efficient portfolios and selection of optimal portfolios.

Project risk   It threatens the operation of a specific project, thereby affecting the repayment of the lender's loan.

Risk-adjusted discount rate   The discount rate applicable to a risky investment. It is equal to the risk-free rate of return plus a risk premium reflecting the risk characterising the investment.

Risk premium   The additional return expected for assuming risk.

Risk   Risk refers to variability. It is measured in financial analysis, generally by standard deviation.

Sensitivity analysis   A technique of risk analysis that can be used to study the responsiveness of a criterion of merit like NPV or IRR to variations in underlying factors such as selling price, quantity sold, etc.

Simulation   A technique for emulating a process, usually conducted a considerable number of times to understand the process better and measure its outcomes under different policies.

Sovereign credit risk   When the debtor is a country, the risk of such default is referred as a sovereign credit risk.

Systematic risk   Risk that cannot be diversified away. It is also referred to as market risk or non-diversifiable risk.

Unsystematic risk   Risk that can be diversified away. It is also referred to as unique risk, specific risk, residual risk, or diversifiable risk.

CONCEPT REVIEW QUESTIONS

1. Explain the difference between risk and uncertainty.
2. Discuss how sensitivity analysis can help management to assess the risk of investment in a project.
3. Discuss the use of risk-adjusted discount rates in the evaluation of investment projects.
4. Explain the meaning of the term 'Monte Carlo simulation'.
5. Differentiate between hard and soft capital rationing.
6. How can portfolio theory and CAPM be used in capital budgeting decision-making process?

NUMERICAL PROBLEMS

1. The Plastic Product of India Ltd is proposing to replace its old bottle-making machinery with more modern equipment. The new equipment costs Rs 100 lakh and the company expects to sell its old equipment for Rs 10 lakh. The attraction of the new machinery is that it is expected to cut manufacturing costs from their current level of Rs 8 per bottle to Rs 4. However, as the following table shows, there is some uncertainty both about future sales and about the performance of the new machinery. Refer to Table E7.16.

Conduct a sensitivity analysis of the replacement decision, assuming a cost of capital of 12%. Ignore taxation.

TABLE E7.16

	Pessi-mistic	Ex-pected	Opti-mistic
Sales (lakh bottles)	4	5	7
Manufacturing cost with new machinery (Rs per bottle)	6	4	3
Economic life of new machinery (years)	7	10	13

2. XYZ company is considering whether or not to invest Rs 1,20,000 in an investment proposal to add a new product to its existing range of products. The management forecasts that the new plant would generate incremental net cash flows, the pattern of which is presented in Table E7.17.

TABLE E7.17

Year	Expected cash inflow (Rs)	Standard deviation (Rs)
1	44,000	8,800
2	40,000	7,600
3	40,000	8,000
4	35,000	6,000
5	30,000	5,000

Assuming normal distribution and an appropriate discounting factor of 10% for evaluating such capital expenditure proposals, compute

(a) The probability that the investment would fetch negative NPV;

(b) The chances that the NPV would be at least Rs 20,000;

(c) Whether the project should be undertaken if the management has laid down a norm that no project should be undertaken unless it has at least 75% chance of fetching an NPV of Rs 25,000.

3. A major munch pulses company is considering the introduction of a new pulse, honey coated oat flakes. Initially, it must decide whether to distribute the goods regionally or nationally. Regional distribution will require an investment of Rs 10,00,000 for a new plant and for marketing efforts. Depending upon the demand in the first two years, the company would decide whether or not to expand to national distribution. If it goes from regional to national distribution, it will need to spend additional Rs 30,00,000. If it does, then it would require Rs 30,00,000 for setting up the plant and for the marketing of the product.

We see that there is an economic benefit associated with distributing nationally at the outset. For one thing, building the large plant is less expensive than building a small one first and then expanding it. Thus, the Rs 10,00,000 buys the company an option to be exercised at the end of two years either to distribute nationally or continue distributing regionally. If the company decides to distribute nationally at the outset, there is a 0.4 probability that the demand will prove to be high, 0.4 probability that the demand will be medium, and 0.2 probability that it would be low. At the end of year 2, the company must decide whether to continue distributing regionally.

In each case, demand will continue to be high, if it was high in the previous two years, and medium if it was medium in the previous years. If it decides to distribute nationally after two years of regional operation, demand may again be high, medium, or low with respective probabilities of (0.6, 0.3 and 0.1), (0.3, 0.4 and 0.3), and (0.1, 0.2 and 0.7).

Expected net present values for various branches of decision tree are given in Table E7.18.

TABLE E7.18

Rs ('000)

Regional distribution throughout	NPV Rs ('000)
High demand	947.4
Medium demand	136.2
Low demand	(637.1)

Region distribution followed by national distribution

High regional demand followed by high national demand	4,096.0
High regional demand followed by medium national demand	1,573.1
High regional demand followed by low national demand	(704.1)
Medium regional demand followed by high national demand	3,377.4
Medium regional demand followed by medium national demand	932.6
Medium regional demand followed by low national demand	(1,426.8)
Low regional demand followed by high national demand	2,411.2
Low regional demand followed by medium national demand	51.9
Low regional demand followed by low national demand	(2,307.5)

National distribution throughout

High demand	3,830.5
Medium demand	851.6
Low demand	(1,927.3)

Which option should be recommended and what is the value of that option?

ASSIGNMENT

Arrange the financials of an upcoming project and then try to find out its accounting break-even point and financial break-even point. Which out of the two should be more and why? Illustrate with suitable calculations.

SELECT REFERENCES

Brealey, R., and S. Myers, *Principles of Corporate Finance,* New York, McGraw Hill Co., 2006, pp. 221–89.

Chandra, P., 'Risk Analysis in Capital Expenditures', *Indian Management,* October, 1975.

Grayson, C., 'The use of statistical techniques in capital budgeting', in Robicheck, A. (ed.) *Financial Research and Management Decisions,* pp. 90–132, New York, Wiley, 1967.

Hammond, J.S., 'Better Decisions with Preference Theory', *Harvard Business Review,* Nov–Dec, 1967.

Hertz, D.B., 'Risk Analysis in Capital Investment', *Harvard Business Review,* Jan–Feb, 1964.

Hiller, F.S., 'The Derivation of Probabilistic Information for the Evaluation of Risky Investments,' *Management_Science,* vol. 9, no. 3, April 1963, pp. 443–57.

Newmann, J.V. and O. Morgenstern, *Theory of Games and Economic Behaviour,* Princeton University Press, 1944.

CASE STUDY
M/s Starlight Enterprise Ltd

M/s Starlight Enterprise Ltd is a medium-scale Indian-based corporate house belonging to the FMGC sector registered in a recognized stock exchange in India. The company was incorporated in the year 1994 and commenced operations in the same year. In course of its functioning in the Indian market since, it has been moderately successful in positioning its products and developing its brand in the Indian market. Over the years, the company has concentrated more on producing and marketing high-quality consumer goods as compared to its efforts in capturing significant marketshare of the product portfolio it deals in. Consequently, although the company may not be regarded as a big player in the industry, its brand of consumer goods are preferred by a selective group of consumers who are reluctant to compromise on quality. In a nutshell, the overall performance of the company has been quite encouraging over the years as is evident from its market reputation and brand image development exercise.

The financials of the company under review also reflect the overall successful performance of the company. The financial statements of the company comprising the profit and loss account for the financial year that ended on 31 March 2008 and the balance sheet as on 31 March 2008 are provided in Exhibits 7.2 and 7.3, respectively. A few indicative financial ratios coupled with a few other financial indicators portraying the performance of the company are also set out in Exhibit 7.4, which also shows the industry standard and its averages with respect to such financial indicators, establishing the observation that the overall performance of the company has been quite satisfactory in the very true sense of the term. Exhibits 7.3, 7.4, and 7.5 are provided herewith for ready reference.

The ruling market price of share (face value Rs 100 each) of M/s Starlight Enterprise Ltd is in the region of Rs 390 per share and for the last three years or so, it has reflected very negligible fluctuations. The market fluctuations vis-à-vis their shares over the years may thus be regarded as quite insignificant.

The Credit

The overall success of the company is primarily attributable to three key executives of the organization, namely VP Operations, VP Marketing, and VP Finance. The team of these three senior executives enjoy a strong backing and support from the Managing Director (MD) of the company who is a leader par excellence. The MD has a lot of trust and faith in this senior management team. Over the years of the existence of the company, he has experienced that the three key executives of his company, as a team, is a well-oiled machine achieving goals and targets with ease and flamboyance. In short, the senior management team as a whole is characterized by all good qualities and traits required and expected of senior managers, which are sought-after virtues in any management team across the globe.

The Vision of the MD

Having strengthened the brand, reputation, and quality of products in the market, the MD felt it was time the company concentrated on expansion and growth, focusing on capturing substantial marketshare in its range of products portfolio. Being a task master, his motto was to translate his dreams into reality and he called for a meeting with his team of key executives. In the meeting, he made the following statement: 'For the last decade of our existence we have been concentrating on consolidation of our brand and market image but now I hope you'll agree that we have essentially operated as a small fish in a big pond. My only ambition is to see that our company now emerges as a big player in the market, enjoying the stature of a big player in the market. I look forward to the day when M/s Starlight Enterprise Ltd will be treated as a market leader and winner rather than a winner alone.

'Gentlemen, it's time we devote adequate time and energy in our expansion plans. I hereby authorize your entire team to develop a business plan incorporating my vision of rapid expansion of our operations through all possible means and opportunities. As it is, we cater to a market where issues such as stagnation and saturation simply don't fit in. There are endless opportunities existing in the market. We simply need to make a breakthrough.'

An exercise to translate the vision into reality

Motivated and convinced by the thoughts and vision of their MD, the senior management team started an exercise of identification of various expansion proposals. After studying and evaluating various investment proposals under consideration, they finally zeroed in on a particular investment proposal, which would call for an initial capital investment of Rs 190 crore. This capital investment proposal would require about one year for commissioning and implementation and was expected to have a useful life of 20 years, approximately. It was also assessed that the same was a high positive NPV project and once the investment crystallized, it would start generating significant operating cash inflows within 4 to 5 years post-implementation stage.

Once the capital project was successfully identified, the team informed the MD about the same, who in turn requested them to draft a proposal to its effect. The MD requested them to provide a technical write-up about the capital investment proposal, which needed to be supplemented with a market demand-cum-sales estimation adequately based on a thorough market survey exercise. He also requested them to prepare the projected financial for the next year incorporating such a capital investment proposal. The MD opined that after going through this draft proposal, he would undertake the exercise of preparation of a complete project report comprising a 10-year financial forecast, which would be placed in front of various financiers for their consideration.

Unfortunately, the team spirit takes a hit

When the team started working on the draft proposal in line with the MD's directives, a major problem suddenly cropped up, which the company could not ignore. There was a significant difference of opinion among the team members, which essentially resulted in a rift between the VP Marketing and VP Operations, on one side, and the VP Finance on the other. The marketing and operations representatives went to the extent of commenting that all the hard work was put in by them in terms of identifying the proposal and they failed to appreciate how a 'finance man' could contribute in such a draft proposal. They had observed that the only thing the VP Finance could contribute was to prepare the one-year financial projections, which was an extremely easy exercise to undertake and hence, anybody could do it satisfactorily without any aid from a so-called finance specialist.

The VP Finance was extremely upset with such sudden turn of events as he felt that he was purposely sidelined by his colleagues as far as this special exercise was concerned. Consequently, he divorced himself from the team and decided that he won't interfere in the preparation of the draft proposal. In fact, he told both of his team mates, 'Gentlemen, it appears that this expansion plan is your baby and hence I suggest that you take care of the drafting of the proposal. I shall not interfere with your work.'

The proposal was still drafted

The VP Operation and VP Marketing had a lot of faith and confidence in their own abilities and they strongly believed that between the two of them, they were adequately equipped to construct the proposal and hence, they were least bothered about the absence of VP Finance. Consequently, they put in a week's effort, which translated in the draft proposal.

This draft proposal comprised of a variety of information, which also included a projected profit and loss statement for the finance year to end on 31 March 2009, along with a projected balance sheet depicting the financial proposal as on 31 March 2009. This projected financials are provided in Exhibits 7.5 and 7.6.

VP Finance takes a good look

The MD came to know about the rift among his senior management and hence, on receipt of the draft proposal he understood that the same did not have the concurrence of VP Finance. Consequently, he sent the draft proposal to him requesting for his comments regarding the financial projection

incorporated as an integral component of such proposal. This action of the MD provided opportunity to the VP Finance to have a thorough look at the projected financials.

After reviewing the financial projections, the VP Finance sent it back to his MD with the following comments:

To,

The Managing Director,

M/s Starlight Enterprise Ltd

Dear Sir,

This is to inform you that I have gone through the financial projections included as an integral component of the draft proposal prepared by my respected colleagues. My observations in respect of the same are as under:

Any kind of financial projections should effectively be treated as a budget simply because the financial projections are constructed with the primary focus that the organization for which it is being prepared should adhere to the same. Unfortunately, if our company proposes to adhere to the financial projections as construed by my esteemed colleagues, the company would land up in a terrible mess in the near future. In view of the same, I am of the opinion that the entire set of financial projections needs to be re-drafted.

The inherent limitations of such financial projections are given below for your reference

....

....

....

EXHIBIT 7.2

**The profit and loss account of
M/s Starlight Enterprise Ltd
for the year ended 31 March 2008**

Income	Rs in crores
Sales	715
Other Income	62
	777
Expense	
Cost of goods sold	468
Establishment expenses	98
Depreciation	54
Interest	37
	657
Profit before taxes	120
Taxation	28
Profit after taxes	92
Dividend	40
Transfers to reserves	10
Retained earnings	42

EXHIBIT 7.3

**The balance sheet account of
M/s Starlight Enterprise Ltd
for the year ended 31 March 2008**

Employment of capital	Rs in crores	Rs in crores
Fixed Assets		182
Current assets		
Inventories	93	
Debtors	125	
Cash and bank balance	60	
	278	
Current liabilities		
Trade creditors	60	
Expense creditors	72	
Bank overdraft	15	
	147	

Employment of capital	Rs in crores	Rs in crores
Net current assets		131
		313
Capital employed		
Share capital		135
Reserves and surplus		115
Loans		63
		313

EXHIBIT 7.4   A few indicators

(All figures given below represent near approximations)

The indicators	M/s Starlight Enterprise Ltd	Industry average
Profitability indicators		
Gross profit ratio (%)	34	30
Net profit ratio (%)	12	10
Return on investment (%)	29	25
Earnings per share (Rs)	68.15	55.00
Price earnings multiple	5.72	5.00
Solvency indicators		
Current ratio	1.89:1	1.50:1
Quick ratio	1.40:1	1.20:1
Debt equity ratio (considering long-term debts only)	0.25:1	1:1
Asset utilization indicators		
Capital turnover ratio	2.28:1	2.50:1
Other indicators		
Debtor velocity (in months)	2.10	1.90
Inventory velocity (in months)	2.38	1.80
Creditors velocity (in months)	1.54	1.00
Cash conversion cycle (in number of days)	100	90

Exhibit 7.5

The projected profit and loss account of M/s Starlight Enterprise Ltd for the year ended 31 March 2009

Income	Rs in crores
Sales	725
Other income	65
	790
Expense	
Cost of goods sold	479
Establishment expenses	103
Depreciation	69
Interest	48
	699
Profit before taxes	91
Taxation	23
Profit after taxes	68
Dividend	40
Transfers to reserves	10
Retained earnings	18

Exhibit 7.6

The projected balance sheet account of M/s Starlight Enterprise Ltd for the year ended 31 March 2009

Employment of capital	Rs in crores
Fixed assets	303
Long-term investment	10

Employment of capital	Rs in crores
Current assets	
Inventories	100
Debtors	135
Cash and bank balance	67
	302
Current liabilities	
Trade creditors	62
Expense creditors	75
Bank overdraft	75
Public deposits	70
	282
Net current assets	20
	302
Capital employed	
Share capital	135
Reserves and surplus	143
Loans	55
	333

Discussion questions

1. Why is VP Finance not happy with the financial projections drafted by his colleagues?

2. 'The inherent limitations of such financial projections are given below for your ready reference …' According to you what can be the limitations of such financial projections? Also, redraft a correct financial projection.

FINANCIAL FORECASTING

An economist is an expert who will know tomorrow why the things he predicted yesterday didn't happen today.

— EVAN ESAR

LEARNING OBJECTIVES

After studying this chapter, you will be able to

- Explain the concept of forecast, including financial forecast and sales forecast
- Know the merits and demerits of the various methods of financial forecasting
- Understand the various techniques of sales forecasting
- Compute the value of external fund requirements
- Prepare projected balance sheets, income statements, and fund flow statements

Projection of Future—Analysing Your Past

The evening was supposed to be a breather for Vijay Sinha and Shyam Rai, best friends and business partners holding equal shares in VS Construction Co. They had decided to discuss everything but business today. But before they could finish sandwich and start with coffee, they found that they had already started discussing business.

SHYAM: See Vijay, after five years in this business, we don't have any other topic of discussion.

VIJAY: That's true, but I like it this way. After all, this business has cemented our friendship. Do you ever wonder where we shall be five years from now?

SHYAM: Yes, I often think about it. I try to visualize the future, but give up after some time. Can anyone speculate the future? I think if we are really interested in knowing about it, we should go to Bhaskaracharya and ask him to read our horoscopes.

VIJAY: You mean you want to go to an astrologer! Are you crazy? Do you think anybody is better placed to visualize our future than ourselves? After all, it is our business and we know every bit of it; where we started, how we stabilized, where we stand now, and where we intend to go.

SHYAM: Yes, we know it all. But still ...!

VIJAY: Listen, we have all the data available with us. We have a detailed history and financial reports of our business for the last five years. If we logically analyse the data using various tools available, we shall definitely arrive at a reasonable forecast of where we would be after five years. We are students of science. We can definitely do a better job than your Bhaskaracharya in forecasting our future.

SHYAM: But how do you guarantee that our speculation will come true in the years to come?

VIJAY: This is forecasting, and there is no guarantee, to be very frank. But I can assure you, if we proceed in a scientific way using forecasting methods, we shall arrive at a fairly reasonable conclusion, and get a sense of our future standing and achievement. It will have, say, 10–15 per cent variation with the actual, but that is quite a good speculation, isn't it?

SHYAM: Well, it sounds interesting. Let us sit with the data tomorrow morning, and start analysing.

VIJAY: Forecasting the future prospects of VS Construction Co., my friend.

8.1 FINANCIAL FORECASTING

As seen in the opening case, the two partners of VS Construction Co. are concentrating on a very important and interesting aspect of business—financial forecasting.

Financial forecasting is a planning process, with the help of which a company's management positions its future activities relative to the economic, technical, competitive, and social environments. Business plans normally show strategies and actions for achieving desired short-term, intermediate, and long-term results. These are quantified in financial terms, in the form of projected financial statements (pro forma statements), and a variety of operational budgets.

Financial forecasting is an integral component of planning a process. Forecasting techniques essentially utilize past data to estimate future financial requirements. Normally, two types of standard forecasting techniques are deployed in the corporate world, namely, the 'percentage of sales method' and the 'pro forma method' of financial forecasting.

8.1.1 Percentage of Sales Method

This method involves a certain deduced correlation between sales and accounts. Different financial statements are calculated, based on the sales forecast. However, the simplicity of the process also makes it vulnerable to mistakes. For example, some novice analysts may assume that the operational capacity can increase in fractional amounts, parallel to increases in sales. But the question arises, for example, can Indian Railways really increase the number of berths which may be equivalent to half or three-fourths of a full compartment? Operational capacity usually increases in lump sum, and not by fractional amounts parallel to increase in sales. Therefore, one must be judicious while determining the percentage of sales using this method.

Advantages This is essentially a simple approach used for financial forecasting, where the items of profit and loss, account, and balance sheet are linked to the turnover figure of the concerned organization. Hence, it is simple in concept and application, and less volume of data and time are required to develop such financial forecasts. As a result, its acceptability by the management may be high, especially in situations where financial projections are developed under acute time constraints.

Disadvantages It is less accurate as it is based on a very simple (and sometimes unfeasible) assumption that all components of a financial statement are linear functions of sales. But it may not be so. That is why not all financial institutions and bankers who are approached to evaluate such proposals usually find these forecasts to be reliable.

It may be noted that reliability and quality are regarded as sought-after virtues as far as the appraisal of proposals are concerned.

8.1.2 Pro forma Forecasting Technique

This method starts with a base year (generally the previous year) of financial statements. To use this method, one needs some kind of forecast about the transactions. These may be available or unavailable to the forecaster, both inside as well as outside the organization. This is the reason why it is considered difficult to deal with. Here, how each account will change and what the resulting new balances will surface are determined through the double-entry book.

Advantages Since it is essentially an elaborate method of financial forecasting, the accuracy achieved is better compared to the other model.

Disadvantages The quantum of data required is quite substantial. The accuracy depends on the assumptions made at various stages of the exercise. Moreover, it is quite tedious and time consuming.

The combination of the two methods forms the most popular approach. For example, the value of units, which varies with sales such as current assets, income statements, etc., is calculated through the percentage of sales method, whereas fixed assets and equity of shareholders are calculated through T-accounts. Tax expenses are usually a percentage of pre-tax income. Dividends and depreciation usually vary with after-tax income and gross fixed assets, respectively.

8.2 GROWTH AND EXTERNAL FINANCIAL REQUIREMENTS

During financial planning, the relationship between a firm's growth objectives and its external financial requirements (EFR) is very useful. In simple terms,

New investments = Existing net assets × Growth rate

Retained earnings invariably provide the fund requirements for investment in new assets. The balance is met by external financing. Theoretically, EFR = Increase in net assets – Increase in retained earnings.

$$EFR = (A - L) \, dS/S - mS_1 (1 - d) \tag{8.1}$$

where,

S = existing sales

A = total assets

L = spontaneous liability

m = net profit margin

dS = expected increase in sales

d = dividend payout

S_1 = projected sales for the next year, i.e., $(S + dS)$

If g represents the growth rate in sales (i.e., S/dS), Eqn (8.1) can take the following shape:

$$EFR/dS = (A/S - L/S) - m (1 + g) (1 - d)/g \tag{8.2}$$

Equation (8.2) distinctly highlights that the amount of external financing depends upon the firm's projected growth in sales. Mathematically, when sales are not growing, no funds are required for expansion, and hence, the entire portion of retained earnings is effectively the surplus funds of the company. As the firm grows in terms of sales, more and more funds would be required for the necessary additional investments in net assets in order to achieve such growth. Essentially, such external financing can be inducted into the business of the firm in the form of short-term borrowings, or through the route of issuing securities or shares.

....

Example 8.1   For the year ended 31 March 2009, the sales for Y Limited was Rs 600 lakh, which was expected to increase by 20% in the next year. The net profit margin and dividend payout ratio are expected to be 5% and 60%, respectively. The balance sheet of the company as on 31 March 2009 is given in Table E8.1.

TABLE E8.1

Liabilities	(Rs lakhs)	Assets	(Rs lakhs)
Share capital	100	Fixed assets	250
Retained earnings	70	Inventories	150
Long-term loans	180	Receivables	120
Accounts payable	60	Cash	30
Provisions	40		
Short-term bank borrowings	100		
Total	**550**	**Total**	**550**

Based on the above data find out the following:

(a) Determine the external financing requirements of Y Limited.

(b) How should the company raise its EFR with the following constraints.

- Current ratio should be at least 1.33

- The ratio of fixed assets to long-term loans should be 1.5

- Long-term loans (*LTL*) to equity should at the most be 1.2

Assume that the company wishes to tap external sources in the following order:

- Short-term bank borrowings

- Long-term loans

- Issue of additional equity share

Solution

(a) External financing requirements $(EFR) = (A - L)\, dS\, /\, S - mS_1(1 - d)$

$$EFR = (550 - 100) \times \frac{120}{600} - 0.05 \times 720 \times (1 - 0.6) = \text{Rs } 75.6 \text{ lakh}$$

(b) Current ratio (CR) = Current assets / Current liabilities = $\dfrac{360}{(120 + STBB)} = 1.33$

Therefore, short-term bank borrowings (*STBB*) = Rs 150.6 lakh

Therefore, additional *STBB* = 150.6 − 100 = Rs 50.6 lakh

Fixed assets / $LTL = \dfrac{250\,(1.2)}{LTL} = 1.5$ or, Rs 200 lakh (LTL = Long-term loans)

Additional LTL = Rs 20 lakh

Therefore, additional equity issue = 75.6 − 50.6 − 20 = Rs 5 lakh

$$\frac{LTL}{\text{Equity}} = \frac{200}{105 + 70 + 0.05 \times 720 \times (1 - 0.6)}$$

$$\frac{LTL}{\text{Equity}} = \frac{200}{105 + 70 + 14.4}$$

$$\frac{LTL}{\text{Equity}} = \frac{200}{105 + 84.4} = 1.05 < 1.2, \text{ hence it is ok.}$$

It is seen in the above calculations that all the three conditions have been satisfied.

8.3 MULTI-YEAR PROJECTIONS—AN ILLUSTRATION

Although the percentage sales method is simple in nature, it needs to be operated with caution coupled with a logical step-by-step approach in order to develop meaningful financial forecasts. In the following pages, we have used a hypothetical case of an organization, Indian Machinery Limited (IML), to illustrate the step-by-step approach along with the suggested approach and solution of multi-year projections.

IML is a large machine tool and machinery manufacturing company that is growing at a high rate. Because of the long-term production cycles of a number of its products, it follows the practice of carrying large inventories. IML has its customers both in public and private sectors. It faces the problem of realizing its credit sales on time from the public sector customers. In the past, the company had to resort to borrowings to meet its fund requirements. This is shown in the profit and loss statement in Table 8.1.

TABLE 8.1 Profit and loss statement (2004–08)

Particulars	2004	2005	2006	2007	2008
Net sales	139.0	152.0	183.0	206.2	238.3
Cost of goods sold	81.2	87.7	104.7	123.7	138.7
Gross profit	57.8	64.3	78.3	82.7	99.6
Administrative expenses	10.3	11.6	12.9	16.8	19.3
Selling expenses	20.1	21.1	23.2	25.0	27.1
Other expenses	11.6	12.9	13.4	15.5	19.1
Total of indirect expenses	42.0	45.6	49.5	57.3	65.5
EBIT	15.8	18.7	28.8	25.4	34.1
Interest	9.8	11.1	16.0	17.8	18.6
PBI	6.0	7.6	12.8	7.6	15.5
Taxation	2.8	3.6	6.2	3.9	8.2
PAT	3.2	4.0	6.6	3.7	7.3
Dividends	1.5	1.5	3.0	3.0	3.0
Retained earnings	1.7	2.5	3.6	0.7	4.3

IML's balance sheet is given in Table 8.2 to help us take the process further.

TABLE 8.2 Balance sheet as on 31st March (2004–08)

Details	2004	2005	2006	2007	2008
Share capital	40.0	40.0	40.0	40.0	40.0
Reserves and surpluses	12.1	14.6	17.9	18.6	22.9
Net worth	52.1	54.6	57.9	58.6	62.9
Borrowings	67.0	69.8	96.0	110.8	114.8
Capital employed	119.1	124.4	153.9	169.4	177.7
Gross block of fixed assets	86.1	92.3	99.3	115.8	141.5
Accumulated depreciation	30.2	34.3	38.7	45.9	54.1
Net block of fixed assets	55.9	58.0	60.6	69.9	87.4
Capital work in progress	3.4	4.6	10.3	17.3	7.0
Net fixed assets	59.3	62.6	70.9	87.2	94.4
Inventories	97.4	110.3	122.5	119.4	122.7
Debtors	47.4	67.8	108.3	126.3	127.9
Cash and bank balances	5.4	2.8	3.9	6.4	11.6
Other current assets	17.0	14.4	17.0	22.2	23.5
Total current assets	167.2	195.3	251.7	274.3	285.7
Current liabilities	107.4	133.5	168.7	192.1	202.4
Net current assets	59.8	61.8	83.0	82.2	83.3

A logical solution to the above case explaining the step-by-step approach The financial strategies adopted by the said organization in order to finance its operations may best be ascertained by developing a fund flow statement. The developed fund flow statement as depicted in Tables 8.3(a) and (b) need to be interpreted in the right spirit as well.

TABLE 8.3(a)　Fund flow statement

Sources of fund	Rs in crores	
PAT	7.3	
Depreciation	8.2	
Funds generated from operations	15.5	
Borrowings	4.0	
Total	**19.5**	
Applications of fund		
Gross fixed assets	25.7	
Capital WIP	(10.3)	
Dividends	3.0	
Increase in working capital	1.1	
Total	**19.5**	

If the above fund flow statement was segregated into long-term and short-term components, it would take the following shape.

TABLE 8.3(b)　Segregated fund flow statement

Sources of fund	Rs in crores	
Sources		
Borrowings	4.0	
Application		
Fixed asset/Capital WIP	15.4	
Dividends		3.0
Working capital increase		1.1
Total of applications	15.4	4.1
(Deficit)	(11.4)	(4.1)
FGFO	15.5	
Net surplus/(Deficit)	4.1	(4.1)

Please note that the company is effectively tapping long-term sources of finance to meet their dividend obligations, which may not be regarded as a wise financial decision. Hence, the financing strategies empl᠄yed by the organization are open to questions.

The fundamental financial analysis (a ratio-based approach) of IML based on its past data (last 5 years) is shown in Table 8.4.

TABLE 8.4　IML's financial ratios for 2004–09

Percentage sales profit	2004	2005	2006	2007	2008	2009
Profit and loss items						
Cost of goods sold	58.4	57.7	57.2	60.0	58.2	58.3
Administrative expenses	7.4	7.6	7.0	8.1	8.1	7.7
Selling expenses	14.5	13.5	12.7	12.1	11.4	12.9
Other expenses	8.3	8.5	7.3	7.5	8.0	7.9
Interest	7.1	7.3	8.7	8.6	7.8	7.9
PAT	2.3	2.6	3.6	1.8	3.1	· 2.7
Balance sheet items						
Net fixed assets	42.7	41.2	38.7	42.3	39.6	40.9
Inventory	70.1	72.6	66.9	57.9	51.5	63.8
Debtor	34.1	44.6	59.2	61.3	53.7	50.6
Cash and bank balance	3.9	1.8	2.1	3.1	4.9	3.2
Other current assets	12.2	9.5	9.3	10.8	9.9	10.3
Current assets	120.3	128.5	137.5	133.0	119.9	127.8
Current liabilities	77.3	87.8	92.2	93.2	84.9	87.1
Net current assets	43.0	40.7	45.4	39.9	35.0	40.8
Net assets	85.7	81.8	84.1	82.2	74.6	81.7
Profitability analysis						
Assets turn over: NS/NA	1.17	1.22	1.19	1.22	1.34	1.23
Profit margin: PBIT/NS (%)	11.4	12.3	15.7	12.3	14.3	13.2
Return on investment: (PBIT/NA)	13.3	15.0	18.7	15.0	19.2	16.2
Leverage factor: (PAT/PBIT) (%)	20.3	21.4	22.9	14.6	21.4	20.1

Contd

Table 8.4   *Contd*

Percentage sales profit	2004	2005	2006	2007	2008	2009
Debt ratio: NA/NW (%)	2.29	2.28	2.66	2.89	2.83	2.59
Return on equity: PAT/NW (%)	6.1	7.3	11.4	6.3	11.6	8.6
Retention ratio: RE/PAT (%)	53.1	62.5	54.5	18.9	58.9	49.6
Growth in equity: RE/NW (%)	3.3	4.6	6.2	1.2	6.8	4.4
Growth in sales (%)	–	9.4	20.4	12.7	15.6	14.5

It may be noted that an attempt has been made to establish a simple relationship between sales and a number of profit, loss, and other balance sheet items. It may aid in our endeavour to develop future financial projection based on the percentage to sales approach.

An analysis of IML's profitability may be developed in the following manner, based on the ratio analysis exercise given above.

IML's sales have been growing at about 15%. The company improved its assets utilization from 1.17 times in 2004 to 1.34 times in 2008. Its profit margin (PBIT/NS) ranged between 11.4% in 2004 to 15.7% in 2006. The company's net margin (PAT/NS) showed more fluctuation because of high proportion interest. IML earned an average net margin of 2.7% during 2004–08.

On an average, the company distributed a little more than 50% of its profits as dividend to its shareholders. IML's net worth did not increase rapidly because of low margins and high payout. As a consequence, the company depended on borrowings to meet its requirement of funds and its debt equity ratio increased from 1.29 in 2004 to 1.83 in 2008. IML has high levels of inventory and debtors. It improved its utilization of current assets in the year 2008. Because of better utilization of fixed assets and improvement in its current assets turnover, the net assets as a percentage of sales declined to about 75% (from 86% in 2004) in 2008. Thus, the company is in a position to improve its assets turnover and profitability, by bringing down the debtors collection period and inventory holding period.

An insight into whether and how much an analysis of past finances may be utilized for future financial projections   Is it possible to develop a feasible financial projection if we assume that the past performance will continue? We may notice that the net margin (except in 2007) showed a gradual improvement. The company's performance improved in 2008 because it could affect cost control and better management of assets. Sales grew at 15.6% in 2008, while the average growth rate was 14.5%. If the company is able to maintain its operating efficiency and financial policies, we can possibly make the following assumptions, which appear to be just and reasonable:

1. Sales growth—15%
2. Net profit margin—3%
3. Net fixed assets to sales—40%
4. Net current assets to sales—35%
5. Hence, net assets to sales ratio—75%
6. Effective tax rate—50%
7. Dividend 10% of paid up capital

The financial forecast of IML during the next five years, on the basis of assumptions as stated above is provided in Table 8.5. Taking the sales of 2008 at Rs 238.3 crore as the basis, the sales for 2009 is calculated as Rs 238.3 × 1.15 = Rs 274 crore. Similar calculations have been made for the following years as well. It may be noted that projected sales have been used to estimate the items of profit and loss account and balance sheet, which are shown in Table 8.5.

This is the essence of the percentage of sales approach to financial forecasting.

TABLE 8.5 Financial projection for the next 5 years

Profit and loss account	2009	2010	2011	2012	2013
Net sales	274.0	315.2	362.4	416.8	479.3
Cost of goods sold	159.5	183.4	210.9	242.6	279.0
Gross profit	114.5	131.8	151.5	174.2	200.3
Non-manufacturing expenses	75.3	86.4	99.3	114.2	131.3
PBIT	39.4	45.4	52.2	60.0	69.0
Interest	22.8	26.4	30.4	35.1	40.1
PBT	16.4	19.0	21.8	24.9	28.9
Tax	8.2	9.5	10.9	12.4	14.5
PAT	8.2	9.5	10.9	12.5	14.4
Dividend	4.0	4.0	4.0	4.0	4.0
Retained earnings	4.2	5.5	6.9	8.5	10.4
Balance sheet					
Share capital	40.0	40.0	40.0	40.0	40.0
Reserves	27.1	32.6	39.5	48.0	58.4
Net worth	67.1	72.6	79.5	88.0	98.4
Borrowings	138.4	163.4	192.3	224.7	261.1

Contd

Table 8.5   *Contd*

Profit and loss account	2009	2010	2011	2012	2013
Capital employed	205.5	236.4	271.8	312.7	359.5
Net fixed assets	109.5	126.1	145.0	166.7	191.7
Net current assets	95.9	110.3	126.8	146.0	167.8
Net assets	205.5	236.4	217.8	312.7	359.5
Funds flow statements					
Retained earnings	4.2	5.5	6.9	8.5	10.4
Funds needed	23.6	25.4	28.5	32.4	36.4
Sources	27.8	30.9	35.4	40.9	46.8
Net fixed assets	15.2	16.5	18.9	21.7	25.0
Net current assets	12.6	14.4	16.5	19.2	21.8
Uses	27.8	30.9	35.4	40.9	46.8

The above projection may be supported by an analytical comment on the same, probably in the following manner.

The fund flow statement shows differences in the balance sheet items. For simplicity, the adjustment for depreciation has not been made. However, in practical life, this invariably becomes a crucial consideration while developing cash flows/fund flows.

The total funds required for financing the net fixed assets and net current assets during 2009 to 2013 is Rs 181 crore (i.e., the 5 years cumulative total of 'sources' as per our projected fund flow statements). Given IML's policy of paying a 10% dividend (Rs 4 crore) each year, retained earnings provide Rs 35.5 crore. The company will have to raise the balance amount (i.e., Rs 145.5 crore) either by issuing equity or debt. If IML does not want to finance its assets by the issue of equity, it will have to borrow funds. IML's forecasted ROE (return of equity) and debt equity ratio are shown in Table 8.6.

TABLE 8.6   Forecasted ROE and debt-equity ratio

Parameters	2009	2010	2011	2012	2013
ROE (%)	12.2	13.1	13.7	14.2	14.6
Debt equity ratio	2.06	2.26	2.42	2.55	2.65

As a final step of the above exercise, a sensitivity analysis may be carried out. As mentioned earlier, a sensitivity analysis is essentially a what-if analysis, and hence, we proceed in the following manner.

What will happen to IML's financial plan if all or some of the assumptions do not hold good? It has been assumed that sales will grow at 15% per annum. Historically, the company has grown in the same years of time at a rate less than 15%. Can IML maintain its profit margin at 3%? The last five years' average is only 2.7%. The margin was as low as 1.8% in 2007. One can also doubt the assumption of an asset ratio of 85%. Except in the most recent year 2008, the net assets to sales ratio has varied from 82% to 87%. If IML cannot improve its profitability and asset utilization, should it continue paying dividends? If it cuts or discontinues paying dividends, what will be the reaction of the shareholders?

The financial manager of IML can answer these and other similar questions if he/she performs a sensitivity analysis to examine the effect of changing assumptions on the firm's fund requirements. He/she may vary one variable at a time and see its effect.

8.4 ESTIMATING FUTURE SALES REVENUES—TRICKS OF THE TRADE

Typically, the starting point of financial projection, i.e., projected profit and loss statement, projected balance sheet, and projected cash-flow statement, is the forecast of sales revenues. While estimating sales revenue, the following should be considered.

- It is not advisable to assume high capacity utilization in the very first year of operation. Technological difficulties and other constraints, such as shortage of raw material, power problem, marketing difficulties, etc., may make it difficult for the firm to achieve a high degree of capacity utilization at the very inception. Thus, it is sensible to assume that capacity utilization would be somewhat low in the first year and, thereafter, increases gradually to reach the maximum level by the end of the fourth or fifth year of operation.
- Typically, it is assumed that the firm manages to sell whatever it produces, and hence finished stock adjustments are usually not done.
- The selling price considered for such estimation should be considered as the net of excise duty and sales tax. Otherwise, if it is treated as the gross of excise duty and sales tax, the excise duty and sales tax payment should be included in the expenditure line.
- Typically, it is assumed that the selling price per unit increases in the same proportion as that of the cost of production.

However, it is to be noted that the above does not represent any hard and fast rule, but simply depicts the standard of industry practices.

8.5 SALES FORECASTING

The prediction of the future sales of a company is termed as sales forecasting. An estimate of various factors, such as profit, cost, price, return, production plan, etc., are calculated in the sales forecast. The accuracy of this kind of prediction varies with the passage of time.

This process consists of the following five basic steps.

1. Determine purpose of focus.
2. Establish a time horizon.
3. Select a forecasting technique.
4. Gather appropriate data and analyse it.
5. Monitor the forecast to see if it will accomplish the desired result.

Sales forecast can be possible through the two following methods.

1. **Quantitative approach (time series)**

   While forecasting, instead of using the qualitative approach, we can also use the statistics based quantitative approach. This approach will be more accurate and methodical and obviously less biased. However, it is more complex and tedious to compute. Some of these quantitative approach techniques are listed below.

   (a) *Moving average method*—A forecast is made for a three or four year period, based on an average sale of recent value. If the data has random variation, a central value is calculated.

   (b) *Weighted moving average method*—Apart from a moving average, weights are also considered. For example, the data of the most recent years are given more weightage than very old data.

   (c) *Naive approach*—This method is considered to be the simplest method, as it uses the last period's actual value as a forecast. This means that the next, or the forecasted value in a series, will be equal to the previous one.

   (d) *Exponential smoothing*—It is the most sophisticated form of averaging random numbers, most widely used, and superior to the weighted moving average method. It is used when a large number of items are to be forecasted. The most recent values receive most of the weights, and it falls exponentially as the age of the data increases. It considers trend, cyclical, or seasonal data. Refer to Eqn (8.3).

   $$F_t = F_{t-1} + \alpha \, (A_{t-1} - F_{t-1}) \tag{8.3}$$

   where,

   F_t = new forecast

   F_{t-1} = old forecast

   α = smoothing constant

   A_{t-1} = old actual data

   t = current period

(e) *Linear regression or method of least square* Regression means dependence. It involves estimating the value of a dependant variable Y from an independent variable X. In simple regression, only one independent variable is used, whereas in multiple regressions, two or more independent variables are involved. Simple regression takes the form as shown in Eqn (8.4).

$$Y = a + bX \tag{8.4}$$

where,

   $Y =$ dependent variable

   $X =$ independent variable

   $a =$ intercept

   $b =$ slope (trend)

The representation for linear regression is shown in Figure 8.1.

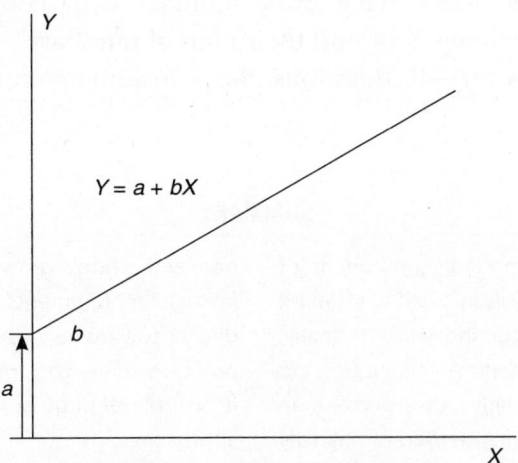

FIGURE 8.1 Linear regression

The model for multiple linear regression is shown in Eqn (8.5).

$$Y = a + b_1X_1 + b_2X_2 + b_3X_3 + b_4X_4 + \ldots + b_nX_n \tag{8.5}$$

Let us restrict our discussion to the linear simple regression of the form $Y = a + bX$.

Consider a model for the simple linear regression that is shown in Eqns (8.6) and (8.7).

$$b = \frac{\Sigma XY - \Sigma \overline{X}\overline{Y}}{\Sigma X^2 - n\overline{X}^2} \tag{8.6}$$

$$a = \overline{Y} -_b \overline{X} \tag{8.7}$$

where,

$$\overline{X} = \frac{\Sigma X}{n} \quad \text{and} \quad \overline{Y} = \frac{\Sigma Y}{n}$$

2. **Subjective or qualitative or judgemental techniques** In forecasting, we can also use the qualitative approach instead of applying numerical figures. By using previous experience, logical analysis, and analysing various feedbacks from various levels like end users, sales force, managers, decision-makers, etc., forecasting can be possible in the following ways.

(a) *Jury of executive opinion*—Finance, marketing, and manufacturing managers at top levels may join to prepare the forecast on the basis of their past experience.

(b) *Delphi technique*—It includes a series of questionnaires answered anonymously by managers and staff, these possessing the knowledge and the ability to contribute meaningfully. Successive questionnaires are based on information obtained from previous surveys. Thus, it enlarges the scope of information and the goal is to achieve a consensus forecast.

(c) *Poll of sales force opinion*—It is a joint estimate obtained from the sales personnel. They have direct contact with consumers and know about consumer behaviour and their plan of purchase.

(d) *Market survey*—It questions the consumers on future plans by random sampling.

SUMMARY

Financial forecasting is an integral component of planning a process. Outside analysts use it to estimate a company's success in the coming year. Normally, two types of standard forecasting techniques are deployed in industries, namely, the percentage sales method and the pro forma method of financial forecasting. In financial planning, the relationship between a firm's growth objectives and its external financial requirements are very useful. Sales forecast directs towards an estimate or plan of production, profit, revenue, cost, price, return, etc. Sales forecast is possible through both qualitative and quantitative approaches.

KEY TERMS

Financial forecasting A financial forecast is normally an estimate of the future financial outcomes for a company. Forecasting techniques essentially utilize past data to estimate future financial requirements.

Percentage of sales method This method starts with a forecast of sales and then estimates other financial statement accounts, based on some presumed relationship between sales and account.

Pro forma forecasting technique This method starts with a base year (generally the previous year) of financial statements. To use this method, one needs some kind of forecast about the transactions.

Sales forecasting Sales forecasting is a prediction about the future sales of a company. It is not a cent percent accurate method, and its accuracy decreases as the time horizon increases.

CONCEPT REVIEW QUESTIONS

1. Show how various financial estimates and projections are inter-related.
2. Define EFR. Derive its formula.
3. Show how the percentage sales method and pro forma forecasting are complementary to each other.
4. Describe different sales forecasting techniques.

5. To what extent is forecasting scientific, in comparison to prediction?
6. 'Estimating future sales revenues—The tricks of the trade'. Explain the various processes to estimate future sales revenues.

NUMERICAL PROBLEMS

1. The balance sheet of Saraswati Limited, as on 31 March 2009, is given in Table E8.2.

TABLE E8.2

(Rs in lakhs)

Liabilities	Rs	Assets	Rs
Share capital	25	Net fixed assets	100
Retained earnings	35	Inventories	50
Term loans	60	Accounts receivable	35
Bank borrowings	30	Cash	15
Accounts payable	40		
Provisions	10		
Total	200	Total	200

Net sales for the year ending 31 March 2009 was Rs 400 lakh, and projected sales for the year 2009–10 is Rs 500 lakh. The net profit margin on sales is 5%, and the dividend payout ratio is 60%. The tax rate for the company is 50%.

Estimate the EFR for the next year (2009–10), and prepare a projected balance sheet, a projected income statement, and a projected fund flow statement for the next five years, assuming that the external funds would be raised equally from term loans and short-term bank borrowings.

2. Zeta Company has the sales pattern during 2000–08 as given in Table E8.3. Compute the sales forecast for 2009.

TABLE E8.3

(Rs in lakhs)

Year	2000	2001	2002	2003	2004	2005	2006	2007	2008
Sales (Rs)	8	10	13	25	35	39	45	50	60

3. The balance sheet of Brunette Enterprise at the end of the year 2007 is given in Table E8.4.

TABLE E8.4

(Rs in lakhs)

Liabilities	Rs	Assets	Rs
Share capital	50	Fixed assets	130
Retained earnings	60	Inventories	90
Long-term loans	80	Receivables	80
Short-term borrowings	60	Cash	20
Trade creditors	50		
Provisions	20		
Total	320	Total	320

Sales for the year just ended (2007) is Rs 400 lakh. The expected sales for the year 2008 is Rs 500 lakh. The profit per cent is 5%, and the dividend payout ratio is 50%.

Find the following:

- Determine the external fund requirement for Brunette Enterprise for the year 2008.
- How should the company raise its external fund requirements, if the following restrictions apply.
  (i) Current ratio should not be less than 1.25.
  (ii) The ratio of fixed assets to long-term loans should be greater than 1.25. Assume that the company wants to tap external funds in the following order: short-term bank borrowings, long-term loans, and additional equity issue.

4. The following information is available on Supersonics Limited:

Sale of this year = Rs 10,000

Projected sales increase for next year = 10%

Profit after tax this year = Rs 600

Dividend payout ratio = 60%

Projected surplus funds available next year = Rs 150

Present level of spontaneous current liabilities = Rs 3,000

What is the level of total assets of Supersonics now?

5. V X Cycles had the following monthly sales figures in its Ranchi area in the year 2008 as shown in Table E8.5.

TABLE E8.5

(Rs in lakhs)

Month	Sales (Rs)	Month	Sales (Rs)
January	1,900	July	800
February	1,800	August	800
March	1,000	September	1,200
April	2,500	October	1,900
May	2,700	November	2,000
June	900	December	2,300

V X expects a 25% growth in the next year's sales. Make a monthly estimate of the sales of the next year.

ASSIGNMENT

Download the last five years' annual reports of any particular BSE listed company from its website, and forecast its coming 5 years, financial performance.

CASE STUDY
Enigma Enterprise

Enigma Enterprise, one of the fastest growing manufacturers of designer garments, had an annual growth rate of 18% in early 2000. It suddenly experienced a sharp decline. By the end of this decade, its growth rate fell to less than 9%. Amidst tough competition, it failed to maintain the brand image.

In 2008–09, the revenue growth was 15%, but the profit before tax declined to 20%. The VP Finance of Enigma was disappointed with the results. However, he was confident that the company would generate better results by implementing a new business strategy. The new strategy focused on three main principles: (a) to increase the image of the Enigma brand through a focused product development approach, and increase investment in stores, (b) to achieve efficiency in, supply chain management by the reduction of input and inventory cost, and (c) to reinforce the confidence of stakeholders.

At the beginning of 2009–10, the CEO of Enigma Enterprise wants assistance in the short- and long-term financial planning for the company. For this, he wants the future earnings and financial needs of the company to be estimated. He desires that the projections should be technically correct, and at the same time should provide practical insights, and be straightforward. Table E8.6 is provided to prepare the next three years' financial statements and demonstrate the debt financing needs of Enigma Enterprise.

A pencil and paper forecast

As an introduction to financial modelling, the forecasted income statement for the entire year, and the balance sheet at the end of the year are to be prepared. It may be prepared first with a pencil and paper, and later by a spreadsheet. The following assumptions may be used as a guide. Refer to Table E8.7.

TABLE E8.6

	2006–07 (Rs)	2006–07 (% sales)	2007–08 (Rs)	2007–08 (% sales)	2008–09 (Rs)	2008–09 .(% sales)
Income						
Turnover	300	100	320	100	368	100
Cost of sales	120	40	130	40.625	140	38.04
Gross profit	180	60	190	59.375	228	61.95
Other costs	150	50	160	50	190	51.63
Exceptional cost 1	4.5	1.5	0.0	0	11	2.98
Exceptional cost 2	16.6	5.53	2.5	0.78	1	0.27
Net interest expense	0.2	0.06	1.6	0.5	4.5	1.22
Profit before tax	8.7	2.9	25.9	8.09	21.5	5.84
Tax expense	8	2.67	10	3.12	4	0.04
Profit / loss after tax	0.7	0.23	15.9	4.96	17.5	4.75
Ordinary dividends	11	3.67	11	3.43	11	2.98
Profit / loss retained	(10.3)	(3.43)	4.9	1.53	6.5	1.76
Balance Sheet						
	2006–07 (Rs)	2006–07 (% sales)	2007–08 (Rs)	2007–08 (% sales)	2008–09 (Rs)	2008–09 (% sales)
Assets						
Cash	34.0	11.33	19.2	6	13.7	3.72
Accounts receivable	27.8	9.26	30.3	9.46	30.3	8.23
Inventories	38.6	12.86	44.7	13.96	51.3	13.94
Other current assets	12.5	4.16	15.6	4.87	17.5	4.75
Net fixed assets	87.8	29.26	104.7	32.71	120	32.60
Other assets 3	0	0	6.0	1.87	6.7	1.82
Total assets	200.7	66.87	220.5	68.90	239.5	65
Liabilities and equity						
Accounts payable	13.0	4.33	20.5	6.40	10.7	2.90
Taxes payable	11.3	3.76	11.7	3.65	7.1	1.92
Accruals	10.8	3.6	15.6	4.87	20.9	5.67
Overdrafts	0	0	0.3	0.09	0.7	0.19
Other current liabilities	21.6	7.2	13.3	4.15	16.9	4.59
Long-term liabilities	28	9.33	36.7	11.46	61.2	16.63
Other liabilities 4	1.7	0.56	1	0.31	0.4	0.10
Shareholder's equity	114.3	38.1	121.4	37.93	121.6	32.88
Total liabilities and equity	200.7	66.87	220.5	68.86	239.5	64.88

TABLE E8.7

Sales	Rs 515,845,000 (a 15% increase over 2008–09)
Cost of goods sold (COGS)	40% of sales
Operating expenses	52% of sales
Interest expenses	7% of debt
Profit before tax	Sales minus COGS minus D&A minus interest 35% of profit before tax
Dividends	Rs 11,000,000 (same as previous three years)
Earnings retained	Profit after tax minus dividend
Current assets	35% of sales
Fixed assets	Rs 12,00,00,000
Total assets	Current assets plus fixed assets
Current liabilities	30% of sales
Debt	Total assets minus current liabilities minus shareholders' equity
Common equity	Rs 12,05,00,000 plus retentions to earnings

Income statement: The sales figure should be used to estimate COGS and operating expenses. As the amount of debt is unknown, the interest expense may be taken as zero. Profit before tax, tax expenses, profit after tax, dividends and earnings retained, are to be estimated.

Balance Sheet

The current assets are to be estimated (35% of sales) and added to Rs 12,05,00,000 to get an estimate of the total assets. Next, the current liabilities (30% of sales) and common equity are to be estimated. Debt becomes the 'plug' figure to balance the two sides of the balance sheet. This 'plug' amount, arrived at by subtracting the current liabilities and common equity from the total assets, is actually the estimate of the external finance needed by The Enigma Enterprise at the end of the year 2009–10.

Iteration

Initially, the interest expense was considered as zero in the income statement. But this is not practical if there is an outstanding debt, or excess cash is invested in interest earning instruments. The income statement and balance sheet are actually dependent on each other. The rate of interest is necessary to estimate the interest expenses, which is necessary to estimate the debts. To deal with this problem, the best estimate of interest expense (7% of debt) may be considered in the income statement. Then the plug figure is to be re-estimated, and the interest expense is to be estimated again, and so on. By iterating five to six times there after, the estimate of interest expense and debt do not change much, and then the iteration is to be stopped.

The financial statement of Enigma Enterprise (Rs in '000,000) for the financial year that ended on 31 March 2006–07 to 2008–09.

1. Exceptional costs in 2008–09 included redundancy costs (Rs 45,00,000), cost of supply chain development (Rs 25,00,000), and impairment of fixed assets and goodwill (Rs 40,00,000).

2. Restructuring cost in 2008–09 and 2007–08 relate to the sale of manufacturing plants in Paharpur, and to the associated re-organization costs.

3. Other assets in 2008–09 and 2007–08 represented receivables relating to the sale of the company's Paharpur manufacturing plants

4. Other liabilities mostly included deferred taxes.

Discussion questions

1. Prepare a forecast, based on the full range of accounts as actually reported by Enigma Enterprise in 2008–09. Table E8.6 presents the result of the past three years. Forecast all the

accounts individually, for the next three years. Make your own assumptions regarding sales growth. Make other assumptions as needed.

2. How did you derive at your forecast?

3. Based on your pro forma projections, how much additional financing will Enigma Enterprise need during this period?

4. What are the most important assumptions in this forecast? What is the effect of the financing by varying each of these assumptions up or down from the base case? Why are these assumptions so important?

5. How will the findings be relevant to the CEO of Enigma?

6. In discussing your analysis with the CEO of Enigma, focus your comments on the results and state them as simply as you can.

FINANCING STRATEGIES

There is only one winning strategy. It is to carefully define the target and direct a superior offering to that target.

— PHILIP KOTLER

LEARNING OBJECTIVES

After studying this chapter, you will be able to
- Understand the various components of the cost of a project and their estimation
- Understand the different components of means of project finance
- Know the merits and demerits of various means of project finance
- Understand the various capital structure theories
- Know about project stakeholders and the different types of project contracts
- Conceptualize how to finance a big project
- Understand the different sources of venture capital in project finance
- Understand and differentiate between leasing and hire purchase

Mr Gilmore's Idea

M/s Purple Haze Limited, an Indian Company, was incorporated in the year 1980 and had started commercial production by early 1981. It manufactured industrial products. Initially, it aimed to establish itself as the primary player in the Indian market, with regard to product range. The Indian market had accepted that the quality of the products offered by M/s Purple Haze Limited was definitely among the best if not the best in the country. It was even said that its products were in no way inferior to that of its global competitors.

By the 1990s it had an average annual turnover of Rs 700 crore, netting an average annual after-tax profit of approximately Rs 150 crore.

However in 1983, the management of the said company (working hand in hand with a number of unscrupulous employees of the same company) started to gradually siphon out the funds through various modes, and the company as a whole fell into a difficult position. Although it was originally known as one of the most cash-rich companies of the country, it started to feel the pinch of an acute cash crunch. The company reported cash losses in 1996 and 1997, and by early 1998 its net worth had become negative. Consequently, the company was declared sick, and accordingly referred to the BIFR.

The mismanagement of the company, coupled with several horror stories of siphoning of funds by the management, became the headline of the Indian newspapers as all related facts became known. Consequently, the company lost its goodwill and image in the market, and its chances of revival and survival were reduced to an impractical dream.

In the view of the above, the entire board was replaced by a new set of directors who were professionally capable, energetic, hard task masters, and quite ethical in their business focus.

The turnaround exercise

The new board of directors drafted a revival plan, which was accepted and passed by the BIFR team. However, they were obviously a little apprehensive about the future prospects of M/s Purple Haze Limited, and decided not to allow the management to go ahead with their proposal on a test-run basis. They were ready to provide financial assistance to the tune of Rs 50 crore, which was estimated as the funds required to restart the operations of the said company, inclusive of the post production of the first month of operations.

The BIFR commented that if the company was able to record a cash profit within a period of six months of their operations (starting from 1 October 2000), then it may be inferred that the revival plan would prove to be successful in future.

The management's decision

The board of directors conducted a meeting involving the top executives of different functional areas of the company. Mr Murray (VP Production) said that his team would perform efficiently and would produce industrial products of excellent quality, as it used to do earlier. He assured the board that as far as the quality of products is concerned, the customers of the company would not have anything to complain about.

Mr Halford (MD) asked Mr Ozborne (VP Marketing) about the existing selling methodology and credit policies of the company. Mr Ozborne commented that all sales of the company used to be through dealers spread over the entire country. It was company policy to give a standard credit term of two months to dealers, with an understanding that if payment is made within a period of one month from the date of sale, the company will allow a cash discount of 3 per cent to the dealers.

Mr Halford told Mr Ozborne to continue with the existing policy of cent per cent sales through the dealers, but advised him to discontinue the credit terms. He explained that if M/s Purple Haze Limited has to survive, it must generate cash resources within a very short span of time. He requested Mr Richards to give discounts up to 8 per cent. He believed that such heavy discounts would motivate dealers to pay early.

Mr Ozborne was convinced that if the company agreed to such generous discounts, his team would not face any difficulty in selling their products to dealers against cash terms. Accordingly, he communicated the idea to his subordinates and gave strict instructions to sell materials only against cash.

The reality

The reaction of the market, however, did not appear to be as rosy as was expected. The marketing team of M/s Purple Haze Limited came up with a completely different picture, as given below.

The marketing professionals said that dealers were ready to accept their materials against strict cash terms. Their reasons were as under:

(a) In the past couple of years, M/s Purple Haze Limited had totally lost their market standing and reputation. Therefore, there were only a few takers for their products, especially since their competitors were doing pretty well, and customers were more or less satisfied with their products and services.

(b) The dealers were not at all confident about selling the products of M/s Purple Haze Limited, and for obvious reasons they could not be rigid with credit terms. Customers would definitely ask for the same credit terms as offered by their competitors.

(c) The dealers were not impressed by the concept of 'cash purchases with heavy discount', and were not ready to take the associated risk, especially when the future of the firm was so uncertain.

Back to square one

Mr Ozborne communicated the same to Mr Halford. The MD was not impressed and commented that it was a complete failure of the marketing team, and unless they could assure cash sales of their products, the company's mission would never be successful.

Mr Halford said, 'I don't know how you will do it Mr Ozborne, but it is very evident that unless you manage to do it, there is absolutely no chance of survival. You must find a way. I don't want our company to suffer because of you and your marketing team.'

An idea

When Mr Ozborne left Mr Halford's room he was very dejected and depressed due to obvious reasons. He had an informal chat with Mr Gilmore (VP – Finance) over coffee. He explained the entire situation to Mr Gilmore and told him that he was totally at a loss, and could not think of a solution.

Mr Gilmore asked him whether it was possible for the company to directly sell their products to the ultimate customers. Mr Ozborne explained that probably that may be considered as a long-term policy decision of the company, but due to various reasons it was not a very feasible option in the current crisis.

After considering the situation for sometime, Mr Gilmore came up with a brilliant idea which could deal with the situation quite well. He was quite confident that the probability of success would be reasonably high if this particular methodology was adapted. He explained the same to Mr Ozborne, who agreed that this was definitely one option worth trying.

What could Mr Gilmore's idea be?

9.1 COST OF PROJECT

Conceptually, the cost of projects represents the total of all items of outlay associated with a project, which are supported by long-term funds. It is the sum of outlay of the following.

- Land and site development
- Building and civil works
- Plant and machinery
- Technical know-how (the engineering fees)
- Technical fees and training expenses
- Miscellaneous fixed assets
- Preliminary expenses and capital issue expenses
- Pre-operative expenses
- Margin money for working capital
- Initial cash losses

Land and site development

In case of land and site development, selection and location of the project are very important. The financial implications of this depend on the availability of central and state government investment subsidy, sales tax deferment or exemptions, and income tax benefits, both during the implementation and operational stage. The elements of cost that determine the cost of land and site development are basic cost of land, transport charges, leveling of the land, laying of roads (internal and approach), construction of boundary wall and main gate, and fixing facilities such as electricity connection, water supply, sewerage, drainage, etc.

Building and civil work

The cost under this head can be divided into main factory building and allied civil work, such as administrative block, storage space for raw materials, and civil work for utilities.

Plant and machinery

The calculation of the cost of plant and machinery needs the integration of the entire plant, machinery, and equipment (both local and imported), and the entire process ordering, i.e., orders which have been placed and orders that are yet to be placed.

Technical know-how (the engineering fees)

It is often necessary to engage technical consultants or collaborates for advice and help in various technical matters, such as preparation of the project report, choice of technology, selection of plant and machinery, engineering advice, and so on. The amount payable for this technical know-how and engineering services to set up the project is a component of the projects cost. This is typically paid as a percentage of sales, which is treated as an operating expense while preparing the statement of profitability.

Technical fees and training expenses

Services of foreign technicians may be required to set up a project and supervise the process of implementation. The expenses incurred with respect to such assistance are usually disclosed under this head. Similarly, expenses on technicians who are being trained abroad to execute such projects are also included under this category.

Preliminary expenses and capital issue expenses

Preliminary expenses comprise expenditure that is incurred on identifying the project, conducting market survey, preparation of the feasibility report, drafting of memorandum and articles of association, and the company incorporation. Sometimes the capital required for a project is derived from public funding. The expenses incurred during this process are called capital issue expenses. Initial advertising and publicity expenses, printing charges, underwriting commission brokerage, and registration are some of the important parts of preliminary expenses.

Pre-operative expenses

Expenses of the following types incurred prior to the commencement of commercial production are referred to as preoperative expenses.
(a) Establishment expenses
(b) Rent, rates, and taxes
(c) Interest on borrowings
(d) Insurance charges
(e) Interest on deferred payments.
(f) Start up expenses
(g) Other miscellaneous expenses

Preoperative expenses are directly related to the project implementation schedule. So, delays in project implementation, which are fairly common, tend to push up these expenses. These expenses are capitalized by apportioning them to fixed assets on an acceptable and fair basis.

Provision for contingencies

Every project is influenced by the normal inflation rate, whose impact is computed in the initial cost estimates. However, the estimated normal inflation rate may be influenced by unpredictable expenses and uncertain price rise in the future. A provision for contingencies is supposed to deal with such unexpected occurrences. It is estimated at about 10 to 12 per cent of the project cost, according to industry standards.

Margin money for working capital

Commercial banks and trade creditors are the main sources of working capital. Long-term sources of finance also contribute to it and are called margin money for working capital. The margin money is a vital component of project cost and is, at times, used to meet capital in case of cost overruns. This process may result in problems with the working capital (or even working capital gap) at a later stage. In order to deal with this problem, the financial institutions suggest that a loan amount, equal to the margin money of working capital, be blocked at an initial stage for as long as the project lasts.

Initial cash losses

Most of the projects incur cash loses in the initial years. Yet, promoters typically do not disclose the initial cash losses because they want the project to appear attractive to the concerned financial institution and public. Failure to make a provision for such cash losses in the project cost generally affects the liquidity position and impairs operations. Hence, it is a prudent practice to provide for such initial cash losses in the project cost estimates.

9.2 MEANS OF FINANCE

The total project cost is usually met by the various sources of finance, namely, share capital, term loans, debenture capital, deferred credits, incentive sources, and other miscellaneous sources. The basic concepts of deferred credit, incentive sources, and miscellaneous source of finance are explained in Table 9.1.

The various means of finance that can be tapped for a project have been described above. The specific means of finance(s) to be utilized for any project is decided upon the following considerations:

- Norms of regulatory bodies and financial institutions (discussed in the 'Project financing' section)
- Key business consideration such as cost, risk, control, and flexibility (described in Table 9.2)

TABLE 9.1 Means of finance

Deferred credits	In quite a few cases, the suppliers of plant and machinery offer a deferred credit facility under which payment for such purchases can be made over a period of time.
Incentive sources	The government and its agencies may provide financial support as an incentive to certain type of promoters or for setting up industrial units at certain specified locations. These incentives may take the form of seed capital assistance provided at a nominal rate of interest or capital subsidy (usually awarded in India when the industrial unit is being set up in some backward locations). These special incentives may also take the form of tax deferment or even tax exemptions in certain cases.
Miscellaneous sources	A small portion of the project finance may come from miscellaneous sources like unsecured loans, public deposits, leasing finance, etc. Unsecured loans are typically provided by the promoters to bridge the gap between the promoter's contribution and the portion of equity capital that the promoters subscribed to as per the pre-specified norms laid down by the financial institution. Public deposit represents unsecured borrowings from the public at large.

TABLE 9.2 Criteria for project financing decision

Cost	The age old concept of 'debts being cheaper than equity' should be given due consideration while deciding on the means of project finances.
Risk	As we already know, the two main sources of risk for a firm are business risk and financial risk.
Control	Proper reviewing or monitoring is the utmost requirement in project financing decision. As it is true that any financing decision cannot be implemented correctly without a proper control mechanism.
Flexibility	This refers to the ability of the firm to raise funds from any source it wishes to tap. This refers to the firm's ability to manoeuvre. For example, if the firm is yet to exhaust its debt capacity, it may enjoy some flexibility in future. In other words, such reserve borrowing power enables the firm to raise debt capital to meet unforeseen future needs.

9.2.1 A Few Innovative Debt Instruments for Project Financing

A project can mainly be financed through the debt route, i.e., borrowed capital. This is because debt is less costly as well as more beneficial for the tax shield. But it is also true that too much debt welcomes financial distress, chances of bankruptcy, etc. Hence a trade off is necessary. Following are a few debt instruments by which companies generate funds and commence work on their projects.

Deep discount bonds Deep discount bonds are issued at a deep discount over its face value. They do not have any coupon rate and, therefore, are also called zero coupon bonds. For instance, SIDBI issued deep discount bonds in 1992 at a deep discounted price of Rs 2,500. Each of these bonds had a face value of Rs 1,00,000. They were to mature 25 years from the date of allotment. However, the investor, as well as SIDBI, could cash in the bond after 5, 9, 12, 15 or 20 years, at the deemed value of Rs 5,300, Rs 9,600, Rs 15,300, Rs 25,000, and Rs 50,000, respectively.

Thus, deep discount bonds allow one to control and conserve the cash flows during the life of the bonds. They also guard the investors against the reinvestment rate risk.

Convertible debentures A debenture that can be partially or wholly converted into equity shares is referred to as a convertible debenture. They are a popular form of debenture around the world. They are a relatively cheaper source of finance. The interest rate on them is lower as compared to that on straight debentures. The conversion price of the convertible debenture is particularly higher than the price at which equity shares can be issued currently. Thus, a company can successfully issue equity shares at a premium, using convertible debentures. These debentures also help in better cash flow matching. Companies usually go for easily serviceable financing instruments. As convertible debentures lower the initial burden, they are an attractive proposition for growing (and risky) firms. However, the firms eventually have to deal with an expensive dilution of control at a later stage.

Floating rate bonds Unlike conventional bonds, floating rate bonds do not involve a fixed interest rate. The rate of interest in floating rate bonds is associated with a benchmark rate, such as the T-Bill interest rate. For instance, the State Bank of India (SBI) introduced floating rate bonds in India in 1993. About 5 million (Rs 1,000 face value) bonds were issued. These were unsecured and redeemable bonds. They were in the form of promissory notes over the bank's maximum term deposit rate, carrying an interest of 3 per cent per annum.

The floating rate bonds have been particularly developed to deal with inflation risk. They are useful for a borrower who has to deal with returns (on assets) that fluctuate with interest rates. They are also suitable for banks and other financial institutions that issue loans at variable interest rates. Besides, floating rate bonds provide the much-desired stability to the principal investment of investors.

Secured premium notes (SPN) SPN is a debt instrument which is issued with a detachable warrant and a maturity of 4 to 7 years. As usual, during the lock-in period no interest is paid. After the lock-in the holder is repaid the principle amount along with additional interest or premium. The specialty of SPN is that return on investment (ROI) would be treated as capital gain, and not as regular income unlike others. The reason why investors gain more advantage is due to lower capital gain tax rate in India.

In 1992, TISCO issued SPN of Rs 300 each. The principal amount of the SPN was to be repaid in four equal installments of Rs 75 each, counted from the end of the fourth year together with an equivalent additional amount of Rs 75 with each such installment. No interest or repayment of principal was due or accrue on the SPN during the first three years after allotment. Each such SPN also had a detachable warrant, against which the holder could get one equity share of TISCO for Rs 80.

Term loans as a source of project finance Financial institutions give rupee term loans as well as foreign currency term loans (for meeting foreign currency expenditure on imports of assets, technical know-how, etc). Term loans typically represent secured borrowing. It is secured by way of first equitable mortgage of all immovable properties of the borrower, and also by hypothecation of all movable properties of the borrower. However, usually the hypothecation of movable properties is only in the nature of a second charge.

Financial institutions, in order to save their interests, put certain restrictions on the borrowers. The exact tenets of the restrictions are determined after considering the financial position of the borrower and the nature of the project. In addition to it, a borrowing firm may also be asked to avoid additional borrowing, complete all registration and clearance process with government agencies, broad base its management team, seek permission from the financing body before starting a new projects, etc.

Debentures They are often better options than term loans, as they offer more flexibility in terms of interest rate, period of maturity, repayment schedule, and security, besides other attractive propositions.

9.2.2 Equity Instruments for Project Financing

Instead of debt instruments, a project can also be financed by taking the equity route. They can be raised by issuing fresh issue, preference share capital, or from retained earnings.

Equity capital The net capital of the equity shareholders is referred to as equity capital. An equity shareholder has to undertake both profits and losses of the firm. Their liability is limited to their contribution to equity capital. Preferential allotment, initial public offering (IPO), right issues, private placements, etc. are various means of collecting equity capital.

Advantages In case of shortage of cash, a firm is not compelled to pay dividends. There is no legal prohibition against skipping equity dividends.
(a) It is not necessary for a firm to redeem equity capital, as it has no maturity date.
(b) Equity capital adds to the creditworthiness of the company as a result of its flexible provisions. The ability of a firm to raise debt finance on favourable terms is directly proportional to the size of its equity base.

Disadvantages
(a) Both, the cost of raising equity capital and the returns demanded by equity investors, are very high.

(b) Since equity dividends are not tax-deductible expenditure, they add to the hidden costs (debt funds).

(c) The control of the existing owners of the firm is weakened by the sale of equity shares to outsiders.

Preference capital   Preference capital is the capital where the fixed amount of dividend is paid with prior claim to that of share holders. No dividend to equity shareholders can be paid unless the claims of preference shareholders are satisfied.

Advantages

(a) Preference shares do not suffer from dilution of control. As usual, these shares do not carry voting rights.

(b) In the absence of any collateral in favour of preference shareholders, the assets of the firm are protected.

Disadvantages

(a) Preference dividend (like equity dividend) is not a tax-deductible expenditure, and hence the implicit cost is higher than that of debts.

(b) If the firm skips preference dividends for three years, it has to grant voting rights to the preference shareholders on matters affecting them, thus, resulting in dilution of control.

Internal accruals as a source of project finance   The internal accruals of a firm consist of depreciation charges and retained earnings. Depreciation represents the allocation of capital expenditure to various periods over which the capital expenditure is expected to benefit the firm.

Advantages

(a) It is readily available with the firm

(b) Utilization of internal accruals does not attract any issue costs.

(c) The question of dilution of control does not arise.

Disadvantages

(a) The amount available in the form of internal accruals may be very limited.

(b) The opportunity cost of internal accruals is quite high (internal accruals denote foregone dividends).

9.3 RAISING FINANCES IN INTERNATIONAL MARKETS

In a global market, project funds are sourced from the international market as well. It is a known fact that interest rates in foreign markets are low. But at the same time, people have to face the risk of fluctuation of the foreign exchange rate. The following are a few instruments by which a company can bring capital from abroad.

Eurocurrency loans   The Government of India has laid down specific guidelines for Indian firms who are interested in borrowing from foreign institutions in order to import machinery and other inputs. Eurocurrency loan is one of the most popular forms of external commercial borrowing. When the local currency of a country is deposited in a foreign bank, it is referred to as Eurocurrency. For instance, a dollar deposited in a bank outside the US is called a Eurodollar.

Let us assume that an American firm purchases some herbal products from an Indian company and pays for it in the form of a cheque drawn on an American bank. The Indian company deposits the cheque in their local bank. Now this deposit (in dollars) in an Indian bank is a Eurodollar deposit. The Indian bank can use such funds to issue Eurodollar loans.

Eurocurrency loans are syndicated loans. This means that for a single loan assignment, a group of banks or financial institutions come together to lend the required amount. The syndicate is represented by a lead bank. A syndicate fee has to be paid by the borrower to the lead bank. The fee includes the management fees of the lead bank, participation fees of the other banks, etc.

The floating rate method is used to compute the interest rate on Eurocurrency loans.

It is usually linked to the LIBOR (London Inter Bank Offer Rate). The spread over the LIBOR is mainly a function of the creditworthiness of the borrower, and the size and maturity period of the loan. For example, Air India obtained a Eurodollar loan of US$88 million in 1982, at an interest rate which was marginally above the LIBOR.

Euro bond   It is issued outside the country in whose currency it is denominated. For example, Eurodollar bonds are sold outside the US and Euroyen bonds, outside Japan. It is usually managed by a syndicate of investment banks and offered to investors in many countries. It is a bearer bond. This means that it is unregistered and payable to the person who carries it. The interest on it is usually paid annually or half yearly.

Global depository receipts   The indirect equity investment in the Euromarkets is represented by global depository receipts (GDRs). A depository (usually a major international bank) holds the shares issued by a company in the depository receipt process. Issues claims, dividends, reports, etc., vis-à-vis these shares are addressed by the depository. Each receipt is a claim on a particular number of shares. These claims are known as depository receipts outside Euromarkets, where they are referred to as global depository receipts.

GDRs have been issued by Indian firms since the early 1990s. The underlying shares are known as depository shares. A convertible currency, such as the US dollar, is used to denominate GDRs. As a result, they can be listed and traded in major stock exchanges. In the depository receipts mechanism, the issuing firm is not obliged to be listed at a stock exchange. The depository converts the dividends that it receives from the issuer firm in its home currency into convertible currency (like the US dollars). It is then distributed among the GDR holders. Thus, listing fees, onerous disclosures, and reporting requirements are avoided by the issuing firm.

Holders of GDRs can convert them into the underlying shares by surrendering the depository receipts to the depository.

Foreign domestic market Direct issuance is another way of raising money at the international platform. It requires the selling of securities directly in the domestic capital markets of foreign countries. For instance, a German company could issue yen-dominated bonds in the Japanese capital market. In Japan, such bonds are called samurai bonds. In the US and the UK, they are referred to as Yankee bonds and bulldog bonds, respectively. In this process, the issuer has to conform to the regulations of the domestic market of the foreign countries. In addition to that, a foreign issuer is bound by special duties that it must undertake.

Indian firms also trade in foreign domestic markets. For example, bonds were issued by Reliance Industries Limited in the US domestic capital market. ICICI and Infosys are some of the other Indian firms that have issued American Depository Shares (ADSs) and have performed well in the US equity market. Similar to GDRs, ADSs represent claim on a particular number of shares. ADSs are different from GDRs in a way that the former is issued in the US domestic market, and the latter in the Euromarket.

9.4 CAPITAL STRUCTURE

An appropriate (optimal) capital structure is an important decision for any business organization. The importance of the decision lies not only in the need to maximize returns to various organizational constituencies, but also because of the impact such a decision would have on the organization's ability to deal with its competitive environment. The most discussed proposition on capital structure is the Miller and Modigliani (M&M) proposition, which was propounded in 1958. It proposes an optimal capital structure which balances the risk of bankruptcy with the tax savings of debt. Once established, the capital structure provides greater returns to stock holders than what they would receive from an all-equity firm.

The discussion below focuses on the capital structure decisions in both perfect and imperfect markets.

Factors affecting the capital structure
1. Cost of capital
2. Cash flow projections of the company
3. Size of the company

4. Dilution of control
5. Floatation costs
6. Leverage

Features of an optimal capital structure
1. Profitability
2. Flexibility
3. Control
4. Solvency

Assumptions of capital structure theories
1. There is no income-tax, corporate or personal
2. A 100% dividend payout ratio
3. NOI is not expected to grow or decline over a period of time
4. No transaction cost
5. Investors are identical

The firm's ultimate objective is to maximize the shareholder's wealth. The capital structure decision should be examined from the point of its impact on the firm's value. The traditional theories believe that the capital structure affects the firm's value, while M&M argue that the capital structure decision is irrelevant. Here, traditional theories are to be discussed initially followed by M&M and other views.

Net income approach In this approach, the cost of equity (k_e) and cost of debt (k_d) remain unchanged when the degree of leverage (B/S) varies.

$$\text{Therefore, } K_o = k_d(B/B+S) + k_e(S/B+S) \tag{9.1}$$

$$K_o = k_d(B/S/(B/S+1)) + k_e(1/(B/S+1)) \tag{9.2}$$

where, K_0 is the cost weighted average of capital of the firm.

TABLE 9.3 Capital structure theories

	Wd	We
B / S = 0.75	0.75 / 1.75 = 0.43	1 / 1.75 = 0.57
B / S = 2	2 / 3 = 0.67	1 / 3 = 0.33
	0.24 increase	0.24 decrease

B is the market value of the outstanding debt.

S is the value of equity.

K_o declines as B/S increases. Refer to Table 9.3.

Net operative income approach The overall capitalization rate and cost of debt remains constant for all degrees of leverage.

$$K_o = k_d(B/B+S) + k_e(S/B+S) \tag{9.1}$$

$$K_e = k_o + (k_o - k_d)(B/S) \tag{9.3}$$

As B/S increases, k_e increases.

Traditional approach Cost of debt capital increases at an accelerating rate, after remaining constant up to a degree of leverage. The cost of equity gradually increases to a certain degree of leverage from an almost constant state. Once it crosses the degree of leverage, it increases at a very fast rate. The average cost of capital drops to a particular limit. A moderate rise in leverage does not affect its state much. However, it increases with significant rise in leverage.

Miller and Modigliani approach The Miller and Modigliani approach is based on the following assumptions.
1. Capital markets are perfect.
2. Information is costless.
3. No transaction cost.
4. Investors are rational.
5. Firms can be grouped into equivalent return classes on the basis of their business risk.
6. There is no corporate or personal income tax.

The M&M approach includes the following propositions.

Proposition I The total market value of the firm is equal to the total of market value of debt and equity, and it is independent of any degree of leverage. It is equal to its expected operating income, discounted at the rate appropriate to its risk class.
Symbolically,

$$Vj = Sj + Bj = Oj/kr \qquad (9.4)$$

where,

V_j is the value of the firm j

S_j is the market value of the equity of the firm j

B_j is the market value of the debt of the firm j

O_j is the expected operating income of the firm j

and kr = discount rate applicable to the risk class r, to which firm j belongs.

Proposition II The expected yield on equity,

$$ke = kr + (kr - i) \, B_j / S_j \qquad (9.5)$$

i = cost of debt or yield on debt

kr = discounting factor of the firm corresponding to its risk class

Proposition III The manner in which an investment is financed does not affect the cut-off rate for the investment's decision-making for a firm in a given risk class. The proposition emphasizes the point that average cost of capital is not affected by the financing decisions or degree of leverage, as both investment and financing decisions are independent.

TABLE 9.4 Proof of M&M hypothesis—The arbitrage mechanism

	Firm X	Firm Y
Risk class	r (same)	r (same)
Expected operating income	O	O
MV of equity	Sx	Sy
MV of debt	–	By
MV of firm	Vx	Vy
Interest rate on debt	–	I
Interest burden	–	iBy

Case 1: When Vx is less than Vy

- Referring to Table 9.4, if an investor holds Sy rupees worth of the equity shares of firm Y ($Sy = wSy$), the return is:

$$Py = w\,(O - iBy) \qquad (9.6)$$

- If the same investor sells shares, i.e., wSy worth of shares of the firm Y, and borrows wBy @ i% on personal account, then the investor can purchase $w\,(Sy + By)\,/\,Sx$ of the equity shares of the firm X ($Vx = Sx$).
- Now the return for the investor will be

$$Px = w\,[(Sy + By)\,/\,Sx]\,O - wiBy \qquad (9.7)$$

- Comparing Eqns (9.6) and (9.7), we find that as long as Vy is greater than Vx, Px will be greater than Py.

- It means that shareholders of firm Y will sell their equity and acquire shares of firm X by resorting to personal leverage, since it is profitable to do so.
- In this process Sy (also Vy) will get depressed, and Sx (also Vx) will rise till the equality between Vx and Vy is established.

Hence, the difference in the values of levered and unlevered firms would be abolished by the personal leverage of the investors.

Case 2: When Vx is greater than Vy

- Let $Vx\,/\,Vy = b$ (b is greater than 1)
- If an investor holds equity shares of firm X worth sx ($= wSx$), the return he gets is:

$$Px = (sx\,/\,Sx) * O = w * O \qquad (9.8)$$

- If he sells his shareholding worth wVx ($Vx = Sx$), he can buy a fraction wb of equity shares and bonds of firm Y, because the market value of firm X is b times the market value of firm Y which will make his return:

$$Py = wb\,(O - iBy) + wb\,(iBy) = wbO \qquad (9.9)$$

- Comparing Eqns (9.8) and (9.9), we find that as long as Vx is greater than Vy (i.e., b is greater than 1), we have Py greater than Px.
- It means that equity shareholders of firm X will sell their shareholding, and buy a portfolio consisting of shares and bonds of firm Y since it is profitable to do so.
- In the process, Vx will get depressed and Vy will rise till the equality between Vx and Vy is established.

9.5 INFRASTRUCTURE FINANCING

Infrastructure projects, which typically provide essential services, have one or more of the following characteristic features:

- They are highly capital intensive.
- They involve huge sunk costs.
- They have a long operating life.

The vital role of the infrastructure in the economy, the essential nature of the goods and services it provides, and the size of the project and its important social dimensions call for the governmental role in planning, promoting, and regulating the sector. When projects are operational, the role of the government can be determined by the ownership and the operational structure of the concerned project.

Traditionally, infrastructure projects in India were owned and managed by the government or government undertakings. Given the massive investments required in infrastructure, which plays a pivotal role in economic development, there is now a broad consensus that private sector participation in this activity must be encouraged.

Infrastructure financing is different from conventional project financing, primarily because most infrastructure projects are in the nature of private–public partnerships, and the evaluation of projects requires a careful understanding and analysis of the complexities inherently embedded in such partnerships. This is especially so in transitional economies, which are attempting to emerge from a historical environment where infrastructure was traditionally planned, developed, financed, implemented, and operated by the government to a newer environment where private initiative in infrastructure holds the key to rapid growth. Project financiers need to carefully evaluate to know if a framework (regulatory, legal, and financing) to support such initiatives exists or not. For a project financier, it is important to understand the risks associated with the project's construction and operation.

Typical configuration for infrastructure projects   Given the complexity of risks that need to be managed during the construction and operations phase of an infrastructure project, project sponsors have tended to follow some simple arrangements while implementing these projects.

(a) Projects are typically in a special purpose vehicle (SPV), which is a distinct corporate entity incorporated with the objective of implementing and operating a project.

(b) Project sponsors typically take an equity stake in the SPV, depending on the project cost, sponsors ability and objectives, as well as the requirements of the project lenders. The stake usually varies from 15 per cent to 30 per cent of the project cost, and is commonly referred to as the 'sponsor's contribution'.

(c) The SPV enters into contractual arrangements with the project contractors, operators, government, and project lenders (i.e., all the project parties). In non-recourse financing (which is commonly the case), project lenders do not enjoy any fallback on the resources/assets of the sponsors if the SPV fails to meet debt obligations.

(d) Infrastructure projects can be financed in relatively higher debts enquiry ratio as compared to conventional projects. For example, for an Indian road project, where private enterprises would construct, operate, and maintain the road during the concession period, and would earn an assured income from the National Highways Authority of India (NHAI) irrespective of the actual level of traffic, lenders may be willing to consider a high-debt equity form of financing structure.

In infrastructure projects, project partners focus their respective individual efforts towards strengthening the contracts. The contract defines the responsibilities and obligations of each participating member. It carefully allocates risky tasks to those parties who are better equipped to deal with it. Financial and legal advisors play an important role in the development and financing stages of the project. They guide the SPV and the sponsors towards proper allocation of risky processes. Besides, the legal and structural framework created by them helps the firm to avoid mismanagement of risky allocation in particular, and the project in general.

9.6 PROJECT STAKEHOLDERS

Major stakeholders of a project are project sponsors, SPV, project lenders, EPC contractors, O&M contractors, and the government. The responsibilities of each party are given in Table 9.5.

TABLE 9.5 Responsibilities of stakeholders

Parties	Responsibilities
Project sponsors	They are responsible for converting a concept into reality. They have an important role in setting up the SPV, identifying and recruiting correct managerial talent to implement and run the project. They have a significant equity participation in the SPV.
SPV	The SPV is responsible for delivering a bankable project during the financing phase, 'implementing the project and thereafter operating it in a manner that is financially viable. It selects and appoints all the project contractors, negotiates such contracts, raises finances, supervises construction and commissioning, and operates the project usually through an O&M contractor.

Contd

Table 9.5   *Contd*

Parties	Responsibilities
Project lenders	They provide loan to finance the construction of the project. Typically a consortium of project lenders led by a 'lead bank' ascertains project cost and in consultation with the SPV and project sponsors decides on the means of finances. Once the debt component is decided upon, they disburse the loan and perform a monitoring role during the construction phase and even beyond till such time the debt is fully repaid. Project lenders are usually secured by project assets and do not normally interfere in the day-to-day operations of the SPV.
EPC contractor	Typically an EPC contractor designs the project, procures all the engineering skills and equipment to construct the project, erects all the project facilities, and ensures that the test and trial runs are completed satisfactorily. Their key objective is to deliver a project within a specified cost and time frame. Normally, they also provide performance guarantee to the SPV.
O&M contractor	As the name indicates, O&M contractors are responsible for operating and maintaining the plant in line with industry best practices. Performance parameters that need to be achieved during operations are predefined in the contract with such contractors. They provide managerial skills and operations experiences to achieve and possibly surpass the agreed parameters.
Government	The government is a key player in an infrastructure project. It ensures that a proper legislative and regulatory framework exists that allows the concerned SPV to compete on a 'level playing field' along with existing entities.

9.7 PROJECT CONTRACTS

The key differentiating feature of infrastructure finance from other kinds of projects is the manner in which project risks are allocated to various parties in an infrastructure project. Through a comprehensive web of contracts, every major risk inherent in the project is allocated to the parties which is best able to assess and manage such risk. The different types of project contracts are shown in Table 9.6.

TABLE 9.6 Types of project contracts

Project contract	Key focus area
Shareholders agreement	An agreement between all shareholders of the SPV, including project sponsors, ensures that equity funding is fully tied up and available to the SPV as per its financing requirements and all major decisions are taken with the concurrence of all shareholders.
EPC contract	An agreement between SPV and EPC contractor is drafted in such a manner so as to ensure reduction of risk of time and cost overruns. By selecting a properly qualified contractor, the SPV can mitigate nonperformance risks to a considerable extent.

Contd

Table 9.6 *Contd*

Project contract	Key focus area
Project loan agreements	An agreement between the SPV and the project lenders ensures that the security and credit enhancement mechanisms are documented and enforceable by contract. It also ensures that lenders have additional rights in the operation and management of the company under conditions of default and can accelerate loan repayments if required.
O&M contract	An agreement with SPV and O&M contractors ensures certain level of mitigation of operating and performance risks.

According to a popular view, the network of contracts that aims at making group effort possible is the key to infrastructure project finance. Discouragement of monopoly and intelligent risk allocation go a long way in ensuring the success of a project.

This view, however, does not take into account the organizational structure, the ownership structure, and the financial leverage of an infrastructure project. In other words, it does not specify why a project is registered and managed as a separate company. It does not explain the involvement of the operators, contractors, suppliers, and consumers in the equity of the project firm. It also fails to question the high dependability of the project company on debt in the form of non-recourse financing.

9.8 PROJECT FINANCE

Project finance is the process of raising required funds for a capital investment proposal. Lenders mainly depend on the estimated future cash flows from that specific project to serve their loans. It is different from traditional financing in the following ways:

- In traditional financing, the utilization of borrowed money is not strictly controlled and monitored by the lenders. But in project finance, it is. Funds are released in stages, as and when assets are created.
- In traditional financing, cash flow from different assets and businesses are accumulated, whereas in project finance, only cash flows from the specific project related assets are considered for evaluating the capacity of repayment.

Evaluating financial soundness of a project (financiers approach) It may be noted that while evaluating the financial viability of a CAPEX proposal, banks and financial institutions based in India (irrespective of whether it is nationalized bank or a foreign bank or even a Indian private bank) depend heavily on an approach guided by 'financial ratios'. Thus, it is needless to comment that till date, the financiers of a CAPEX proposal treat the 'financial ratio approach' as the most effective and powerful tool to measure the financial viability cum strength of CAPEX proposals, in spite of its simplicity.

A list of financial ratios, which are widely used by financiers while evaluating and assessing the financial viability of CAPEX proposals, are provided in Table 9.7.

TABLE 9.7 Financial ratio analysis

The ratio	How do I compute this ratio	What do I assess through this ratio
Current ratio	Known to all of us	Short-term solvency position
Quick ratio	Known to all of us	Immediate solvency position
Net worth to TA	Net worth/total assets	Long-term solvency position
Debt equity ratio	Known to all of us	Measures long-term solvency and the leverage in the capital structure
Fixed assets to fixed liabilities	Fixed assets/Fixed liabilities	Indicates amount of financing done to finance fixed assets of the company. The financiers would always expect this ratio to be on the higher side
Gross profit ratio	Known to all of us	Measures profitability and growth
Operating profit ratio	Net operating profit expressed as a percentage of turnover	Measures profitability and growth
Return on capital employed (ROCE)	Net operating profit as a percentage of capital employed	Measures profitability and effective utilization of resources Incidentally, ROI effectively measures the same parameter as well
EPS	Known to all of us	One of the most important profitability measurement yardsticks
Sales to net worth	Sales/net worth	Effective utilization of shareholders resources
Capital turnover ratio	Sales/capital employed	Effective utilization of total resources
Sales to working capital	Sales/working capital	Effective utilization of working capital pool
Inventory turnover	Known to all of us	Measures effective inventory management
Debtors turnover	Known to all of us	Measures effective receivables management
Interest coverage ratio	Net cash accruals/ interest payments during the year	One of the most important ratios from the view point of the financier. Measures whether the party would be in a position to meet the interest liabilities from its operating cash flows
Debt service coverage ratio	PAT + interest + noncash charges upon loan installment (Principal + Interest)	Perhaps the crucial ratio from the viewpoint of the financiers. It measures the ability of the party to meet the debt obligations from operating cash flows

Other parameters invariably measured by financiers On the basis of the computation of the above ratios, the financiers would invariably assess whether the proposal is showing symptoms of under- or over-capitalization, or symptoms of under- or over-trading. In such cases, the financier will not be inclined to put valued resources in the proposal until adequate remedial measures are chalked out by the organization as a safeguard for the same.

The banks and financial institutions financing CAPEX proposals will have a look at the project IRR and break-even analysis before investing. The computation of project IRR is followed up by a detailed exercise of sensitivity analysis to visualize the extent of the various risks encompassing the proposal under review. In spite of the inherent limitations of IRR and sensitivity analysis techniques, these parameters happen to be the hot favourite evaluation yardsticks as far as Indian financiers are concerned.

From the discussion above, we will now try to understand Mr Gilmore's idea from the opening case. Refer to Exhibit 9.1.

....

EXHIBIT 9.1 Solution to the opening case—What could Mr Gilmore's idea be?

Mr Gilmore's idea
In view of the facts of the case, it appears that Mr Gillmore, VP Finance of M/s Purple Haze Limited, is considering the option of 'bill discounting.' In order to understand the significance and utility of the sam, it is necessary to understand the salient features of 'bill discounting' transactions.

Bill Financing
Analogically, a 'bill of exchange' is like a post dated cheque. It is an instrument containing an unconditional order, signed by a drawer, directing a certain person (the drawee) to pay a certain amount of money to the bearer of the instrument (the payee). Thus, there are three parties in a bill of exchange transaction, namely, the drawer, the drawee, and the payee. The method of operation of the same is quite simple. The drawer, through the instrument, asks the drawee to pay the specified amount after the lapse of a predetermined period. The drawee accepts the same and, thus, gets the desired credit facilities. Once accepted, it becomes a negotiable instrument and can be bought or sold in the market.

However, as per the standard practice, the drawer sells it at a discounted value to the concerned banker and obtains immediate money. Thus, both the drawer and the drawee derive benefits out of such arrangements. It may be noted that a bill of exchange moves in the money market on the strength of the creditworthiness of the drawer and the drawee. Once the bill is accepted, the credit of the drawer is substituted by the credit of the drawee.

Thus in the given case, an arrangement of 'bill discounting' may sort out the problems which are being encountered by M/s Purple Haze Limited. The company may act as the drawer of the bill, and the dealers (i.e., the drawee) may accept the same. In the process, the dealers will get the desired credit terms, and M/s Purple Haze Limited may obtain ready cash by discounting the bill with the bankers. It is needless to mention that the discounting charges may be quite high, but it may also be appreciated that the said company should be ready to accept such high charges in view of the acute cash crunch it is encountering at present.

Moreover, the company had already taken a decision to offer very generous discounts to its dealers (against cash terms), and hence, logically it should be prepared to bear the high bill discounting charges of the bank as well. The bankers may be interested in the deal, simply because it will effectively be providing credit facilities to the dealers, who are expected to have a better market standing as compared to M/s Purple Haze Limited. Thus, it is interesting to note that the above arrangement may satisfy all concerned parties, and there is a high possibility that the deal will be successful.

It may be noted that in the above solution, it has been assumed that the concerned parties will not face any difficulties in obtaining such facilities. In other words, the administrative aspects of bill financing, such as working capital limits, etc., have not been taken into consideration in the above mentioned solution, because the 'case facts' do not help us in developing a concrete opinion in those lines.

It may be noted that the concerned company may also consider the option of 'factoring', in order to resolve the problem at hand.

Factoring

The motto of factoring is to 'produce, sell, and forget'. It is an arrangement under which a business sells its receivables to a specialized agency, known as factor. Functionally, the credit department of a business is substituted by a factor. The factor undertakes collection, accounting, and management of debts. The customer, at the time of sale, is informed about the arrangement, so that they make the payment directly to the factor. Normally a factor agrees to pay substantial advance against the receivables. The business thus gets the benefit of the immediate availability of cash. A factor may purchase receivables without recourse or with recourse. If the arrangement is without recourse, then the factor becomes liable to bear the loss of bad debts. In the case of with recourse factoring arrangements, such loss is borne by the business firm itself. The fees charged by the factor, in case of without recourse arrangement, is much more than the other variety, for obvious reasons. Thus, it is needless to mention that from the cash flow point of view, factoring is an extremely valuable arrangement. Other benefits include elimination of collection costs, and costs associated with credit investigation and analysis.

In view of the above, it may be commented that M/s Purple Haze Limited may consider the option of 'factoring' (with or without recourse, as considered appropriate by the management of the company). Thus, the dealers will get their desired credit terms, and the concerned company will then get ready cash simultaneously. M/s Purple Haze Limited should be in a position to accept the high factoring fees which may be charged by the factor, since the company is as it is ready to bear the burden of generous discounts against cash terms of sale.

9.9 FINANCING IN A BIG PROJECT

It may be noted that all infrastructure projects are not of a similar type, and hence a power project may be completely different in substance and form as compared to a telecommunications project. However, certain features are common.

Large project costs, a virtually continuous project implementation, long gestation period, and a widely dispersed customer base that exposes the project to commercial risks and requires significant marketing and selling efforts characterize telecommunication projects. This would be further explained through an example on telecommunications projects.

Financing telecommunications projects In telecom projects, companies typically commercialize certain areas where the equipment is installed as the company's reach expands with time, so that each geographical territory can be commercialized. In telecom, gestation periods are significant (could range from 3 to 5 years). As the project adds subscribers over a period of time, revenue increases and the project turns profitable. Unlike a power project, which generates reasonably flat revenues and profitability over its continued implementation of strategy, and increase in subscriber base, it demonstrates increase in profitability over a period of time.

Usually, telecom projects require funding at their initial stage, as they are prone to suffer losses at this stage. The 'peak negative cash flow period' concept is adopted by lenders in order to compute the cost of a telecom venture. This concept calculates the net external funding required by the project, along with the maximum duration for which the project would require external support. In this duration, hardware cost, land and construction cost, entry charges, preoperative expenses, interest payment during the construction period, working capital finances, net cash losses, and various other contingencies comprise the project cost. These needs are met through debt, connection charges, customer deposits, and equity investments.

Private telecom cannot function in the country without a license from the Department of Telecom. With exception to variation due to the demand for particular territory coverage, a standard license is applicable to various operators. The guidelines of the license play an important role in shaping the project framework. The license fee includes a one-time entry fee and a revenue share. The telecom project is also obliged to pay special attention to extend the network to rural areas and manage the same within the specified project cost.

Apart from the license itself, project financiers in telecom projects evaluate parameters as given in Table 9.8.

TABLE 9.8 Parameters of project finance

Parameters	Explanation
The equipment supply contract	Such contracts are judged for pricing competitiveness, flexibility for renegotiation, etc. (primarily because global telecom equipment prices have tended to fall significantly over the years).
The financial strength of the project sponsors	On an account of unforeseen circumstances, business plans could go awry leading to higher than envisaged losses and hence, greater than anticipated equity financing requirements.
The business plan assumptions	As the telecom markets become more and more de-regulated and competitive, telecom services are anticipated to cost lesser over a period of time. Project financiers need to be aware of the experiences in other countries that have de-regulated telecom markets and test the project's assumptions against empirical evidences available from these markets.
The competitive environment	Several de-regulated telecom markets, unless constrained by availability of spectrum, allow unlimited number of participants. In such a scenario, early movers almost always find project financiers easier to secure while subsequent entrants may either not be able to secure financing at all or may have to agree to limited or full recourse financing arrangements. In a competitive environment, lenders need to have clarity on projects that they would consider for financing.

9.10 VENTURE CAPITAL IN PROJECT FINANCE

Venture capital may be described as pools of capital constituted for investing in relatively high risk opportunities, in anticipation of potentially high risk adjusted rates of return. Investors in these funds are usually interested in long-term capital appreciation (7 to 12 years), and neither short-term gains or periodic yields by way of dividend and interest. Most venture capital funds are not listed on any exchange nor have an alternative secondary market mechanism worth mentioning. Investors in venture capital funds are institutional investors and high net worth individuals who have the ability and preparedness to accept the liquidity. A variety of financial institutions, corporations, and individuals participate in the venture capital industries as investors.

The popular impression is that venture capital is the same as financing or technology centric business or innovative business ideas. In reality, venture capital is broader and a much more flexible form of financing business enterprises. The following are some typical examples of venture capital investments.

- A national or regional chain of stores across India, based on a new retailing concept such as retailing of IT infrastructure suppliers in offices.
- An infrastructure company that has developed a state-of-the-art telecommunication switch.

9.11 SECURITIZATION

Securitization is the process by which financial assets such as loan receivables, mortgage backed receivables, credit card balances, hire purchase debtors, lease receivables, trade debtors, etc. are transformed into securities. Securitization is different from 'factoring' because 'factoring' involves the transfer of debts without transforming such debts into securities. A securitization transaction normally has the following features.

(a) Financial assets such as loan assets, mortgages, credit card balances, trade debtors, etc. are transferred fully or partly by the owner (known as the originator) to a special purpose entity (SPE) in return for immediate cash payment or other forms of consideration. The assets so transferred are the 'securitized assets', and the assets or rights, if any, which are being retained by the originator are called the 'retained assets'.

(b) The security investment manager (SIM) finances the assets transferred to it by issue of securities such as pass through certificates (PTC) or debt securities issued to investors.

(c) The originator may continue to service the securitized assets (e.g., initiating collections, etc.) with or without charging servicing fees for the same.

(d) The originator may securitize or agree to securitize future receivables (i.e., receivables that do not exist at the time of agreement but which would arise in future). In case of such securitization, the future receivables are estimated at the time of entering into the transaction, and the originator receives the purchase consideration for the same in advance. Securitization can also be in the form of 'revolving period securitization' where future receivables are transferred as and when they arise or at specified intervals, such transfers being on prearranged terms.

9.11.1 Credit Enhancement Feature in Securitization

This is an arrangement designed to protect the holders of the securities issued by the SPE from losses or cash. Applying the following techniques ensures avoidance of any mismatch arising from shortfall or delays in collections from securitized assets.

(a) SPE creates a cash deposit which it can use under specified circumstances to discharge financial obligations in respect of the securities held by the investors.

(b) In certain cases, the assets which are made available to the SPE are in excess of the securitized assets, the realization from which may be utilized to fund the shortfalls or cash.

(c) In a few cases, the originator accepts recourse obligation.

(d) A third party may give a guarantee by accepting the obligation to fund any shortfall on the part of the SPE in meeting its financial obligation, in respect of securitization transactions.

9.11.2 Structuring Securitization Instruments

Securitization instruments are issued by SIM. (Certain standard terms in relation to securitization transactions are explained in Table 9.9.) They may be categorized into senior and subordinated securities, such that the senior securities (issued to investors) are cushioned against the risk of shortfalls in realization of securitized assets by the subordinated securities (issued normally to the originator). Payments on subordinated securities are due only after the amounts due on senior securities are discharged.

A specific securitization deal (in the nature of partial de-recognition)

An originator does not require transferring the complete financial asset in a securitization transaction. Only a part of this asset can be transferred. There are two different modes of doing so. First, only a proportionate share of asset is transferred. For example, the originator may transfer a proportionate share of loan along with

TABLE 9.9 Terminology in securitization

Terms	Brief explanation
Call option	This is an option that entitles the originator to repurchase the financial assets transferred under a securitization arrangement from the SIM. The option may be at a predetermined price or at a value to be determined (e.g., fair value on the date of exercise of the call option).
Interest trip	This is a contractual agreement to separate the right to all or part of the interest due on a bond, mortgage loan, or the other interest bearing financial asset from the financial asset itself. By this agreement right of the original financial asset and its interest are separated.
Investor	Investor is the person who finances the acquisition of the securitized assets by subscribing to PTC (explained below) or debt securities issued by the SPE.
Originator	Originator is an entity that owns the financial assets proposed to be securitized and initiates the process of securitization in respect of such assets.
Pass through certificates	These are instruments acknowledging a beneficial interest in the securitized assets such that the payment of interest on such instruments and the repayment of the principal are directly or indirectly linked or related to realizations from the securitized assets.
Principal strip	This is the right to the remainder of the financial asset, which is net of all rights that have been stripped, thereby one or more contractual arrangements.
Recourse (obligation)	This is an obligation of the originator to reimburse or compensate fully/partly the investors for shortfalls in payments arising out of failure of debtors to pay or pay within the specified time frame or shortfalls due to some other defects in the securitized assets.
Servicing assets	Servicing assets is a contract to service financial assets under which the estimated future revenues from contractually specified servicing fees, late charges, etc., are expected to more than adequately compensate the servicer (who may be the originator as well) for providing such services.
Special purpose utility	SPE is an entity, which acquires the financial assets under securitization and normally holds them till maturity. SPI is an independent entity, usually constituted as a trust or a limited company, formed with small capital for the specific purpose of funding the transaction by issue of PTC or underlying debt securities.

the right to receive the interest and principal, vis-à-vis the loan amount. But the nature of transfer should ensure that the originator and the SPE would share all future cash flows, profit or loss, etc. arising on a deal.

Second, if the financial asset of the originator includes rights on two or more benefit streams, it can retain one of the benefit streams and transfer the other. For example, an originator may retain the interest strips and servicing assets of a loan while transferring the principal strip of the same.

9.12 LEASING AND HIRE PURCHASE

Project financing can be possible through leasing and hire-purchase mechanism. The following section deals with various aspects of leasing and hire-purchase.

9.12.1 Leasing

An important source of medium term financing is leasing. It is a system in which the user of an asset is different from the party that owns and finances it. The user is known as a lessee and the owner as a lessor. To use an asset, the lessee is required to make sequential payment to the lessor at particular intervals of time, as specified in the lease agreement. Lease is an ascribed form of debt. It is similar to borrowing a certain value in kind, instead of cash. The 'kind' in case of the lease is the asset. Just as in any loan guidelines, the lease has to follow a particular repayment schedule for a certain period of time, depending upon the kind of lease and the nature of the asset borrowed.

Lease can be provided both directly (by the asset owner) and indirectly (by financing companies, merchant bankers, or even subsidiaries of commercial banks). The agents of the indirect method are part of the leasing business. They acquire an asset from its owner, and lease it to the contending user. Thus, one can say, an asset user gets exclusive rights over the asset from its owner, at a payment of a certain rental over a period of time.

Appropriate discount rate while evaluating leasing proposals As a lessee is bound by a lease contract to pay a certain rental comprising of interest and principal repayment at scheduled intervals, a finance lease option is considered safer by the financial analysts as compared to a borrow option.

The different tax shields may involve enough risk to require a higher discount rate. For instance, a lessee may be sure of making the lease payments; however, it may not be confident regarding its earning of taxable income to utilise the tax shields. In such a situation, a higher discount rate (instead of the standard after tax borrow rate) would be required to be applied to the cash flows generated by the tax shields. The cash flows associated with maintenance costs and salvage value realization, would also require higher discount rate as they too are difficult to foresee.

It may be observed that evaluation of a lease might in principle end up using a separate discount rate for each type of cash flow affecting the decision making process. Logically, each such discount rate should be chosen in a manner to ensure that it exactly captures the risk exposure of that particular line of cash flow. But, established profitable firms usually find it reasonable to simplify the calculations by discounting the related cash flows at a single, rate based on the rate of interest the firm would have effectively paid if it borrowed rather than leased. Herein lies the rationale for discounting lease cash flows by an after-tax borrowing rate.

Various forms and features of lease agreements

Period   Probably no other form of financing has such a large variation in terms of time. Lease can be for any period, ranging from a day to hundreds of years. The lease period is finally determined on the basis of the requirements of the lessee, and sometimes on the basis of the active useful life of the asset under lease.

Payment   The payments for the use of leased assets are made in a sequential pattern. These payments can be made on a daily, weekly, monthly, quarterly, or usually on a yearly basis, depending upon the terms of the lease agreement.

Security   Generally, a lease transaction does not emphasise the security, since the asset remains under the ownership of the lessor. In the event of a default, the asset can always be taken back. Even in the case of bankruptcy of the lessee, the leased asset is returned to the lessor who stands with other creditors in respect of defaulted lease payments.

The advantages and disadvantages of leasing are listed in Table 9.10.

TABLE 9.10   Advantages and disadvantages of leasing

Advantages	Disadvantages
Leasing is a very simple and convenient method of financing. For example, it is quite simple for a construction company to take a concrete mixer on lease for a short duration, rather than going for an outright purchase of the same. The asset may simply be returned to the lessor after the objective has been satisfied. There will be no need to keep the mixer idle when other activities are in progress.	It is usually costlier than the normal purchase of an asset. However, the true cost of a lease needs to be carefully analysed. Such an analysis takes into account opportunity costs associated with buying the asset and net present values of the sequential future repayment obligations.
At the time of tight money conditions in the market, it may be difficult to raise funds for buying certain equipment. Again if the amount required is not very substantial, it may not be economical to raise a loan from the money-market. In such cases, leasing will be a handy tool for short-term financing.	Tax authorities sometimes provide some extra advantages for buying and owning new equipment. These are not available to the lessee, since the equipment is under the ownership of the lessor. However, quite often the lessor passes such tax benefits to the lessee in form of reduced lease rentals.
In the case of short-term leases, the lessee is free from the fear of technological obsolescence, and on the contrary, keeps on acquiring the latest model of equipment from time to time.	The rigidity of periodic payment obligations may cause some problems in subsequent years, especially in case of long-term lease agreements. As such long-term leases are generally cancelable. The lessee, therefore, needs carry the asset till maturity of the contract even if very advanced technological models have entered the marketplace.

Forms of lease

Operating lease Operating lease is for a shorter duration, much less than the useful life of the asset. The amount of the asset is thus not fully amortised from one specific lease. In such cases, the lessor either releases or sells the equipment after a specific lease agreement expires. Another important feature of an operating lease is that the agreement is cancelable. A common example is the lease of a dwelling unit where the lessee can give a notice of the cancellation of the lease as per the terms of the lease agreement, and the lessor has to make arrangements for the release of the premises. Due to these features, the lessor of the equipment is always exposed to the risk of technological obsolescence in an operating lease.

Financial lease The period of a financial lease is stretched to the useful commercial life of the asset. The amount due is fully amortised during the tenure of the lease period. The lessor holding the title of the equipment owns the residual value as well. Financial lease is usually not cancelable. The risk of obsolescence in such cases is borne by the lessee.

Net lease Both operating and financial leases can be gross or net leases. To be gross or net, a lease depends upon the fact as to who will bear the costs of maintenance, insurance, and other levies associated with the leased asset. In the case of a net lease, the lessee bears those costs, whereas under gross lease, such costs are borne by the lessor. A finance lease is commonly a net lease. Justifiably, because the lease agreement is non-cancelable, a lessee is more careful of its maintenance.

Sale and leaseback transaction When a firm buys an asset from its owner and leases it back to its earlier owner, it is referred to as the sale and leaseback arrangement. Generally, the asset is sold at the market value. At the initial sale, the original owner of the asset receives the asset cost from the buyer. As a result of leaseback, it is also entitled to the commercial use of the asset during the scheduled lease period. In return, the firm (ex-owner, who is now a lessee) has to pay the periodic rentals, and give up the ownership of the asset, and thereby also the residual value of the asset.

Direct leasing Under direct leasing, a company acquires the use of an asset it did not own previously. For example, a vendor sells the asset to the lessor who in turn leases it to the lessee. Alternatively, the manufacturer of the asset can directly lease it to the lessee.

Leveraged leasing A special form of leasing is sometimes used in financing assets requiring large capital outlays. It is known as leveraged leasing. There are three parties involved in these deals

- The lessor
- The lessee
- The lender

From the perspective of a lessee, all the types of leases discussed above are more or less similar. It is the lessor who experiences change due to different lease types. The lessor acquires an asset by an equity investment of say 20 per cent. The lenders finance the remaining 80 per cent of such a purchase price.

Whether the given asset is mortgaged, lease rental payments are assigned, or if it is the case of period interest payments, this loan remains secured. It is important to note that in this case the lessor is the borrower. The depreciation charges associated with the asset under consideration can be claimed by the lessor or the owner of the asset.

Although a lease agreement brings particular benefits for the lessee, scientific research suggests that financers also prefer lease financing over ordinary loan disbursement.

Let us discuss the factors that contribute to such a preference. The position of a lessor is superior to that of the supplier of capital. In case the lessee (or the borrower) liquidates, the lessor is the owner of the asset and can take it back from the lessee if the latter defaults on any tenet of the lease agreement. However, it is a convenient process for a lender if the borrower defaults. Even the loans secured against an asset are not of any particular help, as there are delays and pocket costs associated with the taking over of assets by the lender. The delay, in turn, affects the opportunity costs. The lessor is immune to such painstaking and costly affairs. Besides, the process of bankruptcy also has some costs associated with it.

Thus, the supplier of capital prefers to make a lease rather than a loan agreement. The incentive for the supplier becomes stronger as the risk associated with the firm seeking finance increases. In case of bankruptcy of a firm looking for finance, a lessor is in a much better position than a lender, and this continues to be one of the primary motivations among the suppliers of capital to choose lease over loan.

Lessor to claim income tax depreciation (Year 2001 Central Board of Direct Taxes (CBDT) Circular) Irrespective of the provision laid down in the accounting standard on leasing, issued by the Institute of Chartered Accountants of India (ICAI), the CBDT circular clarifies that depreciation (for the purpose of income tax computation) would continue to be claimed by the lessor for all income tax purposes. It states: 'It has come to the notice of the CBDT that the new accounting standard of ICAI on leasing requires capitalization of the asset by the lessees in financial lease transactions. It is hereby being clarified that, by itself the accounting standard will have no implication on depreciation treatment as per Income Tax provisions and hence, depreciation will be continued to be claimed by the lessor only.'

9.12.2 Hire Purchase Transaction

The hire purchase (HP) system refers to that system where the buyer undertakes to pay the price of the goods/assets bought by installments (inclusive of interest) to acquire the possession immediately, but the title passes to the buyer only on payment of the last installment. Usually, under the terms, a provision for the payment of an initial amount on the date of delivery is made. This payment is called the 'down payment' or 'initial payment'.

Hire purchase agreement as distinguished from ordinary sale transaction   Under a sale, the title of goods passes to the buyer as soon as the transaction is complete, whereas under HP agreement, the legal title passes to the buyer only on payment of the last installment.

The seller under HP agreement can repossess the asset in case of default of installment(s) payments by the buyer. In that case, the payments made before such repossession can be forfeited by the seller, in lieu of rent/hire charges for the use of such goods. Hence the name hire purchase, meaning that the HP agreement effectively boils down to the purchase of the asset, or alternatively taking it on hire (depending on circumstances).

Depreciation on assets acquired under hire purchase agreement   The argument for providing depreciation in cases of assets acquired under HP agreement is that since it is the intention of the purchaser to be the owner of the asset ultimately by making regular payments, depreciation should be provided in the same way as in the case of an on the asset acquired 'ownership on acquisition' basis.

As per the CBDT circular which clarifies the income tax impact of depreciation in the case of an HP contract, if the assessee acquires an asset for the purpose of business and profession, depreciation can be claimed by the concerned assessee by capitalizing such an asset.

Asset acquired under HP agreement to appear in the balance sheet of the buyer   There is a strong argument that unless the ownership of any asset is acquired, it should not be shown in the balance sheet. In the case of an asset purchased under the HP system, the ownership is acquired only after the payment of the last installment. If the buyer defaults in the payment of the installment(s), the asset can be repossessed by the seller. Such being the case, the asset acquired should not appear in the balance sheet at any time before the ownership is acquired. However, in the practical field, this argument is ignored and the asset is shown in the balance sheet before the ownership is legally acquired, on the contention that acquiring the ownership is the ultimate intention of the buyer, and hence there is least possibility of default in payment.

Actually, this is based on the basic accounting principle, namely, 'substance over form', meaning that the substance of the transaction is more important than its legal form.

Example 9.1 **Leasing**

Sobisco Enterprises wants to purchase a new machine of Rs 1 crore. Its useful life is 10 years, and at the end its scrap value will be Rs 15,00,000. The company can use either lease or debt financing. Lease payments will be Rs 15,00,000 each for ten years to be paid at the beginning of each year. For debt financing the interest rate will be 11%, and debt payments would be due at the beginning of each year. The company is in the 25% tax bracket. Which method of financing can be recommended—lease or debt?

Solution

Annual debt payment (Refer Table E9.1).

$$10,000,000 = \sum_{t=0}^{9} \frac{X}{(1.11)^t}$$

$$10,000,000 = X + 5.537 \times X$$

Therefore,

$X = 10,000,000 / 6.537 = Rs\ 15,29,754$

TABLE E9.1

End of year	Debt payment	Amount owing at end of year	Annual interest
0	15,29,754	84,70,246	0
1	15,29,754	5,98,026.94	9,31,727.06
2	15,29,754	14,63,971.037	65,782.9634
3	15,29,754	13,68,717.186	1,61,036.814
4	15,29,754	13,79,195.11	1,50,558.8905
5	15,29,754	13,78,042.538	1,51,711.462
6	15,29,754	13,78,169.321	1,51,584.6792
7	15,29,754	13,78,155.375	1,51,598.6253
8	15,29,754	13,78,156.909	1,51,597.0912
9	15,29,754	0	1,51,597.26

Discount factor = After tax interest rate = 11% × (1 − 25%) = 8.25%. Table E9.2 gives the present value of cash outflow in cash of debt financing.

TABLE E9.2

End of year	Debt payment (2)	Amount owing at end of year	Annual interest (3)	Depre-ciation (4)	(5) Tax shield = (3 + 4) * 25%	After tax cash flow = (2 − 5)	Present value of cash flow (8.25%)
0	15,29,754	84,70,246	0	0	0	15,29,754	15,29,754
1	15,29,754	5,98,026.94	9,31,727.06	8,50,000	4,45,431.765	10,84,322.235	9,97,576
2	15,29,754	14,63,971.037	65,782.9634	8,50,000	2,28,945.741	13,00,808.259	11,05,687
3	15,29,754	13,68,717.186	1,61,036.814	8,50,000	2,52,759.204	12,76,994.796	10,02,441
4	15,29,754	13,79,195.11	1,50,558.89	8,50,000	2,50,139.723	12,79,614.277	9,21,322

Contd

Table E9.2 *Contd*

End of year	Debt payment (2)	Amount owing at end of year	Annual interest (3)	Depre-ciation (4)	(5) Tax shield = (3 + 4) * 25 %	After tax cash flow = (2 – 5)	Present value of cash flow (8.25 %)
5	15,29,754	13,78,042.538	1,51,711.462	8,50,000	2,50,427.866	12,79,326.134	19,09,442
6	15,29,754	13,78,169.321	1,51,584.679	8,50,000	2,50,396.17	12,79,357.83	7,86,805
7	15,29,754	13,78,155.375	1,51,598.625	8,50,000	2,50,399.656	12,79,354.344	6,65,264
8	15,29,754	13,78,156.909	1,51,597.091	8,50,000	2,50,399.273	12,79,354.727	6,52,471
9	15,29,754	0	1,51,597.26	8,50,000	2,50,399.315	12,79,354.685	6,26,884
10	–15,00,000		Residual value	0	–3,75,000	–11,25,000	–5,06,250

Present value of cash outflow = Rs 96,91,397

Table E9.3 gives the present value of cash out flows in case of leasing.

TABLE E9.3

End of year	Lease payment (1)	(2) Tax shield = 1 * 0.25	(3) After tax cash flow = (1 – 2)	Present value of cash outflow (8.25 %)
0	15,00,000	0	15,00,000	15,00,000
1 to 9	15,00,000	3,75,000	11,25,000	68,62,500
10		3,75,000	–3,75,000	–16,50,000

Present value of cash outflow = Rs 67,12,500

By comparing the two modes of finance, we conclude that lease finance will be beneficial.

Example 9.2 IRR (internal rate of return) approach for evaluating a lease

Suppose a company has found it financially worthwhile to get an equipment costing Rs 8 crore, which is financed through a loan bearing at an interest of 14 %. The equipment is estimated to last eight years. Instead of buying, the company can lease the equipment for eight years at an annual lease rental of Rs 1.60 crore from its manufacturer. In case the company purchases the equipment, it needs to pay for the annual maintenance cost, amounting to Rs 0.60 lakh per annum.

However, in case of the lease agreement, the maintenance cost will be borne by the lessor. The estimated salvage value of the equipment at the end of the eighth year is equal to Rs 18 lakh. You may assume a written down value depreciation rate of 25 % on this category of asset, and the same is allowable for income tax purposes. The effective tax rate of the concerned company is 35 %. Comment whether the company will prefer the leasing option over the buying option. Use the IRR approach for decision-making purposes.

Solution

Instead of computing the present value of cash outflows for two financing alternatives (as we had done under the NPV approach discussed earlier), we could compute the internal rate of return (IRR). This approach avoids the problem of having to choose a rate of discount. Moreover, managers feel more comfortable in comparing percentages, in contrast to comparing NPV figures.

In Example 9.2, the after tax cost of lease financing (IRR) from the view point of the lessee is 8.71% (refer to the workings in respect of the example above).

This figure needs to be compared with the after tax cost of alternative debt financing, which is in the tune of 9.10% as in the example.

$$14\% (1 - T) = 14\% (0.65) = 9.10\%$$

Thus, it may be commented that the cost of lease financing is lower than the debt financing option in the example. Hence, the lessee will prefer the leasing alternative in this case.

In summary, the IRR method of analysis permits a simple comparison of the after tax cost of different financing options (i.e., lease financing and debt financing options). The alternative with the lowest rate would be selected according to this method. These calculations are given in Tables E9.4 and E9.5.

TABLE E9.4

	Bristol Enterprise (all amounts in thousand rupees)	Winger Enterprise (all amounts in thousand rupees)
Annual dividends	500	1,000
Annual interest	–	200
Annual cash flow	500	1,200
Equity market value	3,125	6,000
Debt market value	–	2,000
Total market value	3,125	8,000
Cost of equity capital	16%	15%
Cost of debt capital	–	10%
WACC	16%	15%
No. of shares in issue	3.25m	5m
Market price per share	96p	120p

TABLE E9.5

(Rupees in lakhs)	
Cost of computer	75
Interest ($75 \times 8 \times 12\%$)	72
Total	147
Annual installment for Rs 147 lakh for eight years	147 / 8 = Rs 18.375 lakh

SUMMARY

The cost of projects represents the total of all items of outlay associated with a project, which are supported by long-term funds. It is the sum of outlay of the deferred credits, deep discount bonds, convertible debentures, floating rate bonds, etc.

Projects can be financed by debt instruments and equity instruments. After globalization, these funds can be generated from the international market too.

Project finance is the process of raising the funds required for a capital investment proposal. From the early 1990s, Indian companies have issued global depository receipts (GDRs) which represent indirect equity investment in the Euromarkets. A second way to raise money internationally is to sell securities directly in the domestic capital markets of foreign countries, which is referred to as direct insurance. Project financing can also be possible through leasing and hire-purchase mechanism.

KEY TERMS

Convertible debentures A debenture that is convertible partially or wholly into equity shares. Convertible debentures enable a company to effectively issue equity shares at a premium, because the conversion price associated with them is typically higher than the price at which equity shares can be issued currently.

Deep discount bonds A deep discount bond does not carry any coupon rate, but is issued at a deep discount over its face value. It is also referred to as zero coupon bonds.

Deferred credits In quite a few cases, suppliers of plant and machinery offer a deferred credit facility, under which payment for such purchases can be made over a period of time.

Euro bonds It is issued outside the country in whose currency it is denominated. It is usually managed by a syndicate of investment banks, and offered to investors in many countries.

Eurocurrency loans Subject to certain terms and conditions, the Government of India permits Indian firms to resort to external commercial borrowings for the import of plant and machinery. The most common instrument of external commercial borrowing is the Eurocurrency loan. A Eurocurrency is simply a deposit of currency in a bank outside the country of the currency.

Floating rate bonds Floating rate bonds earn an interest rate that is linked to a benchmark rate, such as the T-Bill interest rate.

Foreign domestic market A second way to raise money internationally is to sell securities directly in the domestic capital markets of foreign countries. This is referred to as direct issuance.

Global depository receipts In the depository receipts mechanism, the shares issued by a firm are held by a depository, usually a large international bank, which receives dividends, reports, etc. and issues claims against these shares. These claims are called depository receipts (in Euromarkets they are called GDRs), with each receipt being a claim on a specified number of shares. The underlying shares are called depository shares.

Leasing Leasing is another important source of medium term financing. It is an arrangement under which an asset is financed and owned by one party, but possessed and used by the other. The lease agreement details out the specific period and amount of the sequential payments to be made by the lessee to the lessor, as consideration for the use of the asset. Lease is an imputed form of debt.

Secured premium notes (SPN) SPN is a debt instrument which is issued with a detachable warrant and a maturity of 4 to 7 years.

CONCEPT REVIEW QUESTIONS

1. What are the components of estimating the cost of a project? Briefly describe each of them.
2. What are the advantages and disadvantages of equity capital and debt capital?
3. Derive the Miller and Modigliani hypothesis of the capital structure theory.
4. Briefly describe each party involved in a project and their responsibilities.
5. What are the important contents and objectives of the EPC contract and the O&M contract?
6. What are the different methods of raising finance? Briefly narrate the pros and cons of each method of raising finance.
7. How do venture capital investors value their investment in a company?
8. What are the salient features of a finance lease, a net lease, and an operating lease?
9. Discuss the features of a hire purchase agreement, and how it differs from leasing?

NUMERICAL PROBLEMS

1. Deccan Paints Limited had 10 lakh equity shares outstanding at the beginning of the year 2002, and these shares were traded in NSE at Rs 150 each. The rate of capitalization appropriate to the risk class to which the firm belongs is 12%. The net income for the year is Rs 2 crore and the investment budget is Rs 4 crore. Assume that no dividend is declared and the additional fund requirements are financed by a new issue of equity shares. If the Miller and Modigliani hypothesis holds good, how many numbers of shares should be issued by the company?

2. The Bristol and the Winger Enterprises both operate in the same industry with the same business risks. Their earnings, capital structure, share prices, and other data are listed in Table E9.6.
   (a) If Dikinson, an investor, holds Rs10,00,000 worth of shares in Winger Enterprise, and can borrow at the same rate at Winger, show how he can increase his wealth as arbitrage.
   (b) If the rate of corporate tax is 40%, calculate an equilibrium price for the shares of the two companies in a modified Miller and Modigliani world (i.e., one which allows for taxation).

TABLE E9.6

	Bristol Enterprise (Rs in thousand)	Winger Enterprise (Rs in thousand)
Annual dividends	500	1,000
Annual interest	–	200
Annual cash flow	500	1,200
Equity market value	3,125	6,000
Debt market value	–	2,000
Total market value	3,125	8,000
Cost of equity capital	16%	15%
Cost of debt capital	–	10%
WACC	16%	15%
No. of shares in issue	3.25m	5m
Market price per share	96p	120p

3. Assume that the Floyds' tax rate is 40% and the equipment's depreciation would be Rs 100 per year. If the company leases the asset on a two year lease, the payment would be Rs 110 at the beginning of each year. If Floyds borrowed and bought, the bank would charge 10% interest on the loan. Should Floyds lease or buy the equipment?

ASSIGNMENT

Study a big upcoming infrastructure project near you and try to find out different sources that are financing the project and then prepare a comparative and analytic statement.

SELECT REFERENCES

Brealey, R.A., I.A. Cooper, and M.A. Habib, 'Using Project Finance to Fund Infrastructure Investments', *Journal of Applied Corporate Finance* 9:3, 1996, pp. 25–38.

Esty, B.C., and I. Christov, 'Recent Trends in Project Finance: A 5-Year Perspective', *Project Finance International,* Special 10th Anniversary Issue, issue 249, 2002, pp. 74–82.

Geltner, D. and N. Miller, *Commercial Real Estate Analysis and Investments,* 1st edn.

Gompers, P., and J. Lerner, *The Venture Capital Cycle,* 2nd edn, MIT Press, 2004.

McKeon, P., 'High-Yield Debt: Broadening the Scope of Project Finance', *Journal of Project Finance,* Fall, 1999, pp. 62–69.

Scheinkestel, N.L., 'The Debt-Equity Conflict: Where Does Project Financing Fit?' *Journal of Banking and Finance Law and Practice.* vol. 8, no. 2, 1997, pp. 103–124.

Simpson, P., and N. Avery, 'The Role of Capital Markets in Project Financings', *Journal of Project Finance,* Spring, 1995, pp. 43–48.

Wynant, L., 'Essential Elements of Project Finance', *Harvard Business Review,* May–June, 1980, pp. 165–173.

Yescombe, E.R., *Principles of Project Finance,* Academic Press, US, 2002.

Other resources

www.altassets.net, accessed 28 September 2010.

www.nvca.org, accessed 28 September 2010.

CASE STUDY
Techkom Engineering Enterprises

Techkom Engineering Enterprises is a medium-sized engineering company. It has a total asset of Rs 270 crore and had sales worth Rs 256 crore in 1998. The company has been growing at an annual rate of 23 per cent during the last five years, and the management expects to maintain this trend for the next few years. The growing operations of the company have led the management to consider the possibility of acquiring a medium-sized, specially designed computer for its CAD CAM functions. The management of the company, therefore, has invited representatives from some leading computer firms to help them in designing a useful and cost-effective system. After an evaluation of the various available alternatives, the company zeroed in on the TECH 2000 computer which would best meet its current and expected future needs. This is supplied by a leading computer manufacturing company.

The finance department evaluated the profitability of buying the TECH 2000 computer, using its normal capital budgeting procedures. The company has a policy of using 12 per cent after tax cut-off rate for modernization, up-gradation, or automation projects. For a higher risk project, a higher cut-off rate is used. It was found that this computer has a positive expected NPV.

The chief finance manager has recently been reading a lot about leasing and hire-purchase business in India. The subsidiaries of a number of banks, private firms as well as manufacturers, have been offering lease and hire purchase finance. He thought that there might be some merit in these options. He therefore decided to talk to the management of the computer manufacturing company, if they could sell the computer on lease or hire purchase basis. He found that the manufacturer was ready to consider supplying the computer on lease or hire purchase.

The purchase price of the computer is Rs 75 lakh. It has an expected life of eight years. The company expects to receive a pre-tax benefit of Rs 18 lakh per year from the use of the computer. The company's tax consultant had indicated that if the computer is purchased, the company can depreciate the computer on written down value basis at 25 per cent per annum. On the other hand, if the company decides to take the computer on lease, it will have to forego tax benefit on depreciation. The company will be required to pay lease rentals of Rs 14 lakh at the beginning of each year, for eight years. If Techkom Engineering Enterprises buys the computer, it will be serviced and maintained by the computer company for no extra cost, but in the case of lease, Techkom Engineering Enterprises will have to incur a maintenance cost of about Rs 1.75 lakh per annum.

The chief financial manager is not sure whether there would be any salvage value. However, he thinks that if the technology does not change drastically, it may be sold for Rs 6 lakh. He knows that if the computer is taken on lease, he will have to forego the salvage value. He believes that the company's after-tax cost of borrowing, estimated to be 9.5 per cent, is the appropriate rate to use to evaluate the cash flows of leasing. The company's marginal tax rate is 35 per cent.

As regards the hire-purchase option, the manufacturer quoted a hire-purchase installment of Rs 18.375 lakh per annum, payable in the beginning of the year. He had calculated the annual installment as follows in Table E9.7:

TABLE E9.7

(Rs in lakhs)

Cost of computer	75.00
Interest ($75 \times 8 \times 12\%$)	72.00
Total	147.00
Annual installment for Rs 147 lakh for eight years	$147 / 8 =$ Rs 18.375 lakh

The finance manager was surprised to find a higher quotation for the hire-purchase installment than the lease rental. But he did realize that under hire-purchase, his company would be entitled to claim depreciation. Therefore, he thought it was appropriate to systematically analyse the economics of both options.

Discussion question

Analyse the economics of both options and discuss their advantages and disadvantages.

REAL OPTIONS

Real options is sometimes a little like an extreme sport. People look at it and say, 'Wow, that's really neat, its fun to watch.' But when you actually sit down and try to do it yourself, it's not so easy.

— TRIANTIS

LEARNING OBJECTIVES

After studying this chapter, you will be able to

- Define real options, and explain the difference between financial options and real options
- Classify the important types of real options such as option to delay, option to expand, and option to abandon
- Understand the need of real options analysis using the DCF methods
- Describe the valuation of real options by applying the binomial model
- Describe the valuation of real options by applying the Black and Scholes option pricing model

Options in Our Life

Akash Sharma, the Area Manager, Marketing, of a leading pharmaceutical company, and Rajiv Gupta, Dy General Manager of a Navratna PSU—both from St Xaviers College—are sitting with coffee and snacks at their favourite joint, on a rainy weekend evening in July.

AKASH: Oh, I'm totally drained out! It was a gruelling week.

RAJIV: Me too. After Fridays I become really tired, and don't feel like getting up the next morning. I sometimes think I am growing old.

AKASH: True. Life has become very boring and monotonous. I feel that we are finished and haven't achieved anything in life.

RAJIV: Don't say that. At least you and I have done our bit to provide a comfortable life for our families, and good education, and career for our children. We have also made sufficient provisions for our old age. Looking at it from that perspective, I am content with myself.

AKASH: Rajiv, what if we call it quits? As you have rightly said, we have fulfilled all obligations required for the well-being of ourselves and our family members. Can't we now spend our time in pursuing something that we can enjoy just for the sake of ourselves? It will involve a lot of risk and hard work, but at the end of the day there will be more satisfaction, and more monetary rewards.

RAJIV: You are right. Remember what we used to discuss during college days? About doing a partnership business? Come, let's go for it now.

- Make a reconciliation of the values of the real options obtained by different real-life case studies
- Understand the use of real options in the real world

Both friends are excited. They order one more round of coffee and go deeper into conversation on the subject. With their combined backgrounds in finance and marketing, and more than 20 years experience, they want to get into something that will suit their tastes and can keep them involved. After a lot of discussion, they settle upon the idea of setting up a management education institute.

RAJIV: OK, but we must weigh the idea on some financial scale to see whether our venture is going to be viable in the long run.

AKASH: There is a demand for MBA courses in the market today, and setting up a management institute will be quite profitable.

RAJIV: True, but that is not all. In this business, we will have many choices and possibilities. We can start in a small way and gradually expand. We can first apply for affiliation from a university, or some apex body for management studies. We can begin with limited seats, and then go on to increase the number as per requirement. We can start with offering only two specializations, and after stabilization, other courses can be offered. We can accelerate the project if we get good response. If the market goes into a slump, we can postpone the project partly or fully, and restart when the market picks up. We can start various short-term courses to earn some extra revenue. Besides, we can think of diversification to other courses such as law, finishing school, etc.

AKASH: Wow! It sounds exciting. We'll have so many options, and to think of it, all without having to constantly think of obliging bosses. I can't wait to submit my resignation and take the plunge.

RAJIV: Same here. It is already 9.30. Let's go home and have a good night's sleep. I will call you tomorrow morning.

Akash, a non-finance manager, has unknowingly coined a magic word—Options.

10.1 INTRODUCTION TO REAL OPTIONS

Literally, options means choices (as is reflected from the opening case) and we shall discuss financial options in this chapter. Real options are also kinds of options on real assets that can be defined as opportunities to respond to the changing circumstances of a project. These opportunities to change circumstances consist of rights, and not obligations, to take some action in the future (Dixit and Pindyck 1995). It means that only if a future situation is positive will the options be exercised, not otherwise. The utility of the analysis of real options is to quantify various future opportunities in today's monetary value, which can be done by using the option pricing model. It is also possible to identify the timings as to when these options would yield optimum results.

Till now, under project evaluation dimensions, cash flows were assumed up to a certain horizon and then discounted to their present value. But investment projects are not necessarily 'set in concrete' once they are accepted. Managers can, and often do, make changes that affect subsequent cash flows and/or the life of the project. These real or managerial options are embedded in the investment projects. The overemphasis on discount cash flow modelling often ignores these options and the future managerial flexibility that accompanies them.

Financial and real options Financial option gives you a right, but not an obligation, to take an action in the future. Financial options are of two kinds—call options and put options. Suppose a call option of a particular company is bought by paying a premium of say Rs 5 per share and an exercise price of Rs 120, then, for a specified future date, the person has the right to buy shares at Rs 120 per share. However, there is no obligation to do the same—the person may or may not buy the shares. When the shares are eventually bought, and if on that specified date, the current market price is Rs 140, the person will exercise the option and make a profit of Rs 20 per share. A premium of Rs 5 has been paid and hence, the net pay off is Rs 15.

Now, if the current market price is Rs 110, the option will not be exercised. The person will go to the open market, as there is no obligation. Thereby, the maximum loss incurred will be the amount of the premium, i.e., Rs 5 per share.

Similarly, a real option is a right, but not an obligation, to take an action that will either help to maximize the upside or limit the downside of a capital investment.

Similar to financial options, there are two kinds of real options, namely, real call option and real put option. A real call option gives an opportunity to a firm to start a project; however, it is not a compulsion. It requires the firm to invest a small premium in the concerned project. The options can be utilized at the right time to avail profits if there is opportunity in the future as per estimation. Or else, it can be postponed for a time in the future when benefits are maximum. In real put options, instead of continuing, a project can be discontinued for a fixed salvage value. Thus, the real option route makes flexibility, adaptability, uncertainty, reversibility, and change possible in capital budgeting mechanism. A firm has to pay extra premium, and face more risk and uncertainty in order to extract more gains from a project.

10.2 HISTORY OF REAL OPTIONS

Real options have been used long before transactions involved money. In 1728 BC, Joseph, a priest to the Pharaoh of Egypt, came to know about a dream of the Pharaoh and advised him to buy all the grains that were available, as he feared that a famine lay ahead of them. This story is an ideal example of exercising real options. The price that they had to pay for exercising real options was that they had to spend their wealth in building huge containers for storage. The real option available to them was to hedge against that risk by saving grain. Nevertheless, the expense paid off as the tale says that the Pharaoh's dream did come true, as a famine struck Egypt for seven years.

We can also find some definite evidence of exercising real options from the ancient city of Marions on the banks of the river Euphrates, in present times somewhere near the border of Syria and Iraq. More than 20,000 ancient tablets were excavated, which gives rich evidence of the practice of real options and parlaying of future contracts between 1800 BC and 1500 BC. This shows that business in those times followed the barter system, where one real asset was being exchanged for another.

Similar use of real options can be noticed in the writings of famous, ancient philosophers such as Thales and Aristotle. In ancient times, philosophers would make predictions about any future calamity or happening from their extensive astrological studies of the extraterrestrial bodies. These predictions played a vital role in taking important business decisions by using real options, which gave the philosophers considerably more accurate results.

Aristotle says, in Book 1 of *Politics,* that Thales once foresaw that the next harvest of olive presses would be outstanding, and he decided to engage in contractual arrangements which would give him the right to rent out olive presses at a nominal premium. The risk Thales faced was the uncertainty surrounding the outcome of the next harvest. If the harvest was not good, then the option of acquisition cost would sink and the option would be out of money. However, taking the risk proved fruitful for him in the end. He was able to make a fortune in subleasing the presses to other users at much higher prices, as the olive harvest was enormous and beyond anticipation (Copeland and Antikarov 2001).

There are many other examples around the world which prove that real options have been in practice from ancient times. Around 1600, in the era of Tokawawa, Japanese merchants bought call options on rice. During the same time, in some other part of the world, Dutchmen operated high on real Tulip options.

In 1668, shortly after Amsterdam Bourse was set up, there originated a new term 'time bargains', which was also used as a common term for both options and futures (Cox, Ross, and Rubinstein 1979). In 1848, the Chicago Board of Trade (CBOT) was opened, which was the first formal futures and options exchange. It started its trading operations of futures and options contracts from 1870. In 1973, trading of the first equity options was concurrent with the publication of the Black–Scholes seminal paper 'The pricing of Options and Corporate Liabilities'.

It was Stewart Myers who pioneered the concept that financial investments generated real options. He also introduced the term 'real options' in the year of 1977. His work sparked intense argument, and in the early 1980s, doubts regarding the applicability of traditional DCF for investment decisions related to risky projects were increasingly coming out of the shell. In 1984, Kester deciphered the theoretical concept of 'growth options' into a more logical and strategic format in a Harvard Business Review article 'Today's Options for Tomorrow's Growth'. By drawing an analogy with options on financial securities, investment flexibility is referred to as real option (Dixit and Pindyck 1994 and 1995; Trigeorgis 1995 and 1996).

In an example suggested by Luehrman (1997 and 1998), options are used by a gardener to reap maximum benefits from his garden. As per the traditional DCF method, once the gardener has made up his mind to cultivate tomatoes, he cannot change his decision. Reversibility, flexibility, and change in the decision-making process are introduced by real options. In this case, climate, weeds, predators, etc. are the different agents of risk and uncertainty. Harvest time is the most crucial time for the cultivation process. A passive gardener follows an obvious path, and at the end of the season collects whatever tomatoes are ripe, whereas, an active gardener would visit his garden often and utilize all existing options (such as different intervals at which ripe tomatoes may be available) to optimize his profits.

Luehrman states, 'In option terminology, active gardeners are doing more than merely making exercise decisions (pick or do not pick). They are monitoring the options, looking for ways to influence the underlying variables that determine option value and ultimately the outcomes.'

In the 1990s, several real options modes and statistical applets were worked out by finance researchers. Most part of this effort was aimed at pricing real options by developing the use of technical tools such as differential equations, dynamic programming, and Monte Carlo simulations. Such researches highlighted the strengths of the real options approach. While discussing an example about the purchase development of an oil field, a study demonstrated how five different real options valuation methodologies would deal with the same case. The result showed a wide range ($19 million to $300 million) of option values. Copeland and Antikarov (2001) explained that the wide range values could be compressed to a great extent by using a mutually consistent set of assumptions among the five different real option valuation methods. The range of values was compressed to about $12 million from $279 million, with an average difference of about 5 per cent. This challenged the stand that there is a wide difference in the results computed by real options.

10.3 CLASSIFICATION OF REAL OPTIONS

The presence of real options enhances the worth of an investment project. Its worth can be viewed as the NPV of the project, calculated in the usual way, together with the value of the option(s).

$$\text{Value of the project} = \text{NPV} + \text{Option value}$$

The greater the number of options and the uncertainty surrounding them, the greater will be the option value, and hence the greater will be the value of the project.

The types of real options available in capital expenditure decision-making processes are broadly classified into the following.

Option to expand   It is the option to expand production if market conditions are favourable, and to curtail productions if conditions turn unfavourable. Intensity or operating scale options refer to the flexibility to expand or downsize the operating scale of the project. The management has the choice of changing the option per unit time, or changing the total length of the production runtime. In order to take a decision on the expansion of production, if there is a sudden increase in demand, a firm may build excess production capacity. In this case, the management has the right, but not the obligation, to expand. It will exercise the option only if the market conditions turn out to be favourable.

Option to abandon   If a project has a high abandonment value, it effectively represents the put option (i.e., the option holder enjoying a right to sell within a pre-defined time frame) for the owner of the project.

In traditional project evaluation techniques, e.g., NPV, IRR, or any other DCF methods, irreversibility cannot be avoided. Once the firm has taken a decision, it has to continue with it.

But real option theory says that decisions can be altered, reversed, and also assessed well in advance. Hence, like American put options, a project can be abandoned at a fixed salvage price if the present value of expected cash flows for the remaining period is lesser than its liquidation value.

Option to postpone   For some projects, there is an option to wait in order to obtain new information or act at the most appropriate moment. This is also known as an investment trimming option. For example, the purchaser of an off-shore lease can choose when, if at all, to develop a property, otherwise it can be postponed. The option to postpone is particularly valuable as the purchaser can delay mining a deposit until market conditions are favourable. If the firm is committed to produce all the resource discovered, it should not explore the areas where the estimated extraction cost exceeds the expected future selling price of the resource.

Financial options are easier to value than real options. Sometimes, the standard real option formula does not help in computing the worth of a project, and hence they are treated as qualitative factors. In such situations, real option methodologies are replaced by decision trees, simulation, and even some ad-hoc approaches. The following is a compilation of common real options and sample scenarios.

Waiting-to-invest options   The value of immediate expansion, in the absence of better market information, may be lower than the value of waiting to build a manufacturing plant with all information about the market. The purchase of an off-shore lease is usually chosen later, when it gives more benefit.

Growth options An entry investment may provide opportunities to take up valuable follow-on projects.

Flexibility options An option to relocate or switch resources carries a certain value. For instance, if instead of only one manufacturing unit, two units are set up to cater to the markets in two continents, there is an option of switching production from one unit to the other.

As illustrated in Figure 10.1, a project, a product, or a unit once started or introduced can remain open with a probability of $p1$ and shut down with a probability of $(1-p1)$, depending on its performance. Now, if the output is good, it can be continued further. But if it is bad, there is an option to shut down the project, product, or unit. There is also a switching option, which means that the venture will be switched over to another product just for taking another chance. After this change, if the bad result recovers to become a good one, the project can be reopened once again. If it continues to result in a negative outcome, the project, product, or unit is abandoned forever.

Exit or abandonment or termination options Sometimes, continuing with a project may result in losses. An option to leave such a project, in response to a new input, adds to the value of the project. Such options are particularly valuable for large capital intensive projects such as railways, nuclear plants, etc. This option also holds good for new or innovative projects that may have an uncertain demand or acceptance in the market.

As illustrated in Figure 10.2, a project once started can remain open with a probability of $p1$, and can be abandoned with a probability of $(1-p1)$, depending on its performance. Now, if the output is good, it can be continued further, and if it is bad, there is an option to shut down the project.

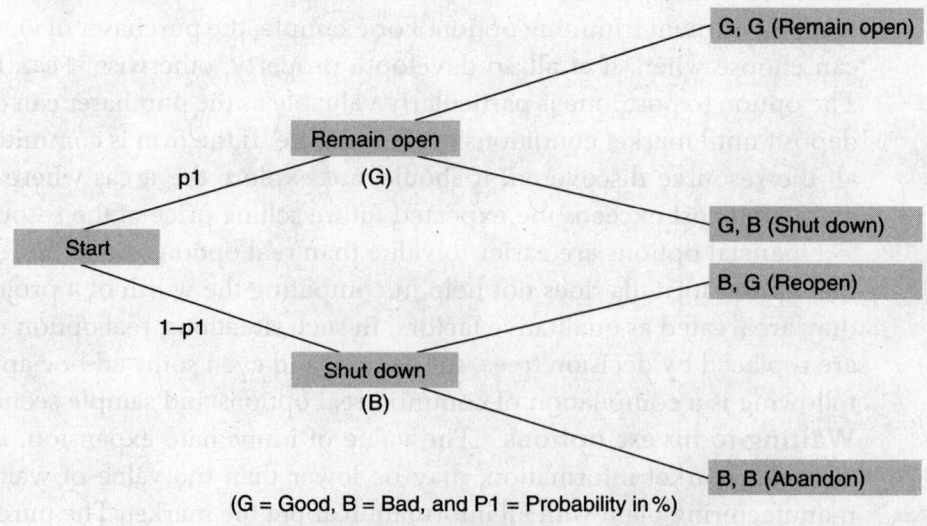

(G = Good, B = Bad, and P1 = Probability in %)

FIGURE 10.1 Flexibility or switching options

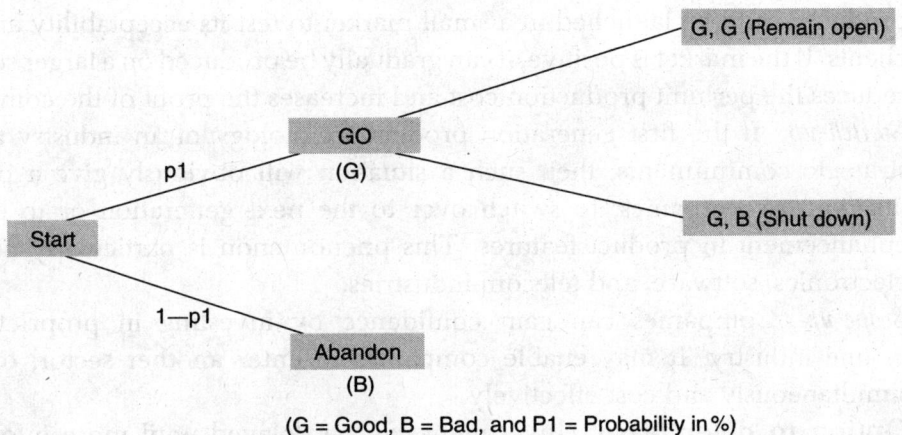

(G = Good, B = Bad, and P1 = Probability in %)

FIGURE 10.2 Abandonment options

Learning options An initial investment is also an opportunity to learn about the market trends. It helps to figure out whether more capacity should be built or not.

Temporary stop or shut down options This is relevant in case of projects that include manufacturing unit(s). There are variable costs associated with a manufacturing plant. The project revenue must cover these costs to ensure that the plant works efficiently. For instance, if the price of a fabric falls below the cost of its production, it may be optimal to temporarily shut down the production. The production can restart once the demand as well as the price of the fabric increases in the market.

10.3.1 American Option vs European Option

The American option is more flexible than the European option because the American option can be exercised at any point of time, at or before its maturity, whereas the European option can only be exercised on the date of maturity. The chances of early exercise make American options more valuable, as well as more risky. This is because the optimal time assessment is a tougher exercise compared to accepting the reality.

10.3.2 Investment Decisions

Copeland and Keenan (1998) further simplify and explain the impact of uncertainty on managerial investment decisions.

Option to invest/grow This can be possible in the following ways.

Scale-up Initial entrants (on a lower scale) can be enhanced through cost-effective sequential investments as the market grows, and also if the market reacts positively. Our basic scale of the economy concept also talks in a similar way. Initially, a new product would be launched in a small market to test its acceptability amongst the clients. If the market is positive, it can gradually be produced on a larger scale, which reduces the per unit production cost and increases the profit of the company.

Switch-up   If the first generation product/technology of an industry accelerates strategic commitments, then such a situation will obviously give a preferential position to companies, to switch over to the next generation or to the further enhancement in product features. This phenomenon is particularly common in electronics, software, and telecom industries.

Scope-up   Companies can gain confidence by investing in proprietary assets in one industry. It may enable companies to enter another sector, or diversify simultaneously and cost effectively.

Option to defer/learn   Investment can be delayed until more information is generated from the market about the customer, competitor, and vendor, or new competencies are acquired. The best example of deferral option would be Tata's Nano car project.

Option to divest/shrink   Like options to invest or grow, there are options to divest or shrink. These are possible through scale-down, switch-down, or scope-down investments.

10.4 BINOMIAL MODEL

The binomial model is particularly important for the evaluation of stock option. It uses a risk-free arbitrage method to compute the option. It requires a discrete time series data for this process. In the absence of any clear formula for the stochastic process, the binomial model helps to calculate the value of derivative securities.

In a single-period model, it is assumed by the investor that at the completion of a period, the stock price (S) will either have a value of S_u (up-state) with probability u, or S_d (down-state) with probability d. If K is the current value of the call option, C_u and C_d will be the corresponding value of the call at the end of a period, as the stock price becomes S_u and S_d, respectively.

In the single period model, the payoff of the call at the expiration date is as follows.

$$C_u = \max\,(0,\, S_u - K) \text{ with probability } u \qquad\qquad (10.1)$$

$$C_d = \max\,(0,\, S_d - K) \text{ with probability } d \qquad\qquad (10.2)$$

where, $S_u = u \times S$ and $S_d = d \times S$

Suppose an investor wants to construct a hedge portfolio of stocks and risk-free bonds. One way of doing this is to let the investor purchase shares and borrow against them in a ratio that replicates the future returns of the call option.

S = price of share

n = number of shares purchased

A = amount of funds to be borrowed to purchase shares by the investors, and $r_f = 1 + r$ = risk-free rate where, r = rate of return

In this environment, an investor should not make any arbitrage profits because here the following relationship is always held in the form of $u > r > d$.

If $u, d > r$, the investor could make a profit by borrowing and investing in the stock. Whereas, if $u, d < r$, the investor would make a profit by investing in bonds.

Cost of the hedge at the current time = $(n \times S + A)$

The value of this portfolio at the end of one period would be either $(n \times S_u + Ar)$ with probability u, or $(n \times S_d + Ar)$ with probability d.

At the end of a single period, replicating the call value, the hedge was selected.

$$C_u = (n \times S_u + A \times r)$$
and
$$C_d = (n \times S_d + A \times r)$$
(10.3)

From the above equations the following expressions for the values of n and A can be formulated

$$n = (C_u - C_d) / (u - d)$$
and
$$A = (u \times C_d - dC_u) / (u - d)\ r$$
(10.4)

Hedge ratio is defined by the number of shares needed to balance the portfolio so that it would be equal to the future payoff of the call. Let n be the hedge ratio.

In the no-arbitrage principle, the call value can never be less than the portfolio. If $C < n \times S + A$, then the investor can make a profit by buying the call and selling the portfolio. Similarly, the call value cannot be higher than the portfolio. Because, if $C > n \times S + A$, the investor sells the call and buys the portfolio. Hence in equilibrium, the call value (C) must be equal to $(n \times S + A)$.

Putting the value of n and A (from Eqn (10.4)), the current or call value can be as follows.

$$C = S \times (C_u - C_d) / (u - d) + (u \times C_d - d \times C_u) / (u - d) \times r = n \times S + A \quad (10.5)$$

Rearranging the formula for the value of the call option, the call value will be:

$$C = [qC_u + (1 - q) C_d] / r,\ where\ q = (r - d) / (u - d) \quad (10.6)$$

But q cannot be zero or equal to one $(0 < q < 1)$. Therefore, q can be viewed as a probability. Call value (C) can be represented as the investor's expectation, with respect to risk-neutral probabilities. When the binomial model is used to derive a value for a call option on a stock, the time to maturity is split into small time intervals Δt, to obtain a better approximation to the Black and Scholes model. The following values are used for the multi-period binomial lattice:

$$u = e^{\sigma\sqrt{\Delta t}}, \; d = e^{-\sigma\sqrt{\Delta t}}, \; q = (e^{r\Delta t} - d)/(u - d) \qquad (10.7)$$

Similarly, by using the risk-free arbitrage principle, the value of a put option can be obtained.

$$\text{Value of put} = P = qP_u + (1 - q) \, P_d \text{ and } q = (e^{r\sigma t} - d)/(u - d) \quad (10.8)$$

One of the key features of an option value is that it is always positive. Table 10.4 describes how variables such as stock price, exercise price, risk-free rates, time to expiration, and risk of return affect the value of a call and a put option.

Binomial models and the abandonment options Another way to view real options is to use a binomial model, first introduced by Cox, Ross, and Rubinstein (1979), that represents the cash flows of a project as points on a lattice. Consider the following project. Refer to Figure 10.3.

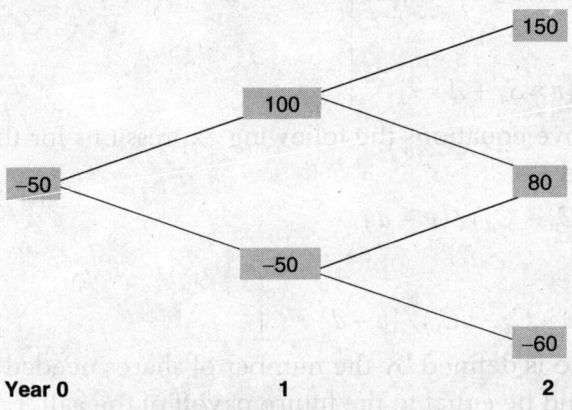

FIGURE 10.3 Project cash flows

In order to value the project, we use the state prices from option pricing. The state price q_u is the price of $1 today, to be paid in the succeeding period in the up-state and similarly for q_d in the down-state.

q_u = price today of $1 in the up-state in period 1

q_d = price today of $1 in the down-state in period 1

State prices are calculated by solving this system of linear equation

$$1 = q_u * u_u + q_d * u_d$$

$$1/(1 + R_f) = q_u + q_d$$

The solution of this system of equation is

$$q_u = (1 + R_f - u_d)/(1 + R_f) * (u_u - u_d) \quad q_d = (u_u - 1 - R_f)/(1 + R_f) * (u_u - u_d)$$

Pricing of an abandonment option: Market data

Expected market return: 12%

Sigma of market return: 30%

Risk-free rate: 6%

One-period up and down of market:

Up: $u_u = EXP$ (Exp market return + Sigma of market return) = 1.521962

Down: $u_d = EXP$ (Exp market return − Sigma of market return) = 0.83527

State prices

$$q_u = (1 + R_f - u_d) / (1 + R_f) * (u_u - u_d) = 0.3087$$

$$q_d = (u_u - 1 - R_f) / (1 + R_f) * (u_u - u_d) = 0.6347$$

Refer to Figures 10.4 and 10.5.

Project cash flows   Project cash flows state dependent present value factors

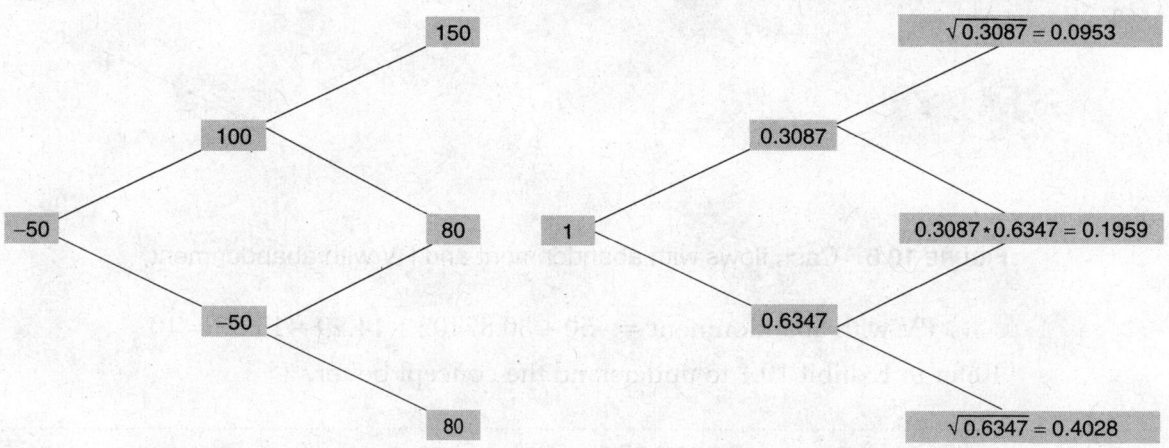

FIGURE 10.4   Project cash flows and state dependent present value factors

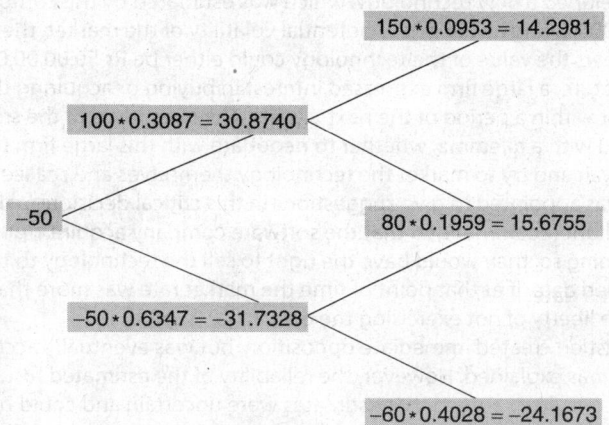

FIGURE 10.5   State-by-state present value

Net present value (NPV)

$$= -50 + 30.8740 + 14.2981 + 15.6755 + 15.6755 - 31.7328 - 24.1673$$

$$= -29.38$$

Now, suppose that we can abandon the project at state 1 if its cash flow threatens to be 50, then the option to abandon the project enhances its value. Refer to Figure 10.6.

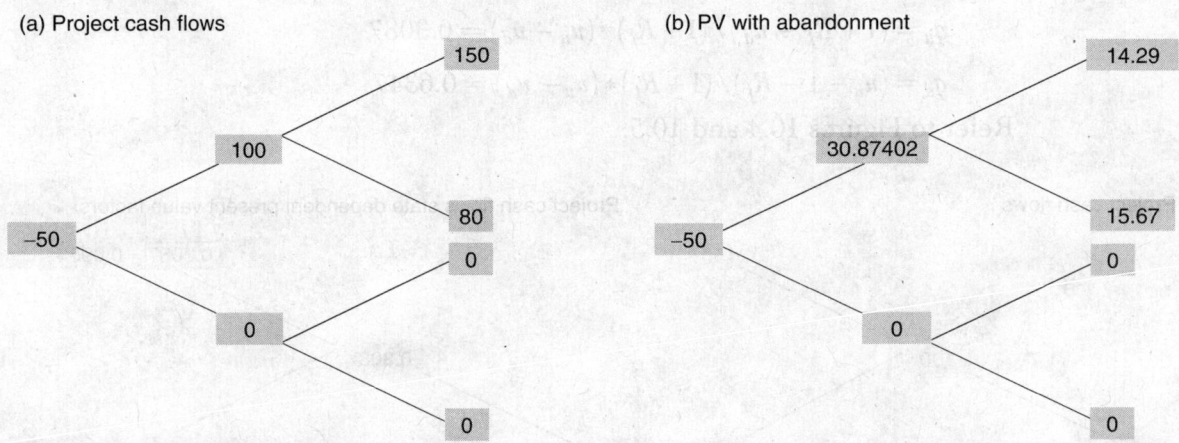

(a) Project cash flows   (b) PV with abandonment

FIGURE 10.6   Cash flows with abandonment and PV with abandonment

PV with abandonment $= -50 + 30.87402 + 14.29 + 15.67 = 10$

Refer to Exhibit 10.1 to understand the concept better.

EXHIBIT 10.1   Real options

In the year 2000, during the waning days of the dot-com boom in the US, a small software company in Bangalore developed a new technology, which was estimated by the company to have a current value of Rs 25,00,00,000. Being aware of the potential volatility of the market, the company believed that in the next five years the value of the technology could either be Rs 50,00,00,000 or Rs 12,50,00,000.

At this juncture, a large firm expressed interest in buying or acquiring the technology—immediately, or within a period of the next 5 years. The executives of the small software company were thus faced with a dilemma, whether to negotiate with this large firm to avoid the risk of market downturn, or wait and try to market the technology themselves and realize the potentially large profit. A consultant was appointed to give suggestions in this critical decision-making process.

The consultant recommended that the software company acquire a put option contract with the large firm. In doing so, they would have the right to sell the technology to the large firm at a fixed price and at a specified date. If at that point of time the market rate was more than the strike price, they would have the liberty of not exercising the option.

This suggestion created immediate opposition, but was eventually accepted after the concept of real options was explained. However, the reliability of the estimated future cash flows was a big question. The consultant agreed that estimates were uncertain and could be made more realistic through market survey and by using the prevailing rate in the market of similar technologies. The value of this put option is governed by market volatility and the strike price (K). A sensitivity analysis could be performed for a range of *u* and *d* together with a parametric analysis for the predetermined exercise price (*K*).

Specifically, four scenarios representing the various degrees of market volatility and levels of pre-agreed sale price were developed as follows.

Scenario 1 Medium market volatility and high pre-agreed sale price
$u = 2.5, d = 0.6, k = $ Rs 25,00,00,000.

Scenario 2 Medium market volatility and medium pre-agreed sale price
$u = 2.5, d = 0.6, k = $ Rs 20,00,00,000.

Scenario 3 High market volatility and high pre-agreed sale price
$u = 3.0, d = 0.4, k = $ Rs 25,00,00,000.

Scenario 4 High market volatility and medium pre-agreed sale price
$u = 3.0, d = 0.4, k = $ Rs 20,00,00,000.

By assuming the risk-free interest rate to be 6%, i.e., $R = 1.06$ for all scenarios, the value of the real put option may be estimated for these four scenarios as follows.

(1) $u = 2.5, d = 0.6, K = 25$
$q = (R - d) / (u - d) = (1.06 - 0.6) / (2.5 - 0.6) = 0.24$
$P = [q (25 - 25) + (1 - q)(25 - 12.5)] / 1.06 = 8.96$

(2) $u = 2.5, d = 0.6, K = 20$
$q = (R - d) / (u - d) = (1.06 - 0.6) / (2.5 - 0.6) = 0.24$
$P = [q (20 - 20) + (1 - q) (20 - 12.5)] / 1.06 = 5.37$

(3) $u = 3.0, d = 0.4, K = 25$
$q = (R - d) / (u - d) = (1.06 - 0.4)/ (3 - 0.4) = 0.25$
$P = [q (25 - 25) + (1 - q) (25 - 12.5)] / 1.06 = 8.84$

(4) $u = 3.0, d = 0.4, K = 20$
$q = (R - d) / (u - d) = (1.06 - 0.4) / (3.0 - 0.4) = 0.25$
$P = [q (20 - 20) + (1 - q) (20 - 12.5)] / 1.06 = 5.30$

From the above calculations, it becomes clear that for the value of put option, the pre-agreed sale price is a more dominating factor than the volatility of the market. It has also become obvious that the net worth of the technology would be from $20 - 5.3 = $ Rs 14.7 crore at the lower end, to $25 - 8.96 = $ Rs 16.14 crore at the upper end. Hence, within these four scenarios, any figure between the above ranges could be an acceptable pre-agreed sale price for this company.

10.5 BLACK–SCHOLES OPTION PRICING FORMULA

This model was developed by Fischer Black and Myron Scholes in 1973, and later on adapted by Garman and Kohlhagen in 1983. It calculates the market price of the call option (or put option). The determinants of this model are exercise price, time remaining before expiration of the option, risk-free rate of interest, and the value of the cumulative normal density function. Various ready-made handy software are available now-a-days to calculate the values of call and put options.

The value of a call option as per the Black and Scholes option pricing formula is,

$$Pc = [Ps] [N(d1)] - [Pe] [antiln(-Rft)] [N(d2)] \qquad (10.9)$$

where,

Pc = market price of the call option

Ps = price of the stock

Pe = striking price of the option

$antiln$ = antilog (base e)

Rf = annualized interest rate

t = time to expiration (in years)

$N(d1)$ and $N(d2)$ are the values of the cumulative normal distribution defined by

$$d1 = [\text{In}(Ps/Pe) + (Rf + 0.5\,\sigma2)t]/\sigma\sqrt{t}, \quad d2 = d1 - (\sigma\sqrt{t}) \qquad (10.10)$$

where, In (Ps/Pe) = the natural logarithm of (Ps/Pe)

$\sigma2$ is the variance of the continuously compounded rate of return on the stock, per time period

Garman and Kohlhagen (1983) used the Black–Scholes model for coping with the presence of two interest rates (one for each currency).

Suppose,

rd = risk-free interest rate to expiry of the domestic currency

r_f = foreign currency risk-free interest rate

where, the currency in which the value of option is obtained is domestic currency.

The formula also requires that forex rates—both strike and current spot—be quoted in terms of 'units of foreign currency per unit of domestic currency'. Then, the value of a call option into the foreign currency has the following value.

$$Pc = exp(-rfT)\,SN(d1) - Kexp(-rdT)\,N(d2) \qquad (10.11)$$

where,

Pc = market price of the call option

S is the current spot rate, K is the strike rate

N is the cumulative normal distribution function

T = time to expiration in years

σ is the volatility of the FX rate

Example 10.1 ABC Manufacturers is thinking of replacing three of its running boilers with new ones. The cost of installing a new boiler is Rs 1 lakh and each boiler has a life of 10 years. The expected cash flows for the new machines are given in Table E10.1.

TABLE E10.1

Year	Expected cash flow (Rs)	Present value of discount factor (10%)	Present value of cash flows (Rs)
0	–1,00,000	1.0	–1,00,000
1	22,000	0.909	19,998
2	24,000	0.826	19,824
3	25,000	0.751	18,775
4	20,000	0.683	13,660
5	10,000	0.620	6,200
6	5,000	0.564	2,820
7	7,000	0.513	3,591
8	8,000	0.467	3,736
9	4,000	0.424	1,696
10	3,000	0.386	1,158
Total			–8,542

Since the above calculation produces negative NPV (–Rs 8,542), as far as traditional discounted cash flow techniques are concerned, the project should not be accepted. Soon after finding out that the purchase of new machines produces a negative NPV, the GM Operation says, 'I want to try one of the new boilers for a year and understand the true realization of its cash flows, rather than going for a greater expansion or a replacement.'

The estimations are:

- Replacing a single boiler produces a negative NPV of Rs 8,542.
- The option of replacing three more boilers in 1 year. Such an option is known as a call option on a boiler that has the current value of S = Rs 91,548 for each boiler
- Variance = 40%
- Initial investment for replacing each boiler = exercise price = K = Rs 1,00,000.

By applying Black and Scholes option pricing model (1973) we can price this call option. If the risk-free rate is 6%, then all the above values (given in Table E10.1) can be calculated as below in Table E10.2.

TABLE E10.2

Symbols	Description of items	Amount
S	PV of cash inflows	91,548
K	Exercise price = Machine cost	1,00,000
Rf	Risk-free rate	6%
T	Time to maturity of option in years	1
σ	Volatility	40%
D1	$(\ln(S/K) + (R_f + 0.5\,\sigma^2)T)/\sigma \times T^{1/2} = [\ln(91,548/1,00,000) + (0.06 + 0.5(0.4)^2 \times 1)]/0.4 \times 1^{1/2}$	1.6041
D2	$D_1 - \sigma \times T^{1/2} = 1.6041 - (0.4 \times 1^{1/2})$	1.2041
N(D1)		0.9463
N(D2)		0.8869

Calculate the total value of the whole project.

Solution

Option Value $= S \times N(D_1) - K \times e^{-R_f T} \times N(D_2) = 91{,}548 \times 0.9463 - (1{,}00{,}000 \times e^{-0.6 \times 1} \times 0.8869) = 37{,}954.6$

Hence, value of the whole project = *NPV* of the first boiler + options for 2 more boilers to be replaced

$= -8542 + 2 \times 37954.6 = 67367.2$

Thus, making one boiler today and in the process acquiring the option to replace two more boilers in one year is a worthwhile project, because it gives a positive NPV of Rs 67,367.2.

10.6 LINK BETWEEN INVESTMENT, AND BLACK AND SCHOLES INPUTS

The following are the determinants of option value (for a call option).

Stock price (S)   The higher the price of the underlying stock, the greater the option's intrinsic value.

Exercise price (K)   The higher the exercise price, the lower the intrinsic value.

Interest rates (r)   The higher the interest rates, the more valuable the call option.

Volatility of the stock price (σ)   The more volatile the stock price, the more valuable the option.

Time to maturity (T)   The time period required to mature the option. Table 10.4 shows the similarity between the determinants used in the Black and Scholes financial investment option and real options inputs. For example, the current market price of the share (*S*) can be related with the present value of the net expected cash flows of the project. Both are associated with uncertainty. Similarly, others such as *K, T, r,* and σ are explained in Table 10.1.

TABLE 10.1   Real options—Link between investment and Black–Scholes inputs

Real Options	Symbol	Investment
PV of project free cash flow	*S*	Stock price
Outlay to acquire project assets	*K*	Exercise price
Time the decision can be deferred	*T*	Time to expiration
Time value of money	*R*	Risk-free rate
Risk of project assets	σ	Risk of returns

Table 10.2 shows how the five determinants (*S, K, T, r,* σ) will affect the call value or put value of an option. For instance, if the strike or exercise price is going to be increased automatically, it will increase the call value and decrease the put value.

TABLE 10.2 Summary of variables affecting call and put prices

Factor / determinants	Symbol	Effect on call value	Effect on put value
Increase in underlying asset's value	S	Increases	Decreases
Increase in strike price	K	Decreases	Increases
Increase in variance of underlying asset	σ	Increases	Increases
Increase in time to expiration	T	Increases	Increases
Increase in interest rates	r	Increases	Decreases
Increase in dividends paid	–	Decreases	Increases

The comparison between financial options and corporate investments that produce benefits is naturally demanding and well accepted (Luehrman 1998). It has been realized that real options will certainly replace NPV as the most widely used method for taking decisions in investment in the next decade (Copeland and Antikarov 2001). The option approach for taking investment decisions is much more advantageous for projects that have uncertain payoffs, whereas the NPV deals with the risk adjusted discounted factor, which itself is not fool-proof.

It is essential to use the NPV analysis correctly, especially when all the options are known from the very beginning of the project. This includes options related to investment and delay. To overcome the issue of using the NPV analysis incorrectly, decision trees were developed. Some proponents of real options, such as Copeland and Antikarov (2001) and Trigeorgis (1995), oppose the NPV analysis. But it should be understood that the NPV analysis is not at fault always; only sometimes does its improper use produce unreliable results.

The main difference between the two is that the real options analysis incorporates uncertainty, whereas decision trees (which rely on the NPV analysis) only compute expected values.

'It took decades for the NPV to become widely accepted in practice,' points out Triantis and Borrison (2001). 'Real option is an even more sophisticated tool. It's going to take a few decades for it as well to be well integrated in corporations.'

Here is a numerical example assuming a discount factor of 10% throughout. For an investment of Rs 5 lakh, there is a 40% chance of earning Rs 2 lakh per annum for 5 years, and a 60% chance of earning nothing per annum. The NPV of the average cash flow $= -5 + 0.4 \times 2 \times PVIFA_{5,10\%} = -5 + 0.4 \times 2 \times 3.791 = -1.97$ (negative NPV, reject the project).

Now, the Rs 0.5 lakh investment is followed by an additional Rs 4.5 lakh investment at the end of the first year of operation if everything is under control. Then, it can be calculated that Rs 2 lakh per annum can be earned for the remaining life of the project (50% likely). The NPV of cash flow, including option $= -0.5 - 4.5/1.1 + 2 \times PVIFA_{4,10\%} = -0.5 - 4.09 + 6.34 = +1.75$ (positive NPV, accept the project).

Though it has been 36 years since the famous Black and Scholes formula made its debut, and nearly 32 years after Myers named it as a real option, it has not been able to become popular in companies. A survey was conducted by Bain & Co. in the year 2000, and 451 senior executives were asked about their preference among various capital budgeting tools. Real option, which stood last in the preference list, was used by only five of them.

In the year 2002, Ryan & Ryan conducted another survey which shows that 85.1% of companies use the sensitivity analysis, 66.8% use the scenario analysis, and more than 90% use the NPV as the basic capital budgeting tool. In comparison, only 11.4% CFOs use real option as an alternative capital budgeting technique.

Options in investment analysis According to traditional DCF techniques, a new project or investment is considered acceptable only if the return is higher than the cut-off rate. In terms of cash flows and discount rate, a positive NPV suggests the feasibility of a project. However, there is a vast difference between estimation and the actual achievement of the desired cash flow. The difference occurs due to a large number of uncertain, unpredictable events that a project may face during its actual execution.

Traditional methods do not consider these unforeseen events. This leads to lack of flexibility in the management of the project. Also, the firm (handling the project) misses out on several options that help in the customization of capital budgeting decisions. There are three options that a firm can utilize in order to achieve the desired NPV in the face of unpredictable hurdles. First, if the firm has exclusive authority to delay the project execution, it should do so. Second, the firm could seek to cater to a bigger market and modify its goals accordingly. Lastly, if continuing the project only results in losses, the firm could consider terminating it.

The real option method is used to deal with a higher degree of uncertainty that is associated with the outcome of a follow-on investment opportunity. The investment opportunity is like a call option. One exercises the call and invests in the follow-on opportunity.

If the investment does not yield the expected results, one can walk away from it. When the call option reaches its expiry date, it is possible to predict the outcome of an investment quite clearly, as the uncertainty associated with the opportunity reduces to a great extent. The NPV of a project and the value of the opportunity of follow-on investment (call option) together determine the value of a project.

Real options vs Financial options

The value of an underlying asset is calculated in case of a real option. This value can be observed in case of a traded option. The present value of the expected cash flows is referred to as the value of the underlying option. The risk of the cash flows should be considered while deciding the discount rate. The estimated investment is the exercise price. The PV of the investment is computed by the risk-free interest rate, as the investment is taken as certain.

Traded option is the financial option traded in stock and derivative markets. Whereas, real option is the same as traded option, the only difference is that it is used for real assets or capital investment projects.

Variance estimation is required to use the Black and Scholes option pricing formula. The probability of different possible results (cash inflows) has to be considered while calculating the expected value or the NPV of the follow-on opportunity. The cash flows used to calculate the expected cash flows can also be used to determine the standard deviation or variance. However, it is more appropriate to use comparables. They are traded stocks with business risks similar to the investment opportunity. The risk of the investment opportunity is analysed against the average standard deviation of two comparable firms. It is essential to reduce the standard deviation to eliminate volatility from the process.

10.7 OPTION TO EXPAND

Sometimes organizations go ahead with certain projects because they might lead to other projects or markets. In such cases, the firm also accepts a project with negative net present value. The organization should be willing to pay for such options, as it would give them an opportunity to work on some other project.

Let us assume that a new product will be launched in the market, and the present value of expected cash inflows out of this product will be Rs X lakh for its entire life. To introduce this new product today, an investment of Rs Y lakh is required.

In this venture, if we consider only the initial few years of expected cash inflows, the NPV of the project might be negative. Hence, as per traditional method, this product should not be introduced.

But it can be considered as an option to expand or grow after a certain point of time, if the present value of cash inflow is more than the cost of launching the product. From that point the NPV starts being positive and the pay off will be Rs $(X-Y)$ lakh as shown in Figure 10.7.

As can be seen in the figure, at the expiration of the fixed time horizon, the firm will enter the new market, or take the new project if the present value of the expected cash flows at that point in time exceeds the cost of entering the market.

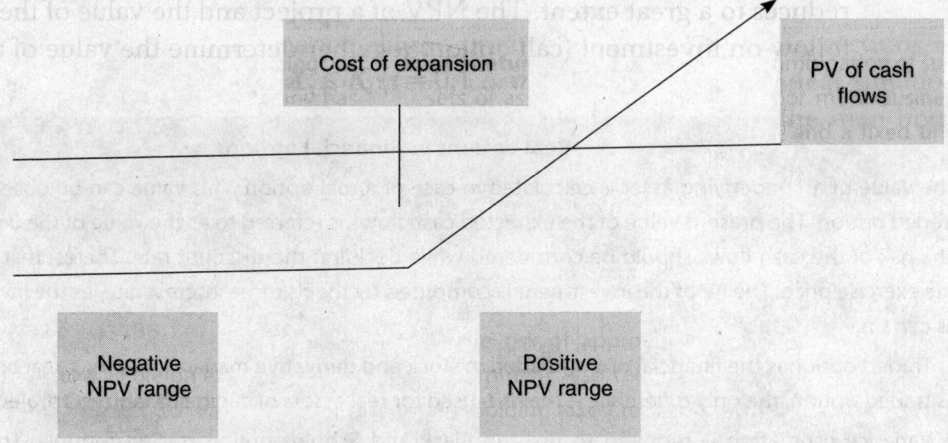

FIGURE 10.7 Options to expand a project

10.8 OPTION TO ABANDON

When the cash flows do not measure up to expectations, the option to abandon a project is the only option left. One way to reflect this value is through decision trees, which have limited applicability in most of the real-world investment analysis. This approach typically works only for multi-stage projects, and requires inputs on probabilities at each stage of the project. One can estimate the value of abandonment by using the option pricing approach, and building it into a value of an option.

Let us assume that the life of an existing machine = N (in years)

Present value of worth of the machine out of its remaining life = Rs Y lakh

If at this juncture this machine is abandoned, then its liquidation value is Rs X lakh.

Now, if X is less than Y, then obviously the machine should be retained. In that case, the option will be not exercised. Payoff will be zero, and chances of maximum loss will be the premium amount.

But if X is greater than or equal to Y, then the option of abandonment will yield a positive payoff.

In that case, the value of put option or payoff = $X - Y$. The machine should be abandoned as shown in Figure 10.8. The option to abandon takes on the characteristics of a put option.

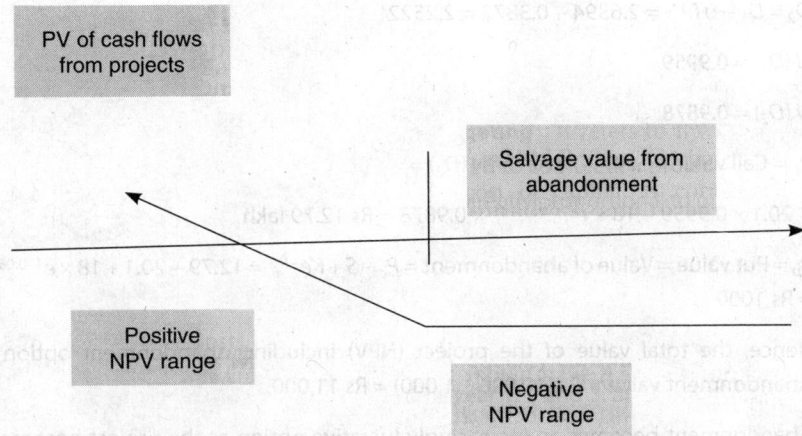

FIGURE 10.8   Options to abandon a project

Valuing an option to abandon—Examples

Example 10.2   A partnership firm is thinking of taking up a 15 year project with an initial outlay of Rs 20 lakh. It is expected that the present value of its expected cash inflow is Rs 20.1 lakh. The NPV of the project is 0.1 lakh. According to the firm's decision, the return of investment is not a significant amount.

That is why the firm thinks that it has the option to abandon this project any time within its life (15years) by selling its share of the ownership for Rs 18 lakh. Calculate the total NPV of the project.

Let us assume that the volatility in the present value of the cash flows = 10%

Solution

As per Black and Scholes option pricing formula,

Value of the underlying assets (S) = Profit of cash inflows = Rs 20.1 lakh

Exercise price (K) = Salvage value = Rs 18 lakh

Risk free Interest rate = R_f = 6%

Time to expiration = T = 15 years

σ = Volatility = 10%

Therefore,

$$D_1 = \frac{\ln (S/K) + (R_f + (0.5 \times (\sigma)^2))\, T}{\sigma \times T^{2/2}} = \frac{\ln \left[\dfrac{20.1}{18}\right] + (0.06 + 0.5 \times (0.1)^2)15}{0.1 \times 15^{1/2}} = 2.6394$$

$D_2 = D_1 - \sigma T^{1/2} = 2.6394 - 0.3872 = 2.2522$

$N(D_1) = 0.9959$

$N(D_2) = 0.9878$

$P_c = $ Call value $= S N(D_1) - Ke^{-R_f T} N(D_2) =$

$= 20.1 \times 0.9959 - 18 \times e^{(-0.06) \times 15} \times 0.9878 = $ Rs 12.79 lakh

$P_p = $ Put value = Value of abandonment $= P_c - S + Ke^{-R_f T} = 12.79 - 20.1 + 18 \times e^{(-0.06) \times 15} = 0.01$ lakhs (positive) = Rs 1000

Hence, the total value of the project (NPV) including abandonment option = NPV of the project + Abandonment value = Rs (10,000 + 1,000) = Rs 11,000.

Abandonment becomes an increasingly lucrative option as the project becomes older, since the present value of the remaining expected cash flows will fall.

Example 10.3 Abandonment using NPV and real options

Zeta Ltd has taken a 3-year lease on an iron deposit mine. The deposit contains a hundred lakh kg of iron. Mining involves a one-year development phase, at a cost of Rs 500 lakh. Extraction cost is Rs 5 per gm. The sale of iron would be at the spot price of iron at the beginning of the extraction phase.

The current spot price of iron is Rs 9 per kg. Changes in iron prices are normally distributed with mean 7% and standard deviation 20% (p.a.). The company's required rate of return for this project is 12%, and the riskless rate is 6%.

Analyse the project and check whether it should be accepted or rejected.

Solution

Analysis using DCF (NPV technique)

Current price of iron $= S_o = $ Rs 9 per kg

Expected rate of return of iron in one year $= 8\%$

Expected price of iron in one year $= S_1 = 9 \times e^{0.08} = 9.749$

Expected $NPV = -500 + \{100 (E[S_1] - 5)\} / 1.12$

Where, $E[S_1]$, expected price of iron in 1 year $= 9.749$

Expected $NPV = -500 + 100 \times (9.749 - 5) / 1.12 = -75.98$

Decision: Negative NPV, hence project should be rejected.

Real options analysis using Black and Scholes option pricing formula

$S = $ current spot price $= 9 \times 100 = 900$

$K = $ exercise price or initial investment $= 5 \times 100 = 500$

$R_f = 6\%$

$T = 1$ year

σ = volatility = Std deviation = 20%

Using option pricing formula,

$D_1 = [\ln (900 / 500) + (0.06 + 0.5 (0.2^2 \times 1))] / 0.2 \times 1^{1/2} = 1.675$

$D_2 = 1.475$

$N (D_1) = 0.9530$

$N (D_2) = 0.9300$

Option value = $900 \times 0.9530 - 500 \times e^{-0.06 \times 1} \times 0.9300 =$ Rs 419.779 lakh (positive)

Decision: The project should be accepted.

Example 10.4   Deferment options

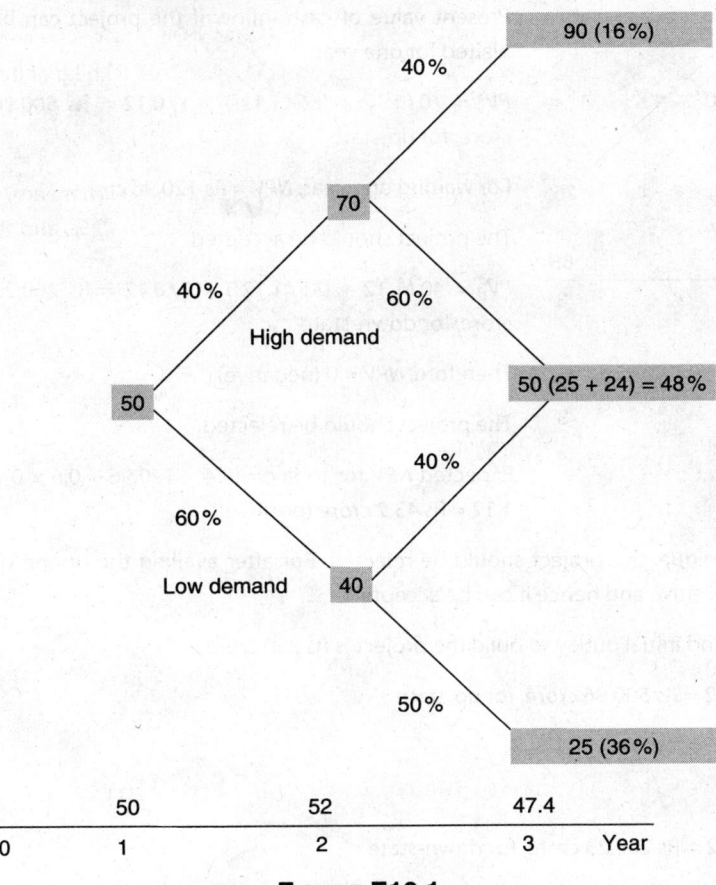

A firm has a green project to start a new manufacturing unit at a new site, for which the initial outlay can be either Rs 380 crore or Rs 350 crore. The expected net cash flow is Rs 50 crore in the first year of operation. The net cash flow depends upon whether the state government gives a special tax benefit or not. There is a 40% probability that the government will do so, and with this benefit, the cost of production will be reduced. The special tax benefit is applicable for price and for that effect the market demand will increase. The net expected cash flow up to three years is shown in Figure E10.1; after three years there will be a perpetual assumption of a discount factor of 12%.

Check if the project should be accepted or not.

Solution

Condition 1a: According to the traditional DCF model

Present value of cash inflow = (50 / 1.12) + (52 / 1.12²) + (47.4 / 1.12³) × (1 / 0.12) = Rs 367.24 crore.

FIGURE E10.1

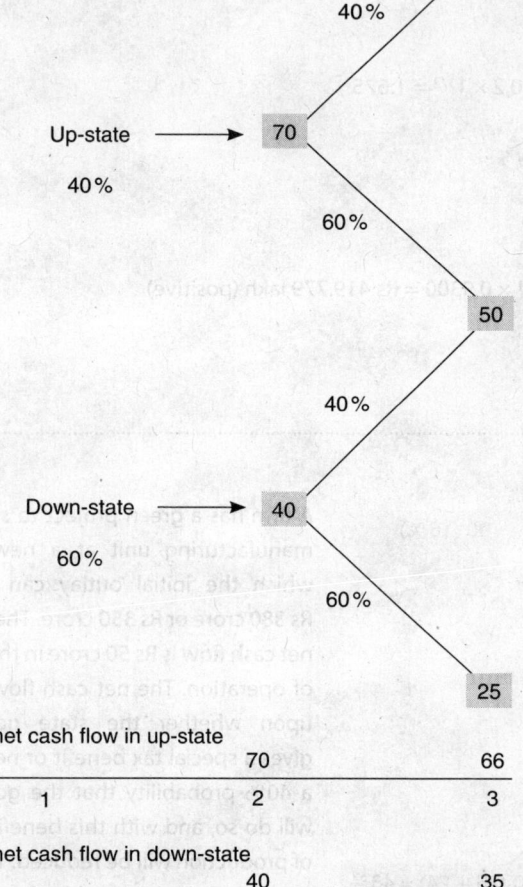

Initial outlay to build the project = Rs 380 crore

Therefore, NPV = Rs 12.76 crore (negative)

Hence, the project is rejected.

Condition 1b: If the initial outlay to build the project = Rs 350 crore, NPV = Rs 17.24 crore (positive). Refer to Figure E10.2.

Hence the project is accepted.

Condition 2a: According to the real option model (option to delay for 1 year)

During this one-year delay, the firm will get new additional information and some more effective links, hence a smarter decision can be made.

Initial outlay to build the project = Rs 380 crore

Present value of cash inflow if the project can be waited for one year:

PV_u = 70/1.12 + (66/1.12²) × 1/0.12 = Rs 500.96 crore, for up-state

For waiting one year, NPV = Rs 120.96 crore

The project should be accepted.

PV_d = 40/1.12 + (35/1.12²) × 1/0.12 = Rs 268.23 crore, for down-state

Therefore, NPV = 0 (negative)

The project should be rejected.

Expected NPV for today = (0.4 × 120.96 + 0.6 × 0)/1.12 = Rs 43.2 crore (positive)

Expected net cash flow in up-state

	70		66
0	1	2	3

Expected net cash flow in down-state

	40		35
0	1	2	3

FIGURE E10.2

Hence, using traditional DCF technique, the project should be rejected. But after availing the option of delay for one year, NPV becomes positive and hence it can be accepted.

Condition 2b: Delay for one year and initial outlay to build the project is Rs 350 crore.

PV_u = 70/1.12 + (66/1.12²) × 1/0.12 = Rs 500.96 crore, for up-state

For waiting one year, NPV = Rs 150.96 crore

The project should be accepted.

PV_d = 40/1.12 + (35/1.12²) × 1/0.12 = Rs 268.23 crore, for down-state

Therefore, NPV = 0 (negative), and the project should be rejected.

Expected *NPV* for today = (0.4 × 150.96 + 0.6 × 0) / 1.12 = Rs 53.2 crore (positive).

Hence, the project should be accepted.

By using both the traditional DCF and real option method, the project can be accepted. But by waiting one year, the NPV of the project can be increased by Rs 53.2 − Rs 17.24, i.e., Rs 35.96 crore.

10.9 LUEHRMAN'S TOMATO GARDEN

Timothy A. Luehrman (1998) compared managing a portfolio of strategic options with growing a garden of tomatoes in an unpredictable climate, in his paper 'Strategy as a Portfolio of Real Options' (Figure 10.9).

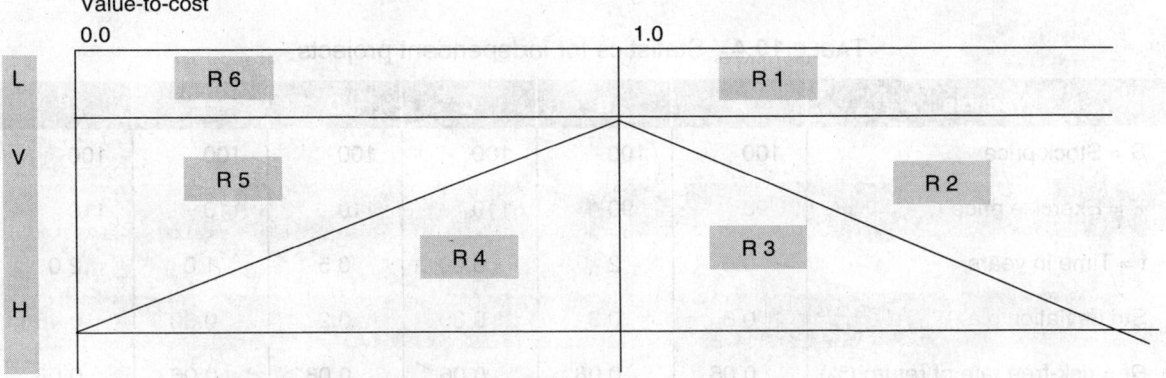

FIGURE 10.9   Relationship between volatility and value cost

V = Volatility (L = Low, H = High) = Standard Deviation $\sqrt{time}$ and Value-to-cost = NPV_q = Stock price / PV of exercise price in Black and Scholes option pricing formula. The horizontal axis of the figure measures value-to-cost and the vertical axis signifies volatility. R 1 to R 6 is defined in Table 10.3.

TABLE 10.3   The tomato garden

Region	Tomatoes	Value-to-cost	Volatility	Remarks
R1	Ripe	>1	Low	Invest now
R2	Imperfect but edible	>1	Low-to-high	May be now
R3	Inedible but very promising	>1	Low-to-high	Probably later
R4	Less promising green tomatoes	<1	Low-to-high	May be later
R5	Late blossoms and small green tomatoes	<1	Low-to-high	Probably never
R6	Rotten	<1	Low	Invest never

In this tomato garden, the Tata Nano project in Singur will fall either in region 4 (may be later) or region 5 (probably never) where,

(a) value-to cost ($NPVq$): <1

(b) volatility ($s.d.\sqrt{t}$): low-to-high

Hence, it can shift to region 3 (probably later) if NPV_q becomes >1, or by increasing the project worth or by decreasing the project cost.

As an example of what can be learnt from the tomato garden, Timothy suggested six hypothetical projects that are entirely unrelated to one another. Table 10.4 shows the statistics for six independent projects labelled A to F. The six projects have different time and volatility profiles and hence different values for their value-to-cost and volatility matrix. Accordingly, all projects will be under different region and different decision levels.

TABLE.10.4   Statistics for independent projects

Variable	A	B	C	D	E	F
S = Stock price	100	100	100	100	100	100
X = Exercise price	90	90	110	110	110	110
t = Time in years	0.0	2	0.00	0.5	1.0	2.0
Std deviation p.a.	0.3	0.3	0.30	0.2	0.30	0.40
Rf = risk-free rate of return (%)	0.06	0.06	0.06	0.06	0.06	0.06
NPVq = Value-to-cost	1.111	1.248	0.909	0.936	0.964	1.021
Std deviation √t	0.00	0.424	0.00	0.141	0.30	0.566
Call value	10	27.23	0.00	3.06	10.42	23.24
S – X	10	10	−10	−10	−10	−10
Region	R1	R2	R6	R5	R4	R3
Decision	Now	May be now	Never	Probably never	May be later	Probably later

Note: Vital statistics for six projects using tomato garden concept (all are in '000,000 Rs)

Source: Luehrman, Sep–Oct 1998.

....

Example 10.5   Increasing project value by delaying the project

Project X has 2 phases. You may invest in the first, in both, or in neither. The first phase requires an investment of Rs 100 m now. One year later, X will deliver either Rs 120 m or Rs 80 m with equal probability.

At that time, you can invest an additional Rs 100 m for phase II. One year later, phase II pays out either 20% more or less than phase I (equally likely). (Assume a 10% hurdle rate) That is why, in phase II, payoff becomes 144 (25% probability), 96(50% probability), and 64 (25% probability). (Refer to Table E10.3.)

TABLE E10.3

Phase	Payoff	Probability	Outflow	Worth	NPV
I	120	0.5	100	90.9	$-9.1_{t=0}$
	80	0.5			
II	144	0.25	100	90.9	$-9.1_{t=1}$
	96	0.5			
	64	0.25			
II (by waiting another year)					$-8.3_{t=0}$
Total					$-17.4_{t=0}$
Wait II					Increases by 0.8
Total					

Project Y has exactly the same structure as earlier but different cash flows. For Rs 100 m invested today, Y delivers either Rs 140 m or Rs 60 m with equal probability in phase I. Phase II requires an additional Rs 100 m investment and delivers either 40% more or 40% less than phase I did. Project Y has the same structure as Project X and the same expected cash flows. If we cannot wait, both have the same value. But Y has higher variance (*s.d.* for X = 0.18 and for Y = 0.34).

Solution

If we can wait to decide about phase II, the higher variance of Y makes the phase II growth option worth more for Y than X. Because of the higher growth option value, the project as a whole is more valuable. The total NPV of project Y is 3.3 (more than project X). Hence, from the above example, it is clear that sometimes the project worth can be increased by waiting and by incorporating more volatility and uncertainty.

10.10 SINGUR—A JOURNEY FROM TRADITIONAL NPV TO REAL OPTIONS

The NPV rule is easy, but it makes the false assumption that the investment is either reversible or that it cannot be delayed. Option value has important implications for managers, because by using them they can rethink about their investment decision as per the market opportunities available. It is often highly desirable to delay an investment decision and wait for more information about market conditions, even though a standard analysis indicates that the investment is economical right now. This may be the case for the Singur–Nano also. According to the NPV rule (now-or-never), there was hardly any hope for the Singur project.

Singur—The Tata Nano story   It may be recalled that in March 2006, Tata Motors announced their intention of establishing an automobile plant at Singur, West

Bengal. The company decided to roll out (by 2008) the small and inexpensive Nano priced at US$2000, with a capacity of 2,50,000 vehicles per annum, with flexibility to raise it to 3,50,000 p.a., targeting both the foreign and domestic markets.

As West Bengal did not have adequate high-quality suppliers, the company thought of inviting some ancillary units to invest in the project along with Tata Motors. These included well-known reputed multinational Indian companies such as Bosch, Behr, Gabriel, Exide, Caparo, Kinetic, Sona, Subros, Rico, Rasandik, Lumax, Tata Ryerson, Tata Auto Components, etc.

In March 2007, the West Bengal government entered into an agreement with Tata Motors through which the Tatas were offered a lot of concessions by the government, which both the parties felt shy of disclosing. A total of 997.11 acres of land spread across mouzas in Singur, district Hooghly, which had been acquired by WBIDC, was handed over to Tata. Almost 23 ancillary units together completed the construction work on the project site.

In response to serious socio-political opposition, Mr Ratan Tata, the chairman of the Tata Group of Companies, made a press statement on 22 August 2008, expressing his willingness to 'pull out' of the Singur project. In response to such an unwarranted statement, it was pointed out that the Tata project management team had done little to address the social impact of the investment.

On 2 September 2008, Tata Motors communicated through an official release that the company was evaluating alternative options for manufacturing the Nano car, and the detailed plan to relocate the plant and machinery to an alternative site was under preparation.

Strategic commitment The strategic effect of a commitment is positive when the commitment alters the market condition, demand, and competitors' behaviour in ways that are advantageous to the firm making the commitment. These strategic effects are often rooted in inflexibility because they are almost always made under conditions of uncertainty about market conditions, costs, pricing, economy, demand, competitors' goals, etc. This may have happened in the case of the Singur project, where the early commitment of Rs 1 lakh for the Nano car might have created flexibility and uncertainty.

Flexibility gives rise to what are called real options Tata Motors had an opportunity to customize their decision to information about the market that would be available in the future. Here, a real option of the Tatas intentionally delaying the investment in the Nano project and awaiting new information about its profitability becomes available.

The above issue can be easily explained by taking a simple hypothetical example. Say the Tata Group invested Rs 2,000 crore (hypothetical figure) in their Nano project to enter the small car market. Given the uncertainties about how the market would accept the new product, the firm forecasts the following two scenarios.

High acceptance ($p = 0.5$): Investment will have a PV of Rs 6,000 crore

Low acceptance ($p = 0.5$): Investment will have a PV of Rs 1,000 crore

Expected $NPV = 0.5 (6,000 + 1,000) - 2000 = 1,500$ crore

Now suppose by waiting a year or so, Tata calculates that Nano would turn out to have a high level of market acceptance, they would invest more, otherwise not.

Then the expected $NPV = (0.5 \times 4000 + 0.5 \times 0) / 1.10 =$ Rs 1818.2 crore (@10% discount rate).

Therefore, from a now-or-never choice, if the Nano project can have the flexibility to delay and gain additional information, the incremental value of real option would be (Rs 1818.2 − Rs 1500 crore) = Rs 318.2 crore.

As per the present hypothetical figures, Tata would be able to tailor their decision-making according to the underlying circumstances. This would help them avoid an important investment mistake, i.e., avoid investing in a new plant when the demand is low. During the worldwide recession, this can be a revival strategy of the Type II error (accepting a project when it should be rejected) of Shah and Stiglitz (1986).

According to Ghemawat (1991), the learn-to-burn ratio is the key determinant of option value. It is a ratio of the learn rate and the burn rate. The former refers to the rate at which a firm receives new information that helps it to make necessary changes in its strategic choices. The latter is the rate at which a firm invests in sunken assets to strengthen its strategies. A strategic choice is highly flexible and uncertain if its learn-to-burn ratio is high. The Tata Nano car project also had a high learn-to-burn ratio. Thus, there was hardly any major investment at their Singur plant, from where they eventually had to pull out. A capacity for high learn-to-burn ratio can be found in several commitment-intensive choices. Developing such a capacity, however, demands efficient management. The Tatas could increase the learn-to-burn ratio of the Nano project by experimenting at Singur and initiating pilot programmes in Gujarat. It also added to the project's uncertainty and flexibility in making a commitment-intensive choice. Finally, it enhanced the overall value of the project.

How is Tata's Nano an example of a hold-up problem? To explain this, some concepts used in Strategic Economy (Coase 1937) must be understood.

Transaction costs These include the time and expense of negotiating, writing, and enforcing contracts. They arise when one or more parties to a transaction can act opportunistically.

Relationship-specific assets These are investments made to support specific transactions. Hence, they cannot be redeployed to another transaction without some sacrifice, such as reducing productivity or some extra cost in adapting the assets to the new transaction.

Fundamental transformation Once the parties invest in relation-specific assets, the relationship changes from a large numbers bidding situation to a small numbers bargaining situation (Williamson 1985).

Rents and quasi-rents These are explained through a numerical example about a hypothetical transaction in Tata's Nano project at Singur.

Let us assume that Caparo Engg contemplates building a factory to produce cup-holders for the Nano project. The factory can make up to one million holders per annum, at a variable cost of Rs v per unit. Caparo finances the construction of their factory with a mortgage from the bank that requires a payment of Rs P.

Total cost p.a. for Caparo (even if they do not do business with Tata) $=$ Rs C

Total production and financial cost of Caparo p.a. $=$ Rs $C + 1000000v$

After the situation held up (September 2008), i.e., the pull out from Singur decision by Tata, Caparo could have the bail-out option. They could sell to other automobile manufacturers or jobbers with suitable modification and a lower price (say, p_m p.u. and $p_m > v$) and $C > 10,00,000 \ (p_m - v)$.

Hence, it would not make sense for one to build the holders factory if they did not expect to sell to Tata. A portion of their investment is specific to their relationship with Tata.

Relationship specific investment (RSI) is the unrecovered investment if any ancillary unit cannot do business with the firm as per earlier contract. $RSI = C - 1000000 \ (p_m - v)$

Rent Holders price p.u. if Tata will generate business $= p_t \ (p_t > p_m)$

Hence, rent is the benefit of Caparo if everything goes as planned. It is the economic profit or NPV.

Rent $= 10,00,000 \ (p_t - v) - C$

Quasi-rent It is the difference between the profit they get from selling to Tata and the profit they get from their next best option if they cannot do business with Tata and are forced to sell to jobbers.

Quasi rent $= 10,00,000 \ (p_t - v) - C - [10,00,000 \ (p_m - v) - C]$

$= 10,00,000 \ (p_t - p_m)$

Holdup problem The expression 'holdup problem' was coined by Goldberg (1976). When a firm invests in a relationship-specific asset, quasi-rent cannot be zero; it must be positive. If the quasi-rent is large, a firm stands to lose a lot. This opens the possibility that its trading partner could exploit this large quasi-rent through holdup. In the Tata case, there may be a possibility of holding up the ancillary partners by attempting to renegotiate the terms of earlier deals. When contracts are incomplete and there are chances of more uncertainty, holdup will be more beneficial for the firm. The potential for holdup raises the cost of market transaction. It can be done by negotiating and renegotiating the contract, and by that it will improve post-contractual bargaining positions for the firm.

If $p_t = 12$, $p_m = 4$, $v = 3$, $C = 70,00,000$

Caparo's rent $= (12 - 3)\ 10,00,000 - 70,00,000 = $ Rs 20,00,000 p.a.

Caparo's quasi-rent $= (12 - 4)10,00,000 = $ Rs 80,00,000 p.a.

If Tata renegotiates the contract down to Rs 8 per unit, Tata will increase its profits by Rs 40,00,000 per annum and it will have transferred half of Caparo's quasi-rents to itself. After the holdup, Caparo will realize that its now making a profit of $(8 - 3) \times 1000000 - 7000000 = -2000000$, which is actually a loss. But they have to continue in this trap, and this will enhance the possibility of Tata making more profit or reducing its cost of production.

As per Timothy Luehrman's Tomato Garden metaphor, the Nano project would be located in region 3 or 4 that corresponds to 'probably later' and 'may be later', respectively. The Singur plant would lie in region 5 ('probably never'). In times of economic meltdown, delaying a project is the best alternative. It also adds to the project's value.

Traditional NPV (now-or-never) will no longer last in the present era that is highly volatile and uncertain. A firm must apply flexibility and take to the real option path in order to avail the opportunity of enhancing the project worth and start investing at the right time after getting the right information.

Tata's Nano story during the Singur days was nothing but a holdup problem; further uncertainty and delay will enlarge the quasi-rent of its ancillaries and will further reduce the production cost of the Nano and enhance project NPV.

10.11 REAL CONCERNS

Why have companies been slow to adopt the real option valuation technique? The reason can be found in the following comment made by Van Putten and MacMillan (2004): 'For all their theoretical attractiveness as a way to value growth projects, real options have had a difficult time catching on with managers. CFOs tell us that real options overestimate the value of uncertain projects, encouraging companies to over-invest in them. In the worst case, they grant excessively ambitious managers a license to gamble with the shareholders' money.'

Conceptually, real option is okay, but the problem lies in its applicability because it involves complex mathematical tools, partial differential equations, and stochastic calculus. These are bottlenecks for a practising manager to view various options by using real options mechanisms (Favato, Mills, and Weinstein 2005).

Owing to the use of sophisticated mathematics, a real option is like a black box. The lack of transparency and simplicity constitutes its major drawbacks. The aim for higher and higher statistical sophistication reached its saturation when Mun (2002) observed that in the limits, the results obtained by the use of bizarre binomial lattices were similar to those obtained from the Black and Scholes model. To further demonstrate his findings, Mun performed a 1,000 simulation tests that included around 5×109 nodal computations. This effort was equivalent to 4.6 GB of computer memory or 299 Excel spreadsheets.

Real options do not consider management realities. A common question is whether the strength of real options is also its greatest weakness? Criticism of real options states that managers cannot be held accountable to shut down a project when needed, as real options do not expire like financial options as per the contract.

Real options is sometimes a little like an extreme sport—people look at it and say, 'Wow, that's really neat.' That is why Triantis says, 'It's fun to watch, but when you actually sit down and try to do it yourself, it's not so easy.'

10.12 CONCLUSION

Theoretically, the concepts of financial option analysis can be readily extended to real options. In fact, real options have historically preceded financial options, and are especially widely used in real estate and equipment leases with an option to purchase. Thus, it would seem that the same valuation approach of the financial options can be applied to real options as well.

However, there is a major difficulty in extending the financial option concept exactly into real options. With the little historical data available and upcoming new trading markets, such as technology development, one can state that effective markets for real options, especially for real properties, often do not exist. As a result, reliable data for estimating S, uS, and dS is lacking ($S =$ a financial stock currently valued by the market, $uS =$ the expected rise of stock valuation with probability p, and $dS =$ the expected fall of stock valuation with a probability $1 - p$). The input data for valuation will largely be based on judgements, thus causing concern and consternation among technology executives who have been trained in hard statistics and engineering precision.

Another major bottleneck is the cultural difference between financial investors and technology developers. Financial investors believe that an efficient market determines the financial value of a technology, whereas technology developers are of the opinion that such a value can be obtained through trend forecasting or subjective judgement and are usually sceptical about the true efficiency of the financial market. As a result, technology developers generally have difficulty in accepting the law of one price, which is actually the corner stone of real option analysis.

SUMMARY

Most 'options' mean financial choices; 'real' means non-financial real assets or capital investments. Real options are options on real assets that can be defined simply as opportunities to respond to the changing circumstances of a project. The trade of options on real assets is much older than transactions involving money. Like financial options, call and put options, real options can also be broadly classified as option to expand, option to abandon, option to postpone, or switching options.

The binomial model for pricing stock options is a discrete time model. It clearly explains the fundamental economic principle of option valuation by the risk-less arbitrage method. The Black and Scholes, option pricing formula, a mathematical model was developed by Fischer Black and Myron Scholes (1973) and later on adapted by Garman and Kohlhagen (1983) for currency options. The Black–Scholes model determines a fair value price based on current price (spot), exercise price, time remaining before expiration of the option, the compounded riskless rate of interest, and the value of the cumulative normal density function.

KEY TERMS

Binomial method   A method to arrive at the value of an option, assuming only two possible future courses to action or values of the asset, is referred as binomial method.

Delta of an option   It is the ratio of spread of payoff of the option to the spread of the price of the asset.

Flexibility options   An option to reallocate resources or switch, has value. For example, building two plants instead of one to serve markets on two continents, creates the option of switching production from one plant to the other.

Option to abandon   The option to walk away from a project in response to new information, increases the value of the project. It is equivalent to a put option.

Option to delay   Option to delay is a decision that rests with the management. They decide when to implement a project. It is also referred to as option to wait, or timing decision.

Option to expand   Option to expand refers to the flexibility to start a project at a lower scale and then expand as time progresses and uncertainties resolve.

Real options   Real options are options on real assets that can be defined as opportunities to respond to the changing circumstances of a project.

CONCEPT REVIEW QUESTIONS

1. What are real options? How they are useful in capital budgeting decisions?
2. What are the different kinds of real options? Illustrate.
3. What are the differences between real option and financial option?
4. Why do you think that the DCF analysis is not an appropriate tool for evaluating capital budgeting proposals involving real options?
5. What is the difference between option to grow and option to abandon?
6. In terms of the Black and Scholes model of valuation of call and put option for option to wait, to expand, and to abandon describe:
   (i)   What the underlying asset would be?
   (ii) What the exercise price would be?
   (iii) How you would find out volatility?

NUMERICAL PROBLEMS

1. AB Technologies Limited is considering a buy out of a firm, Sydney Software, for a price of Rs 500 crore. It is expected to provide an annual cash flow of Rs 50 crore for the next 25 years. The cost of capital of AB Technologies is 11%. Should it go ahead with the acquisition? The annual cash inflow estimate has been prepared on the basis of a 50% chance of getting a cash flow of Rs 75 crore and a 50% chance of having only Rs 25 crore as the annual cash inflow.

   Meanwhile, the original promoters of Sydney Software have offered to buy back the firm for Rs 450 crore two years later, but they would have to pay Rs 525 crore now instead of Rs 500 crore. Should it go ahead with such proposition?

   Find the value of the option in the above case as per Black and Scholes Option Pricing Model. Assume the standard deviation of returns at 45%.

2. Use the Black–Scholes model to price the following call option. (You may use the Black and Scholes formula and a computer, or other published tables.)

   (a) A one-year European call option on 100 shares of XYZ Corporation. The exercise price is Rs 50 per share. The standard deviation of returns on XYZ's shares is Re 0.2 per year. The current stock price is Rs 35 per share. The risk-free rate of return is 3%.

   (b) Now vary the terms of the call on XYZ one at a time. What happens to the value of the call as

   (i) The standard deviation of returns on shares goes from Re 0.2 to Re 0.5

   (ii) Maturity goes from 0 to 3 years

   (iii) The exercise price goes from Rs 25 to Rs 35 to Rs 50

   (iv) The stock price goes from Rs 35 to Rs 60

   (v) The risk-free rate goes from 3% to 6%

   (c) (i) What is the value of a European put on 100 shares of XYZ, with terms identical to those given in 2 (b)(i)?

   (ii) Repeat the calculations from part (b) for the European put on XYZ. What are the intuitive explanations for the changes in value you computed?

3. Project alpha has two phases. You may invest in the first, in both, or in neither. The first phase requires an investment of Rs 100 today. One year later, Alpha will deliver either Rs 120 or Rs 80, with equal probability. At that time (after the phase 1 payout has been received), you can invest an additional Rs 100 for phase 2. One year later, phase 2 pays out either 20% more cash than phase 1 actually delivered, or (equally likely) 20% less. For investments in this business, your company normally applies a 10% hurdle rate.

   (a) How much would project Alpha be worth if it offered only phase 1 cash flows, without the phase 2 opportunity?

   (b) How much would phase 2 opportunity be worth if you had to choose today, once and for all, whether or not to invest in it?

   (c) Assuming you can wait to decide about phase 2, what is the total value of project Alpha? Should you invest the first Rs 100?

   (d) Project Omega has exactly the same structure as project Alpha, and the same systematic risk, but somewhat different cash flows. For Rs 100 invested today, Omega delivers in phase 1 either Rs 140 or Rs 60, with equal probability. Phase 2 requires an additional Rs 100 investment and delivers either 40% more or 40% less than phase 1 did. What is the total value of project Omega? Should you invest the first Rs 100?

   (e) Compare these two projects. Which is riskier? Which is more valuable? Which has a higher fraction of its value accounted for by 'growth options', i.e., the phase 2 opportunity? Assuming both were undertaken, would you finance Alpha and Omega differently? How and why?

ASSIGNMENT

You have been shortlisted as a prospective vendor to supply tyres for a new automobile model being developed by an auto manufacturer. The initial outlay of the project is Rs 6 crore and the NPV of the project is Rs 4.5 crore, having a life of 3 years. The success of the new model can be known only after 2 years. The chances of success are 70%. These raised volumes would generate cash flows of Rs 1 crore annually for next 25 years. No additional investment is required.

(i)   Would you accept the project?

(ii) Is there any real option available in this situation? If yes, describe it.

(iii) What is the exercise price?

(iv) How would you value the option, if such an option exists?

SELECT REFERENCES

Amaram, M. and N. Kulatilaka, *Real Options: Managing strategic investments in an uncertain world,* HBS Press, Cambridge, MA, 1998.

Black, M. and M. Scholes, The Pricing of Option and Corporate Liabilities, *Journal of Political Economy,* University of Chicago Press, vol. 81, no. 3, May–June 1973, pp. 637–654.

Coase, R., 'The Nature of the Firm', *Economica,* no. 4, 1937, pp. 386–405.

Copeland, T. and V. Antikarov, *Real options: A practisioner's guide,* New York: Texere LLC, 2001.

Coval, J.E., and T. Shumway, 'Expected Option Returns,' *Journal of Finance,* vol. 56, no. 3, 2001, pp. 983–1009.

Cox, J.C., S.A. Ross, and M. Rubinstein, 'Option pricing: A simplified approach', *Journal of Financial Economics,* vol. 7, October, 1979, pp. 229–64.

Dixit, A.K. and R.S. Pindyck, *Investment under uncertainty,* Princeton University Press, 1994.

Dixit, A.K., and R.S. Pindyck, 'The options approach to capital investment', *Harvard Business Review,* May–June, 1995, pp. 105–115.

Favato, G., R.W. Mills, and B. Weinstein, 'Real Option Taxonomies', *Henley Management College Discussion Paper Series,* HDP 10, 2005.

Ghemawat, P., *Commitment: The Dynamic of Strategy,* New York: Free Press, 1991.

Goldberg. V., 'Regulation and Administered Contracts', *Bell Journal of Economics,* no. 7, Autumn, 1976, pp. 426–48.

Kester, W.C., 'Today's option for tomorrow's growth', *Harvard Business Review,* March–April, 1984, pp. 153–60.

Luehrman, T.A., 'Investment Opportunities as Real Options: Getting Started on the Numbers', *Harvard Business Review,* July–August, 1998, pp. 51–67.

Luehrman, T.A., 'Strategy as a Portfolio of Real Options', *Harvard Business Review,* Sep–Oct, 1998, pp. 89–99.

Luehrman, T.A., 'What's It Worth? A General Manager's Guide to Valuation,' *Harvard Business Review,* May–June, 1997, pp. 132–42.

Myers S.C., 'Finance theory and financial strategies' in D. Chew Jr (ed.) 'The New Corporate Finance', 2nd ed., p. 119, McGraw Hill 1998.

Myers. S.C., 'Determinants of Corporate Borrowing', *Journal of Financial Economics,* no. 5, 1977, pp. 34–46.

Rendleman, R. and B. Bartter, 'Two State Option Pricing', *Journal of Finance,* vol. 34, 1979, pp. 1092–1110.

Ryan, P.A. and G.P. Ryan, 'Capital Budgeting Practices of the Fortune 1000: How Have Things Changed?', *Journal of Business and Management,* vol. 8, no. 4, 2002, pp. 355–64.

Shah R.K. and J. Stiglitz, 'The Architecture of Economic Systems: Hierarchies and Polyarchies', *American Economic Review,* vol. 76, September 1986, pp. 716–727.

Triantis, A. and A. Borrison, 'Real Option, State of Practice', *Journal of Applied Corporate Finance,* vol. 14, 2001, pp. 8–24.

Trigeorgis, L., *Real Options in Capital Investment: Models, Strategies, and Applications,* Westport, Conn: Praeger, 1995.

Trigeorgis, L., *Real Options: Managerial Flexibility and Strategy in Resource Allocation,* Cambridge, MA: MIT Press, 1996.

Van Putten, A.B. and I.C. MacMillan, 'Making real options really work', *Harvard Business Review,* vol. 82, no. 12, 2004, pp. 234.

Williamson, O., *The Economic Institutions of Capitalism,* Chap. 2, New York: Free Press, 1985.

CASE STUDY
Valuing an Expansion Strategy—The Vijayandra & Co. Case

Overview

In 2006, Vijayandra & Co. was negotiating with a biotechnology research company regarding the marketing rights for a new compound, PICASSO. This was indicated to be useful for the treatment of a disease of coronary arteries after the intervention of percutaneous transluminal coronary angioplasty (PTCA). Coronary artery disease causes the narrowing or obstruction of the blood vessels, which is caused by fatty deposits. Angioplasty, a common non-invasive procedure, reshapes the blood vessel, opening the occluded artery with a balloon catheter. In some patients, re-narrowing may occur a few days after the PTCA. Controlled clinical studies showed that PICASSO was effective in reducing the risk of that disease after transluminal catheterization.

Initial evaluation of the approved indication seemed clearly to indicate a negative NPV value. The NPV projection for the three indications, considered separately, was really discouraging:

- Base case indication (PTCA) *NPV* = Rs 1,00,00,000
- First expansion (angina)   *NPV* = Rs –11,80,000
- Second expansion (cardiac infarction)
                                 NPV = Rs –73,00,000

According to the management of Vijayandra & Co., the forecast of future patients suitable for PTCA was highly uncertain. Subsequent extensions would depend on the PTCA performance of PICASSO. The overall assessment should account for the possibility of expanding the marketing of the drug into related indications. By purchasing the marketing and development rights of PICASSO and launching it in the market, Vijayandra was clearly acquiring a future options at the same time, but important questions still needed to be answered.

Discussion questions

- Should angina and second treatments be developed in parallel (independently) or in sequence (staging the investment)?
- What is the total value of the investment opportunity when management can choose the optimal situation between the available expansion strategies within the next two years?
- How is the value of synergy and the opportunity affected if the second treatment is less correlated with angina?
- What is the total value breakdown?
- Which input variables have the most significant impact on total value?

A brief analysis of the above case

It is important to note that the basic scenario plots identified by the Vijayandra management focused exclusively on one dimension, which was the future positive clinical effects of the product, failing even to consider alternative scenarios determined by competitive pressures. It was known at the time that Berk was in the late clinical development stage of a similar drug (AGGRA-STAT), and Schering was considering acquiring the marketing rights of INTEGRILIN, an anticlotting agent with features very similar to PICASSO.

The scenarios envisaged by Vijayandra completely ignored the possible likelihood and turbulences generated by near and future competitive pressures. This short-sighted approach to a complex investment decision proved to be very costly to Vijayandra: the use of a broader integrated approach to risk management would have identified the potential risk earlier, probably leading the management to take a different position about the investment risk embedded in the PICASSO investment decision. In retrospect, widening the content for possible scenarios should have been a part of the analysis undertaken by Vijayandra. Attempting scenarios does not, of course, guarantee that all relevant opportunities and threats will be on the radar screen, but narrowness of vision is diminished and potential disasters may be avoided.

What were the options?

Managers and investors who understand the value of available options will gain the greatest insight into true business potential, but undoubtedly the initial hurdle was to identify the right options (Trigeorgis, 2005). Real options thinking highlights the point that management intervention—call it 'strategic action'—often creates valuable options. Once identified, these options can be assessed and exercised (if appropriate), starting the cycle of value creation and new options all over again. The approach adopted by the academicians was to assess the options available to Vijayandra in terms of flexibility, contingency, and volatility. As is illustrated in the above case, all three were highly relevant. What is meant by them?

- *Flexibility* is the ability to defer, abandon, or expand an investment. Within the next two years, Vijayandra's management could have decided to exercise an expansion option, paid the necessary development costs then, and proceeded to the drug's extension to other applications.

- *Contingency* here means that future investments are contingent on something happening in the future. Managers can make investments today, even in those where it is presently showing a negative NPV value. But in future, it will give much higher NPV investment opportunities. It can be evaluated by using the deterministic budgeting model. Building on the experience with PICASSO in a low-risk therapeutic segment such as PTCA, Vijayandra researches could have expanded the clinical development to two more competitive sectors, such as angina and acute myocardial infraction, significantly reducing the cost of entry.

- *Volatility* is a factor that somewhat counter intuitively increases the value of options. In option theory, higher volatility—because of the asymmetric payoff schemes—leads to higher option value. For example, the uncertainty related to the actual number of patients eligible for PICASSO treatment after PTCA procedure would increase NPV than its initial projections.

In the above case, the main value drivers in the uncertainty of the number of PTCA patients (main risk driver) were identified, as well as the upside potential enhanced by two expansion options (angina and second treatments). A decision map was built specifying the following two options:

1. Expand into angina within the following two years if the present value of the expanded market was higher than the development costs, to obtain the product approval from FDA.

2. Expand into second treatment between years two and four, either directly if the present value of that was higher than development costs, or indirectly to exploit synergies from first developing the angina treatment.

HANDLING MULTIPLE PROJECTS—CONSTRAINTS AND SOLUTIONS

Beware of the time-driven project with an artificial deadline.

— M. DOBSON

LEARNING OBJECTIVES

After studying this chapter, you will be able to

- Understand the kind of issues involved in prioritizing multiple projects by a firm
- Know about conflict in ranking various cases and be able to find suitable solutions
- Understand capital rationing and choose a project amidst many
- Understand approaches to select more than one project from numerous alternatives
- Explain the linear, integer, and goal programming approach

Handling Multiple Projects

Just before Lent, the government of Rio de Janeiro embarked on a project to build a combined school and carnival stadium to house the crowd that comes to see the Lent parades and annual festivities for four days in March every year. The stadium had to seat 7,000 Samba fans, with the whole facility accommodating 2,00,000 people overall for rock concerts and like events. The rest of the year, the structure would operate as a school for 4,000 students. Since the annual cost of facilities for the festival was $10 million a year, and the project would only cost $15 million, the project had to be completed very quickly in order to avoid any time or cost overrun. Groundbreaking took place in October and the project had to be finished by the following Lent, only four-and-a-half months later.

The challenges of completing such a mammoth task in such a short time were severely exacerbated by a project environment that included political uncertainty, rampant inflation, governmental bureaucracy, and local contractor politics. However, extreme public pressure and strong desire to finish the project on time led to a successful project completion, not only on time but of high quality standards within the budget. Moreover, the short time span actually contributed to the success in some way.

At the same time, the government of Rio de Janeiro was involved in many other infrastructure projects. Some of them were already in progress and many of them were soon to be started on priority basis. Out of the lot, the combined school and carnival stadium project was placed high on the priority list. During that time, the government of Rio de Janeiro faced many challenges while handling multiple projects simultaneously.

Source: Adapted from Dinsmore and Bizola 1993.

When project managers are simultaneously handling more than one project, their first job is to prioritize them because their resource pool might be similar but of limited use. The major challenge is how to handle multiple projects at a time with limited resources. During prioritization, managers might struggle to figure out which project should be ranked first.

11.1 CONFLICT IN RANKING—VARIOUS CASES

It is usual practice for a firm to manage a number of projects at the same time. As resources (capital, man power, equipment, etc.) are limited and the ROI from each project is different, a firm has to prioritize all the available projects. In the process of ranking the various projects, using the NPV or IRR methods, conflicting results are often obtained. This leads to a dilemma as to which project to consider as the first one in the priority list.

In the following cases, we will discuss three aspects that deal with the handling of multiple projects when there is a conflicting opinion of ranking these projects using NPV and IRR—projects with different life spans, projects with different cash flows, and projects with different initial investment. These are described as under.

Projects with different life spans

If projects have different useful lives (maturity periods), it is perfectly possible that their rankings may vary under the NPV and IRR methods.

Example 11.1   There are two projects A and B. A has a service life of one year while B's useful life is five years. The initial cash outlay for both projects may be assumed to be Rs 25,000 each. The cash proceeds from project A (at the end of the first year) amount to Rs 30,000. The one-time cash generated from project B at the end of the fifth year is Rs 50,000. Assume that the appropriate discount rate for both the projects is 10% (as shown in Table E11.1).

TABLE E11.1

Project	Life (year)	Initial outlay (Rs)	Cash inflows in year 1 (Rs)	Cash inflows in year 2 (Rs)	Cash inflows in year 3 (Rs)	Cash inflows in year 4 (Rs)	Cash inflows in year 5 (Rs)	Present value of cash inflows (discount rate 10%) (Rs)	NPV (Rs)	IRR
A	1	25,000	30,000					27,272.72	2,272.72	20%
B	5	25,000					50,000	31,046.06	6,046.06	15% (approx.)

Solution

As per the calculations shown in Table E11.1, the results are clear.

Hence, as per the NPV rule, project B is better, whereas, as per the IRR rule, project A is better.

Projects with different cash flows

Mutually exclusive proposals have identical initial investments. However, their pattern of cash flows generation is different. These different patterns result in a conflict when the given proposals are ranked by the IRR and NPV methods. This conflict is also referred to as the time disparity problem.

The examples below help explain the concepts better.

Example 11.2   The initial investment of projects A and B is Rs 1,00,000 each. The useful service lives in both these cases is 5 years and the appropriate discounting rate in both cases can be taken as 10%. The expected cash flows for the above projects for those 5 years are shown in Table E11.2.

TABLE E11.2

Project	Initial investments (Rs)	End of year 1 (Rs)	End of year 2 (Rs)	End of year 3 (Rs)	End of year 4 (Rs)	End of year 5 (Rs)
A	1,00,000	60,000	45,000	30,000	15,000	10,000
B	1,00,000	15,000	30,000	45,000	75,000	15,000

Solution

NPV of project A = $-1,00,000 + (60,000 \times 0.9091) + (45,000 \times 0.8264) + (30,000 \times 0.7513) + (15,000 \times 0.6830) + (10,000 \times 0.6209) = 30,727$

NPV of project B = $-1,00,000 + (15,000 \times 0.9091)) + (30,000 \times 0.8264) + (45,000 \times 0.7513) + (75,000 \times 0.6830) + (15,000 \times 0.6209) = 32,775.5$

Hence, project B is better as per the NPV rule, but the IRR of project A is higher than that of project B.

Example 11.3   The life of projects A and B is two years and the appropriate rate of discount for both projects can be taken as 10%. The other details are given in Table E11.3.

TABLE E11.3

Projects	Initial Investment (Rs in lakhs)	Cash inflows (Rs in lakhs)		NPV	IRR
		Year 1	Year 2		
A	100	200	0	81.82	100%
B	100	0	400	230.58	100%

Solution

Going by the calculations in Table E11.3 given above, we can state that:

As per the NPV rule, B is better, whereas, as per the IRR rule, both are indifferent.

Projects with different initial investment

The NPV and IRR methods of ranking give conflicting results in the case of projects that have different initial investments. However, the use of incremental approach in the calculation of incremental IRR can help resolve the contradiction in ranks. As per this approach, only projects with higher initial investment are chosen when incremental IRR is more than the required rate of return expected by the investors. Thereby, the results of incremental IRR would be identical to those derived from the NPV calculation.

Example 11.4   A and B are two mutually exclusive projects of one year each involving different outlays. The effective rate of discount for both the projects can be taken as 10%. Relevant details of the projects are as in Table E11.4.

TABLE E11.4

Project	Initial investment (Rs)	Cash inflow (Rs)
A	7,500	10,100
B	10,000	13,000

Solution

NPV of project A = –7,500 + 10,100 / 1.1 = 1,681.81

NPV of project B = –10,000 + 13,000 / 1.1 = 1,818.18

IRR of project A = 10,100 / 7,500 – 1 = 0.34, i.e., 34%

IRR of project B = 13,000 / 10,000 – 1 = 0.3, i.e., 30%

Hence, as per the NPV rule, project B is better and as per the IRR rule, project A is better.

The IRR decision rule does not always rank projects in the same way as the NPV method. This we have seen in the earlier cases of projects with different life spans, projects with different cash flows, and projects with different initial investments. Sometimes it is not only important to find out which project gives a positive return, but which one gives the higher positive return as well. For instance, projects may be mutually exclusive and a choice needs to be made because only one such project needs to be selected. Now, in such cases, the use of the IRR method alone sometimes leads to ambiguity.

For instance, study the projects in Table 11.1 with given cash flows, IRRs, and NPVs.

TABLE 11.1 Details of projects

Projects	Cash flows (Rs in lakhs)		IRR (%)	NPV
(1 year life)	Year 0	Year 1		18% discounting rate
A	(20)	40	100%	13.89
B	(40)	70	75%	19.32

As per the NPV rule, project B is superior and as per the IRR rule, project A is superior.

The ranking by the NPV decision criteria would theoretically be more correct, as it is consistent with the goal of maximization of the shareholders' wealth in absolute terms. Further, the reinvestment rate of funds released by the project is based on certain assumptions which are more logical as compared to the implicit assumptions in the case of IRR calculations. In certain cases of conflict between the NPV and IRR, the modified IRR technique proves to be quite handy, but as explained earlier, it involves additional computation and is finally bound to give the same results as NPV.

Thus, in view of the above, NPV emerges as a superior tool.

TABLE 11.2 Computation of NPV applying different discount rates

Discount rate (%)	Project A	Project B
0	20	30
20	13.33	18.33
50	6.67	6.67
75	2.86	0
100	0	(5)
125	(2.22)	(8.89)

Table 11.2 clearly shows that the NPV ranking depends on the discount rate applied. Thus, if the discount rate used in the NPV calculation is higher than 50%, project A is superior. When the discount rate is 50%, both the projects are indifferent. If the discount rate falls below 50%, project B is invariably a better choice as per the NPV criterion.

One of the major elements leading to the theoretical dominance of the NPV is that it takes into account the scale of investment as well. NPVs are measured in absolute terms.

11.2 SOLUTION OF THE CONFLICT IN RANKING

One problem of the IRR centres on the reinvestment assumption (as mentioned earlier in Chapter 5). With the NPV, it is assumed that cash inflows arising during the life of the project are reinvested at the opportunity cost of capital or discount factor, whereas the IRR implicitly assumes that the cash inflows can be reinvested elsewhere at a rate equal to the IRR. This is intuitively unacceptable and absurd. In the real world, if a firm invested in a very high-yielding project and some cash was returned after a period, then it is unlikely that the firm would be able to deposit this cash elsewhere and reach the same extraordinary high yield. That is why the firm's normal discount rate is the better estimate of the reinvestment rate. Due to this wrong assumption, the estimated IRR of the project will be more inflated or hyperbolic and far from reality.

If, for reasons of pragmatism and communication within the firm, it is necessary to describe a project appraisal in terms of percentage, then instead of the IRR, it is recommended modified internal rate of returns (MIRR) should be used. It is the rate of return m, which, if used to compound the initial investment amount (i.e., the original cash outlay), produces the same terminal value as the project cash inflows.

Here we are trying to find out the compounding rate, which will equate the terminal value of the intra-project cash inflows with the terminal value of the initial investment or cash outflows.

The following example would clarify the concept.

Example 11.5 A firm has been working towards selecting between two projects in the coming year. Both the projects have the same initial investment (Rs 25,000) and a life of 4 years. On the basis of the IRR and NPV, the firm has conflicting results towards the acceptance of the project. In this situation, which project should the firm select if the opportunity cost of capital is 10%? Table E11.5 shows cash flows of both the projects.

TABLE E11.5

Year	A (Rs)	B (Rs)
0	−25,000	−25,000
1	10,000	0
2	10,000	5,000
3	10,000	10,000
4	10,000	30,000

Solution

TABLE E11.6

NPV IRR and MIRR values of projects (Discount factor −10%)

Project	IRR	NPV (Rs)	MIRR
A	22%	6,090	16.73%
B	18%	6,487	17.13%
Decision	A is better	B is better	B is better

MIRR calculations for project A

$$10,000 \times (1 + 0.1)^3 + 10,000 \times (1 + 0.1)^2 + 10,000 \times (1 + 0.1)^1 + 10,000 \times (1 + 0.1)^0 = 25,000 \, (1 + \text{MIRR})^4$$

MIRR = 16.73 %

MIRR calculations for project B

$0 \times (1 + 0.1)^3 + 5,000 \times (1 + 0.1)^2 + 10,000 \times (1 + 0.1)^1 + 30,000 \times (1 + 0.1)^0 = 25,000 (1 + MIRR)^4$
MIRR = 17.13 %

(For both the cases, r = opportunity cost of capital = 10 %).

Therefore, MIRR and NPV have given the same solution. B should be acceptable.

11.3 CAPITAL RATIONING

Our entire discussion of capital budgeting has rested on the proposition that the wealth of a firm's shareholders is highest if every project that the firm accepts has a positive NPV. However, suppose there are certain limitations on the investment programme of the company that prevent it from undertaking all such projects. This is known as the capital rationing problem. When capital is rationed, we need a method of selecting a packet of projects that is within the company's resources yet gives the highest possible NPV.

Example 11.6   A company has a 10 % opportunity cost of capital and has the following options to evaluate, where the life of three projects is 2 years and each project is divisible in nature (this would mean that if only 50 % of project B is undertaken, then its NPV would be Rs 98 lakh, which is half of Rs 196 lakh). Refer to Table E11.7 for details.

TABLE E11.7

Figures in Rs in lakhs

Projects	Cash flow year 0	Cash flow year 1	Cash flow year 2	NPV @ 10 % DF	P/I at 10 % DF
A	−12	32	10	+25.35	3.1
B	−6	10	20	+19.6	4.26
C	−6	5	20	+15.06	3.51

Note: All three projects are attractive, but suppose the firm can spend the Rs 12,00,000 only and can invest in any one of the projects. Although individually B and C have lower NPV than A, when taken together they generate a higher NPV. Thus, in this case the project cannot be chosen solely on the basis of NPV. When funds are limited it is essential to get the maximum out of the investment. In other words, the project chosen should give the highest NPV per rupee in the initial outlay, i.e. on the basis of the profitability index.

Solution

P/I of the three projects are as follows:

Project A = 3.1

Project B = 4.26

Project C = 3.1 (as computed).

Thus, project B has the highest P/I and project C has the next highest P/I. Hence, these two projects should be accepted under a situation of resource constraints in order to achieve maximum possible NPV.

The above method of ranking suffers from certain deficiencies. For example, if the projects are not divisible by nature, the decision parameter is not P/I but NPV once again.

Moreover, the ranking methodology as mentioned above fails when more than one resource is rationed, which (as we would agree) is a common phenomenon under real-life circumstances.

Such capital rationing issues can be dealt with by using linear programming techniques (discussed later in the chapter). Students should know that in practical dealings we are mainly concerned with non-divisible capital investments. Fractional or divisional projects are rather rare. Also, the P/I method assumes that in case of divisible propositions, the cash flow stream is divisible up to the magnitude of the project. This may not be true in real-life situations.

LPP models may be very effective in dealing with capital budgeting issues during short supply of resources. But, due to certain prominent shortcomings, they are not put to practice in industrial processes. These models demand the concerned manager to have information regarding all future investment prospects. However, it is not practical as investment issues and opportunities are not constant but are continuously changing. Also, these models are usually expensive. Adding to that, the inability to gather quality data retards the functioning of long range planning tools like these. Use of expensive methods to process poor quality data puts to question the viability of the entire process.

11.4 TECHNIQUES FOR SELECTING MORE THAN ONE PROJECT FROM A GROUP

This section discusses various approaches for selecting multiple projects at a given point of time from a bunch of alternatives on the basis of different features such as NPV, P/I, ROI, etc. Various resource constraints will also be discussed.

Choosing the capital budget on the basis of individual ranking has a problem of indivisibility of capital expenditure. This is explained using Example 11.7.

Example 11.7 A firm has an option of choosing from the following set of six new projects that are available for a given year. Each of these project's initial outlay and NPVs are given and accordingly their individual ranks are evaluated. This year the firm has a capital budget constraint of Rs 27,00,000. Refer to Table E11.8.

TABLE E11.8

Project	Initial investment (Rs)	NPV (Rs)	Rank
A	15,00,000	1,50,000	1
B	12,00,000	1,25,000	2
C	8,00,000	1,20,000	3
D	7,00,000	1,05,000	4
E	7,50,000	95,000	5
F	5,00,000	90,000	6

Solution

If the selection is based on individual ranking on the basis of NPV, projects A (rank 1) and B (rank 2) would be selected for this year's capital budgeting. For this, the total initial investment will be Rs 27,00,000 and the NPV will be Rs 2,75,000. However, this exhausts the capital budget. A close examination suggests that the selection of B, C and D (ranks 2, 3, and 4) will be more profitable, as these projects can be accommodated within the capital budget (Rs 27,00,000) and also because the NPV of the three combined together would yield a total NPV of Rs 3,50,000, which is Rs 75,000 more than the earlier choice.

If projects B, D, and E are chosen, the entire amount of Rs 27,00,000 will be not exhausted (Rs 26,50,000) and the NPV will also be less. Similarly, if we select projects C, D, E and F, then the initial capital budget constraint (Rs 27,00,000) cannot be maintained, because this combination of projects needs Rs 27,50,000.

Hence, the combination of projects B, C, and D, would be the ideal choice.

Feasible combination approach

This approach can be used for selecting a set of investments under capital budgeting constraints or capital rationing. This can be done by the following steps:
- Given the capital budget restriction and project interdependence, all feasible combinations of projects are defined.
- The feasible combination with the highest NPV is selected.

Example 11.8 Five projects M, N, O, P, and Q are available to a company. Refer to Table E11.9 for details.

TABLE E11.9

	M	N	O	P	Q
Initial investment (Rs)	20,000	50,000	75,000	1,00,000	1,50,000
Annual cash flow (Rs)	6,000	8,000	15,000	15,000	25,000
Life (years)	5	10	8	12	7
Salvage value (Rs)					

Project N is a prerequisite of project Q, and projects O and P are mutually exclusive. Otherwise, the projects are independent. If the cost of capital of the firm is 10%, which projects should be chosen at the budget levels of Rs 1,25,000? Assume that the decision criterion is the NPV. Use the feasible combinations approach.

Solution

The net present values of the five projects M to Q are calculated below:

$$NPV\ (M) = \sum_{t=1}^{5} \frac{6,000}{1.1^t} - 20,000$$

$$= 6,000 \times PVIFA_{(10.5)} - 20,000 = Rs\ 2,746$$

$$NPV\ (N) = 8,000 \times PVIFA_{(10.10)} - 50,000 = -Rs\ 840$$

$$NPV\ (O) = 15,000 \times PVIFA_{(10.8)} - 75,000 = Rs\ 5,025$$

$$NPV\ (P) = 15,000 \times PVIFA_{(10.12)} - 1,00,000 = Rs\ 2,210$$

$$NPV\ (Q) = 25,000 \times PVIFA_{(10.7)} - 1,50,000 = -Rs\ 28,300$$

Since the projects N and Q reveal negative NPVs, they are rejected. Therefore, the projects to be considered in the feasible combinations are M, O, and P.

Given the capital budget constraint of Rs 1,25,000 and the constraints relating to their mutually exclusive nature of projects O and P, the feasible combination along with their respective NPVs and outlays are tabulated in Table E11.10.

TABLE E11.10

Combination	Outlay (Rs)	NPV (Rs)
M	20,000	2,746
O	75,000	5,025
P	1,00,000	2,210
M & O	95,000	7,771
M & P	1,20,000	4,956

Heuristic approach

The heuristic approach effectively deals with problems related to multi-project scheduling with limited resources. There are several challenges in the analytic computation of practical problems. By using the heuristic approach, some of the practical problems can be solved.

There are many theoretical processes based on the heuristic technique. Some good sources of this process include Davis and Patterson (1975), Pascoe (1965), and various commercial programmes. The simple extensions of popular approaches to job-shop scheduling are represented by them. Certain other heuristics have also been developed. They are meant for resource allocation and are accessed directly from PERT/CPM. These are commercially available in the market. Software vendors can also purchase most of these in slightly different versions such as the Primavera and MS Project among others.

Resource scheduling   Activity with minimum value of D_{ij} should be taken up first during the computation of the priorities among various activities. When activity i is followed by activity j, there is an increase in the project duration, which is a maximum of 0 and $(EFT_i - LST_j)$. This is referred to as D_{ij}

where,

EFT_i = early finish time of activity i

LST_j = latest start time of activity j

Finally, pair-wise comparison is conducted among all the activities in the conflict set.

Minimum late finish time   As per this rule, the earliest late finishers are given priority. The schedule is formulated with reference to late finish times.

Greatest resource demand   High-priority projects and processes are given preference in their demand for resources. This rule helps set priorities considering the total resource requirement. Project or task priority is calculated as:

$$\text{Priority} = d_j \sum_{i=1}^{m} r_{ij}$$

where,

d_j = duration of activity j

r_{ij} = per period requirement of resource i by activity j

m = number of resource types

Greatest resource utilization   This rule gives priority to those activities that result in maximum resource utilization or minimum idle resources. The rule is implemented by solving the 0–1 integer programming problem (will be discussed later on). Variations of this rule are found in commercial computer programs such as RAMPS (Moshman, Johnson, and Larsen 1963).

Most possible jobs   Priority is given to the set number of activities resulting in the greatest number of activities being scheduled in any period. This rule also requires the solution of a 0–1 integer programme. It differs from the earlier one in that the determination of the greatest number of possible jobs is made purely with regard to resource feasibility and not with respect to resource utilization.

Mathematical programming approach

Combination procedures for a few projects have been discussed till now. It however becomes very difficult to handle a large number of projects with longer lives with the aid of the above discussed procedures. Mathematical programming is a better method to be used to ease this problem. The most advantageous feature of this method is obtaining the optimal or the best-fit combination of investment.

Untill now, we have been discussing feasible combination procedures for a few projects on hand. However, as the number of projects along with the planning year increases, it is quite difficult to use the above procedures as it becomes cumbersome. Hence, in order to overcome this problem, mathematical programming becomes inevitable. The basic advantage of this mathematical programming is that the optimal solution (the most desirable combination of investments) without all the possible feasible combinations can be obtained.

Mathematical programming has its base in two broad categories of equations:

(a) The objective functions representing the goal or objective which is to be achieved by the decision-makers.

(b) The constraints equation representing restrictions arising out of certain limitations such as managerial policies, resources and production, etc.

Mathematical models enhance the utility of the objective function and keep a check on the various limitations faced by the project. The objective functions and the constraints are also referred to as the parameters and decision variables. Parameters correspond to the factors decision environment. Decision variables get their designation from their highly decisive nature. In the end, appropriate decision is the prerogative of the decision-makers. Although a number of mathematical programming models are available, the three models given below are highly useful and are discussed in detail.

- Linear programming model
- Integer programming model
- Goal programming model

11.5 LINEAR PROGRAMMING APPROACH

A linear objective function is prone to limitations regarding the number of linear equality and inequality. The method of reducing such a function is called linear programming. For example, in problems associated with complex processes (that involve several variables and limitations) such as military logistics planning and airline crew scheduling, the linear programming approach helps in reaching a solution.

Stigler's diet problem (1945) was the first to put linear programming to use. Significant use of the linear programming method can be found in Koopman's transportation problem (1947). Leontif (1963, 1970) adapted linear programming during the process of input–output analysis. The primary process to work out a linear programming model is called the simplex method.

The linear programming model is an entirely mathematical approach. It is a premium process for project selection. It acts on the key relationships (represented through straight lines) to work out the most appropriate solutions.

Using linear programming, let us deal with a hypothetical example of Stigler's diet problem. An Indian snack shop, Sweet & Sour, operates with limited capacity. Its menu includes only four preparations–veg roll, pao bhaji, rasgulla, and samosa. The manager has decided that the quantity of the given food items prepared each day should be the same. This would reduce the cooking time and aid other decision-making processes. However, people who visit the restaurant need to strike a balance between their intake of vitamins and calories to maintain their weight and overall health. Table 11.3 is the resolution of the given problem—an attempt to minimize the number of calories consumed but simultaneously satisfy the minimum nutritional requirements.

TABLE 11.3 Sweet & Sour's menu

Food Item	Vitamin A	Vitamin B	Vitamin C	Vitamin D	Calories
Veg. roll (V)	100	200	60	65	250
Pao bhaji (P)	120	240	80	75	450
Rasgulla (R)	130	260	80	80	500
Samosa (S)	90	180	60	60	350
Requirements	600	1200	300	400	

All of us want to minimize the number of calories consumed but simultaneously want to satisfy the minimum nutritional requirements.

Hence, our objective is to minimize the function.

$$Z = 250X_V + 450X_P + 500X_R + 350X_S$$

Subject to constraints:

$$100X_V + 120X_P + 130X_R + 90X_S \geq 600$$

$$200X_V + 240X_P + 260X_R + 180X_S \geq 1200$$

$$60X_V + 80X_P + 80X_R + 60X_S \geq 300$$

$$65X_V + 75X_P + 80X_R + 60X_S \geq 400$$

$$X_V \geq 0, \ X_P \geq 0, \ X_R \geq 0, \ X_S \geq 0$$

In a linear programming model, three things should be specified. These have been mentioned below, keeping in mind the example above:

1. Decision variables (X_V, X_P, X_R, X_S): These are considered to be continuous.
2. Objective functions (Z = $250X_V + 450X_P + 500X_R + 350X_S$): These are uni-dimensional, i.e., they either minimize or maximize.

3. Constraints (e.g., $100X_V + 120X_P + 130X_R + 90X_S \geq 600$ and others): These equations are always linear.

Let us take the case of a poultry farm where the farm owner has to decide the number of eggs and chickens that are to be produced. Here, the decision variables will be the number of eggs produced, say P_1, and the number of chickens produced, say P_2. After defining the decision variables, the farm owner has to now identify the objective function. In this case, the objective of the firm owner is to maximize profit. If the profit per unit from eggs is Rs 4 and from the chickens is Rs 7, then the objective function can be written as:

Maximize $Z = 4P_1 + 7P_2$

In this example, the constraints might be labour hours, food availability for chickens, space, etc. Suppose that three labour hours are required per unit of egg production and 4 labour hours for every unit of chicken. The total number of labour hours available is 40 per day.

Then, this constraint can be written as:

$3P_1 + 4P_2 \leq 40$

The next step is to find the optimal solution.

After going through the basic formulation of a linear programming model, we move on to projects. In projects, the objective function is to optimize the net present value or internal rate of return or payback period, etc. The decision variables are regarding the project selection and also the extent of investment. The constraints can be the cash availability, man power, machine hours, availability of raw material, fuel, etc. The general formulation of a linear programming model for a capital rationing problem is as in Figure 11.1.

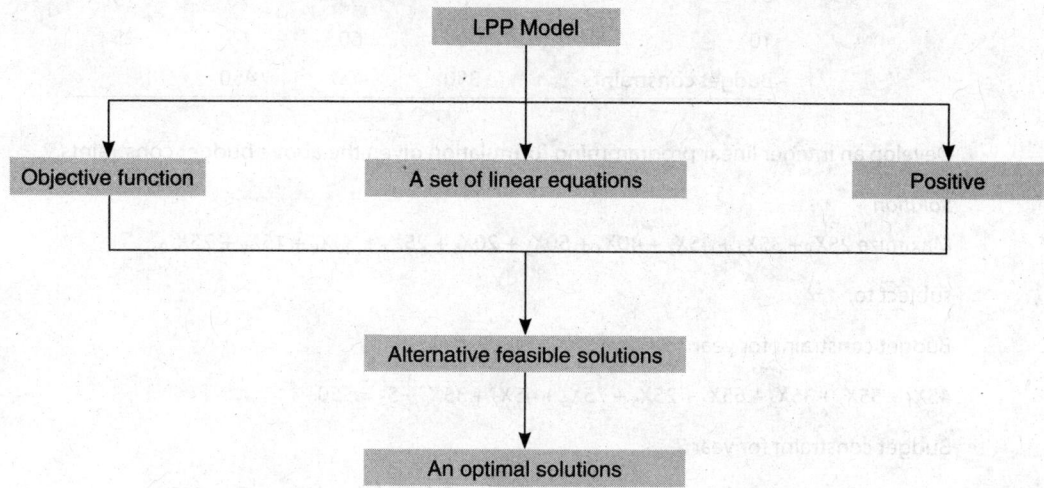

FIGURE 11. 1   Ingredients of a linear programming problem model

$$\text{Maximize} \quad \sum_{a=1}^{n} X_a\, NPV_a$$

$$\text{Subject to} \quad \sum_{a=1}^{n} CF_{at}\, X_a \le K_t \ (t = 0, 1 \dots m)$$

$$\text{and} \quad 0 \le X_a \le 1$$

where, NPV_a = Net present value of project A

X_a = Amount of project A accepted

CF_{at} = Cash outflow required for project A in period t

K_t = Capital budget available in period t

....

Example 11.9   Consider the projects listed in Table E11.11.

TABLE E11.11

Rs in lakhs

Project	Cash outflow			NPV
	Year 1	Year 2	Year 3	
1	45	65	10	25
2	55	70	0	35
3	35	45	55	45
4	65	60	0	40
5	25	40	45	50
6	75	70	0	20
7	45	55	35	25
8	35	45	0	35
9	0	55	75	15
10	0	60	65	25
Budget constraints	350	400	450	

Develop an integer linear programming formulation given the above budget constraints.

Solution

Maximize $25X_1 + 35X_2 + 45X_3 + 40X_4 + 50X_5 + 20X_6 + 25X_7 + 35X_8 + 15X_9 + 25X_{10}$

subject to,

Budget constraint for year 1

$45X_1 + 55X_2 + 35X_3 + 65X_4 + 25X_5 + 75X_6 + 45X_7 + 35X_8 + S_1 = 350$

Budget constraint for year 2

$65X_1 + 75X_2 + 45X_3 + 60X_4 + 40X_5 + 70X_6 + 55X_7 + 45X_8 + 55X_9 + 60X_{10} + S_2 = 400$

Budget constraint for year 3

$$10X_1 + 55X_3 + 45X_5 + 35X_7 + 75X_9 + 65X_{10} + S_3 = 450$$

$$X_1 + S_4 = 1 \qquad\qquad X_2 + S_5 = 1 \qquad\qquad X_3 + S_6 = 1$$

$$X_4 + S_7 = 1 \qquad\qquad X_5 + S_8 = 1 \qquad\qquad X_6 + S_9 = 1$$

$$X_7 + S_{10} = 1 \qquad\qquad X_8 + S_{11} = 1 \qquad\qquad X_9 + S_{12} = 1$$

$$X_{10} + S_{13} = 1$$

$$X_a \geq 0 \ (a = 1, 2, \dots 10)$$

$$S_i \geq 0 \ (i = 1, 2, \dots 13)$$

where S_i represents the slack variables which are added to inequality constraints to make them equal constraints. S_1, S_2 and S_3 represent the amount unallocated in year 1, 2 and 3, and S_4 to S_{13} represents the proportion of project not accepted.

Example 11.10 Consider the 10 investment projects in Table E11.12:

TABLE E11.12

Rs in lakhs

Project	Cash outflow in year 1	Cash outflow in year 2	NPV
A	45	65	25
B	55	70	35
C	35	45	45
D	65	60	40
E	25	40	50
F	75	70	20
G	45	55	−25
H	35	45	35
I	10	55	15
J	10	60	25

- The budget constraints for years 1 and 2 are 350 and 275, respectively.
- Of the set of projects B, F, and H, at least one must be accepted.
- Projects C and I are mutually exclusive.
- Project D cannot be accepted, unless project G is accepted.
- Surplus funds in year 1 can be shifted to year 2 and the shifted funds can earn a 10% return.
- Of the set of projects A, F, and J, at the most two can be accepted.
- Project E can be delayed by a year. Though the cash outflow required will be the same, the net present value will reduce to Rs 40 lakh.

A. Formulate the above problem as an integer linear programming model.

B. After formulating the model, the management decides that project i will definitely be taken up. One way to modify the model is to include the constraints $X_i = 1$. In what other ways can the model be modified?

Solution

A. The integer linear programming formulation

Let X_k be the decision variable to represent the delay of project e by one year.

Maximize $25X_a + 35X_b + 45X_c + 40X_d + 50X_e + 20X_f - 25X_g + 35X_h + 15X_i + 25X_j + 40X_k$

subject to,

1. $45X_a + 55X_b + 35X_c + 65X_d + 25X_e + 75X_f + 45X_g + 35X_h + 10X_i + 10X_j + 0.X_k + S_1 = 350$

2. $65X_a + 75X_b + 45X_c + 60X_d + 0.X_e + 70X_f + 55X_g + 45X_h + 55X_i + 60X_j + 25.X_k + S_2 = 275 + S_1 \times 1.1$

3. $X_e + X_k \leq 1$

4. $X_b + X_f + X_h \geq 1$

5. $X_c + X_i \leq 1$

6. $X_d \leq X_g$

7. $X_a + X_f + X_j \leq 2$

8. $X_z = \{0,1\}\ z = (a, b \ldots k)$

9. $S_y \geq 0\ y = (1, 2)$

B. We have to modify the objective function and also constraints no. 1 and 2. Constraint no. 5 will not be required.

Maximize $25X_a + 35X_b + 40X_d - 50X_e + 20X_f + 25X_g + 35X_h + 25X_j + 40X_k$

subject to,

1. $45X_a + 55X_b + 65X_d + 25X_e + 75X_f + 45X_g + 35X_h + 10X_j + 0.X_k + S_1 = 350 - 10$

2. $65X_a + 75X_b + 45X_c + 60X_d + 0.X_e + 70X_f + 55X_g + 45X_h + 55X_i + 60X_j + 25.X_k + S_2 = 275 + S_1 \times 1.1 - 55$

Merits of linear programming

1. The linear programming model is the best possible method for the utilization of available resources such as time, labour, and machine.

2. The linear programming model can be useful in handling the 'bottleneck' situations of an organization where some resources are over-utilized and some are under-utilized.

3. As the decisions are made objectively the quality of decision is much better.

4. Resources can be utilized judiciously.

Demerits of linear programming

1. It is only applicable for the situations where the objective functions and their constraints are linear or straight line in nature. But in reality, most of the problems are not linear at all.

2. In this approach of problem solving, factors such as risk or uncertainty are not taken into account.

11.6 INTEGER PROGRAMMING APPROACH

This is a class of linear programming model which is used for optimization. Only integer variables are considered while finding out the optimal solution by imposing additional requirements. It is applicable to those problems which deal with only integer numbers for the final solution. The regions of application of the integer linear programming model are allocation of sales personnel, capital budgeting, research and development, etc. The maximization or minimization of the objective function depends upon the type of application. The model can be in the form of equalities or inequalities. The aim of applying this model is to find the solution for the problems related to partial projects, as this method deals only with 0 and 1 values for the decision variables. It can be very useful for handling interdependent projects. The basic advantage of the integer programming model over the linear programming model is that it ensures the complete rejection ($X_a = 0$) or complete acceptance ($X_a = 1$) of a project.

The formulation of the integer linear programming model for the capital budgeting under capital rationing can be represented as:

$$\sum_{a=1}^{n} X_a \, NPV_a$$

subject to

$$\sum_{a=1}^{n} CF_{at} \, X_a \leq K_t \, (t = 0, 1, \dots m)$$

$$X_a = (0,1)$$

Features of integer programming approach

Project interdependencies Integer linear programming deals with 0s and 1s. It is perfect for dealing with various kinds of interdependency such as mutual exclusiveness, contingency, and complementarities.

Mutual exclusiveness Mutually exclusive projects are a set of projects where the inclusion of any one prevents the rejection of other projects in the set. This is shown as:

$$\sum_{a \in A} X_a \leq 1$$

where,

A = the set of mutually exclusive projects under consideration

$a \in A$ = an expression means that project a belongs to set A

Contingency It states that the relationship between two projects, say S and T, is such that the acceptance of one is highly dependant on the other. In such a situation, we can say that project S is contingent on another project T. This can be represented as follows:

$$X_S \leq X_T$$

A project can be contingent on more than one project such as project K can be contingent on project I and J which can be written as:

$$2X_K = X_I + X_J$$

Mutual exclusiveness and contingency At times, the above mentioned project dependencies can exist simultaneously.

Let us take two projects R and W that are mutually exclusive. There is another project F which is contingent on the acceptance of either R or W. It can be reflected as follows:

$$X_R + X_W \leq 1$$
$$X_F = X_R + X_W$$

Complementariness Complementariness is a situation where acceptance of a certain project affects positively the cash flow of another one. Therefore, these two projects can be complementary projects. Let there be two projects H and U, and both of them are independent. Now, if both are accepted (H and U), more benefits will be obtained.

$$X_H + X_U + X_{HU} \leq 1$$

Demerits of this model are as follows:

1. The time consumed to solve a problem in this model is more than the linear programming model.
2. The time taken for solving a problem is not fixed and also not proportional to the size of the problem.
3. Integer linear programming models cannot be generalized by a single solution algorithm.

Example 11.11 Formulate the integer programming model for the following 10 projects whose inter dependencies are given as follows. Refer to Table E11.13

TABLE E11.13

Rs in lakhs

Project	Cash outflow			NPV
	Year 1	Year 2	Year 3	
1	45	65	10	25
2	55	70	0	35
3	35	45	55	45
4	65	60	0	40
5	25	40	45	50
6	75	70	0	20
7	45	55	35	25
8	35	45	0	35
9	0	55	75	15
10	0	60	65	25
Budget constraints	350	400	450	

- Project 4 and 5 are mutually exclusive.

- Project 9 and 10 are complementary. If the two are accepted together, the total cash outflow will be less by 6%, whereas NPV will increase by 10%.

- Out of the set of projects 3, 4, 5, and 6, at least one must be accepted.

- Project 6 cannot be accepted unless project 1 is accepted.

- Project 2 can be delayed by 1 year. Such a delay would not change the cash outflows but reduce the NPV to 30.

Solution

Integer linear programming formulation

As usual, X_1 to X_{10} are the decision variables for the original 10 projects.

X_{11} is the decision variable representing the delay of project 2 by one year.

X_{12} is the decision variable representing the combined project of 9 and 10.

Maximize $25X_1 + 35X_2 + 45X_3 + 40X_4 + 50X_5 + 20X_6 + 25X_7 + 35X_8 + 15X_9 + 25X_{10} + 30X_{11} + 44X_{12}$

subject to,

Budget constraint for year 1

$45X_1 + 55X_2 + 35X_3 + 65X_4 + 25X_5 + 75X_6 + 45X_7 + 35X_8 + 0 \times X_9 + 0 \times X_{10} + 0 \times X_{11} + 0 \times X_{12} \leq 350$

Budget constraint for year 2

$65X_1 + 75X_2 + 45X_3 + 60X_4 + 40X_5 + 70X_6 + 55X_7 + 45X_8 + 55X_9 + 60X_{10} + 55X_{11} + 108.1X_{12} \leq 400$

Budget constraint for year 3

$10X_1 + 0 \times X_2 + 55X_3 + 0 \times X_4 + 45X_5 + 0 \times X_6 + 35X_7 + 0 \times X_8 + 75X_9 + 65X_{10} + 75X_{11} + 131.6X_{12} \leq 450$

NPV of X_{12} = (*NPV* of X_9 + *NPV* of X_{10}) × 1.1 = (15 + 25) × 1.1 = 44

Cash outflow of X_{12} of year 1 = (0 + 0) × 0.94 = 0

Cash outflow of X_{12} of year 2 = (55 + 60) × 0.94 = 108.1

Cash outflow of X_{12} of year 3 = (75 + 65) × 0.94 = 131.6

$X_4 + X_5 \leq 1$

$X_9 + X_{10} + X_{12} \leq 1$

$X_3 + X_4 + X_5 + X_6 \geq 1$

$X_6 \leq X_1$

$X_2 + X_{10} \leq 1$

Similarly, suppose there are five projects with conditions as given in Table E11.14.

TABLE E11.14

Conditions	Constraint equations using integer programming model
Project 3 can only be done if 1 is also done	$X_3 < X_1$
We must invest in at least one of the first three projects	$X_1 + X_2 + X_3 > 1$
Only one of projects 2, 4, and 5 can be done	$X_2 + X_4 + X_5 < 1$
Any two of the last 3 projects must be invested	$X_3 + X_4 + X_5 = 2$

Merits of the integer linear programming model
1. It can overcome the problems related to partial projects as it permits only 0 and 1 values of the decision variables.
2. This model is well-equipped to handle various kinds of project interdependencies.
3. It can be applied to problems such as allocation of salesman, capital budgeting, and R&D.
4. Integer programming techniques can be applied to both the conditions of inequalities and equalities.
5. By applying this model, whether a project is either fully accepted or not can be calculated.

Demerits of the integer linear programming model
1. The technique is too time-consuming compared to other mathematical programming approaches and the solution time is highly uncertain.
2. A small variation in the observations or values causes a considerable amount of increase in solution time.
3. There is no generalized solution algorithm available for different kinds of problems.

11.7   GOAL PROGRAMMING APPROACH

After the goal of a project—minimization of cost or maximization of profit—has been chosen by the management, the linear programming model can be put into practice. However, project goals may have more variables (such as high-quality product, employee retention, etc.) in the face of economic instability and other reasons.

In the face of multiple project goals, a new method called goal programming technique is put to practice. This technique was first used in 1961 by Charnes and Cooper to deal with a single or multi-dimensional objective function, with a set of limitations that was expressed in linear form. In the goal programming model, all management goals are used with the aim of minimizing the deviation from the set goals, priority-wise.

In a set of project goals, every goal has an estimated target (set by the management) and they are ranked according to their significance. The goal programming technique ensures minimum deviation from the set target.

Generally, the goal programming format is represented as shown below:

Minimize

$$Z = \{Q_1[f_1(a_1^+, a_1^-)] + Q_2[f_2(a_1^+, a_1^-)] - \ldots + Q_m[f_m(d_m^+, d_m^-)]\}$$

subject to,

$$\sum a_{j1}X_j \leq C_1$$

$$\sum a_{j2}X_j \leq C_2$$

.

.

.

.

$$\sum a_{jk}X_j \leq C_k$$

$$\sum b_{j1}X_j + d_1^-, d_1^+ = G_1$$

$$\sum b_{j2}X_j + d_2^-, d_2^+ = G_2$$

.

.

$$\sum b_{jm}X_j + d_m^-, d_m^+ = G_2$$

$$X_j, d_1^-, d_1^+ \geq 0$$

This model also has three basic components:
1. Objective function
2. Economic constraints
3. Goal constraints

Objective function The objective of the following function is to minimize the deviation from the set targets of various goals as per the priority basis. It is as follows:

$$\text{Minimize } P_1 d_1^- + P_2 d_2^- + P_3 d_3^- + P_4 (d_4^- - d_4^+)$$

In this equation, we have used d_1^+ to indicate a positive deviation from the goal sought to be achieved and d_1^- to indicate a negative deviation from the goal.

The term $P_1 d_1^-$ indicates the negative deviation from the required goal that has to be minimized for the goal accorded first priority. Similarly, both $P_2 d_2^-$ and $P_3 d_3^-$ can be interpreted. $P_4(d_4^- - d_4^+)$ relates to the goal with priority number four. The requirement is to minimize the negative deviation $-d_4^-$ and maximize the positive deviation $-d_4^+$.

Economic constraints

They represent limits, restrictions, or boundaries beyond which the decision cannot be violated. They are also known as hard constraints. Like LPP, they also require slack (deficit) or surplus (excess) variables.

Goal constraints

They represent the target levels of various goals according to their priorities. Defined as strict equalities, goal constraints contain, in addition to an expression showing the impact of decision variables on goal attainment, two deviational variables denoted by d_1^- and d_1^+ (Figure 11.2).

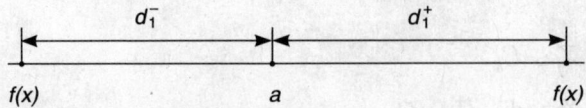

Source: Charnes and Cooper 1961.

FIGURE 11.2   Goal constraints

where,

$f(x) =$ objective value, $a =$ target value, $d_1^- = a - f(x)$, $d_1^+ = f(x) - a$

d_1^+ indicates that desired levels of the goal have been overachieved, and d_1^- indicates that desired levels of the goal have been underachieved. When the desired levels of the goal are overachieved, d_1^+ is non-zero and d_1^- is zero. When the desired levels of the goals are underachieved, d_1^+ is zero and d_1^- is non-zero.

Merits of goal programming
1. Allows multiple objectives.
2. Allows slack in the constraint (not hard).
Demerits of goal programming
1. The method is not simple or candid.
2. Must elicit goal values from the decision maker.
3. Must find a way to homogenize these goal values.

Example 11.12 Formulate the goal programming model for the information given below. The target for the net profit in years 1 and 2 are 5 and 6, respectively, and the sales growth target is 10% for the first and 11% for the second year. Refer to Table E11.15.

TABLE E11.15

Project (X_j)	NPV	Cash outflow in year 1 (C_{j1})	Cash outflow in year 2 (C_{j2})	Fuel requirement (F_j)	Man power requirement (M_j)
1	10	6	6	20	6
2	12	10	8	30	5
3	5	10	10	40	8
4	6	5	15	30	9
5	10	8	15	50	5
	$\Sigma NPV = 43$	$\Sigma X_j C_{j1} \leq 30$	$\Sigma X_j C_{j2} \leq 20$	$\Sigma X_j F_j \leq 100$	$\Sigma X_j M_j \leq 25$

The contribution of the project to the net profit and sales growth is shown in Table E11.16

TABLE E11.16

Project	Net profit		Sales growth	
	Year 1	Year 2	Year 1	Year 2
1	1	1.5	0.01	0.2
2	2	1.5	0.02	0.1
3	1.1	2.6	0.025	0.3
4	2.4	0.9	0.03	0.2
5	1.2	1	0.1	0.2

The priorities assigned to various goals are as follows:

Priority 1 (P_1): Sales growth

Priority 2 (P_2): Net profit

Priority 3 (P_3): NPV

Solution

At priority level 1, the sales growth for year 1 is weighted 2.5 times as important as the sales growth for year 2.

At priority level 2, the net profit for year 1 is weighted 1.5 times as the net profit for year 2.

Minimize

$$Z = [P_1 (2.5d_1^- + d_2^-) + P_2 (1.5d_3^- + d_4^-) + P_3 (d_2^- - d_5^+)]$$

Economic constraints:

Fund constraints for year 1 = $6X_1 + 10X_2 + 10X_3 + 5X_4 + 8X_5 + S_1 = 30$

Fund constraints for year 2 = $6X_1 + 8X_2 + 10X_3 + 15X_4 + 15X_5 + S_2 = 20$

Fuel requirement constraints = $20X_1 + 30X_2 + 40X_3 + 30X_4 + 150X_5 + S_3 = 100$

Man-power requirement = $20X_1 + 30X_2 + 40X_3 + 30X_4 + 150X_5 + S_4 = 25$

Upper limit on project acceptance

$X_1 + S_5 = 1$

$X_2 + S_6 = 1$

$X_3 + S_7 = 1$

$X_4 + S_8 = 1$

$X_5 + S_9 = 1$

$X_j \geq 0$ ($j = 1, 2 \ldots 5$)

$S_i \geq 0$ ($l = 1, 2 \ldots 9$)

Goal constraints

Sales growth for year 1 = $0.01X_1 + 0.02X_2 + 0.025X_3 + 0.03X_4 + 0.1X_5 + d_1^- - d_1^+ = 0.1$

Sales growth for year 2 = $0.2X_1 + 0.1X_2 + 0.3X_3 + 0.2X_4 + 0.2X_5 + d_2^- - d_2^+ = 0.11$

Net profit for year 1 = $X_1 + 2X_2 + 1.1X_3 + 2.4X_4 + 1.2X_5 + d_3^- - d_3^+ = 5$

Net profit for year 2 = $1.5X_1 + 1.5X_2 + 2.6X_3 + 0.9X_4 + X_5 + d_4^- - d_4^+ = 6$

NPV = $10X_1 + 12X_2 + 5X_3 + 6X_4 + 10X_5 + d_5^- - d_5^+ = 43$

Example 11.13 The ABN Group of companies manufactures three types of boilers:

Boiler type	Profit/item (Rs in thousands)	Labour	Material (steel in tonnes)	Minimum qty
A	15	27	3	3
B	30	40	5	5
C	50	45	6	4

Find the highest profit combination of items to make given labour hours available = 400 and steel available = 30 tonnes.

Formulize the maximum profit.

Solution

Maximize $Z = 15X_A + 30X_B + 50X_C$

subject to

$27X_A + 40X_B + 45X_C \leq 400$

$3X_A + 5X_B + 6X_C \leq 30$

$X_A \leq 3, X_B \leq 5, X_C \leq 4$

Say the profit aspiration level = Rs 3,00,000

Assign penalty for deviation:

Labour—pay overtime @ Rs 15 per hour, maximum of 8 hours in a day

Material emergency order—extra Rs 50,000 per tonne with no limit

Minimize $n_1 + 15P_2 + 50P_3$

$15X_A + 30X_B + 50X_C + n_1 - P_1 = 300$

$27X_A + 40X_B + 45X_C + n_2 - P_2 = 400$

$3X_A + 5X_B + 6X_C + n_3 - P_3 = 30$

$X_A \leq 3, X_B \leq 5, X_C \leq 4, P_2 \leq 8$

$n_j, P_j \leq 0, \in j$

So, in short, one can see that linear programming is a process that helps to minimize a linear objective function which is subject to the constraints of a number of linear equality and inequality. Integer programming is another LPP where only integer variables are considered. Goal programming is used to find out the optimum solution of a single or a multi-dimensional objective function with a given set of linear constraints. In this way, by using these three methods, various constraint functions in case of multiple projects are formulated and objective function can be optimized.

SUMMARY

Usually a firm deals with too many projects at a time. It generally encounters a conflict between projects with different return on investment, as the available resources are limited and it often needs to prioritize and rank the projects accordingly. While ranking projects with different life spans, with different cash flows, and with different initial investment through the process of NPV or IRR, a firm can have conflicting results.

Capital rationing method is used when there are certain limitations on the investment programme of the company that prevents it from undertaking all such projects. Some of the approaches for selecting multiple projects at a given point of time from a bunch of alternatives on the basis of different features, such as NPV, P/I and ROI, are feasible combination approach, heuristic approach, mathematical programming approach, linear programming approach, and goal programming approach.

KEY TERMS

Capital rationing problem It occurs when there is a limitation to the firm's investment capacity to all such projects that earn a positive NPV. While solving this problem, i.e., when capital is rationed, only those projects are selected that come within the company's resources yet give the highest possible NPVs.

Feasible combination approach This approach can be used for selecting the set of investments under capital budgeting constraints or capital rationing. This is done by defining all the feasible combinations of projects after knowing the capital budget restriction and project interdependence. After the combinations have been defined, the one with the highest NPV would be selected.

Goal programming model In order to maximize the multiple goals of a firm, a new method is introduced, known as goal programming technique. It is to find out an optimum solution to a single or multi-dimensional objective function with a given set of constraints that is expressed in linear form.

Heuristic approach The difficulties in the analytical formulation of multi-project scheduling with constraint resources can be overcome by using heuristic techniques.

Integer programming approach This is a class of linear programming models used for optimization, where only integer variables are considered while finding out the optimal solution by imposing additional requirements.

Linear programming approach Linear programming is a process to minimize a linear objective function which is subject to the constraint of number of linear equality and inequality. In the case of solving problems with too many variables and constraints, the linear programming approach is used to find a solution.

Mathematical programming approach There are mathematical models to optimize the objective function, keeping a close eye on the various constraints. They are linear programming, integer programming, and goal programming.

Modified internal rate of return (MIRR) It is the rate of return which is used to compound the initial investment amount (i.e., the original cash outlay). It produces the same terminal value as the project cash inflows. It is used when there is a conflict between project ranking by using different project appraisal methods such as NPV or IRR.

CONCEPT REVIEW QUESTIONS

1. Why do different opinions arise on using different financial appraisal techniques in the case of a project selection process? How can this problem be sorted out?
2. Describe a situation, with numerical examples, where the above problem or conflict arises.
3. What is capital rationing? In case of rationing of capital amongst multiple projects, what factors should be considered and why?
4. What are the techniques available for selecting more than one project from multiple choices? Explain a few of them.
5. Describe three mathematical programming approaches discussed in this chapter and also give a comparative analysis of these three methods.
6. The linear programming method can be used for selecting projects when there are many projects to choose from and the selection is subject to various constraints. But this model gives an output which consists of partial projects and certain project inter-dependencies that cannot be incorporated into it. Is there a model which can overcome these problems? Describe it.

NUMERICAL PROBLEMS

1. Mr Madhavan, the CEO of Aura Limited, is analysing the following capital expenditure proposals as shown in Table E11.17 given by Director–Finance, Mr Kumaran.

TABLE E11.17

Rs in lakhs

Project	NPV	Cash outflow in year 1 (CF1)	Cash outflow in year 2 (CF2)
1	30	50	35
2	40	50	60
3	35	55	30
4	40	40	60
5	60	30	80
6	10	45	5
7	40	15	10
8	30	80	0
9	20	40	10

Mr Kumaran had commented that the funds available for year 1 and year 2 will be Rs 200 lakh and Rs 250 lakh, respectively. Mr Mehera, Director–Operations, has provided the following information:

- Project 1 and 5 are mutually exclusive.
- Out of the set of projects 4, 7, and 9, at least one must be accepted.
- Project 4 is prerequisite for project 1.
- Project 8 can be delayed by one year. Such a delay would shift the cash outflow for one year and reduce the NPV of the project by Rs 12 lakh.
- Project 4 and 6 are complementary. If the two are accepted together, the total cash outflow would increase by 10%, whereas the NPV will be less by 10%.

Confronted with all the information Madhavan said 'Kumaran, I had difficulty in understanding the first set of figures. Now I am totally confused.' Offering helpful advice, Kumaran said 'while the problem appears to be very complicated, I believe that the technique of mathematical programming can be applied to determine the optimal capital budget. We can seek the help of professional financial analysts'.

They seek your help in developing a suitable mathematical programming formulation of their capital budgeting problem.

2. Consider the following 10 investment projects in Table E11.18.

TABLE E11.18

Rs in lakhs

Project	Cash outflow in year 1	Cash outflow in year 2	Cash outflow in year 3	NPV
1	30	70	0	20
2	40	60	0	28
3	35	45	10	30
4	50	38	8	40
5	58	32	0	18
6	65	41	10	60
7	28	80	4	15
8	14	30	60	42
9	2	56	10	12
10	6	78	15	25

The budget constraints for year 1, 2, and 3 are Rs 250 lakh, 350 lakh, and 100 lakh, respectively.

Develop the integer linear programming formulation for the above problem if the following project inter-relationships exist:

- Of the set of projects 3, 4, and 8, at the most two can be accepted.
- Projects 5 and 9 are mutually exclusive, but one of the two must be accepted.
- Project 6 cannot be accepted unless both project 1 and 10 are accepted.
- Project 2 can be delayed by a year. Though the cash flows required will be the same, the net present value will drop to 22.
- Project 3 and 7 are complementary. If two are accepted together the total cash flow will be reduced by 10% and the NPV will be increased by 10%.

3. For the next financial year, the CEO of Rosemary Pharmaceuticals Ltd, Mr Amar Kaul has been allotted Rs 1 million for capital expenditure. The company's project manager has supplied him with information regarding the following projects listed in Table E11.19.

TABLE E11.19

Project	Investment (Rs in thousands)	NPV (Rs in thousands)	IRR (%)
A	350	60	18.2
B	250	−5	9.3
C	300	40	17.2
D	145	18	12.9
E	170	11	11.0
F	360	77	10.0
G	430	53	15.5

Opportunity cost of capital for each project is 10%. Assume that all projects are independent. You are requested to answer the following:
(a) Which of these projects should the company accept to stay within the Rs 1 million budget?
(b) How much does the budget limit cost the company in terms of its market value?
4. An engineering company is planning to diversify its operations during 2008 and 2009. The company has allocated a capital expenditure budget of Rs 515.5 lakh for 2008 and Rs 615.5 lakh for 2009. The company has five projects under consideration. The estimated NPV and expected cash expenditure of each project for the two years are given in Table E11.20.

TABLE E11.20

Rs in lakhs

Project	Expected NPV	Cash expenditure (2008)	Cash expenditure (2009)
1	220	100	300
2	370	500	585
3	60	108	200
4	140	230	30
5	162	320	470

Assuming that the net return from a particular project is directly proportional to the investment in it, formulate the above as a linear programming model.
5. Hammond Sportswear Ltd, is evaluating three projects. The following information is available regarding the projects. Refer to Table E11.21.

TABLE E11.21

Project	Economic constraints			Managerial goals		
	Cash outflow		Managerial supervision	NPV	Net income	
	Year 1	Year 2			Year 1	Year 2
1	12	15	5	12	60	90
2	32	20	12	17	93	124
3	35	52	20	14	115	137
4	55	57	18	13	100	144
Amount available/ desired goal	80	90	30	maximum	245	315

The management wants to give the highest priority to the achievement of NPV and the second and third priorities to the achievement of net income in the first and second years respectively. You are required to formulate the above as a goal programming problem.
6. Five projects are available to a company. Refer to Table E11.22.

TABLE E11.22

	Project I	Project II	Project III	Project IV	Project V
Initial investment (Rs)	15,00,000	65,00,000	70,00,000	80,00,000	1,00,00,000
Annual cash flow	6,00,000	9,00,000	11,00,000	9,00,000	12,00,000
Life years	5	10	8	12	7
Salvage value (Rs)	1,50,000	–	–	1,50,000	50,000

Project II is a prerequisite for project V and project III and IV are mutually exclusive. Otherwise the projects are independent. If the cost of capital for the firm is 12%, which project should be chosen at the following budget levels: Rs 1,50,00,000 and Rs 2,00,00,000. Using the feasible combinations approach, find out the optimal solution if decision criteria is NPV only.

ASSIGNMENT

Suppose that your father will retire next month and he will receive Rs 50 lakh as his total retirement benefits. You, as a financial analyst, recommend him about/on how he can optimally utilize his life savings and get the maximum benefit out of it. While analysing this optimization problem, use any suitable mathematical programming approach and consider all available avenues with their practical constraints that prevail in the Indian financial market.

SELECT REFERENCES

Charnes, A., and W.W. Cooper, *Management Models and Industrial Applications of Linear Programming*, John Wiley, 1961, New York.

Davis, E.W. and J.H. Patterson, 'A comparison in heuristic and optimum solution in resource constrained project scheduling', *Management Science*, April 1975.

Dinsmore, P.C. and J.O. Bizola, 'PM under Rampant Inflation', *Project Management*, 1993, New York.

Koopman T.C., 'Optimum Utilization of the Transportation System', *Proceedings*, International Statistics Conference, 1947, Washington D.C.

Leontif, W., 'The Dynamic Inverse, in Carter A.P. Brody A., et al. (eds), *Contribution to input output analysis*, 1970, North Holland, Amsterdam.

Leontif, W. and A. Strout, 'Multiregional input-output analysis', in Barna T. (ed.) *Structural Interdependence and Economic Development*, St. Martin's Press Inc, 1963, New York.

Moshman, J., J.R. Johnson, and M. Larsen, 'RAMPS —A technique for resource allocation and multiple scheduling', *Proceedings*, Spring Joint Computer Conference, 1963.

Pascoe, T.L., 'An experimental comparison of heuristic methods for allocating resources', PhD. dissertation, Department of Engineering, Cambridge University Press, 1965.

Stigler's G., 'The Cost of Subsistence', *Journal of Economics*, vol. 25, 1945, pp. 303–314.

CASE STUDY
Precision Machinery Company

The CMD of Precision Machinery Company has recently finalized a modernization package for the company product line, which will be mostly technology oriented. Rajiv Saxena, the Executive Director, Works, is concerned about providing adequate resources to this multi-project modernization programme. Saxena is apprehensive that the concerned department, though sufficiently equipped to run the overall engineering activity of the company, will fall short of providing adequate technical support as required by the project head.

The Executive Director, Projects, has under him five project managers handling five segments of the modernization programme. Each group functions as per its own suitable schedule.

Saxena is not conversant with resource allocation techniques in case of multiple project constraints. But he knows that an important technique is to work first on the activity with the minimum slack. So he has instructed his people to use this approach and proceed as per the job assigned by the project manager.

Discussion questions

1. Is working fast on the minimum slack approach a reasonable way to schedule the engineering resources at Precision Machinery Company? Analyse why or why not?
2. Do you think that undertaking these five separate projects simultaneously may lead to some kind of complications? Give reasons.

INTERNATIONAL PROJECT APPRAISAL

In any military operation it is important to first know the lay of the land. When you know the distance to be travelled then you can plan whether to proceed directly or by circuitous route. When you know the ease or difficulty of travel, then you can determine the advantages of the infantry or mounted troops. When you know the dimensions of the area then you can assess how many troops you need, many or few. When you know the relative safety of the terrain, then you can discern whether to do battle or disperse.

— SUN TZU in the *THE ART OF WAR*

LEARNING OBJECTIVES

After studying this chapter, you will be able to

- Understand project appraisal in the international context
- Understand the reasons for cross-border investment
- Know about the foreign exchange exposure from FDI and cost of capital
- Understand the adjusted present value approach
- Discuss about exposure of FDI to political risk

What Makes a Company Global?

The current worldwide economic crisis has shown just how global the economy has become. Financial and product markets have become far more interconnected than ever before. Even in the early part of the twentieth century, a supposed heyday of globalization, only a small number of countries handled most of the currencies and goods being traded. As we enter the next century, it is fair to say that nearly all countries are navigating a single economic sea.

It is one thing to say that the markets of the world are coming together. But are global markets creating global-minded companies? Are we seeing the emergence of rootless corporations guided only by market opportunities, not by allegiance to their home countries? As managers look for growth outside their home regions, are they shaking off traditional operating rules in favour of supposed global ideals of behaviour? Are company practices matching the grand rhetoric of globalization? In the political realm, are global companies overwhelming the efforts of nations to preserve their distinctive identities?

For the authors of *The Myth of the Global Corporation* (1998), the clear answer of these questions is a no. They see enormous differences among multinational companies, which they trace to the unique political economic characteristics of

- Understand the relationship between the CAPM and Black and Scholes option pricing formula
- Discuss international joint ventures

their home countries. When it comes to corporate behaviour, the authors show convincingly that nationality is destiny.

'The national debates over globalization now taking place, from the streets of France to the villages of Indonesia, should not be dismissed. They raise not only powerful concerns over the survival of national cultures and the unfairness of the rapid change but also complex questions about the nation's advantages. Globalization is a powerful force not just because influential political and economic interest groups, frustrated with national institutions, have made it their war cry. Globalization is powerful because it is an idea that has seeped into the imagination of ambitious individuals in all corners of the world, even though many find the concept alarming. Trying to create the right balance between the national policies that undergird competitiveness and the aspirations of a globally conscious world citizenry is a major challenge for managers and their companies.'

Source: Kogut 1999.

12.1 PROJECT APPRAISAL IN INTERNATIONAL CONTEXT

A project is a set of functions that have a specific direction. It has one or more set targets to achieve within a predetermined budget and schedule. An international project is one which involves multiple locations, entities, organizations, and business units across several countries. With the onset of globalization, international projects have become more frequent. War against terrorism, international police efforts, or foreign aid can be examples of international projects that are executed together by the governments of different countries. International profit-making companies are also often engaged in international projects to expand their customer base and enter new markets.

Mergers and acquisitions have always been an important part of international projects. Companies are increasingly engaging in profitable merger and acquisition deals. The primary objective of a company for engaging in a merger and acquisition of international projects is to standardize the technological systems used in all locations of the firm and to seek new customers and markets. They also work towards selling their existing and new products to different parts of the globe.

Over the past few years, the world has experienced a large number of international and large-scale projects. And the positive results coming out of these projects have encouraged many multi-national companies to engage in such projects. The factors that have affected the increase in the number of the international projects are expansion of individual firms to include a wider market for their range of products, realization by governmental bodies around the world of the benefits of expanding business by standardizing its rules and simplifying its regulations through free trade zones, merger and acquisition of smaller companies by a larger one aiming for global presence, standardization of parts manufactured and sold around the world, etc.

There are many benefits for organizations that seek to plan and execute complex international projects. They are as follows.

Scale of economy   By centralizing the entire administration, a company achieves administrative economics of scale. By centralizing similar types of manufacturing activities, it increases the benefit of scale of economy and decreases the cost of production.

Volume   A larger firm enjoys more benefit due to its size and bulk purchasing of raw material, etc. Retail is a good example. A Wal-Mart or a Carrefour can purchase bulk amounts at lower prices and consequently become more competitive. When a company undertakes an international project, there are opportunities of growth in production and sales, leading to the rise in profits.

Entry in new markets and increased sales   By pursuing foreign projects, a company can get a chance to penetrate a new market. The time required to enter new markets has been reduced. In addition, a company can enter a market on a test basis and later withdraw or retrench if conditions are not favourable.

Access to human resources   Many firms are facing the struggle of unavailability of skilled labour for a specific task in their countries. This problem can be resolved if human personnel can be accessed internationally.

Lower cost of operations   The cost of operations is reduced in international projects due to high production value and lower cost of procuring materials and human resources.

International projects are complex

There are many complex aspects of an international project. They are as follows.

Lack of control   As international projects occur across several countries in a large, complex dimension, it is difficult to control such projects with a centralized approach. It might happen that the objective of a particular international project does not fit with the overall agenda of the company and the project leader starts losing control.

Different cultures   An organization handling an international project must be careful of the difference in cultures because it can greatly affect the work environment. It is a challenge to run a project consisting of people from different countries and cultures. The differences slowly show a difference of opinion, which is harmful for the success of the project.

Different time zones Handling different time zones is a very important aspect of international projects, as it often happens that two sectors in different geographical locations have different working hours and therefore the project suffers from a severe communication problem.

Different currencies Money can be a critical issue in executing international projects, as the values of currencies of different countries vary and there can be legal issues in carrying money across international borders.

Variety of regulations and rules Countries have their own rules and regulations, not only nationally but regionally as well. A company engaging in an international project must take care of these local systems and rules. It should give proper respect to local laws, customs, and regulations. Otherwise, it cannot get the desired support from the locals and the country as a whole.

Political upheaval and uncertainty This can be a major hindrance to the success of a project and can even change the scope of work.

Visibility of the project to the outside world These projects are generally seen with a wider perspective rather than just the organization. Such projects are usually large in size and scope, and involve a large variety of workforce, which automatically gives birth to complexity.

12.2 REASONS FOR CROSS-BORDER INVESTING

A project is selected only if it creates wealth for its investors. This is applicable to both domestic and international investments. Some additional benefits of foreign projects are as follows.

Wage rate Labour cost is one of the crucial motivations for cross-border investment. It is particularly important for labour intensive industries. However, when the emphasis is on the skills (particularly technical skills) of the workforce, the concerned company may have to pay higher wages.

Transport costs Most manufacturing firms require extensive, efficient, and cost-effective transport facilities. Therefore, it is an important consideration for cross-border investment. There are various methods of cost control vis-à-vis transport services. For instance, proximity of the manufacturing unit to the market or the source of raw material can significantly cut down the overall transport costs.

Diversification Cross-border investment, in different countries, helps in the diversification of the cash flows. As the socio-economic and political situations of various nations are different, the return generated and the risk associated with investment in these regions are also diverse. Investment in different countries should be done in such a manner that the risk and returns from various regions are balanced.

Operational constraints In some cases, a company interested in cross-border investment may be compelled to set up a local manufacturing unit in the region. It is because certain governmental policies restrict the outflow of raw material from their country. Also, sometimes due to rigid policies and regulations in the domestic environment, a company may find that investing in a foreign land is more attractive and feasible. Banks also prefer to invest in foreign lands in order to avoid reserve requirements and gain insurance and tax benefits on the deposits.

Special constraints There are unique incentives for MNCs that invest in foreign lands. These include exemption or tariff reduction on imported goods, investment grants, and local loans at preferential interest rates, along with various other subsidies. They can also avail tax concession on sales, exports, and license fees.

Market considerations According to the product life cycle hypothesis by Vernon and Wells (1976), a new product will be produced in the country that developed the innovation regardless of cost because of its price insensitive demand. Foreign investment decisions can turn futile if they are done without proper market analysis. Researches show that the decision to invest abroad by major US firms have been driven by their analysis of the concerned markets (Polk et al. 1966 and Spithaller 1971). A proper market analysis, and the aim to dominate it, is directly proportional to the long-term benefits (Gale 1972). Another reason to explore foreign markets could be the poor condition of the domestic market.

12.3 FOREIGN EXCHANGE EXPOSURE FROM FOREIGN DIRECT INVESTMENT AND COST OF CAPITAL

In case of international projects, relative prices of inputs vary and the inflation rate differs across countries. Foreign exchange rates also move constantly with respect to various foreign currencies and time. They discrepancies can cause an imbalance in the demand and supply of forex. These have a serious impact in the occurrence of cash flows in case of the foreign project as well as the parent company. These unpredictable differences in cash flows due to disequilibrium in the demand and supply of foreign currency are known as foreign exchange exposure.

Relation between foreign exchange risk and cost of capital

Exchange risk and capital market segmentation Cash flows in international projects involve dealing in foreign currencies. The change in the foreign exchange rate would also affect the cash flow. This is referred to as exchange risk, which is an important concern during foreign project evaluation. Since the domestic market and the foreign markets are not integrated, the computation of weighted average cost of capital (WACC) is a major issue in international project appraisal.

International taxation When subsidiary companies do international business, they not only pay taxes to the foreign countries (host) but also remit taxes to the parent countries on dividends and other income. Parent companies can reduce their tax burden by the amount of tax paid abroad. This is known as double avoidance treaty. Transfer pricing can be used as another mechanism for tax reduction by multinationals where they have priced intra-corporate exchange of goods and services in such a manner that it maximises overall tax profit.

Blocked funds   Sometimes funds are accumulated in a foreign country and they cannot be taken out due to tax-related issues. These are called block funds. It makes sense to invest the block funds locally (in the foreign country) in some joint venture or associated projects to generate profits.

Accounting exposure   If the assets, liabilities, and profit and loan accounts of a firm are denominated in a foreign currency, there is a risk of accounting or balance sheet exposure. This risk occurs as these accounts need to be reassessed in terms of the firm's (reporting) currency, at regular intervals of time. The following methods can be used for translating a foreign entity's balance sheet into the parent's currency of reporting.

Closing rate or current rate method   In the process of converting foreign currency into domestic currency, the exchange rate can vary with different dates. The problem of multiple dates (and thereby multiple exchange rates) can be dealt with by using the closing rate or current rate method. For all kinds of transactions, this method takes into account the forex rate prevailing on the parent's balance sheet date.

Current-noncurrent method   Using this method, the current and noncurrent assets and liabilities can be differentiated in order to find out the exchange rates of various dates. It uses the closing rate for current assets and liabilities, i.e., the balance sheet date for the parent company and historical rates for noncurrent assets and liabilities.

Temporal method   In this method, all items are computed at historical rates, except cash receivables and payables that are considered at the closing rate.

Monetary-non-monetary method   In this method, the monetary assets and liabilities, which include sundry creditors, debtors, cash in hand, cash at bank, and bank loans, are translated at the closing rate. Historical rates are considered for the translation of other items.

Economic exposure   Due to the changes in the exchange rates, a certain risk factor is associated with companies that are involved in foreign investment. This risk factor is determined by economic exposure during the assessment of the concerned company's economic value. It takes into account the present value of future operating cash flows. Also, it monitors the change in the present value (expressed in parent currency) as a result of exchange rate movements. This concept can also be used in the operation of cash flows of a firm in its domestic projects. For instance, the weakening of the competitors currencies can influence the income of the domestic firm.

Computation of economic exposure This is done on the basis of a subjective assumption of the future cash flows over the life of the project. The profitability of a company, along with its long-run sustainability, can be achieved through efficient management of its economic exposure. Planning economic exposure is not a short-term initiative. It requires the interaction of different high-level strategies in marketing, finance, and production.

Cost of capital The WACC can be used as the rate of return in a situation where a parent company has the same risk as its foreign project. However, the similarity in the risk may not always be there. A company can determine the risk differential in its capital budgeting process in many ways. It can accommodate the weighted average cost of capital for the risk differential, or calculate NPVs based on WACC.

12.4 ADJUSTED PRESENT VALUE APPROACH

In traditional NPV methods we cannot segregate the value of a project according to its capital mix. The APV approach derives the impact of financing effects and other special features of a project from its operating cash flows. It is determined according to value additivity principle.

APV = Base-case value (value considering full equity finance) + Value of all financing side effects (e.g., interest tax shields, costs of financial distress, subsidies, hedges, issue costs, etc.)

APV dismantles each component which contributes to the value of a project and analyses each one separately. On the contrary, WACC sums up all financing side effects into the discount rate.

Steps in a basic APV analysis (Luehrman 1997)

Step 1: Prepare performance forecasts and base-case incremental cash flows for the business.

Here the components of values are bundled together.

Prepare a valuation spreadsheet for each component of value.

Step 2: Discount base-case cash flows and terminal value to present value.

Step 3: Evaluate financing side effects (for example, interest tax shield).

Here, they are unbundled.

Add the components of value.

Step 4: Add the pieces together to get an initial APV.

APV = Base-case value + Value of financing side effects

Step 5: Tailor the analysis to fit managers' needs.

Finally, they are rebundled.

Companies have to distinguish between project and parent cash flows in the analysis of international projects. This cannot be done using conventional capital budgeting methods. Apart from various domestic issues, these methods deal with changes in the exchange rates. Now, these changes may or may not represent the exchange transactions, rates of inflation, or credit controls. Also, it is uncertain whether the exchange rate's changes would provide a detailed use of financial subsidies including concessionary credit and guarantees, incomplete capital markets, and different tax systems. Moreover, variable economic and political conditions result in differences between the risk classes of the foreign and domestic projects of the same company.

The APV approach is a better option than conventional methods, in this context. The former is more flexible and condition specific as compared to the latter. It enables the identification of unique cash flows for different risk classes. The APV method also helps in dealing with misconceptions in the basic assumption of the NPV equation. This method accounts for a wide variety of investment-financing interactions, in ways that are more relevant with the capital market theory. It is a simple and effective method to deal with large complex projects with various project-specific needs.

Details of adjusted present value approach

The most prominent method of project appraisal is to discount expected after-tax project cash flows by a weighted average cost of capital.

$$NPV = \sum_{t=0}^{t} \frac{CF_t}{(1+k)^t} \tag{12.1}$$

where, NPV is net present value, CF_t is the expected total after-tax project cash flow in period t, and k is the weighted average cost of capital.

$$k = (E / (E+D)) k_e + (D / (E+D)) k_d (1-t) \tag{12.2}$$

where, D/E is the weight of debt in the total capital structure, k_e is the required rate of return on equity, k_d is the pre-tax interest rate on debt, and t is the corporate tax rate.

The advantage of the orthodox method is its simplicity. It considers a single discount rate for all cash flows; it enables planners to focus only on the project's investment features. However, different discount rates are required for projects that differ from a firm's typical project in terms of either business risk or contribution to debt capacity.

Differences in project debt capacity can be incorporated in an alternative weighted average formula developed by Modigliani and Miller (1963):

Weighted average cost of capital $= k = k_e \{1 - t(1 - D/E)\}$ (12.3)

Further, it can be represented in the cases where business risk differs. The required rate of return k_j is given by:

$$K_j = \{1 + \beta_j (k_m - r)\}\{1 - t(1 - D/E)\} \qquad (12.4)$$

where, β_j is the project's beta coefficient and $(k_m - r)$ is the risk premium on the market portfolio.

Myers and Pogue (1974) suggest a return to the basic Modigliani–Miller equation.

$$APV = \sum_{t=0}^{T} \frac{CF_t}{(1 + k_e)^t} + \sum_{t=0}^{T} \frac{TS_t}{(1 + k_d)^t} \qquad (12.5)$$

where, the first term is the present value of the total expected operating cash flows discounted by k_e (all equity financed), also known as base-case NPV, and the second term is the present value of the tax shields arising from debt, discounted at the cost of debt k_d.

Applying APV in foreign projects

The APV approach implies a bundled, unbundled, and re-bundled approach in capital budgeting. The present value is the sum of the present values of the basic project cash flows. The various financing side effects can be incorporated readily for evaluating a foreign project. APV can be calculated in the following ways, considering all financing side effects.

Adjusted present value (APV) = Capital outlay (I)

$$+ \quad \text{Remittable after-tax operating cash flows} \quad \sum_{t=0}^{T} \frac{CF_t(1 + t)}{(1 + k_1)^t}$$

$$+ \quad \text{Depreciation tax shields} \quad \sum_{t=0}^{T} \frac{DEP_t(t)}{(1 + k_2)^t}$$

$$+ \quad \text{Interest tax shields} \quad \sum_{t=0}^{T} \frac{INT_t(t)}{(1 + k_3)^t}$$

$$+ \quad \text{Financial subsidies} \quad \sum_{t=0}^{T} \frac{\Delta INT_t}{(1 + k_4)^t}$$

$$+ \quad \text{Tax reduction} \quad \sum_{t=0}^{T} \frac{TR_t}{(1 + k_5)^t}$$

$$+ \quad \text{Additional remittances} \quad \sum_{t=0}^{T} \frac{REM_t}{(1 + k_6)^t} \qquad (12.6)$$

Appropriate discount rates with the APV approach

With the APV approach, discount rates no longer carry the burden of implicitly capturing all the effects of a project's financial structure on its value. However, they continue to reflect the risk involved in each APV term, as well as the implicit assumptions incorporated in the cash flows vis-à-vis inflation and exchange rate changes.

It does not take into account the effects of financial structure in the discount rate. The discount rate for each term must reflect both the rate of interest and a risk premium. According to the current capital market theory, this risk premium should reflect only the systematic risk of the project. As shown by Lessard (1976), the discount rate serves a dual purpose. First, it is used to adjust cash flows. Second, it can discount the cash flows by a risk premium. Appropriate discount rates for each category of the APV terms are discussed below.

Operating cash flows (k_1)   These are not contractually fixed in any currency, but vary depending on the interactions among inflation, exchange rates, and a number of other factors. They should be stated in terms of units of constant purchasing power. Also, they should be discounted at the real rate of interest, including a risk premium reflecting their systematic risk.

Depreciation tax shields (k_2)   This is a normal cash flow in either the parent currency or the foreign currency, depending on which country's tax rate results in a higher tax bill. If the foreign tax rate is lower than the domestic tax rate, the term will include the additional taxes levied by the domestic currency, and the incremental tax rebate will be that which is provided by the domestic tax law. The risk involved in this case is that the firm cannot utilize the depreciation tax shields.

Interest tax shields (k_3)   The risk associated with the interest tax shields is that the firm is not able to obtain them. It either defaults on its debt, fails, or has no profits against which it can offset the deductions.

Financial subsidies or premiums (k_4)   These are nominal flows which should be discounted at the nominal interest rate on the firm's debt in the corresponding currency.

Tax reduction or deferrals (k_5)   These are nominal flows in domestic currencies. They should be discounted at the firm's nominal interest rate.

Additional remittances (k_6)   To find the exact discounting factor for these is very difficult. They are real flows, but the risks are to be highly systematic. The amount available for these will depend directly on the project operating cash flows. That is why the discount rate applied to operating flows, k_1, should be a sensible choice.

Hence, the APV approach is not stagnant like other methods. It is highly flexible and situation based. A skilled analyst can configure a valuation in whatever way it makes most sense for the people involved in managing its separate parts. The basic skeleton can be highly refined or customized according to tastes and situations, but a simple hypothetical example explains the essential idea.

12.5 MANAGING EXPOSURE OF FDI TO POLITICAL RISK

Assets located abroad are exposed to the risk of appropriation by the host country. Also, there may be changes in applicable withholding taxes, restrictions on remittances by the subsidiary to the parents, etc. These will create a risk in the case of evaluation of foreign projects, which is known as political risk.

Managing political risk While investing in a project in foreign countries, a firm should first assess the political environment of the country in which it desires to invest. The structure of the investment should minimize the political risk. The bigger the firm's investment, the more susceptible it is to the change in government policies.

Pre-investing planning Given the recognition of the political risk, an MNC can follow at least four separate, though not necessarily mutually exclusive, policies.

Avoidance The easiest way is to handle any difficult issue is to avoid it. It applies to the prevention of political risk also. Hence, firms can filter out the politically uncertain or risky countries where investment should be avoided.

Insurance An alternative to risk-avoidance is to insure the risk. Most developed countries sell political risk insurance to cover the foreign assets of domestic companies. The Overseas Private Investigation Corporation (OPIC) provides US investors with insurance against loss due to the specific political risk of expropriation, currency inconvertibility, and political violence, such as war, revolution, and/or insurrection.

Negotiating the environment In addition to insurance, some firms try to make an agreement with the host government before undertaking the investment defining rights and responsibilities of both the parties. This is known as concession agreement.

Structuring the investment Once a firm decides to invest in a country, it tries to minimize its political risk by increasing the host government's cost. This involves adjusting the operating and financial policies so that the value of the foreign project of the multinational firm is under control.

12.6 RELATIONSHIP BETWEEN CAPM AND BLACK–SCHOLES OPTION PRICING FORMULA

Chapter 10 of this book describes how the Black and Scholes option pricing formula can be used for project evaluation. Similarly, it might also be applicable for evaluating international projects. In this section, CAPM and Black and Scholes models are used simultaneously to find out the risk premiums, using the concept of option value.

In Chapter 10, it has been shown how the equity in the levered company can be valued as a call option on the firm's assets. If, at the debt's due date, the value of the firm's asset is higher than the amount of the debt to be paid, the debt is paid and the shareholders keep the difference. In the opposite case, the shareholders walk away and leave the firm's assets to the debt-holders. In this scenario, where the firm issues only one class of zero-coupon debt, the Black and Scholes option pricing formula gives the firm's equity value. In such cases,

$$P_c = [P_s][N(d_1)] - [P_e][antiln(-Rft)][N(d_2)] \tag{12.7}$$

where,

P_c = market price of the call option

P_s = price of the stock

P_e = striking price of the option

antiln = antilog (base e)

Rf = annualized interest rate

t = time to expiration (in years)

$N(d_1)$ and $N(d_2)$ are the values of the cumulative normal distribution defined by

$$d_1 = [ln(P_s / P_e) + (Rf + 0.5 \ \sigma2)t]/\sigma\sqrt{t}, \ d_2 = d_1 - (\sigma\sqrt{t}) \tag{12.8}$$

where,

$In(P_s/P_e)$ = the natural logarithm of (P_s/P_e)

$\sigma2$ is the variance of continuously compounded rate of return on the stock per time period

It was in 1983 that Garman and Kohlhagen used the Black–Scholes model for coping with the presence of two interest rates (one for each currency).

Suppose,

r_d = risk-free interest rate to expiry of the domestic currency

r_f = foreign currency risk-free interest rate

where, the currency in which the value of option is obtained is domestic currency.

The formula also requires that the FX rates—both strike and current spot—be quoted in terms of 'units of foreign currency per unit of domestic currency'.

Following this, the value of a call option in foreign currency has the following value.

$$P_c = exp \ (- \ r_f T)SN(d_1) - Kexp(- \ rdT)N(d_2) \tag{12.9}$$

where,

P_c = market price of the call option

S is the current spot rate, and K is the strike rate

We can express the required rate of return on risky bonds in the continuous time version of the CAPM derived by Merton (1973).

$$\overline{R}_b = r_f + \beta_b (\overline{R}_m + r_f) \tag{12.10}$$

where,

$\overline{R}_b$ = required rate of return on a risky bond

$\overline{R}_m$ = required return on the market portfolio

$\beta_b = cov\,(R_b,\,R_m) \div var\,(R_m)$

$\overline{R}_m + r_f$ = the financial risk premium expressed in CAPM

In order to link the Black and Scholes formula (Eqn (12.9)) to the CAPM (Eqn (12.10)) we can write

$$dB = \frac{\partial B}{\partial V}dV + \frac{\partial B}{\partial B}dt + \frac{1}{2}\frac{\partial^2 B}{\partial V^2}\sigma^2 V^2 dt \tag{12.11}$$

Taking the limit of the Eqn (12.11) as dt goes to zero and dividing by B

$$\lim_{dt \to 0} \frac{dB}{B} = \frac{\partial B}{\partial B}\frac{dV}{B} = \frac{\partial B}{\partial V}\frac{dV}{V}\frac{V}{B} \tag{12.12}$$

dB/B is the bond's rate of return, R_b, and dV/V is the rate of return on the firm's assets R_v. Therefore,

$$dB = \frac{\partial B}{\partial V}\frac{V}{B}R_v \tag{12.13}$$

Using Eqn (12.13) and the definition of β, we can write the instantaneous covariance as:

$$\beta_b = \frac{\partial B}{\partial V}\frac{V}{B}\beta_v \tag{12.14}$$

Taking the first partial derivative of Eqn (12.9) with respect to V

$$\frac{\partial B}{\partial V} = N(-d_1) \tag{12.15}$$

so that the equation becomes,

$$\beta_v = N(-d_1)\frac{V}{B}\beta_v \tag{12.16}$$

Substituting Eqns (12.11) and (12.9) gives

$$\overline{R}_b = rf + \beta_v N(-d_1)\frac{V}{B}(\overline{R}_m + r_f) \tag{12.17}$$

From the CAPM, we know that $\overline{R}_v - r_f = \beta_v (\overline{R}_m + r_f)$

Substituting these with Eqn (12.17) and rearranging gives the risk premium in terms of the option pricing formula:

$$\overline{R}_b = r_f N(-d_1)\frac{V}{B}(\overline{R}_v + r_f) \tag{12.18}$$

Hence, from the above discussion, it can be seen that the required rate of return on risky bonds now is $\overline{R}_b = r_f N(-d_1)\dfrac{V}{B}(\overline{R}_v + r_f)$, which is the combined output of Black and Scholes and the CAPM approach.

12.7 INTERNATIONAL JOINT VENTURES

A joint venture is a combination of sub-sets of assets contributed by two or more business enterprises for a specific objective and a fixed time period. Each of the venture partners continue to exist as a separate firm. The joint venture between these partners represent a completely new business entity. All entities in this joint venture can be from the same country, or one of them can be from a different country. The latter is known as an international joint venture.

The growth of international joint ventures over the last 20 years has been dramatic. Prior to 1973, there was such little activity in this area that the US Department of Commerce did not even bother to systematically collect data on foreign transactions. The foreign purchases of American companies in 1968 accounted for a mere 16 transactions (Khoury 1980) out of 4,462 joint venture announcements for that year (*Mergerstat Review* 1985).

Table 12.1 provides information about Indian merger and acquisition (M&A) events. It gives the deal size in USD of major joint ventures in the Indian telecom sector during 1998 and 2006.

Rationale behind international joint ventures

Many of the reasons for international joint ventures are similar to those of domestic transactions, while others are unique to the international arena. These motives include the following.

Growth Companies pursue international joint ventures in order to achieve long-term strategic goals, to enhance the growth rate beyond the capacity of the saturated domestic market, to extend the market abroad, and to protect the existing domestic market.

Technology International collaboration is required to utilize technological knowledge advantage, and also to acquire new and advanced technology.

Extend advantages in differentiated products There is always a strong correlation between multi-nationalization and product differentiation. International business may lead a company towards increasing its scope in differentiating products.

Government policy Companies enter international joint ventures to circumvent protective tariffs and quotas, as well as to reduce dependence on export.

Exchange rate International joint ventures have an impact on the relative cost of foreign versus the domestic acquisitions, and on the value of repatriated profits.

Political and economic stability Companies look to international joint ventures so that they can invest in a politically safe and predictable environment.

Diversification Companies need to diversify in product lines for geographical expansion and reduction of systematic risk.

TABLE 12.1 Major joint venture deals in the Indian telecom sector

Company/service name	Stake sold (%)	Buyer	Seller	Year	Deal size (US$)	Indicative enterprise value (US$)	Per sub value (US$)
Orange, Mumbai	41	Hutchison Group, Hong Kong	Max Group, Delhi	1998	560 m	1.36 b	NA
Modi Telestra, Calcutta	100	Bharti Group, India	B.K. Modi and Telestra	2000	NA	160 m	–
Command Cellular, Kolkata	100	Hutchison & Indian Group	Usha Martin and others	2000	–	138 m	–
Reliance CDMA	–	Qualcomm San Diego, US	Reliance Infocomm	2002	–	10 b	–
Aircel, Chennai	79.24	Sterling Group, Chennai	RPG Group	2003	210 m		
Hutch Essar	3.17	Essar Group	Max India	2005	146 m	–	570
Idea Cellular	48.14	Aditya Birla Group	Tata Group	2005	NA	2 b	400
BPL Mobile and BPL Cellular	–	Promoters		2005	1.15 b	NA	–
Bharti Airtel	10	Vodaphone	Bharti Group	2005	1.5 b	16 b	1000
Aircel, TN, Chennai and NE	74	Maxis, Malaysia	Sterling Group	2006	750 m	1.07 b	496
Spice (Punjab and Bangalore)	49	Telekom Malaysia, Malaysia	NA	2006	178 m	363 m	–
Hutch, India	8.33	Max India	Kotak Mahindra, India	2006	225 m	–	NA
Hutch Essar, India	5.1	Hutchison Group, Hong Kong	Hinduja	2006	450 m	9 b	NA
Bharti	9.3	Private investors	Warburg Pincus	NA	873 m	NA	1000

Source: Banka 2006.

A merger is a fusion of two or more companies to become a single company or to form a completely new company altogether. Similarly, acquisition refers to the process in which one firm takes over another and makes it a part of its existing enterprise. Mergers and acquisitions may be broadly classified into the following three categories.

Horizontal   A horizontal acquisition or merger is one that takes place between companies which are essentially operating in the same market. Their products may or may not be identical. The merger of the Tata Oil Mills Company Limited (TOMCO) with Hindustan Lever Limited (HLL) is an example of a horizontal merger. Both companies have similar products. Mahindra & Mahindra's acquisition of the Reva Electric Car Company is also an example of a horizontal merger or takeover.

Vertical   A vertical acquisition or merger is one in which a company expands backwards by acquiring or merging with a company supplying raw materials, or expands forward in the direction of the ultimate consumer. For example, the merger of Reliance Petrochemical Limited (RPCL) with Reliance Industries Limited (RIL) is an example of a vertical merger with a backward linkage, as far as RIL is concerned.

Conglomerate   In a conglomerate acquisition or merger, the concerned companies operate in totally unrelated lines of business. For example, Motha Steel Industries Limited merged with Vardhaman Spinning Mills Limited.

On 2 April 2007, Tata Steel, India's largest steel producer, acquired Corus, which is four times bigger than Tata and the largest steel producer in the UK. After this acquisition, Tata became the world's fifth largest steel producer. The political and economic stability of India greatly helped to make the deal possible. Other reasons, such as the government policies of both countries and the exchange rate, also created an amicable situation which helped materialize this international joint venture.

SUMMARY

With the onset of globalization, international projects have become more frequent. Wars against terrorism, international police efforts, and foreign aid can be examples of international projects that are executed by the governments of different countries. International profit-making companies also engage in international projects to expand their customer base and enter new markets. Merger and acquisition has always been an important part of international projects. Foreign exchange risk from FDI can occur due to the exchange risk and capital market segmentation, international taxation, blocked funds, accounting exposure, and economic exposure.

Some reasons for cross-border investment are cost of labour, transport costs, diversification, operational constraints, special incentives, and market considerations. Companies go for international joint ventures to avail the benefits of scale of economy, enhancing growth, differentiating products, advancing of technology, enjoying the benefit of exchange rates and different types of financial incentives such as tax concession, subsidies, etc. A company must assess a country's political environment before getting into an agreement with it over an international joint venture.

KEY TERMS

Accounting exposure This risk of accounting or balance sheet exposure arises when a company has assets and liabilities, and profit and loss accounts denominated in a foreign currency.

Blocked fund A fund that is not freely convertible to other currencies due to exchange and other controls.

Economic exposure It refers to the extent to which the economic value of a company may decline due to changes in exchange rates.

Foreign exchange exposure Foreign exchange rates move constantly with respect to various foreign currencies and time. These unpredicted differences in cash flows, due to disequilibrium in the demand and supply of foreign currency, are known as foreign exchange exposure.

Joint venture A joint venture is a combination of sub-sets of assets contributed by two or more business enterprises for a specific objective and a fixed time period. Each of the venture partners continues to exist as a separate firm. The joint venture between these two or more partners represents a completely new business entity.

Political exposure Assets located abroad are subject to the risk of appropriation by the host country's government. Also, there may be changes in applicable withholding taxes, restrictions on remittances by the subsidiary to the parents, etc. These will incorporate a risk during the evaluation of foreign projects. This is known as political risk or exposure.

CONCEPT REVIEW QUESTIONS

1. Why do corporates want to invest abroad?
2. How is APV becoming more useful than NPV in the case of international capital budgeting decisions?
3. How can a foreign exchange risk arise from a foreign direct investment?
4. What are the different types of translation or accounting exposures? Describe each of them.
5. How can the cash flows of the parent company be different from the project cash flows in an international project?

CRITICAL THINKING QUESTIONS

1. Assume that funds of project X are blocked at the central bank of a host country without any interest up to the end of the project. The fund can be fully repatriated only after the project is completed. Is project X acceptable?
2. 'The United States is a real testing ground. If you make it here, you establish your credentials for the rest of the world.' What do you understand by this statement? How would you measure the benefits of investing in the United States?
3. Multi-national firms are riskier than domestic firms in the same industry because of additional political and economic exposures that appear to exist overseas. What should an MNCs strategy be to overcome these risks and become more competitive in the global market?

ASSIGNMENT

1. Following is a list of international projects:
   - Merger of Tata Corus
   - Merger of Hutch and Vodaphone
   - Merger of Chrysler and Daimler-Benz

Out of the above list, choose one and find out if it is a success or a failure and discuss the reasons behind the same.

SELECT REFERENCES

Banka, S., 'Mergers & Acquisitions (M&A) in Indian Telecom Industry—A Study', *The Chartered Accountant,* December 2006, p. 935.

Doremus, P.N., W.W. Keller, L.W. Pauly, and S. Reich, 'The Myth of the Global Corporation', Princeton University Press, New Jersey, 1998.

Gale, B.T., 'Market share and rate of return', *Review of Economics and Statistics,* December 1972.

Khoury, S.J., *Transnational Mergers and Acquisitions in United States,* Lexinton, Lexinton Books, 1980.

Kogut, B., 'What Makes a Company Global?' *Harvard Business Review,* Jan–Feb, 1999.

Lessard, D.R., 'World, Country and Industry Relationships in Equity Returns: Implications for Risk Reduction through International Diversification', *Financial Analysts Journal,* Jan–Feb, 1976, pp. 74–98.

Luehrman, T.A., 'What's it worth? A general manager's guide to valuation', *Harvard Business Review,* May–June, 1997, pp. 132–42.

Mergerstat Review, Chicago, IL: The W.T. Grim and Co., 1985.

Modigliani, F. and M. Miller, 'Corporate income taxes and the cost of capital: A correction', *American Economic Review,* June 1963, pp. 433–43.

Myers, S.C. and G.A. Pogue, 'A Programming Approach to Corporate Financial Management', *Journal of Finance,* 1974, vol. 29, pp. 579–99.

Polk, J. et al., *US Production Abroad and Balance of Payments,* National Industrial Conference Board, New York, 1966.

Spithaller, E., 'A Survey of Recent Quantitative Studies of Long-term Capital Movements', *Staff Papers,* IMF, March 1971.

Tzu, S., *The Art of War,* OUP, 1963.

Vernon, R. and L.T. Wells, *Managers in the International Economy,* 4 edn, Englewood Cliffs, New Jersey, Prentice Hall, 1976.

CASE STUDY
Evaluation of Foreign Investment

Technocom Industries is a fast-growing software company based in Hyderabad, catering to the US and European markets, besides the Indian market. The MD of Technocom Industries is in a dilemma as he has to decide whether the US or Europe should be selected to open up a new unit. In his opinion Europe might be a better choice, but the Head-Finance feels that the Euro-zone is not the right choice for investment as it is dependent on business from the US. On the other hand, the US is facing a recession and due to that the economic condition of the Euro-zone is not rosy either.

The MD agrees with what the Head-Finance feels and they jointly decide to open a manufacturing unit in the US.

The following estimates and projections are made by the Head-Finance of the company.

Initial investment required for the project to commence is US$250 million. This is required to set up the plant, machinery and other facilities, including US$30 million as working capital margin. The project would be operational within a year. Capacity utilization of the project after being operational is projected as follows in Table E12.1:

TABLE E12.1

Year	1	2	3	4	5
Capacity utilization (%)	60	70	80	90	100

At 100% capacity utilization, the sales revenue of the current prices is estimated at $220 million. Technocom Industries presently exports software products worth $120 million annually to the US. If the project is carried out, these exports will cease to exist. The net profit margin on these exports is currently 15% in dollar terms, which is expected to grow to keep pace with inflation rates in the US.

Technocom Industries has an accumulated blocked fund of $15 million that can be used in this project. The life of the project is 5 years and its salvage value is nil.

The contribution is expected to be 60% of the sales. The fixed cost excluding depreciation for the five years of operation is estimated to be $30 million at the current prices. Selling expenses constitute 5% of the sales. Due to this project, Technocom Industries is able to generate a profit worth $15 million without paying any taxes at current prices each year.

Due to this project, Technocom Industries has increased its borrowing in the Indian market by Rs 5000 million. The US government has also offered a concessional loan for 5 years of $60 million at 6%, which is available in the US market at 8.5%. The rest is being financed through Technocom Industries' own funds in India. Technocom Industries faces a borrowing rate of 11% in India. The risk-free rate in India and the US are 6.0% and 2.0% respectively.

The effective corporate income tax rate in the US and India are 30% and 35% respectively. The current exchange rate is Rs 44.44/$ and the required rate of return of Indian shareholders of Technocom Industries is 15%.

Table E12.2 shows the expected inflation rates in the US and India

TABLE E12.2

Year	Inflation rate in India (%)	Inflation rate in US (%)
1	3.75	1.20
2	4.00	1.30
3	3.50	1.50
4	4.20	1.75
5	4.70	2.00

Discussion question

Evaluate the US investment proposal of Technocom Industries using the Adjusted Present Value (APV) Method, according to the estimates and projections presented by the Head-Finance of the company.

Will you accept the opinion of the Head-Finance? While making your analysis, assume the following:

1. Working capital margin can be realized at the whole amount of initial injection.

2. Plan and machineries are to be depreciated within the life of the project and on straight line basis.

3. There is a double taxation avoidance treaty between India and the US, under which full credit is given to Indian companies for taxes paid in the US, subject to the condition that the rate does not exceed the Indian tax rate.

4. It is considered that purchasing power parity (PPP) between India and the US holds good.

5. All expenses and revenues and the net profit margin of the company will go up as per inflation in the US.

PART III

PROJECT PLANNING, EXECUTION, AND CONTROL

PROJECT PLANNING

Plans are only good intentions unless they immediately degenerate into hard work.

— PETER DRUCKER

LEARNING OBJECTIVES

After studying this chapter, you will be able to

- Define project plan and understand its importance
- Know the process of planning and the components of a good plan
- Conceptualize reasons for the failure of a project
- Understand the reasons for time overrun and cost overrun

Project In, Project Out

'Hello … check … mike testing … 1 … 2 … 3 … check!'

Villagers of Ranipur, old and young alike, are excited and waiting since morning in their best attire at the central market place. The chief minister's convoy will arrive any moment. He is scheduled to lay the foundation stone of the Ranipur Power Project, a 2.5 MW power plant, today. The power plant will be considered a top priority and will start its operations within 12 months. A lot of local people will get jobs and the standard of living of the people of Ranipur will improve significantly—that is what the local panchayat chief has made them understand.

The chief minister arrives, he is greeted with flowers and garlands, the foundation stone-laying ceremony follows in grandeur, and there is excitement in the air. Lots of promises fill peoples' minds with anticipation and hope.

The following year passes by, uneventful.

The place around the foundation stone lies covered with grass and weeds. The engravings on the stone—the name of the chief minister and the date of stone-laying is no longer readable from a distance.

However, the children of the village are very happy. The stone now serves the purpose of a wicket—for their cricket practice.

13.1 WHAT IS PROJECT PLANNING?

Planning can be stated as the function of fulfilling a firm's objectives by developing the policies, procedures, and programmes necessary to accomplish them. Planning, in a project environment, may be defined as preparing a predetermined flow of action within a pre-assumed environment. The milestones of a project, which the line managers are expected to achieve, are set according to project requirements. The project manager must make goals which are feasible and achievable by line managers. Planning is an integrated function that involves both upper and lower level management, as all levels of management are equally affected if an alternative plan is to be executed over the predetermined ones. Planning is one of the most important management functions, as it is necessary to solve the most complex problems that are faced by the management during the execution of a project.

According to Dilworth et al. (1985), planning, and integration and execution of plans, comprise the most important functions of a project manger. Various functional units are together responsible for the successful completion of a project; therefore, different plans must be appropriately integrated. Otherwise, the project would be reduced to a set of discrete initiatives. Proper and extensive planning helps in efficient integration and execution of a project against limited and conditional availability of time and resources.

The planning process is expected to be equipped to handle any adverse situation that a project may face, either in the triggering stage or anywhere during the course of action. Project managers must be fully involved with the project, right from the initiation stage to the completion. They must realize and abide by the realization that project planning is an iterative process and must be continued till the completion of a project.

Important aspects of project planning

One of the objectives of project planning is to define and classify all work required, so that all members of the project team become aware of their specific role in a particular project. Project planning is very essential in a project environment. If the task is well understood prior to starting it, then almost half the work can be completed without any trouble. Otherwise, during its actual execution, it is sometimes found that some change may be needed that would result in reallocation, rescheduling, and re-prioritizing of resources such as time, funds, material, manpower, etc. The riskier the task, the greater is the amount of exercise and effort that must be devoted in order to ensure effective performance.

Successful project management, whether involved in an in-house project or in a customized one, must put to use effective planning techniques with the aid of the quantitative and qualitative tools of project planning. From a system's point of view, the management must make effective utilization of resources. This can be done only if the utilization of the resources is planned in a foolproof manner, i.e., while scheduling and allocating resources, the management must treat the whole organization as a whole network subdivided into smaller sections.

First, the management should identify the project objectives. These goals or objectives may be used to develop expertise in a given area, to become competitive, to modify an existing facility for later use, or simply to keep key personnel employed.

The objectives of a particular project are both implicitly and explicitly interrelated. It often happens that the management is not able to satisfy all the desired objectives of a project. Then it must prioritize, based on the strategic importance of a particular project objective.

Once they are clearly identified, there are a few factors that are to be taken care of and understood, i.e., the interrelationship of the working elements to fulfil the objectives, the functional division that will be responsible for fulfilling the objectives, the availability of the corporate and organizational resources, and the level of information flow required for the project.

For a too large and complex project, project planning must be tight and flawless. This can be achieved by keeping in mind some key factors, such as designing of the project organizational structure in accordance with project requirement, optimizing available resources, and a well-developed accounting and management information system.

An exclusive and complete plan cannot be possible until all necessary information is available at the project initiation. These information requirements are as follows.

Statement of work (SOW)   It is a broad description of a project. It includes the objectives of the project, a brief schedule of the work to be done, various resource constraints such as capital, time, manpower, machinery, material, etc.

Project specifications   This refers to the special requirements of the clients. It can vary from client to client.

Milestone schedule   This schedule is a gross schedule which includes things such as start date, end date, major milestones, and written reports (data items).

Work breakdown structure (WBS)   It defines the various project sub-activities in relation to the project's final outcome. It creates a framework for project control and provides the basis for insight into the time and cost status of a project through various management tools. (Refer to section 2.2.2 in Chapter 2.)

13.2 THE PROCESS OF PLANNING

A project manager must continuously analyze the external environment in order to envision the future of the project and strategize accordingly. It has to be done so that the project becomes well structured and can be executed under pressure. These environmental factors become an integral part of planning. The project manager must be able to identify and assess these strategic factors to meet future problems keeping in mind the resource constraints (Kerzner 1977).

A horizontal hierarchy level is maintained in strategic project planning environment. As in other cases, the final decision is taken by the top level. Following are the three basic guidelines for strategic project planning:

1. It is a task that should be executed by the project managers and decided by the top level.
2. The fulfilment of the plan is entirely dependent on the relationship between the top-level management and the various project teams.
3. Success of a strategic plan depends on how well it explains the nature of the job, job responsibility, and the specific roles played by the members of the different project teams.

Project teams must be clearly informed about all the strategic variables that can have a direct impact on the success or failure of a project. The analysis begins with environment, which is subdivided as internal, external, and competitive, as shown in Figure 13.1.

Once all three variables are defined for a particular project, the planning process consists of the following steps, as illustrated in Figure 13.2.

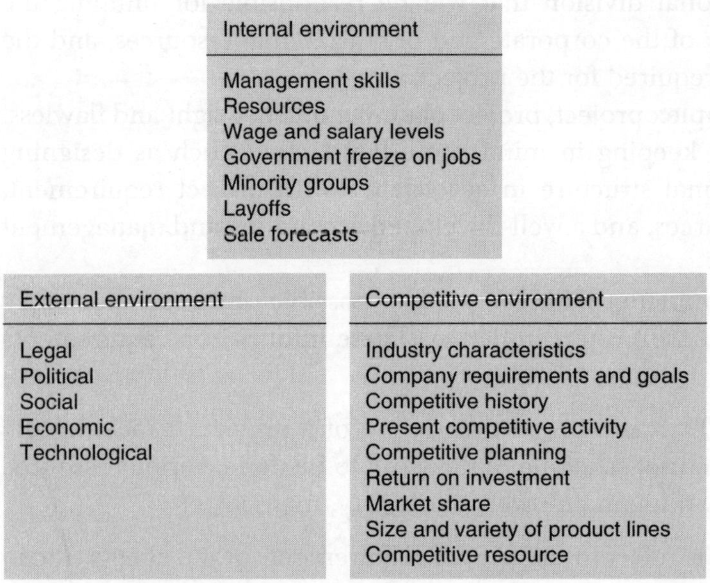

It is not at all easy to identify the complete set of strategic variables at the initiation level. The programme personnel can easily get hold of the internal or operating variables by studying the organizational structure. The external variables are usually read with a top management perspective. In most cases, those who are in the horizontal hierarchy of the proposed programme ignore external factors. They tend to be more and more ignorant about the changing external variables as the programme rolls on. In order to bring these changing external variables under constant surveillance of the top management,

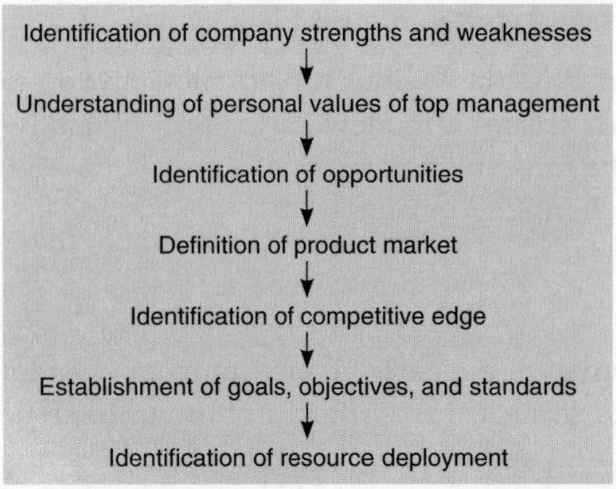

Internal environment

Management skills
Resources
Wage and salary levels
Government freeze on jobs
Minority groups
Layoffs
Sale forecasts

External environment

Legal
Political
Social
Economic
Technological

Competitive environment

Industry characteristics
Company requirements and goals
Competitive history
Present competitive activity
Competitive planning
Return on investment
Market share
Size and variety of product lines
Competitive resource

FIGURE 13.1 Environment analysis

Identification of company strengths and weaknesses
↓
Understanding of personal values of top management
↓
Identification of opportunities
↓
Definition of product market
↓
Identification of competitive edge
↓
Establishment of goals, objectives, and standards
↓
Identification of resource deployment

FIGURE 13.2 The planning process

there must be strong and clear communication between the management and the project office.

Top-management support must be available for the identification of strategic planning variables. This initiative helps in making an effective decision at the programme or the execution level. In strategic decision-making, the top management's role, maturity, experience, and knowledge cannot be ignored or replaced. At the end of the day, decisions are always finalized at the top level, regardless of the organizational structure. Exhibit 13.1 shares a few findings regarding managerial priorities while planning for projects.

EXHIBIT 13.1 Planning variables across industry

IBS Kolkata Research Centre (2006) surveyed about fifty manufacturing companies, to determine if the lower and middle-level project managers knew which variables were considered as important planning variables in their own industry by top management. The results of the above survey shows:

1. Top executives within the same industry differed vis-à-vis the identification of strategic variables, even with companies having almost identical business bases.
2. Very little attempt was made by the top management to quantify the risks involved with strategic variable, as it is a very difficult process.

For example, in the field of education, one house may be struggling for long-term survival, whereas another may be game for quick, easy, and short-term benefit. Hence, for the same type of ventures, strategic variables for their respective top executives are different.

The study also found that the differences between the project manager and top-level management mainly boils down to the following six strategic variables:

1. Business markets and business cycles
2. Product features
3. Pricing and advertisement policies
4. Technical know-how
5. Labour force and inter-personal skills
6. Customer organization restructuring

The top-level management, as well as the project manager, usually agree upon the first four factors after some discussion. But the last two clauses, i.e., labour force and interpersonal skills and customer organization restructuring, require further discussion because many customers perform a make-or-buy analysis before contracting with specified companies.

Source: Survey report by IBS-K 2006.

13.3 ATTRIBUTES OF A GOOD PLAN

The basic requirements of a good project plan (Doran 1981) would include the following:

1. *Goal/objectives*—They must be defined at the system level as well as at the company level.
2. *Work description and instructions*—It consists of project specifications, statement of work (SOW), work breakdown structure (WBS), and organizational breakdown structure (OBS).

3. *Network scheduling*—This can be done by preparing a milestone schedule, using PERT or CPM, start date, end date, and major milestones.

4. *Master or detailed schedules*—Each project plan must consist of a detail or master schedule and plan regarding how a project should be executed, so that it can achieve its desired goal. For the success of the project, a detailed breakup of work schedule is required.

5. *Budgets*—The budget is prepared by trading off time and cost.

6. *Time/cost/performance tracking*—This helps in capturing the planned and actual time frame, effort, resources required, and duration of projects, and it provides a model for estimating workloads for a variety of projects.

7. *System reports*—It contains information about time, cost, performance, reliability, maintenance, and effectiveness of a specific project.

8. *Feedback*—Based on the feedback and input from the project managers and stakeholders, the acceptance of the final project deliverables and project scope are defined.

9. *Management decision-making*—The decision of project managers will play an important role in the success of a project's initiation, development, and implementation.

Figure 13.3 illustrates the relationships between the various requirements for any project.

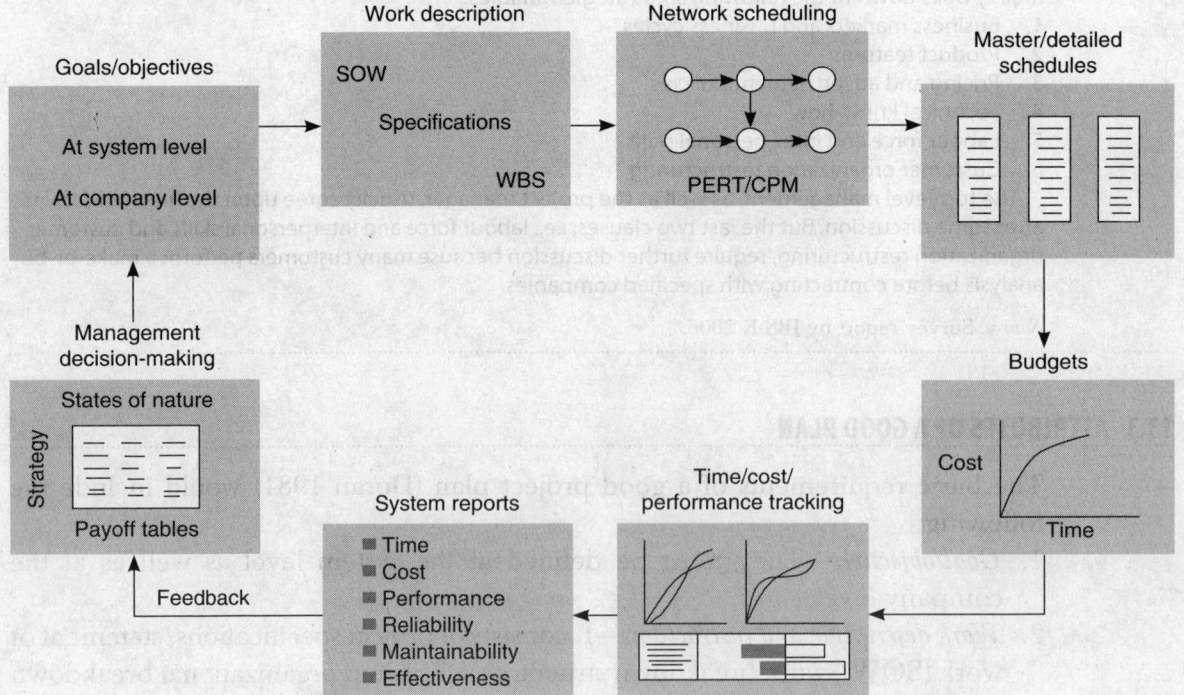

FIGURE 13.3 Requirements of a prescribed project plan

13.4 PROJECT LIFE CYCLE PLANNING

Project life cycle planning is a new approach towards planning for a project, to ease the task of the project manager. It is the methodological procedure to bring a certain amount of uniformity in the planning of project phases. In this methodological approach, the project is sub-divided into different phases and each phase is dealt with one at a time. It is done by holding a meeting of all the personnel who are concerned with the specific phase of the project. To control the different phases of the project, companies prepare project management policies and procedure manuals, subdividing the information according to the life cycle of the project.

The various phases in the life cycle of a project are described below.

Initialization   Through brainstorming and using common sense, project ideas are initiated. At this stage, the exact problem is identified and potential solutions are also prescribed.

Feasibility or appraisal study   After evaluating and considering all technical aspects, a project manager has to decide about the acceptability of the project. The other objective of the feasibility phase is to plan the project development, to find out the probable completion time, and also estimate the required human resource, machinery, and cost.

Preliminary planning   In this stage, the project manager has to define the various requirements of the project. He/she should consider the following: scope of the project, project goals, documentation and specifications, specific information, schedule of performance, exhibits, attachments, and appendices.

Detailed planning   The preliminary plan is prepared in more detail and depth considering the cost factor as well.

Execution   Planning does not happen on paper alone. The project has to be executed or implemented according to its plan. (This will be discussed in detail in Chapter 14.)

Testing and commissioning   Finally, a project should take its original shape as per the plan. In this last phase, project managers must take a re-look at their work and if there are any discrepancies, alternative ways to mend them must be found. (This will be discussed in detail in Chapter 15.)

13.5 VARIOUS COMPONENTS OF PROJECT PLANNING

For a successful project plan, a project manager requires certain information. This is mainly of two types—customer and environmental input (Figure 13.4).

Customer input   It consists of work schedules, i.e., a listing of activities, the possible interrelationships between activities, activity time estimates, activity cost estimates, project specifications, and appropriate project schedules (bar charts, milestone charts, PERT/CPM network, etc.).

Environmental input It consists of the following appraisals from various departments.

Legal appraisal This is to check whether the proposed project is being executed within the specified legal conditions. It is the first prerequisite input for preparing a project plan.

Social appraisal This is a social cost-benefit analysis which is concerned with judging a project from a larger social point of view. In such an evaluation, the focus is on the social cost and benefit of a project, which may often be different from its monetary costs and benefits.

Technological appraisal This reviews the technological aspects of projects, such as location, size processes, site selection, etc. It also screens the incorporation of all factors responsible for effective formulation of a given project.

Economical appraisal It reviews the economic sustainability of a given project, along with its market value. A project involves several economic processes, such as the loan value, the expected returns, and so on. These processes must be resolved in favour of the project for it to become successful.

Political appraisal The influence and impact of political power cannot be ignored during project planning. It is important to position the project in such a manner that it does not suffer from any political hindrance during its term of execution or later.

Ecological appraisal Today, environmental issues are of paramount importance. An ecological appraisal looks into the feasibility of certain kinds of projects, such as irrigation set ups, power plants, chemical industries, leather processing, etc., which pose significant threat to the environment.

After integrating customer and environmental input, a project manager formulates the plan, which is finalized after several iterations (Cleland and King 1975), as shown Figure 13.4.

13.6 PROJECT SUCCESS AND FAILURE—ATTRIBUTES AND MEASURES

Sometimes a certain project, even after meeting its standard goals, is perceived as a failure. The reason behind this consideration is that either it is not completed within the estimated time period or within the budgeted cost, or all the technical specifications have not been met. Whereas at other times, a project is considered a success even if it fails to meet the two important objective standards related with success, i.e., time and cost.

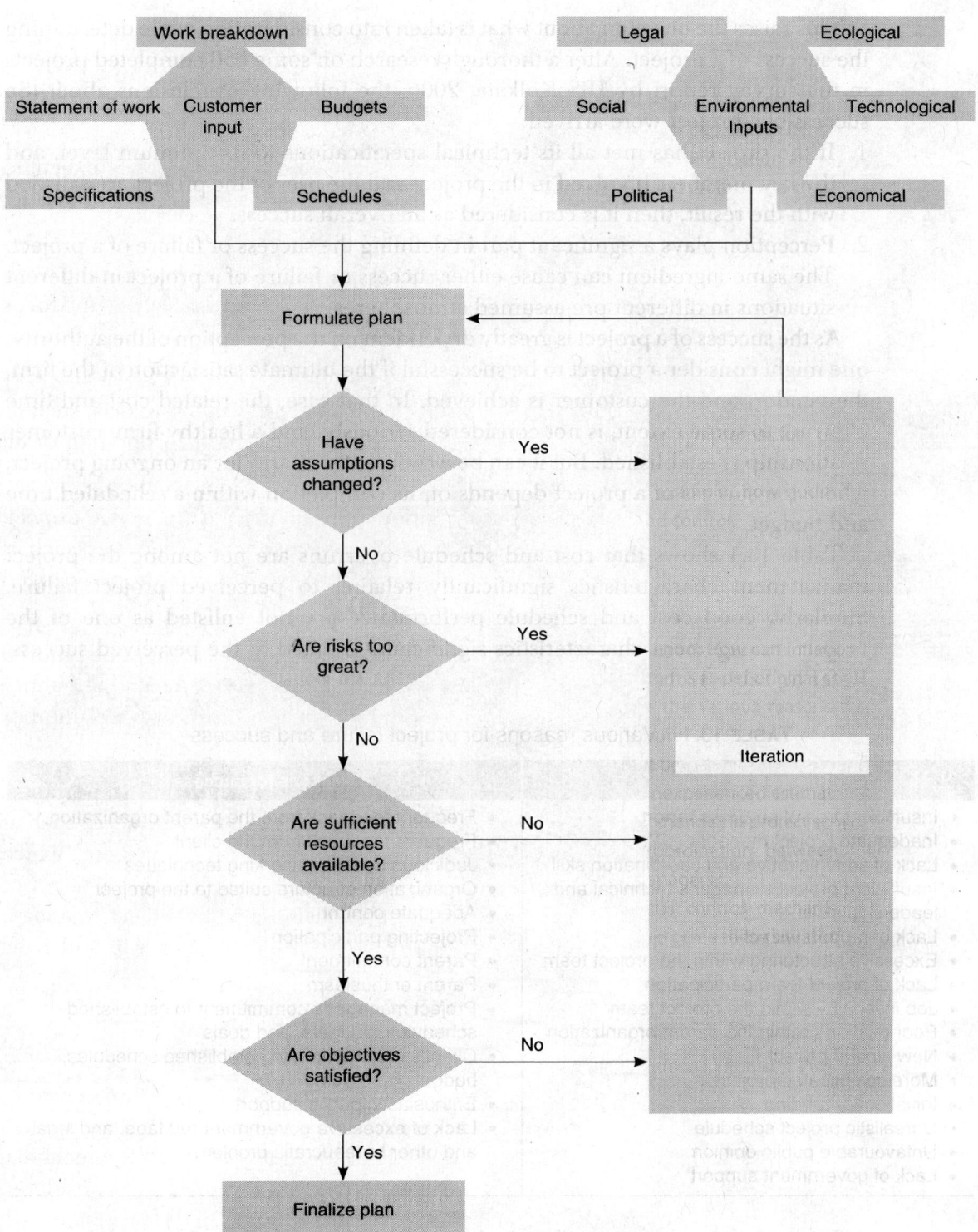

FIGURE 13.4   Various inputs required for project planning

This raises the question about what is taken into consideration while determining the success of a project. After a thorough research on some 650 completed projects in the survey report by IBS Kolkata, 2006, the following conclusions about the success of a project were arrived:

1. If the project has met all its technical specifications to its optimum level, and the key members involved in the project and the user of the project are satisfied with the result, then it is considered as an overall success.

2. Perception plays a significant part in defining the success or failure of a project. The same ingredient can cause either success or failure of a project in different situations in different pre-assumed atmospheres.

As the success of a project is greatly dependent on the perception of the authority, one might consider a project to be successful if the ultimate satisfaction of the firm, the vendor, and the customer is achieved. In that case, the related cost and time overrun, to some extent, is not considered seriously, and a healthy firm–customer relationship is established. But it can be a different scenario for an ongoing project, where the success of a project depends on its completion within a scheduled time and budget.

Table 13.1 shows that cost and schedule overruns are not among the project management characteristics significantly relating to perceived project failure. Similarly, good cost and schedule performance are not enlisted as one of the project management characteristics significantly related to the perceived success. Refer to Table 13.1.

TABLE 13.1 Various reasons for project failure and success

Reasons for failure	Reasons for success
• Insufficient use of progress report	• Frequent feedback from the parent organization
• Inadequate project manager	• Frequent feedback from the client
• Lack of administrative and coordination skill	• Judicious use of networking techniques
• Insufficient project manager's technical and leadership skills	• Organization structure suited to the project
• Lack of rapport with client	• Adequate control
• Excessive structuring within the project team	• Projecting participation
• Lack of project team participation	• Parent commitment
• Job insecurity within the project team	• Parent enthusiasm
• Poor relations within the parent organization	• Project manager's commitment to established schedules, budgets, and goals
• New type of project	• Client's commitment to established schedules, budgets, and goals
• More complicated project	• Enthusiastic public support
• Initial under funding	• Lack of excessive government red tape, and legal and other bureaucratic problems
• Unrealistic project schedule	
• Unfavourable public opinion	
• Lack of government support	

In conclusion, we can say that the key contributors to project failure and success are:

1. Goal commitment
2. Accurate initial cost estimates
3. Adequate project team capability
4. Adequate funding to completion
5. Optimum planning and control techniques
6. Minimal start-up difficulties
7. Task vs social orientation
8. Absence of bureaucracy
9. On-site project manager

A study conducted on an aerospace project showed that it had taken into consideration only 20 per cent of the whole list of reasons mentioned above for the success of its project. It has also been seen that to a project personnel who has always been under tremendous pressure of completing a task within the scheduled time and cost, the negative outcome certainly comes as a surprise.

13.7 TIME OVERRUN AND COST OVERRUN

For any project to be effective, the scheduled time of completion as well as the allocated cost needs to be maintained. These two terms—time overrun and cost overrun—determine how a project is managed, and help identify remedial measures for future projects for any organization to undertake.

When a specific project requires more time than it is budgeted for, the situation is known as leading to time overrun. Whereas, cost overrun would involve a specific project requiring more cost than it is budgeted. In an inflationary economy, generally, time overrun leads to cost overrun.

Time overrun or cost overrun may lead to stopping and even abandoning of projects.

Some of the reasons for time overruns and cost overruns:
1. Final achievement of the objectives
2. Poor initial planning and market prognosis
3. Better alternative being found
4. Change in the company interest and strategy
5. Allocated time being exceeded
6. Budgeted cost being exceeded
7. Key people having left the organization
8. Personal whims of management
9. Problem too complex for the resources available

The construction of the Vivekananda Setu or the Second Hoogly Bridge on the River Ganga and the Kolkata Metro Rail project are examples of time and cost overrun which happened due to poor initial planning, insufficient allocated time, and project complexity. In both cases, as time exceeded, the cost also increased due to inflation and other related reasons.

The statistics for the period starting from April 1992 to March 2009 by the Ministry of Statistics and Programme Implementation (MOSPI), India, shows that a total of 894 infrastructure projects are running with both cost and time overrun in the country at various sectors such as petroleum, railways, power, road and transport, coal, shipping and ports, etc. The percentage of projects with cost overrun is 40.72, whereas the percentage of projects with time overrun is 82.3, and the percentage of projects running with cost, but not time, overrun, is 3.13 (Singh 2009).

The Kabul 105 Mega Watt Power Plant Project is a very famous example for cost and time overrun. Table 13.2 enumerates various reasons for the delaying of the Kabul project in detail.

Source: Black and Veatch.

Kabul Power Plant as of 21 October 2009

Instead of quantitative reasons, it is behavioural patterns, such as low labour productivity, lack of encouragement, etc., that are the most prominent reasons why projects are not completed within the framework of limited time and cost.

It is important to put a closure on a project, once reasons for its termination are analysed and accepted. Withdrawal and reassigning of the human resources to some higher priority, and stopping the inflow of capital, are some of the methods of planned termination of projects. Three important areas to be considered while putting an end to a project are as follows:

1. *Morale of workers*—When a project is to be terminated before completion, the workers' morale and psychology, and basic human values should be considered as topmost priority.

TABLE 13.2 Factors contributing to Kabul 105 MW Power Plant Project delays

Factors	USAID Inspector General's findings
Land issues	The project was partly delayed by a land ownership issue which took almost a year to resolve due to USAID/Afghanistan's failure to obtain an advanced commitment from the host government.
Ambiguous statement of work	Under the pressure of political urgency, the mission wrote a vague statement of work.
Delays in subcontract award and mobilization	Numerous delays occurred in the award and mobilization of subcontract. According to the USAID Inspector General's report, Black and Veatch told Symbion Power that its subcontract will be awarded in April 2008, and that its mobilization effort could begin in May 2008. However, the final subcontract was not signed until early June 2008.
Subcontractors performance problem	Caterpillar, the firm that manufactured 18 generators, notified Black and Veatch that a quality control problem would delay delivery of the generators of block B and C. The delivery schedule of block B slipped by 88 days and for block C by 15 days.
Lack of timely approval	Black and Veatch contended that the approval for the critical tasks required, for a fast-track project like this, was delayed at the mission. The mission agrees that all parties to the process should have been involved from the beginning in deciding how to transport the generators. This particular approval was taking longer than expected. This one contract modification took two months to approve—a critical delay for a fast-track project
Lack of on site quality assurance	Quality assurance construction activities is normally conducted on site, either by independently contracted engineers or missions local staffs. However, USAID/Afghanistan have this practice documented in its procedures, and in this case the mission did not have an on-site presence.
Inconsistent communication between USAID and Black and Veatch	Specifically, a contractor's internal report dated December 2008 and detailing problems in delivering the completed facility on time was not provided until mid-January. Further delays in custom clearance as well as the inability to obtain work visas were not communicated promptly to the mission. The mission contended that had it known of all the problems the contractor was experiencing, it could have intervened sooner to help resolve the problems.
Transport and Custom Delays	The project also suffered from a series of transportation delays. Especially, there were problems with clearing items through customs at border crossing and finding drivers wiling to transport items from the borders of Pakistan to Kabul. Also items such as transmission towers and raw materials were delayed at border crossings.

Source: Office of the USAID Inspector General's report, 2010.

2. *Reassignment of workforce*—The existing pool of workforce should be relocated to another project and their jobs reassigned at the earliest.

3. *Wrap up*—When a particular project comes to an end, the entire unit should be packed up and migrated to the next destination.

A project can be cancelled at any point during its lifetime. Cost overrun is usually not the reason why projects are terminated, as the project under consideration may not entirely be responsible for the cost overrun. For example, if project A appears to be successful, the resources of A are used for another less successful project, say B. The cost of project A increases drastically because all remaining activities now become critical to complete project A. The increasing cost for project A is linked with time and other factors. Costs for project B are directly related to time, and more activities are being carried out as more manpower is available. Though the manpower is working for project B, the cost for it is charged to project A, because the money is allocated from the budget of project A.

The net output is that both projects exceed the authorized budgets by about the same percentage, due to undue circumstances. That is why the top management neither pats nor blames any of the project teams, either for success or for failure. To achieve an anticipated wholesome target, corporate management will distribute success and failure uniformly, rather than increase the performance level of a particular project only.

13.8 ENHANCING THE SUCCESS OF A PROJECT—KEY AREAS AND ISSUES

In section 13.6, we have discussed that various attributes act as catalysts, either for the success or failure of a project, or even both. This section focuses on the key areas which appear to be most significant for reaching a high level of perceived success.

Going back to the points provided in Table 13.1, which discuss the variables responsible for the failure of a particular project, it is found that most of them revolve around the poor level of coordination and human relation prototypes. Therefore, to avoid these, project managers should stress upon improving human relationships and networking. Also, they should try to make the working environment more cordial and friendly. Though such amendments may eliminate the risk of failure of a project, they cannot increase the probability of its success. The factors that are important to achieve success for a project have been discussed in Table 13.1.

Effective project planning is absolutely essential for a project to succeed. Of the items listed in Table 13.1, more than half of the variables, such as insufficient use of progress report, administrative and coordination skills, new type of project, unrealistic project schedule, etc., are associated with perceived failure. They can be avoided through effective project planning. The role of project planning is even more apparent in Table 13.1. Finally, all items discussed earlier in section 13.7

are highly correlated to the project planning process. For example, absence of bureaucracy is an obvious and valid reason for project success. It also acts as a check point for the progress of the project. Similarly, it can be applicable for other cases also. In conclusion, we can say that the reasons for project success or failure are not mutually exclusive.

SUMMARY

Planning, in a project environment, may be described as establishing a predetermined course of action within a forecasted environment. It is important in a project environment to avoid tasks of reallocation, rescheduling, and re-prioritizing of resources. The attributes of a good plan should include proper definitions of goals, work description, schedule, budget, etc. The various components of project planning basically include customer inputs and environment inputs. Time overrun and cost overrun help managers determine ways of identifying and managing factors for future projects.

KEY TERMS

Cost overrun   When a project needs more money than the allocated budget, it is known as cost overrun. In an inflationary economy, generally time overrun leads to cost overrun. Due to time overrun or cost overrun, sometimes projects have to be stopped.

Milestone schedule   The schedule is a gross schedule and includes things such as start date, end date, major milestones, written reports (data items), etc.

Project life cycle planning   The project life cycle planning approach provides a method for uniformity in project planning. It consists of conceptualization, feasibility, preliminary planning, detail planning, execution, testing and commissioning of a project.

Statement of work (SOW)   A narrative description of the work to be accomplished, which includes the objectives of the project, a brief description of the work, the funding constraints (if any), and the specification and schedule.

Time overrun   When a project needs more time than what it is allocated, it is known as time overrun.

CONCEPT REVIEW QUESTIONS

1. What is project planning and why is it necessary?
2. What are the components of a good plan?
3. What is SOW? Under what conditions it is necessary for initial planning?
4. What are the customer inputs and environmental inputs those are required for project planning?
5. What is project life cycle planning? Describe it with an example that consists of all the different phases of project life cycle.
6. Define time overrun and cost overrun. Enumerate various reasons for time overrun and cost overrun.

CRITICAL THINKING QUESTIONS

1. All management books state that you should plan your work by doing one thing at a time. Can it be true for a project manager's plan also? Justify.

2. The project start up phase is complete and you are now ready to finalize the operational plan. Below are six steps that are often part of the finalization procedure. Place them in correct order:

   (i)   Integrate diagrams in each level until only one exists, then begin integration into higher WBS levels until the desired plan is achieved.

   (ii) Draw diagrams for each individual's WBS element.

   (iii) Create a network diagram and decide upon the WBS.

   (iv) Define the diagram by combining all logic into one plan, then decide upon the work appointments.

   (v)   Establish the WBS and identify the reporting elements and levels.

   (vi) Try to condense the diagram as much as possible without losing clarity.

ASSIGNMENT

A major functional company has a planning group that prepares budgets and selects the projects to be completed within a given time period. As a project manager you are assigned a project which you find should have been started 'last month' in order to meet the completion date. What can you, as a project manager, do about this? Should you delay the start of the project to re-plan the work?

SELECT REFERENCES

Cleland, D.I. and W.R. King, *Systems Analysis and Project Management,* New York, McGraw-Hill, 1975, pp. 371–80.

'Contract Delays Led to Cost Overruns for the Kabul Power Plant and Sustainability Remains a Key Challenge', Special Inspector General for Afghanistan Reconstruction (SIGAR) audit report, USAID, January 2010.

Dilworth, J.B. et al., 'Centralized Project Management', *Journals of Systems Management,* August 1985, pp. 30–35.

Doran, G.T., 'There's a smart way to write management goals and objectives', *Management Review,* November 1981, pp. 35–36.

Kerzner, H., 'Survey of strategic planning variables', Project/Systems Management Research Institute, 1977.

'Search for reasons of successful projects', a survey report prepared by ICFAI Business School Research Centre, Kolkata, 2006.

Singh, R., 'Delays and Cost Overruns in Infrastructure Projects: An Enquiry into Extents, Causes and Remedies', working paper no. 181, Centre for Development Economics, Department of Economics, Delhi School of Economics, August 2009.

CASE STUDY
Royal Park Flyover—It's Still a Dream for Its Residents

The entire locality of Royal Park is discussing only one issue. The municipality has issued a notice to all residents, informing that a flyover will be constructed to connect Royal Park to the city centre. The notice further states that to facilitate the construction, all balconies facing the main road will have to be demolished and owners of all such houses and flats have to sign and submit a consent letter to the chairman within seven days.

There is a mixed reaction to this notice. Most people are unhappy that their balconies will be demolished and their houses will lose the beautiful getup, which is a matter of pride to the residents of Royal Park. However, the proposed flyover would make life easier for everybody; they can reach the city centre within twenty minutes, which presently takes more than one and half hours.

The executive engineer incharge of the project is also a resident of Royal Park. His wife is quite displeased at having to sacrifice her well-maintained balcony with potted plants and a bird's cage. Her son's tricycle and toys are also kept on one side of the balcony, and she does not know where to accommodate them. The executive engineer tries to show his wife some reason—the flyover will help him save time reaching office, and give her more than an hour of extra time in the morning to cook and pack his tiffin. Most importantly, it will make life much easier for their son Rahul—he can sleep half an hour more in the morning and get ready for school leisurely.

Years passed. Rahul is now the executive engineer, and he is in a meeting negotiating with the contractors' union representatives over the progress of the flyover project. The union leaders are bargaining for increased wages, otherwise the workmen will not report for duty. Rahul tries to make them understand that the project is already many years overdue, and cost overrun is unimaginable, and thus, no further wage increase is admissible. The union leaders shout at the top of their voices and leave the meeting room, announcing that the municipality is not interested in completing the project, and hence, they are abandoning the job.

The picturesque Royal Park still stands, its buildings with demolished balconies, and some concrete pillars and unfinished structures. While old residents like Rahul's parents still remember what it is all about, others look at it with surprise and pity.

Discussion questions

1. In your opinion, what could be the possible reasons of time overrun and cost overrun of the flyover projects.

2. With this example, establish that cost overrun and time overrun may even stop the project.

PROJECT EXECUTION

My project has critical time constraints, and the requirements are evolving constantly during the project. Because of turbulence in the market, generating and maintaining the range of documentation required for a typical corporate project would doom this one. We're still disciplined, in rigorous testing for example, but in different ways.

— JIM HIGHSMITH

LEARNING OBJECTIVES

After studying this chapter, you will be able to

- Understand project organization
- Understand the matrix form of project organization
- Explain the recruitment procedures for a project
- Understand the attributes of an effective project manager
- Define various costs involved in a project and budget procedures
- Understand project scheduling and estimation
- Explain various steps in project estimation

Individual or Team Work

Rajiv returned home on Saturday evening wearing a bright smile. Reena, his wife, was more than surprised—she was used to seeing the tired irritated appearance of her husband after a gruelling week. Rajiv explained, 'I am the only one in my department who has been selected for the additional responsibility of looking after the modernization project of my shop. From Monday I shall start my new assignment.' 'Additional responsibility!' exclaimed Reena. 'That means more work, and you will have to deal with a lot more stress and strain. How come you are so glad about it?'

'It is a great achievement, Reena. I shall get an opportunity to put my innovative ideas to do the work better, and my contribution will be noticed by the higher management. I know best how the job can be done,' said Rajiv proudly.

Mr Shaha, the project manager, however, had a tough time handling an over-charged Rajiv. Rajiv always had his own way of doing a job, and considered it the best way. Mr Shaha's instructions were often neglected. What Mr Shaha failed to make Rajiv understand was that the success of the project is more important than any individual achievement.

After bearing with it for a month, Mr Shaha recommended that Rajiv be removed from the project team and be sent back to his original place of work.

Rajiv is back to his old job profile, but he still spends a lot of time glorifying his achievements in the project to his friends and at home.

14.1 PROJECT ORGANIZATION

Project organization is the representation of the different levels of functions and responsibilities assigned to different persons involved in a project. Project organization is also referred to as an organization chart in a particular project. Project organization is represented in a tabular (matrix) form. This form is best suited for project driven companies, such as construction companies. Figure 14.1 shows a typical matrix structure. Each level in the organization has a fixed responsibility and represents a potential profit centre. The project is headed by the general manager, who holds the total authority, responsibility, and accountability for the project. This is passed on by the general manager to the respective project managers. The project manager utilizes this authority to discharge responsibility and is accountable for the success of his/her profit centre. Parallelly, the functional managers have the functional responsibility of maintaining the technical excellence of the project. Each functional manager or departmental manager has the prime responsibility of maintaining a unified technical base and exchanging information for each project. They should also keep their team aware of the latest technical accomplishments of the industry.

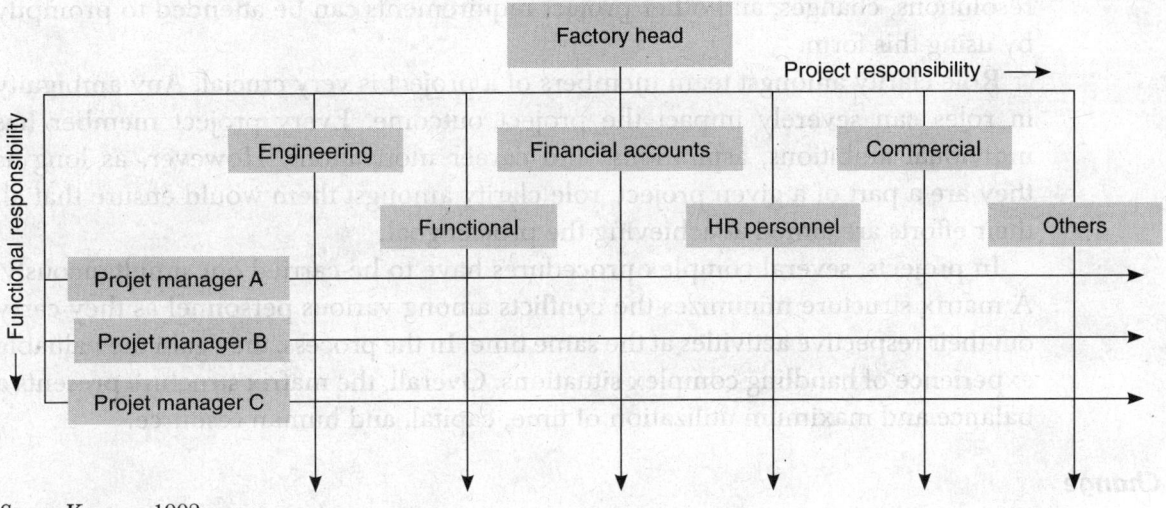

Source: Kerzner 1992.

FIGURE 14.1   Pure matrix structure

A project organization is the effect of the collaboration of different project management tools, which in turn are coordinative functions. In this approach of project management, the work or the task assigned to an individual or a team is specific. The matrix form of the organization is purely collaborative, where information sharing is a must. One of the unique and advantageous features of this form is that the decision-making authority is within the working team.

The following ground rules are laid down for the development of an effective matrix:

1. Participants must spend full time on the project. This ensures the required degree of loyalty.
2. Horizontal as well as vertical channels must exist for making commitments.
3. There must be good communication channels and very quick and effective methods for conflict resolution.
4. All managers must contribute to the planning process.
5. Managers must be ready to negotiate for resources.
6. The horizontal line of the matrix must be permitted to operate as a separate entity except for the administrative process.

These ground rules are the ideal conditions that a matrix structure should possess. Each rule has its advantages and disadvantages.

The matrix form is one of the best modes of project organization. It empowers the project manager to regulate project costs and exercise better control over various team members. Also, this form enables him/her to access and check various procedures and policies of the company. The matrix structure ensures careful and efficient management of the company's resources. The various conflicts, their resolutions, changes, and other project requirements can be attended to promptly by using this form.

Role clarity amongst team members of a project is very crucial. Any ambiguity in roles can severely impact the project outcome. Every project member has individual ambitions, aspirations, and career motivations. However, as long as they are a part of a given project, role clarity amongst them would ensure that all their efforts are aimed at achieving the project goal.

In projects, several complex procedures have to be carried out simultaneously. A matrix structure minimizes the conflicts among various personnel as they carry out their respective activities at the same time. In the process, they gain the valuable experience of handling complex situations. Overall, the matrix structure presents a balance and maximum utilization of time, capital, and human resource.

Change

The matrix form also has a set of shortcomings. It does not offer unidimensional communication. The workforce has to report to multiple managers. As a result, their personal objectives suffer and there is a prevalence of role ambiguity. Also, the management does not share the same goals as the project. Functional managers may place functional priorities over project priorities. Unlike traditional forms, the formulation of policies and processes demand more attention and efforts in the matrix form. Proper balance of power between the project and the functional organizations is another issue of concern. Because of such disadvantages, the matrix form demands a regular monitoring of time, capital, and performance.

Modification of a matrix structure

With a limited number of projects, smaller organizations practise unidimensional reporting. The project manager directly communicates with the general manager, who coordinates the activities of various projects and resolves the conflicts, if any, among them. As there are a limited numbers of projects to be handled, it is supposed that the general manager would have enough time to attend to every project manager.

However, such an arrangement becomes unfeasible with the increase in the size of the company. A general manger can no longer handle the various project issues alone. A new designation, called manager or director of programmes, is created to take over the responsibility from the general manager. The manager of programmes (MPMs) now, on the whole, looks after the various projects and their associated processes. The primary role of project managers is explained by Wysocki, Beck, and Crane (2000).

Unlike project managers, the MPMs are not supposed to involve themselves with the minute details of the projects. They are responsible for the overview of the projects under them. They have to make sure that project goals align with the organization goals. Also, they have to check the interrelation amongst various projects and resolve conflicts.

An MPM is a project manager, resource manager, a change manager, and a systems manager. This means that MPMs manage the project, manage the fund, implement changes, provide physical and IT infrastructure, etc. All these roles are equally important. The role of an MPM is the overall management of projects, which involves leading and instructing the workforce. They have to plan changes in the organization, along with management of different project initiatives. They are also responsible for facilitating communication amongst the higher management, the project management department, and the system department.

14.2 PROJECT STAFFING

Project management can only be successful if the individuals who are in charge of the key functions meet expectations. It is not a one person affair; it requires a group of individuals dedicated to the achievement of a single goal. It includes a project manager, a project office, and a project team. Project office personnel are assigned full time to the project and report directly to the project manager; they may be attached to their line function only for administrative control. The project team also comprises members who work from outside the project office. In small projects, project team members often manage the entire show. Sometimes one person may be filling in all the project office positions.

The staff functions begin with the following five basic questions:

1. What are the requirements of an individual to become a successful project manager?
2. Who should be a member of the project team?
3. Who should be a member of the project office?
4. What are the problems that can occur during recruiting activities?
5. What can happen downstream to cause loss of a key team member?

Initially, it may appear that these questions are not so difficult to answer. But as they are placed against a project environment, they can take a very complex shape. This is true especially if the organization is not equipped with able and adequate staff. Initially, there may be a conflict between project members, which needs to be resolved first. However, the primary and the most important factor that works in project staffing is the priority that is set for the given number of staff.

The staffing environment

To understand staffing environment, and more importantly the problem encountered during project staffing, it is important to analyse problems related to the project environment. The major problem in project environment is that of 'personal performance problem'. This problem is encountered because project environment includes a change in the way of working. Individuals, regardless of their competence, find it difficult to continuously adapt to changing situations and reporting to multiple managers. Projects, by definition, are temporary assignments. Most individuals prefer a stable situation to work efficiently. However, there are many individuals who look at such temporary assignments as their 'chance of glory'. Such people are highly creative and enjoy challenging jobs. To them, challenge is more important than the cost of failure.

Unfortunately, some people often tend to consider the chance of glory more important than the project itself. They may perform a task in their own way, without following the instructions of the project manager, because they think that they know the job better. The objective of the project and its ultimate success is immaterial to them. They only want to be recognized for their individual achievements. In case the project fails, such individuals still have a functional area to go back to. (As in the case of Rajiv in the opening case of this chapter.) In cricket and other sports, the team performance matters more than the individual efforts.

The next major performance problem that lies in project and functional interface is where an individual suddenly finds himself/herself reporting to two bosses—the functional manager and the project manager. If the functional manager and the project manager are in total agreement, the performance of the interface is satisfactory. But if the individuals at the interface receive conflicting directives, they are left in a compromising situation and their performance suffers. In this situation, the employee's performance is controlled by the manager who holds the purse strings.

Successful project management

The achievement of a set of goals through a project is made possible through proper project management. Administrative processes require inter-linkages among various projects. But other than that, project management allows the autonomous functioning of each project. Under the larger goals and guidelines of the higher management, projects are allowed to chart and follow their own policies, processes, rules, and standards. Top management bestows the authority to handle these unique project activities on the respective project managers.

Project management is successful only if the project manager and his/her team are totally dedicated to the goal of the project. This requires each team member, of the project team and office, to have a good sense of the primary target of the project. Successful project completion requires fulfilment of the activities such as customer liaison, project direction, project planning, project control, project evaluation, and project reporting.

Every individual involved in the project, i.e., each member of the project office and the project team, must be convinced to satisfy these requirements. To fulfil these requirements, all the participants, including functional representatives, must work together as a team. Team work is vital for the success of a project.

Attributes of a project manager

The person who plays the most important role in the successful completion of the project is the key project manager. Personal attributes and abilities of a project manager either attract or deter other potentially competent team members. Hence, certain qualities are mandatory for a good and effective key project manager, such as

- Honesty and integrity
- Ability to evaluate risk and uncertainty
- Understanding of project technology
- People management capability and understanding of the human element of a project
- Competence in business management principles and good communication
- Versatility
- Alertness
- Energy and toughness
- Prompt decision-making ability

A project manager must exhibit honesty and integrity with subordinates as well as line personnel and foster an atmosphere of trust. He/she should not make false or impossible promises, such as immediate promotions. Honesty, integrity, and handling of human issues of the project team can eliminate problems and conflicts and lead to a creation of a truly dedicated project environment.

Project mangers are required to have both business and technological knowledge. They must understand the fundamentals of business management and effective communication channels. Project managers should have knowledge about the technical implications of a problem, as they are ultimately responsible for proper decision-making. They may have a group of technical professionals to assist them. However, the project manager's role is basically management oriented. Many technically competent project managers have failed because they became more involved in the technical side of the project rather than the management side. Technical expertise is ideal. But if the individual tends to become a generalist without a sense of business management, it can become a major problem. This eventually leads to the failure of the project in the extreme case.

As a project is a relatively short duration affair, a prompt decision-making ability of the project manager is pivotal to its success. The project manager must be alert and quick. Versatility and toughness, in order to keep subordinates dedicated to the achievement of the project goal, is essential. The primary objective of the project manager, with regard to staffing, is to acquire the best available human resource and try to improve them. Project managers should provide a good working environment to personnel and make sure that all resources are applied effectively, so that constraints can be met to the extent possible.

14.3 PROJECT BUDGETING

A budget refers to a broad plan regarding quantitative utilization of resources over a period of time. In the case of a project, this process is called project budgeting. Preparing a project budget basically concerns the estimation of its net cost. Project cost is always directly proportional to time. Therefore, a project is divided into different temporal phases.

Time-phased budget

Cost estimates alone do not make a budget. A cost estimate takes the shape of a budget only when it is time determined. It is very important to make a cost estimate which is linked with time, which makes it possible to get full control over the budget. Suppose a budget is estimated at Rs 10,00,00,000, there must be a definite procedure for the distribution of this amount. The whole project is divided into work packages, and all these work packages require a time-phased budget (as shown in Table 14.1). The work packages generally have a duration of three weeks. At this stage it is not possible to assess the allocation of the money at every level. This work package duration, and other factors, are used to prepare the project network schedule. The time-phased budgets are then allocated according to the scheduled time period over the life of the project. In this way, the total capital need of the project can be determined. The time-phased budget should show how, when, and what amount of the real cash is needed in a project.

TABLE 14.1 Work packages estimates

Work package description		
Work package ID: 1.3.45 Deliverable: Engine Organization unit: Automobiles Work package: 3 weeks		Project: Conversion into LPG engine Date: 15/01/2010 Estimator: KPMG Total budget: Rs 758

Time-phased budget (Rs in lakhs)							
Direct costs	Rate	Work periods					Total
		1	2	3	4	5	
Material costs	@ Rs x/hr	30	40	50			
Labour costs							
Skilled	@ Rs y1/hr	20	30	30			
Semi-skilled	@ Rs y2/hr	20	20	20			
Unskilled	@ Rs y3/hr	15	20	20			
Total labour costs		55	70	70			
Overheads costs	@ Rs z/hr	20	35	35			
Other costs		15	15	20			
Total costs		120	160	175			Rs 455

Source: Kerzner 1992.

Every project manager has his/her own perception of cost and budget. Figure 14.2 describes the various perceptions and three different possibilities of the cost structure of a particular project. Before actual resources are used, a project manager can anticipate and assign costs for a particular job much ahead of that. It helps the finance manager to estimate future cash flows. The project manager is actually interested in three types of timings. They are

1. The time when budgeted cost is anticipated to occur (committed cost)
2. When the estimated cost is actually spent (scheduled budgeted cost)
3. Finally, at the end, when the actual cost evolves (actual cost)

Cost variances and project schedule should be prepared on the basis of these three cost figures.

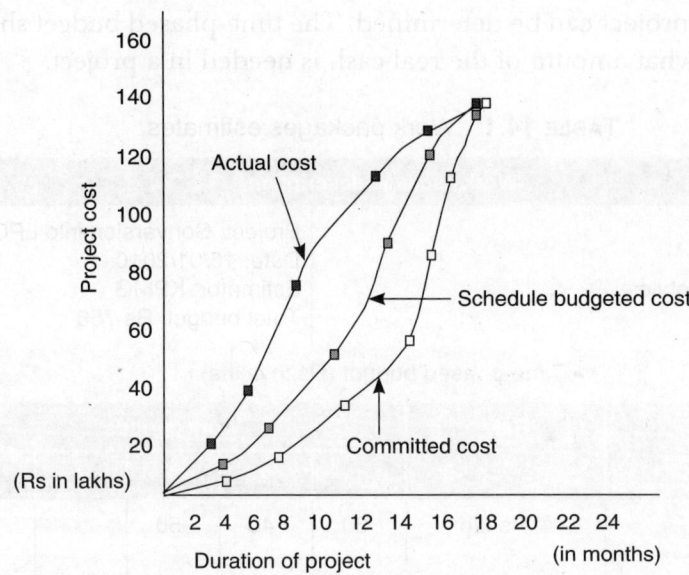

FIGURE 14.2 Three different views of cost and cost variance

Types of costs

The precision of cost estimates improves as one moves from the conceptual stage to the next level where individual work packages are defined. Detailed cost estimates can only be made when the work packages are defined. Costs that are usually involved in a project are direct costs, and direct and indirect project overheads. The reason for breaking up the total cost estimation is to tighten the grip over the process and improve decision-making.

Direct costs In cost accounting concept, direct costs are directly related to the production, or operation, or the main business of the firm. They include direct material and labour costs. In the case of project budgeting, direct costs can be defined as those costs that are related to some particular work package. It clearly depends upon the project manager, the teams, or the individuals involved in that particular work package of the concerned project. These costs are the main cash outflow that must be paid as the project starts rolling. Lower level projects usually have only direct costs.

Direct project overhead costs In management accounting, overheads are considered as the cost excluding material and labour. They can be cost for fuel, electricity, etc.

Project overhead rates more specifically show the resources of the organization that are to be used in a particular project. Direct overhead costs can be related to project work packages. Examples of direct overhead costs can be the salary of the project manager and rent for the space required by the project team. These are not immediate expenses but they are plausible and must be taken care of in the long run.

Indirect project overhead costs These costs are usually those organizational costs that are not directly related to the project. These costs are borne during the project duration. These expenses are spent commonly on all the products or projects of the organization such as advertising, accounting, administration, and other commercial purposes. These costs are usually a percentage of the total direct cost and generally vary for different organisations.

For a given direct cost and direct overhead cost for a specific job, indirect cost will generally be given a percentage of total direct cost. After that, a percentage margin out of the total cost will be considered as a profit for a contractor. A break up of an entire cost sheet for a proposed agreement is depicted in Table 14.2.

TABLE 14.2   Cost summary for a contract bid

	Rs
Direct costs	100,000
Direct overhead costs	30,000
Total direct costs	130,000
Indirect overhead costs (25%)	32,500
Total costs	162,500
Profit (15%)	24,375
Total bid	186,875

14.4 PROJECT SCHEDULING

It is a process by which a detailed breakup of project activities is listed, so that the final goal or objectives can be achieved. It helps in clearly stating what activities are to be performed and by whom. When the team members are well aware of their responsibilities, the movement of the project towards its completion is faster.

A schedule should have a specific start and end time. During this entire journey, it requires resources such as time, cost, and labour. The effectiveness of project scheduling depends on the optimal use of resources without compromising quality. The various types of project scheduling processes, such as CPM, PERT, GERT, etc., have been already discussed in detail in Chapter 2. It has also been elaborately explained how project scheduling can be done with constraint resources.

Project estimation

Project implementation demands careful utilization of three important resources, namely, human resource, material resource, and time. It helps in avoiding time and cost overrun in projects. Therefore, proper estimation of resource requirement in a project is a must. Post-resource estimation, a comprehensive programme cost should be prepared. It involves estimation of the cost and time required to carry out different project-related activities. Activities are priced out over the scheduled period of performance. These pricing units (various units, sections, or departments) present the real and usable cost information. In an ideal situation, historical standards determine the man hours required to carry out a particular task.

Hence, it will not be a logical idea to consider these historical data as standard at the time of estimation.

During the implementation of any project, special caution must be taken against various uncertain factors such as inflation, cost escalation, risks, etc. Project management is greatly influenced by its environment, which is not constant. In such a situation, it is essential to consider the above mentioned factors for estimation vis-à-vis the project.

Project management involves optimum usage of resources within limited time and cost. The eleven steps in Figure 14.3 comprise a logical project estimation technique. They are dependent upon the company type.

Project estimation mainly means scheduling of projects. Project scheduling can be done by PERT, CPM, Gantt chart, etc., which have been discussed in Chapter 2. Besides time and activity scheduling, estimation also includes manpower, monetary, material, and machinery resources. That is why it is very useful to curb the problem of project overrun and underrun through effective and efficient project estimation.

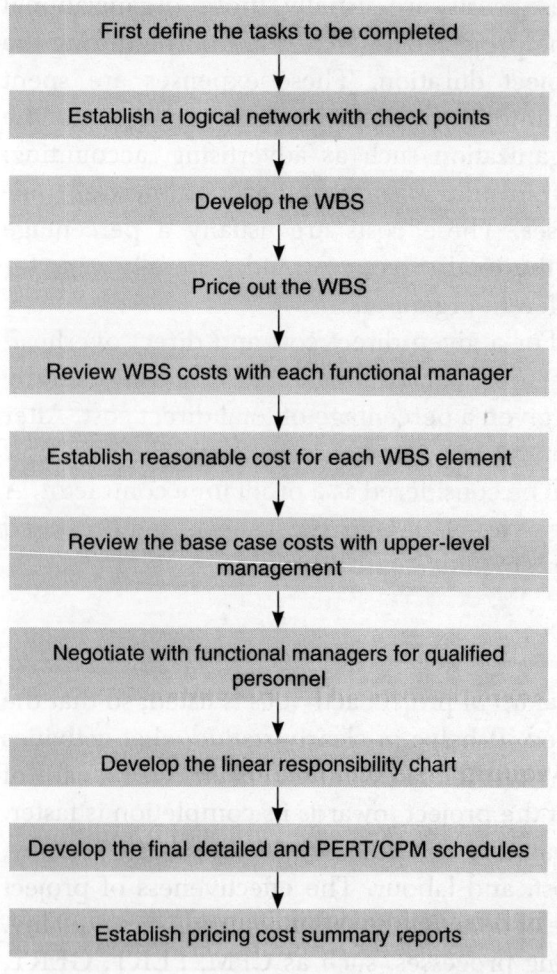

FIGURE 14.3 Steps in project estimation

First define the tasks to be completed

Establish a logical network with check points

Develop the WBS

Price out the WBS

Review WBS costs with each functional manager

Establish reasonable cost for each WBS element

Review the base case costs with upper-level management

Negotiate with functional managers for qualified personnel

Develop the linear responsibility chart

Develop the final detailed and PERT/CPM schedules

Establish pricing cost summary reports

SUMMARY

Project organization is the representation of the different levels of roles and responsibilities assigned to different people involved in a specific project. Successful project management is not a one-person affair; it requires an efficient leader and a group of individuals working as a team, dedicated to the achievement of the project goal. Costs that are usually involved in a project are direct costs, and direct and indirect project overheads. A proper estimation of resource requirement in a project is also vital as it helps in avoiding time and cost overrun in projects.

KEY TERMS

Direct costs In the cost accounting concept, direct costs are the costs which are directly related to the production, operation, or the main business of the firm. They include direct material and labour cost.

Direct project overhead costs In management accounting, overheads are considered as other costs excluding material and labour. They can include costs for fuel, electricity, etc.

Indirect project overhead costs These costs are usually those organizational costs that are indirectly related to the project. These costs are revealed over the project duration. These expenses are spent commonly for all products or projects of the organization, such as advertising, accounting, administration, and other commercial purposes.

Project budgeting It refers to the estimation of the cost required to complete a project. But the cost of a project is directly proportional to project time. Hence, project budgeting is a totally time bound estimation.

Project scheduling It is a process by which the detailed break up of the project activities are listed, so that finally final goal or objectives are achieved. Hence, it should have a specific start and end, and during this entire journey it requires resources such as time, cost and performance.

CONCEPT REVIEW QUESTIONS

1. Define project organization. Differentiate it from any formal organizational structure.

2. How can a matrix structure of organization be modified in the case of project organization?

3. Who is more important for the success of a project—the leader, his team members, or both? Justify your answer with illustrations.

CRITICAL THINKING QUESTIONS

1. Consider pursuing your two years of management study as a project of your life. Then prepare a time phased budget with numerical figures for this project. Do a variance analysis also, considering all the three types of costs which are discussed in this chapter.

2. Suppose that your mother wants to start the construction of a duplex apartment after retirement for residential purpose. Advise her with all the necessary steps required for estimating costs, time, and resources, for this particular project.

ASSIGNMENT

From the concept of work breakdown structure (WBS) (discussed in Chapter 2) design a project budget for that institute building project. Organize it according to its hierarchy by specific job, tasks, etc.

SELECT REFERENCES

Kerzner, H., *Project Management—A Systems Approach to Planning, Scheduling and Controlling*, 4e., New York, International Thomson Publishing, 1992.

Wysocki, R.K., R. Beck, and D.B. Crane, *Effective Project Management*, 2e, New York, John Wiley, 2000.

CASE STUDY
Hazra's Dilemma

Sumit Hazra has been appointed project manager of the Widal Company's new boiler manufacturing process project. Boilers are extremely price sensitive. But Widal has done a great deal of quantitative work. So it can accurately forecast changes in sales volume, relative to changes in pricing.

The CEO of the company, Mr J.K. Iyer, has enough faith in the firm's sensitivity model. He insists that all projects that affect the manufacturing cost of boilers be run against the sensitivity model, in order to gather information for calculating the ROI.

The output is that the project manager, Hazra, is under tremendous pressure to submit realistic budgets. Also, he needs to work towards taking a decision on whether the project would be continued or not.

In this process, Iyer has cancelled several projects which overestimated the project cost. Out of them, one particular project was stopped by Iyer in its initial stage. He also fired the concerned project manager, Mr Ranade. But after eight months or so, BDR Companies, a competitor of Widal, launched a similar boiler and became highly successful.

Hazra is considering how to prepare a budget which exactly reflects the cost of the original project. He has an experience of more than ten years in project evaluation, and feels quite confident while doing it. Simultaneously, he also remembers Ranade's case.

Only one stage out of the traditional four stages of boiler manufacturing process will be changed, for which he needs the cost information. Further, this new modification may cause some minor changes in the three later stages. This particular first stage consumes roughly around half of the total project cost.

Discussion question

In this scenario, discuss whether Hazra would pursue the same conventional budgeting mechanism or a completely different one. Or would he consider the cost effect of respective changes of the first stage?

PROJECT CONTROL AND AUDIT

External audits are routine in the financial area. I fail to understand why non-profitable organizations don't use them more in the vital programme areas also.

— E. STOESZ

LEARNING OBJECTIVES

After studying this chapter, you will be able to

- Understand how to monitor, review, and control project cost
- Explain the termination of a project, its types, and symptoms
- Understand the requirement and process of project audits

Need for Programme Control System

A few years back, DXL Lab took a decision to create a research project management system, including a programme control segment, for projects costing over Rs 1 crore. As a part of the management information and support function, the programme control specialists are charged with development, implementation, and maintenance of programme control system for DXL Lab's research programmes. These systems are not the usual monitoring systems used to provide information to top management for decision-making. Their main objective is to look after the lower level project managers, contract administrator, personnel specialists, and others who have a direct impact on project success or failure.

The objective of the programme control segment is to assure a quality product, on schedule and within budget. In some government projects, such as with DRDO or National Productivity Council, the implementation of a full cost-schedule control system criteria is required for control purposes. For many other projects, particularly R&D projects, such control is not required. With a good system in place, chances of cost overruns, time overruns, and missing of scheduled milestones are reduced. Hence, there is a need for a proper programme control function like that of DXL Lab.

Since its introduction, the benefits of this function in their project management system have only increased. In a Rs 18-crore telephone line alignment and development programme under the Ministry of Telecommunications, DXL's programme control function is credited with achieving a high level of success and an overall performance rating of 'excellent'. Again, in another power sector programme, 'outstanding' performance rating was achieved. Paying attention to the control aspect of project management appears to be highly beneficial.

Source: Adapted from Johnson 1985.

15.1 PROJECT MONITORING AND CONTROL

From a philosophical perspective, 'control' can never be defined in a nut shell. There has been an age-old opinion that control can only be exercised where there is an authority for making decisions. In this case, it lies with the project managers, line supervisors, and design engineers. The fundamental units of control are cost estimate and project schedule. Often, a cost and schedule engineer only provides information and does not exercise control. It actually depends on the execution and delivery of works. If a task is performed as per schedule, monitoring and control will then be an automatic and obvious process. However, reporting, trending, and analysis are the main ingredients of control.

Often, project managers jump to conclusions regarding projects, without having discussions with its functional arms. This can have an adverse effect on the project. In the case of large projects, resource requirements, control systems, and organizational arrangements should be discussed, to ensure the availability of the estimated manpower and resources during the execution of the project. Whatever may be the project size, the proposed plan and execution strategy are the most important factors for considering the basis of control.

The effectiveness of a project control programme is mainly dependent on the reliability of the following information and guidance:
- Estimating project schedules
- Manpower planning
- Determining productivity level
- Developing a cost schedule
- Trend analysis
- Evaluating the performance of the work
- Identifying the scope of the work

Figure 15.1 shows the over-scheduling relationship of an EPC (engineering, procurement, and construction) project. This figure contains only the execution phase; a conceptual design phase precedes this phase where the exact planning is done. The entire schedule is demonstrated with a trapezoid and the entire complex work is executed in three phases—a build up (20% of overall duration), a peak period (another 20%), and a rundown (the remaining 60% of the overall duration) of the engineering schedule. The engineering schedule is the same schedule as the overall project duration. The schedule ratios are based on historical experience and specific standards.

The second part of Figure 15.1 shows the trapezoid for the construction schedule. To determine the peak duration (X), the following information is either known or is to be assumed (Kerzner 1992):
1. Scope in man hours
2. Effective monthly hours per man

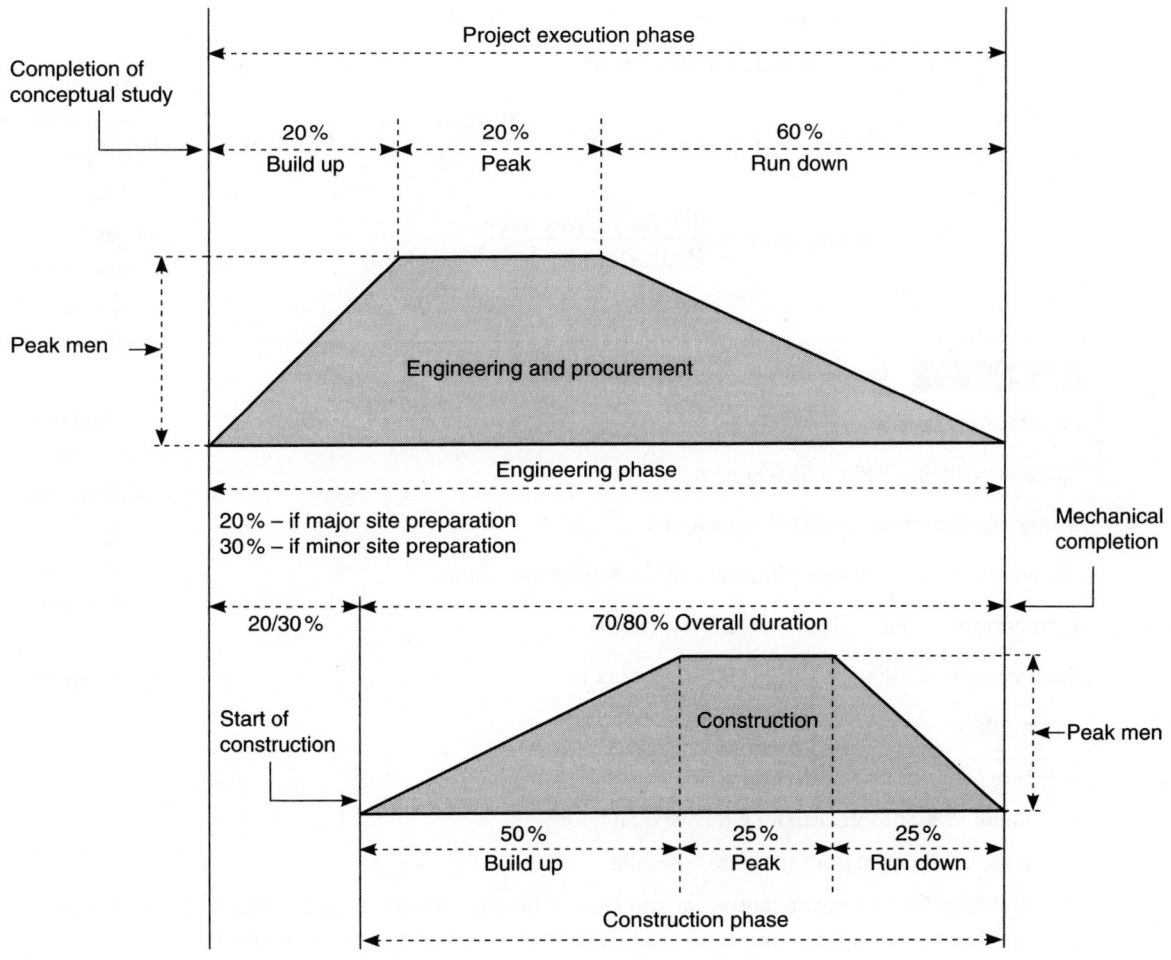

Source: Kerzner 1992.

FIGURE 15.1 Overall project scheduling in execution phase

3. Build up (standard schedule) in months
4. Peak in months
5. Rundown (half of build up) in months
6. Peak men (explained in Example 15.1)

If the limit area or the plot plan is known, then by evaluating a labour density level (generally in the range of 150 to 300 sq. ft per man), one can determine the peak number of men (refer to Figure 15.2).

The calculation for the construction duration will be as follows (trapezoidal technique):

$$\text{Area} = \text{Scope}\left(\frac{M}{H}\right) \tag{15.1}$$

$$\frac{\text{Scope in man hours}}{\text{Effective monthly man hours}} = \left[\frac{\text{Build up}}{2}\right]$$

$$\times \text{Peak men} + [\text{ X. Peak men }] + \frac{\text{Build down}}{2} \times \text{Peak men} \quad (15.2)$$

$$\text{Peak manpower} = \frac{\text{Battery limit area}}{\text{Peak density level}} \quad (15.3)$$

Example 15.1   Labour density

For a foundry unit, let

Plot area = 300ft × 220ft = 66,000 sq. ft

Scope (direct higher) = 6,00,000 man hours

Allowance for indirect labour in area + 10% = 50,000 man hours

Estimating allowance + 15% = 70,000 man hours

Total scope for evaluation = 7,20,000 man hours

Assumptions

1.   Due to criticality, use density of 300 sq. ft per man

2.   Allow 15% absenteeism for effective man hours

3.   Build up duration from standard schedule

4.   Consider the case of subcontract labour instead of direct hired labour, because it has been observed that local subcontractors are more productive than prime contractors or direct hires

Solution

Scope = 7,20,000 (man hours for direct hire) – 72,000 (10% productivity adjustment for local subcontractor labour) = 6,48,00 man hours

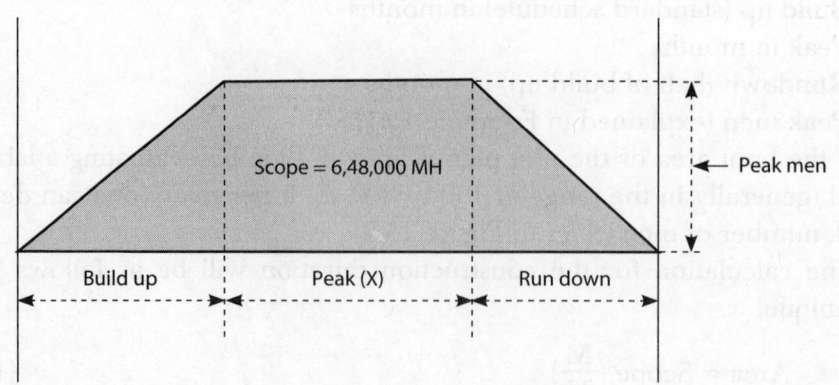

1. Labour availability = no constraints

2. Peak density level = 250 sq. ft per man

3. Peak manpower = plot area / peak density = 66,000 sq. ft / 250 sq. ft per man = 264 men

4. Effective man hour per man-month = 26 × 85 % × 8 = 177 hours

5. Build-up (by judgement) = 2 + 3 + 5 = 10 months

6. Rundown (by judgement) = 7 months

Therefore, putting all the values in Eqn (15.2), we get:

$$\frac{648,000}{177} = \left[\frac{10}{2}\right] \times 264 + [\,X\,.264] + \frac{7}{2} \times 264 = 5.63 \text{ months} \approx 6 \text{ months}$$

Therefore, total construction duration (subcontract labour) = 10 + 6 + 7 = 23 months

---

Example 15.2   A fabrication task of 430 hours is required to be completed within three weeks (six days per week). How many men are required if the calculation method is:

$$\frac{\text{Man hours}}{\text{man hours per week} \times \text{no of weeks}} = \text{Number of men} \tag{15.4}$$

According to Equation 15.4, the number of men = 430 / (6 × 8 × 3) = 3 men

If the task increases 60 times in size, i.e., 25,800 hours, it should be completed within 24 weeks.

Therefore, as per earlier method, in this case the number of men required = 25,800 / (6 × 8 × 24) = 24 men.

But this is not a correct solution. The calculation should be done by the trapezoidal method and by using Equation 15.2.

Solution

25,800 / (6 × 8) = (5X / 2) + (5X) + (14X / 2)

Therefore, peak men = X = 37 men

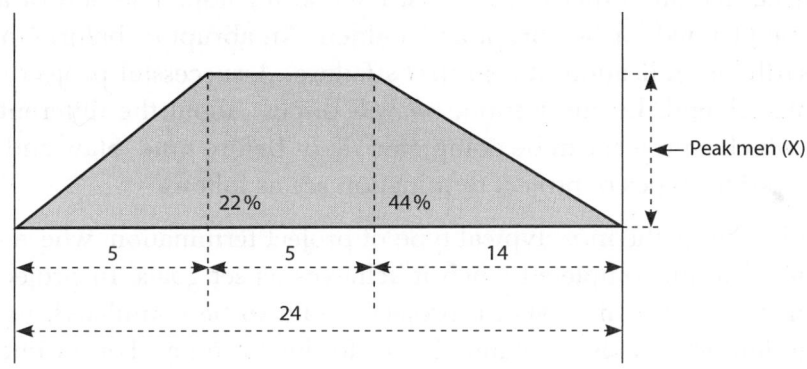

In the earlier chapters, we have already defined WBS (work breakdown structure). WBS is the total project split into successive unitary levels until the expected control levels are achieved. Hence, WBS serves as a tool for the project cost monitoring and control. As work progresses, WBS provides the format on which cost, time, and performance can be compared against its plan and budget for each level of WBS. By this comparison, the first purpose of control, i.e., verification process or variance analysis, has been accomplished. The next objective of the control is that of decision-making out of actual reality. It is the most crucial challenge for the project manager, or else he/she might 'win the battle but lose the war'.

The key terms used in control mechanism is cost reduction. It can be possible, usually more readily, in the early project phases. But the chances of cost reduction will be reduced as the project proceeds further into its life cycle (Figure 15.2).

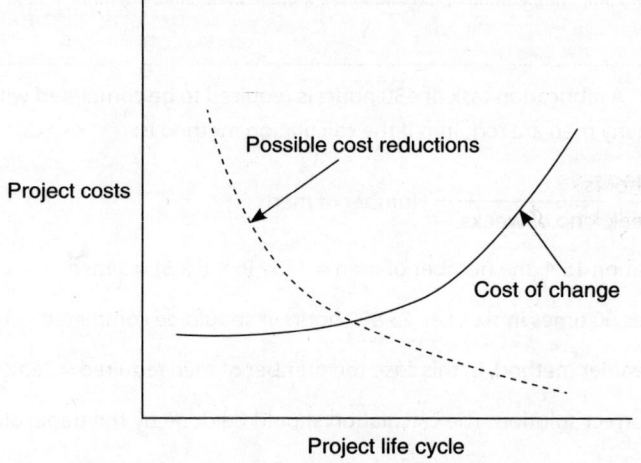

FIGURE 15.2   Cost reduction analysis

15.2 TERMINATION OF A PROJECT

A project, like any other event, must have a full stop. The end of a project can either be planned, or be abrupt and sudden. An abrupt or before-time end is not necessarily an indication of a project's failure. A successful project too can have a premature end. In this section, we will discuss about the different possibilities under which a project can be completed on or before time (Staw and Ross 1987).

The various types of project termination are as follows.

Normal   This is the most typical type of project termination, where the project is considered to be completed when it achieves its set goals. In projects where the customer is directly involved, a project is said to be completed, usually, on the day the finished goods are handed over to the customer. For an internal project, such as upgrades or creating new alterations in the system, the project is generally terminated when the result can be successfully incorporated into the existing system.

Advanced A premature end of a project often occurs when the project priority has changed, mainly due to marketing reasons. This means that the time for the completion of the finished goods, and not their features, becomes the primary factor. In this type of project termination, price escalation can be a major determining factor. Ending a project prematurely becomes a matter of great concern for the management, and so it should have the full support of the project stakeholders. The decision of shutting down a project well in advance should be taken jointly by the audit team, project team, and the top management. For example, in the year 2005, a sewerage water project of Suez water, Aguas de Barcelonas at Buenos Aires City, Argentina, was terminated due to great increase in tariff for compensating the devaluation of currency (http://www.manthan-india.org).

Everlasting Some projects seem to be never-ending and the end is generally forced upon it by the project managers or the audit group. One of the very common examples of such projects is software projects, where the demand for adding some new features, both by the users as well as the makers, is constant. It is generally terminated by forcing a budget and time limit by the senior management and the audit team.

Failed project There are circumstances where a project seems to fail. A project fails mainly because of unrealistic planning, change of market or demand, and also due to the project's unviability. For example, Enron's Dabhol Power Plant, a 740-megawatt power project in India, was terminated in the month of April 2001 due to various reasons like high power tariff, environmental hazards, lack of competitive bidding or procurement method, lack of transparency, incremental cost, not satisfying the taste of least cost power, socio-political resistance, central and state government policy, and economic non-viability.

Changed priority A project team may change the priority of a project at any time during its lifetime due to change in circumstances, change in the goals of the top management, and/or abrupt changes in the market. These changes can be both small and big, occurring periodically. At times, changes in project priorities become so large that it may require serious alteration, or even termination, in order to start a new project. For example, the dissolution of the small car project (NANO) of Tata Motors at Singur, West Bengal, can be an example of project termination due to priority changes. In September 2008, Tata actually felt the impact of world recession on the automobile industry, along with opposition from local landowners and political parties. Due to such opposing circumstances, the entire project decision was reshaped and shifted to Gujarat with some new priorities.

Symptoms for early project termination

An inexperienced auditor must go through some of the studies on the factors that were responsible for the success, failure, or delay of earlier projects of a firm (Ashley, Lurie, and Jaselskis 1987; Pinto and Slevin 1988). It would definitely help the auditor to identify the nature and the location of problems associated with the present project and how they can be mended. Coincidentally, most of these studies state that poor project definition (whose goals are not properly defined) is a major reason for project failures. There are some difficulties specifically related to particular tasks that have been listed in Table 15.1 (Gobeli and Larson 1986).

TABLE 15.1   Reason for early project termination related with specific task

Task	Difficulties
Planning	Absurd concept, poor decision-making, wrong information, alteration in methods or systems
Scheduling	Tight schedule, unable to reach fixed schedules
Organizing	Lack of responsibility or accountability, inefficient project manager, interference of top management
Staffing	Insufficient manpower, high attrition rate, poor manpower
Directing	Inefficient leadership and coordination, low commitment and involvement
Controlling	Poor feedback and monitoring system, absence of problem identification, and strong control mechanism

Source: Gobeli and Larson 1986.

15.3 PROJECT AUDIT

A periodic check up has become routine, whether for the health of an individual or for any highly complex operation. It helps in the diagnosis of a physical problem that may have occurred. It is also applicable for the management of a project. A periodic inspection is necessary to assure safe and proper performance by team members. It ensures that the organisation is running in good health as well as meeting all its objectives.

A periodic audit of a project has always been an effective tool for the management, in order to maintain effective control. The management's only source of getting the actual status of an ongoing project is periodic reporting. The effectiveness of this reporting depends upon the frequency and genuineness of the supplied data.

It has been seen earlier that projects have failed even in the advanced stage of completion because of the reluctance of the project manager to inform the management of the defects, thereby delaying an early possibility of recovery.

Another factor that becomes prevalent in the failure of a mature project is the overconfidence of the project personnel, which gives a false sense of security and ultimately leads to the crashing of the project.

Audit rules and regulations

There are well-defined corporate policies for every business function. Audit, being one of the major business functions that are performed by most corporate organisations, has established procedures and policies of its own. Rules and procedures for an audit should cover all the responsibilities and the general approaches associated with it. It must justify the reason for the selection of a particular project for auditing. It should state the team for auditing a project, the respective responsibilities of the team members, functional organizations, and their reporting structure.

Preparation of audit plan

Preparing a detailed audit plan is necessary both from the perspective of the audit team, as well as the project team. The plan informs the project team about their relevance and areas on which they must focus. It should be a detailed outline of the subject areas that are covered by the audit team. While making an audit plan, the organization can take the shortcomings of a previous project as the scale to judge project performance. The purpose of an audit plan is to give equal priority to the shortcomings and areas of excellence of a project, in order to measure the overall performance of the project team. An original audit plan has been provided in Annexure 15.1 at the end of this chapter.

Audit execution

Auditing is a very organized process. The normal procedure of executing an audit is to conduct meetings with the project manager, along with the project team and the supporting functional managers. Generally, a member of the project team is assigned the task of fixing the meeting schedules with different functional teams. This tells the project team the sequence of audit areas and lets them prepare for the same. The interviews generally follow the organizational structure, starting from the top and gradually descending to the lower levels. Auditors, being outsiders to the project team, must maintain the code of ethics while taking audit interviews and should not be disrespectful to any project member.

Scanning of audit findings

Before the audit of a concerned project is finalized, there are some general findings, like appropriate bills, vouchers, invoices, specifications, and necessary documents that are sought by the audit team. Generally, during auditing the audit team goes back to the persons responsible for the concerned areas, to find out what may have gone wrong. Sometimes a little confrontation may occur between the audit team and the person involved, but most of the time the concerned person is happy to help out the audit team with the findings. If project team personnel accept evidence of their errors found by the audit team, they are on a safer side, as now they become part of the solution.

Audit report preparation

The audit report is the end product of all efforts made by the audit team and the project team. Much depends upon the presentation of an audit report. The report should be sleek and the findings should be stated clearly. The discussion must contain factual information to support every finding. Credits and flaws should be treated equally. While writing a report it may happen that the drafting of findings may be iterated five times or more, before the final version is achieved to make the draft actual, accurate, and flawless. The content of the report should not be hyperbolic or exaggerated. During the preparation of the report, an auditor should follow his or her professional ethics and bindings, so that window dressing is avoided. An original audit report is provided in Annexure 15.2 at the end of this chapter.

As with the project itself, after the audit is completed, the audit process must be ended. When the final report and recommendations and suggestions for improvement are published, there should be a review of the audit process. This is done to improve the methods of auditing. When this review is finished, the audit is actually completed. After that, the audit team may be formally disbanded.

For example, all the World Bank's projects are subject to an ex-post audit, done by the bank itself. This is based on a review of the materials and activity pertaining to the project, and if required on the basis of survey or field review. This completes the audit process.

SUMMARY

Control and audit are the fundamental units of any project. The effectiveness of a project control programme is dependent on the reliability of information and guidance such as project schedules estimation, human resource planning, productivity level determination, cost-schedule development, trend analysis, work performance evaluation, identification of scope of work, and so on. These, if kept in mind and conducted regularly every now and then, lead to satisfactory results. WBS is an important instrument which helps in monitoring and controlling projects.

Every project eventually comes through a termination stage. The types of project termination are normal, advanced, everlasting, failed project, and changed priority.

A periodic audit has always been an effective tool for management, in order to maintain effective control. An audit usually covers all responsibilities and general approaches associated with it.

KEY TERMS

Audit rules and regulations   There are well-defined corporate policies for every business function. The rules and procedures for an audit should include preparation of an audit plan, audit execution, scanning of audit findings, and audit report preparation.

Project audit   Periodic project audit is required for efficiently maintaining control mechanism.

Termination of a project   A project, like any other event, must have a full stop. The end of a project can be either planned, or can be abrupt and sudden. Types of project termination are normal, advanced, everlasting, failed project, and changed priority.

CONCEPT REVIEW QUESTIONS

1. Explain with a suitable example how cost control can be possible for an ongoing project, through the trapezoidal technique.
2. Why is the possible cost reduction curve downward sloping as a project progresses?
3. Enumerate and explain the different types of project termination.
4. What are the symptoms for premature project termination?
5. Explain, with example, how audit helps in project monitoring and control.

CRITICAL THINKING QUESTIONS

1. Following are the various conditions which might cause an out-of-control situation for an ongoing project:
   (a) Accepting unrealistic terms and conditions
   (b) Overestimation and over-confidence about self-ability
   (c) Misinterpretation of client's requirement
   (d) Lack of time to research specification
   In which phase can the above situations be identified? Suggest remedial measures for each situation.
2. Generally, infrastructure projects are undertaken for a long-term period. How can inflation rate influence the payment terms as per original contract?
3. Following are the various reasons for project time and cost overrun:
   (a) Unrealistic benchmark
   (b) Poor and inexperienced estimation
   (c) Too many changes in project scheduling
   (d) Lack of coordination between functional and project managers
   Suggest various control mechanisms that can be adopted to overcome these situations.

SELECT REFERENCES

Ashley, B.D., C.S. Luri, and E.J. Jaselskis, 'Determinants of Construction Project Success', *Project Management Journal*, vol. 18, no. 2, June 1987, p. 72.

Chilstrom, K.O., 'Project Needs and Techniques for Management Audits', *Project Management Handbook*, 2e, edited by D.I. Cleland, and W.R. King, New York, International Thomson Publishing, 1988, pp. 620–637.

Gobeli, D.B., and E. Larson, 'Barriers Affecting the Project Success', 1986 Project Management Institute: Measuring Success', Upper Derby, PA: Project Management Institute, 1986, pp. 22–29.

Johnson, R.K., 'Program control from the bottom up—exploring the working side', *Project Management Journal*, March 1985.

Kerzner, H., *Project Management—A Systems Approach to Planning, Scheduling and Controlling*, 4e, New York, International Thomson Publishing, 1992.

Pinto, J.K. and D.P. Slevin, 'Critical Success Factor across the Project Life Cycle', *Project Management Journal*, vol. 19, no. 3, June 1988, p. 72.

Staw, B.M. and J. Ross, 'Knowing when to put the plug', *Harvard Business Review*, March–April 1997, pp. 68–74.

Other resources

http://www.manthan-india.org/IMG/pdf/FailedPrivatisationProjects_July_08.pdf, accessed 22 April 2010.

CASE STUDY
The Crisis in a Slow-down Period of SRM Industries

Hindustan Corporation awarded a prestigious contract to SRM industries on 1 January 2007. The project was a eleven-month endeavour to develop a new product for Hindustan Corporation. While awarding the contract, SRM Industries was informed that if the initial R&D effort was satisfactory, a single-source production contract would follow for at least seven years, and this contract would be negotiated on a year-to-year basis.

Rakesh Sharma, a young and enthusiastic engineer, was appointed project manager. He was given eight very efficient people for his project office. In addition, there were six people from operations, as functional project team members.

The progress was fine till 31 July 2007, when Hindustan Corporation informed SRM Industries that they were envisaging a cash flow problem, and hence, a follow-on contract could not be awarded till the beginning of the next financial year (April 2008).

Rakesh Sharma now had a big problem. He did not want to damage the project office and let the key people of the project be assigned to some other project, as there was no surety that they would be available at the beginning of the follow-on contract.

Rakesh estimated that Rs 1 lakh per month was required to maintain his key personnel for the slow-down period of 4 months (December 2007 to March 2008). With the Puja and Diwali holidays of 18 days and some short-term assignments in hand, he estimated that Rs 2–8 lakh were needed as excess fund.

Rakesh conveyed to the programme team members that they would have to generate a management reserve of Rs 3 lakh. The contract being a firm-fixed-price contract, all schedules for the project office and project team were extended to 31 March 2008. Rakesh also kept his boss Shankar Choudhury informed about his plans.

Shankar initially agreed to Rakesh's approach. But just before the Pujas, he advised Rakesh to book the management reserve as excess profit, and close the contract as per the original schedule of 30 November 2007. He informed him that this would help increase their Puja bonus. He also assured Rakesh that the key personnel would be reassigned to the follow-on project when it materialized. Rakesh was furious.

Discussion questions

1. Why was Rakesh furious? What aspects of project control can be identified here?

2. Suggest some remedial measures for the above crisis. Compare this with any other organizational project that you may have come across.

ANNEXURE 15.1

Pro forma of an Audit Plan for a Project

An audit plan will be prepared in the following format:

(i) Purpose

(ii) Scope

(iii) Approach for conduct

    (a) Team assignment

    (b) Schedule/itinerary

(iv) Audit areas

(v) Interview questions by area

In the case of a new project, an audit plan is usually developed to cover all management areas that could affect the success of the project. In this event, a typical plan would include the following areas to be audited:

Audit areas for a project:

(a) Organization

(b) Policies and procedures

(c) Master planning and control

(d) Work authorization

(e) Contract administration

(f) Engineering

(g) Manufacturing

(h) Quality control

(i) Test

(j) Logistic support

(k) Customer requirements

(l) Vendor support

ANNEXURE 15.2

An Audit Report Format

Part I: Introduction

Section I: Purpose

             (Give a brief explanation of any special reason for which the audit is being conducted.)

Section II: Scope

             (Give a description of the scope of auditing including the limitation imposed.)

Section III: Audit team
(List team membership by name, title and organization)
Section IV: Audit interviews
(List all persons interviewed by name, title and organization)

Part II: Audit results

Section I: Summary and recommendations
The summary of results should be a one page abstract of the major findings and recommendations. Following each specific recommendation will be the action office responsible for that recommendation.

Section II: Findings, discussion and recommendations
This portion of the report will contain the detailed findings, discussions and recommendations that pertain to the programme.

1. Subject: Use a short descriptive title 'Overtime'.
2. Findings: The finding should be brief, but include (1) a statement that describes the condition, i.e., problem or outstanding condition; (2) the cause or reason for this condition or problem; and (3) the effect or impact resulting from the condition. Summarized, the finding should reflect a condition, a cause and the effect.
3. Discussion: Mention the pertinent factors collected during the discussion with others, or revealed through your personal investigations. Present as thorough and comprehensive analysis of the condition as necessary, to prove the statement of your findings.
4. Recommendation: If corrective actions are suggested by the finding, they should be recorded at the end of the discussion. Following each recommendation, note the action assignments.

Part III: Supplementary data

Note: The appendices listed are only for guidance and will not necessarily apply to each audit report. Conciseness should be employed. For example, data under appendices for programme history and a description of the system should not normally exceed one page each.

Annexure

A – Project history
B – Description of system
C – Documentation and reporting
D – Programming and funding history
E – Customer organization
F – Programme organization and management controls.

PART IV

PROJECT MANAGEMENT—
THE FUTURE

MANAGING E-PROJECTS

In this era of computers, the solutions to projects are just a few clicks away—
you just have to find the right tab.

— ANONYMOUS

LEARNING OBJECTIVES

After studying this chapter, you will be able to

- Define e-project and understand its various features
- Understand the merits and demerits of an e-project
- Identify the future trends of e-projects
- Know the role of computers in project management

Migration towards Web-based Project

The advent of the e-era has brought about a revolution in the way businesses are conducted across the globe. Many firms dedicate resources and funds to e-business, e-learning, e-commerce, e-consultant, etc. Over the last few years, there has been a radical change in the effective execution of projects. Emphasis is put on the development of soft skills to get better output amongst project team members. We are now moving towards a virtual world, where the traditional concept of team is often not relevant. More projects are being executed with most team members not physically present at one place. In many cases, the team is fragmented across different countries and continents. The requirement from present-day project managers is that they must be more computer savvy and get involved in e-business, and eventually in e-projects.

16.1 WHAT IS AN E-PROJECT?

As per the definition given by AACE International (2001), 'project management is the utilization of skills and knowledge in coordinating, organizing, planning, scheduling, directing, controlling, monitoring, and evaluating the prescribed activities to ensure that the stated objectives of a project, product for manufacture, or services are achieved.' The focus of e-project management is to use electronic tools to enhance the handling of projects. Due to e-project management, there is a tendency to move towards a paperless work environment. Though many communications can be accessed electronically, there are still some essential documents such as contracts, delegation of power, acceptance of the offer, etc., for which we depend on traditional hard copy for legality and tangibility.

E-project is an application designed for managing working relationships with end costumers. The application helps project managers in all phases of a project including project planning, estimation, pricing, scheduling, activity tracking, project completion, and customer satisfaction. It is an extensive application of electronic technology to project management. Electronic technology uses the following tools: personal computer, cellular phone, digital camera, network server, e-mail, voice mail, telephonic or video conference, the Internet, intranet, extranet, application service provider, fax, computer-based projector, knowledge database, electronic message board, electronic agents, parallel processing computers, etc.

As technology evolves, new tools will be available and the journey of e-project will expand beyond our expectation.

16.2 FEATURES OF AN E-PROJECT

Today the execution of a project, irrespective of its size, is mostly dependent on how quickly or ably project managers can absorb the technology that it involves. With the varying size and complexity of projects, it is a must for an organization to implement the essentials of e-project to make their business successful. Managers should take a closer look at e-project attributes to stay updated in the changing technological environment so that they can run projects successfully. Features of e-projects should be studied, understood, and implemented correctly in the right sequence and manner.

Attributes of e-projects consist of the following.

Project planning and management Project planning and management is made up of various parts that help the project manager organize the project into definite phases. These parts are as follows.

(a) *Cost estimation and pricing*—Here, the whole project is divided into several tasks and for each task an associated cost is estimated and allocated.

(b) *Scheduling and calendars*—E-projects allow managers to assign specific jobs for specific employees in a given span of time. It also helps them in scheduling calendar dates for the given jobs so that no conflict of dates occur.

(c) *Managing the project customers*—It helps project managers to handle multiple customer location and contacts on a single project.

(d) *Activity management*—An e-project allows project managers to create a new activity, or recreate an existing one whenever it is required to speedup work in order to finish the project within the estimated time, cost, and resources.

(e) *Documentation and accession of external customers*—An e-project allows the project team to keep an updated documentation of the progress of the project. It also allows project managers to be in touch with end users while the project is still in progress. Managers can make amendments to baseline estimation depending on the feedback from the end customers.

(f) *Setting up of benchmark*—An e-project can be configured by setting up milestone dates to ensure that the project is heading in the right direction and is on time.

Managing of several requests for change in various aspects of the project An e-project enables the management to simultaneously handle several requests for modification of various aspects of the projects by different users.

Multi-tasking It allows project managers to view and edit information on various projects at the same time.

Individual work management tools and equipment It allows project managers to manage project activities by viewing only the relevant projects in the system.

Resource management tools and equipment It empowers the project manager with the required resources, such as time, funds, material, manpower, machinery, etc., in a scheduled manner.

Communications in e-project It delivers e-mail notifications to all involved in a particular project about the events that occur in the system.

Administration details An e-project provides the ability to manage various resource levels or job types. Customized text, date fields, customer's name, address, and other information can be administered through it.

Monitoring and control Every project and its outcome are unique in nature. Hence, its success depends on day-to-day monitoring and using a strong control mechanism. Through e-project, the managing and controlling of different issues becomes much easier.

Providing feedback Like communication, e-project management is also a two-way process. Unless a realistic feedback is available, its applicability cannot be developed.

16.3 MERITS AND DEMERITS OF AN E-PROJECT

Due to globalization and the rise of MNCs, trendy terms such as 'virtual teaming' and 'virtual organization' are gaining popularity. Virtual team members 'must go an extra mile' to keep others informed (Biglow 2000). It demands a new management approach and a keen awareness of the potential problems and challenges from the entire team. In e-environment, e-project management enhances the effectiveness and efficiency in the handling of a project. Table 16.1 lists key merits and demerits of an e-project.

TABLE 16.1 Merits and demerits of an e-project

Merits	Demerits
• Using and sharing data and information is easier. • Communication becomes easier, faster, and more streamlined. • Standardized or generalized management processes. • Establishing or importing model project templates. • Using common and proven applications. • Minimizing development and maintenance cost of data. • Minimizing time to plan, execute, and share information within team members. • Removing problem of distance or absenteeism.	• There is a chance of information loss due to data insecurity. • Generally people are not ready to accept changes easily. • Legal considerations that need some adjustments and special attention are not fully taken care of. • Use of mainframe software requires strong internal communications lines for support. • Software implementation is less likely to succeed if the organization does not have sufficient training in project management principles.

Source: Kerzner, H., *Project Management—A Systems Approach to Planning, Scheduling and Controlling*, 4e, New York, International Thomson Publishing, 1992.

16.4 FUTURE OF E-PROJECTS

Project management software helps to analyse, optimize, and manage projects. It also supports decision-making regarding the right mix of project. Further, it helps in estimating the resources that fulfil strategic objectives. Without project portfolio management software, it is almost impossible to manage portfolios of too many projects and the interdependencies among them simultaneously. Computer and software can be the only means to make this happen.

On the management side, firms are slowly but surely adapting to the software-based project management approach to reduce cost and add value. The concept of centralized procurement system once again comes into picture. It demands a stronger base for project management software.

Given the potential benefit of software and use of computers along with economic and technological improvement, the demand for project management and project portfolio management will increase. This means that the concept of e-project will certainly be more popular in the coming decade.

A survey was conducted by a group of researchers—Froese, Waugh, and Pouria (2001)—to understand the future of e-projects. The results indicated a positive and increasing usage of IT in project management. Not just this survey, but other research studies also suggest that within ten years from now, computers will be much more powerful and user interfaces are likely to be significantly different from those of today. IT issues will register an increase in their importance vis-à-vis project management, and will become fundamentally inherent in our work practices. IT will be ready to provide access to all information at all times. Today, according to the Right to Information Act, communication and information sharing is a must and it gives a platform to work competitively and efficiently.

Global recession (2008) hit IT industries massively across the world. Their initiatives in innovating and improving value-added services in their organization have become curtailed. However, during the recession, industrial countries around the world are investing billions on infrastructure and other projects to stimulate the economy. This has created considerable demand for software in project management. In fact, the market for project portfolio management (PPM) software was around $2.9 billion in the year 2008, according to Forrester Research. It is expected that the market for PPM will increase with a multiplying factor in the near future.

16.5 ROLE OF COMPUTERS AND SOFTWARE IN PROJECT MANAGEMENT

Project management can be a very complex process, requiring a great deal of expertise in many fields. The processes involved must be very structured and organized. It requires development and processing of large volumes of data and frequent reporting of plans and progress.

Overall, project management requires much more than planning, scheduling, tracking, and control. There are some specific complex functions that can only be done with the aid of a computer. It was thirty years ago that the old lumbering mainframes were put into service to support project management. For most of those years, access to computerized project management was reserved for large organizations: those with 'management information system operations' and an army of dedicated project control specialists and lots of money to spend on both hardware and software. But because computer technology has changed over the years, the benefits of computerized project management have been put within the range of any potential user, for any project application.

During the last few years, there has been immense development in the world of automation through the success of microcomputers and their acceptance in the business community. This acceptance comes through the development of computer programs that help solve business problems. Now, with a minimum investment, and bypassing the MIS bureaucracies, the doors to the computer utilization in the business place have been opened to even small business organizations.

Who would have believed, just a few years ago, that there would be this abundance of project management software available for the casual as well as the serious user, and at prices that are surprisingly low? Microcomputers have given us accessibility to sophisticated programs that only recently were the private domain of the information system gurus. The nature of project management systems—a combination of simple algorithms, calculations, and database management—is natural for computers. The need to do what-if analysis in the typical project management environment was an additional driver of the microcomputer explosion.

These products address the entire range of the product management market-place. There are programs for the local theatre group that can help them plan their next production. There are programs for bankers and researchers. Programs exist at every level for the assignment and tracking of resources, and for cashflow planning and monitoring. Even formal project management organizations, with mainframe computer systems, are finding it advantageous to supplement, or even replace, their extensive batch systems with some of the very sophisticated professional level project management software programs that are available for the microcomputer.

In this section, we will discuss the various functions of computer software packages in project management and how they can help to carry out the required project functions. Table 16.2 outlines the various parameters of project functions and the role of computers.

TABLE 16.2   Role of computers in various project functions

Project functions	Role of computers
To fix a project goal or plan This is the first stage to begin any project. The objective here is to set the basis of time line, budget, and technical know-how, keeping in mind the organizational objectives and policies for the project.	There are several software packages that provide some guidance for this function in their users' manuals. Most of these tasks can be easily processed on computer.
To identify the work To develop a baseline or a standard way to carry out the task. Here, the work that is to be done is identified, and the resource and the budget for the work are specified. Keeping all this in mind, the time duration for the work is fixed as well.	Major portion of the project planning process is not done by the computers.
To set up the work period One of the most essential project objectives is to determine the timing parameters and prepare a schedule for the completion of the project.	Usually, at this point of the project, one builds up a critical path network. Thorough analysis of this network path is done with the aid of computers to initiate an early start and finish. The task schedule can be drawn in three typical formats: a tabular listing, a bar (Gantt) chart, or a network diagram.
To set up resource availability and requirements The need for resource allocation and costing sets the perspective towards resource and cost functions of project management software. These resources consist of manpower and materials.	Since the variations involved in the resource theme are not limited, they cannot be determined by a simple review. Therefore, there is a need to determine the type of project management software on the basis of the level of details required by the organization to run the project successfully.

Contd

Table 16.2 *Contd*

Project functions	Role of computers
To set up a baseline for the cost of the project To control the cost of a specific project, one has to set up a work-scope-oriented budget. This can be done at the task level or at the work package level. This also helps in getting an idea about the profit margin for any project.	To make this process easier, a table of resource and its cost is established with the aid of computers by entering the task durations, resources, and fixed costs. The budget is created. At the resource area, costing can be approached through various levels of details.
To evaluate the baseline plan Here, an evaluation of the relation between the schedules of individual tasks and milestone tasks is done. This is the first opportunity in the project wherein one validates the earlier assumptions and decides the need for additional resources, more work per week, or adjusting of relationships to meet the overall timing objectives.	The computer is the best tool available for performing the evaluation and optimization of the baseline plan. The computer works upon logic to calculate the earliest start and finish. It also performs a backward pass to determine the latest start for an activity so as to finish within the budgeted timing. The computer marks the difference between the earlier dates and the late ones. This helps in identifying an activity as 'float' or 'slack'. Therefore, ones attention can easily be drawn towards the activities having least floats (the most critical activities).
To keep a track of the progress of the work Keeping track of a project also includes changes that are to be made in the network plan and the budget along with the changes that comes in the work scope.	In this part of project management, computers play a very important role as some programs, such as QWIKNET, are equipped with auto-progressed settings. When the program runs in the auto-progress mode, the system assumes that any activity scheduled to start prior to the data date has actually been progressed as planned, although no progress has been entered.
To evaluate the performance There are two important factors on which the project performance depends. They are project completion date and the project margin.	Computers play the most imperative role. The project management software is usually equipped with analytical data that is required to evaluate and report on project performance. A very good example of such a software is QWIKNET.
To report and export data Here, the final report regarding the progress of different activities conducted for the completion of the project is made.	The computer is equipped with programs that not only match the data formats, environments, and needs, but also help with the preparation of hard copy (reports and graphics) for presentation to the various project stakeholders. Programs such as Artemis 2000 actually allow the user to modify the project database structure and add extensions to that structure.

Source: Project Management Handbook, 2e, edited by David I. Cleland and William R. King, Van Nostrand Reinhold, New York, 1988.

All functions described above are of little value unless they are used. It has been generally found that the discipline of computer-based project planning and control system leads to a more cohesive and supportable project management and reporting. It helps project managers to be more efficient and get better output.

SUMMARY

The focus of e-project management is to use electronic tools to enhance the handling of projects. Using an e-project helps in project planning and management, managing several requests to change project schedule at a time, multi-tasking, accessing individual work management tools and equipment, resource management tools and equipment, better communication, administration details, monitoring and control, and providing feedback. Project management software helps to analyse, optimize, and manage projects, and it also aids in decision-making vis-à-vis the right mix of project. Moreover, it also estimates the resources required to fulfil the strategic objectives of a project.

As computer technology has developed over the years, the benefits of computerized project management have been put within the range of any potential user for any project application.

KEY TERMS

E-project An application of using updated software designed to manage a task more effectively and efficiently. It involves all stakeholders of the project on a similar platform, where everybody can interact and share information and also be able to provide their feedback.

Activity management A process that helps managers speedup their work in order to finish their project, keeping in mind the estimated schedule and cost.

CONCEPT REVIEW QUESTIONS

1. Define e-project and establish the relation between using a software in project management and its success.

2. Describe the various functions in project management and also the corresponding roles of computers in those specific functions.

3. Describe attributes of e-projects with examples.

CRITICAL THINKING QUESTIONS

1. 'If a computer works well, it always gives better output.' Is this always true? While answering the question, list the various advantages and disadvantages of an e-project.

2. A survey report says that the project portfolio management (PPM) software market will become 1.5 times its present size, or may be more, within 5 years from now. Comment on this particular report. Draw the worldwide trends and positions of the PPM software market in the year 2020 on the basis of today's projections and expectations. Your analysis should be supported by an analytical report.

ASSIGNMENT

Consider a hypothetical organization that is not yet fully automated and prepare a draft report for making it fully computerized.

SELECT REFERENCES

Biglow, B., 'Challenges to the virtual organization', *PM. Network*, July 2000, pp. 17–20.

Chen, M.T., 'Key learning from e-project management', AACE International Transactions, 2001.

Froese, T., L. Waugh, and A. Pouria, 'PM 2020— Future trends in IT for project management', AEC Conference Proceedings, May 2001.

Vandersluis, C., 'Web-based project management system for every man', *PM Network,* May 2000, pp. 32–35.

CASE STUDY
Differentiating between Relevant and Not-so-relevant Information

'Oh! Too many reports!' reacted Joseph Mathew, GM–Projects of Modi Industries. He was going through the reams of printed stationary neatly stacked on his table, trying to take some notes before the important meeting at the CEO's office.

'Why can't they make specific reports? We should get the requisite information handy and not waste time searching for details in so many reports.'

Yadav, the senior project engineer, tried to convince Mathew, 'Sir, every report that we receive is necessary for us to take effective decisions with regard to planning, organizing, and controlling each project. We are the biggest users of these reports, and we just can't do without them.'

'OK, but I don't think that all the information in these reports is useful. Also, since reports are not required frequently, say on a daily or a weekly basis, if we can ask the IT department to generate these reports fortnightly, or monthly, we shall have fewer papers to handle. We can also strike off the not-so-relevant information in each report to make the report easier to interpret.'

Just before the CEO's meeting, Mathew and Yadav had a brief talk with Kamalesh, GM–IT. 'I have thought about this, Joseph. I fully agree that we are generating more papers than necessary. It is making your job more complicated, and at the same time, significantly increasing the cost. Each report seems to be a one-shot deal. So, I have thought of sitting with your people and the manufacturing group to identify which reports are required in detail/summary, how many copies are required, and at what frequency. We can also review the structure of each report to make them more user-friendly.'

They met the CEO, and shared their views with him. He advised that they work on reducing the reports, but without compromising on the necessary information needed for effective functioning and control.

Discussion questions

1. Do you think the approach taken by the management of Modi Industries is correct?
2. What is, in your opinion, the function of today's project manager? Is it just about following the plan and control chalked out by the computer software, or use of one's own brain wherever necessary?

FUTURE OF PROJECT MANAGEMENT

The best way to predict the future is to create it.

— PETER DRUCKER

LEARNING
OBJECTIVES

After studying this
chapter, you will be
able to

- Identify the different
  career opportunities
  available and become
  familiar with the various
  training courses in
  project management
- Discuss recent trends in
  project management
- Conceptualize the
  project management
  maturity model
- Know various
  contemporary issues in
  project management

17.1 CAREER PATH IN PROJECT MANAGEMENT

Career opportunities are not fixed at any point of time. The number of opportunities fluctuate from company to company, industry to industry, and also from field to field. It also depends on the country's economic trend and the available opportunities. It is a dependent variable for demand–supply relationship as well. The career path in project management is neither a straight well-established line, nor is it applicable to everyone. But definitely every project manager's career path has a starting point. Each path guides the managers in a certain direction to get a clear idea about what they are required to know. This is based on their interests and where they are placed at present. Depending upon the consequences of following a particular path, the manager can go further along the path, retrace steps, or discover a new path and explore a new career. There is no single, well-defined path for making a successful career in project management. Thus, managers learn on the job and then further enhance their skills as time progresses.

It is important to note that holding a degree in the related field is not enough. A person also requires significant exposure in the field of management to become a successful project manager. Exhibit 17.1 discusses the ways of developing project leaders. There are different associations and professional bodies who offer various certificate courses in project management. But certification alone does not help one to become an efficient project manager. Strong interpersonal skills are needed. For instance, a manager should be able to work simultaneously with completely opposite type of people. A manager should have the ability to keep calm and maintain cool when things go wrong, and must be competent to take the right decision during a crisis to avoid the failure of the project.

EXHIBIT 17.1   Harvesting project leaders

'Executives do not have a clue about how to develop project managers', says Gopal Kapur, president of the Centre of Project Management, a consulting agency in San Ramon, California. 'Project managers do not grow on trees. You have to understand the process of gardening before you can grow something.' Kapur advocates that corporations develop internal programmes to develop project managers.

The Federal Reserve Bank of St Louis has had such a programme for more than a year. It helped the bank develop forty-five new project managers. It combines hands-on work in medium to low-risk projects with classroom training. A new project manager is guided by a veteran leader who acts as a coach or mentor. Gary Arnold, manager of learning and developement services, calls it a very critical piece of the programme. The coach/mentor can offer advice based on experience.

Typically, Arnold says, project manager wannabes are sent to the classroom for a few days before they apply skills in a practical environment. But the federal reserve bank found that the opposite works better and starts them off in the trenches. This way they directly experience and understand the need to master key project management tools and concepts.

Source: Saia 1997.

In addition to being able to handle crises, a project manager has to be very diplomatic when dealing with clients and making people understand the exact work to be carried out. A project manager should also be careful about the progress of work, as time is a crucial determinant of project cost and overall success.

As every project is unique in nature, a project manager's job is very interesting, challenging, and exciting. In the recent economic downturn, this was the only field where good lucrative packages were still being offered. One great thing in this field is that once a qualified individual has gained experience, any type of project can be handled. For example, if a person chooses to work as a construction project manager, they may get a chance in the future to be a senior project manager of mega events such as Olympics, Football World Cup, etc.

Career advancement in project management   Like other professions, for a career in project management, sky is the limit. A career in project management requires learning through various on-the-job training, workshops, seminars, in-house management development programmes, etc. Several universities are offering various courses on project management. Regardless of the level of training, one needs to supplement it with further education in project management.

Generally, big companies have their own in-house training module on project management. For instance, HP has more than 32 modules in project management curriculum. As given in Exhibit 17.1, many companies have combined classroom instruction with on-the-job training. Those which cannot provide training programmes send their managers to other consulting and training firms or institutes. Figure 17.1 outlines the courses offered by ESI International.

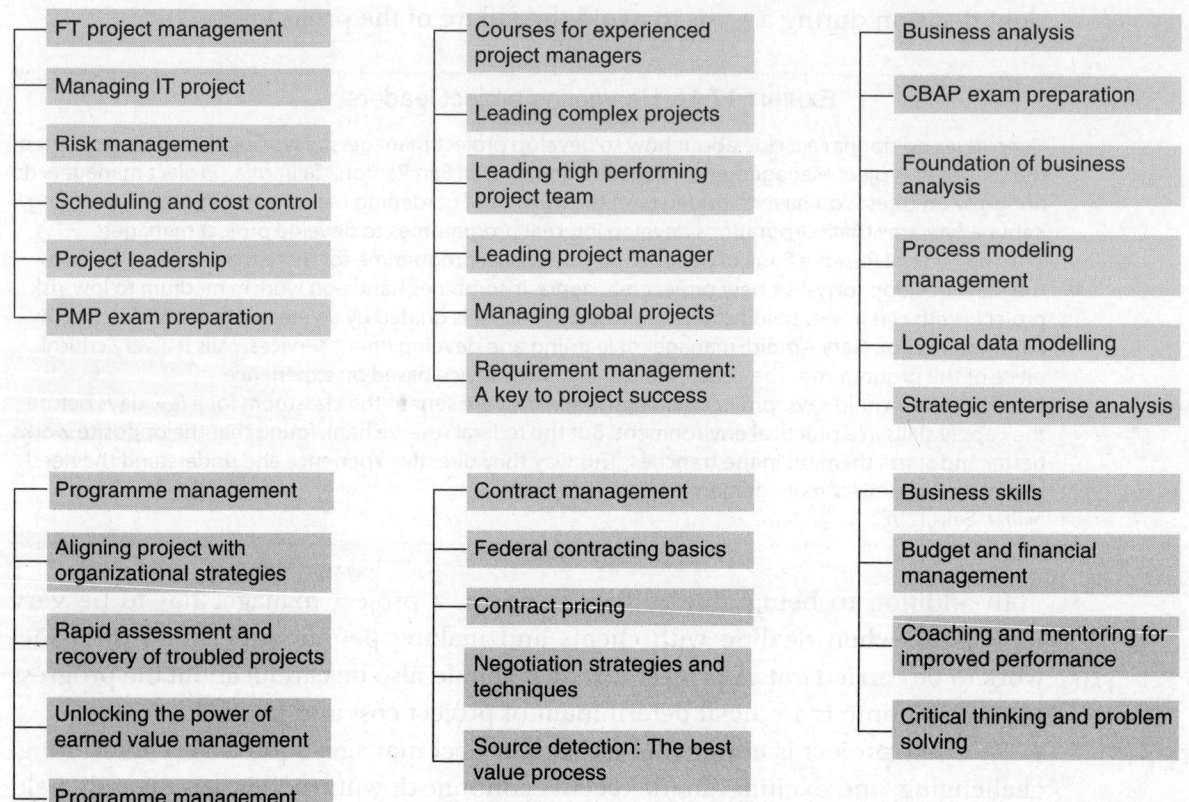

FT project management	Courses for experienced project managers	Business analysis
Managing IT project	Leading complex projects	CBAP exam preparation
Risk management	Leading high performing project team	Foundation of business analysis
Scheduling and cost control		
Project leadership	Leading project manager	Process modeling management
PMP exam preparation	Managing global projects	Logical data modelling
	Requirement management: A key to project success	Strategic enterprise analysis
Programme management	Contract management	Business skills
Aligning project with organizational strategies	Federal contracting basics	Budget and financial management
Rapid assessment and recovery of troubled projects	Contract pricing	Coaching and mentoring for improved performance
Unlocking the power of earned value management	Negotiation strategies and techniques	Critical thinking and problem solving
Programme management	Source detection: The best value process	

Source: ESI International 2010 Program (www.esi-intl.com).

FIGURE 17.1 Project management training courses

Efficient project managers require strong interpersonal skills. These skills can be enhanced by their participation in workshops on team building, soft-skills development, and other personal development programmes (Exhibit 17.2). Some technical people are returning to universities to pursue an MBA or part-time management courses to strenghten their profile. Many others find it beneficial to join the PMI (Project Management Institute).

If despite all efforts the project manger is not satisfied with the results and is craving to achieve more, then a switch to a different company or industry where the project manager is exposed to many more opportunities and opportunities for learning must be considered. A good work experience aids in the advancement of career.

EXHIBIT 17.2   Works well with others

The phrase 'works well with others' has long been a staple remark on grade school report cards; now, in the IT world, it is the number one criteria for a management candidate. In a nationwide survey conducted in 1999, 27% of chief information officers (*CIOs*) cited strong interpersonal skills as the single most important quality for reaching management levels. Advanced technical skills came in second, receiving 23% of the response.

The project was sponsored by RHI Consulting, which provides information technology professionals on a project basis. An independent research firm was hired by RHI Consulting to administer the survey. More than 1400 CIOs responded to the questionnaire. Survey respondents were also asked: 'in 2005, how frequently will employees in your IT department work on project-based teams with members of the other teams (of other departments) throughout the company?'
Their responses:

Very frequently   57%
Somewhat frequently   26%
Somewhat infrequently   10%
Very infrequently   6%
Never   1%

Greg Scileppi, RHI Consulting's Executive Director, recommends that IT professionals develop their interpersonal skills. 'The predominance of project teams has created a corresponding need for strong communication and team-player abilities. Technical staff put these skills to test daily as they work with employees at all levels to create and implement IT solutions ranging from simple troubleshooting to corporate web initiatives and system-wide upgrades.'

Source: Nellenbach 1999.

17.2 EMERGENCE OF PROJECT MANAGEMENT—CURRENT TRENDS

Bredillet (2008) defines new project management trends in the form of nine schools of thoughts (Figure 17.2). These are as follows.

Governance   It includes issues related to the legal, social, ethical, government policies, and environmental impacts of projects. It talks about the dos and don'ts in project management. It directs the guidelines, rules, and regulations for a specific project. It explores the importance and dependence of other management disciplines, such as operation, commercial, finance, HR, marketing, etc., on project management.

Marketing   Market research can be conducted on the scope of project management, both in traditional industries and in newly developed industries. Traditional project management areas include construction, engineering, IT, and utilities and the non-traditional project management areas include banking, pharmaceuticals, consulting, advertising, legal, healthcare, safety, etc.

Behaviour   This is also known as the sociology of project management. It studies and shows the empirical results on the effects of social network position, structure, and ties on the performance of workers in diversified occupational communities on the performance of a particular project.

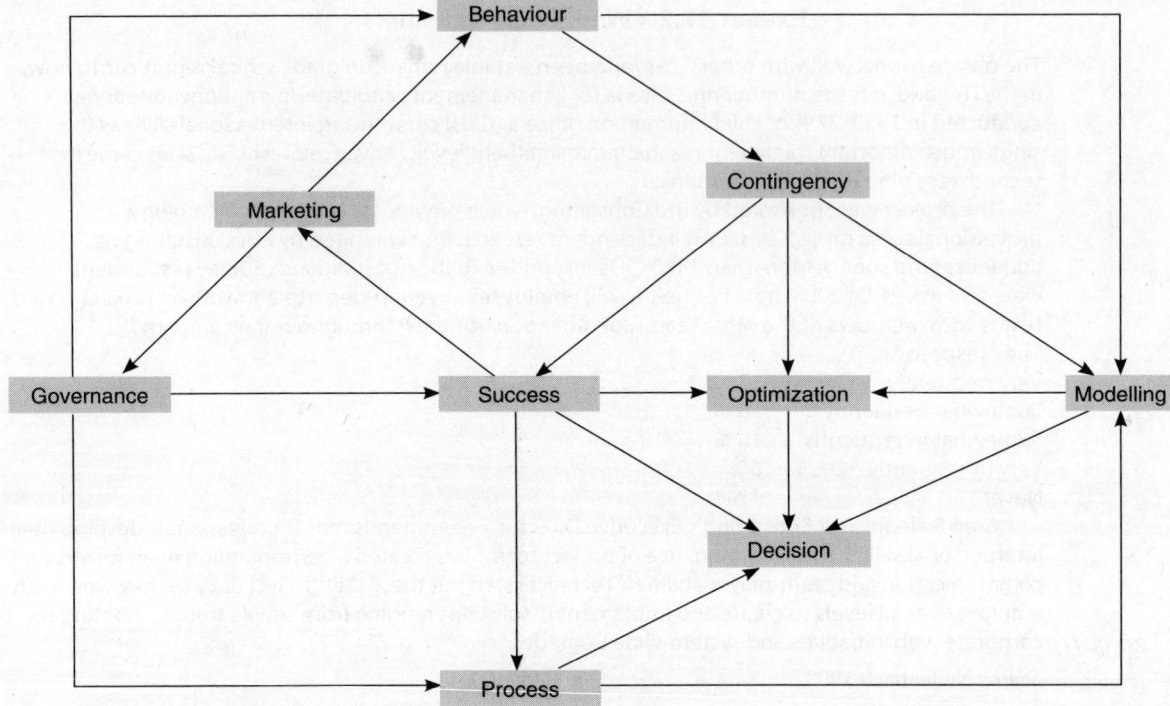

FIGURE 17.2 Nine schools of project management thoughts

Contingency The project management discipline is also known as the 'allied discipline framework' (Kwak and Anbari 2009). The allied disciplines are defined and categorized into eight groups and are listed below.

- Operations research, decision sciences, operation management, and supply-chain management
- Organizational behaviour and human resources management
- Information technology and information systems
- Technology, innovation, new product development, and research and development
- Engineering construction, contracts, legal aspects, and expert witness
- Strategy, integration, portfolio management, value of project management, and marketing
- Performance management, earned-value management, project finance, and accounting
- Quality management, Six Sigma, and process improvement

Success In the era of globalization, success in project management is typically dependent on areas such as communication, risk, standardization, and programme management (Levin 2009).

Optimization This dimension shifts project management from operation to strategic level. It gives importance to the interdependencies and the trading of the concepts amongst project management, strategic management, portfolio management, etc., so that ultimately the goal of the firm is optimized (Kwak and Anbari 2009).

Modelling Every project is unique in nature and the goals or objectives to be fulfilled by this project are also different for different stakeholders. Hence, it should be designed in such a way that all stakeholders work on a similar platform for a common objective.

Decision Today, many firms are investing more time and money to deal better with the increasing complexity of projects. It helps them in taking the final decision and in deriving greater efficiency from their valuable resources.

Process Now-a-days, process is defined as 'the accepted way of getting work done in a flexible, outsourced, and projectized environment'. The ultimate challenge of a project manager is to make this happen and achieve success.

Ten current trends in project management

In the current project management era, following are the top ten trends assessed by the top management and practitioners of ESI International (Baseline, July 2008):

Investment in project management training Investment in project management training is particularly important when a country's economy is in doldrums. Strategic organizations recognize this condition as an opportunity to invest in project management training and development to optimize performances.

Better, faster project decision-making A project manager should be determined enough to take fast and prompt decisions while choosing projects and should know which project to decline and which to accept, keeping in mind the return on investment in each case.

Critical thinking as a key project management competency Technical competency alone cannot ensure success of a project. It demands considerable amount of brainstorming and critical thinking.

Emerging relevance of the project management office The importance of project management office (PMO) has increased over the period of time with the increase in complexity and number of projects. Through this office, it becomes more convenient to control and coordinate the processes of a project. It also enables more efficiency in day-to-day project management.

Co-dependency between project management and enterprise analysis Through the exchange of knowledge between project managers and functional managers, experienced project managers who have an interest in risk management are taking over the responsibilities of traditional business analysts, including enterprise analysis.

Leadership roles in project management   In present times, when there are unending changes in the project organizations, project managers are gradually building leadership characteristics. Today, project managers need to understand the project implications and their role as leaders in a project. They must be proactive in bringing positive organizational changes through effective project portfolio management (PPM).

Communication challenges within a team   Most of the communication is done through emails, telephone, or video conferences as the numbers of projects conducted through global outsourcing have increased over the years. To maintain the quality of communications among different sectors of such virtually networked projects, it is vital for the project managers to find and put to use the technology available.

Earning certification   PMI is a professional body offering various certificate courses in project management. Obtaining a certificate from the PMI, which is a pioneer and an internationally accepted organization, helps in increasing the credibility of the managers.

Navigating the overlap between project management and business analysts   Now-a-days the role of a project manager and a business analyst are interdependent. Project managers and business analysts should follow their own responsibilities in the areas where their job profile overlaps.

Talent management's impact on return on investment   Organizations need to develop a talent management strategy, such as offering high incentives, which will help to recruit and retain talented professionals for improving business performances.

17.3 PROJECT MANAGEMENT MATURITY MODEL

The term 'maturity model' was first coined in the late eighties by a research group of the US government and the Software Engineering Institute (SEI) at Carnegie Mellon University. The government was looking for a tool that could anticipate the success rate of development work undertaken by contractors. The output of this research was the Capability Maturity Model (CMM). The Project Management Maturity Model (PMMM) is a formal tool developed by PM Solutions that is used in measuring the maturity of an organization's project management abilities. Once the initial levels are identified, it shows the required steps to be taken for further advancement and improvement. As shown in Figure 17.3, PMMM has five evolutionary maturity levels and examines nine knowledge areas published in *A Guide to the Project Management Body of Knowledge (PMBOK Guide)* in 2002 by PMI.

PM Solutions' Project Management Maturity Model combines SEI-type maturity measurement and PMI's *PMBOK Guide*'s industry standard in identifying key areas of project management. This unique approach to measure project management maturity gives an organization a firm understanding of their strenghts and areas for improvement. It also provides a sound and structured way for plan improvement.

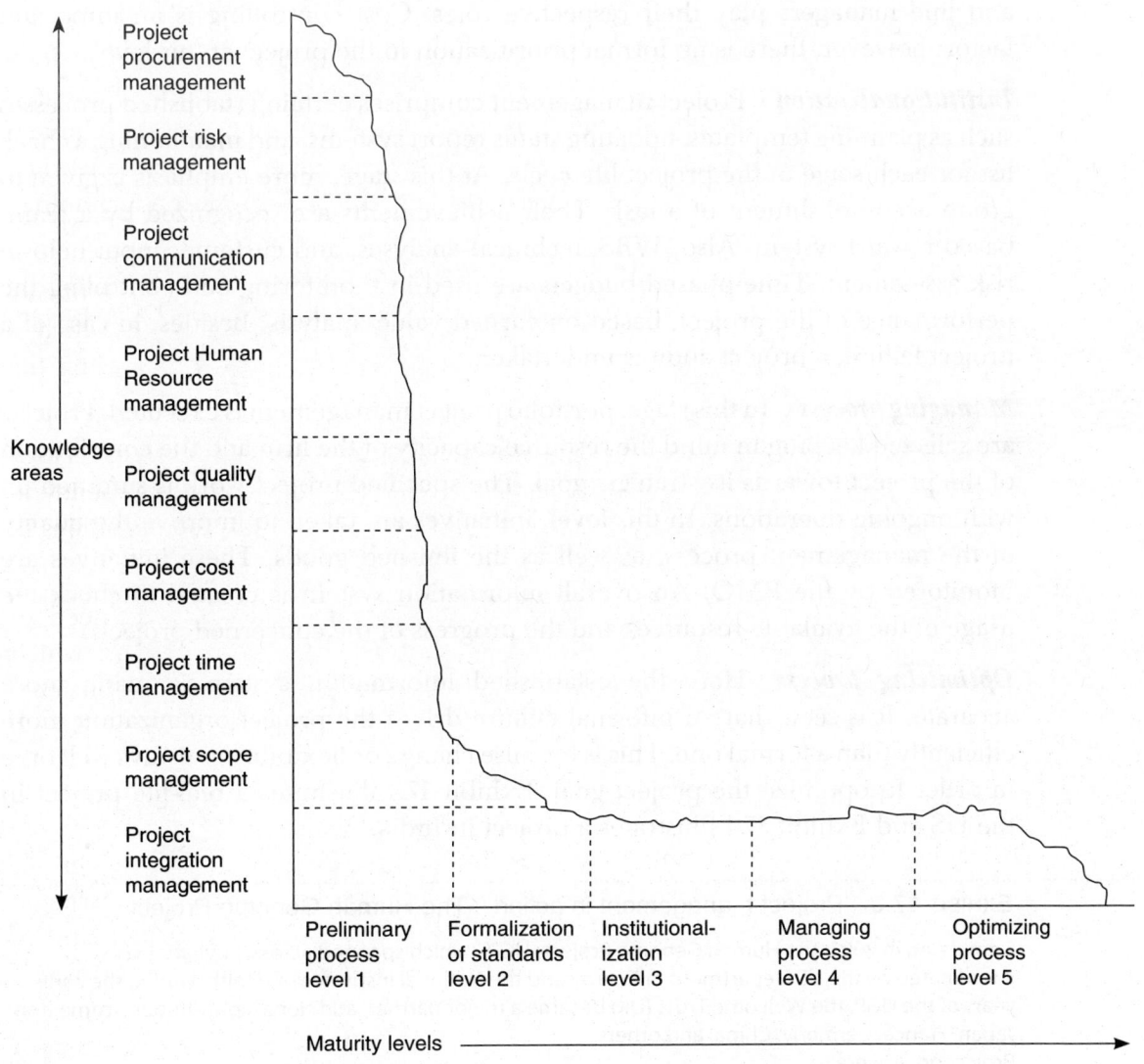

Source: www.pmsolutions.com.

FIGURE 17.3   Project management maturity model

Attributes of each level of PMMM are as follows.

Preliminary process   There's no specific criterion for undertaking a project. It is selected on the basis of the decisions made by the higher authorities. Initially, working on a new project becomes difficult as things are not streamlined and are often against the established rules of the company.

Formalization of standards   There are standard methods of handling a project. These include preparation of scope statements, WBS, and activity lists. At this level, organizations usually follow a stronger matrix structure in which project managers and line managers play their respective roles. Cost controlling is an important factor; however, there is no formal prioritization in the project at this level.

Institutionalization   Project management comprises certain established processes such as planning templates, updating status report systems, and maintaining a check list for each stage of the project life cycle. At this stage, more emphasis is given to group accomplishment of a task. Their achievements are recognized by a team-based reward system. Also, WBS, technical analyses, and customer input help in risk assessment. Time-phased budgets are used in monitoring and controling the performance of the project, based on earned value analysis. Besides, in case of a project failure, a project audit is undertaken.

Managing process   In this stage, portfolio project management is executed. Projects are selected keeping in mind the resource capacity of the firm and the contribution of the project towards its strategic goal. The specified project work is summed up with ongoing operations. In this level, initiatives are taken to improve the quality of the management process, as well as the finished goods. These initiatives are monitored by the PMO. An overall information system is created to check the usage of the available resources and the progress of the concerned projects.

Optimizing process   Here the established information system is made more accurate. It is seen that an informal culture drives the project organization more efficiently than a formal one. This is because change or flexibility is always welcome in order to optimize the project goal. Exhibit 17.3 illustrates a real-life project in the US and Exhibit 17.4 illustrates a project in India.

EXHIBIT 17.3   Project management in action—The Human Genome Project

Completed in 2003, the Human Genome Project (HGP), which spanned across 13 years, was coordinated by the US Department of Energy and the National Institutes of Health. During the early years of the HGP, the Welcome Trust (UK) became a major partner; additional contributions came from Japan, France, Germany, China, and others.
Project goals were to
- Identify all the approximately 20,000–25,000 genes in the human DNA
- Determine the sequences of the 3 billion chemical base pairs that make up the human DNA
- Store this information in databases

- Improve tools for data analysis
- Transfer related technologies to the private sector
- Address the ethical, legal, and social issues (ELSI) that may arise from the project

Though the HGP is finished, analyses of the data will continue for many years. An important feature of the HGP project was the federal government's long-standing dedication to the transfer of technology to the private sector. By licensing technologies to private companies and awarding grants for innovative research, the project catalysed the multibillion-dollar US biotechnology industry and fostered the development of new medical applications.

Source: www.ornl.gov/TechResources/Human_Genome/home.html, accessed 2 July 2010.

EXHIBIT 17.4   Dabhol project

'It makes a history in project management issues in India'
An MOU was signed in 1992 on Dabhol combined cycle plant project between Enron and the Maharashtra State Electricity Board (MSEB). Even seven years from the initial MOU, proper construction did not start. Because of making such a huge plant at a remote site, the project faced enormous unexpected difficulties, oppositions, and challenges. *Frontline* (November–Decemebr 2004) projected that the Dabhol project had been mired in controversy for the past several years. Prashant Bhushan's article

'Enron's Montek Connection' (*Frontline*, 19 November 2004) ignited this controversy to a larger extent. Challenges that were experienced in Dabhol Project are as follows (Larson, Gray and Gopalarathinam 1999):

1. Getting clearance from central and state government on issues such as techno-economic clearance (TEC) etc., before executing the power purchase agreement.
2. There was a major change in the site layout, which involved relocation of 2000 families. The relocation of the LNG jetty was necessary to avoid serious ecological problems involving the river estuary.
3. Litigations were proposed to be issued against the company by the high court in public interest.
4. The Maharashtra Industrial Development Corporation (MIDC) had many problems regarding the acquisition of land as the demand of the landholders had to be resolved.
5. After the elections in 1995, the new government issued a stay order and work could not be resumed for over a period of 12 months.
6. After the suspension order was lifted in August 1996, the new fuel for the project was decided to be naphtha. This required considerable amount of modification in its engineering design and specifications. However, these processes were already at an advanced stage of completion.

Dabhol was clearly a flawed project selection by the Maharashtra government. But it is important to learn the right lessons from this experience. There is nothing inherently wrong with private investment and foreign investment infrastructure. Rather, it should be welcomed. Practically, it needs a strong regulatory system capable of determining the tariff in a transparent manner. From the consumer's viewpoint, what matters is the tariff. Unfortunately, the techno-economic clearance system did not give emphasis to this issue. This lacuna has been filled since then and all generating stations today have been approved by an independent regulator.

17.4 CONTEMPORARY ISSUES IN PROJECT MANAGEMENT

With the increase in price of the resources, organizations must find and adapt to new procedures for executing projects by staying within the cost boundary. They must develop better methods to control the increasing resource cost to stay competitive.

The frequent hikes in the cost of fuel have become a concern for organizational heads. Senior and experienced project leaders must find a way out to absorb this hike in the project process or to increase the price of the finished product. The present project management procedures are fighting hard with this increasing price of resources. The emphasis is also on the ways in which consumption of the resources can be minimized. Often project managers are assigned the job of finding out better ways through which an organization can deliver its product concentrating little on cost and more on the schedule and technical accuracy of the product. Today, the need of the hour is to have effective and efficient project managers.

Trends in project management

Organizations are switching their focus from surviving to showing business value. The major key to this approach is maintaining matrices, i.e., keeping management informed about project performance and its impact on the bottom line and end users. A global panel of consultants and senior executives assembled by ESI identified the following trends that are being followed.

Uncertainty   Success of a project cannot be guaranteed. This is because a project develops in an environment of variable social, economical, and political situations. Uncertainty in project management also occurs due to its finite inputs that include capital, time, and other resources. The principles of PPM play a very important role in selecting the right project and ensuring favourable results. In the future, risk assessment methods would be critical to project management across the globe. Project Management Risk Assessment Principles (PMRAP) would also help in dealing with the interdependencies between programme and portfolio components. Organizations would prefer to categorize systematic and non-systematic risks that threaten the success of a project.

More tech-savvy   With the advancement of web-based services, particularly among small companies, the business models of large monolithic companies have come under serious threat. Small companies with limited resources but professional competence are offering specialised web-based solutions to customers in a much more cost-effective way. This greatly affects the business of established vendors. Therefore, the established have to match the competitors in the field of web-based services.

PM learning In recent times, many organizations have executed first-time learning initiatives focused on project management maturity. This has been done in order to have an edge over competitors. To survive in the present competitive era, organizations must provide customized training to project managers, which not only gives inputs and instructions, but also assesses progress and demonstrates performance improvement.

Correlation between project management and operation management Earlier it was believed that project management was an issue of concern for only the techies, the field-level workers, and the lower level managers. But with the increase in competition, the high-level executives are equally involved in taking decisions to make project management processes effective and fruitful. Hence, the communication and cooperation among project managers and top-level executives such as CEO, CFO, COO, etc., should be strong and clear for the overall success of the project.

Coherence between PMO and CFO In recent times, especially in a project-based service-oriented economy, customer engagement and billing arrangements are becoming more complex. It has to consider the internal customer satisfaction as well. Even internal departments have to justify their cause, deliver services efficiently, satisfy the next level internal customer and earn business within the firm. As a consequence, estimating project value and identifying revenue with various GAAP (generally accepted accounting principles) are becoming more challenging for CFOs. Under the global project management scenario, IFRS (International Financial Reporting System) will be applied to the evaluation of projects as well. The complexity and intricacy involved in the assessment of project value have resulted in cooperation and collaboration between CFOs and project managers, and it is expected to grow stronger with time.

Varied customers and varied expectations Every project is unique. Therefore, each project has to be customized and designed to satisfy its own requirements and expectations. Customer's requirements vary not only due to their specific interests, but also because of their demographic, socio-economic, and cultural locations.

Transfer from project management to workforce management Although there has been an increase in the number of highly qualified project personnel who are sincere towards the institutional guidelines, it is observed, statistically, that many projects have failed to produce the desired results. It is being predicted that greater involvement of stakeholders and better project management and communication will be advantageous and will reduce the project failure rate. The success of a project is dependent on the team that runs the project. According to *Build to Last* (Collins and Porras 2004), the need of the hour is to have 'the right people on the bus', that is, the best practices and better tools cannot be more important than selecting the right people and the most suitable resources for running a project.

Vendor management and outsourcing Outsourcing will play a leading role in the near future as organizations are looking forward to doing more business without increasing the number of permanent employees. Organizations will guide their outsourcing companies through project management principles.

Interrelationship between PMO and business analysis centres of excellence In the recent past, we have seen that the PMO's had a considerable positive effect on the business. In the future, PMO's will definitely use this position to set up business analysis centres of excellence to improve project outcomes.

Leadership A ship cannot move an inch without its captain. It is applicable to project management as well. One of the major reasons for project failure is the incompetency of its leader. It does not matter how strong a project is with regard to resource, time, and cost, it can never be successful until it is headed by someone who has the ability to take prompt and effective decisions, especially in times of crisis. In the near future, organizations will be looking forward to such competent, smart, and efficient leaders who can get the maximum out of a project.

Russell D. Archibald has commented that following three major project management trends will continue in future:

- Linking strategic and project management through PPM practices.
- Broadening the application of project management to include the total project life cycle, from concept through to full realization of project benefits.
- Continued discovery of new application areas for the project management discipline.

Today, project management is not only a means for the successful completion of a project, but also a strategic tool to it in the right direction according to the changing demands of time. Hence, the traditional project management field is now aspiring to become strategic project management in the near future.

SUMMARY

Project management has given way to new career opportunities for professionals in organizations. Project managers, today, have become the most important managers in any firm. Their type and profile varies from organization to organization and project to project.

Regardless of the level of training, one needs to supplement it with further education in project management. Universities and institutions now offer specialized courses on project management. Some of the institutes like PMI are well-known institutes for people studying to become project managers. In-house training of project managers is another way of providing training in organizations.

Project management maturity model measures the maturity of an organization's project management abilities and identifies the required steps for further advancement. To overcome the increase in competition among firms and the price of resources, ESI has identified new trends to help organizations adapt to new and complex circumstances for executing projects by staying within the cost boundary.

CONCEPT REVIEW QUESTIONS

1. Why are careers in project management very challenging?
2. What are the recent and future trends in project management?

3. Describe Project Management Maturity Model.

ASSIGNMENT

Study five Indian and five international ongoing and upcoming projects — their features, utilities, and uniqueness. Give your insight about the changes in project management as a field.

SELECT REFERENCES

Bredillet, C.N., 'Exploring Research in Project Management: Nine Schools of Project Management Research', *Project Management Journal*, vol. 39, no. 3, Septemebr 2008, pp. 2–4.

Bhushan, P., 'Enron's Montek Connection', *Frontline*, vol. 20, Novemebr 2004.

Kwak, Y.H., and F.T. Anbari, 'Impact on Project Management of Allied Disciplines: Trends of Future of Project Management Practises and Research', *Project Management Journal*, vol. 39, no. 2, June 2008, pp. 111.

Larson, E.L., R.J. Gray, and R. Gopalarathinam, 'Dabhol Phase I: Project Management Issues', *Modern Power Systems*, July 1999, pp. 37–39.

Levin, G., 'Fundamentals of Effective Program Management: A Process Approach Based on the Global Standards', *Project Management Journal*, vol. 40, no. 2, June 2009, pp. 105.

Saia, R., 'Harvesting Project Leaders', *Computer World*, vol. 31, no. 29, July 1997, pp. 1.

Nellenbach, J.M., 'People Skills Top Technical Knowledge, CIO Insists', *PM Networks*, August 1999, pp. 7–8.

Other resources

www.pmi.org, accessed 2 July 2010.

www.ornl.gov/TechResources/Human_Genome/home.html, accessed 2 July 2010.

www.esi-intl.com, accessed 2 July 2010.

www.baselinemag.com, accessed 2 July 2010.

www.pmsolutions.com, accessed 2 July 2010.

www.sei.cmu.edu/activities/sema/profile.html, accessed 2 July 2010.

APPENDIX 1

REGULATORY FRAMEWORK IN PROJECT APPRAISAL

Introduction

In India, projects need to be planned and implemented within the large framework provided by the industrial policy statement, through which the government indicates its attitude towards the industry. Various aspects of relevance such as industrial licensing, mergers, acquisitions, transactions involving the use of foreign exchange, incentives for small-scale sector, the government's concern for environmental protection, and so on are provided in this.

The New Industrial Policy, 1991, tabled on the 24 July 1991 (amended in 2001), envisaged drastic changes in the government's attitude towards the industry. While reiterating the objectives of employment generation, reduction of socioeconomic disparities, removal of poverty and such others, the policy also has brought: about considerable changes in the areas as licensing, monopolistic practices, private sector participation in various areas, foreign companies, and participation in the equity of Indian companies in order to enable the Indian industry to graduate from being protected to being on their own, taking on global competition and meeting demands there from competently.

The new industrial policy not only represents the restrictions imposed, but also throws up a lot of opportunities which are to be availed. The discussion that follows dwells on the following aspects, which are related to planning and control of projects:

• The changes in the IDRA
• The changed procedure for licensing
• The incentives provided for EOUs/EPZ units
• Incentives for units in the industrially backward areas
• Incentives for units in the small-scale sector
• Environmental guidelines for industries

    Foreign collaborations including Foreign Technology Agreements and Foreign Investments.

    Some of the notifications issued since, introducing newer changes have also been incorporated.

Industrial Licensing Policy

Industrial licensing is governed by the Industrial Development and Regulation Act (IDRA). In keeping with the changing industrial scenario, the process of licensing has been considerably liberalized. The Industrial Policy Statement (IPS) tabled on the 24 July 1991 (amended in 2001), has removed the requirement of licensing in various sectors of the economy in order to actively encourage and assist entrepreneurs to exploit and meet the emerging domestic and global opportunities and challenges.

In order to enable entrepreneurs make investment decisions on the basis of their own commercial judgement and to facilitate the attainment of technological dynamism and international competitiveness through swift responses to the demands of the last changing industrial environment, the Industrial Development and Regulation Act (IDRA), was changed substantially. According to the notification issued, industrial undertakings have been exempted from the operation of Sections 10, 11, 11A and 13 of the IDR Act, 1951, subject to the fulfilment of certain conditions.

Section 10 refers to the requirement of registration of existing industrial units.

Section 11 refers to the requirement of licensing of new industrial undertakings.

Section 11A refers to the licenses for production of new articles.

Section 13 refers to the requirement of licensing for substantial expansion.

The notification has three schedules:

Schedule I: List of industries reserved for the public sector and includes mineral oils, railways, defence related industries, and atomic energy.

Schedule II: List of industries subject to compulsory licensing

Schedule III: Lists the articles reserved for the small sector such as ancillary sector including textiles, food and allied products, wood, paper, leather products, rubber, plastic products, chemicals, dyes, tiles, glass, and ceramics.

Provision of the New Policy

Industrial licence requirement has been progressively reduced. At present industrial licence for manufacturing is required only for the following:
(i)   Industries retained under compulsory licensing
(ii) Items reserved for small-scale sector
(iii) When the proposed location attracts locational restriction

Industries Retained Under Compulsory Licensing

The list of items requiring compulsory licensing is reviewed on an ongoing basis. At present, only six industries are under compulsory licensing mainly on account of environmental, public health, safety, and strategic considerations. Similarly, there are only three industries' reserved for the public sector.

A. The following industries require compulsory industrial license:
1.   Distillation and brewing of alcoholic drinks
2.   Cigars and cigarettes of tobacco and manufactured tobacco substitutes
3.   Electronic aerospace and defence equipment: all types
4.   Industrial explosives including detonating fuses, safety fuses, gun powder, nitrocellulose, and matches;
5.   Hazardous chemicals
     • Hydrocyanic acid and its derivatives
     • Phosgene and its derivatives

- Isocyanates and di-isocyanates of hydrocarbon, not elsewhere specified (for example, methyl isocyanate)
6. Drugs and pharmaceuticals (according to modified Drug Policy issued in September 1994 and subsequently amended in February 1999)

B. A list of industries reserved for the public sector:
1. Atomic energy
2. The substances specified in the schedule to the notification of the Government of India in the Department of Atomic Energy Number S.O. 212 (E), dated the 15 March 1995
3. Railway transport.

Items Reserved for Small-scale Sector

The government took some steps to support the small-scale sector. One of the steps is reservation of items of manufacture exclusively for the small-scale sector. Since 24 December 1999, industrial undertakings with an investment up to Rs 1 crore are within the small-scale and ancillary sector. A differential investment limit has been adopted since 9 October 2001 for 41 reserved items where the investment limit up to Rs 5 crore is prescribed for qualifying as a small-scale unit. The investment limit for tiny units is Rs 25 lakh. Small-scale units can get registered with the Directorate of Industries/District Industries Centre of the State Government. 749 items are reserved for manufacture in the small-scale sector. All undertakings other than the small-scale industrial undertakings engaged in the manufacture of items reserved for manufacture in the small-scale sector are required to obtain an industrial licence and undertake an export obligation of 50% of the annual production. This condition of licensing is, however, not applicable to those undertakings operating under 100% Export Oriented Undertakings Scheme, the Export Processing Zone (EPZ) or the Special Economic Zone Schemes (SEZs).

Liberalization of the Locational Policy

A significantly amended locational policy in tune with the liberalized licensing policy is in place. No industrial approval is required from the government for locations not falling within 25 km of the periphery of cities having a population of more than one million except for those industries where industrial licensing is compulsory. Non-polluting industries such as electronics, computer software, and printing can be located within 25 km of the periphery of cities with more than one million population. Permission to other industries is granted in such locations only if they are located in an industrial area so designated prior to 25 July 1991. Zoning and land use regulations as well as environmental legislations have to be followed.

Exempted Industrial Licensing

Licensing is abolished for all industrial undertakings including MRTP/FERA companies and small-scale and ancillary industries provided,
I. The proposed article(s) of manufacture is not included in Annexure I or II or is not reserved for the small-scale/ancillary sector.

II. The proposed project is not located within 25 km from the periphery of the standard urban area limits of a city having a population of more than 10 lakh according to the 1991 census.

This condition will not apply to electronics, computer software, printing and other non-polluting industries as notified from time to time, as also to those industries not located within the areas designated as 'industrial areas' by the state government(s) before 25 July 1991.

Notwithstanding the above, the location of industrial projects will also be subjected to central or state government environmental laws or regulations including local zoning and land-wise laws and regulations.

Small-scale and ancillary undertakings are exempted from industrial licensing requirements for all items of manufacture except those listed in Annexure I and Annexure II. They are also exempted for articles of manufacture exclusively reserved for the small-scale/ancillary sector even if they happen to be included in Annexure II. Further, they are exempted from locational conditions subject to the provisions of any central/state environmental laws or regulations including land zoning and land-wise laws and regulations.

Substantial Expansion

Substantial expansion of units involved in the manufacture of articles other than those listed in Annexure I and Annexure II or reserved for small-scale/ancillary sector is exempt from licensing requirements subject to the locational conditions already discussed.

The term 'annexure', wherever mentioned in this supplementary note, has reference to the Annexures, three in number, of the New Industrial Policy Statement, 1992. These are appended to the note.

Broad Banding/Manufacture of New Articles

Existing units would be permitted to manufacture any new article without additional investment if the article is not otherwise subject to compulsory licensing. This is notwithstanding any locational conditions. This is an additional facility to existing units.

Guidelines for Industrial License Applications Received for Industries falling Outside Compulsory Licensing but Involving Locational Angle

Industrial licensing is exempt for all except 16 specified categories of industries, subject to certain locational restrictions. The proposed project should not be located within 25 km from the periphery of the standard urban area limits of a city having a population of more than 10 lakh according to 1991 census. However, if the unit was located in an area designated as an 'Industrial area' by the concerned state government before 25 July 1991, this restriction will not apply. Industrial units other than electronics, computer software or printing, which lie outside 'industrial areas', but within the 25 km limit specified above, require industrial licenses even if they are otherwise delicensed.

Procedure for Scrutiny of IEM and follow up Action

- Under the existing procedure, an acknowledgement is given on filing of the IEM with the minimum of scrutiny. But, this is not conclusive evidence that the proposed unit confirms to the conditions of delicensing.
- To further simplify existing procedures, it has been decided that hereafter only one copy of the IEM be filed with the SIA.
- Locational conditions being one of the important aspects of delicensing, the concerned ministries, technical authorities, state governments, etc., furnish their comments to SIA only if, in their opinion, the proposed item of manufacture requires licensing under the IDRA, 1951, and/or the location of the proposed unit does not confirm to the locational policy of the government.

In case no comments are received within the stipulated period of two weeks, it will be presumed that the proposed unit satisfies the conditions of delicensing and location.

Abolition of Existing Registration Schemes

As a consequence of the new industrial policy, existing registration schemes, namely, the Delicensed Industries Registration Scheme (DIR), Exempted Industries Registration Scheme (EIR), and Registration with DGTD, which office has since been abolished, and other technical authorities, namely the Textile Commissioner and the Development Commissioner from Iron and Steel, have been abolished.

Procedural Requirements for Delicensed/Licensed Sectors

- All exempted industries, including those undertaking substantial expansion shall file information in the prescribed Industrial Entrepreneurs Memorandum (Form IEM) with the Secretariat for Industrial Approvals (SIA) along with a crossed demand draft of Rs 1,000 drawn in favour of the Pay and Accounts Officer, Department of Industrial Development, Ministry of Industry.
- Industrial undertakings shall also file information in another prescribed memorandum at the time of commencement of commercial production with the SIA.
- Small-scale and ancillary units are not required to file an IEM with the SIA. They may get themselves registered with the Director of Industries of the concerned state government/ union territory.

The receipt of the memorandum will be acknowledged by the SIA and a reference number will be issued.

New Classification System

The description of articles exempted from compulsory licensing should also be stated according to the Indian Trade Classification System in the IEM with the SIA. In other applications for industrial approvals also the description of article(s) to be manufactured should be stated, where required, according to the classification.

Phased Manufacturing Programme

The system of Phased Manufacturing Programme (PMP) has been abolished for both new as well as existing projects.

Industries Subject to Compulsory Licensing

Whereas the process of licensing has been considerably liberalized, some industries continue to be subject to compulsory licensing for reasons related to security and strategic concerns, social reasons, problems related to safety overriding environmental issues, manufacture of products of hazardous nature and articles of elitist consumption.

The industrial policy statement has specified that the following sectors shall continue to be subject to compulsory industrial licensing.

- The proposed article(s) of manufacture is included in the list of industries reserved for the public sector (Annexure I) or those in respect of which licensing is compulsory (Annexure II).
- The proposed project is within 25 km from the periphery of the standard urban limits of a city having a population of more than 10 lakh according to the 1991 census.
- Items reserved for exclusive development in the small-scale sector.

Procedure for Processing Pending Industrial License Application

The pending applications for issue of letters of intent are scrutinized by the SIA who advise the concerned parties to file IEMs along with the prescribed fee. Where the request of the party for conversion of letter of intent into industrial License is pending with the administrative ministry and the item of manufacture is exempt from licensing, according to the new industrial policy, if steps have already been taken by the LOI holder to implement the project, the LOI holder need only file part 'B' of the memorandum required to be submitted at the time of commencement of commercial production. However, entrepreneurs may file-an initial memorandum if they so desire, whenever any deviations from the conditions stipulated in the LOI are contemplated upon.

Industrial undertakings covering the project for manufacture of articles requiring compulsory license are required to apply in Form IL with 8 spare copies with a covering letter to the SIA, Department of Industrial Development, with a Demand Draft for Rs 2,500 drawn in favour of Pay and Accounts Officer, Department of Industrial Development, Ministry of Industry.

Industrial Licensing Procedure for Industries subject to Licensing Requirements

As per the provisions of the new industrial policy, all entrepreneurs setting up manufacturing facilities for products included in Annexure to this note are required to obtain industrial license for all or any one of the following purposes:

(i)   Setting up of a new industrial undertaking
(ii) Manufacturing of a new article
(iii) Substantial expansion of the licensed capacity of the undertaking
(iv) Carrying on business
(v)   Change of location

The entrepreneurs are required to apply in Form IL in a set of 10 copies with a covering letter to the Secretariat for Industrial Approvals (SIA). A special Form IL (NRI) has been prescribed for Non-Resident Indians (NRIs). This form should be submitted in a set of 11 copies. Application for carrying on business license should be made on Form EE in a set of 8 copies. Application for license or permission on change of location should be made in Form E in a set of 13 copies. An application for a license for: (i) establishment of a new undertaking (ii) for the manufacture of new article or (iii) for effecting substantial expansion in capacity should be made before–

(a)   Issue of capital to the public
(b)   Commencing construction of factory building
(c)   Placing order for plant and machinery

An application for change of location of an industrial undertaking should be made before

(a)   Acquisition of land at the new site
(b)   Construction of premises for housing the industrial undertaking at the new site
(c)   Dismantling any machinery at the existing site

In cases where an application needs capital goods clearance and/or foreign collaboration clearance, in addition to an industrial license, the entrepreneur may file applications for all the approvals required simultaneously. Such 'composite applications' would enable the government to give a composite or simultaneous clearance.

Where an application for grant of license is approved by the government, a letter of intent/industrial license is issued. In case where neither foreign collaboration approval nor capital goods clearance is involved, an industrial license, instead of a letter of intent is issued. The initial validity period, from the date of issue of the letter of intent would be twelve months. The concerned administrative ministry can grant two extensions of not more than six months on each occasion. Similarly, the initial validity period of two years for industrial license may be extended by the administrative ministry for one year, on each occasion. Subsequent extensions, if necessary, would be decided upon by the approval committee.

To avoid the delay in converting the letter of intent into industrial license, letter of intent is automatically converted into industrial license when the subsequent clearances are finally given, namely, foreign collaboration approval, capital goods clearance and certificate relating to environmental pollution.

Entrepreneurs holding industrial licenses are required to submit returns in Form G within one month after the expiry of every half-year ending 30 June, and 31 December, commencing from the date of issue of the license, until such time as the industrial undertaking commences production.

Processing of Application for Industrial License

The normal stages through which an application for industrial license passes are as follows:

- Receipt's of application.
- Registration and acknowledgement of the application (indicating registration number and date).

- Scrutiny of the application and seeking of clarification for any minor deficiency/ discrepancy.
- Circulation of the application to members of the Approval Committee for comments.
- Receipt of the comments from the members.
- Preparation of the summary for the approval committee.
- Submission of the summary for recommendation of the approval committee
- Consideration by the approval committee
- Preparation of minutes of the recommendations of the approval committee.
- Approval of the minutes incorporating the recommendations of the approval
- Committee by the Ministry of Industry.
- Circulation of approved minutes to concerned ministries/departments.
- Issue of letter of intent/industrial license or prima facie rejection letter.
- Consideration of representation, if any, against prima facie rejection.
- Reconsideration by approval committee, wherever necessary.
- Issue of final rejection letter or letter of intent/industrial license after recon-sideration.

The SIA scrutinizes the application to ensure that it is complete in all respects. Any deficiency or mistake is brought to the notice of the applicant for rectification. The SIA may also return the application for resubmission after rectification of deficiencies. It may also call for such additional information as it may consider necessary and such additional information must be furnished within the time period specified. If the additional information or clarification is not received within the specified time limit, a prima facie rejection of the proposal is communicated to the applicant.

When copies of the application are circulated to the members of the approval committee, such members are required to send their comments within a specified time period. It must also be noted that a summary is required to be prepared for the consideration of the approval committee. The preparation of such summary will not normally be held up if the comments are not received in time. When comments are not received, the views of the members are expressed orally at the meeting of the committee and followed up with written confirmation of their views. The application for grant of industrial license is brought before the approval committee after 35 days of its receipt.

The central government has evolved a set of guidelines to be adhered to by the approval committee for scrutiny of applications and grant of industrial licenses.

These guidelines are as follows:

- The application must be scrutinized with reference to the priority accorded to the industry for which the application is being made as outlined in the relevant Five-year Plan.
- The proposed investment conform to the policies outlined in the industrial policy statements made by the government from time to time.
- The planned or projected demand, including export demand, for the proposed items of manufacture and the scope for further licensing in the light of capacity already licensed and likely to materialize must be scrutinized.
- The committee must consider the net effect on balance of payments having regard to export possibilities, import savings and the outgo on import of capital goods, raw materials and components, and on payments for import of technology.

- The committee must consider the locational aspects in the light of regional demand and whether the project will be, or is capable of being, set-up in a backward area with special reference to the policy consideration spelt out in the statements on industrial policy, as amended from time to time.
- The committee must evaluate the extent to which and the time period over which the continued dependence on imports is sought to be reduced through a phased programme for progressive indigenous manufacture of components and raw materials.
- The committee must examine the extent to which the proposal postulates the utilization of indigenous know-how, design and consultancy services, and research and development.
- It must evaluate the potential created for direct and indirect employment.
- The committee must examine whether the components are proposed to be sub-contracted to small-scale and ancillary units to the extent that is appropriate and feasible.
- Whether the processes proposed to be adopted are efficient from a techno-economic viewpoint must be examined.
- The committee must evaluate the extent to which diversification and expansion proposals will result in fuller utilization of capacity and economies of scale.
- The committee must also examine whether adequate attention in preparing the proposal has been given to the market, availability of raw materials, utilization of by-products, availability of water, power, transport and fuel, arrangements to ensure the-safe disposal of effluent, and other relevant factors.
- The committee must scrutinize the competence of the entrepreneur as evidenced by the preparatory work done, his technical qualifications, etc., and his record in implementing other licenses which might have been issued to him.
- The committee must examine whether commercial production is proposed to be achieved in a realistic time-period.

A technical appraisal of the license application by DGTD is necessary for a decision by the licensing committee. The technical appraisal should consider the following aspects:

- Does the production capacity offer scope for economic production?
- Are the assumptions made for investment on plant and machinery adequate?
- Is the provision for raw material consumption reasonable?
- Has the investor ensured adequate supply of electricity, power, water, and fuel?
- Is the phased manufacturing programme (in respect of indigenization) sound and practicable?
- If obnoxious by-products/effluents are likely to arise, are satisfactory arrangements being made for their disposal in a safe manner?
- Is the proposed unit at an economic distance from another unit making the same product to ensure reasonable market when the unit commences production?
- Is the location of the unit satisfactory with respect to raw materials' supply, power, water, and fuel supplies, and also regional distribution of industries and development of backward areas?
- Is there potential for developing exports of the product?
- Is there any need for foreign collaboration?
- Are there identifiable areas which lend themselves to ancillarization?

The approval committee after a due deliberation either recommends approval or rejection of the application. In case it is not able to formulate the recommendation for any reason, the committee can defer the case for reconsideration at a subsequent meeting on the basis of any additional material either from the applicant or from the concerned administrative ministry to come to a decision on the application.

The minutes of the committee containing the recommendations is prepared for approval by the Ministry of Industry. It is for the ministry to accept or reject the recommendation. However, the decision of the ministry is final. the minutes as approved by the ministry are circulated to the concerned ministries/ departments.

If the applicant's proposal is approved and if the proposal does not involve import of capital goods, then a letter of intent or industrial license is issued. If the proposal is rejected, a prima facie rejection letter is issued giving a period of three weeks within which an applicant can represent against the prima facie rejection. If any representation is made by the entrepreneur, then the proposal is again submitted to the approval committee for reconsideration. If on reconsideration, the proposal is approved, then the letter of intent/ industrial license is issued and if rejected, a final rejection letter follows. If no representation is received against prima facie rejection within the time specified, then the proposal would be finally rejected.

It is pertinent to note here that the application for industrial license is considered in two stages:

1. If on the basis of the facts mentioned in the application it is found prima facie that the party would also be able to implement the scheme, a letter of intent is issued.
2. When the applicant satisfies the conditions laid down in the letter of intent, an industrial license is issued.

The above procedure also ensures that the capability of the applicant to complete the various steps involved in the setting up of the industrial undertaking is tested.

Applications for grant of industrial license are generally rejected on the following grounds only:

(a) Adequate capacity already exists in the country
(b) Constraints in availability of raw material
(c) Proposed location is not in conformity with governments' locational policy
(d) Ill-conceived proposal or improper formulation of the proposal
(e) Proposal not being in line with the current licensing policy.

Earlier a scheme of re-endorsement of capacity up to 49% under modernization/ replacement/renovation of equipment was available. After the announcement of the new industrial policy, since the requirement of licensing has been done away with for all but 16 industries, the government has withdrawn the scheme. The withdrawal of the re-endorsement scheme implies that an entrepreneur will have to apply for grant of letter of intent for substantial expansion of capacity if the article to be manufactured is subject to compulsory licensing irrespective of the location of the industrial undertaking. Even if the article of manufacture is not under compulsory licensing, but the undertaking is located within a radius of 25 km from the periphery of the standard urban area limits of a town with a population of more than one million, then any proposal for substantial expansion would require a license.

Electronic Hardware Technology Park (EHTP)/Software Technology Park (STP) Scheme

To build up a strong electronics industry and to enhance export, two schemes, viz., Electronic Hardware Technology Park (EHTP) and Software Technology Park (STP) are in operation. Under EHTP/STP scheme, the inputs are allowed to be procured free of duties.

The Directors of STPs have powers to approve fresh STP/EHTP proposals and also grand post-approval amendment in respect of EHTP/STP projects as have been given to the development commissioners of export processing zones in the case of export oriented units. All other applications for setting up projects under these schemes, are considered by the Inter-Ministerial Standing Committee (IMSC) chaired by secretary (Information Technology). The IMSC is serviced by the SIA.

Exported Oriented Units/Export Processing Zones Scheme

The new industrial policy statement has established a system of automatic approvals for EOU/EPZ units within certain parameters. Import of capital goods which are new is cleared if the foreign equity covers their cost or where they are less than 50% of the value of plant and equipment subject to a limit of Rs 3 crore.

While those which deserve automatic approvals shall be granted within two weeks. The others shall be submitted to the board of approvals and granted license within 45 days.

Automatic Approvals

The SIA shall grant automatic approvals to 100% EOUs, and the respective development commissioners for units to be set-up in the EPZ/FTZ, if:
- The product is not included is Schedule I or II of the 1D
- The locational conditions are satisfied, whether they are located within or outside an EPZ
- The project satisfies the export obligation prescribed
- The conditions for import of capital goods are satisfied
- The foreign technology agreement is restricted to a lump sum payment of Rs 1 crore or 8% royalty, over a period of 5 years from the commencement of production
- The exports by the unit are to be physically made to the general currency area
- The unit meets the requirements of the customs authorities
- The conditions relating to DTA sale are adhered to
- The unit has an annual turnover of at least Rs 50 crore if it is for manufacture of gems and jewellery and is located outside EPZs/other designated areas.

The following specific concessions to 100% EOUs/EPZs units have also been extended:

1. Allowing entry of imported raw material on 'provisional assessment' basis, to expedite customs clearance
2. Permitting units under the EPZ and 100% EOU schemes to supply/transfer finished goods among themselves
3. Replacement of a multiple bond by a single bond, for obtaining import clearance

4. Increasing the list of items under the 'Special Import License Scheme'
5. Clarifying that container stuffed in EPZs and 100% EOUs are not to be re-inspected at other points, as long as the seals are intact
6. Simplified rules for clearance of goods from EOU/EPZ unit into Domestic Tariff Area (DTA)
7. Liberalizing the import policy for export oriented units and EPZ units by way of reducing physical control on such units and to rely on their self-declaration and to adopt single window clearance
8. Software units being allowed to use the computer systems for training purpose including commercial training

The government has also decided to allow private parties to establish bonded warehouses within EPZ for stocking and sale of duty-free raw materials, components, consumables, and spares to EPZ units arid 100% EOUs. This will cut down delay in obtaining supplies of duty-free materials which are in constant and regular demand by exporters.

The following points deserve discussion.

Import of Capital Goods

EOUs/EPZs may import free of duty all types of goods including capital goods required for manufacture, production, or processing except those in the negative list of import. All second-hand capital goods having a minimum residual life of greater than 5 years may be imported by the actual users, without a license. A self-declaration shall be provided by the actual user that the goods imported have a minimum residual life of 5 years in the prescribed form. Where the CIF value of the goods being imported exceeds Rs 1 crore, a certificate from an internationally reputed Inspection and Certification Agency to the effect that the purchase price is reasonable, shall be furnished to the customs, at the time of clearance of goods.

Leasing of Capital Goods

An EOU/EPZ unit may, on the basis of a firm contract between the parties, source capital goods from a domestic leasing company. The domestic leasing company is eligible to import the capital goods free of duty and supply it to the EOU/EPZ units. The capital goods shall remain in part of the capital assets of EOU/EPZ until the export obligation is discharged by the unit and they shall not be diverted for any other use.

Value addition and Export Obligation

The EOU/EPZ shall achieve a minimum value addition of 20%, but units engaged in the manufacture of articles mentioned in Annexure II shall achieve the norms mentioned therein. Items of manufacture for export specified in the letter of intent/letter of permission above shall be taken into account for calculation of value addition and discharge of export obligation. Notwithstanding the above, projects shall be allowed to be set-up without minimum value addition stipulation in such sectors as electronics hardware.

Domestic Tariff Area Sales

The entire production of EOU/EPZ units shall be exported except:

- Rejects up to 5% or such percentage as may be fixed by the board of approval, which may be sold in the DTA subject to payment of applicable duties, and 25% of the production in value terms may be sold in the DTA subject to fulfilment of minimum value addition. DTA sale of jewellery, diamonds, precious and semi-precious stones/gems, motor cars, alcoholic liquors, silver bullion and such other items as may be stipulated by the Director General of Foreign Trade by a public notice issued in this behalf.
- However, EOU/EPZ units involved in agriculture, animal husbandry, floriculture, horticulture, pisciculture, poultry and sericulture, may sell up to 50% of their production in DTA in accordance with the DTA sale guidelines subject to fulfilment of minimum value addition.
- Electronic hardware products may be sold in the DTA on the following basis:
  1. If the value addition is less than 15%, nil.
  2. If it is between 15% and 25%, 30% of the production including components may be sold.
  3. If it is above 25%, up to 40%, including components may be sold.
- EOUs/EPZ units may be permitted to sell finished products which can be freely imported under the policy, in the DTA, over and above the levels permissible against payment of full duties on annual basis provided they have achieved the stipulated NFEP (Net forex earnings as per cent of exports) and export obligation.

DTA sale of software items up to 50% is permitted.

Benefits for EOU/EPZ Units

1. **Concessional rent**

   Units set-up in EPZs will be eligible for concessional rent for lease of plots and standard design factory sheds and buildings allotted for the first three years at the following rates:

   For plots

   The concession is 75% in the first year, 50% in the second and 25% in the 3rd year only if production had commenced in the first or second years.

   For SDF buildings/sheds

   The concession is 50% in the first year and 40% in the second year if production had commenced in the first year. The concession is 25% in the third year if production had commenced in the first year. No concession is given if production had not commenced by the end of first year.

2. **Tax holiday**

   EOUs/EPZ units are exempted from corporate income tax for a block of 10 years. MAT scheme is not applicable to these units.

   FOB Value of an EOU/EPZ unit may be clubbed with that of the parent company in the DTA for the purpose of according Export House/Trading House/ Star or Super Star Trading House for the latter.

3. 100% foreign equity

   100% foreign equity participation is permissible in the case of EOUs/EPZs. No restrictions on repatriation of capital and remittance of profits and dividends.

4. 100% EOUs or units in EPZ, amounts up to 70% of the inward remittances in convertible foreign currencies can be credited to their Exchange Earners Foreign Currency (EEFC) Account.

5. Supplies made in DTAs by EOUs/EPZ units against payment in foreign exchange shall be counted towards fulfilment of the export obligation.

6. Duty free import of second hand capital goods.

7. Sub-contracting or outside processing is also permitted subject to customers regulations.

8. Capital subsidy on investment in fixed assets and exemption from payment of sales tax on inputs procured from within the state.

Incentives for Units in Industrially Backward Areas

Balanced regional development, the process of industrialization of backward areas, through the locational dispersal of industries has been one of the primary objectives of the successive five-year plans. Various incentives and concessions have been provided for the purpose. The new industrial policy 1991, reiterates this commitment and envisages the achievement of this objective through appropriate incentives, institutions, and infrastructure investments, the important among which are the 'Transport Subsidy Scheme' and the new 'Growth Centre Scheme'.

Transport Subsidy Scheme

This scheme, introduced to promote industries in hilly, remote, and inaccessible areas in the states of Himachal Pradesh, Jammu and Kashmir, the North Eastern States, Sikkim, Union Territories of Andaman and Nicobar Islands, Lakshadweep, Darjeeling district of West Bengal, the hill districts of Uttar Pradesh comprising Almora, Chamoli, Dehra Dun, Naintal, Pansi Garhwal, Pithoragarh, Tehri Garwal and Uttar Kashi Provides subsidy ranging from 50% to 90% on the transport costs incurred for movement of raw material and finished goods from designated rail heads/ports up to the location of the industrial units and vice versa. The scheme, introduced in 1971, shall remain operation till 31 March 2007.

Growth Centre Scheme

The government had announced this scheme in June 1988, to develop growth centres in an area of 400–800 hectares at a cost of Rs 25-30 crore, and endowed with basic infrastructure such as power, water, telecommunication, and banking to attract industries.

Criteria for Selection of a Growth Centre

The criteria followed are:

- The growth centres shall not be located within 50 km from the boundary of the seven cities with a population above 25 lakh, 30 km from the boundary of the 2 cities with a population above 15 lakh, but below 25 lakh, and 15 km from the boundary of the cities with a population above 7.5 lakh, but below 15 lakh.
- The growth centres shall be located close to district/sub-divisional/block/taluk head quarters or developing urban centres.
- The growth centres shall have access to rail-heads, national or state highways, water supply, adequate and dependable source of power, telecommunication facilities, reasonable educational and health facilities, and sufficient land for housing facilities.
- The growth centres should not lead to undue diversion of fertile and available agricultural lands should not be located in ecologically sensitive areas except if permitted by the Department of Environment, and should not lead to denudation of the forests.
- The growth centre's sphere of influence should cover a radius of about 20–25 km.

Financing Pattern for the Growth Centres

Each growth centre would be jointly funded by the centre, state, and the financial institutions as follows:

	Rs in crore
Central government (equity)	10
State government (equity)	5
All India financial institutions (including Rs 2 crore as equity)	4
Nationalized banks	1
Market borrowings	10
Total	30

When the requirement is lesser, file financing pattern is determined on their special conditions.

The government planns to offer the development of growth centres to the private sector throughout the country due to the paucity of funds with state governments. The first privately funded growth centre to be developed over 300 acres in NOIDA, UP has already been awarded to an NRI.

Administration of the Growth Centre Scheme

For the selected sites, the state governments are requested to send detailed project reports which are appraised and approved by the government of India. On approval of the project reports, the first instalment of the central government's share is released. The release of subsequent instalments is subject to the release of proportionate share of funds by the state governments and financial institutions. Physical progress made in the implementation of the projects by the state governments is also taken into account.

Tax Holiday for Industries Located in the Backward Areas

All industrial undertakings, whether small, medium or large, located in the backward areas have been granted a 5-year, tax holiday under Section 80-IA, even if they manufacture articles listed in the eleventh schedule of the Income Tax Act, which articles were earlier reserved for the small sector. The clarification issued with regard to this on 29 July 1993, further clarifies that this tax-holiday is independent of the requirement of industrial licensing under the provisions of the IDRA, 1951. Industrial license, wherever necessary, will require to be obtained, and in respect of delicensed industries an IEM shall be filed with SIA.

New Policy for Small Scale Industrial Sector

24 December 1999, the government announced a new industrial policy for small-scale sector. The primary objective of the Small-scale Industrial Policy is to impart more vitality and growth impetus to this sector to enable it to contribute its mite fully to the economy, particularly in terms of growth of output, employment and exports. The following are the highlights of the policy:

1. The investment limits in plant and machinery of small-scale industries, ancillary units and export-oriented units have been increased to Rs 1 crore. The investment ceiling of these units have been raised to offset erosion in the value of rupee due to domestic inflation, devaluation or realignment of exchange rates with foreign currency, erosion in the value of rupee due to increase in the international price of capital goods, and to enable the SSIs to meet the growing needs of technology up gradation and modernization and also due to anti-pollution measures introduced.

2. In order to provide access to the capital market and to encourage modernization and technological up gradation, it has been decided to allow equity participation by other industrial undertakings in the small-scale industries, not exceeding 24% of the total shareholding.

3. Regulatory provisions relating to the management of private limited companies are being liberalized. A Limited Partnership Act will be introduced to enhance the supply of risk capital to the small-scale sector.

4. Efforts are being made to solve the problem of delayed payment to small industries by setting up of factoring services through Small Industries Development Bank of India (SIDBI). Network of such services would be set-up throughout the country and operated through commercial banks. A suitable legislation will be introduced to ensure prompt payment of small industries bills.

5. To facilitate location of industries in rural/backward areas and to promote stronger linkages between agriculture, and industry, a new scheme of integrated infrastructural development (including technological back-up services) for small-scale industries would be implemented with the active participation of the state governments by financial institutions.

6. A Technology Development Cell (TDC) would be set-up in the Small Industries Development Organization (SIDO) which would provide technology impetus to improve productivity and competitiveness of the products of small-scale sector.

7. Market promotion would be undertaken through co-operative/public sector institutions, other specialized/professional marketing agencies and consortia approach, backed by necessary incentives. National Small Industries Corporation (NSIC) would concentrate on marketing mass consumption items under common brand name.

8. An export development centre would be set-up in SIDO to serve the small-scale industries through its network of field offices to further augment expert activities of this sector.

9. Procedures would be simplified, bureaucratic controls effectively reduced, unnecessary interference eliminated, and paperwork cut down to the minimum to enable the entrepreneurs to concentrate on production and marketing functions.

10. Entrepreneurship Development Programme (EDP) will be given to entrepreneurs. Large number of EDP trainers and motivators will be trained to conduct such programmes. Women entrepreneurs will receive support through special training programmes.

11. Definition of women enterprises would be simplified. The current rule of employment of majority of women workers would be dispensed with and units in which women entrepreneurs have a majority shareholding and management control would be defined as women enterprises.

The Incentive Scheme

The government of India has been operating an incentive scheme of reimbursement of expenses of acquiring Quality Management System (QMS) ISO-9000 certification in the small scale sector to the extent of 75% of the amount limited to Rs 75,000 to each unit. The scope of this scheme now has been extended to provide reimbursement of expenses incurred on acquiring EMS -ISO 14001 certificate. The salient features of the scheme are as under:

1. The scheme envisages reimbursement of charges of acquiring ISO-9000/ISO-14001 certifications to the extent of 75% of the expenditure subject to a maximum of Rs 75,000 in each case. The scheme is valid up to 31 March 2007.

2. The permanent registered small-scale/ancillary/tiny/small scale service business enterprises (SSSBE) units are eligible to avail the incentive scheme.

3. The scheme is applicable to those SSI/ancillary/tiny/SSSBE units, which have already acquired ISO-9000/ISO-14001 certification.

4. It is an all India scheme administered by the Development Commissioner (SSI), Ministry of SSI, Government of India. A screening committee under the chairmanship of AS&DC (SSI) has been set-up to consider the applications for the approval of reimbursement.

5. The scheme shall provide one time reimbursement only against a permanent SSI registration certificate. The amount of incentive/subsidy/grant already availed for acquiring ISO 9000 or ISO 14001 certification under any central government (including DCSSI incentive scheme), state government, and financial institution shall be adjusted against the entitlement of reimbursement.

6. It means the total entitlement of reimbursement of acquiring one or more than one certification shall be up to the maximum, limit of Rs 75,000 only. In case a unit has

received reimbursement/subsidy/grant from central government/state government/ financial institution against any one of the certifications for an amount less than the maximum limit of Rs 75,000, the unit shall be eligible to receive the balance amount only.

7. Only one time reimbursement is allowed against a permanent SSI registration for acquiring ISO-9000/1SO-14001 certification irrespective of the fact whether the concerned SSI has one or more than one unit(s) within the same premises/location or outside.

8. In case an ISO-9000/ISO-14001 certificate is obtained jointly by SSI units (even having a separate permanent SSI registration certificates) under the corporate/group of industries category, the total reimbursement shall be limited to 75% of the total expenditure incurred by the concerned units or Rs 75,000 whichever is less and each SSI unit shall get the amount on prorata basis.

10. The scheme contemplates norms of reimbursement as under:
   • Payments made to certification agency = Full amount (excluding travel and hotel expenses, and surveillance changes)
   • Payments made towards consultancy up to Rs 3,000
   • Training and calibration (Rupees thirty thousand only) The entitlement for reimbursement = 75% ((a) full amount + (b) up to Rs 30,000) up to Rs 75,000

Policy for Foreign Direct Investment

Promotion of foreign direct investment (FDI) forms an integral part of India's economic policies. The role of foreign direct investment in accelerating economic growth is by way of infusion of capital, technology, and modern management practices. The department has put in place a liberal and transparent foreign investment regime where most activities are opened to foreign investment on automatic route without any limit on the extent of foreign ownership. Some of the recent initiatives taken to further liberalize the FDI regime, inter alia, include opening up of sectors such as insurance (up to 26%); development of integrated townships (up to 100%); defence industry (up to 26%); tea plantation (up to 100% subject to divestment of 26% within five years to FDI); enhancement of FDI limits in private sector banking, allowing FDI up to 100% under the automatic route for most manufacturing activities in SEZs; opening up B2B e-commerce; Internet Service Providers (ISPs) without gateways; electronic mail and voice mail to 100% foreign investment subject to 26% divestment condition.

Foreign Collaborations

All agreements, whether involving financial or equity participation or not, outright purchase of technology, licensing agreement, purchase of designs and drawings refer to foreign collaborations. The agreement may be for financial or technical reasons or for both.

Foreign collaborations are normally entered into in industries where a sophisticated technology is required or where an up gradation of the existing technology is necessary. Some agreements may be entered into for the import of both technology as well as capital, by capital intensive industries such as petrochemicals and fertilizers. Agreements that involve only the transfer of technology are known as technical collaborations and those that involve both finance as well as technology are known as financial-cum-technical collaborations. Pure financial collaborations can also be found.

Foreign collaboration projects are different from others in that they require the approval of the government and in that these have special tax implications which are assessed taking into account such aspects as royalty payments, dividend remittances and so on.

Foreign collaborations have always been welcome in India as may be gauged from the fact that over 10,000 agreements have been approved since 1957, in various areas including electrical equipment, industrial machinery, chemicals other than fertilizers, mechanical and engineering industry, machine tools, telecommunications, automobiles and so on. The collaborators, experience has been very good given that they have earned returns which are superior to those offered even by some developed countries. This may be gauged from the fact that the maximum number of technology transfers and financial investments over the past few years have been from the United States.

In the past few years, the Indian Economy has been considerably liberalized. Further, the sweeping changes occurring world over have led to the government thinking in terms of opening up the economy through such measures as the removal of restrictions, simplification of procedures, opening up of several areas to the private sector and encouraging global competition and foreign investment in many areas. The Industrial Policy Statement (IPS) 1991, bears testimony to this. Some of the changes which have been brought about thereafter only confirm this opinion.

Policy Highlights with Reference to Foreign Collaborations

The new Industrial Policy Statement 1991, incorporates radical changes in matters relating to foreign investment and technology agreements in India. For this, now automatic approvals are given to foreign equity investments up to 51% in high priority industries. Further, in order to promote exports, to attract investment and to gain access to high technology, the government has set-up a special empowered board to negotiate with large multinational firms so as to develop industries and technology in the national interest.

Further, in order to establish a continuous relationship between the users of technology and its suppliers, and to induce technological dynamism, the government will provide automatic approval for technology agreements in the high priority industries within specified parameters. Similar facilities are being extended to other industries as well, provided these do not require the expenditure of free foreign exchange. This, it is hoped, would lead to the development of indigenous competence for the absorption of foreign technology, to greater investments in research and development. For this, the need for prior clearance for the hiring of foreign technicians and foreign testing of indigenously developed technologies has been removed.

New Policy on Foreign Investment

The new foreign investment policy aims at the installation of simplified mechanisms for providing expeditious approvals. Hence, the Reserve Bank of India accords automatic approval to all proposals–

1. Where the foreign investment in the equity capital of the Indian company is up to 50%/51%/74% and 100% where such investment is proposed in the high priority industries listed in the Annexure III of the Statement and where such investment covers the foreign exchange requirements for the import of capital goods needed for the project.
2. The industries referred to in Annexure III have been recast into 4 parts. Part A lists industries/activities for which automatic approval is available for foreign equity up to 50%, Part B for foreign equity up to 51% and Part C for foreign equity up to 74%, and Part D for F E up to 100%.

Items not eligible for automatic approval are–

1. Items reserved for SSIs
2. Items which require industrial license
3. All items of aerospace and defence equipment whether specifically mentioned or not
4. All items related to production or use of atomic energy under Atomic Energy Act.

It is to be noted that

1. The import of components, raw materials, and intermediate goods and payment of know-how fees and royalties are governed by the domestic policies applicable to other domestic units
2. The plant and machinery proposed to be imported must be new and not second-hand
3. The outflow on account of dividend payments is to be balanced by export earnings over a period of time in respect of industries in the consumer goods sector (list annexed).

Of existing companies wishing to raise foreign equity up to 51% as part of an expansion programme provided the expansion is in the high priority sectors listed in the Annexure III of the IPS.

Of existing companies wishing to raise foreign equity up to 51% without an expansion programme provided they are predominantly engaged in the high priority sectors listed in Annexure III of the IPS.

It is to be noted that

In case of the former, the equity should be part of the financing of the expansion programme. Further, in both the cases, the increase in the equity level must result from the expansion of the equity base of the existing company and the foreign equity must be from remittance of foreign exchange. Moreover, in case of the former, the proposed expansion must be predominantly in the high priority sectors and the company itself need not be exclusively engage in the activity listed in Annexure III.

For majority foreign equity holding up to 51% in trading companies primarily engaged in export activity. While the thrust would be on export activity, such trading houses would be on par with domestic trading and export houses in accordance with the import and export policy.

Applications for such foreign investment proposals should be in Form FC (RBI) to the Reserve Bank of India, exchange control department. Where a company undertakes expansion programme, the articles to be manufactured need be stated in Indian trade classification (harmonized system). The proposal should be a composite one including detailed information on the capital goods to be imported for the expansion programme.

Where the company is not undertaking expansion programme the application must state the existing products of the company in the ITC (HS Classification).

The automatic approval for foreign investment proposals inter alia, includes exemption from the operation of Section 26(7), 28, 29 and 31 of FERA. The approval for investment in trading houses includes inter alia, exemption from the operation of Section 26 (7), 28, 29 and 31 of FERA.

Dividend Balancing

The outflow of foreign exchange on account of dividend payments, which are to be balanced by export earnings over a period of time, shall be monitored by the RBI. Dividend balancing shall be done on the following basis:

The Dividend balancing will be done over a period of seven years from the date of commencement of production for companies raising foreign equity for expansion, and, if not, from the date of allotment of shares for raising foreign equity.

Remittance of dividends should be covered by earnings on the company from export of items given under list of industries, 51% foreign investment which is given automatic approval. The export earnings for dividend payment may be of years prior to the payment of dividend or of the same year.

Dividend balancing shall apply only to approvals for investment in industries of the consumer goods sector. The condition shall also not be applied to investments by approved international organizations such as the International Finance Corporation and the Asian Development Bank, Common Wealth Development Corporation (CDC), Deutsche Entwicklungs Gescllschaft (DEG).

All other proposals which do not fulfil the aforesaid conditions specified for automatic approval are considered for approvals, on merits, by the government.

Under the new industrial policy, proposals for foreign investment need not be accompanied by foreign technology agreements. All such proposals including those for investment by NRIs or in 100% EOUs are considered by the foreign investment promotion board for approval. Even composite proposals seeking approvals for industrial license, technical collaborations, etc., besides foreign investment are cleared by the Foreign Investment Promotion Board (FIPB).

The Foreign FIPB will

- provide a single-window clearance for all aspects of proposals considered by it
- prepare a short list of international firms which have evinced interest in investing in India and draw up detailed plans in respect of these firms
- identify sectors for such investment in keeping with the programmes of the eighth plan and maintain close liaison with the Indian industry.

The FIPB, located in the Prime Minister's Office comprises of the Principal Secretary to the Prime Minister, as Chairman, the Finance Secretary, the Commerce Secretary, and Secretary, Industrial Development. The FIPB is empowered to engage in purposive negotiation, and is totally free from predetermined parameters or procedures in considering proposals, which is done in totality.

Applications are to be submitted to the FIPB, or the Government of India's missions abroad which forwards them to the SI A for further process.

Foreign Investment in Hotel and Tourism-related Industry

Foreign equity holdings up to 51% will also be permitted in hotels and tourism related industry. NRIs can invest up to 100% in a hotel. Applications shall be filed with the RBI in the prescribed form.

Other Foreign Investment Proposals

All other investment proposals will be subject to existing procedures. Applications will be made to the SIA in the department of industrial development in the prescribed form. All these proposals including those involving 51% foreign equity which do not satisfy all the criteria shall be considered according to the usual procedure. Proposals of foreign investment, foreign technology agreements not covered by the automatic facility and import of capital goods, may, if desired, continue to be made on a composite basis.

New Policy on Foreign Technology Agreements

The New Industrial Policy 1991, has simplified mechanisms of approval in order to induce technological dynamism in the Indian industry to smoothen the process of technological transfers. For this the Reserve Bank of India accords automatic approval to

- all industries for foreign technology agreements within prescribed monetary royalty, i.e., up to a lump sum payment of US $2 million, 5% royalty for domestic sales and 8% for exports, subject to total payments of 8% of sales over a 10-year period from date of agreement or 7 years from commencement of production.
- foreign technology agreements for hotel and tourism related industry, provided the following conditions relating to payments are satisfied:
  1. *Technical and consultancy services*   Lump sum fee not more than $2,00,000.
  2. *Franchising and marketing/publicity support*   Up to 3% of gross room sales support.
  3. *Management fees*   Up to 10% of the foreign exchange earnings provided the foreign party puts in 25% of the equity. This will also cover payment for marketing/publicity support.

The government has now decided to prescribe the following norms for grant of automatic approval of the RBI for foreign technical collaborations in the hotel industry.

1. Technical and consultancy services including fees for architects, design supervision, etc., up to 3% of the capital cost of the project (less cost of land and finance).
2. Franchising and marketing/publicity support fee: Up to 3% of the net turnover (net turnover is gross receipts less credit card charges, travel agents commission, sales tax, statutory payment, etc).
3. Management fees (including incentive fees) up to 10% of the gross operating profit.

Applications should be submitted in Form FC (RBI), to the RBI, Exchange Control Department.

All other proposals are considered for approval, on merits, by the government.

The application for such proposals should be in form FC (SIA) to the SIA Department of Industrial Development, Ministry of Industry. Approvals are provided within 4 to 6 weeks of filing the application.

Extension of FTA Extension of foreign technology agreements requires government approval even if automatic approval had been granted in the first instance.

Hiring of foreign technicians Irrespective of whether the collaboration is approved or not, no permission is required to hire foreign technicians. The RBI, which has full powers, has empowered authorized dealers for release of foreign exchange payments in this regard.

Deputation of Indian technicians abroad For deputing Indian personnel for training and other purposes abroad, dealers may be approached directly for permission as per RBIs guidelines and procedures.

Foreign testing of indigenous raw materials and products and indigenously developed technology The RBI, which has received full powers from the government, has empowered authorized dealers for foreign exchange payments in this regard.

Use of foreign brand names/trade marks for internal sale The restriction prohibiting the use of foreign brand names/trade marks on goods for sale within the country shall no longer be imposed while granting letters of intent and approvals.

Electronics hardware technology park/software technology park scheme The Department of Electronics, Government of India, to develop the industry, provides impetus and to enhance its export potential, has provided a scheme of incentives/facilities.

The following discussion deals with the regulatory framework that governs Indian companies planning to establish a base abroad.

Indian companies are now permitted to establish joint ventures abroad, since the section 27 of FERA, which dealt with the same, is abolished. However, certain conditions need to be fulfilled and some regulations considered.

The application for direct investment in a foreign concern needs to be made to the Ministry of Commerce (Overseas Investment Division), in Form PFC-I in 11 copies, automatic approval for which shall be given 21 days provided either if:

(i)   The total value of the direct investment does not exceed US $4 million. In respect of Indian rupee investments in Nepal, the total value of the investment does not exceed Rs. 25 crore.

(ii) The amount of investment is up to 25% of the annual average export/forex earnings of the Indian company (other than equity exports to existing JVs abroad) in the preceding three years. (Not applicable to Indian rupee investments in Nepal.)

(iii) The amount of investment should be repatriated in full by way of dividends, royalty, technical services fee, etc., within a period of 5 years with effect from the date of first remittance of equity to the foreign concern or the date of first shipment of equity exports or the due date for receipt of entitlements which are to be capitalized whichever is earlier.

The investment may, beside cash remittance at the discretion of the Indian party, be contributed by capitalization in full or part of:

1. Indian made plant, machinery, equipment, and components supplied to the foreign concern (second-hand or reconditioned indigenous machinery may be supplied by the Indian party as its contribution)
2. The proceeds of goods exported by the Indian party to the foreign concern
3. Fees, royalties, commissions, or other payments made by the foreign concern for the supply of technical know-how, consultancy, managerial, or such other services.

Automatic approval is given to the Indian party in respect of the same foreign concern only once in a block of three financial years including the one in which the investment is made.

These guidelines will apply to direct investments, which is to be understood as investment in the equity of the foreign concern made for the purpose of acquiring long-term interest in that concern which may also be reflected through representation on the board of directors and/or the supply of technical know-how, capital goods, components, raw materials, etc., made in joint ventures and wholly-owned subsidiaries abroad. This may be the initial or additional investment in firms engaged in commercial, industrial, trading or services activity or in hotel or tourism industry.

Portfolio investments and investments in the financial sector such as banking, insurance, mutual funds, etc., are considered on merits by the Ministry of Commerce.

Remittance of Income

The Indian party has to remit to India, within 60 days of payments becoming due, all entitlements due to it from the foreign concern on account of royalty, technical fees, management fees, and so on, in free foreign exchange. So also, dividends/profits after tax, within a period of 60 days of their declaration.

Some other conditions which are stipulated for automatic approval are:

- An annual performance report along with certified true copy of annual report containing annual accounts shall be furnished within 30 days of the expiry of the time period stipulated for the purpose in the country of investments, to the Ministry of Commerce.
- Approval to implement the project is generally valid for two years.
- The Indian party shall not give any guarantee or undertake any financial liability or commitment in respect of any loan, etc., raised by the joint venture or wholly–owned subsidiary except with the prior approval of the Government of India. Where the proposal does not qualify for automatic approval, it shall be considered by an inter-ministerial committee of the Ministry of Commerce and the decision made within the 90 days of the receipt of application. The direct investment may also be in the form of:
  (i)   External borrowing subjects to the approval of appropriate authorities.
  (ii) Payment out of blocked funds arising out of export receivables or returns from investments made in the host country not being transferred to the Indian party due to reasons beyond the control of the Indian party.
  (iii) Such other sources as many as permitted by the government of India.

Taxation

Income of the joint ventures, being taxable entities by themselves, shall be taxed in the country of its location. But dividends, royalties, fees for technical services and so on receivable by the Indian party shall be taxed in India.

Guidelines for Foreign Collaboration

Comprehensive guidelines on general policy and procedure for handling foreign investment and technical collaboration proposals were issued by the Government in January 1969. These guidelines hold good even now with some changes as per the New Industrial Policy 1991, and RBI instructions in the revised form.

The following are the guidelines which the entrepreneurs are normally required to take note of in negotiating proposals for foreign collaboration so as to ensure that such proposals conform to the policies of the Central Government.

1. Non-resident Shareholding

   The total non-resident shareholding in the undertaking should not exceed the percentage(s) specified in the approval letter. In case of any change in the amount of foreign/NRI investment, or the paid-up capital, an intimation to this effect may be given to Secretariat for Industrial Approvals (SIA), RBI and the Administrative Ministry, subject to the percentage of foreign/NRI equity shareholding remaining unchanged.

2. Royalty

   (a) The royalty will be calculated on the basis of the net ex-factory sale price of the product, exclusive of excise duties, minus the cost of the standard bought-out components and the landed cost of imported components, irrespective of the source of procurement, including ocean freight, insurance, custom duties, etc. The payment of royalty will be restricted to the licensed capacity plus 25% excess thereof for such items requiring industrial license or on such capacity as specified in the approval letter. This restriction will not apply to items not requiring industrial license. In case of production in excess of the quantum, prior approval of government would have to be obtained regarding the terms of payment of royalty in respect of such excess production.

   (b) The royalty would not be payable beyond the period of the agreement if the orders had not been executed during the period of agreement. However, where the orders themselves took a long time to execute, then the royalty for an order booked during the period of the agreement, but executed after the period of agreement, would be payable only after a chartered accountant certifies that the orders in fact have been firmly booked and execution began during the period of agreement, and the technical assistance was available on a continuing basis even after the period of agreement.

   (c) No minimum guaranteed royalty would be allowed.

   Royalty is the consideration for transfer of technical know-how on an annual basis over the duration of the agreement. Sometimes the foreign collaborator may also require lump sum payments to be made as consideration for the transfer of drawings and designs and assistance rendered in erecting and commissioning the plant. While determining the quantum of lump sum royalty payments to be made to the collaborator, the entrepreneur prior to the announcement of the New Industrial Policy 1991 had to keep in view the following norms laid down by the government.

1. The payment of royalty is normally restricted to the amount determined by the following formula:

$$ARP = 0.05 \, (SP_{ex} \cdot ED - C_{be} - C_{ic}) \times 1.25 \, LC$$

where,

ARP = Annual royalty payment

SPex = Ex-factory selling price per unit

ED = Excise duty per unit

Cbc = Cost of standard bought-out components per unit

Cic = Landed cost of imported components per unit

EC = Licensed (restricted) capacity.

2. In case the production exceeds the annual licensed capacity plus 25% in excess thereof, prior approval of the government must be sought for payment of royalty in respect of such excess production.

3. The lump sum payment is permitted to be made provided the payment is divided into three equal instalments and remitted as follow: (i) first instalment on filing the collaboration agreement with RBI; (ii) second instalment on obtaining technical documentation from the collaborator; (iii) final instalment on the commencement of commercial production or 4 years after the agreement is filed with RBI whichever is earlier.

4. The duration of the agreement is to be restricted to a period of 8 years and royalty can be paid for a maximum period of 5 years, allowing 3 years for commercial production. The total lump sum and royalty payments should not be more than 8% of total expected sales (calculated on an ex-factory value basis) over a period not exceeding 10 years. The government may allow the duration of the agreement to be extended to 10 years in certain cases.

5. The collaboration agreement must not provide for the payment of a minimum guaranteed royalty irrespective of the quantum and value of production. The royalty will be payable at the market rate of exchange prevailing at the time of remittance.

6. All royalty and lump sum payments are subject to deduction of Indian taxes. The New Industrial Policy 1991, as mentioned earlier, envisages automatic permission for foreign technology agreements in high priority industries for a lump sum payment of Rs 1 crore, 5% royalty for domestic sales and 8% for exports, subject to a total payment of 8% for exports, subject to a total payment of 8% of sales over a 10-year period from date of agreement of 7 years from the commencement of production. The above prescribed rates are net of taxes and will be calculated according to standard procedure (as specified in (i) above). In respect of industries other than those in high priority areas, automatic permission will be given subject to the same guidelines if not free foreign exchange is required for any payments. From reading the above guidelines on royalty payments included in the New Industrial Policy 1991, it is clear that except in cases of high priority industries and agreements in industries which are not in high priority areas, but for which no free foreign exchange would be required, the norms mentioned in (1) to (6) above would continue to hold good.

3. The lump sum shall be paid in three instalments as detailed below, unless otherwise stipulated in the approval letter:

- First 1/3rd after the agreement is filed with Reserve Bank of India/authorized dealer in foreign exchange.

- Second l/3rd on delivery of technical documentation.
- Third and final l/3rd on commencement of commercial production, or four years after the agreement is filed with Reserve Bank of India/authorized dealer in foreign exchange, whichever is earlier.

4. All remittances to the foreign collaborator shall be made as per the exchange rates prevailing on the date of remittance.

5. For undertaking the export obligation, if any, specified in the approval letter, the requisite guarantee, i.e., legal undertaking/bank guarantee, as may be required, should be furnished according to the detailed instructions issued by the Chief Controller of Imports and Exports (E.O. Cell), Ministry of Commerce (EP) and the administrative ministry, who may be contacted in the matter.

6. There should be no provision in the agreement for payment of interest on delayed payments.

7. Import of capital equipment components and raw materials will be allowed as per the import policy prevailing from time to time.

8. No permission will be necessary for the hiring of foreign technicians. Release of foreign exchange, if any involved, will be regulated in accordance with the Reserve Bank of India guidelines. Reserve Bank of India may be approached accordingly in the matter. Also for deputing Indian personnel for training and other purposes abroad, RBI may be approached.

9. The agreement shall be subject to Indian Laws.

10. A copy of the collaboration agreement signed by both the parties may be furnished to the following authorities:
    (a) The concerned administrative ministry/department.
    (b) Directorate General of Technical Development, Udyog Bhavan (in duplicate), New Delhi.
    (c) Secretariat for Industrial Approvals (Foreign Collaboration II Section).
    (d) Department of Scientific and Industrial Research, New Delhi.
    (e) Ministry of Finance (Department of Economic Affairs), New Delhi.

11. All payments under the collaboration agreement including rupee payments (if any) to be made in connection with engagement/deputation of foreign technical personnel such as passage fare, living expenses, etc., of foreign technicians, would be liable for the levy of cess under the Research and Development Cess Act, 1986, and the Indian company while making such payments should pay the cess prescribed under the Act to Industrial Development Bank of India.

Terms and Conditions of Collaboration Agreements

While structuring the foreign collaboration agreement, the entrepreneur must take into consideration the following guidelines issued by the government. The guidelines have a bearing on the inclusion/exclusion of certain clauses in the agreement.

Technical Assistance/Collaboration Agreement

A collaboration agreement is a written document embodying comprehensive provisions as to the rights and obligations of the contracting parties as also other particulars relating to the subject matter on which the foreign collaborator and the local concerns in the developing countries seek to collaborate. The agreements generally provide for the establishment or setting up of new industrial unit based on the technical know-how of the foreign collaborator. It may also provide for financial collaboration or for import of plant and machinery or for rendering technical services. It may also contain terms and provisions for assignment of or license for working patents, sharing of the results of the research and development and training of the technical personnel by the foreign collaborator in the developing country.

Technical assistance agreement is primarily an agreement for transfer of technical know-how which may on long-term be as that of procuring equipment or continuing services or short-term for the designs and constructing of manufacturing facilities. Short-term services can be classified to cover assessment of markets, definition of products, investment analysis ensuring raw materials availability, recommendation of plant location, choice of technology, identification of equipment suppliers.

Drafting an Agreement

While drafting a technical assistance agreement, the following factors should be kept in mind. It is pertinent to note here that it is difficult to prepare a set frame of the terms and conditions relevant in all cases as the conditions may differ according to requirements. However, the following things should be kept in mind while drafting an agreement for technical assistance:

1. Capability of the collaborator and the requirement of the party are clearly indicated.
2. Definitions of technical terms are given.
3. Exclusive and non-exclusive rights and privileges relating to manufacturing, assembly and sale of the product to be manufactured in the territory.
4. Terms and conditions regarding nature of technical know-how, disclosure of drawings, specifications and other documents, furnishing of technical information in respect of processes with flow charts, etc., plant outlay, list of equipment, machinery and tools with specification have to be provided.
5. Provisions for making available the engineers and/or skilled workers of the collaborator on payment of expenses relating to their stay per diem, etc., are given.
6. Details regarding specification and quality of the product to be manufactured are given.
7. Quality control and trademarks to be used are also specified.
8. Responsibility of the collaborator in establishing or maintaining assembly plants should be clearly defined.
9. In case the final product of manufacture is such which may require manufacture of some components on sub-contracting basis for the assembly of product, it may be clarified whether there would be any restrictions from the side of the collaborator for such sub-contracting.
10. The rate of royalty is in accordance with the conditions of approval.
11. Use of information and industrial property rights should also be provided for in the agreement.
12. The terms of the agreement should be as per the policy of the government.

13. A clause on force majeure should be included.

14. A clause that the collaborating company has to train the personnel of Indian company within a specified period is added. The clause should also specify the terms and conditions of such assistance, place of training, period of training and fees payable.

15. A comprehensive clause on arbitration should be included containing a clear provision as to the kind of arbitrator and place of arbitration.

16. There should be provision in the agreement for payment of interest on delayed payments.

RBI/Government—Approval to form Part of the Agreement

Under the revised procedure for approval of foreign collaboration/investment it has been prescribed that the RBI/Government approval should form part of foreign collaboration investment agreement.

Important Clauses in Collaboration Agreements

Based on the foregoing ingredients in the proposal for a collaboration agreement, each agreement should generally contain the following comprehensive clauses –

1. In case of agreement for provision of technical know-how:
    (i)   Definition and characteristics of the subject matter of the know-how
    (ii)   The mode of transfer of technical know-how, i.e., the time and place of transfer, and whether the transfer is absolute or for a specified period
    (iii)   Clause safeguarding secrecy of the technology
    (iv)   Training of the technical personnel of the Indian company by the foreign collaborator
    (v)   Performance guarantee in regard to the achievement of the required qualities, standard of the product, quantities to be produced and minimum standard of performance with suitable indemnity clause
    (vi)   Conferring of license or patent right for the technical know-how and the product to be manufactured
    (vii)   Mode and method of payment, i.e., whether a lump sum or by way of royalty or technical fees
    (viii) Right on the future improvements in the technology by transfer made by transfer of the technology
    (ix)   Termination clause of the agreement
    (x)   Force majeure clause
    (xi)   Arbitration clause
    (xii)   Jurisdiction, in case of dispute

2. In case of agreement for supply of plant and machinery:
    (i)   The agreed date of shipment of plant and machinery
    (ii)   The place of delivery, i.e., whether F.O.B. Indian port or the port shipment
    (iii)   Mode of payment, whether payable in India or outside India
    (iv)   Whether the supplies will be made through the agents of the foreigner in India or directly by the foreign principal to the Indian firm, so as to avoid the complications on payment of income tax in India; similarly, the provision of technical personnel by the foreigner for erection of the plant and machinery in India should be carefully drafted so as to avoid an element of continuity and consequential.

3. In case of agreement for a joint venture:
    (i) Since in India a foreign company is not allowed (except in exceptional circumstances) to hold more than 51% shares in any company in India, care must be taken to provide for the equity participation by the foreign company under a joint venture agreement; the agreement should also provide for the type of share capital and the mode of payment for acquiring the shares.
    (ii) The constitution of the board of directors with election, number of directors and the powers of the board
    (iii) The mode of declaration and distribution of the dividends
    (iv) The area of marketing of the products
    (v) Restriction on any change in the ownership ratio
    (vi) Other provisions as incorporated under an agreement for supply of technical know-how
4. In case of agreement for a specific project in India:
    Since this type of agreement involves more than one foreign party to the transaction according to the nature of their respective responsibility, for example, one supplying the technical know-how and design, another supplying the plants and machinery, the other supplying the technical services for erection or installation of the plants and machineries, while another undertaking the civil engineering jobs, etc., it may pose problems to finalize any one single document of this nature. However, the problem may be resolved by adopting any one of the following measures:
    (i) By executing separate agreements with each party, according to the nature of the responsibility
    (ii) By making a comprehensive agreement, where there will be only one main party, usually the supplier of the plant and machinery, who usually awards sub-contracts with other foreign/Indian parties
    (iii) By concluding a turnkey agreement in which a single contracting party shall be responsible for all or for a large part of the work.

Investments by Non-Resident Indians (NRIs)/Over Seas Corporate Bodies (OCBs)

For allowing investments in India by NRIs and OCBs predominantly owned by them, a wide-range of facilities for investments in firms and companies has been provided. The limits for investments in industrial ventures by NRIs and OCBs have been raised and the approval procedures modified.

Approvals for NRIs/OCBs Investment up to 100% Equity

NRIs and OCBs predominantly owned by them will be permitted to invest up to 100% foreign equity in high priority industries with full benefits of repatriation of capital invested and income accruing thereon provided:

• The foreign equity covers the foreign exchange requirement for import of new, and not second hand, capital goods.
• Outflow on account of dividend payments is balanced by export earnings over a period of seven years from the commencement of commercial production. Balancing will not be required beyond this period.

- The project lies 25 km beyond the periphery of the standard urban area limits of a city populated by more than 10 lakh people according to the 1991 census.

The said facility is available for new investments including those for expansion and diversification of existing industrial undertaking and will apply to investments in private/ public limited companies as well as in partnership firms.

The scheme for 100% NRI investments in 100% EOUs as also the scheme for revival of sick units by NRIs will continue.

Existing or new companies (private or public limited) can issue up to 100% of the new issue with repatriation benefits if the companies are engaged in development of plots, townships, roads, highways and other infrastructure facilities, manufacturing of building material, or financing of housing development. Overseas corporate bodies predominantly owned by NRIs are not eligible to invest on repatriation basis in these areas.

The application for approval of the proposal, a composite one with detailed information on the capital goods to be imported for the project, will be filed in 10 copies with the RBI stating the item of manufacture in the 1TC (harmonized system).

The RBI grants permission under the FERA, 1973, which will include exemption from the operation of Sections 26 (7), 28, 29 and 31of FERA. Based further on the confirmation by the RBI that the foreign equity covers the import of capital goods, the Director General of foreign trade shall issue the relevant license.

Approval for Investment up to 100% by NRIs/OCBs in Other Industries

NRIs/OCBs will be permitted to invest up to 100% equity with full repatriation benefits in industries requiring compulsory licensing, those reserved for the small-scale sector, provided the export obligation criterion is satisfied, as well as other industries excepting those reserved for the public sector. So also in hotels and tourism industry, hospitals, advanced diagnostic centres, shipping, export-oriented deep-sea fishing industry and oil exploration services with full repatriation benefits.

For the import of new capital goods, financed fully by NRIs out of their own resources abroad, no indigenous clearance is required, provided the items are not a part of the negative list of imports. Import of second-hand goods is allowed on a case to case basis.

Licensing

The procedures relating to industrial licensing issued under IDRA, 1951 are equally applicable to NRIs also.

Tax System in India

India has a well-developed tax structure. The main taxes/duties that the Union Government is empowered to levy are income tax (except tax on agricultural income, which the state governments can levy), customs duties, central excise and sales tax and service tax. The principal taxes levied by the state governments are sales tax, stamp duty, state excise, land revenue, tax on professions and the like. The local bodies are empowered to levy tax on properties, octroi and for utilities such as water supply, drainage, etc.

Tax Incentives Available in India

1. Tax incentives, i.e., deduction of 100% of the profits from business for a period of 10 years available for those engaged in development of infrastructure are listed below:
   (i) Development or operation and maintenance of ports, airports, roads, highways, bridges, rail systems, inland waterways, inland ports, water supply projects, water treatment systems, irrigation projects, sanitation and sewage projects, solid waste management systems.
   (ii) Generation, distribution and transmission of power, which commence before 31 March 2006.
   (iii) Development, operation and maintenance of an industrial park or special economic zone established before 31 March 2006.
2. Income by way of dividend, interest, or long-term capital gain of an infrastructure capital company or an infrastructure capital fund is 100% tax-exempt. Income of a venture capital company or venture capital fund set-up to raise funds for investment in a venture capital undertaking is also tax-exempt.
3. Special packages for special category states offer the following:
   (i) Deduction of 100% of profits derived by undertakings set-up in certain notified areas or in certain thrust sector industries in the North-Eastern states and the State of Sikkim, for a period of ten years.
   (ii) Deduction of 100% of profits derived by undertakings set-up in certain notified areas or in certain thrust sector industries in the States of Uttaranchal and Himachal Pradesh for the first five years and 25% (30% in the case of companies) for the next five years.
4. Units located in specified zones have the following tax exemptions:
   (i) Deduction of 100% of profits, derived from the export of articles or things or computer software is available for undertakings set-up in free trade zones, electronic hardware technology parks, software technology parks for 10 years, up to 31 March 2009.
   (ii) Deduction of 100% of profits derived from the export of articles or things or computer software, is available for undertakings set-up in Special Economic Zones (SEZs) for a period of five years followed by 50% for the next two years. An additional deduction of 50% of the profits credited to a reserve account to be utilized for the purposes of the business is also available to such undertakings for the next three years.
   (iii) Deduction of 100% of profits, derived from the export of articles or things or computer software, is available for 100% Export Oriented Units for ten years,-up to 31 March 2009.
   (iv) Deduction of 100% of income of an off shore banking unit situated in a Special Economic Zone from business activities with undertakings located in the Special Economic Zone, for a period of three years followed by 50% of such income for the next two years.
5. Tax incentives for certain specified sectors are also available as explained below:
   Multiplex theatres and other convention centres
   (i) Deduction of 50% of profits derived from the business of building, owning and operation of multiplex theatres or convention centres constructed before 31 March 2005, for a period for five years. Building housing projects.

(ii) Deduction of 100% of profits derived by undertakings engaged in the business of developing and building housing projects which are approved by the local authority before 31 March 2005. Handling, storage and transportation of food grains.

(iii) Deduction of 100% profits derived by an undertaking from the integrated business of handling, storage and transportation of food grains for the first five years and 25% (30% in the case of companies) for the next five years. Refining of mineral oil.

(iv) Deduction of 100% of profits derived by an undertaking engaged in the commercial production or refining of mineral oil for a period of 7 years.

(v) Export of wood-based handicraft.

(vi) Deduction of 100% of profits derived from export of wood based handicraft is available to undertakings up to 31 March 2009.

Annexure I

List of industries reserved for the public sector
1. Atomic energy.
2. The substances specified in the schedule to the notification of the Government of India in the Department of Atomic Energy Number S.O. 212 (E), dated the 15 March 1995.
3. Railway transport.

Annexure II

List of industries for which industrial licensing is compulsory
1. Distillation and brewing of alcoholic drinks.
2. Cigars and cigarettes of tobacco and manufactured tobacco substitutes.
3. Electronics, aerospace and defence equipment; all types.
4. Industrial explosives including detonating fuses, safety fuses, gun powder, nitrocellulose, and matches.
5. Hazardous chemicals.
6. Drugs and pharmaceuticals (according to modified Drug Policy, 1994 as amended in 1999).

Annexure III

Part A

List of industries/items for automatic approval for foreign equity up to 50%

Sl. no.	NIC Code	Description
A-1	12	Mining of Iron Ore
A-2	13	Mining of metal ores other than Iron Ore (Mining of Uranium group ore is not covered)
A-3	15	Mining of non-metallic minerals not elsewhere classified (n.e.c.)

Part B
List of industries/items for automatic approval for foreign equity up to 51%

Sl. no.	NIC Code	Description
B-1	00	Agriculture Production (n.e.c)
B-2	01	Plantations (n.e.c)
B-4	23	Manufacture of cotton textiles
B-6	24	Manufacture of wool, silk, and manmade fibre textiles
B-5	26	Manufacture of textile products
B-7	28	Manufacture of paper and paper products, printing and publishing and allied industries
B-10	32	Manufacture of non-metallic mineral products (n.e.c)
B-11	34	Manufacture of metal products and parts, except machinery and equipment
B-12	35/36	Manufacture of machinery and equipment other than transport equipment
B-13	37	Manufacture of transport equipment and parts
B-15	70	Land transport (support services)
B-16	71	Water transport (support services)
B-17	73	Services incidental to transport (n.e.c)
B-18	85	Renting and leasing (n.e.c)
B-19	89	Business services (n.e.c)

Part C
List of industries/items for automatic approval for foreign equity up to 74%

Sl. no.	NIC Code	Description
C-1	19	Mining services
C-2	33	Basic metals and alloys industries.
C-3	38	Other manufacturing industries
C-5	43	Non conventional energy generation and distribution construction
C-6	50	Construction
C-7	70	Land transport
C-8	71	Water transportation
C-9	74	Storage and Warehousing services

The above is an abridged version of Annexure III. Each division is normally classified into group and class to identify the activities more specially.

Part D

List of Sectors under automatic route for FDI up to 100%

The government has reviewed the existing guidelines for automatic approval for foreign equity for electric generation, transmission and distribution projects, and has decided to enlarge the provisions for automatic approval for such projects. Accordingly, projects for electric power generation, transmission, and distribution will be permitted foreign equity participation up to 100% on the automatic approval route provided the foreign equity in any such project does not exceed Rs 1,500 crore. The categories, which would qualify for such automatic approval, are:

(i)   Hydro-electric power plants
(ii)   Coal/lignite based thermal power plants
(iii) Oil-based thermal power plants
(iv)   Gas-based thermal power plants

The following sectors are under automatic approval route for foreign equity up to 100%.

Non-banking financial services

- Drugs and pharmaceuticals that do not attract compulsory licensing or involve use of recombinant DNA technology
- Food processing
- Electronic hardware
- Software development
- Film industry
- Advertising
- Hospitals
- Private oil refineries
- Pollution control and management
- Exploration and mining of minerals other than diamonds and precious stones Management consultancy Venture capital funds/companies
- Setting up/development of industrial park7model town/SEZ
- Petroleum products pipeline
- Mass rapid transport system
- Roads and highways
- Toll roads
- Vehicular bridges
- Ports and harbours
- Hotel and tourism
- Township, housing, build up infrastructure construction projects

SEVERAL DISCOUNTED AND COMPOUNDED FACTORS FOR VARIOUS RATES AND TIME PERIODS

TABLE X Present value interest factor
$$PVIF_{(k,n)} = 1/(1+k)^n$$

Period n	1%	2%	3%	4%	5%	6%	7%	8%	9%
0	1.000	1.000	1.000	1.000	1.000	1.000	1.000	1.000	1.000
1	0.990	0.980	0.971	0.962	0.952	0.943	0.935	0.926	0.917
2	0.980	0.961	0.943	0.925	0.907	0.890	0.873	0.857	0.842
3	0.971	0.942	0.915	0.889	0.864	0.840	0.816	0.794	0.772
4	0.961	0.924	0.889	0.855	0.823	0.792	0.763	0.735	0.708
5	0.951	0.906	0.863	0.822	0.784	0.747	0.713	0.681	0.650
6	0.942	0.888	0.838	0.790	0.746	0.705	0.666	0.630	0.596
7	0.933	0.871	0.813	0.760	0.711	0.665	0.623	0.583	0.547
8	0.923	0.853	0.789	0.731	0.677	0.627	0.582	0.540	0.502
9	0.914	0.873	0.766	0.703	0.645	0.592	0.544	0.500	0.460
10	0.905	0.820	0.744	0.676	0.614	0.558	0.508	0.463	0.422
11	0.896	0.804	0.722	0.650	0.585	0.527	0.475	0.429	0.388
12	0.887	0.788	0.701	0.625	0.557	0.497	0.444	0.397	0.356
13	0.879	0.773	0.681	0.601	0.530	0.469	0.415	0.368	0.326
14	0.870	0.758	0.661	0.577	0.505	0.442	0.388	0.340	0.299
15	0.861	0.743	0.642	0.555	0.481	0.417	0.362	0.315	0.275
16	0.853	0.728	0.623	0.534	0.458	0.394	0.339	0.292	0.252
17	0.844	0.714	0.605	0.513	0.436	0.371	0.317	0.270	0.231
18	0.836	0.700	0.587	0.494	0.416	0.350	0.296	0.250	0.212
19	0.828	0.686	0.570	0.475	0.396	0.331	0.276	0.232	0.194

Contd

Table X   *Contd*

Period n	1%	2%	3%	4%	5%	6%	7%	8%	9%
20	0.820	0.673	0.554	0.456	0.377	0.312	0.258	0.215	0.87
25	0.780	0.610	0.478	0.375	0.295	0.233	0.184	0.146	0.116
30	0.742	0.552	0.412	0.308	0.231	0.174	0.131	0.099	0.075

Period n	10%	11%	12%	13%	14%	15%	16%	17%	18%
0	1.000	1.000	1.000	0.885	1.000	1.000	1.000	1.000	1.000
1	0.909	0.901	0.893	0.783	0.877	0.870	0.862	0.855	0.847
2	0.826	0.812	0.797	0.693	0.769	0.756	0.743	0.731	0.718
3	0.751	0.731	0.712	0.613	0.675	0.658	0.641	0.624	0.609
4	0.683	0.659	0.636	0.543	0.592	0.572	0.552	0.534	0.516
5	0.621	0.593	0.567	0.480	0.519	0.497	0.476	0.456	0.437
6	0.564	0.535	0.507	0.425	0.456	0.432	0.410	0.390	0.370
7	0.513	0.482	0.452	0.376	0.400	0.376	0.354	0.333	0.314
8	0.467	0.434	0.404	0.333	0.351	0.327	0.305	0.285	0.266
9	0.424	0.391	0.361	0.295	0.308	0.284	0.263	0.243	0.226
10	0.386	0.352	0.322	0.261	0.270	0.247	0.227	0.208	0.191
11	0.350	0.317	0.287	0.231	0.237	0.215	0.195	0.178	0.162
12	0.319	0.286	0.257	0.204	0.208	0.187	0.168	0.152	0.137
13	0.290	0.258	0.229	0.205	0.182	0.163	0.145	0.130	0.116
14	0.263	0.232	0.181	0.160	0.160	0.141	0.125	0.111	0.099
15	0.239	0.209	0.183	0.141	0.140	0.123	0.108	0.095	0.084
16	0.218	0.188	0.163	0.125	0.123	0.107	0.093	0.081	0.071
17	0.198	0.170	0.146	0.111	0.108	0.093	0.080	0.069	0.060
18	0.180	0.153	0.130	0.098	0.095	0.081	0.069	0.059	0.051
19	0.164	0.138	0.166	0.087	0.083	0.070	0.060	0.051	0.043
20	0.149	0.124	0.104	0.047	0.073	0.061	0.051	0.043	0.037
25	0.092	0.074	0.059	0.026	0.038	0.030	0.024	0.020	0.016
30	0.057	0.044	0.033	0.885	0.020	0.015	0.012	0.009	0.007

Contd

Table X   *Contd*

Period n	19%	20%	24%	28%	32%	36%	40%
0	1.000	1.000	1.000	1.000	1.000	1.000	1.000
1	0.840	0.833	0.806	0.781	0.758	0.735	0.714
2	0.706	0.694	0.650	0.610	0.574	0.541	0.510
3	0.593	0.579	0.524	0.477	0.435	0.398	0.364
4	0.499	0.482	0.423	0.373	0.329	0.292	0.260
5	0.419	0.402	0.341	0.291	0.250	0.215	0.186
6	0.352	0.335	0.275	0.227	0.189	0.158	0.133
7	0.296	0.279	0.222	0.178	0.143	0.116	0.095
8	0.249	0.233	0.179	0.139	0.108	0.085	0.068
9	0.209	0.194	0.144	0.108	0.082	0.063	0.048
10	0.176	0.162	0.116	0.085	0.062	0.046	0.035
11	0.148	0.135	0.094	0.066	0.047	0.034	0.025
12	0.124	0.112	0.076	0.052	0.036	0.025	0.018
13	0.104	0.093	0.061	0.040	0.027	0.018	0.013
14	0.088	0.078	0.049	0.032	0.021	0.014	0.009
15	0.074	0.065	0.040	0.025	0.016	0.010	0.006
16	0.062	0.054	0.032	0.019	0.012	0.005	0.007
17	0.052	0.045	0.026	0.015	0.009	0.005	0.003
18	0.044	0.038	0.021	0.012	0.007	0.004	0.002
19	0.037	0.031	0.017	0.009	0.005	0.003	0.002
20	0.031	0.026	0.014	0.007	0.004	0.002	0.001
25	0.013	0.010	0.005	0.002	0.001	0.000	0.000
30	0.005	0.004	0.002	0.001	0.000	0.000	0.000

TABLE Y Future value interest factor
$$FVIF_{(k,n)} = (1+k)^n$$

Period n	1%	2%	3%	4%	5%	6%	7%	8%	9%
0	1.000	1.000	1.000	1.000	1.000	1.000	1.000	1.000	1.000
1	1.010	1.020	1.030	1.040	1.050	1.060	1.070	1.080	1.090
2	1.020	1.040	1.061	1.082	1.102	1.124	1.145	1.166	1.188
3	1.030	1.061	1.093	1.125	1.158	1.191	1.225	1.260	1.295
4	1.041	1.082	1.126	1.170	1.216	1.262	1.311	1.360	1.412
5	1.051	1.104	1.159	1.217	1.276	1.338	1.403	1.469	1.539
6	1.062	1.126	1.194	1.265	1.340	1.419	1.501	1.587	1.677
7	1.072	1.149	1.230	1.316	1.407	1.504	1.606	1.714	1.828
8	1.083	1.172	1.267	1.369	1.477	1.594	1.718	1.851	1.993
9	1.094	1.195	1.305	1.423	1.551	1.689	1.838	1.999	2.172
10	1.105	1.219	1.344	1.480	1.629	1.791	1.967	2.159	2.367
11	1.116	1.243	1.384	1.539	1.710	1.898	2.105	2.332	2.580
12	1.127	1.268	1.426	1.601	1.796	2.012	2.252	2.518	2.813
13	1.138	1.294	1.469	1.665	1.886	2.133	2.410	2.720	3.066
14	1.149	1.319	1.513	1.732	1.980	2.261	2.579	2.937	3.342
15	1.161	1.346	1.558	1.801	2.097	2.397	2.759	3.172	3.642
16	1.173	1.373	1.605	1.873	2.183	2.540	2.952	3.426	3.970
17	1.184	1.400	1.653	1.948	2.292	2.693	3.159	3.700	4.328
18	1.196	1.428	1.702	2.026	2.407	2.854	3.380	3.996	4.717
19	1.208	1.457	1.754	2.107	2.527	3.026	3.617	4.316	5.142
20	1.220	1.486	1.806	2.191	2.653	3.207	3.870	4.661	5.604
25	1.282	1.641	2.094	2.666	3.386	4.292	5.427	6.848	8.623
30	1.348	1.811	2.427	3.243	4.322	5.743	7.612	10.063	13.268

Period n	10%	11%	12%	13%	14%	15%	16%	17%	18%
0	1.000	1.000	1.000	1.000	1.000	1.000	1.000	1.000	1.000
1	1.100	1.110	1.120	1.130	1.140	1.150	1.160	1.170	1.180
2	1.210	1.232	1.254	1.277	1.300	1.322	1.346	1.369	1.392

Contd

Table Y   *Contd*

Period n	10%	11%	12%	13%	14%	15%	16%	17%	18%
3	1.331	1.368	1.405	1.443	1.482	1.521	1.561	1.602	1.643
4	1.464	1.518	1.574	1.630	1.689	1.749	1.811	1.874	1.939
5	1.611	1.685	1.762	1.842	1.925	2.011	2.100	2.192	2.288
6	1.772	1.870	1.974	2.082	2.195	2.313	2.436	2.565	2.700
7	1.949	2.076	2.211	2.353	2.502	2.660	2.826	3.001	3.185
8	2.144	2.305	2.476	2.658	2.853	3.059	3.278	3.511	3.759
9	2.358	2.558	2.773	3.004	3.252	3.518	3.803	4.108	4.435
10	2.594	2.839	3.106	3.395	3.707	4.046	4.411	4.807	5.234
11	2.853	3.152	3.479	3.836	4.226	4.652	5.117	5.624	6.176
12	3.138	3.498	3.596	4.335	4.818	5.350	5.936	6.580	7.288
13	3.452	3.883	4.363	4.898	5.492	6.153	6.886	7.699	8.599
14	3.797	4.310	4.887	5.535	6.261	7.076	7.988	9.007	10.147
15	4.177	4.785	5.474	6.254	7.138	8.137	9.266	10.539	11.974
16	4.595	5.311	6.130	7.067	8.137	9.358	10.748	12.330	14.129
17	5.054	5.895	6.866	7.986	9.276	10.761	12.468	14.426	16.672
18	5.560	6.544	7.690	9.024	10.575	12.375	14.463	16.879	19.673
19	6.116	7.263	8.613	10.197	12.056	14.232	16.777	19.748	23.254
20	6.728	8.062	9.646	11.523	13.743	16.367	19.461	23.106	27.393
25	10.835	13.585	17.000	21.231	26.462	32.919	40.874	50.658	62.669
30	17.449	22.892	29.960	39.116	50.950	66.212	85.850	111.065	143.371

Period n	19%	20%	24%	28%	32%	36%	40%
0	1.000	1.000	1.000	1.000	1.000	1.000	1.000
1	1.190	1.200	1.240	1.280	1.320	1.000	1.400
2	1.416	1.440	1.538	1.638	1.742	1.360	1.960
3	1.685	1.728	1.907	2.097	2.300	1.850	2.744
4	2.005	2.074	2.364	2.684	3.036	2.515	3.842
5	2.386	2.488	2.392	3.436	4.007	3.421	5.378
6	2.840	2.986	3.635	4.398	5.290	4.653	7.530

Contd

Table Y *Contd*

Period n	19%	20%	24%	28%	32%	36%	40%
7	3.379	3.583	4.508	5.629	6.983	6.328	10.541
8	4.021	4.300	5.590	7.206	9.217	8.605	14.758
9	4.785	5.160	6.931	9.223	12.166	11.703	20.661
10	5.695	6.192	8.594	11.806	16.060	15.917	28.925
11	6.777	7.430	10.657	15.112	21.199	21.647	40.496
12	8.064	8.916	13.215	19.343	27.983	29.439	56.694
13	9.596	10.699	16.386	24.759	36.937	40.037	79.372
14	11.420	12.839	20.319	31.961	48.757	54.451	111.120
15	13.590	15.407	25.196	40.565	64.359	74.053	155.568
16	16.172	18.488	31.243	51.923	84.954	100.712	217.795
17	19.244	22.186	38.741	66.461	112.139	136.969	304.914
18	22.901	26.623	48.039	85.071	148.023	186.278	426.879
19	27.252	31.948	59.568	108.890	195.391	253.33s	597.630
20	32.429	38.338	73.864	139.380	1.320	344.540	836.683
25	77.388	95.396	216.542	478.905	1.742	468.574	4,499.880
30	184.675	237.376	634.820	1,645.504	2.300	2,180.081	24,201.432

TABLE Z1 Present value interest factor for an annuity
$$PVIFA_{(k,n)} = \{1-1/(1+k)^n\}/k$$

Period n	1%	2%	3%	4%	5%	6%	7%	8%	9%
0	1.000	1.000	1.000	1.000	1.000	1.000	1.000	1.000	1.000
1	0.990	0.980	0.971	0.962	0.952	0.943	0.935	0.926	0.917
2	1.970	1.942	1.913	1.886	1.859	1.833	1.808	1.783	1.759
3	2.941	2.884	2.829	2.775	2.723	2.673	2.624	2.577	2.531
4	3.902	3.808	3.717	3.630	3.546	3.465	3.387	3.312	3.240
5	4.853	4.713	4.580	4.452	4.329	4.212	4.100	3.993	3.890
6	5.795	5.601	5.417	5.242	5.076	4.917	4.767	4.623	4.486
7	6.728	6.472	6.230	6.002	5.786	5.582	5.389	5.206	5.033
8	7.652	7.325	7.020	6.733	6.463	6.210	5.971	5.747	5.535

Contd

Table Z1   *Contd*

Period n	1%	2%	3%	4%	5%	6%	7%	8%	9%
9	8.566	8.162	7.786	7.435	7.108	6.802	6.515	6.247	5.995
10	9.471	8.983	8.530	8.111	7.722	7.360	7.024	6.710	6.418
11	10.368	9.787	9.253	8.760	8.306	7.887	7.499	7.139	6.805
12	11.255	10.575	9.954	9.385	8.863	8.384	7.943	7.536	7.161
13	12.134	11.348	10.635	9.986	9.394	8.853	8.358	7.904	7.487
14	13.004	12.106	11.296	10.563	9.899	9.295	8.745	8.244	7.786
15	13.865	12.849	11.938	11.118	10.380	9.712	9.108	8.559	8.061
16	14.718	13.578	12.561	11.652	10.838	10.106	9.447	8.851	8.313
17	15.562	14.292	13.166	12.166	11.274	10.477	9.763	9.122	8.544
18	16.398	14.992	13.754	12.659	11.690	10.828	10.059	9.372	8.756
19	17.226	15.678	14.324	13.134	12.085	11.158	10.336	9.604	8.950
20	18.046	16.351	14.877	13.590	12.462	11.470	10.594	9.818	9.129
25	22.023	19.523	17.413	15.622	14.094	12.783	11.654	10.675	9.823
30	25.808	22.397	19.600	17.292	15.373	13.765	12.409	11.258	10.274

Period n	10%	11%	12%	13%	14%	15%	16%	17%	18%
0	1.000	1.000	1.000	1.000	1.000	1.000	1.000	1.000	1.000
1	0.909	0.901	0.893	0.885	0.877	0.870	0.862	0.855	0.847
2	1.736	1.713	1.690	1.668	1.647	1.626	1.605	1.585	1.566
3	2.487	2.444	2.402	2.361	2.322	2.283	2.246	2.210	2.174
4	3.170	3.102	3.037	2.974	2.914	2.855	2.798	2.743	2.690
5	3.791	3.696	3.605	3.517	3.433	3.352	3.274	3.199	3.127
6	4.355	4.231	4.111	3.998	3.889	3.784	3.685	3.589	3.498
7	4.868	4.712	5.564	4.423	4.288	4.160	4.039	3.922	3.812
8	3.335	5.146	4.968	4.799	4.639	4.487	4.344	4.207	4.078
9	5.759	5.537	5.328	5.132	4.946	4.772	4.607	4.451	4.303
10	6.145	5.889	5.650	5.426	5.216	5.019	4.833	4.659	4.494
11	6.495	6.207	5.938	5.687	5.453	5.234	5.029	4.836	4.656
12	6.814	6.492	6.194	5.918	5.660	5.421	5.197	4.988	4.793

Contd

Table Z1 *Contd*

Period n	10%	11%	12%	13%	14%	15%	16%	17%	18%
13	7.103	6.750	6.424	6.122	5.842	5.583	5.342	5.118	4.910
14	7.367	6.982	6.628	6.302	6.002	5.724	5.468	5.229	5.008
15	7.606	7.191	6.811	6.462	6.142	5.847	5.575	5.324	5.092
16	7.824	7.379	6.974	6.604	6.265	5.954	5.669	5.405	5.162
17	8.022	7.549	7.120	6.729	6.373	6.047	5.749	5.475	5.222
18	8.201	7.702	7.250	6.840	6.467	6.128	5.818	5.534	5.273
19	8.365	7.839	7.366	6.938	6.550	6.198	5.877	4.584	5.316
20	8.514	7.963	7.469	7.025	6.623	6.259	5.929	5.628	5.353
25	9.077	8.422	7.843	7.330	6.873	5.464	5.097	5.766	5.467
30	9.427	8.694	8.055	7.496	7.003	6.566	6.177	5.829	5.517

Period n	19%	20%	24%	28%	32%	36%	40%
0	1.000	1.000	1.000	1.000	1.000	1.000	1.000
1	0.840	0.833	0.806	0.781	0.758	0.735	0.714
2	1.547	1.528	1.457	1.392	1.332	1.276	1.224
3	2.140	2.106	1.981	1.868	1.766	1.674	1.589
4	2.639	2.589	2.404	2.241	2.096	1.966	1.849
5	3.058	2.991	2.745	2.532	2.345	2.181	2.035
6	3.410	3.326	3.020	2.759	2.534	2.339	2.168
7	3.706	3.605	3.242	2.937	2.678	2.455	2.263
8	3.954	3.837	3.421	3.076	2.786	2.540	2.113
9	4.163	4.031	3.566	3.184	2.868	2.603	2.379
10	4.339	4.193	3.682	3.269	2.930	2.650	2.414
11	4.486	4.327	3.776	3.335	2.978	2.683	2.438
12	4.611	4.439	3.851	3.387	3.013	2.708	2.456
13	4.715	4.533	3.912	3.427	3.040	2.727	2.469
14	4.802	4.611	3.962	3.459	3.061	2.740	2.478
15	4.876	4.675	4.001	3.483	3.076	2.750	2.484
16	4.938	4.730	4.033	3.503	3.088	2.758	2.489

Contd

Table Z1   *Contd*

Period n	19%	20%	24%	28%	32%	36%	40%
17	4.990	4.775	4.059	3.518	3.097	2.763	2.492
18	5.033	4.812	4.080	3.529	3.104	2.767	2.494
19	5.070	4.844	4.097	3.539	3.109	2.770	2.496
20	5.101	4.870	4.110	3.546	3.113	2.772	2.497
25	5.195	4.948	4.147	3.564	3.122	2.776	2.499
30	5.235	4.979	4.160	3.569	3.124	2.778	2.500

TABLE Z2   Future value interest factor for annuity

$$\text{FVIFA}_{(k,n)} = [(1+k)^n - 1]/k$$

Period n	1%	2%	3%	4%	5%	6%	7%	8%	9%
1	1.000	1.000	1.000	1.000	1.000	1.000	1.000	1.000	1.000
2	2.010	2.020	2.030	2.040	2.050	2.060	2.070	2.080	2.090
3	3.030	3.060	3.091	3.122	3.152	3.184	3.215	3.246	3.278
4	4.060	4.122	4.184	4.246	4.310	4.375	4.440	4.506	4.573
5	5.101	5.204	5.309	5.416	5.526	5.637	5.751	5.867	5.985
6	6.152	6.308	6.468	6.633	6.802	6.975	7.153	7.336	7.523
7	7.214	7.434	7.662	7.898	8.142	8.394	8.654	8.923	9.200
8	8.286	8.583	8.892	9.214	9.549	9.897	10.260	10.637	11.028
9	9.369	9.755	10.159	10.583	11.027	11.491	11.978	12.488	13.021
10	10.462	10.950	11.464	12.006	12.578	13.181	13.816	14.487	15.193
11	11.567	12.169	12.508	13.486	14.207	14.972	15.784	16.645	17.560
12	12.683	13.412	14.192	15.026	15.917	16.870	17.888	18.977	21.141
13	13.809	14.680	15.618	16.627	17.713	18.882	20.141	21.495	22.953
14	14.947	15.974	17.086	18.292	19.599	21.015	22.550	24.215	26.019
15	16.097	17.293	18.599	20.024	21.579	23.276	25.129	27.152	29.361
16	17.258	18.639	20.157	21.825	23.657	25.673	27.888	30.324	33.003
17	18.430	20.012	21.762	23.698	25.840	28.213	30.840	33.750	36.974
18	19.615	21.412	23.414	25.645	28.132	30.906	33.999	37.450	41.301
19	20.811	22.841	25.117	27.671	30.539	33.760	37.379	41.446	46.018

Contd

Table Z2 *Contd*

Period n	1%	2%	3%	4%	5%	6%	7%	8%	9%
20	22.019	24.297	26.870	29.778	33.066	36.786	40.995	45.762	51.160
25	28.243	32.030	36.459	41.646	47.727	54.865	63.249	73.106	84.701
30	34.785	40.568	47.575	56.805	66.439	79.058	94.461	113.283	136.308

Period n	10%	11%	12%	13%	14%	15%	16%	17%	18%
1	1.000	1.000	1.000	1.000	1.000	1.000	1.000	1.000	1.000
2	2.100	2.110	2.120	2.130	2.140	2.150	2.160	2.170	2.180
3	3.310	3.342	3.374	3.407	3.440	3.473	3.506	3.539	3.572
4	4.641	4.710	4.779	4.850	4.921	4.993	5.066	5.141	5.215
5	6.105	6.228	6.353	6.480	6.610	6.742	6.887	7.014	7.154
6	7.716	7.913	8.115	8.323	8.536	8.754	8.977	9.207	9.442
7	9.487	9.783	10.089	10.405	10.730	11.067	11.414	11.772	12.142
8	11.436	11.859	12.300	12.757	13.233	13.727	14.240	14.773	15.327
9	13.579	14.164	14.776	15.416	16.085	16.786	17.518	18.285	19.086
10	15.937	16.722	17.549	18.420	19.337	20.304	21.321	22.393	23.521
11	18.531	19.561	20.655	21.814	23.044	24.349	25.733	27.200	28.755
12	21.384	22.713	24.133	25.650	27.27!	29.002	30.850	32.824	34.931
13	24.523	26.212	28.029	29.985	32.089	34.352	36.786	39.404	42.219
14	27.975	30.095	32.393	34.583	37.581	40.505	43.672	47.103	50.818
15	31.772	34.405	37.280	40.417	43.842	47.580	51.660	56.110	60.965
16	35.950	39.190	42.753	146.672	50.980	55.717	60.925	66.649	72.939
17	40.545	44.501	48.8S4	53.739	59.118	65.075	71.673	78.979	87.068
18	45.599	50.396	55.750	61.725	68.394	75.836	84.141	93.406	103.740
19	51.159	56.939	63.440	70.749	78.969	88.212	98.603	110.285	123.414
20	57.275	64.203	72.052	80.947	91.025	102.44	115.380	130.033	146.628
25	98.347	114.413	133.334	155.620	181.871	212.793	249.214	292.105	342.603
30	164.494	199.021	241.333	293.199	356.787	434.745	530.321	647.439	790.948

Contd

Table Z2   *Contd*

Period n	19%	20%	24%	28%	32%	36%	40%
1	1.000	1.000	1.000	1.000	1.000	1.000	1.000
2	2.190	2.200	2.240	2.280	2.320	1.000	2.400
3	3.606	3.640	3.778	3.918	4.062	2.360	4.360
4	5.291	5.368	5.684	6.016	6.362	4.210	7.104
5	7.297	7.442	8.048	8.700	9.398	6.725	10.946
6	9.683	9.930	10.980	12.136	13.406	10.146	16.324
7	12.523	12.916	14.615	16.534	18.696	14.799	23.853
8	15.902	16.499	19.123	22.163	25.678	21.126	34.395
9	19.923	20.799	24.712	29.369	34.895	29.732	49.153
10	24.709	25.959	31.643	38.592	47.062	41.435	69.814
11	30.404	32.150	40.238	50.399	63.122	57.352	98.739
12	37.180	39.580	50.985	65.510	84.320	78.998	139.235
13	45.244	48.497	64.110	84.853	112303	108.437	195.929
14	54.841	59.196	80.496	109.612	149.240	148.475	275.300
15	66.261	72.035	100.815	141.303	197.997	202.926	386.420
16	79.850	87.442	126.011	181.868	262.356	276.979	541.988
17	96.022	105.931	157.253	233.791	347.310	377.692	759.784
18	115.266	128.117	195.994	300.252	459.449	514.661	1064.697
19	138.166	154.740	244.033	385.323	607.472	700.939	1491.576
20	165.418	186.688	303.601	494.213	802.863	954.277	2089.206
25	402.042	371.981	898.092	1,706.803	3,226.844	1,293.817	1,1247.199
30	966.712	1,881.882	2,640.916	5,873.231	12,940.859	6,053.004	60,501.081

TABLE W   Normal distribution

No. of Standard deviation from the Mean (Z)	Area to the left or right (One tail)	Number of Standard deviation from mean (Z)	Area to the left or right (One tail)
0.00	0.5000	1.70	0.0446
0.05	0.4801	1.75	0.0401
0.10	0.4602	1.80	0.0359
0.15	0.4404	1.85	0.0322

Contd

Table W   *Contd*

No. of Standard deviation from the Mean (Z)	Area to the left or right (One tail)	Number of Standard deviation from mean (Z)	Area to the left or right (One tail)
0.20	0.4207	1.90	0.0287
0.25	0.4013	1.95	0.0256
0.30	0.3821	2.00	0.0228
0.35	0.3632	2.05	0.0202
0.40	0.3446	2.10	0.0179
0.45	0.3264	2.15	0.0158
0.50	0.3085	2.20	0.0139
0.55	0.2912	2.25	0.0122
0.60	0.2743	2.30	0.0107
0.65	0.2578	2.35	0.0094
0.70	0.2420	2.40	0.0082
0.75	0.2264	2.45	0.0071
0.80	0.2119	2.50	0.0062
0.85	0.1977	2.55	0.0054
0.90	0.1841	2.60	0.0047
0.95	0.1711	2.65	0.0040
1.00	0.1587	2.70	0.0035
1.05	0.1469	2.75	0.0030
1.10	0.1357	2.80	0.0026
1.15	0.1251	2.85	0.0022
1.20	0.1151	2.90	0.0019
1.25	0.1056	2.95	0.0016
1.30	0.0968	3.00	0.0013
1.35	0.0885	3.05	0.0011
1.40	0.0808	3.10	0.0010
1.45	0.0735	3.25	0.0006
1.50	0.0668	3.50	0.00023
1.55	0.0606	4.00	0.00003
1.60	0.0548	4.99	0.0000003
1.65	0.0495		

TABLE U   Value of call option as percentage of share price
Share price divided by PV (exercise price)

	0.40	0.45	0.50	0.55	0.60	0.65	0.70	0.75	0.80
0.05	0.0	0.0	0.0	0.0	0.0	0.0	0.0	0.0	0.0
0.10	0.0	0.0	0.0	0.0	0.0	0.0	0.0	0.0	0.0
0.15	0.0	0.0	0.0	0.0	0.0	0.0	0.1	0.2	0.5
0.20	0.0	0.0	0.0	0.0	0.0	0.1	0.4	0.8	1.5
0.25	0.0	0.0	0.0	0.1	0.2	0.5	1.0	1.8	2.8
0.30	0.0	0.1	0.1	0.3	0.7	1.2	2.0	3.1	4.4
0.35	0.1	0.2	0.4	0.8	1.4	2.3	3.3	4.6	6.2
0.40	0.2	0.5	0.9	1.6	2.4	3.5	4.8	6.3	8.0
0.45	0.5	1.0	1.7	2.6	3.7	5.0	6.5	8.1	9.9
0.50	1.0	1.7	2.6	3.7	5.1	6.6	8.2	10.0	11.8
0.55	1.7	2.6	3.8	5.1	6.6	8.3	10.0	11.9	13.8
0.60	2.5	3.7	5.1	6.6	8.3	10.1	11.9	13.8	15.8
0.65	3.6	4.9	6.5	8.2	10.0	11.9	13.8	15.8	17.8
0.70	4.7	6.3	8.1	9.9	11.9	13.8	15.8	17.8	19.8
0.75	6.1	7.9	9.8	11.7	13.7	15.8	17.8	19.8	21.8
0.80	7.5	9.5	11.5	13.6	15.7	17.7	19.8	21.8	23.7
0.85	9.1	11.2	13.3	15.5	17.6	19.7	21.8	23.8	25.7
0.90	10.7	13.0	15.2	17.4	19.6	21.7	23.8	25.8	27.7
0.95	12.5	14.8	17.1	19.4	21.6	23.7	25.7	27.7	29.6
1.00	14.3	16.7	19.1	21.4	23.6	25.7	27.7	29.7	31.6
1.05	16.1	18.6	21.0	23.3	25.6	27.7	29.7	31.6	33.5
1.10	18.0	20.6	23.0	25.3	27.5	29.6	31.6	33.5	35.4
1.15	20.0	22.5	25.0	27.3	29.5	31.6	33.6	35.4	37.2
1.20	21.9	24.5	27.0	29.3	31.5	33.6	35.5	37.3	39.1

Standard deviation times square root of time

Contd

Table U *Contd*

		0.40	0.45	0.50	0.55	0.60	0.65	0.70	0.75	0.80
Standard deviation times square root of time	**1.25**	23.9	26.5	29.0	31.3	33.5	35.5	37.4	39.2	40.9
	1.30	25.9	28.5	31.0	33.3	35.4	37.4	39.3	41.0	42.7
	1.35	27.9	30.5	33.0	35.2	37.3	39.3	41.1	42.8	44.4
	1.40	29.9	32.5	34.9	37.1	39.2	41.1	42.9	44.6	46.2
	1.45	31.9	34.5	36.9	39.1	41.1	43.0	44.7	46.4	47.9
	1.50	33.8	36.4	38.4	40.9	42.9	44.8	45.5	48.1	49.6
	1.55	35.8	38.4	40.3	42.8	44.8	46.6	48.2	49.8	51.2
	1.60	37.8	40.3	42.2	44.6	46.5	48.3	49.9	51.4	52.8
	1.65	39.7	42.2	44.0	46.4	48.3	50.0	51.6	53.1	54.4
	1.70	41.6	44.0	45.9	48.2	50.0	51.7	53.2	54.7	56.0
	1.75	43.5	45.9	54.6	50.0	51.7	53.4	54.8	56.2	57.5
	2.00	52.5	54.6	62.5	58.2	59.7	61.1	62.4	63.6	64.6
	2.25	60.7	62.5	69.4	65.6	66.8	68.0	69.1	70.0	70.9
	2.50	67.9	69.4	75.4	72.0	73.1	74.0	74.9	75.7	76.4
	2.75	74.2	75.4	80.5	77.5	78.4	79.2	79.9	80.5	81.1
	3.00	79.5	80.5	88.3	82.2	82.9	83.5	84.1	84.6	85.1
	3.50	87.6	88.3	93.3	89.3	89.7	90.1	90.5	90.8	91.1
	4.00	92.9	93.3	96.4	93.9	94.2	94.4	94.6	94.8	94.9
	4.50	96.2	96.4	98.2	96.7	96.9	97.0	97.1	97.2	97.3
	5.00	98.1	98.2	98.8	98.3	98.4	98.5	98.5	98.6	98.6

Contd

Table U   *Contd*

	0.82	0.84	0.86	0.88	0.90	0.92	0.94	0.96	0.98	1.00
0.05	0.0	0.0	0.0	0.0	0.0	0.1	0.3	0.6	1.2	2.0
0.10	0.1	0.2	0.3	0.5	0.8	1.2	1.7	2.3	3.1	4.0
0.15	0.7	1.0	1.3	1.7	2.2	2.8	3.5	4.2	5.1	6.0
0.20	1.9	2.3	2.8	3.4	4.0	4.7	5.4	6.2	7.1	8.0
0.25	3.3	3.9	4.5	5.2	5.9	6.6	7.4	8.2	9.1	9.9
0.30	5.0	5.7	6.3	7.0	7.8	8.6	9.4	10.2	11.1	11.9
0.35	6.8	7.5	8.2	9.0	9.8	10.6	11.4	12.2	13.0	13.9
0.40	8.7	9.4	10.2	11.0	11.7	12.5	13.4	14.2	15.0	15.9
0.45	10.6	11.4	12.2	12.9	13.7	14.5	15.3	16.2	17.0	17.8
0.50	12.6	13.4	14.2	14.9	15.7	16.5	17.3	18.1	18.9	19.7
0.55	14.6	15.4	16.1	16.9	17.7	18.5	19.3	20.1	20.9	21.7
0.60	16.6	17.4	18.1	18.9	19.7	20.5	21.3	22.0	22.8	23.6
0.65	18.6	19.3	20.1	20.9	21.7	22.5	23.2	24.0	24.7	25.5
0.70	20.6	21.3	22.1	22.9	23.6	24.4	25.2	25.9	26.6	27.4
0.75	22.5	23.3	24.1	24.8	25.6	26.3	27.1	27.8	28.5	29.2
0.80	24.5	25.3	26.0	26.8	27.5	28.3	29.0	29.7	30.4	31.1
0.85	26.5	27.2	28.0	28.7	29.4	30.2	30.9	31.6	32.2	32.9
0.90	28.4	29.2	29.9	30.6	31.8	32.0	32.7	33.4	34.1	34.7
0.95	30.4	31.1	31.8	32.5	33.2	33. 9	34.6	35.2	35.9	36.5
1.00	32.3	33.0	33.7	34.4	35.1	35.7	36.4	37.0	37.7	38.3
1.05	34.2	34.9	35.6	36.2	36.9	37.6	38.2	38.8	39.4	40.0
1.10	36.1	36.7	37.4	38.1	38.7	39.3	40.0	40.6	41.2	41.6
1.15	37.9	38.6	39.2	39.9	40.5	41.1	41.7	42.3	42.9	43.5
1.20	39.7	40.4	41.0	41.7	42.3	42.9	43.5	44.0	44.6	45.1
1.25	41.5	42.2	42.8	43.4	44.0	44.6	45.2	45.7	46.3	46.6

Standard deviation times square root of time

Contd

Table U   *Contd*

		0.82	0.84	0.86	0.88	0.90	0.92	0.94	0.96	0.98	1.00
Standard deviation times square root of time	1.30	43.3	43.9	44.5	45.1	45.7	46.3	46.8	47.4	47.9	48.4
	1.35	45.1	45.7	46.3	46.8	47.4	47.9	48.5	49.0	49.5	50.0
	1.40	46.8	47.4	47.9	48.5	50.7	51.2	51.7	52.2	52.7	53.2
	1.45	48.5	49.0	49.6	50.1	52.3	52.8	53.3	53.7	54.2	54.7
	1.50	50.1	50.7	51.2	51.8	53.8	54.3	54.8	55.3	55.7	56.2
	1.55	51.8	52.3	52.8	53.3	55.4	55.9	56.3	56.8	57.2	57.6
	1.60	53.4	53.9	54.4	54.9	56.9	57.3	57.8	58.2	58.6	59.1
	1.65	54.9	55.4	55.9	56.4	58.4	58.8	59.2	59.7	60.1	60.5
	1.70	56.5	57.0	57.5	57.9	59.8	60.2	60.7	61.1	61.5	61.8
	1.75	58.0	58.9	58.9	59.4	66.6	66.9	67.3	67.6	67.9	68.3
	2.00	65.0	65.4	65.8	66.2	72.5	72.8	73.1	73.4	73.7	73.9
	2.25	71.3	71.6	71.9	72.2	77.7	78.0	78.2	78.4	78.7	78.9
	2.50	76.7	77.0	77.2	77.5	82.2	82.4	82.6	82.7	82.9	83.1
	2.75	81.4	81.6	81.8	82.0	85.9	86.1	86.2	86.4	86.5	86.6
	3.00	85.3	85.4	85.6	85.8	91.6	91.6	91.7	91.8	91.9	92.0
	3.50	91.2	91.3	91.4	91.5	95.2	95.3	95.3	95.4	95.4	95.4
	4.00	95.0	95.0	95.1	95.2	97.4	97.4	97.5	97.5	97.5	97.6
	4.50	97.3	97.3	97.4	97.4	97.4	97.4	95.3	95.4	97.5	97.6
	5.00	98.6	98.6	98.7	98.7	98.7	98.7	98.7	98.7	98.7	98.8

		1.02	1.04	1.06	1.08	1.10	1.12	1.14	1.16	1.18
Standard deviation times square root of time	0.05	3.1	4.5	6.0	7.5	9.1	10.7	12.3	13.8	15.3
	0.10	5.0	6.1	7.3	8.6	10.0	11.3	12.7	14.1	15.4
	0.15	7.0	8.0	9.1	10.2	11.4	12.6	13.8	15.0	16.2
	0.20	8.9	9.9	10.9	11.9	13.0	14.1	15.2	16.3	17.4
	0.25	10.9	11.8	12.8	13.7	14.7	15.7	16.7	17.7	18.7

Contd

Table U   *Contd*

		1.02	1.04	1.06	1.08	1.10	1.12	1.14	1.16	1.18
	0.30	12.8	13.7	14.6	15.6	16.5	17.4	18.4	19.3	20.3
	0.35	14.8	15.6	16.5	17.4	18.3	19.2	20.1	21.0	21.9
	0.40	16.7	17.5	18.4	19.2	20.1	20.9	21.8	22.6	23.5
	0.45	18.6	19.4	20.3	21.1	21.9	22.7	23.5	24.3	25.1
	0.50	20.5	21.3	22.1	22.9	23.7	24.5	25.3	26.1	26.8
	0.55	22.4	23.2	24.0	24.8	25.5	26.3	27.0	27.8	28.5
	0.60	24.3	25.1	25.8	26.6	27.3	28.1	28.8	29.5	30.2
	0.65	26.2	27.0	27.7	28.4	29.1	29.8	30.5	31.2	31.9
Standard deviation times square root of time	0.70	28.1	28.8	29.5	30.2	30.9	31.6	32.3	32.9	33.6
	0.75	29.9	30.6	31.3	32.0	32.7	33.3	34.0	34.6	35.3
	0.80	31.8	32.4	33.1	33.8	34.4	35.1	35.7	36.3	36.9
	0.85	33.6	34.2	34.9	35.5	36.2	36.8	37.4	38.0	38.6
	0.90	35.4	36.0	36.6	37.3	37.9	38.5	39.1	39.6	40.2
	0.95	37.2	37.8	38.4	39.0	39.6	40.1	40.7	41.3	41.8
	1.00	38.9	39.5	40.1	40.7	41.2	41.8	42.4	42.9	43.4
	1.05	40.6	41.2	41.8	42.4	42.9	43.5	44.0	44.5	45.0
	1.10	42.3	42.9	43.5	44.0	44.5	45.1	45.6	46.1	46.6
	1.15	44.0	44.6	45.1	45.6	46.2	46.7	47.2	47.7	48.2
	1.20	45.7	46.2	46.7	47.3	47.8	48.3	48.7	49.2	49.7
	1.25	47.3	47.8	48.4	48.8	49.3	49.8	50.3	50.7	51.2
	1.30	48.9	49.4	49.9	50.4	50.9	51.3	51.8	52.2	52.7
	1.35	50.5	51.0	51.5	52.0	52.4	52.9	53.3	53.7	54.1
	1.40	52.1	52.6	53.0	53.5	53.9	54.3	54.8	55.2	55.6
	1.45	53.6	54.1	54.5	55.0	55.4	55.8	56.2	56.6	57.0
	1.50	55.1	55.6	56.0	56.4	56.8	57.2	57.6	58.0	58.4

Contd..

Table U   *Contd*

		1.02	1.04	1.06	1.08	1.10	1.12	1.14	1.16	1.18
Standard deviation times square root of time	1.55	56.6	57.0	57.4	57.8	58.2	58.6	59.0	59.4	59.7
	1.60	58.0	58.5	58.9	59.2	59.6	60.0	60.4	60.7	61.1
	1.65	59.5	59.9	60.2	60.6	61.0	61.4	61.7	62.1	62.4
	1.70	60.9	61.2	61.6	62.0	62.3	62.7	63.0	63.4	63.7
	1.75	62.2	62.6	62.9	63.3	63.6	64.0	64.3	64.6	64.9
	2.00	68.6	68.9	69.2	69.5	69.8	70.0	70.3	70.6	70.8
	2.25	74.2	74.4	74.7	74.9	75.2	75.4	75.6	75.8	76.0
	2.50	79.1	79.3	79.5	79.7	79.9	80.0	80.2	80.4	80.6
	2.75	83.3	83.4	83.6	83.7	83.9	84.0	84.2	84.3	84.4
	3.00	86.8	86.9	87.0	87.1	87.3	87.4	87.5	87.6	87.7
	3.50	92.1	92.1	92.2	92.3	92.4	92.4	92.5	92.6	92.6
	4.00	95.5	95.5	95.6	95.6	95.7	95.7	95.7	95.8	95.8
	4.50	97.6	97.6	97.6	97.6	97.7	97.7	97.7	97.7	97.8
	5.00	98.8	98.8	98.8	98.8	98.8	98.8	98.8	98.8	98.9

		1.20	1.25	1.30	1.35	1.40	1.45	1.50	1.75	2.00	2.50
Standard deviation times square root of time	0.05	16.7	20.0	23.1	25.9	28.6	3.10	33.3	42.9	50.0	60.0
	0.10	16.8	20.0	23.1	25.9	28.6	31.0	33.3	42.9	50.0	60.0
	0.15	17.4	20.4	23.3	26.0	28.6	31.1	33.3	42.9	50.0	60.0
	0.20	18.5	21.2	23.9	26.4	28.9	31.2	33.5	42.9	50.0	60.0
	0.25	19.8	22.3	24.7	27.1	29.4	31.7	33.8	42.9	50.0	60.0
	0.30	21.2	23.5	25.8	28.1	30.2	32.3	34.3	43.1	50.1	60.0
	0.35	22.7	24.9	27.1	29.2	31.2	33.2	35.1	43.5	50.2	60.0
	0.40	24.3	26.4	28.4	30.4	32.3	34.2	36.0	44.0	50.5	60.1
	0.45	25.9	27.9	29.8	31.7	33.5	35.3	37.0	44.6	50.8	60.2

Contd

Table U   *Contd*

		1.20	1.25	1.30	1.35	1.40	1.45	1.50	1.75	2.00	2.50
	0.50	27.6	29.5	31.3	33.1	34.8	36.4	38.1	45.3	51.3	60.4
	0.55	29.2	31.0	32.8	34.5	36.1	37.7	39.2	46.1	51.9	60.7
	0.60	30.9	32.6	34.3	35.9	37.5	39.0	40.4	47.0	52.5	61.0
	0.65	32.6	34.2	35.8	37.4	38.4	40.3	41.7	48.0	53.3	61.4
	0.70	34.2	35.8	37.3	38.8	40.3	41.6	43.0	49.0	54.0	61.9
	0.75	35.9	37.4	38.9	40.3	41.7	43.0	44.3	50.0	54.9	62.4
	0.80	37.5	39.0	40.4	41.8	43.1	44.4	45.6	51.1	55.8	63.0
	0.85	39.2	40.6	41.9	43.3	44.5	45.8	46.9	52.2	56.7	63.6
Standard deviation times square root of time	0.90	40.8	42.1	43.5	44.7	460	47.1	48.3	53.3	57.6	64.3
	0.95	42.4	43.7	45.0	46.2	47.4	48.5	49.6	54.5	58.6	65.0
	1.00	44.0	45.2	46.5	47.6	48.8	49.9	50.9	55.6	59.5	65.7
	1.05	45.5	46.8	48.0	49.1	50.2	51.2	50.2	56.7	60.5	66.5
	1.10	47.1	48.3	49.4	50.5	51.6	52.6	53.5	57.9	61.5	67.2
	1.15	48.6	49.8	50.9	51.9	52.9	53.9	54.9	59.0	62.5	68.0
	1.20	50.1	51.3	52.3	53.3	54.3	55.2	56.1	60.2	63.5	68.8
	1.25	51.6	52.7	53.7	54.7	55.7	56.6	57.4	61.3	64.5	69.6
	1.30	53.1	54.1	55.1	56.1	57.0	57.9	58.7	62.4	65.5	70.4
	1.35	54.6	55.6	56.5	57.4	58.3	59.1	59.9	63.5	66.5	71.1
	1.40	56.0	56.9	57.9	'58.7	59.6	60.4	61.2	64.6	67.5	71.9
	1.45	57.4	58.3	59.2	60.0	60.9	61.6	62.4	65.7	68.4	72.7
	1.50	58.8	59.7	60.5	61.3	62.1	62.9	63.6	66.8	69.4	73.5
	1.55	60.1	61.0	61.8	62.6	63.3	64.1	64.7	67.8	70.3	74.3
	1.60	61.4	62.3	63.1	63.8	64.5	65.2	65.9	68.8	71.3	75.1
	1.65	62.7	63.5	64.3	65.0	65.7	66.4	67.0	69.9	72.2	75.9
	1.70	64.0	64.8	65.5	66.2	66.9	67.5	68.2	70.9	73.1	76.6

Contd

Table U   *Contd*

		1.20	1.25	1.30	1.35	1.40	1.45	1.50	1.75	2.00	2.50
Standard deviation times square root of time	**1.75**	65.3	66.0	66.7	67.4	68.0	68.7	69.2	71.9	74.0	77.4
	2.00	71.1	71.7	72.3	72.9	73.4	73.9	74.4	76.5	78.3	81.0
	2.25	76.3	76.8	77.2	77.7	78.1	78.5	78.9	80.6	82.1	84.3
	2.50	80.7	81.1	81.5	81.9	82.2	82.6	82.9	84.3	85.4	87.2
	2.75	84.6	84.9	85.2	85.5	85.8	86.0	86.3	87.4	88.3	89.7
	3.00	87.8	88.1	88.3	88.5	88.8	89.0	89.2	90.0	90.7	91.8
	3.50	92.7	92.8	93.0	93.1	93.3	93.4	93.5	94.0	94.4	95.1
	4.00	95.8	95.9	96.0	96.1	96.2	96.2	96.3	96.6	96.8	97.2
	4.50	97.8	97.8	97.9	97.9	97.9	98.0	98.0	98.2	98.3	98.5
	5.00	98.9	98.9	98.9	98.9	99.0	99.0	99.0	99.1	99.1	99.2

DETAILED PROJECT REPORT

Introduction

A detailed project report (DPR) is a report that covers various aspects of a project. It gives information about the details of the company undertaking the project, financial projection, market demand analysis, technical analysis, environmental aspects, appraisal, expected cash flows, profitability, socio-economic aspects, etc. This report is generally submitted to the financial institution from where the project is to be financed.

Generally, each financial institution has its own format and there is no fixed pattern in which the DPR has to be presented. But one should keep in mind the analyses and feasibility studies—market and demand, technical, socio, economical, environmental, and mainly financial aspects of the project should be systematically presented in it. Along with this, some other related information such as promoters' background and profile, location of the site, etc., is also included in the DPR

A firm usually submits a DPR when it applies for a loan from a financial institution for a new project. This report should comprise of the project's viability and its projected profitability and forecasted return on investment. Only after analysing DPR, i.e., various pros and cons of the proposed project does the financial institution sanction the loan.

Contents of DPR

Though each financial institution has its own style of filling up the DPR forms, the following are some of the essentials common to all DPRs.

1. General information:
    1.1 Name of the venture
    1.2 Constitution and sector
    1.3 Location
    1.4 Nature of industry and product
    1.5 Promoters and their contributions
    1.6 Cost of project and means of finance
2. Promoters' profile
3. Marketing and selling plan
4. Project particulars

Structure of DPR

In this section, we are providing a general format of a DPR, which generally covers all the components of a standard DPR, followed by any financial institution.

Format of Application of All India Financial Institution

PROJECT LOAN APPLICATION FORM

Date of Loan Application	General Background Information

Name of the Industrial Concern (in block letters)	

Constitution		Public Ltd Co.	Sector		Public Sector
		Private Ltd Co.			Joint Sector
		Co-op Society			Private Sector
		Others, please specify			Co-operative Sector

Industry Classification	

Date of Incorporation/Registration	
Date of Commencement of Business	

	Village	Tehsil	District	State
Registered Office				
Controlling (Head) office				
Project Location				

PROJECT PROFILE

Project Type		Greenfield		Diversification		Others (specify)
		Expansion		Modernization		

Description of proposed product(s)	Licensed capacity	Existing installed capacity	Proposed installed capacity	Maximum envisaged production

Briefly describe the project (product, process, technology, special features in regard to any specific advantage, etc.)

Indicate section-wise capacity for the major sections of the plant along with detailed calculations. Explain the reason for excess/inadequate capacity, if any, in any of the sections.

Give Specifications of Major Products and By-products

Products/ by-products	Size	Weight	Chemical/physical properties	Industrial Uses

Part I Promoter/Company Information

A. **Promoter background** (required only if applicant is new)

I–1 Provide the following information on the main promoter

Name and Address	
Age	
Educational qualification	
Relevant industry experience	

Name of the company promoted/affiliated with	Brief description of the company	(for the past 5 years)	1	2	3	4	5
1.		Sales, net profit, net worth					
2.		Sales, net profit, net worth					
3.		Sales, net profit, net worth					

Name of the bankers with whom enquiries can be made	

Defaults on existing commitments to:

	Amount (Rs in lakhs)				Period of default
	Principal	Interest	Other	Total	
IDBI					
Other FIs					
Banks					

I–2 Provide a brief write-up on the activities and past performance of the company (only required if promoter is a limited company)

Activities					
Performance	20____	20____	20____	20____	20____
Sales Gross Profit Operating Profit Net Profit Share Capital Net Worth					

I–3 Describe any other expansion programme(s) contemplated (only required if promoter is a limited company)

B. **Company background** (only required if the applicant is an existing company)

I–4 Provide a brief history of the concern including any change in the names, business management, etc. and indicate any merger or reorganization which took place

I–5 Provide a list of all subsidiary/ancillary company

Name of subsidiaries	Percentage of holding

I–6 Provide the following information on the holding companies

Name of the holding company:	

Other subsidiary companies under the holding company	Paid up capital of subsidiaries		Percentage held by holding company	
	Equity share	Preference share	Equity share	Preference share

I–7 Is the company regular on crediting its contribution and the contribution of its employees to the Employees' Provident Funds and meeting other statutory obligation

	Yes		No

I–8 Describe manufacturing facilities separately at each plant as follows:

Plant	Dates of installation and major remodelling	Paid up capital of subsidiaries		Specification of products manufactured
		Design capacity	Normal capacity	

I–9 Provide information on each major product/product group as follows:

Major product/ product groups	Licensed capacity	Installed capacity	Production	Sales quantity	Sales value

I–10 Provide reasons for under utilization of capacity and significant variation in production and sales

I–11 Describe locational advantages of the plant

I–12 Indicate the existing requirements of raw materials, utilities, and services

I–13 Describe export sales over last 5 years as follows:

Export product	Main destination	Physical volume	Proceeds of export sales

I–14 Provide the details of insurance carried on/by fixed assets and inventories

Covered item	Basis of insurance	Name of insurer	Risk type covered

I–15 Provide the details of litigation either by or against the company

I–16 Furnish information on R&D activities

Nature of R&D activities	

Total amount of the capital expenditure incurred	
Annual budget	
Number of scientists/technical personnel employed	

Lit of new products/process developed	Extent of commercial exploitation

I–17 Describe any assets that may have been revalued or written off at any time during the existence of the company

Revalued or written off assets	Reasons

I–18 Provide the following information over the company's tax status

Year up to which the company has been assesse for income tax	
Estimated unassessed liability	
Concessions available	
Basis of tax provision	
Details of unclaimed tax benefits	

I–19 Provide details of any other new/expansion projects which are under implementation or are planned to implemented by the company

Project description	Estimated cost	Means of financing	Present status

I–20 Provide the following particulars for all existing debentures:
(Use additional sheets of paper if necessary)

	#1	#2	#3
Date of debenture trust deeds			
Purpose for which debenture was raised			
Security charge and nature of charge			
Trustees of debenture holders			
Original amount of issue			
Amount outstanding			
Rate of interest			
Amortization schedule			
Conversion or other special provision			
Main holders of debentures			
Restrictive covenants			

I–21 Provide the following particulars for all existing long term secured loans:
(Use additional sheets of paper if necessary)

	#1	#2	#3
Name of the institution granting the loan			
Purpose of the loan			
Original amount			
Amount outstanding			
Rate of interest			
Amortization schedule			
Security charge and nature of charge			
Date of creation of charge			
Any defaults in interest and principle payments			
Restrictive covenants			

I–22 Provide the following particulars for existing cash credit/overdraft agreements: (Use additional sheets of paper if necessary)

	#1	#2	#3
Name of the bank			
Nature of facility			
Maximum limit			
How and when repayable			
Particulars of security			

Stipulated margin percentage			
Particulars of guarantees			
Rate of interest			
Value of security and drawing power			
Amount outstanding on date of application			
Negative charge on fixed assets			

C. Management structure

I–23 Provide the following details for each member of the board of directors:

(Use additional sheets of paper if necessary)

Director's name		Age:	
Address		Existing shareholding	%
		Proposed shareholding	%
Educational qualification			
Relevant industry expertise			

Affiliated/group companies	Nature of business	Any financial dealings with the company	Size of turnover/net worth

I–24 Provide a list of key executive and technical staff

Key executive/technical staff	Age	Qualification and experience	Salary	Length of service

I–25 Provide a list of key administrative and accounting staff

Key administrative/accounting staff	Age	Qualification and experience	Salary	Length of service

I–26 Furnish the number of personnel employed in each existing plant

Plant	Supervisory	Skilled	Semi-skilled	Unskilled

I–27 Describe the proposed arrangement of the executive management of the concern both during the construction period and for the regular operations thereafter.

D. Shareholding pattern

I–28 Provide the list of shareholders owning or controlling 5% or more of equity shares

Shareholder's name	Amount owned	Business relationship

I–29 Total number of shareholders

Equity	
Preferences	

I–30 Provide detail on the distribution of shareholdings (only required for existing companies)

Indian promoters	Equity	Preference
1.		
2.		
3.		
4.		
5.		
Foreign collaborators		
Central		
State government		
State industrial development corporation		

Financial Institutions	Equity	Preference
IDBI		
IFCI		
ICICI		
LIC		
UTI		
GIC		
Banks		
Others (please specify)		
Public		

I–31 In respect of shares issued for consideration other than for cash, furnish the following particulars:

Name of the party	No. of shares Issued	Value of shares issued	Date of Issue	Consideration for which Issued

Part II Technical Information

A. Technical arrangement

II–1 Explain the technical process proposed to be employed, including reasons for adopting this particular process

II–2 Whether the proposal has ever been tried in this country? If yes, what were the results? Please indicate the performance of concerns adopting similar technology

II–3 Explain the technical arrangements made/proposed for implementation of the project

II–4 In case any collaboration is involved, furnish the following information

Collaborator Company		Size and turnover	

Describe major activities and performance of the collaborator company

List particulars of existing plants

Describe other projects in India and abroad set-up with same collaboration

II–5 Provide particulars for consultants employed

Consultant	Scope of work assigned	Fees payable	Particulars of consultants

II–6 Provide particulars for architect employed

Architect/firm	Scope of work	Fees payable	Past experience and bio-data of previous personnel

II–7 Provide the particulars for the main plant that was imported/to be imported for the project (Please furnish similar detail for each equipment separately in annex)

Description with board specification					
Name of manufacturer					
Country of origin					
Basis of selection of equipment					
Source(s) of supply					
Has the machinery already been imported?			Yes		No
If no, has the order has been placed?			Yes		No
If yes, what is the order placement date?					
What is the expected delivery date?					
Port of landing					
Fob value					
Basis of valuation					
Insurance and freight	Rs	Import duty			%

II–8 Provide the following particulars for the main plant that was acquired/to be acquired indigenously (Please furnish similar detail for each equipment separately in annex)

Description with board specification				
Name of the manufacturer:				
Basis of selection of equipment				
Source(s) of supply				
Has the machinery already been imported?		Yes		No
If no, has the order been placed?		Yes		No
If yes, what is the order placement date?				
What is the expected delivery date?				
Ex works for price				
Basis of valuation				

B. Location and site

II–9 Indicate location of plant, requirements of land for the project, and the arrangement made therefore. Describe the location advantages.

II–10 Give the following particulars in respect of the land acquired/proposed to be acquired for the project:

Describe the extent of the land and its cost:	
what is the basis of evaluation?	

Has entire sale consideration lease premium being paid?	Yes	No

If yes, describe instalments.	

What is the tenure of the land?	

What is the expected delivery date?	/ /

Has possession of the land being taken?	Yes	No
If yes, when was the possession taken?	/ /	

Give the particulars of the sales/lease deeds obtained

Most likely execution date if not already executed	/ /

Any restrictions against the mortgage of the land?	Yes	No
If yes, has permission been obtained?	Yes	No
Is name of company/society mutated in records?	Yes	No
Is the land subjected to any restrictions under local land ceiling laws?	Yes	No
Is land directly connected to the public road?	Yes	No
If no, has the company/society acquired or purchased the land on which to construct the approach road connecting the land to the public road?	Yes	No

Has the land been acquired by the company society under the land acquisition act?	Yes	No
If yes, have all the requirements under the act complied with?	Yes	No

Give particulars

Are all the title deeds/documents, receipts, etc., available?	Yes	No

If no, give reasons

```


```

Are the provisions of Urban Land (Ceiling and Regulation) Act applicable to the land?		Yes		No
If yes, have the exemption under Section 20 and permission to transfer under Section 26 and 27 of the Act been obtained?		Yes		No
Are there any restrictions under local laws against the land being used for non-agricultural/industrial purposes?		Yes		No
If yes, then has requisite permission for non-agricultural use been obtained?		Yes		No
Is the land free from encumbrances?		Yes		No

If no, provide details

```


```

Are any suit/appeal or other proceedings pertaining to the land pending in any court?				
Are any proceedings taken for recovery of land revenue, rents, royalties or other taxes and dues of public nature?				

If yes, provide details

```


```

Describe the type of soil and load bearing capacity

```


```

Describe water table

```


```

II–11 Explain the arrangement made/proposed for constructing each building as follows:
(Please furnish the details of other civil works in the following format, separately)

Description of the building	
Type of construction	

No. of floors		Length		Breadth	
Avg. floor height		Total floor area		Rate per sq. m.	
Estimated cost					

Name of contractor				
Contract	/	/	Contract amount	

Expected date of completion	/	/

Remarks (indicate the reasons for higher/lower construction costs such as heavy foundation, special construction, etc.).

C. Inputs of production

II–12 Describe indigenous raw materials requirements

Name of material/ chemical component	Specifications	Requirement per tonne of final production	Total annual requirements	Unit cost	Basis of cost estimate

II–13 Describe imported raw material requirements

Name of material/ chemical component	Specifications	Requirement per tonne of final production	Total annual requirements	Unit cost	Basis of cost estimate

II–14　Indicate principle trade suppliers who have contracted/agreed to supply

Name of supplier	Address	Material(s) agreed to supply

II–15　Provide details on any price or distribution controls on any of the raw materials, if any

II–16　Indicate the arrangements made/proposed for obtaining raw materials which are in short order or to be imported

II–17　In case of mining lease, provide the following details:

Location and area of mineral bearing land	
Particulars of mineral	
Principle terms of the mining lease	
Estimated future reserves and quality of reserves for each of the minerals and basis thereof	
Means of transport from the mines to the factory	

II–18　Describe the requirements and availability of labour, as well as training and development programmes

	Total	Availability	Training programmes	Manpower development programmes
Skilled				
Semi-skilled				
Unskilled				

II–19　Furnish existing and proposed arrangements for housing the staff and workers

	Senior executives	Other executives	Supervisors	Labour
No. of quarters (existing)				
No. of quarters (proposed)				

Floor area (existing)				
Floor area (proposed)				
Unit cost (existing)				
Unit cost (proposed)				
Amount to be met from industrial housing scheme				

II–20 Furnish the following details regarding power requirements:

Sources of power and supply voltage	
Purchased	
Own generation	
Stand-by arrangements	
Maximum demand	
Connected	
Peak hour requirements	
Contract load	
Power tariff	
Cost of power per annum at maximum capacity utilization	

Provide calculations

II–21 Furnish the following details regarding conservation of energy (only required for hotel projects). Indicate the efforts proposed for utilizing alternate sources of energy for the following:

Improving power factor

Improving heating efficiency in kitchens, toilets, etc.

Describe the use of solar energy for low temperature heating requirements and whether sitting/ orientation of the hotel building has been made to optimize the use of solar energy for the following:

Bringing down air conditioning loads

```

```

Optimizing illumination from lighting fixtures

```

```

Indicate the efforts proposed for better power load management, including for evening out peak demand requirements and cutting down non-essential loads.

```

```

Indicate the efforts proposed for generally cutting down losses in the use of various utility services, namely power, water and stream, and maximum and efficient utilization of waste heat

```

```

Indicate any other measures considered necessary or proposed to be taken in the context of energy conservation

```

```

Give particulars of the monitoring system to acquire the desired economy in use of energy

```

```

Indicate the savings achieved/proposed to be achieved by utilizing alternative sources of energy

```

```

II–22 Furnish the following details regarding water requirements:

Requirements of water

Circulating	
Make-up	
Process	
Boiler feed	
Drinking	
Cooling	
Sources of water arrangement proposed	
Water charges payable	
Capacity of tanks	
Capacity of reservoirs	

Describe proposed water treatment arrangements

II–23 Furnish the following details regarding the steam requirements:

Steam required	
Steam balance	
Types of boiler	
Capacity	

Provide detailed specification

Consumption station	Total energy generated/ purchases	Theoretical requirements of energy	Expected actual requirements

If alternative processes are available, provide comparative energy consumption figures for the various processes.

If the project is energy intensive, discuss the possibility of choosing alternative processes

Describe the steps proposed to be taken by the company to improve energy efficiency and reduce energy losses (such as power factor improvement, power load management, optimizing illumination, waste heat utilization, etc.)

Describe the scope of usage of solar and other renewable sources of energy

Describe any other measures contemplated in the in the direction of energy conservation and management

II–24 Furnish the following details regarding compressed air and fuel requirements

Requirement	Sources	Arrangements proposed	Cost at site	Detailed cost calculation

II–25 Describe the arrangements proposed for carrying raw materials and finished goods, provisions for own trucks, railway siding, etc. and arrangements with private truck operators

D. Implementation schedule

II–26 Complete the following implementation schedule:

Item	Commencement date	Completion date
Acquisition of land		
Development of land		
Civil works		
Factory building		
Machinery foundation		
Auxiliary building		
Administrative building		
Miscellaneous buildings		
Arrangements for power		
Arrangements for water		
Erection of equipment		
Commissioning		
Procurement of raw materials and chemicals		
Training of personnel		
Trial balance		
Commercial production		

	Placement and order date	Delivery at site date
Plant and machinery imported		
Indigenous		

Part III Market Information

A. Demand outlook

III–1 Provide a brief note on the market of the proposed products

Proposed product	Major uses	Scope of market	Substitute products	Special features

III–2 Provide estimates of historic demands for each of the products proposed to be manufactured (please mention source of information)

Product	Year 5	Year 4	Year 3	Year 2	Year 1

III–3 Provide information regarding export possibilities and the nature of competition to be faced in foreign countries

III–5 If there are any export commitments assumed by the company as a part of the government requirements, indicate the arrangement proposed for meeting the same and the export incentives available

B. Supply outlook

III–6 Provide estimates of history supply of each of the products proposed to be manufactured

Product	Year 5	Year 4	Year 3	Year 2	Year 1

III–7 Give an assessment of likely competition in the future and indicate any special feature of the project that may enable it to meet the competition

III–8 Specify the particulars of government controls and restrictions, if any, on the sale price, distribution, import, export of each of the products proposed to be manufactured

Proposed products	Government controls and restrictions

C. Market potential

III–9 Provide estimate of the projected demand for each of the products proposed to be manufactured

Product	Year 5	Year 4	Year 3	Year 2	Year 1

III–10 Provide estimate of the projected supply for each of the products proposed to be manufactured

Product	Year 5	Year 4	Year 3	Year 2	Year 1

III–11 Provide current prices of proposed products

Proposed products	International	CIF	FOB	Landed cost

III–12 Give details regarding trends of prices during the last five years. If the prices are controlled by the government or on a voluntary basis, indicate the basis on which the prices were fixed

D. Selling arrangements

III–13 List principal customers and particulars of any firm arrangements entered into with them

Principal customers	Particulars of firm arrangements

III–14 If sales are o be made directly by the company, provide information on the nature of the proposed selling organization for each product

Principal customers	Nature of proposed selling organization

III–15 If sales are to be made by distributors or selling agents, please provide the following particulars on the selling arrangements

Proposed product	Proposed selling arrangements in india and abroad	Proposed commission	Description of selling agent's organization

III–16 If sales are to be made through any sole selling agents, please provide a description of remuneration, reason for appointment, relationship of directors with selling agent, the agents past experience, and the adequacies of storage facilities for each sole selling agent

Part IV Financial Information

A. Project cost

IV–1 Provide the following breakdown project cost:

Items	Rupees cost	Rupee equivalent of FE cost
Land and site development		
Buildings		
Plant and machinery		
Imported		
Indigenous		
Technical know how fees*		
Expenses on foreign technicians and training of Indian technicians abroad *		
Miscellaneous fixed assets*		
Preliminary and preoperative expenses*		
Provision for contingencies*		
Margin money for working capital*		
Total		

*Calculations for estimation of these costs may be given in separate sheets and attached to the application.

B. Means of financing

IV–2 Provide a breakdown of the proposed means of financing

	Rupee cost	Rupee equivalent of FE cost
Promoter's capital		
Public issue of capital		
Rupee loan		
Debentures		
Foreign currency loan		

Guarantee of foreign currency loan/deferred credit
(Rs equivalent at market rate)

	Rupee cost	Rupee equivalent of FE cost
Principal		
Interest		
Total		
Guarantee to be issued in favour of		
Internal cash accruals		
Other (specify)		

IV–3 Provide details on proposals for raise in share capital, loans and debentures

	Subscription/Underwriting of share capital		Loans			
	Equity	Preference	Rupee	Foreign currency	Debenture	Remarks
Indian promoters						
In cash						
Other than cash						
Foreign collaborators						
State government						
SIDC						
IDBI						
IFCI						
ICICI						
LIC						
UTI						
Banks (specify)						
Insurance cos (specify)						
Brokers						

IV–4 Briefly describe the arrangements so far made for raising the finance and proposed arrangements

IV–5 List the particulars of foreign currency loans/guarantees applied for

	Currency	Rate of exchange		Rupee equivalent at	
		Parity rate	Market rate	Parity rate	Market rate
Loan					
Guarantee of foreign currency loan/deferred credit					

IV–6 Indicate sources of foreign exchange and arrangements, if any, made from obtaining foreign exchange

IV–7 Indicate sources from which expenditures already incurred have been financed

	Amount (Rs 000)	Rate of interest payable	Other terms and conditions
Share capital			
Equity			
Preference			
Long/medium term loans from banks			
Loans from financial institutions			
Loans/deposits from promoters, directors, etc.			
Public deposits			
Other sources (specify)			

IV–8 Calculate the following for the promoter's contribution

Promoter's contribution to project cost	Rs
Promoter's contribution as % of total cost	%

IV–9 List the persons/firms who/which would be contributing to the promoter's share of the capital

Person/firm contributing to promoters share	Amount

IV–10 Details of assistance sought from IDBI   (Rs lakh)

Types of assistance	Loan	Underwriting	Guarantee
Rupees			
Foreign currency			

IV–11 Provide the details of security proposed

Loan	
Guarantee for deferred payments on plant and machinery	
Guarantee for foreign currency loans	

Do you propose to offer a bank guarantee instead of mortgage of fixed assets?		Yes		No
If yes, please specify the bank name				

C. Sources and its uses of funds

IV–12 In the case of internal accruals are taken as a source of finance, explain the basis of estimation of internal accruals by means of a suitable statement

D. Performance indicators

IV–13 Give estimates of cost of production for the first five years of operations

Cost of manufacturing	Years +1	Years +2	Years +3	Years +4	Years +5
1) Raw materials					
2) Chemical					
3) Component					
4) Consumable stores					
Total material costs (a)					

Utilities					
Power					
Water					
Fuel					
Total utilities (b)					
Labour and plant overheads					
Wages					
Factory supervisor					
Salaries					
Bonus					
Provident fund					
Total labour (c)					
Factory overheads					
Repair and maintenance					
Light					
Rent and taxes on factory					
Assets					
Insurance					
Miscellaneous expenses					
5% Contingency					
Total factory overhead (d)					
Estimate of cost of manufacturing (f) = (A) + (b) + (c) + (d)					

IV–14 Provide estimates of production and sales for the first five years of operation (if more than one product, prepare response for each product)

	Years + 1	Years + 2	Years + 3	Years + 4	Years + 5
Installed capacity					
No. of working days					
No. of shifts					
Estimate production per day (quantity)					
Estimated annual production (quantity)					
Estimated output as % of plant capacity					
Sales after adjusting stock (quantity)					
Unit selling price					
Value of sales					

IV–15 Give estimates of working results of first 5 years of operation.

	Years +1	Years +2	Years+3	Years + 4	Years + 5
Cost of production – from question IV-12(a)					
Administrative expenses					
Administration salaries					
Remuneration of directors					
Professional fees					
Office supplies					
Insurance and taxes					
Miscellaneous					
Total administration expenses(b)					
Total sales expenses (c)					
Royalty/know how (d)					
Total cost of production (E) = (a) + (b) + (c) + (d)					

Expected sales – from question IV-13(f)					
Gross profit before interest(g) = (f) – (e)					
Financial expenses					
Interest on term loan					
Interest on working capital loan					
Guarantee commission					
Total financial expenses (h)					
Depreciation (i)					
Operating profit (j) = (g) + (h) + (i)					
Other income (if any) (k)					
Preliminary expenses written off (l)					
Profit/loss before tax (m) = (j) + (k) + (l)					
Provision for taxation (n)					
Profit after taxation (m) – (n)					

IV–16 Give the estimates of profitability for the project (only required for expansion/diversification of existing companies)

	Years +1	Years + 2	Years + 3	Years + 4	Years + 5
Cost of production – from question iv-12 (a)					
Administrative expenses					
Administration salaries					
Remuneration to directors					
Professional fees					
Office supplies					
Insurance and taxes					
Miscellaneous					
Total administration expenses (b)					
Total sales expenses (c)					
Royalty/know how (d)					
Total cost of production (e) = (a) + (b) + (c) + (d)					
Financial expenses					
Interest on term loans					
Interest on working capital loan					
Guarantee commission					

Total financial expenses(h)					
Depreciation (i)					
Operating profit (j) = (g) + (h) + (i)					
Other income, if any (k)					
Preliminary expenses written off (l)					
Profit/loss before tax (m) = (j) + (k) + (l)					
Provision for taxation (n)					
Profit after taxation (m) – (n)					

IV–17 Provide a cash flow statement for the company as a whole for the first five years of operation.

Sources of funds	Years + 1	Years + 2	Years + 3	Years + 4	Years + 5
Share issue					
Profit before interest and tax					
Depreciation provision					
Development rebate reserve					
Increased in secured medium and long-term borrowing for projects					
Other medium/long-term loans					
Increase in unsecured loans and deposits					
Increase in working capital loan					
Increase in liabilities for the deferred payments to machinery suppliers					
Sale of fixed assets					
Sale of investments					
Other income					
Total sources					

Disposition of funds	Years + 1	Years + 2	Years + 3	Years + 4	Years + 5
Capital expenditure of the project					
Other normal capital expenditures					
Increase in working capital					
All-india institutions					
SFCS					
Banks					
Decrease in unsecured loans and deposits					
Decrease in working capital loan					
Decrease in liabilities for deferred payments to machinery suppliers					
Increase in investments in other companies					
Interest on term loans					
Interest on working capital loan					
Taxation					
Dividends					
Equity					
Preferences					

Other expenditures					
Total dispositions					
Opening balance of cash in hand and cash at bank					
Net surplus/deficit					
Closing balance of cash in hand and at bank					

IV–18 Provide a projected balance sheet for ten operating years for the company as a whole

IV–19 At what capacity will the plant break-even? Provide detailed calculations

Part V Socio-Economic Impact Informaion

A. Economic consideration

V–1 Provide prices of competing import/export products

Competing export/ import product	FOB	CIF	Landed cost (incl. import duty)	Selling Price

V–2 Provide detailed explanations for differences in selling prices of the product and those of imported goods with qualitative data on differences in cost of production (such as scale of operation, differences in costs of inputs, and various local duties and taxes)

V–3 Provide prices inputs which can be imported or exported

Inputs	International	CIF	FOB

V–4 Explain in details the various duties, taxes, and incentives

Excise duty	
Import duty	
Export duty	
Export assistance	
Replenishment loan	
Duty drawback	
Cash subsidy	
Other	

V–5 Provide a brief write-up on the economic benefits to the country in general and the region in particular on account of the proposed project

V–6 How far does the unit contribute to the establishment of ancillary industries in the region?

B. Environmental Considerations

V–7 Furnish details on the nature of the atmospheric, soil, and water pollution likely to be created by the project

Nature of pollution	Measures proposed for control of pollution	Necessary permission for disposal of effluents obtained
Atmosphere		
Soil		
Water		

C. Status of Government Consent

V–8 Indicate whether the various license/consents required for the project have been obtained from the respective authorities

	Date of issue	Present status if not already issued
Letter of intent		
Industrial license		
Capital goods clearance		
Import license		
Foreign exchange permission		
Approval of technical/financial collaboration		
Clearance under MRTP Act		
Consent of the Controller of Capital Issue		
Other (specify)		

V–9 Specify any special condition attached to the license/consents and the undertakings given by the company in connection with them

Source: www.idbi.com/IDBI/doc/tufsapp.doc, accessed 30 March 2010.
www.cityofnewhaven.com/SmallBusiness/.../SBIapplicationform.pdf; accessed 30 March 2010.
www.hudco.org/prapp.pdf, accessed 30 March 2010.

INDEX